Co]

G000069635

EASY READ
LONDON

Contents

Police
Police st

Post offic
office

Library

King's
Cross

Camden
Town   ISLIN

35   **36**   **37**   **38**

gent's
ark   ST. PANCRAS

THE
VENUE
EMPIRE   BEA

LEICESTER
SQ   HUN.CT

ODEON
Thistle   Sch
Pastoria SQ
IRVING

als Gate, SE10 . **1**
miral Sq, SW10....**162**
dmiral St, SE8......**177** D
Admirals Way, E14...**125** D1
★ Admiralty Arch,
   SW1.............**87** D4
Admiralty Cl, SE8 ....**176** C3
Admiral Wk, W9 ......**53** D3
Adolphus St, SE8 ....**176** B1
dpar St, W2.........**54** C
ian Ms, SW10 ....**137**
ic Bldg, E14 ....**9**
Ct E14

Published by Collins
An imprint of HarperCollins Publishers
77-85 Fulham Palace Road, Hammersmith, London W6 8JB

www.collinsworld.com

Copyright © HarperCollins Publishers Ltd 2008

Collins® is a registered trademark of HarperCollins Publishers Limited

Mapping generated from Collins Bartholomew digital databases

London Underground Map by permission of Transport Trading Limited
Registered User No. 07/4668

The grid on this map is the National Grid taken from the Ordnance Survey map with the permission of the Controller of Her Majesty's Stationery Office.

The contents of this publication are believed correct at the time of printing. Nevertheless, the publisher can accept no responsibility for errors or omissions, changes in the detail given, or for any expense or loss thereby caused.

The representation of a road, track or footpath is no evidence of a right of way.

Printed in China

ISBN   978 0 00 725763 8   Imp 001   VM12347 / NDL

e-mail: roadcheck@harpercollins.co.uk

Key to map symbols

A4 Dual	Primary route
A40 Dual	'A' road
B504	'B' road
173	Address number ('A' & 'B' roads only)
	Other road
→	One way street
	Street market
	Pedestrian street
	Access restriction
··············	Long distance footpath
-------- -------	Track/Footpath
	Borough boundary
	Postal district boundary
	Extent of London congestion charging zone.
---⊖---	Pedestrian ferry with landing stage
⇄	Main national rail station
⊛	Other national rail station
⊖	Underground station
⊖	Overground station
⊖	DLR station
⬤	Bus/Coach station
P	Car park
👫	Public toilet
i	Information centre for visitors
i	Other information centre

Pol **TPol**	Police station/Transport Police station
PO **PO**	Post office/Postal delivery office
Lib	Library
🎥	Cinema
⛩	Theatre
🏨	Major hotel
m	Historic site
⌐USA	Embassy
+	Church
☾ ✡	Mosque/Synagogue
■ Mormon	Other place of worship
⬤	Community centre/Hall
■ Amb Sta	Ambulance station
	Leisure/Tourism
	Shopping
	Administration/Law
	Market
	Health/Welfare
	Education
	Industry/Commerce
	Major office
	Other landmark building/ Tower block
	Public open space
	Woodland
	Park/Garden/Sports ground
	Cemetery

0 ············ ¼ ············ ½ mile

0 ············ 0.25 ············ 0.5 ············ 0.75 kilometre

Scale 1:7,500   8.5 inches (21.5cm) to 1 mile / 13.3 cm to 1 km

Key to map pages

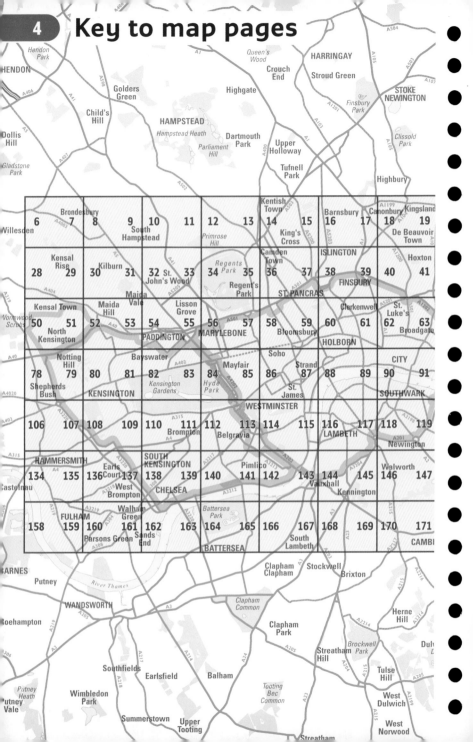

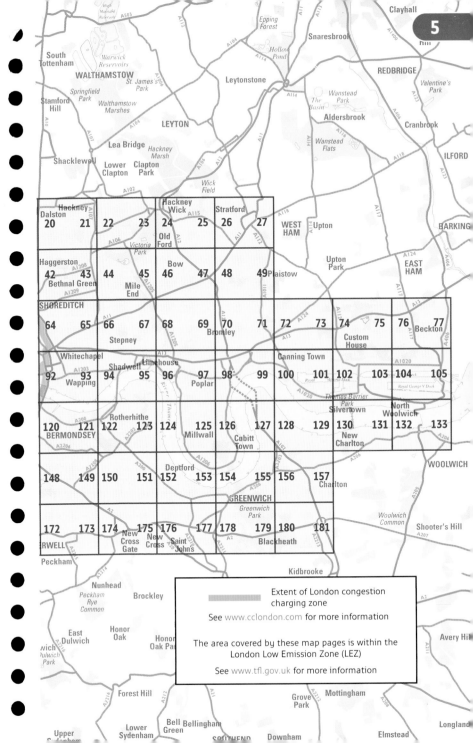

Clayhall
Epping Forest
Snaresbrook
hill
REDBRIDGE
Valentine's Park
South Tottenham
Warwick Reservoirs
A503
Hollow Pond
WALTHAMSTOW
St. James's Park
Leytonstone
Springfield Park
Stamford Hill
Walthamstow Marshes
The Basin
Wanstead Park
Aldersbrook
Cranbrook
LEYTON
Wanstead Flats
ILFORD
Lea Bridge
Hackney Marsh
Shacklewell
Lower Clapton
Clapton Park
Wick Field
A102

Hackney Dalston 20	21	22	23	Hackney Wick 24	25	Stratford 26	27	WEST HAM	Upton		BARKING
Haggerston 42	43 Bethnal Green	44	Mile End 45	Bow 46	47	48	49 Plaistow	Upton Park		EAST HAM	
SHOREDITCH 64	65	66	67 Stepney	68	69	70 Bromley	71	72	73	74 Custom House	75	76	77 Beckton
Whitechapel 92	93 Wapping	Shadwell 94	Limehouse 95	96	97 Poplar	98	99	Canning Town 100	101	102	103	104	105
120 BERMONDSEY	121	Rotherhithe 122	123	124	125 Millwall	126	127 Cubitt Town	128	129	Silvertown 130 New Charlton	131	North Woolwich 132	133
148	149	150	151	Deptford 152	153	154	155	156	157 Charlton				WOOLWICH
172	173	174	New Cross 175 Gate	New Cross 176 Saint John's	177	178	Greenwich Park 179 Blackheath	180	181	Woolwich Common		Shooter's Hill	

Victoria Park
Old Ford
WEST HAM
Upton
GREENWICH
Peckham
Kidbrooke
Nunhead
Peckham Rye Common
Brockley
East Dulwich
Honor Oak
Honor Oak Park
Avery Hil
wich Dulwich Park
Forest Hill
Grove Park
Mottingham
Longland
Upper S...denham
Lower Sydenham
Bell Green
Bellingham
SOUTHEND
Downham
Elmstead

Extent of London congestion charging zone

See www.cclondon.com for more information

The area covered by these map pages is within the London Low Emission Zone (LEZ)

See www.tfl.gov.uk for more information

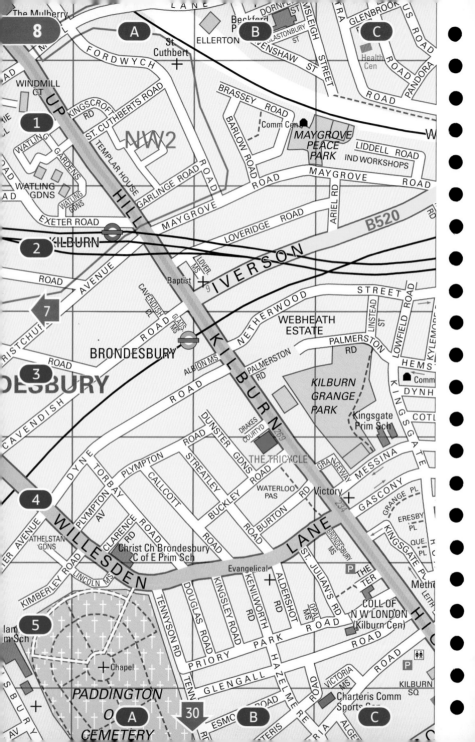

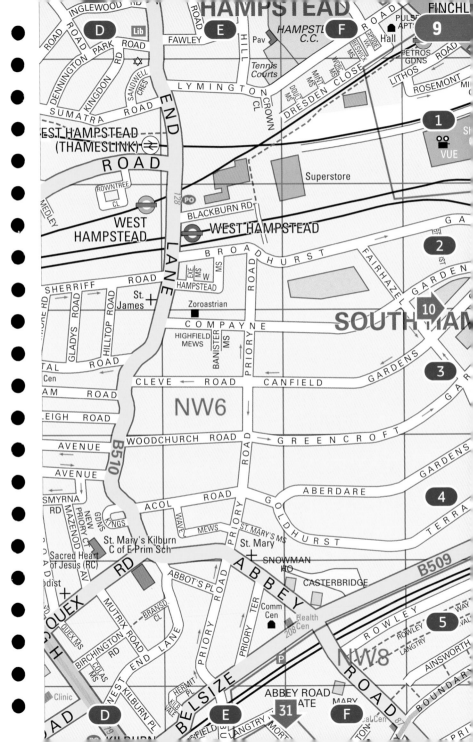

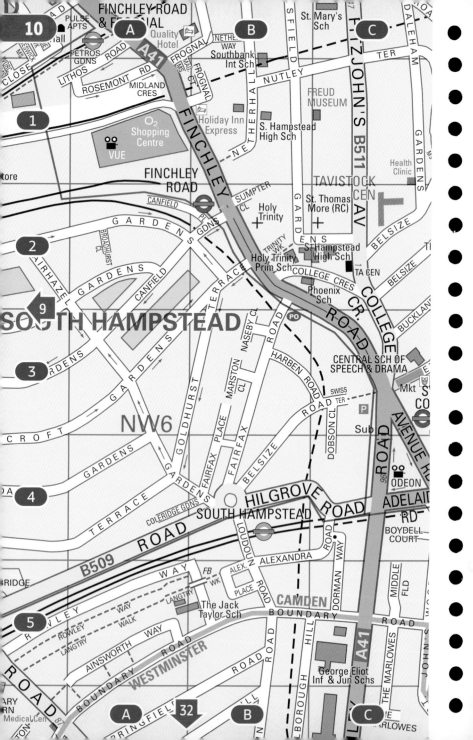

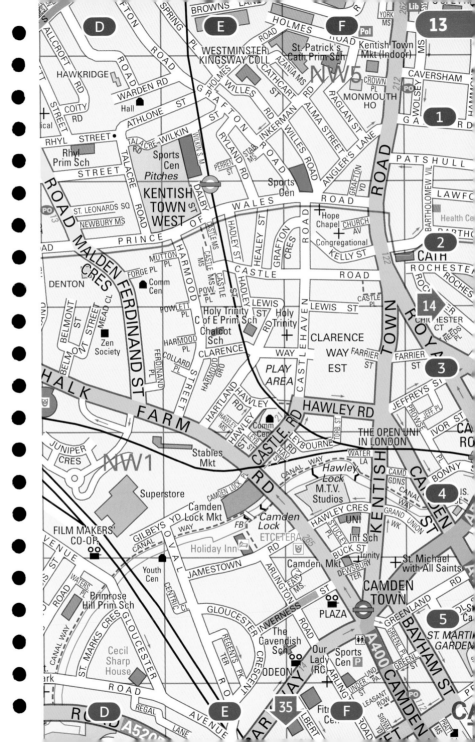

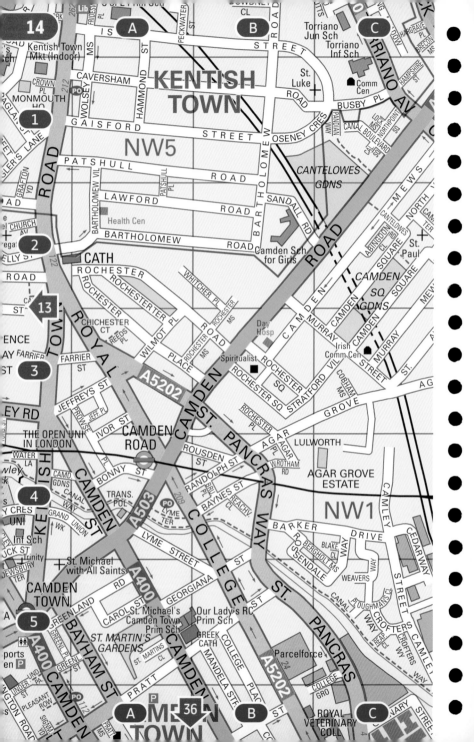

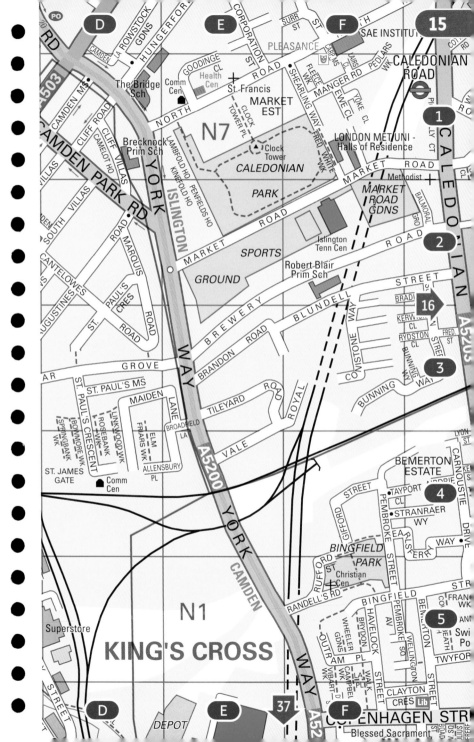

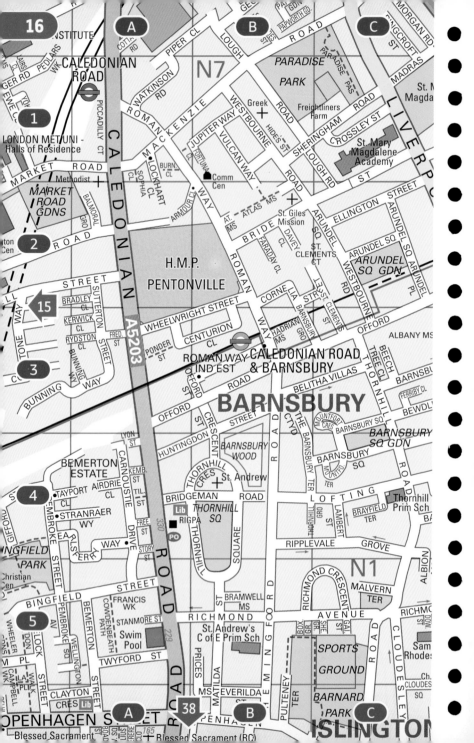

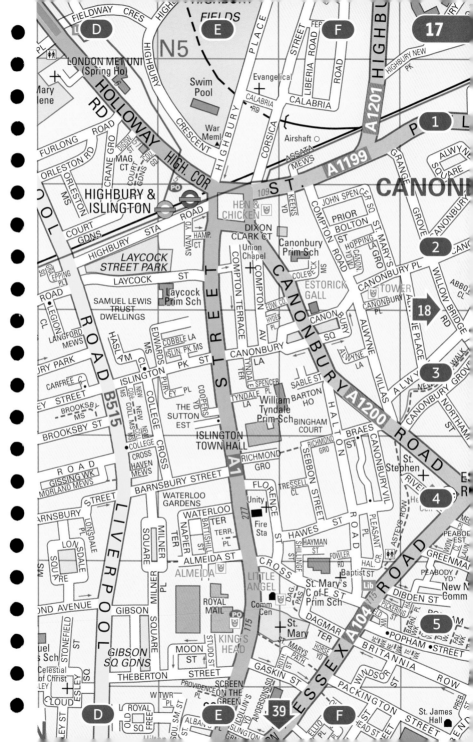

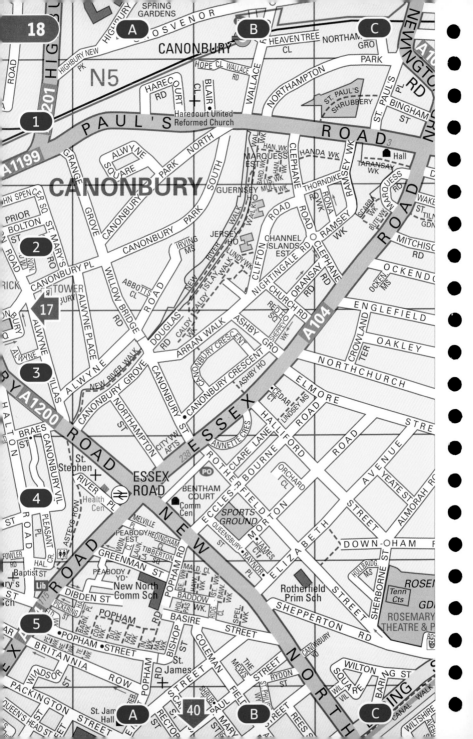

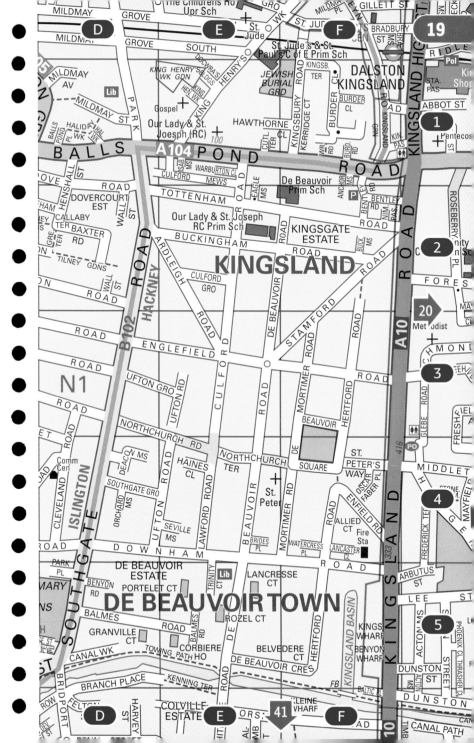

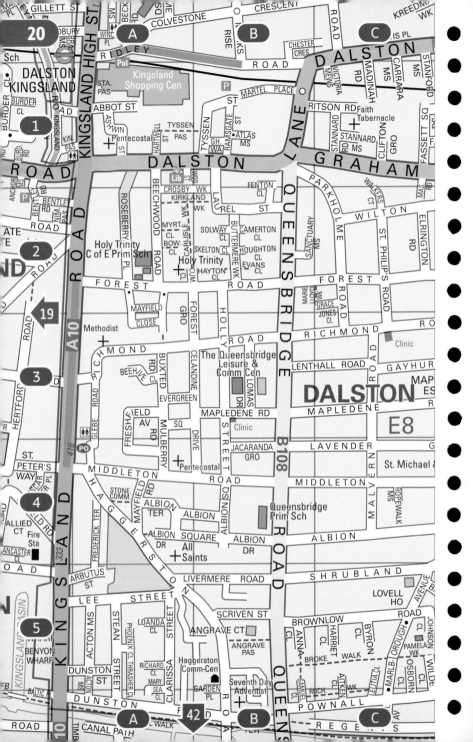

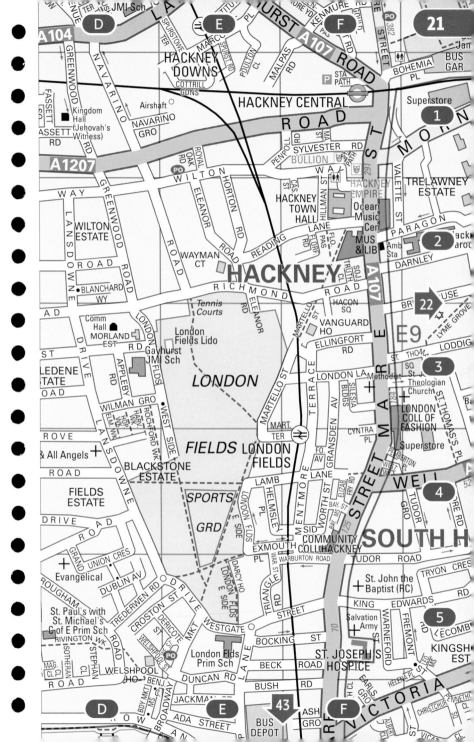

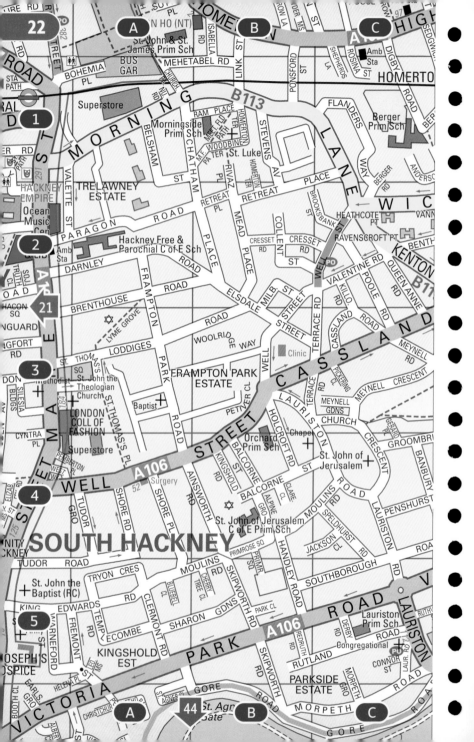

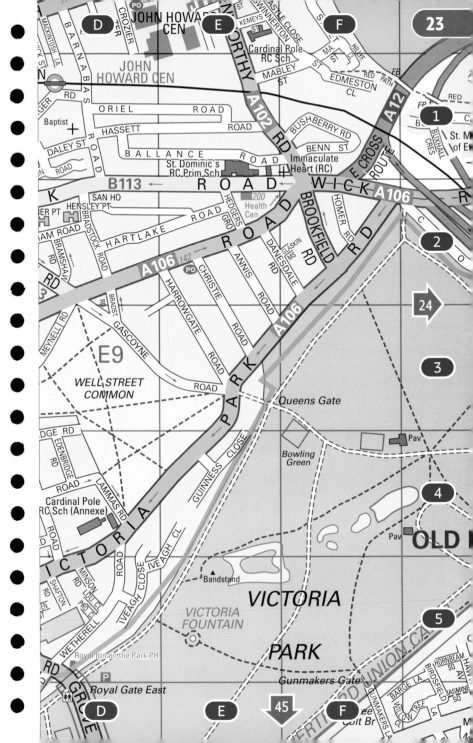

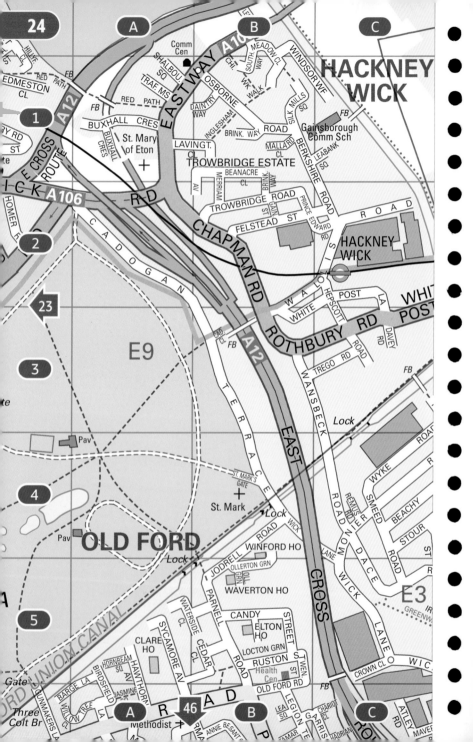

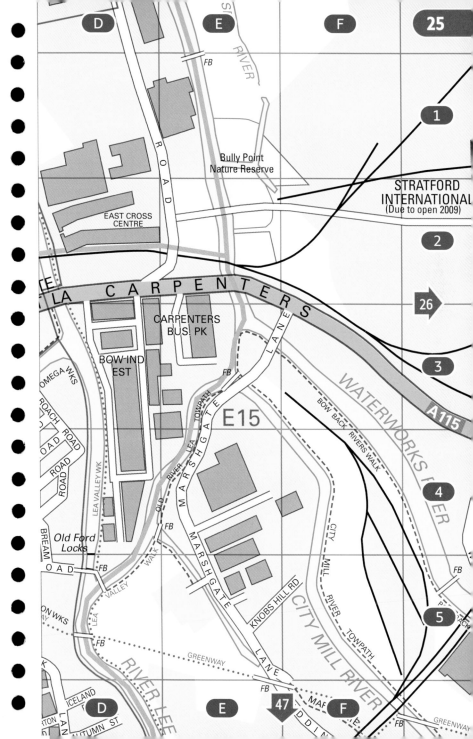

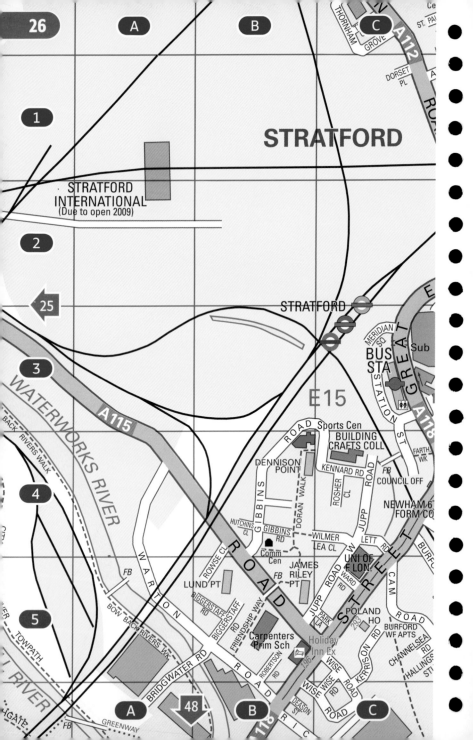

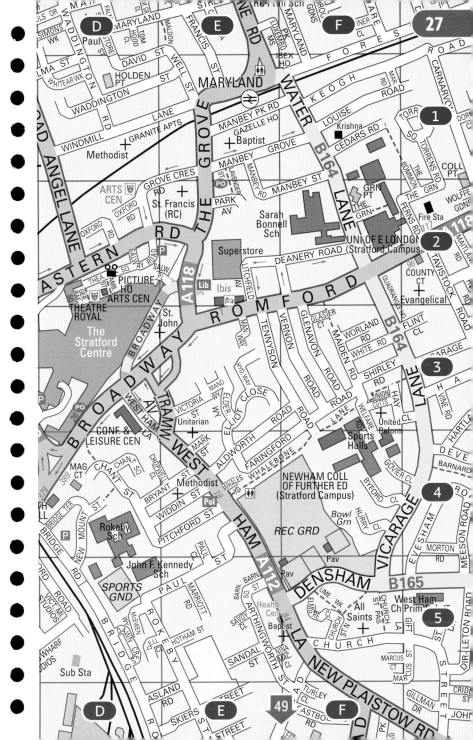

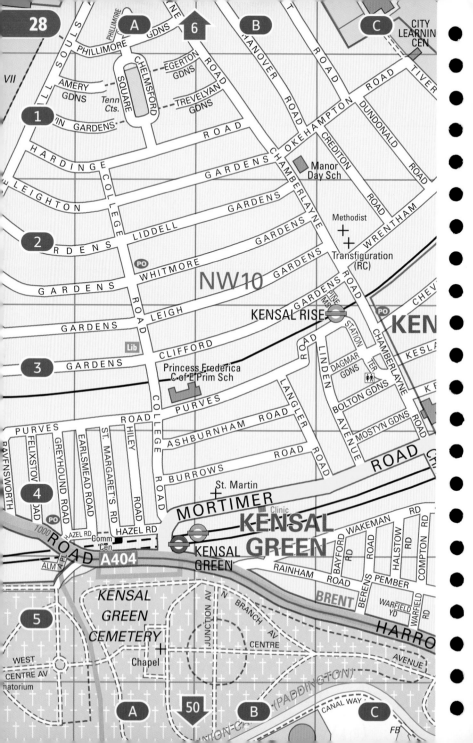

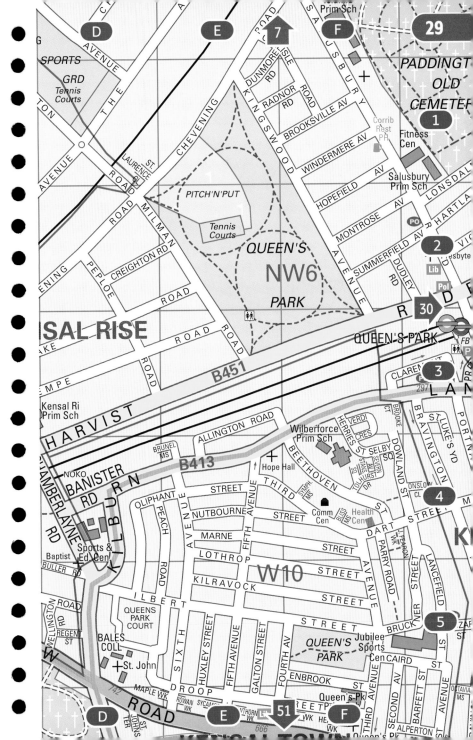

D E 7 F

SPORTS
GRD
Tennis
Courts

PADDINGT
OLD
CEMETEF
1

Corrib
Rest
PH

Fitness
Cen

Salusbury
Prim Sch

LONSDAL

HARTLA

VIC

PO

2
esbyte

Lib

Pol

30

FB

QUEEN'S-PARK

CLARE
3
297
LAN

Kensal Ri
Prim Sch

HARVIST

ALLINGTON ROAD

Wilberforce
Prim Sch

VERDI
HERRIES CRES
SELBY
SQ

BROOKE

ST LUKE'S YD

BRAVINGTON

PORTN

B413

Hope Hall

BEETHOVEN

THIRD

DOWLAND ST

ONSLOW
CL

4

M

NOKO

BANISTER

BRUNEL
MS

STREET

SYMPH
MS

Comm
Cen

BLISS
MS

Health
Cen

DART

ST

STREE

K

OLIPHANT

NUTBOURNE

FIFTH AVENUE

STREET

FEHRON
WK

PARRY ROAD

LANCEFIELD

Sports &
Ed Cen

Baptist

BULLER RD

PEACH

MARNE

LOTHROP

ROAD

KILRAVOCK

W10

STREET

STREET

STREET

AVENUE

KNER

STREET

5
ZAF
ST

WELLINGTON
RD

REGENT
ST

QUEENS
PARK
COURT

ILBERT

STREET

S
STREET

BRUCK

BALES
COLL

St. John

SIXTH

HUXLEY STREET

FIFTH AVENUE

GALTON STREET

FOURTH AV

QUEEN'S
PARK

Jubilee
Sports
Cen CAIRD

ST

SECOND AV

ST

BARFETT

AVENUE

OCTAVIA
MS

MAPLE WK

DROOP

ROWAN SYCAM
WK WK

ENBROOK

Queen's-Pk

ST

THIRD

ALPERTON ST

742

D

ROAD

ST
JOHNS
TER

E

51

THORN
WK HE

666

F

Queen's Pk

AVENUE

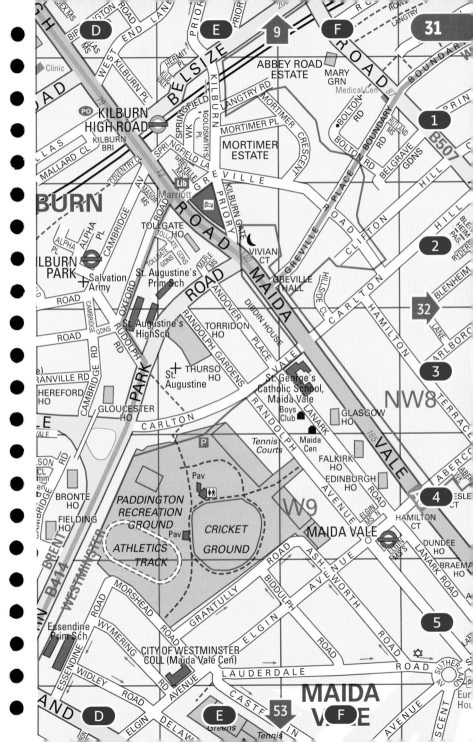

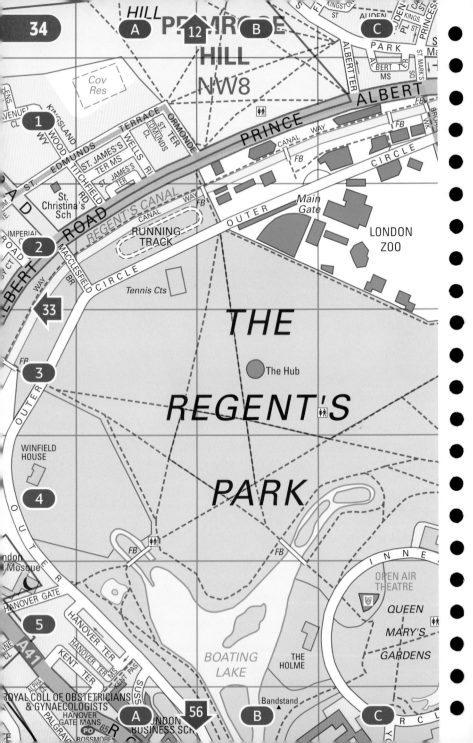

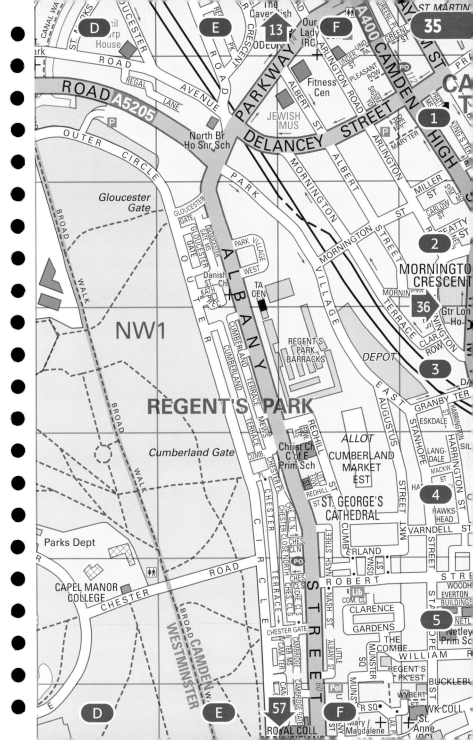

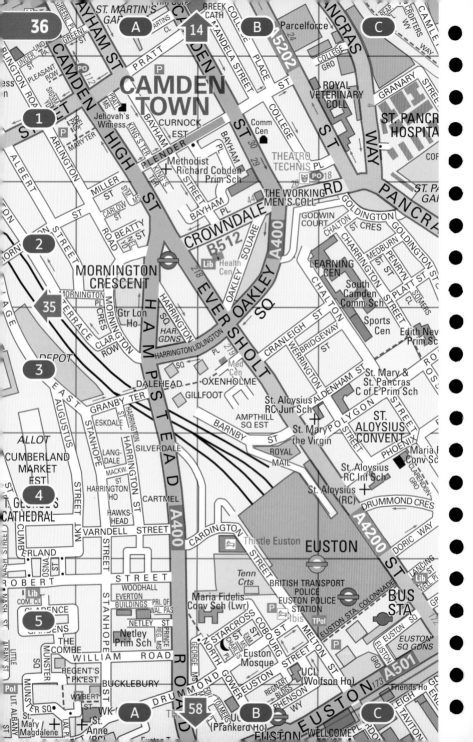

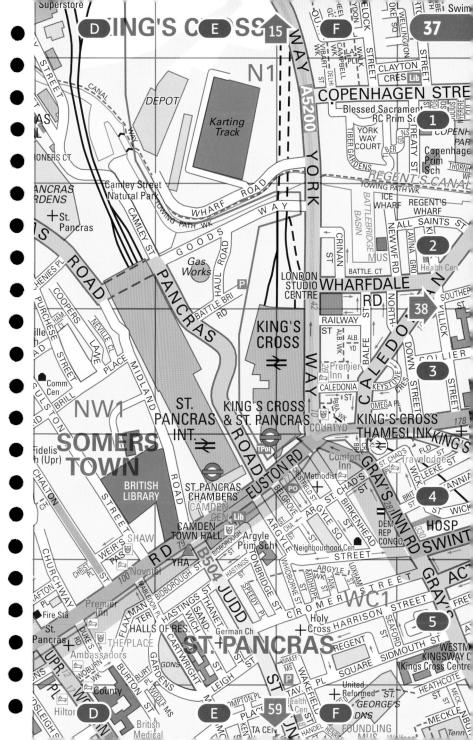

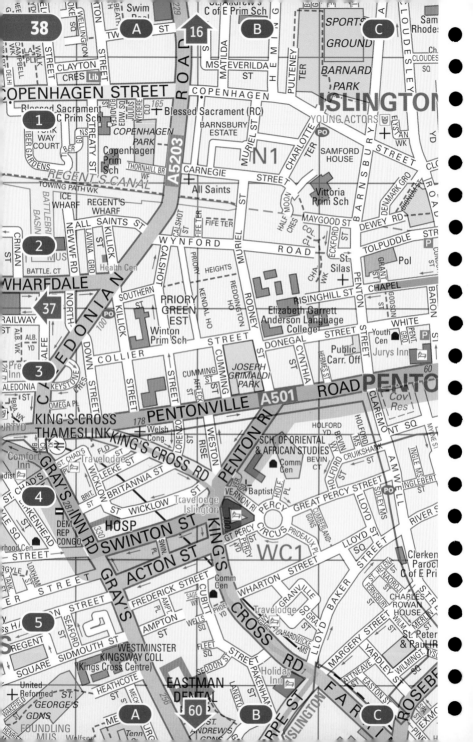

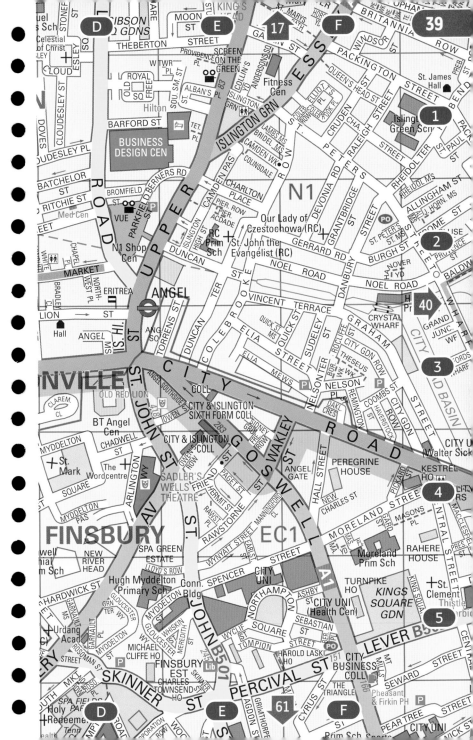

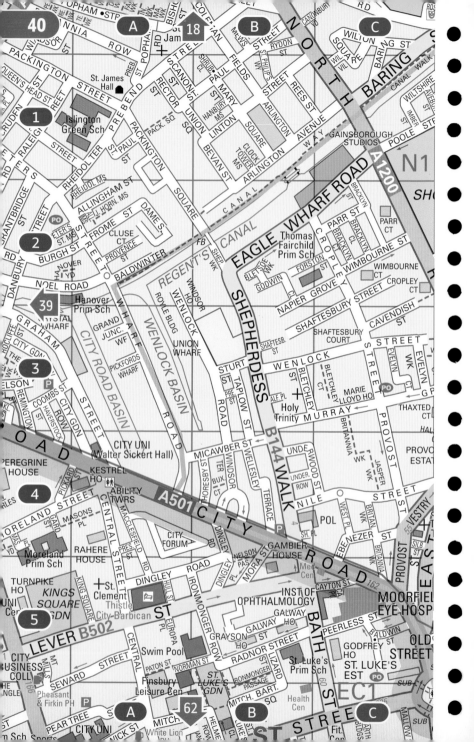

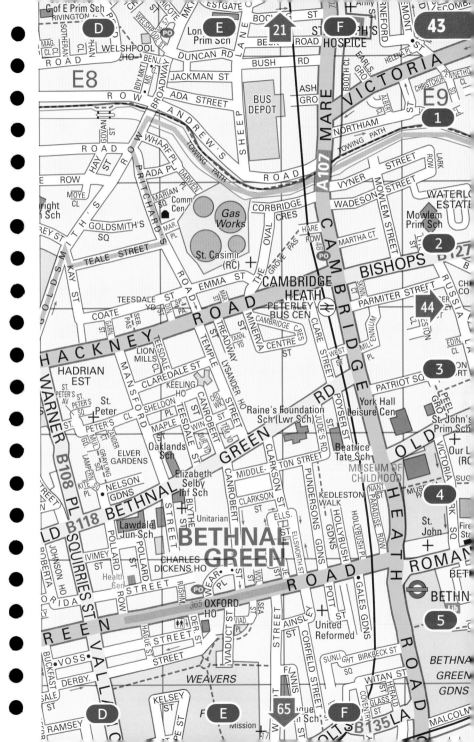

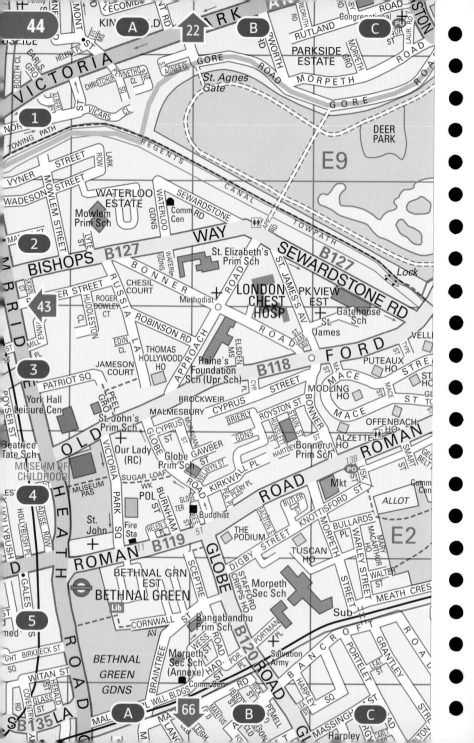

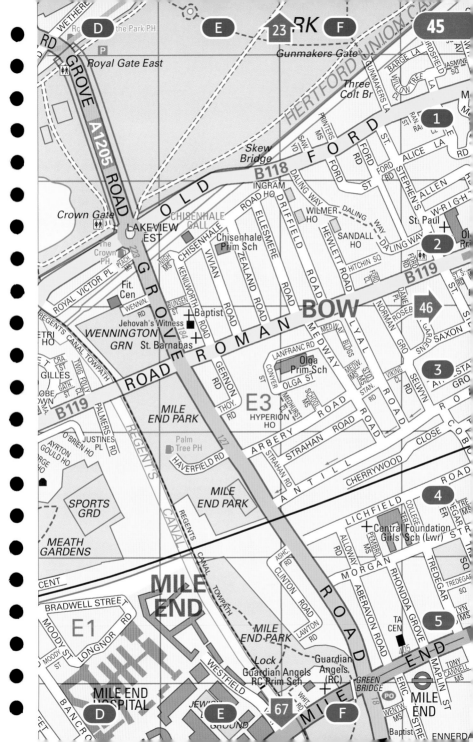

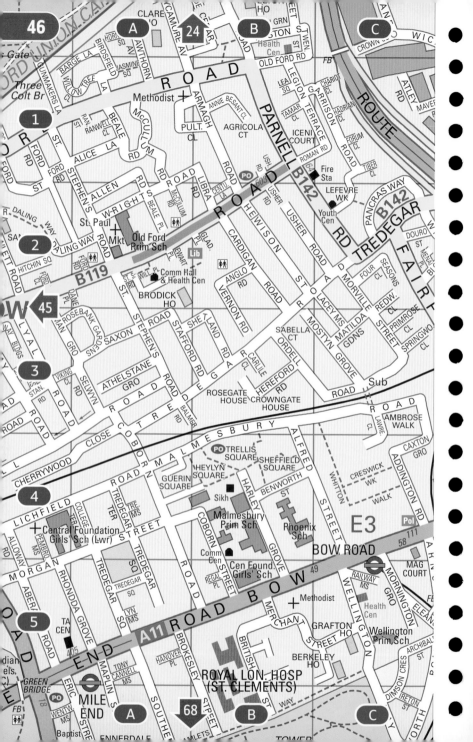

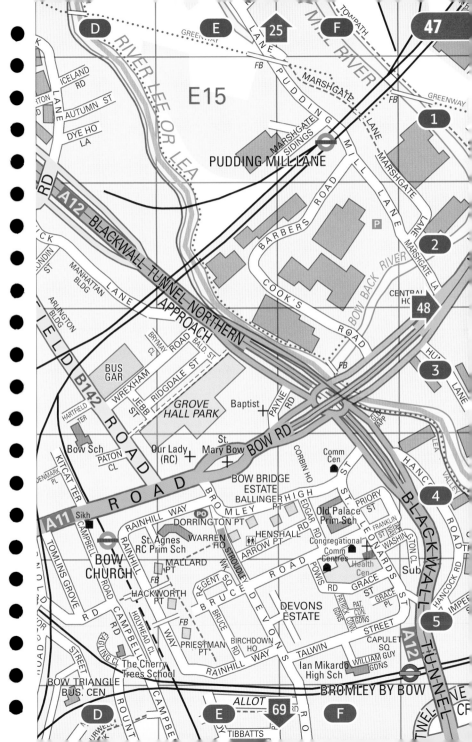

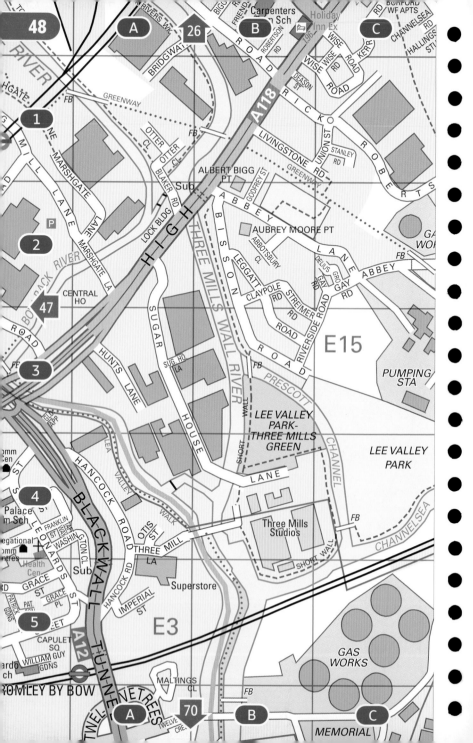

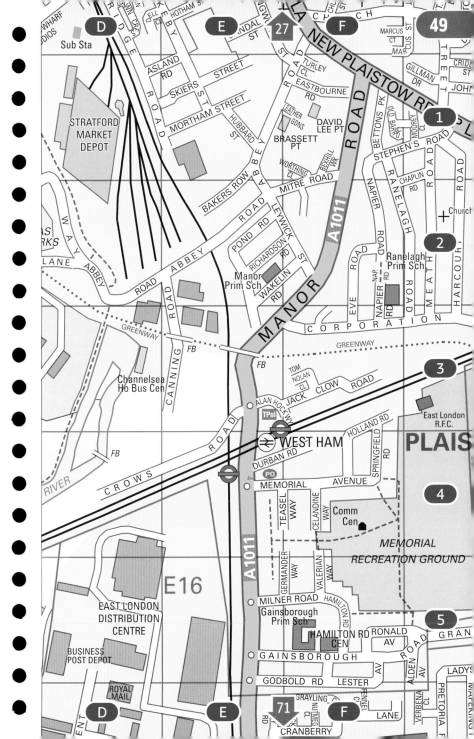

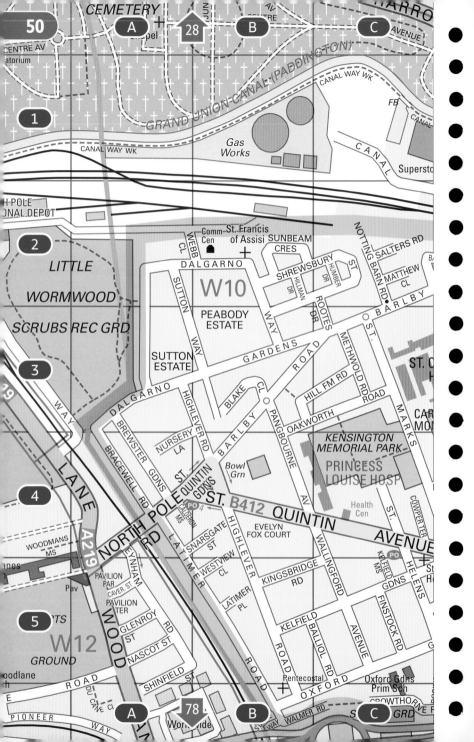

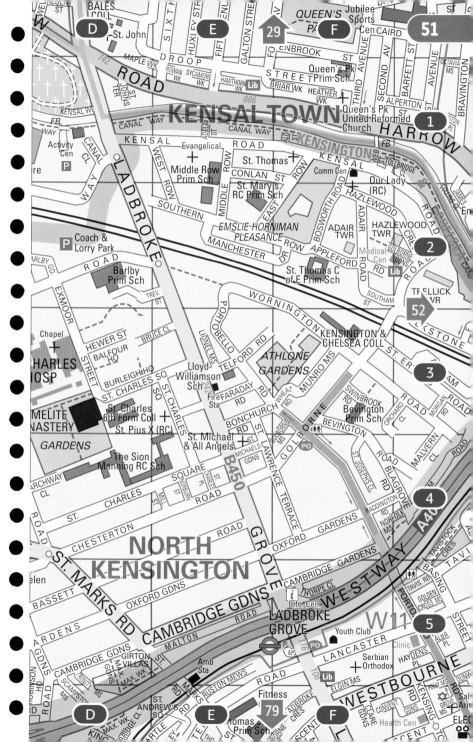

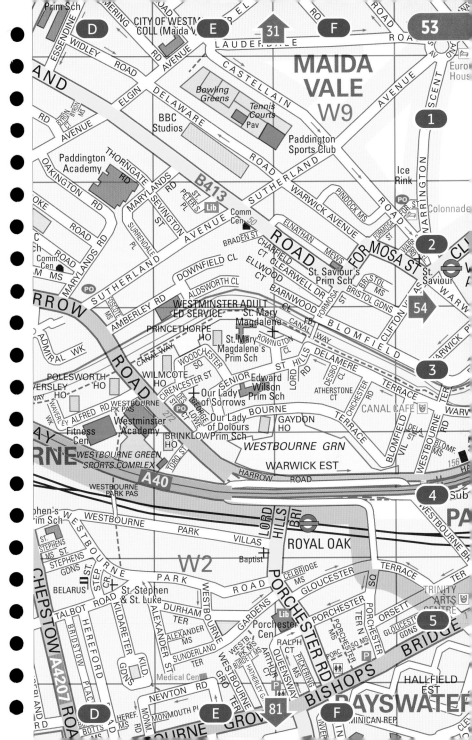

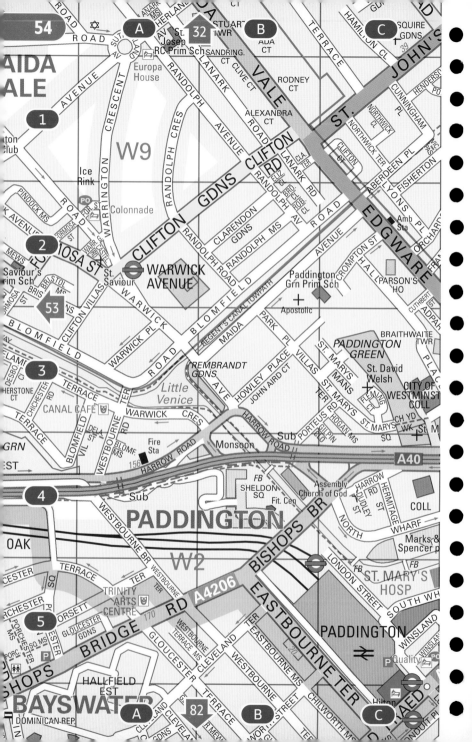

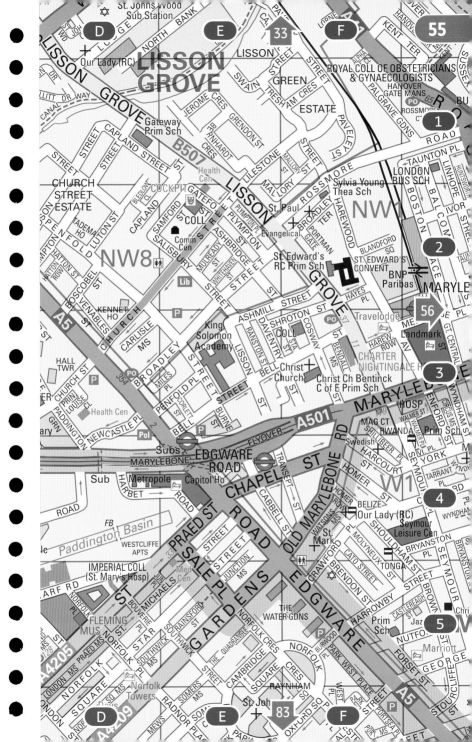

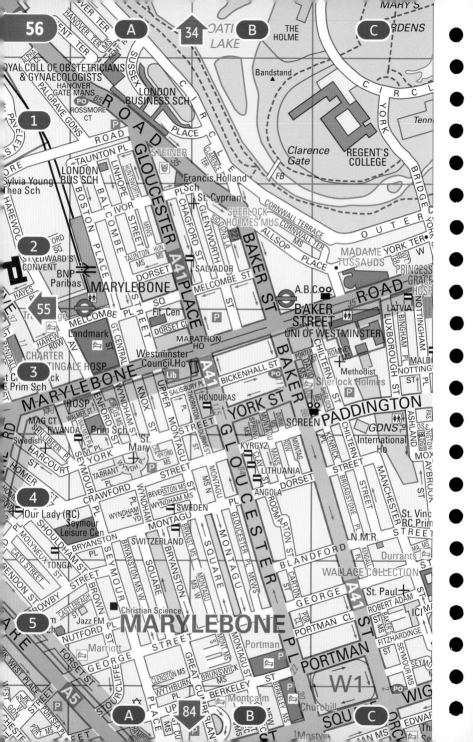

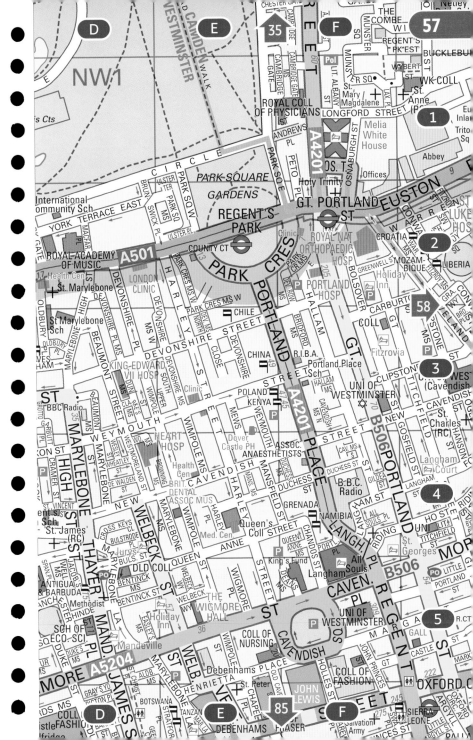

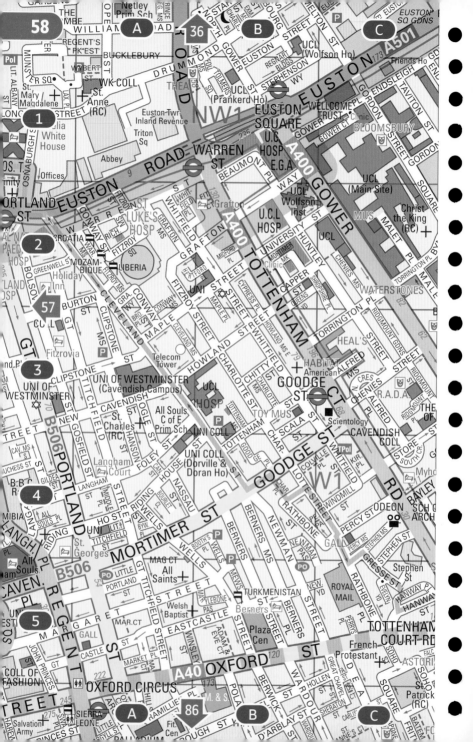

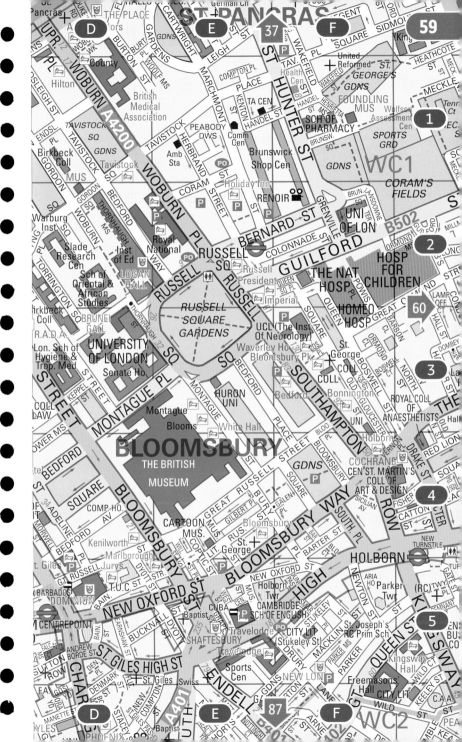

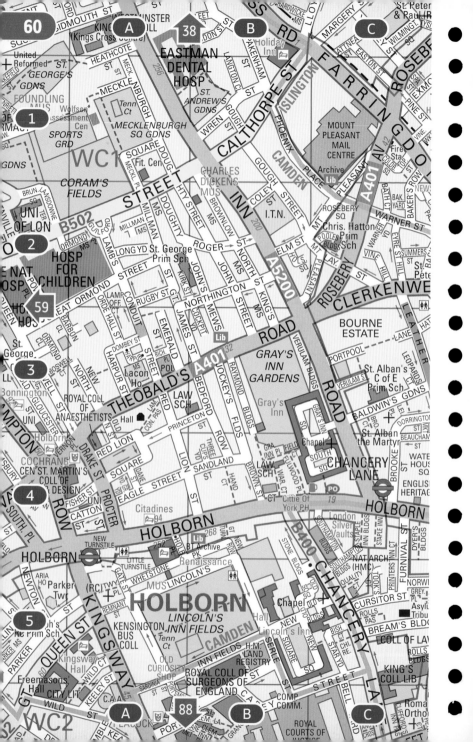

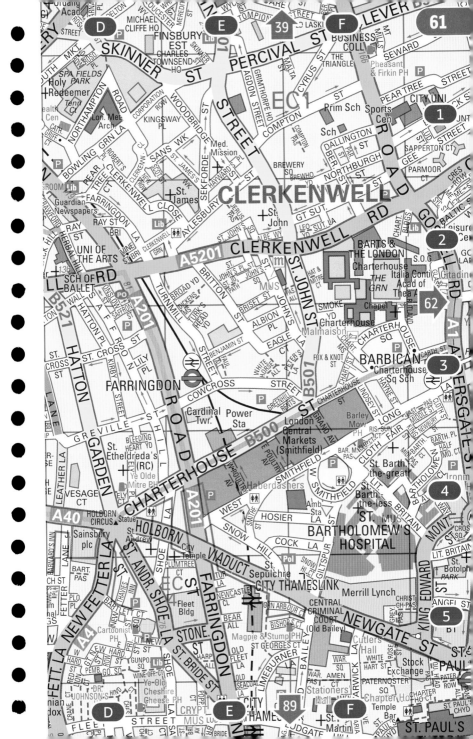

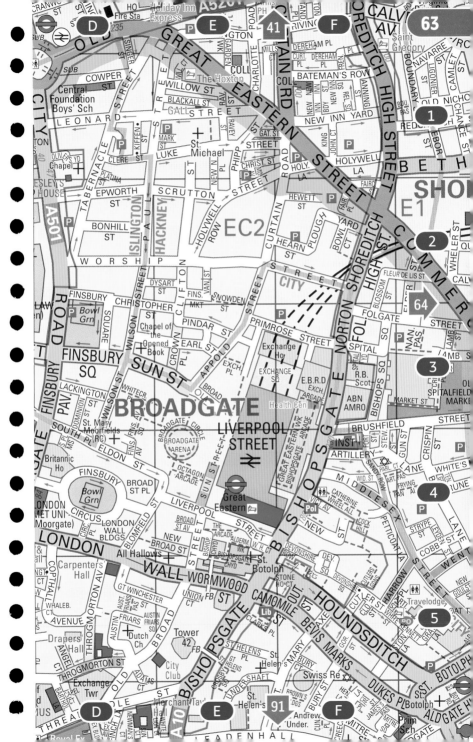

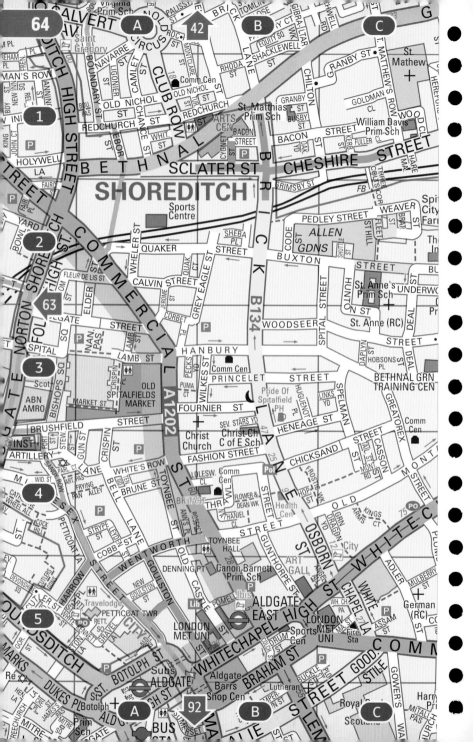

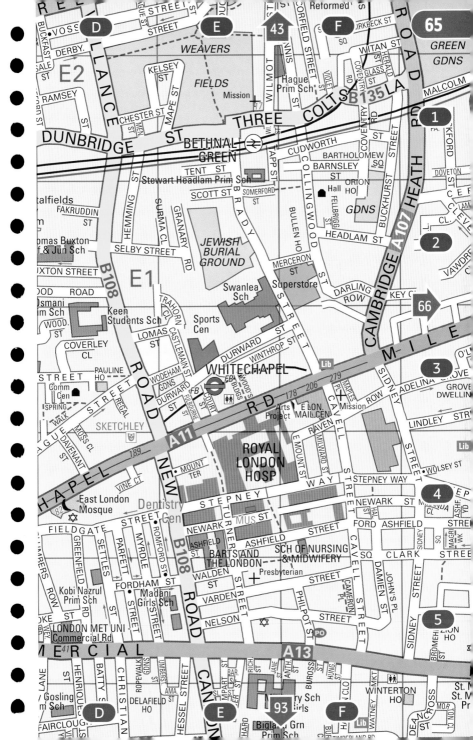

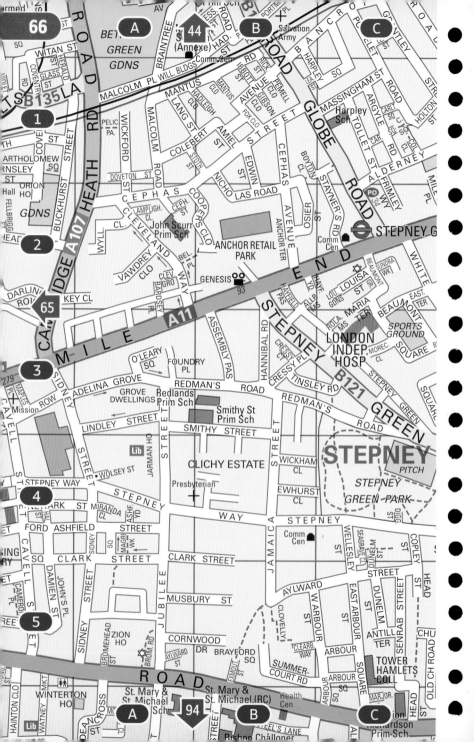

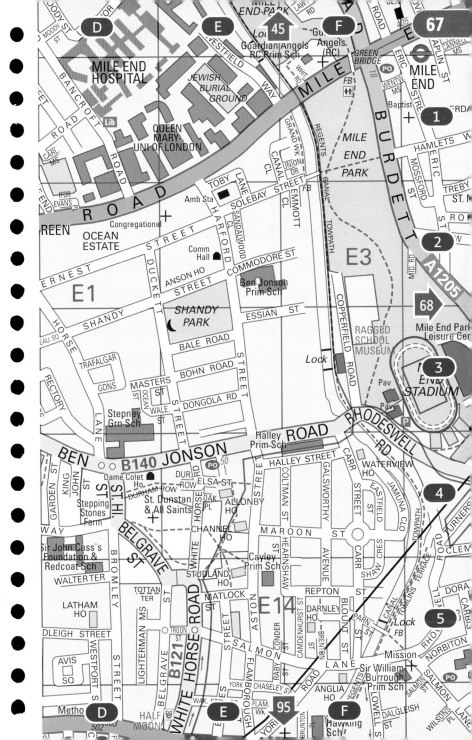

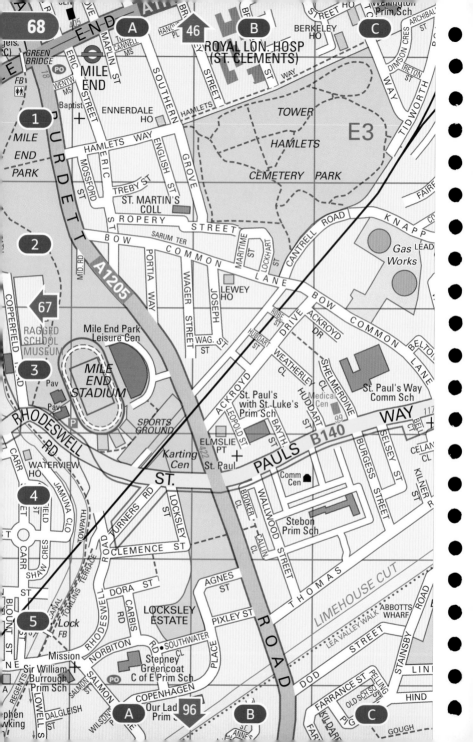

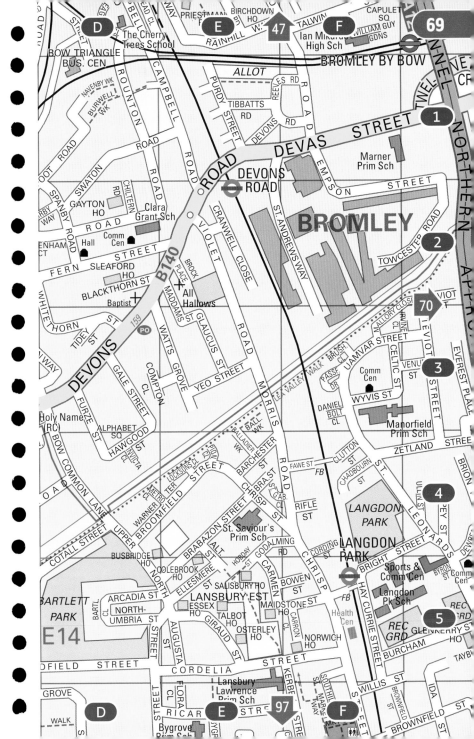

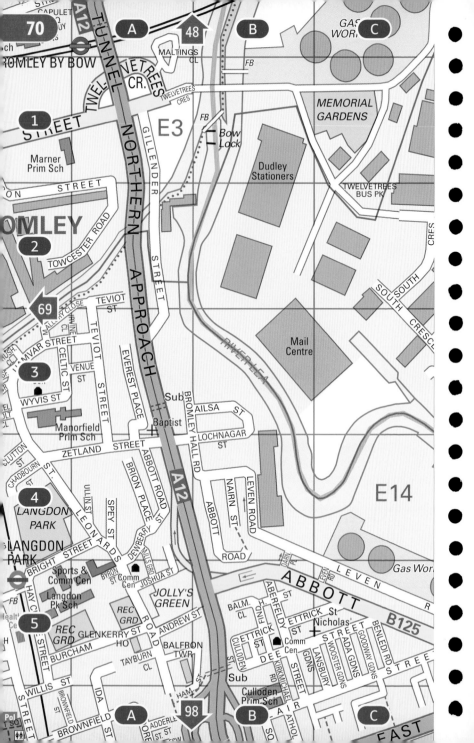

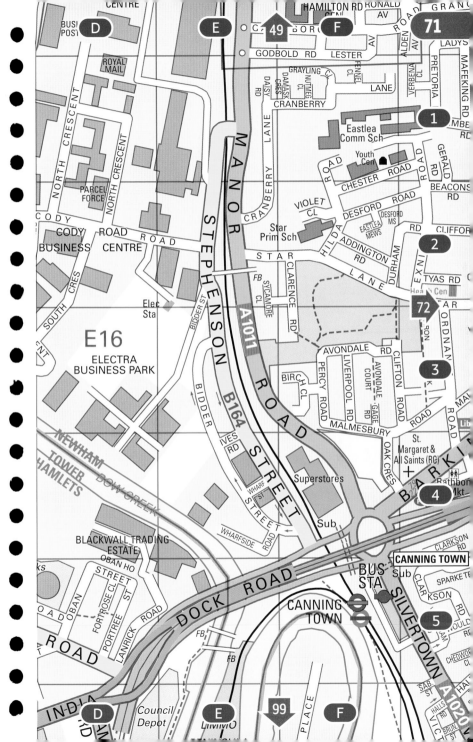

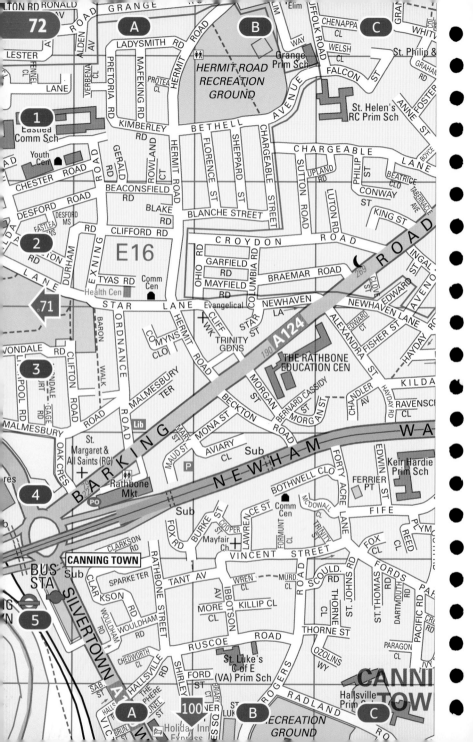

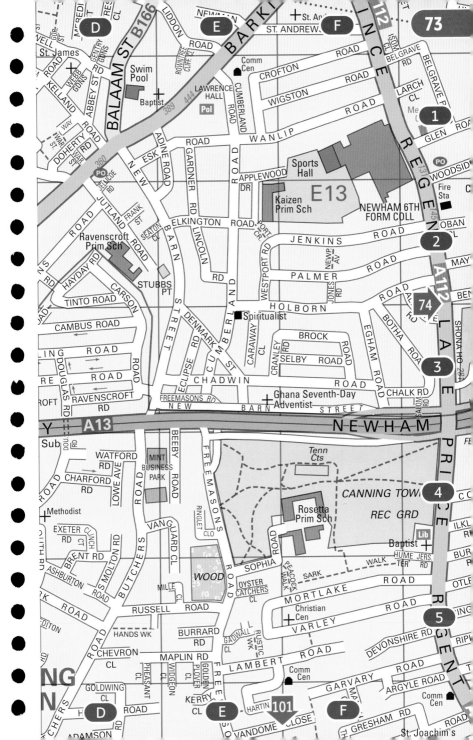

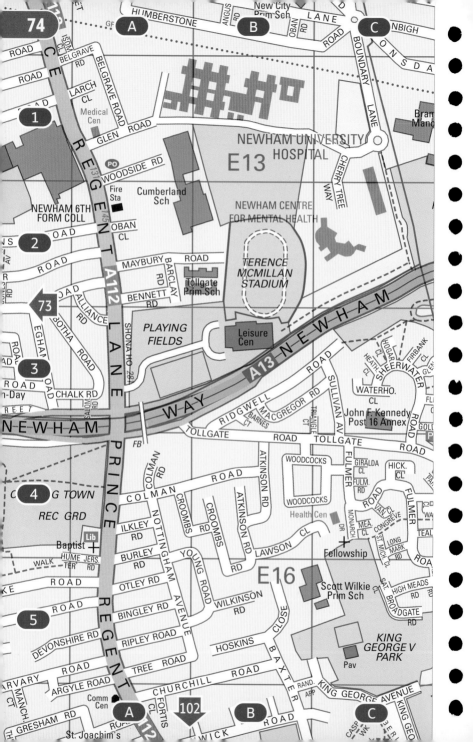

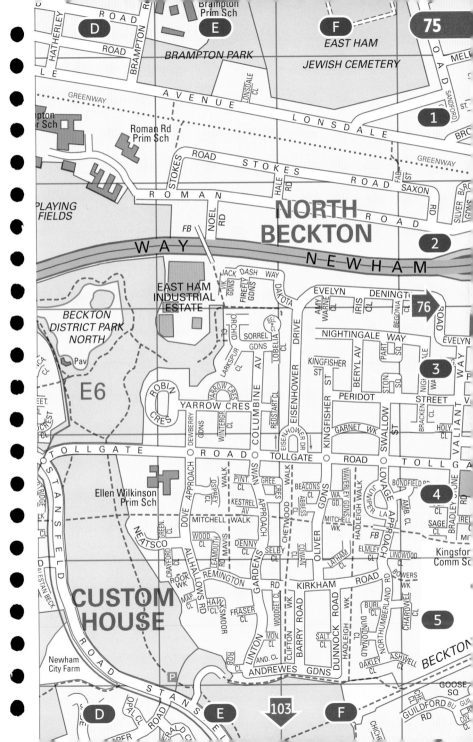

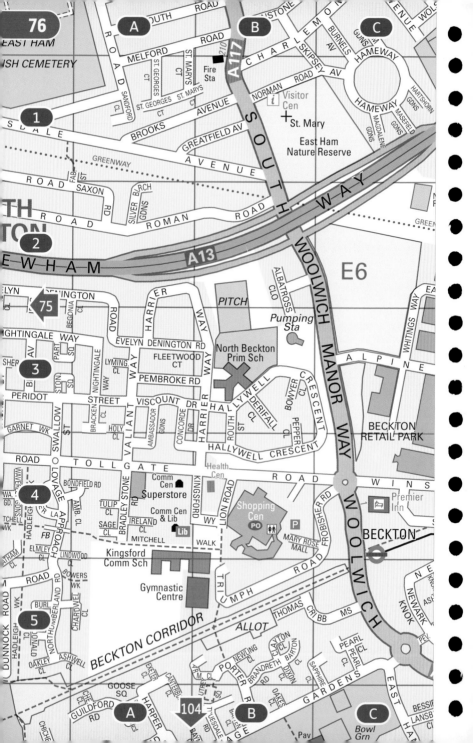

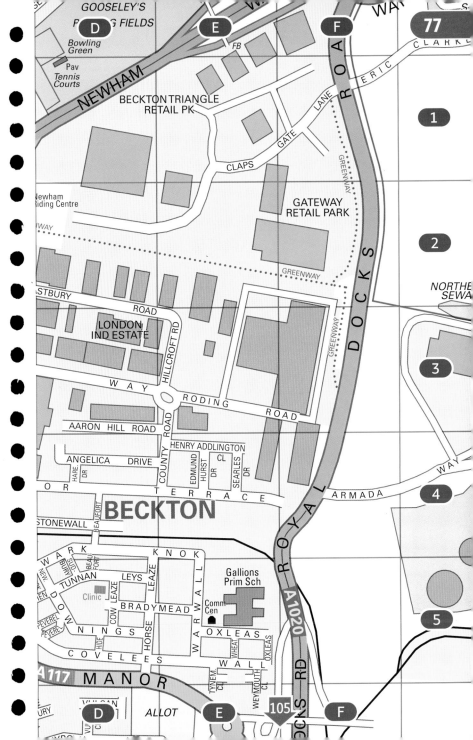

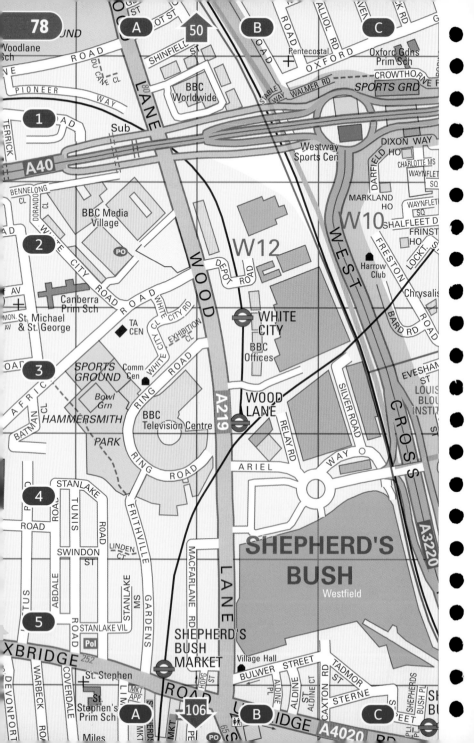

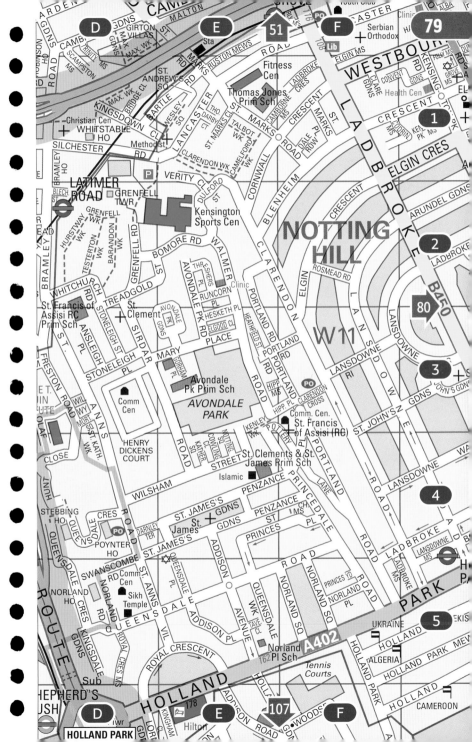

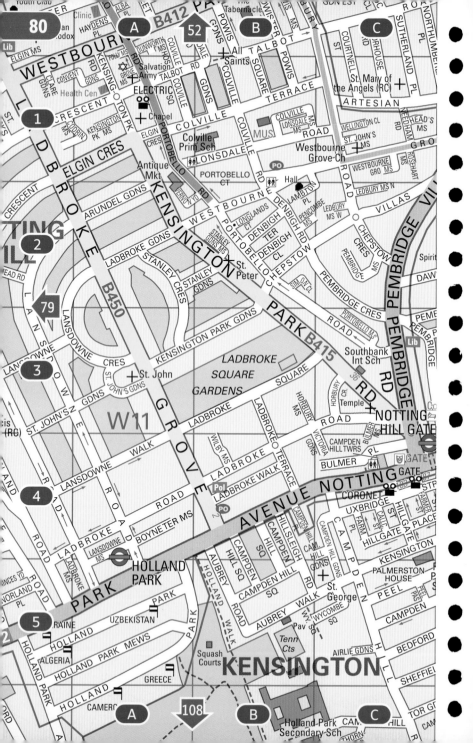

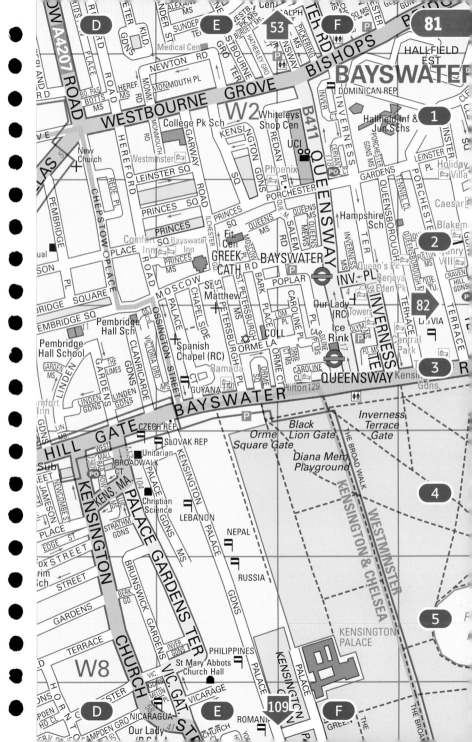

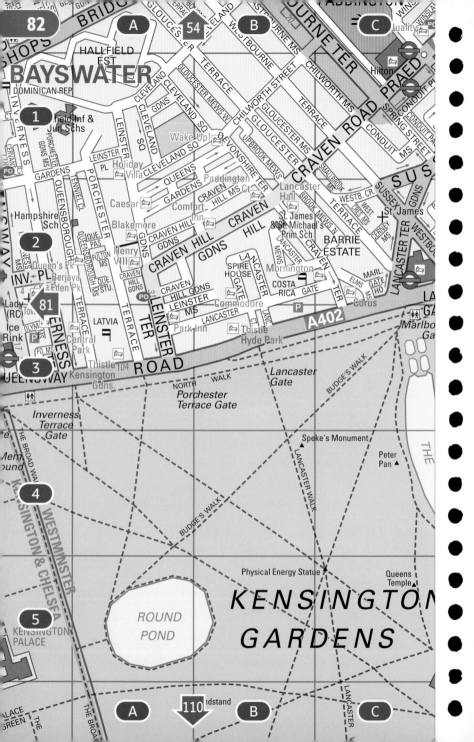

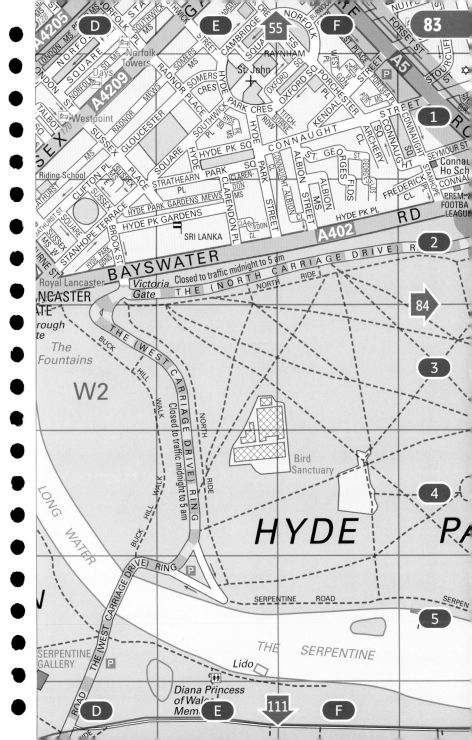

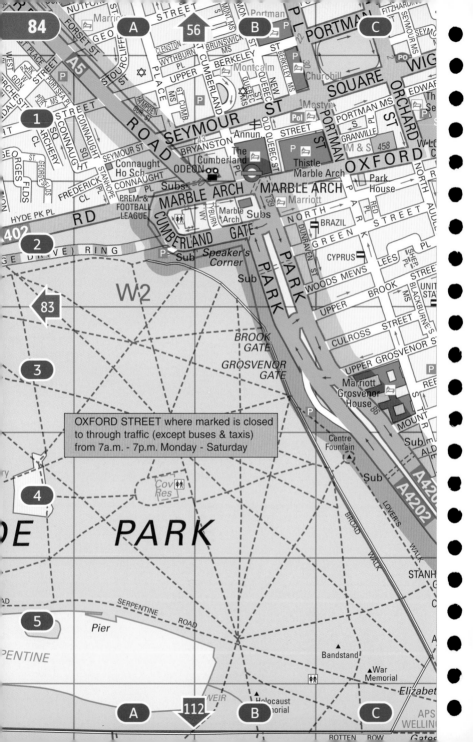

OXFORD STREET where marked is closed
to through traffic (except buses & taxis)
from 7a.m. - 7p.m. Monday - Saturday

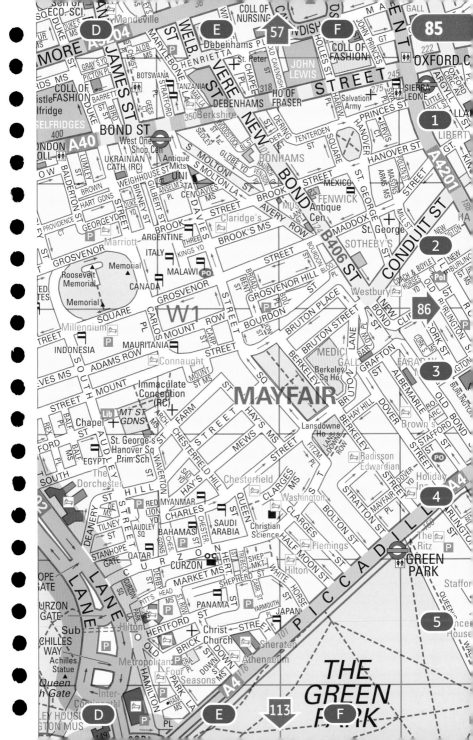

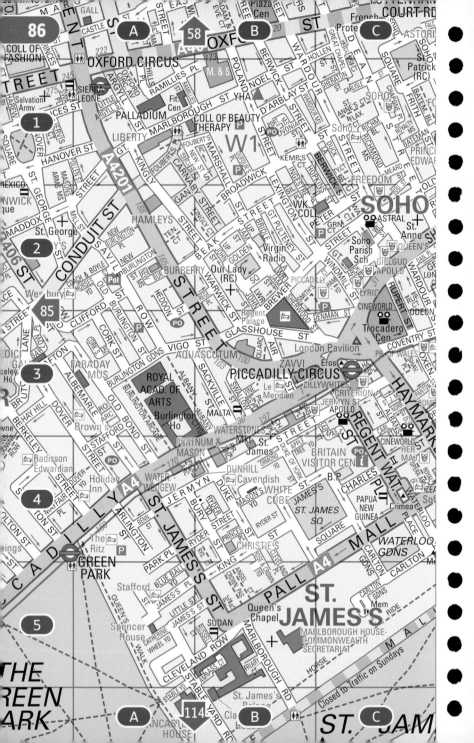

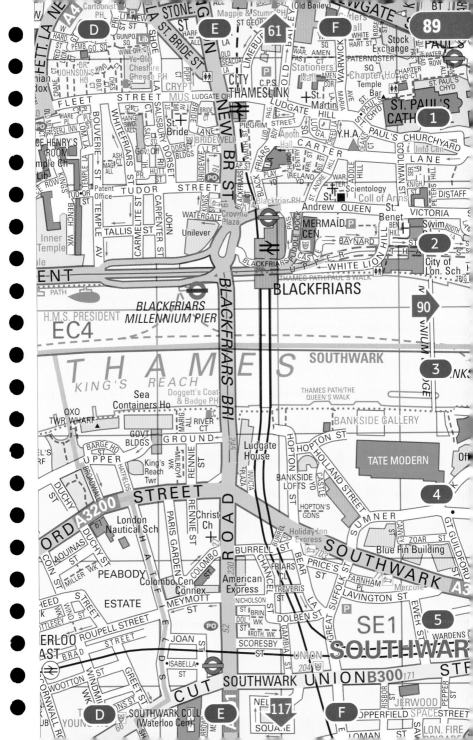

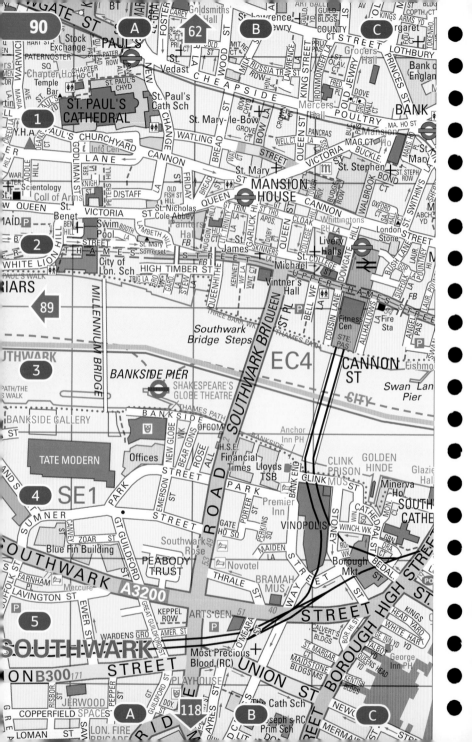

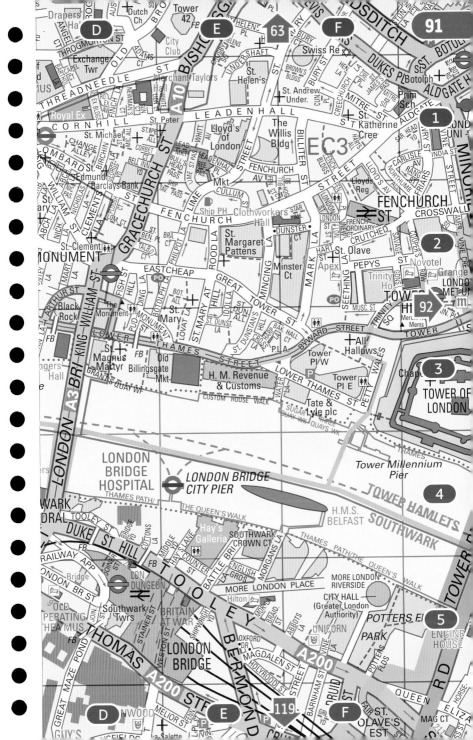

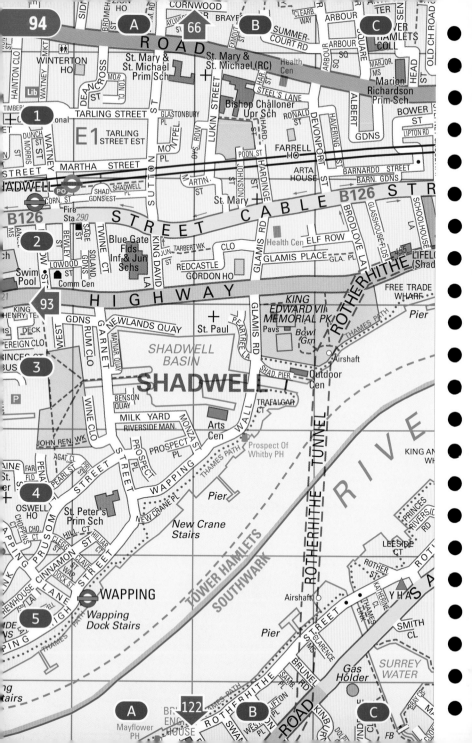

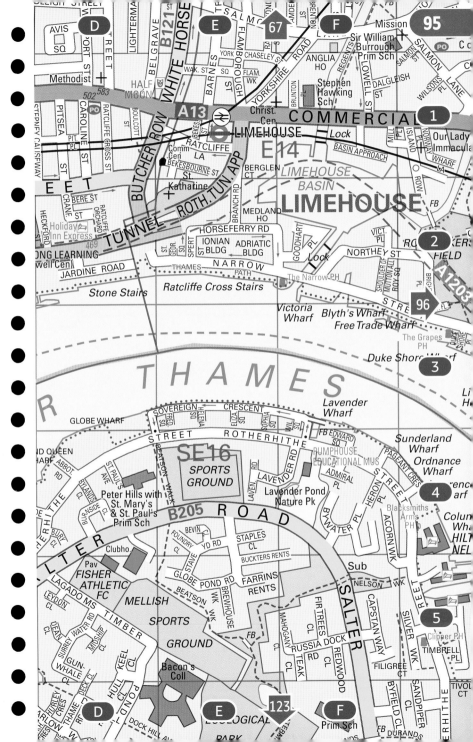

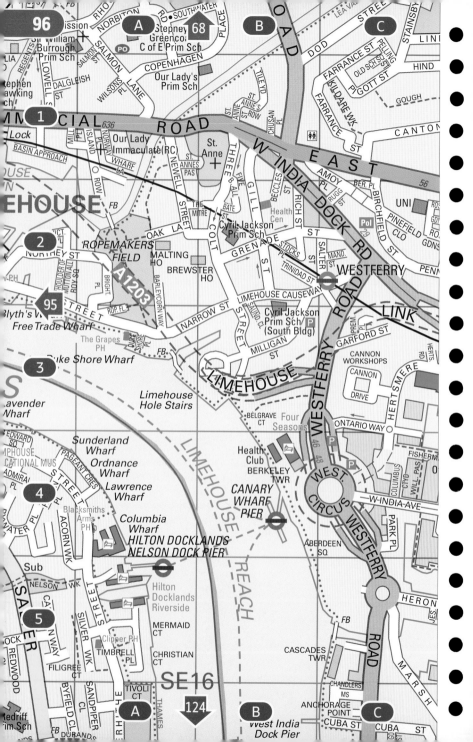

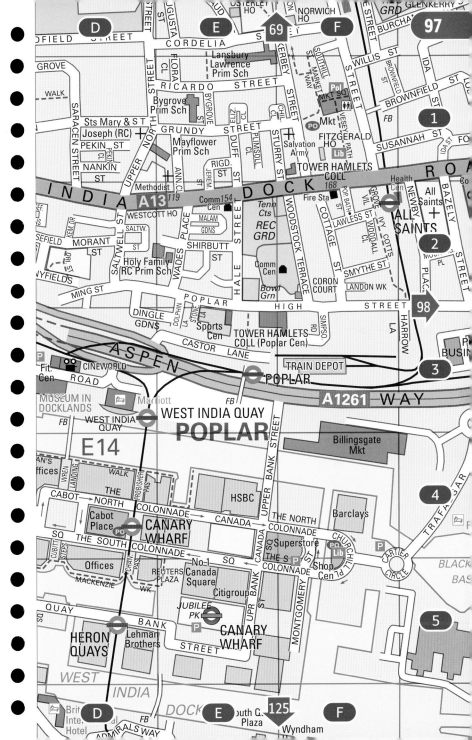

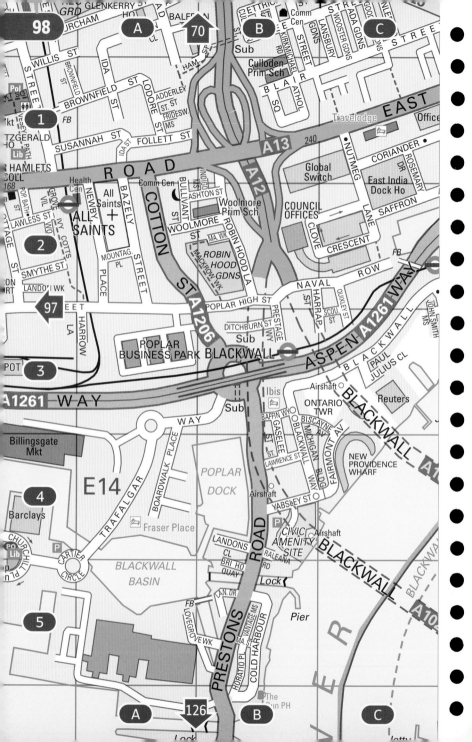

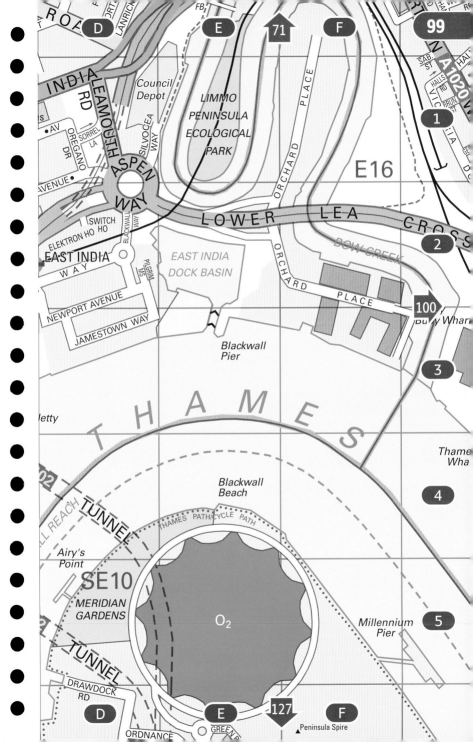

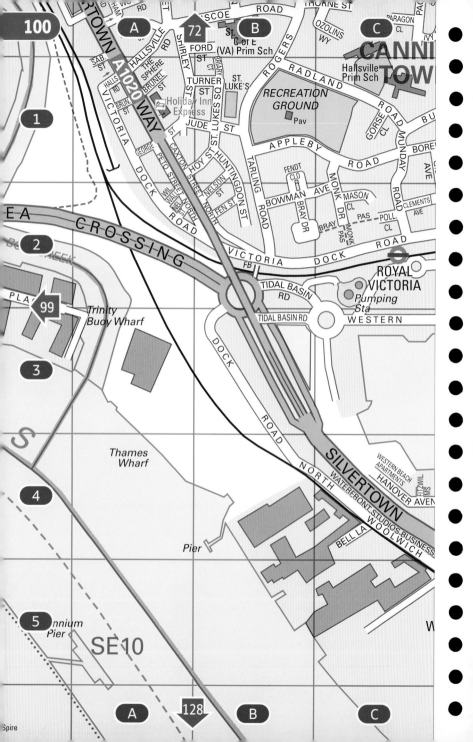

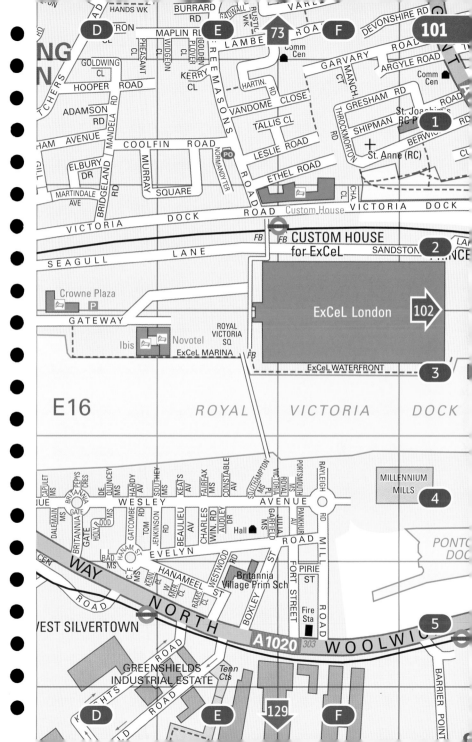

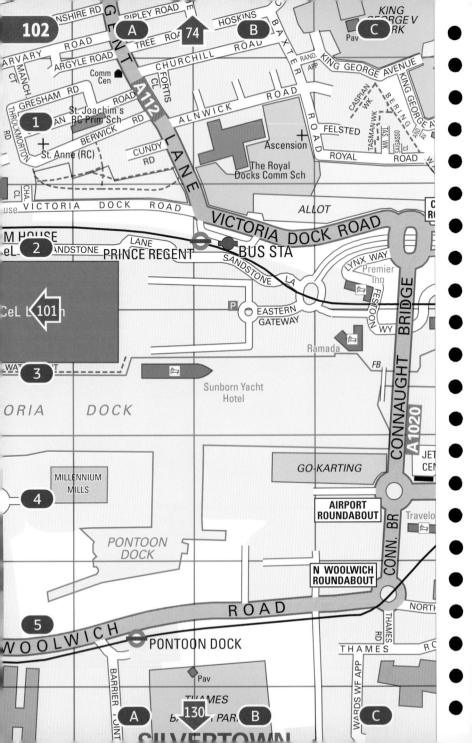

D Newham City Farm

E

F

75

1

JADE CL
OPAL CL
JASPER CL
AGATE CL
EMERALD CL

STANSFELD ROAD

RICHARD HOUSE DRIVE

Calverton Prim Sch

Hospice

CONNAUGHT ROUNDABOUT

FB

ALLOT

ROYAL ALBERT ROUNDABOUT

E6

BECKTON DISTRICT PARK SOUTH

GOOSE SQ

GUILDFORD RD

CHICHESTER CL

BOULT

YORK

STRAIT

ROYAL ———— ALBERT

ROYAL ALBERT

DOCKSIDE

ROAD

THE ROYALS BUSINESS PARK

Boathouse

London Regatta Centre

2 A-

BECKTON PA ROUNDABO

104

3 RC

E16

4 KIN

NTRE

dge

London City Airport

TERMINAL BUILDINGS

HARTMANN ROAD

CAMEL RD

DREW ROAD

CONNAUGHT ROAD

ORIENTAL RD

MUSIC HALL

WOOLWICH ROAD

Etap

AD

LONDON CITY AIRPORT

Drew Prim Sch DREW

Sub

PARKER ST
CONSTANCE RD
PAR CL
PO
WYTHES RD
SAVILLE RD
LEONARD ST

HARTMANN RD

P

P

N E W L A N D

HOLT RD
LORD ST
TATE RD
TATE RD
MU ST

Healtl Cen Comm Cen

5 RAW CL

A112

A L B E R T

F A C T O R Y

ROAD

THAMESIDE INDUSTRIA

131

D

E

F H WOOLW

NORTH WOOLW

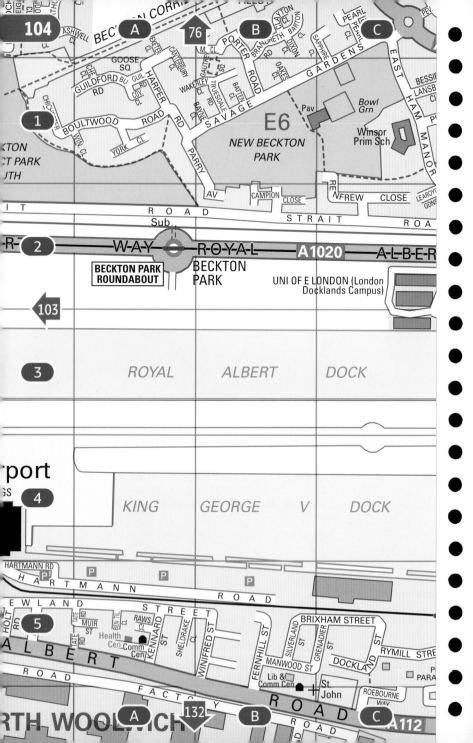

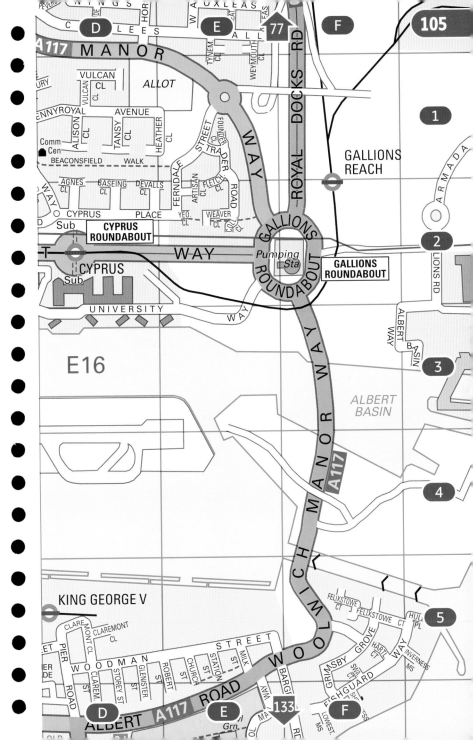

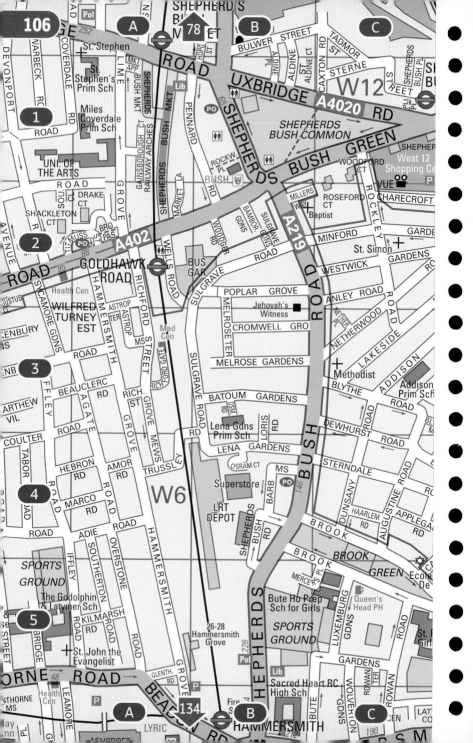

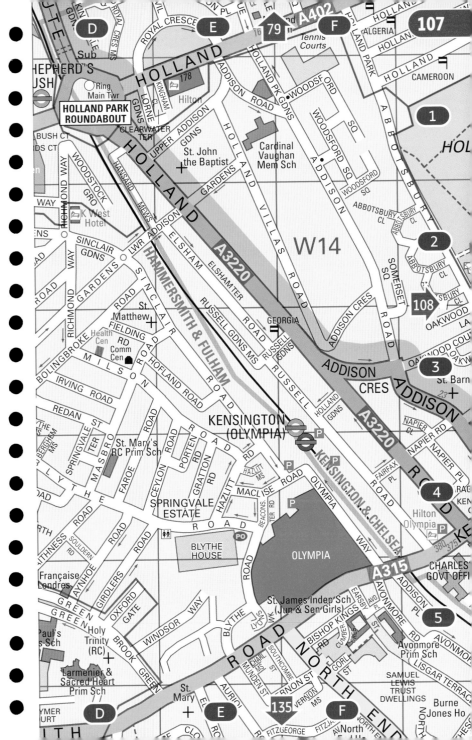

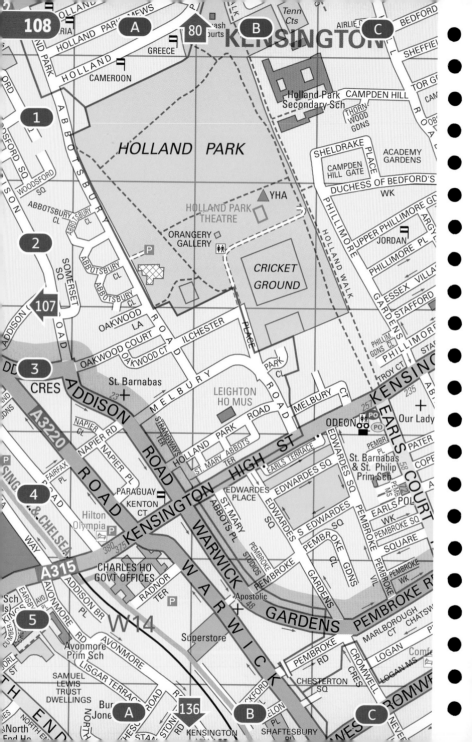

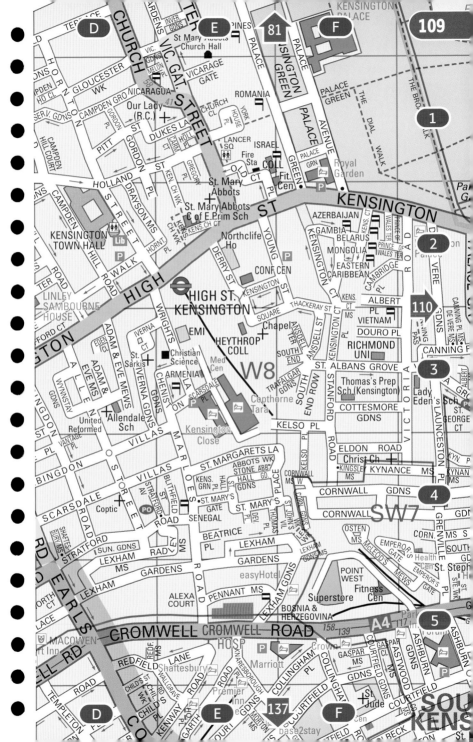

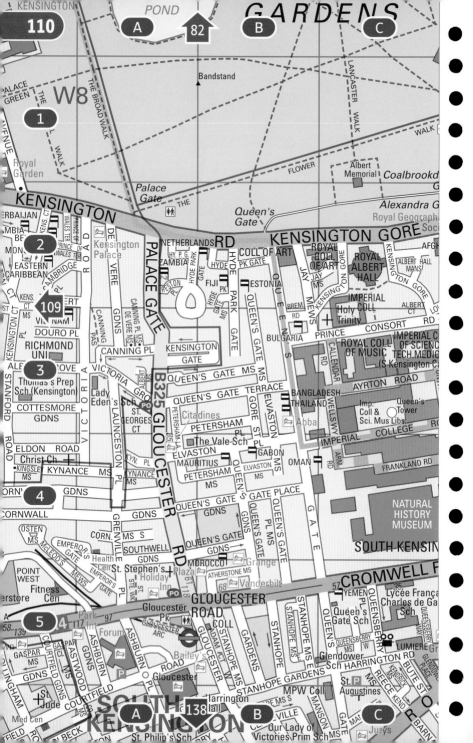

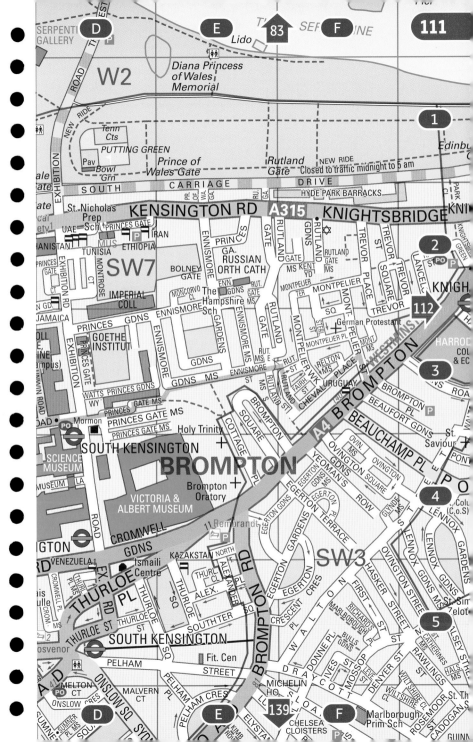

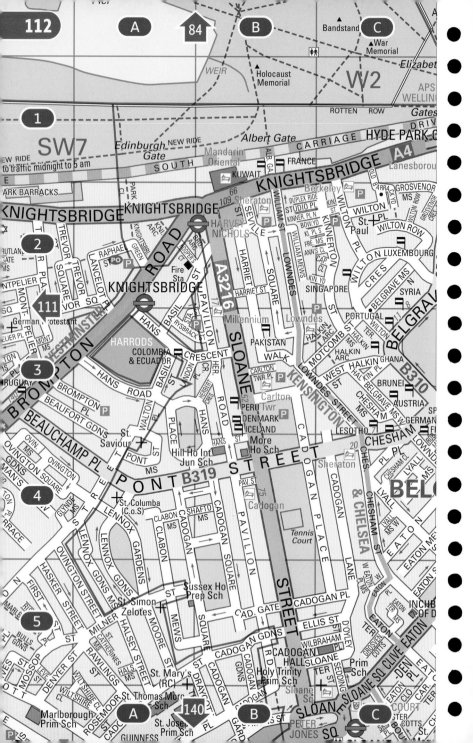

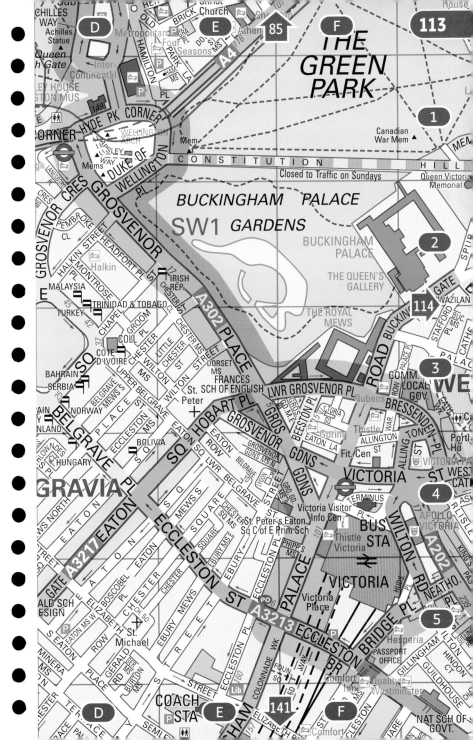

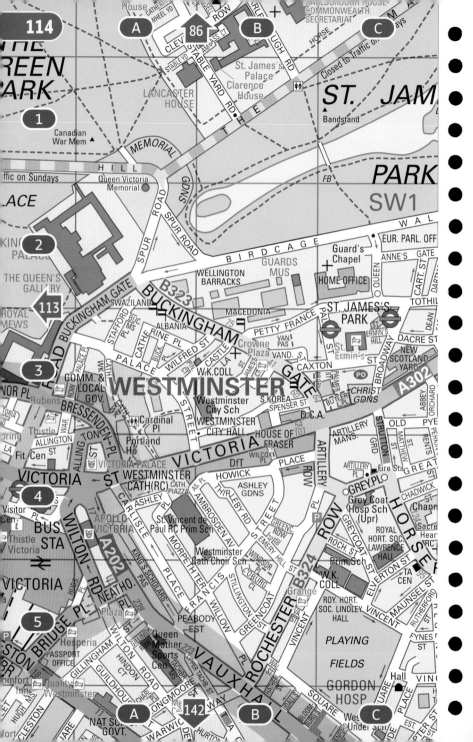

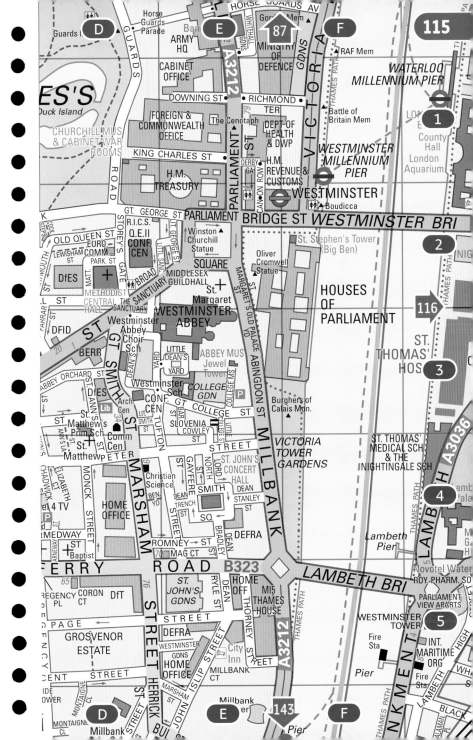

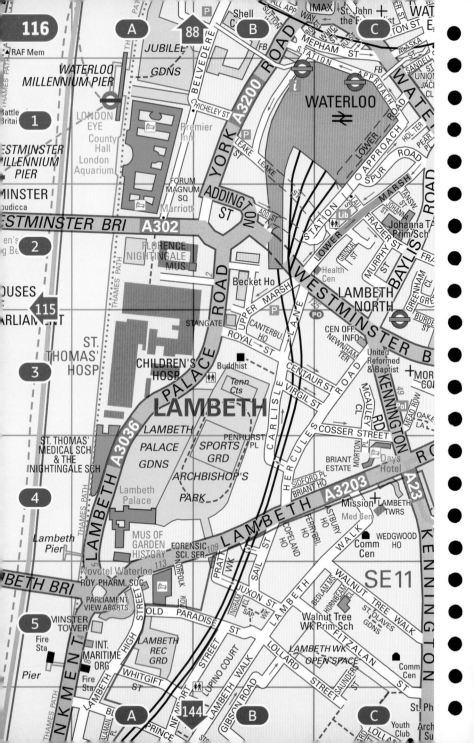

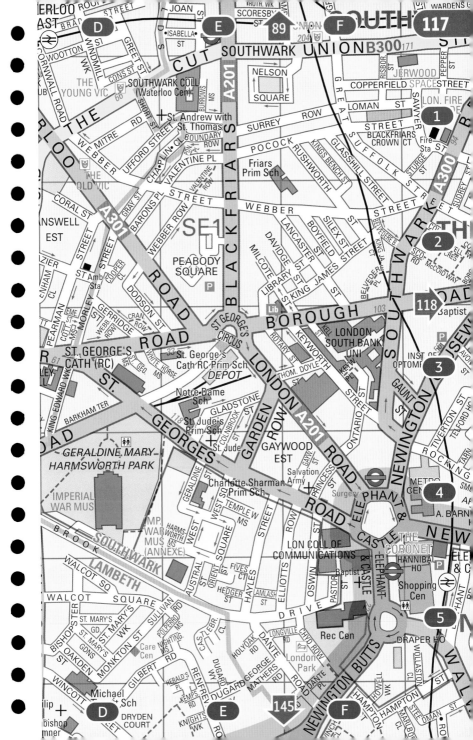

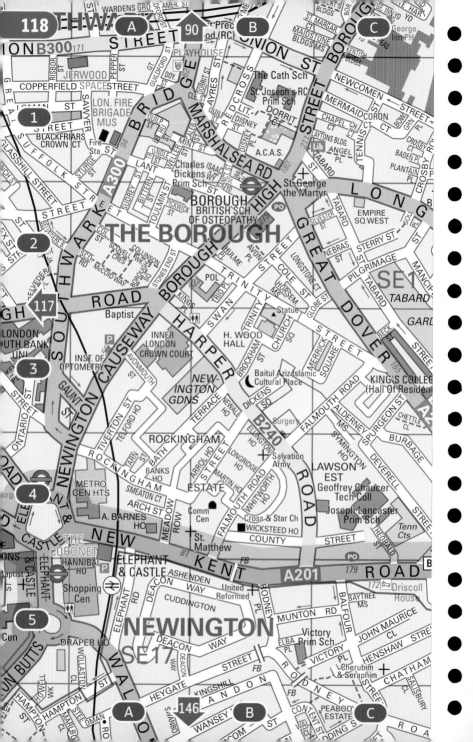

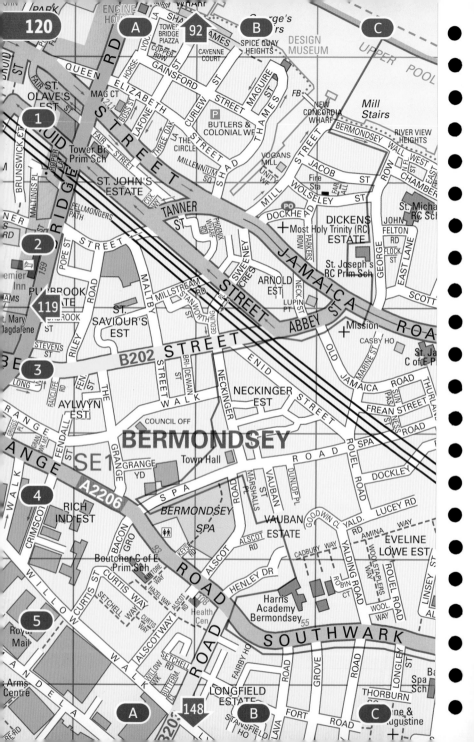

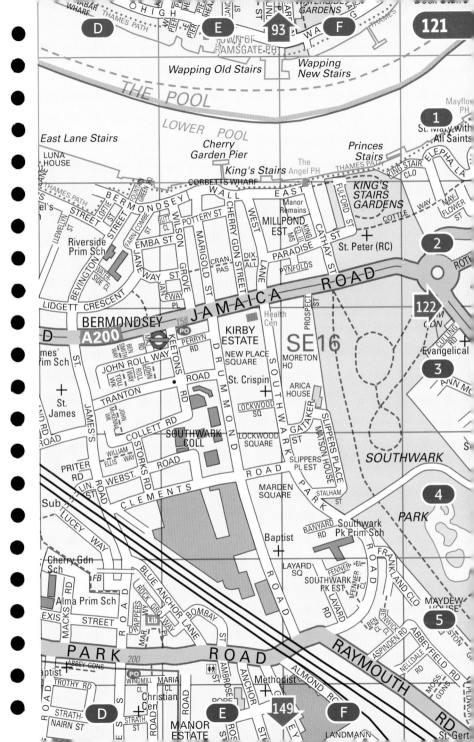

THAMES PATH

HIGH

D

E

93

F

Wapping Old Stairs

Wapping New Stairs

THE POOL

LOWER POOL

TOWN OF RAMSGATE PH

Mayflower PH

1

St. Mary with All Saints

East Lane Stairs

LUNA HOUSE

Cherry Garden Pier

The Angel PH

Princes Stairs

THAMES PATH

KING STAIR CLO

ELEPHA LA

2

ROTH

KING'S STAIRS GARDENS

COTTLE

WAY

MAYFLOWER ST

el's

THAMES PATH

BERMONDSEY STREET

LOFTIE ST

FARNCOMBE ST

FOUNTAIN GREEN

BUTLER CL

WILSON GROVE

POTTERY ST

MARIGOLD ST

WALL

CHERRY GDN STREET

CRANK PAS

DIX ALL

WEST LANE

EAST

Manor Remains

MILLPOND EST

KING MS MS

PARADISE

PYNFOLDS

CATHAY ST

FULFORD ST

St. Peter (RC)

Riverside Prim Sch

LLEWELLYN STREET

BEVINGTON

WATERSIDE CL

JANEWAY

EMBA ST

JANEWAY PL

LIDGETT CRESCENT

JAMAICA ROAD

PROSPECT ST

122

CDN

CULLING RD

Evangelical

3

ANN MO

BERMONDSEY

A200

D

158

PO

KIRBY ESTATE

Health Cen

SE16

ames' rim Sch

JOHN ROLL WAY

BEN SMITH WAY

JOHN ROLL WK

KEETONS RD

PERRYN RD

DRUMMOND

NEW PLACE SQUARE

St. Crispin

SOUTHWARK

MORETON HO

ARICA HOUSE

GATAKER ST

MATSON HOUSE

SLIPPERS PLACE

St. James

JAMES'S ST

TRANTON

JOHN MCKENNA WK

ROAD

LOCKWOOD SQ

ROTHEND RD

ROAD

COLLETT RD

STORKS RD

SOUTHWARK COLL

LOCKWOOD SQUARE

SLIPPERS PL EST

STALHAM ST

SOUTHWARK

PRITER RD

WILLIAM ELLIS WAY

WEBST.

ROAD

CLEMENTS

MARDEN SQUARE

PARK

4

PARK

LIN. ST

Sub

TUCEY WAY

Baptist

BANYARD RD

Southwark Pk Prim Sch

FRANKLAND CLO

Cherry Gdn Sch

FB

BLUE ANCHOR LANE

ROCK GRO WAY

PAPPERS WK

Lib

BOMBAY ST

LAYARD SQ

SOUTHWARK PK EST

FENNER CL

FENNER RD

LAYARD RD

MAYDEW HOUSE

5

BENWICK RD

ASPINDEN RD

Alma Prim Sch

MACKS RD

EXISS

STREET

MAR

ROAD

PARK

200

ROAD

RAYMOUTH RD

ABBEYFIELD RD

NELLDALE RD

MOSS GDNS

aptist

TROTHY RD

STRATH NAIRN ST

D

WINDMILL CL

MARIA CL

Christian Cen

STRATH. ROAD

MANOR ESTATE

E

AMBROSE

ANCHOR ROAD

149

Methodist

ALMOND RD

LEY

F

LANDMANN

St Gert

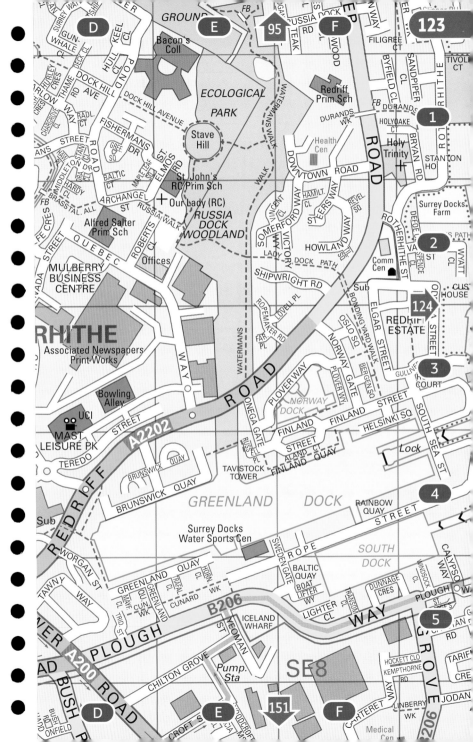

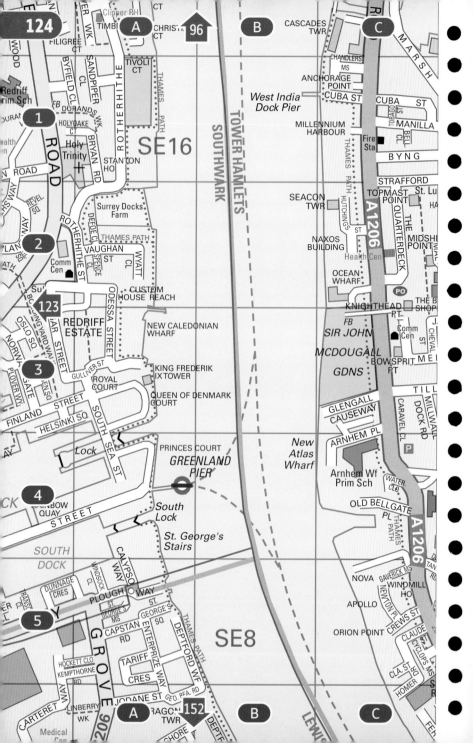

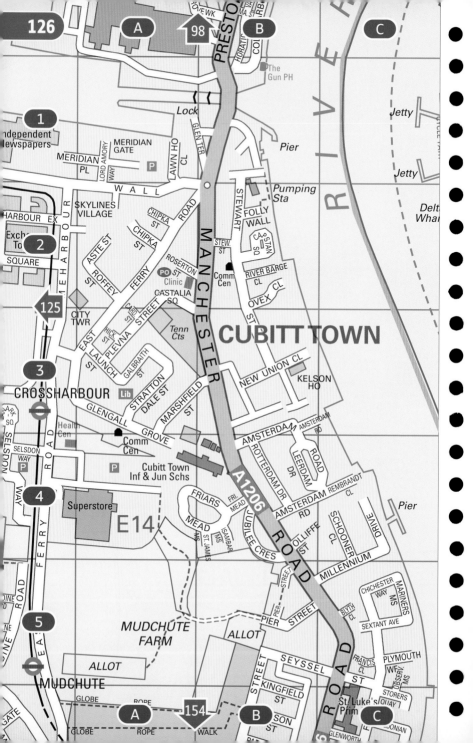

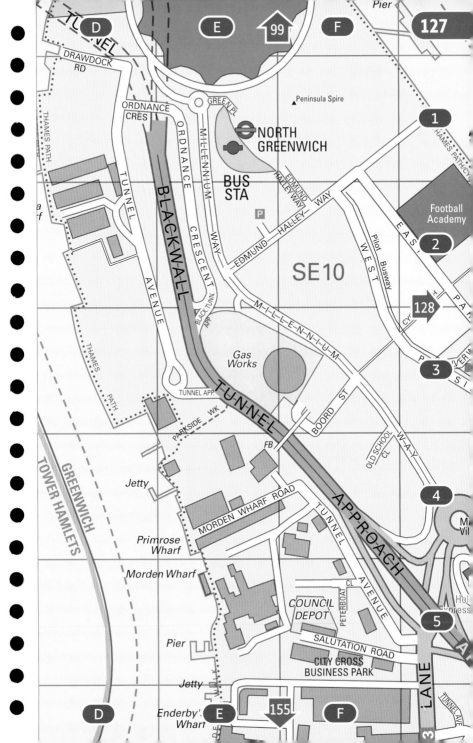

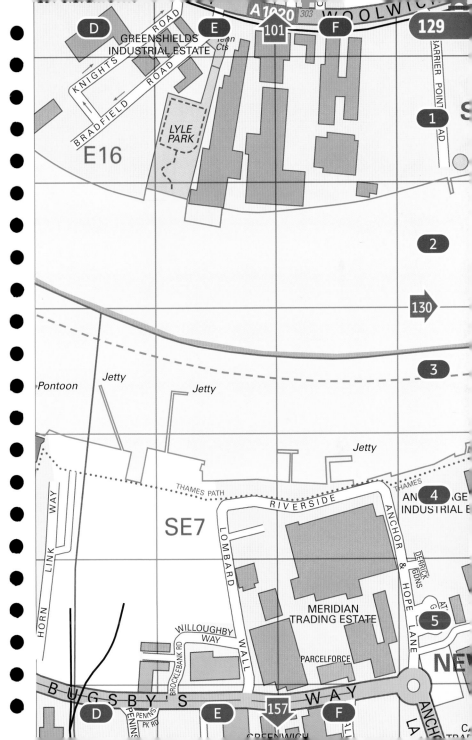

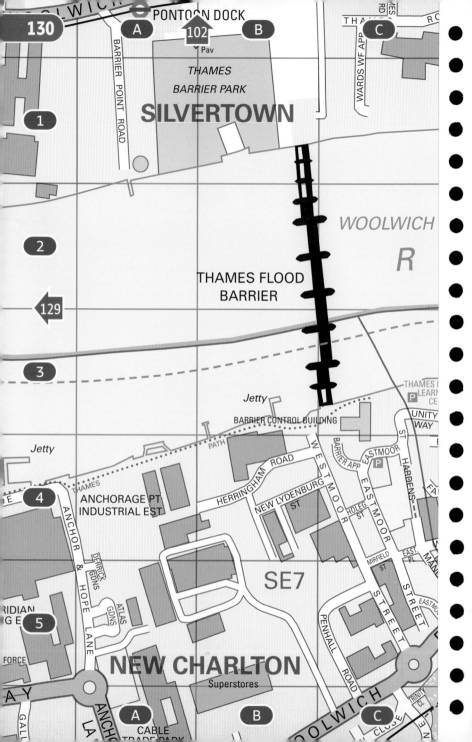

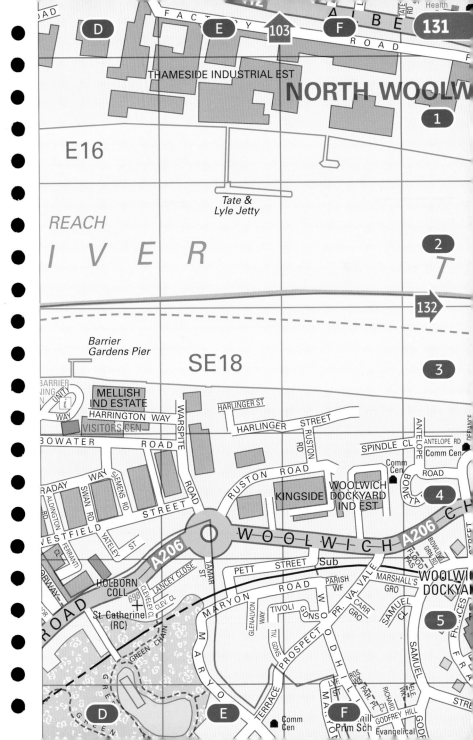

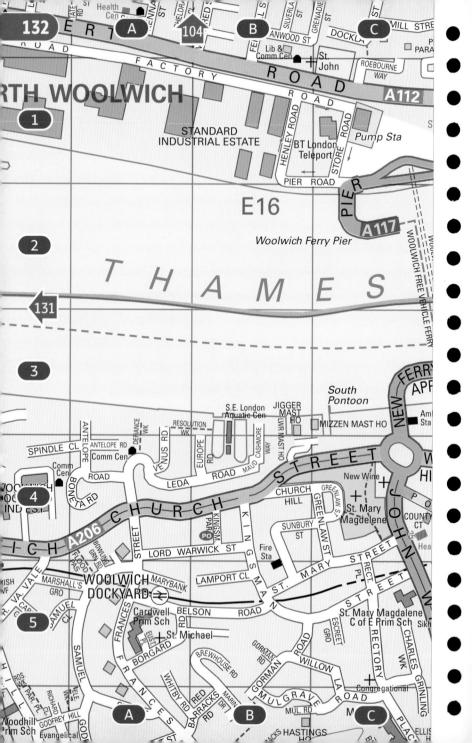

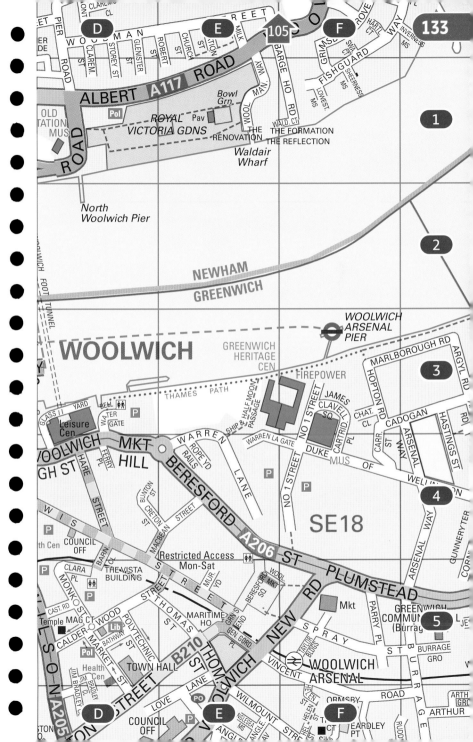

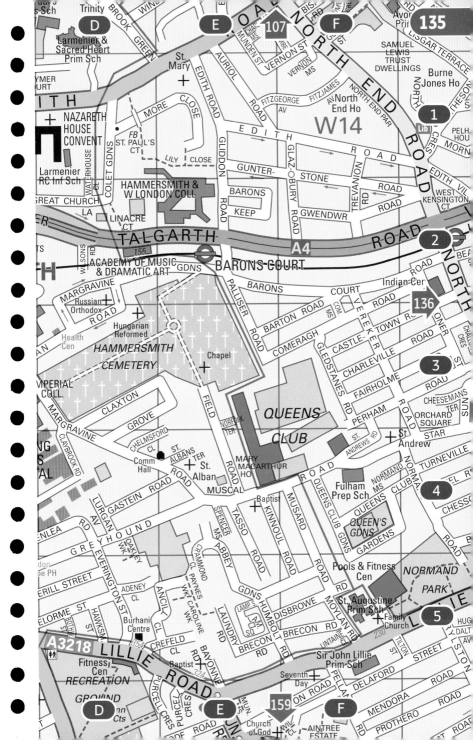

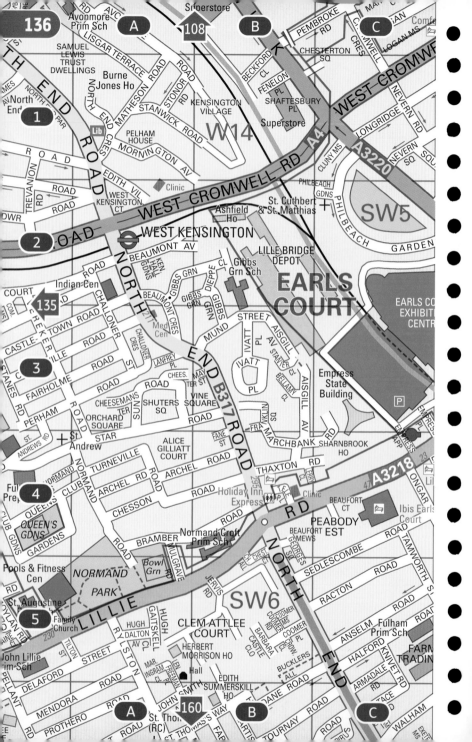

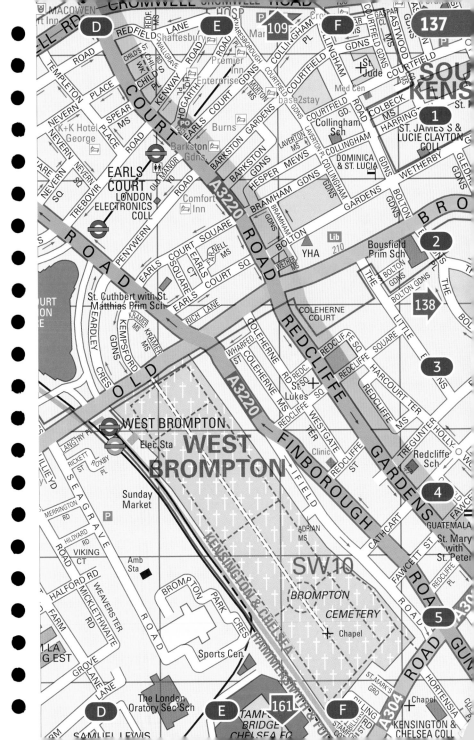

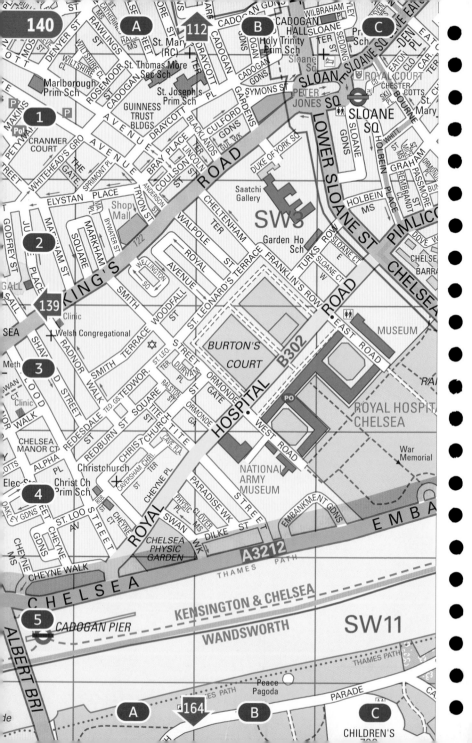

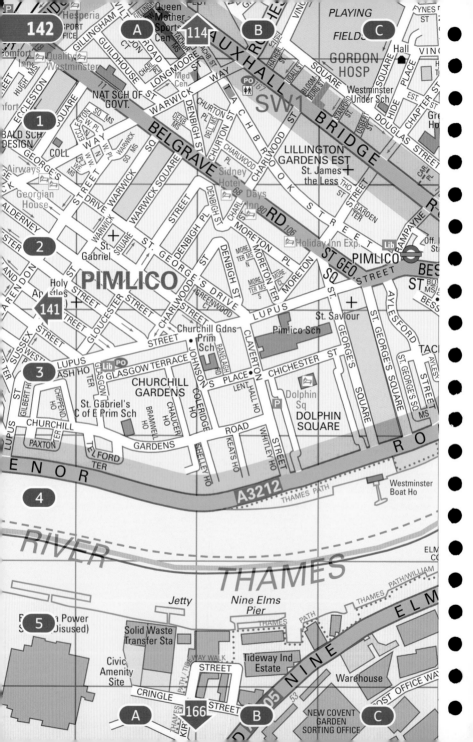

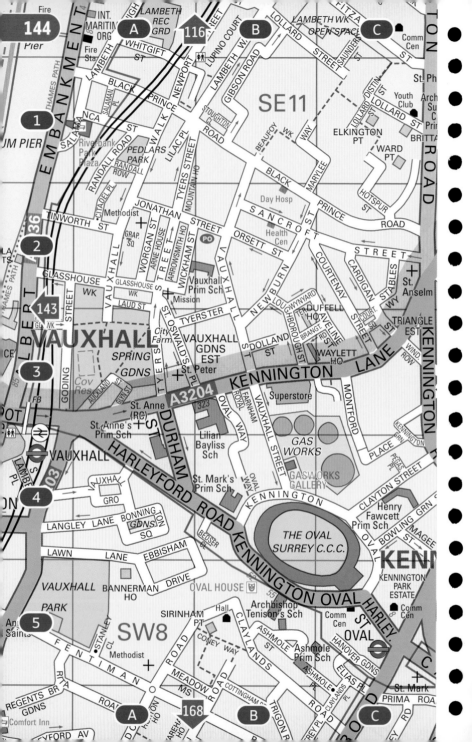

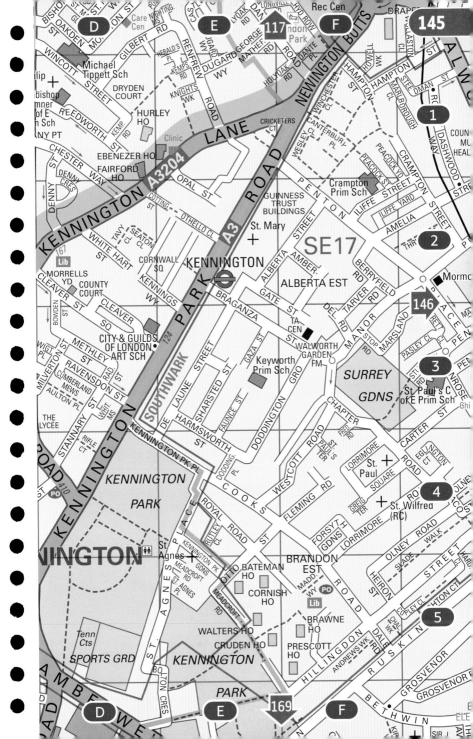

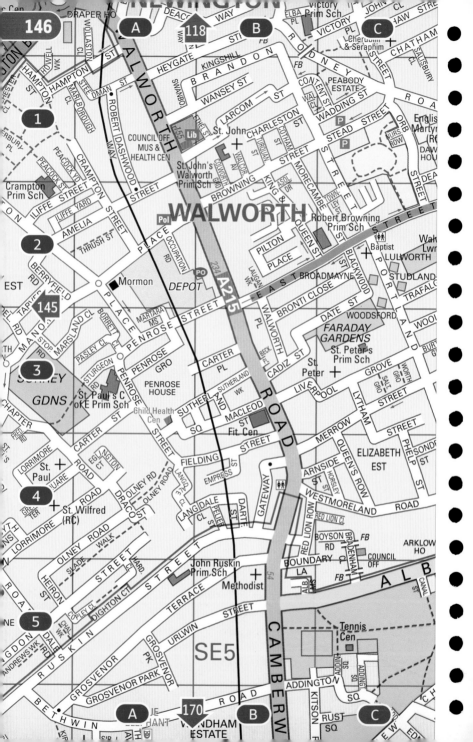

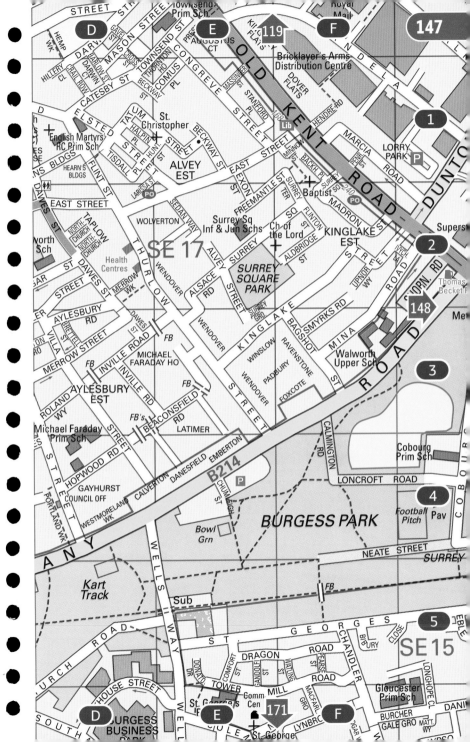

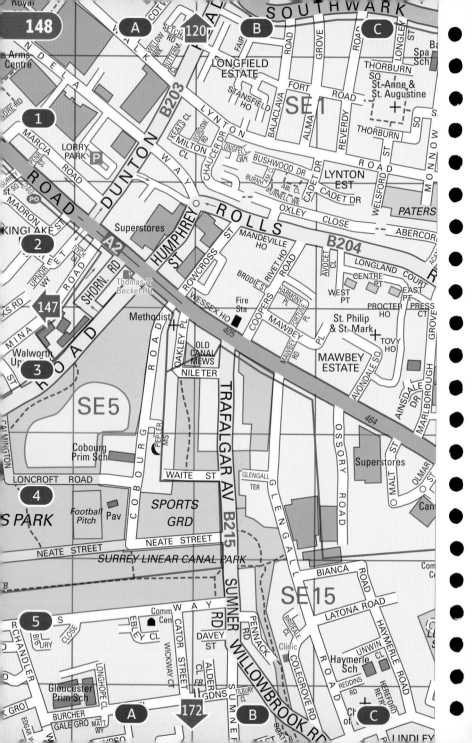

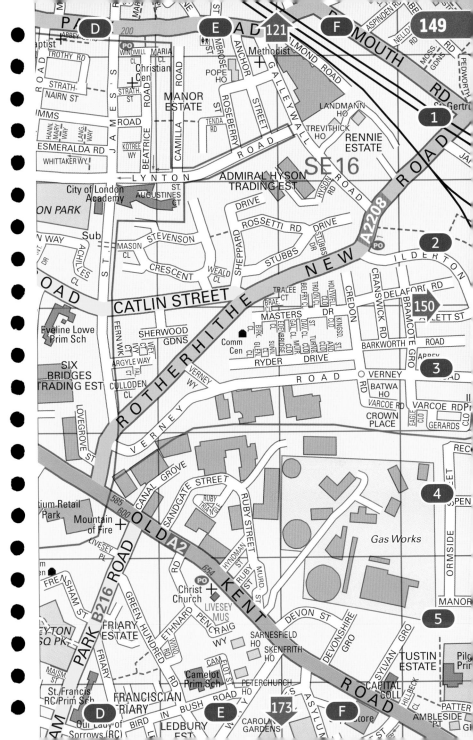

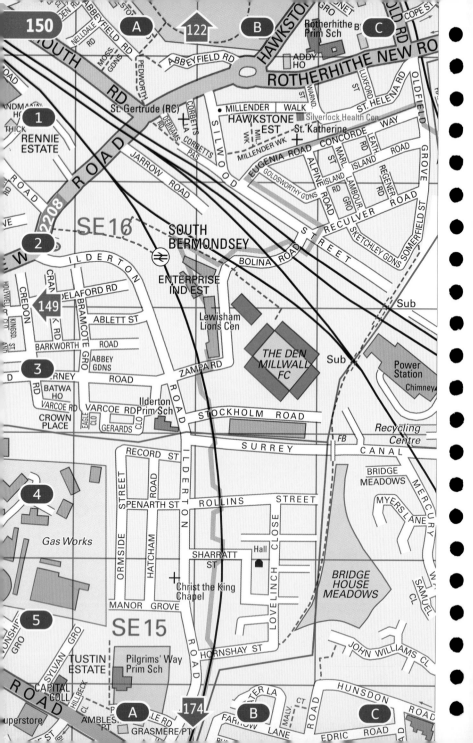

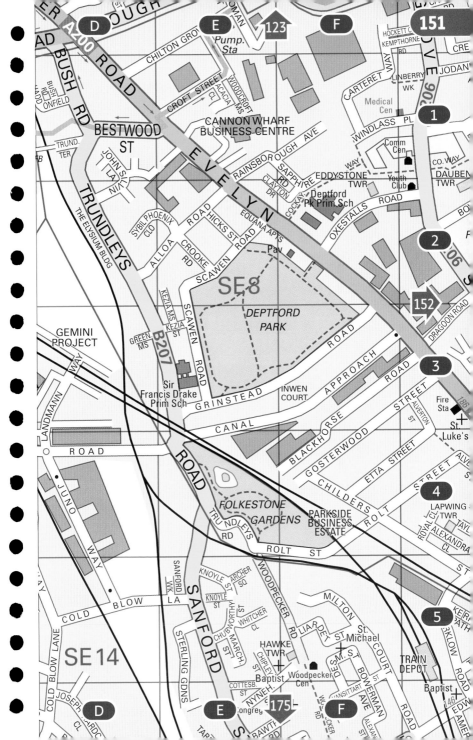

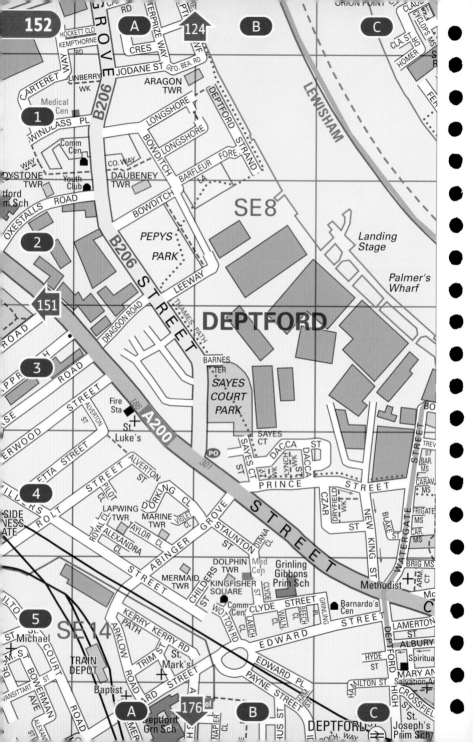

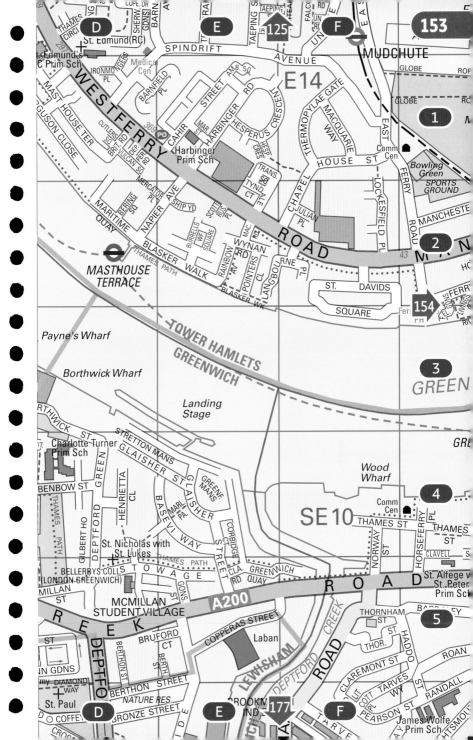

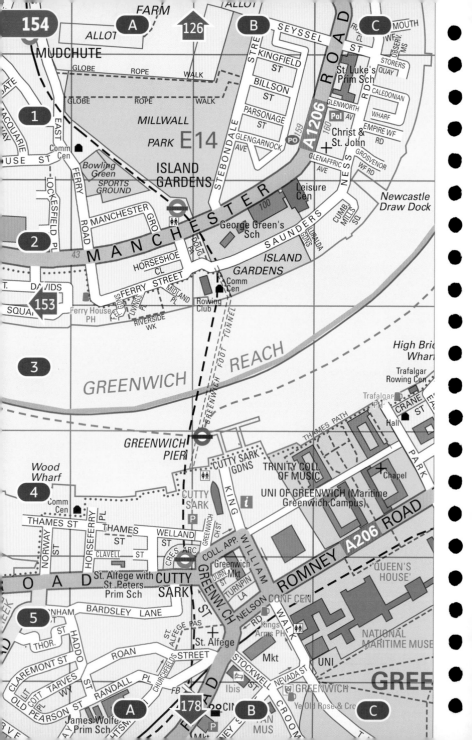

Pier

SALUTATION ROAD
CHAPEL'S
BUSINESS PARK

LANE

Jetty

Enderby's
Wharf

Piper's
Wharf

TUNNEL AVE

MAURITIUS ROAD

1

BLACKWALL A2

AZOF STREET

CHRISTCHURCH STREET

DAVERN CLO

CLO

ELIUS

HEV

TWYCROSS
Christchurch MS
C of E Prim Sch

BELLOT STREET

CALLISONS
PL

FLAVELL MS

ARMITAGE ROAD

Granite
Wharf

CADET
PL

DERWENT
ST

KOSSOL ST

BELLOT ST

BELLOT
GDNS

COMMERELL ST

St. Joseph's
RC Prim Sch

HATCLIFFE
ST

2

GL

Lovell's
Wharf

PATH

PELTON

ROAD

WAY

WHITWORTH ST

+
St.
Joseph
(RC)

CHRISTCHURCH

PO

WOO

VANBRUGH

156

BALLAST
QUAY

ENDERBY
ST

CARADOC
ST

HADRIAN ST

Comm
Cen

United

+
191

ROMERO
ST

COLOMB

P

3

CALVE

BANNING

BRADDYLL
ST

THORPL

GIBSON R

KING WILLIA

dge

LASSELL

HOSKINS

STREET

ORLOP
ST

MELL

WOOL
WK

ROAD

TYLER
ST

EARLSWOOD

WALNUT TREE
RD

ANNA

Power
Sta

HIGH
BRIDGE

WOOLWICH ST

GREENWICH

WOODLAND
GRO

HILL

Meridian
Prim Sch

TRENCHARD
ST

A206

TUSKAR
ST

WOODLANDS

FROBISHER
ST

STREET

TYLER ST

WOODLANDS PK RD

DINS

The
Arches
Leisure
Cen

AXIS
CT

WAL.
TR. RD

STREET
PK

RD

ANNA

STNEY
LD

ST

P

TRAFALGAR

CORVETTE
SQ

THALIA
CL

TRAFALGAR
GRO

PARK STREET

WOODLAND CRES

MAZE HILL

LEMMON RD

NORFOLK
HO

WOODLAND
HTS

RESTELL CL

4

U

FEATHE
ROW

RS PLACE

VISTA

TOM SMITH
CL

MAZE
HILL

LASSETER
PL

VANBRUGH

PARK

ULUNDI ROAD

HILL

SE3

SE 10

AVENUE

MAZE HILL

SE3

5

CROSS

ONE TREE
HILL

WESTCOMBE

PARK

FOYLE

VANBRUGH

NWICH

UM

LOVERS

GREENWICH

179

WALK

HIGHMORE RD

John Roan
Sec Sch

ROYAL OBSERVATORY

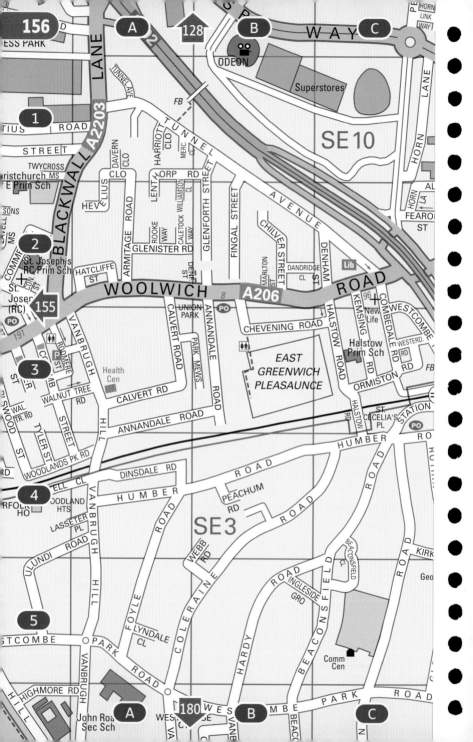

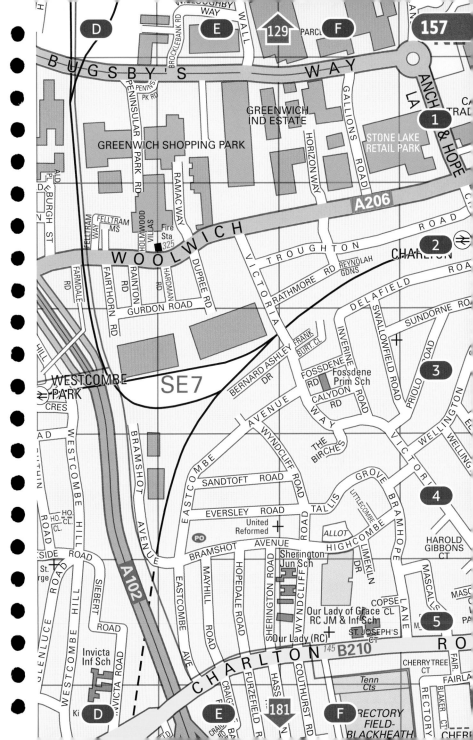

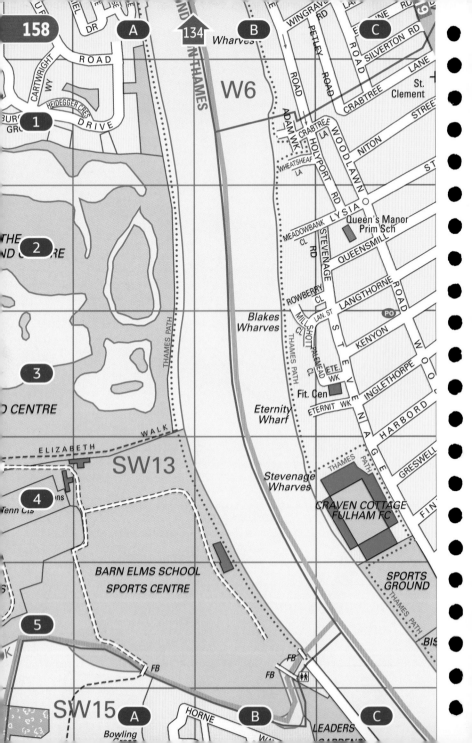

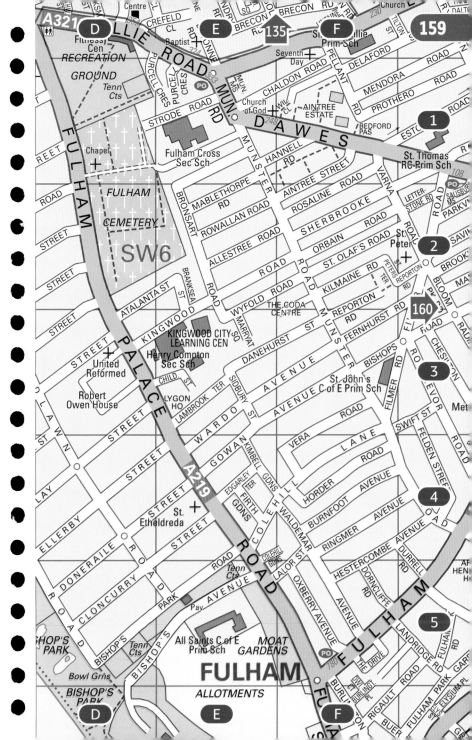

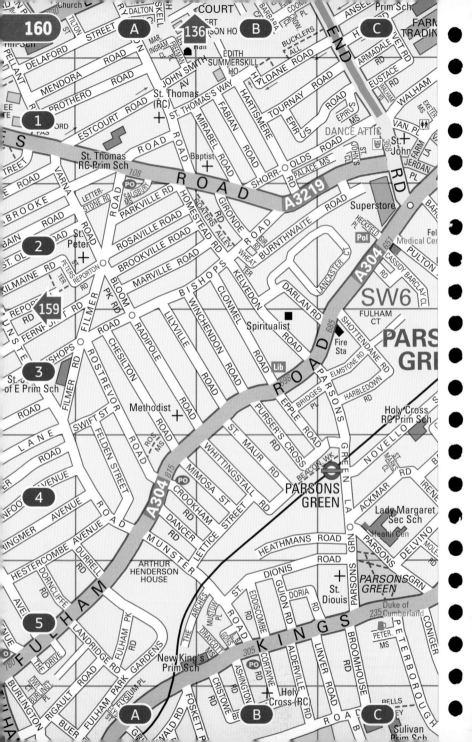

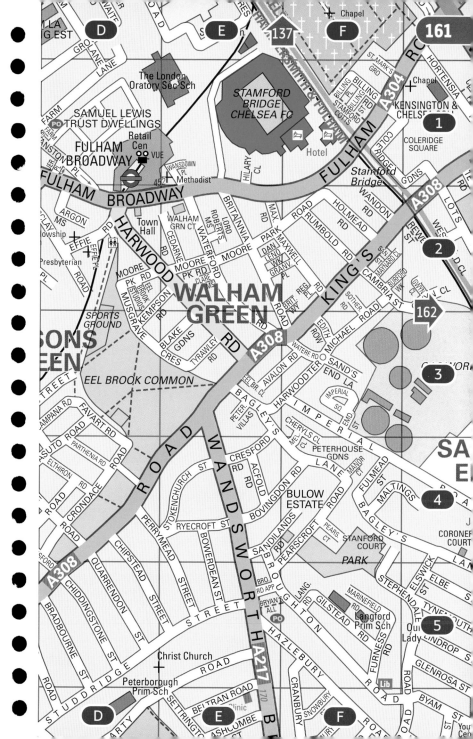

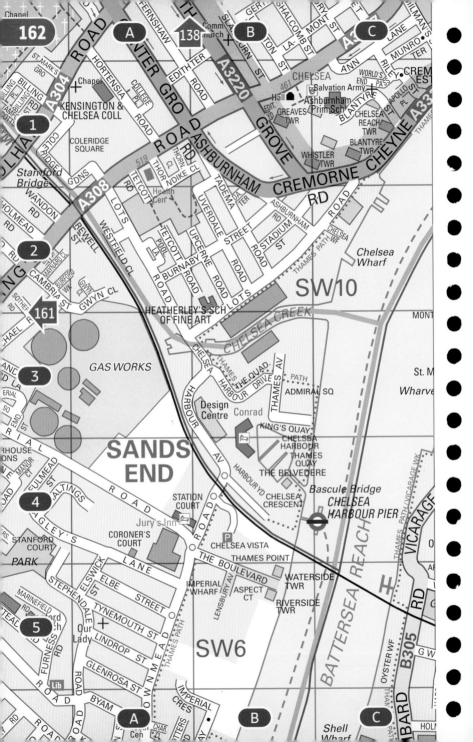

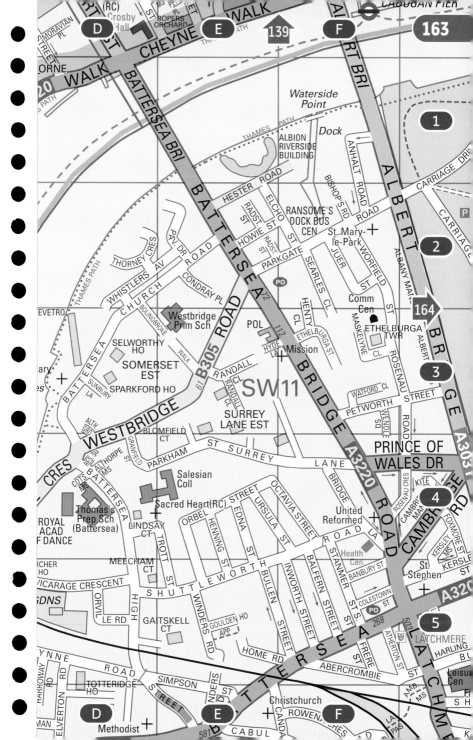

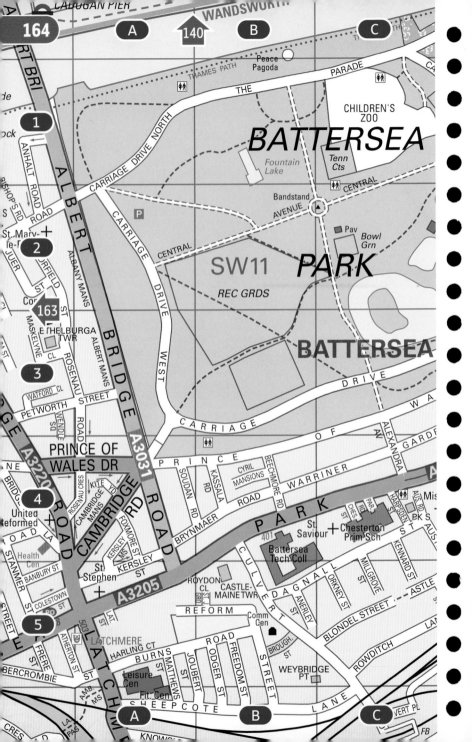

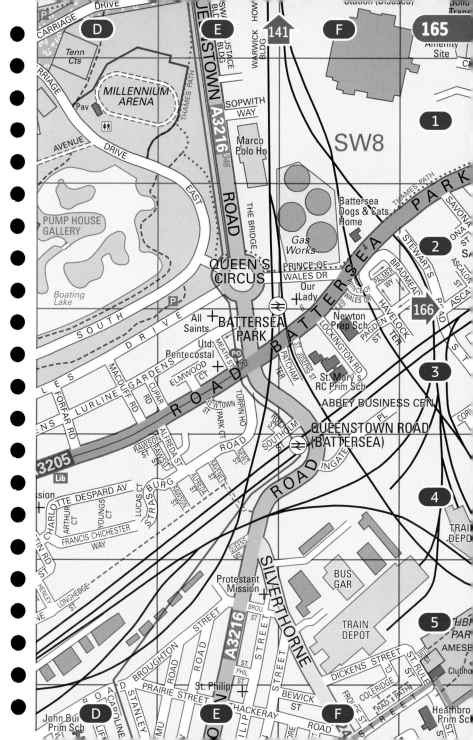

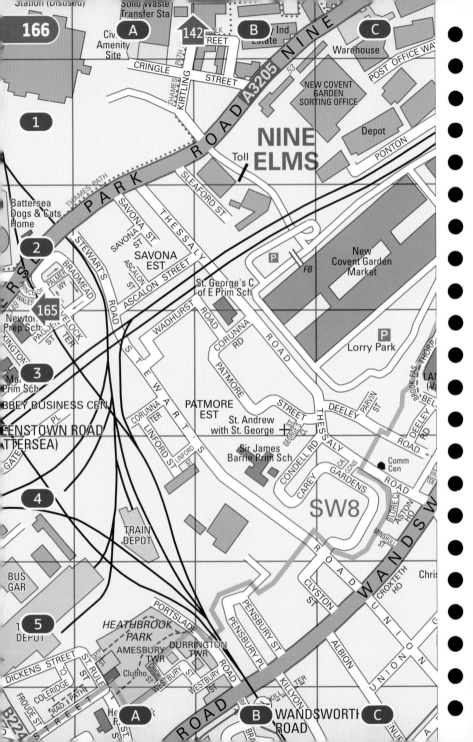

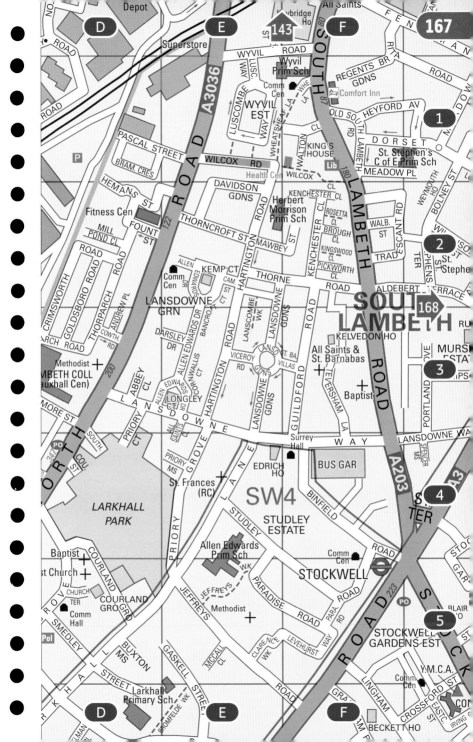

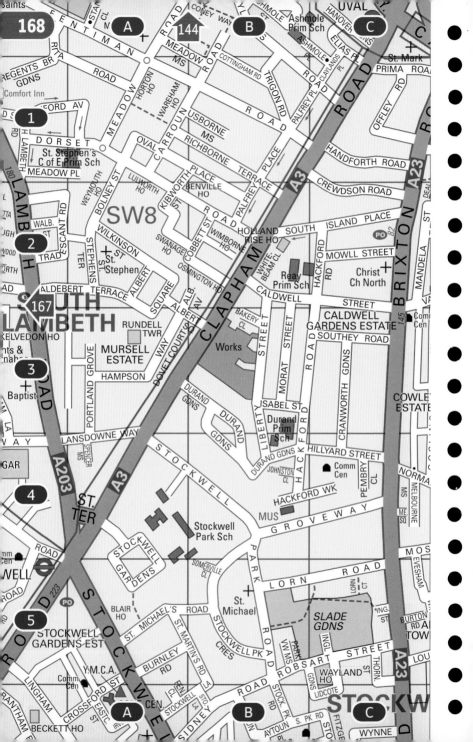

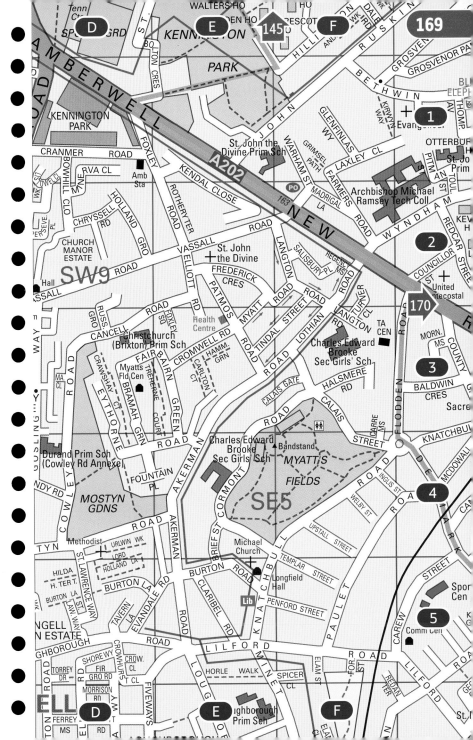

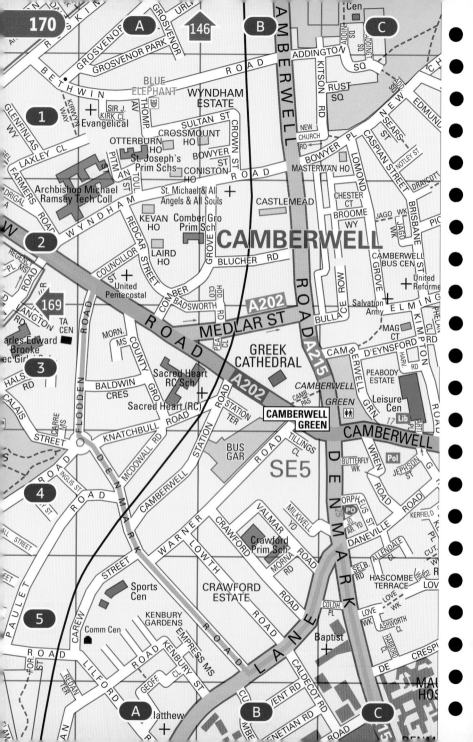

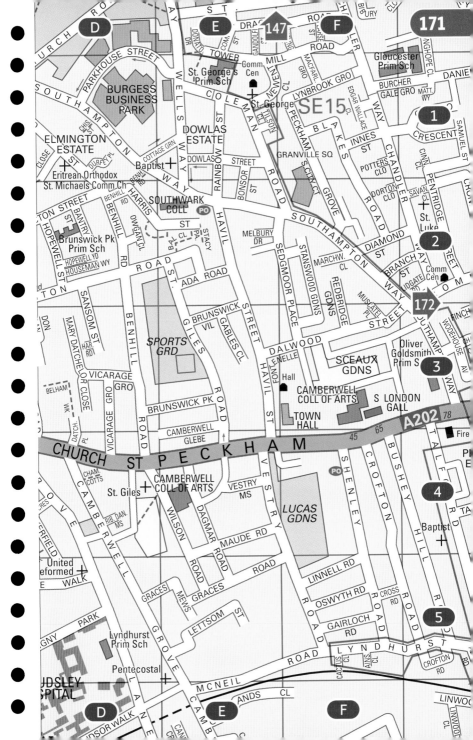

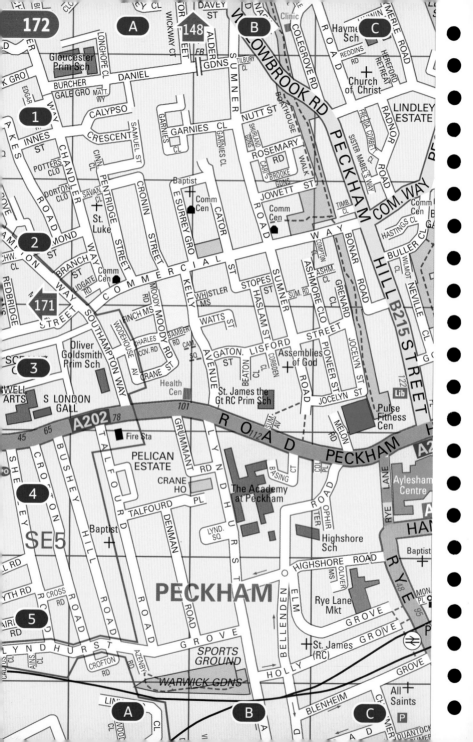

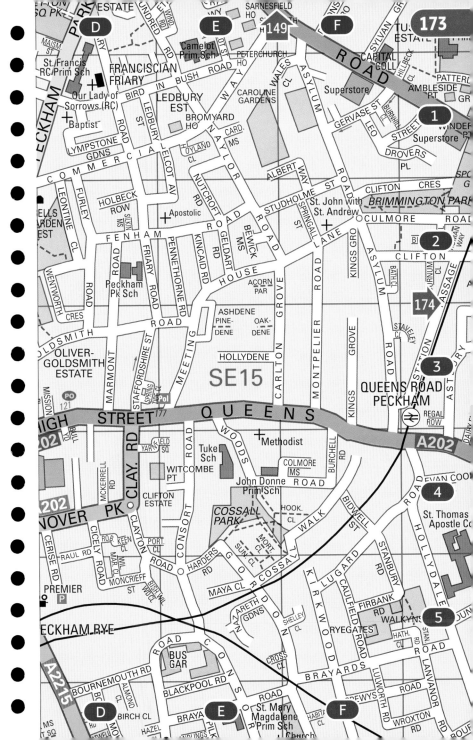

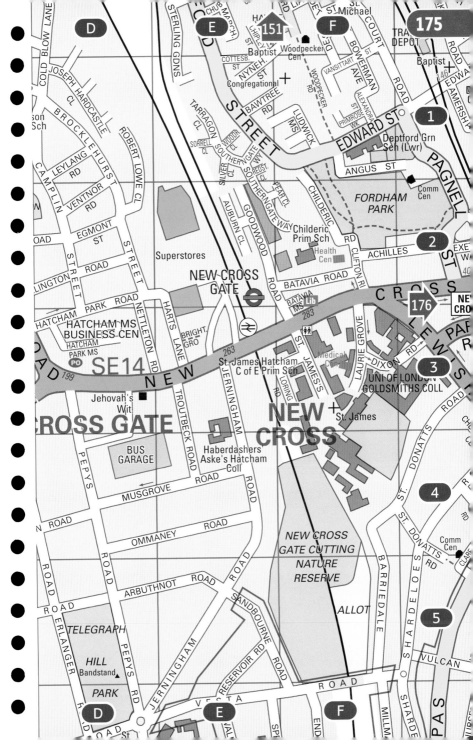

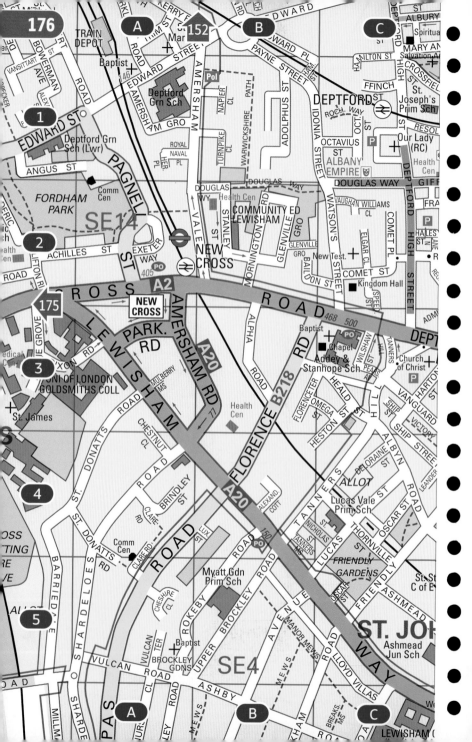

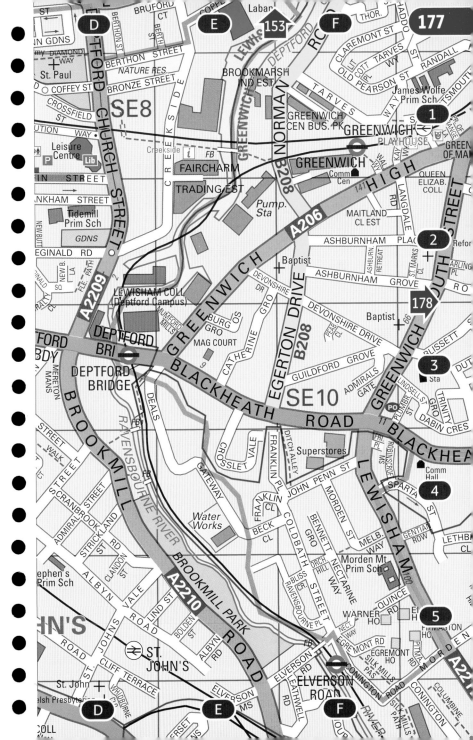

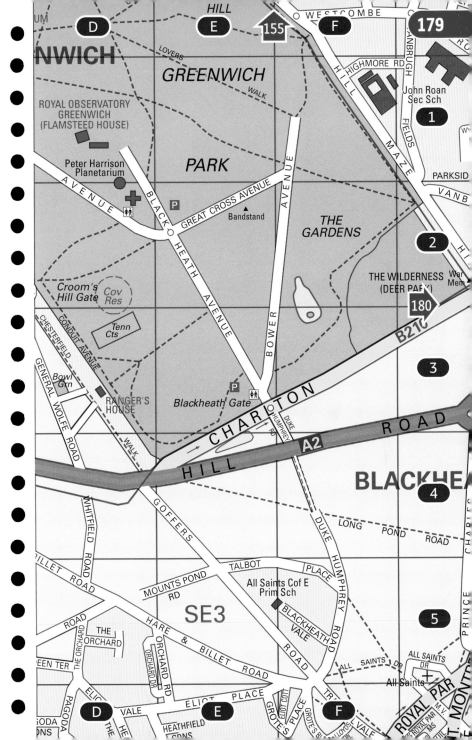

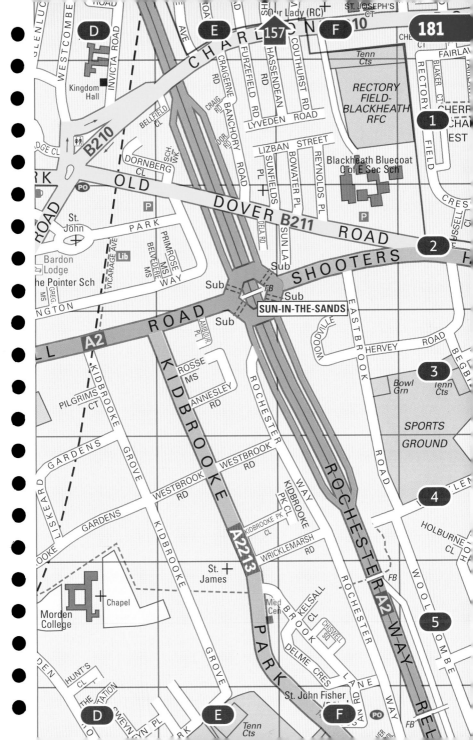

Index & abbreviations

The figures and letters following a name in the index indicate the Postal District, page and map square where the name can be found.

Acad	Academy	FC	Football Club	Pav	Pavilion
All	Alley	Fld	Field	Pk	Park
Allot	Allotments	Flds	Fields	Pl	Place
Amb	Ambulance	Fm	Farm	Pol	Police
App	Approach	GM	Grant Maintained	Poly	Polytechnic
Apts	Apartments	Gall	Gallery	Prec	Precinct
Arc	Arcade	Gar	Garage	Prep	Preparatory
Assoc	Association	Gdn	Garden	Prim	Primary
Av	Avenue	Gdns	Gardens	Prom	Promenade
BUPA	British United	Gen	General	Pt	Point
	Provident	Govt	Government	Quad	Quadrant
	Association	Gra	Grange	RC	Roman Catholic
Bdy	Broadway	Gram	Grammar	Rd	Road
Bk	Bank	Grd	Ground	Rds	Roads
Bldg	Building	Grds	Grounds	Rbt	Roundabout
Bldgs	Buildings	Grn	Green	Rec	Recreation
Boul	Boulevard	Grns	Greens	Rehab	Rehabilitation
Bowl	Bowling	Gro	Grove	Res	Reservoir,
Br	Bridge	Gros	Groves		Residence
C of E	Church of	Gt	Great	Ri	Rise
	England	HQ	Headquarters	S	South
Cath	Cathedral,	Ho	House	SM	Secondary Mixed
	Catholic	Hos	Houses	Sch	School
Cem	Cemetery	Hosp	Hospital	Schs	Schools
Cen	Central, Centre	Hts	Heights	Sec	Secondary
Cft	Croft	Ind	Industrial	Sen	Senior
Cfts	Crofts	Indep	Independent	Shop	Shopping
Ch	Church	Inf	Infant(s)	Spec	Special
Chyd	Churchyard	Inst	Institute	Sq	Square
Cin	Cinema	Int	International	St	Street
Circ	Circus	JM	Junior Mixed	St.	Saint
Cl	Close	JMI	Junior Mixed &	Sta	Station
Co	County		Infant(s)	Sts	Streets
Coll	College	Jun	Junior	Sub	Subway
Comb	Combined	Junct	Junction	Swim	Swimming
Comm	Community	La	Lane	TA	Territorial Army
Comp	Comprehensive	Las	Lanes	TH	Town Hall
Conf	Conference	Lib	Library	Tech	Technical,
Cont	Continuing	Lit	Literary		Technology
Conv	Convent	Ln	Loan	Tenn	Tennis
Cor	Corner	Lo	Lodge	Ter	Terrace
Coron	Coroners	Lwr	Lower	Thea	Theatre
Cors	Corners	Mag	Magistrates	Trd	Trading
Cotts	Cottages	Mans	Mansions	Twr	Tower
Cov	Covered	Med	Medical	Twrs	Towers
Crem	Crematorium	Mem	Memorial	Uni	University
Cres	Crescent	Met	Metropolitan	Upr	Upper
Ct	Court	Mid	Middle	Vet	Veterinary
Cts	Courts	Mkt	Market	VA	Voluntary Aided
Ctyd	Courtyard	Mkts	Markets	VC	Voluntary
Dep	Depot	Ms	Mews		Controlled
Dept	Department	Mt	Mount	Vil	Villas
Dev	Development	Mus	Museum	Vil	Villa
Dr	Drive	N	North	Vw	View
Dws	Dwellings	NHS	National Health	W	West
E	East		Service	Wd	Wood
Ed	Education,	NT	National Trust	Wds	Woods
	Educational	Nat	National	Wf	Wharf
Elec	Electricity	Nurs	Nursery	Wk	Walk
Embk	Embankment	PH	Public House	Wks	Works
Est	Estate	PO	Post Office	Yd	Yard
Ex	Exchange	PRU	Pupil Referral Unit		
Exhib	Exhibition	Par	Parade	POST TOWN ABBREVIATIONS	
FB	Footbridge	Pas	Passage	Bark.	Barking

The index contains some street names which are not shown on the maps because there is not enough space to name them. In these cases the adjoining or nearest named thoroughfare to such streets is shown in the index in *italics*, and the reference indicates where the unnamed street is located *off* the named thoroughfare.

★ Place of interest ⇌ Railway station ↻ London Overground station ● London Underground station

1 Canada Sq, E14 . . . . . **97** E5
30 St. Mary Axe, EC3
  off St. Mary Axe . . . **63** F5
99 Bishopsgate, EC2
  off Bishopsgate **63** E5
Uni200 Pentonville Rd,
  Halls of Res, N1 . . . . . **38** A3

A

Aaron Hill Rd, E6 . . . . . **77** D3
Abady Ho, SW1
  off Page St **115** D5
Abbess Cl, E6 . . . . **75** F4
Abbey Business Cen,
  SW8 . . . . **165** F3
Abbey Cl, SW8 . . . . **167** D3
Abbeyfield Rd, SE16 . . **122** A4
Abbey Gdns, NW8 . . . . **32** A3
  SE16 . . . . **121** D5
  SW1 *off Great Coll St* **115** D3
  W6 . . . . **135** E4
Abbey Orchard St,
  SW1 . . . . **115** D3
Abbey Rd, E15 . . . . **49** D2
  NW6 . . . . **9** E4
  NW8 . . . . **32** A1
Abbey Rd Est, NW8 . . . **31** E1
Abbey St, E13 . . . . **73** D1
  SE1 . . . . **119** F3
Abbot Ct, SW8
  off Hartington Rd . . **167** E2
Abbotsbury Cl, E15 . . . **48** B2
  W14 . . . . **107** F2
Abbotsbury Rd, W14 . **107** F1
Abbots Gdns, W8 . . . . **109** E4
Abbotshade Rd, SE16 . . **95** D4
Abbots La, SE1 . . . . **91** F5
Abbots Manor Est,
  SW1 . . . . **141** E1
Abbot's Pl, NW6 . . . . **9** E5
Abbot St, E8 . . . . **20** A1
Abbott Rd, E14 . . . . **70** A4
Abbotts Cl, N1 . . . . **18** A2
Abbotts Wf, E14 . . . . . . **68** C5
Abchurch La, EC4 . . . . . **91** D2
Abchurch Yd, EC4 . . . . . **90** C2
Aberavon Rd, E3 . . . . . . **45** F5
Abercorn Cl, NW8 . . . . **32** A3
Abercorn Pl, NW8 . . . . **32** A4
SchAbercorn Sch, NW8 . **32** B3
Abercorn Wk, NW8 . . . **32** A4
Abercorn Way, SE1 . . **148** C2
Abercrombie St,
  SW11 . . . . **163** F5
Aberdale Ct, SE16
  off Garter Way **122** C2
Aberdare Gdns, NW6 . . **9** F4
Aberdeen Pl, NW8 . . . . **54** C2
Aberdeen Sq, E14 . . . . . **96** B4
Aberdeen Ter, SE3 . . **178** C5
Aberdour St, SE1 . . . . **119** E5
Aberfeldy St, E14 . . . . **70** B5

Ability Twrs, EC1 . . . . . **40** A4
Abingdon Cl, NW1 . . . . **14** C2
  SE1 . . . . **148** B2
Abingdon Rd, W8 . . . . **108** C3
Abingdon St, SW1 . . . . **115** E3
Abingdon Vil, W8 . . . . **108** C4
Abinger Gro, SE8 . . . . **152** A5
Abinger Ms, W9 . . . . . . **52** C1
Ablett St, SE16 . . . . . . **150** A3
Acacia Cl, SE8 . . . . **151** E1
Acacia Gdns, NW8 . . . . **33** D2
Acacia Pl, NW8 . . . . . . **33** D2
Acacia Rd, NW8 . . . . . . **33** D2
SchAcademy at Peckham,
  The, SE15 . . . . **172** B4
Academy Gdns, W8 . . **108** C1
Acanthus Dr, SE1 . . . . **148** C2
Acfold Rd, SW6 . . . . . **161** E4
Achilles Cl, SE1 . . . . . **149** D2
Achilles St, SE14 . . . . **176** A2
Achilles Way, W1 . . . . . **84** C5
Acklam Rd, W10 . . . . . . **52** A4
Ackmar Rd, SW6 . . . . **160** C4
Ackroyd Dr, E3 . . . . **68** B3
Acol Rd, NW6 . . . . **9** D4
Acorn Par, SE15 . . . . **173** E2
Acorn Wk, SE16 . . . . . . **95** F4
Acton Ms, E8 . . . . **20** A5
Acton St, WC1 . . . . **38** A5
Ada Ct, W9 . . . . **32** B5
Ada Gdns, E14 . . . . **70** C5
Adair Rd, W10 . . . . **51** F2
Adair Twr, W10 . . . . **51** F2
Adam & Eve Ct, W1 . . . **58** B5
Adam & Eve Ms, W8 . **109** D3
Adam Ct, SW7 . . . . . . **110** B5
Adam Meere Ho, E1
  off Tarling St **94** A1
Adams Ct, EC2 . . . . **63** D5
Adams Gdns Est,
  SE16 . . . . **122** A1
Adamson Rd, E16 . . . . **101** D1
  NW3 . . . . **11** D3
Adams Row, W1 . . . . . . **85** D3
Adam St, WC2 . . . . **87** F3
Adam Wk, SW6 . . . . . **158** B1
Ada Pl, E2 . . . . **43** D1
Ada Rd, SE5 . . . . **171** E2
Ada St, E8 . . . . **43** E1
Adderley St, E14 . . . . . . **98** A1
SchAddey & Stanhope Sch,
  SE14 . . . . **176** C3
Addington Rd, E3 . . . . . **46** C4
  E16 . . . . **71** F2
Addington Sq, SE5 . . . **170** B1
Addington St, SE1 . . . . **116** B2
Addison Av, W11 . . . . . **79** E4
Addison Br Pl, W14 . . **108** A5
Addison Cres, W14 . . **107** F3
Addison Gdns, W14 . . **106** C3
Addison Pl, W11 . . . . . . **79** E5
SchAddison Prim Sch,
  W14 . . . . **106** C3
Addison Rd, W14 . . . . **108** A3
Addle Hill, EC4 . . . . **89** F2
Addle St, EC2 . . . . **62** B4
Addy Ho, SE16 . . . . . . **150** B1

Adelaide Rd, NW3 . . . . . **11** D4
Adelaide St, WC2 . . . . . **87** E3
Adela St, W10 . . . . **51** E1
Adelina Gro, E1 . . . . **66** A3
Adeline Pl, WC1 . . . . . . **59** D4
Adelphi Ct, SE16
  off Garter Way **122** C2
Adelphi Ter, WC2 . . . . . **87** F3
Adeney Cl, W6 . . . . **135** D5
Adie Rd, W6 . . . . **106** A4
Adine Rd, E13 . . . . **73** E1
Adler St, E1 . . . . **64** C5
Admiral Hyson Trd Est,
  SE16 . . . . **149** E1
Admiral Pl, SE16 . . . . . . **95** F4
Admirals Gate, SE10 . **177** F3
Admiral Sq, SW10 . . . . **162** B3
Admiral St, SE8 . . . . . **177** D4
Admirals Way, E14 . . . **125** D1
★ **Admiralty Arch**,
  SW1 . . . . **87** D4
Admiralty Cl, SE8 . . . . **176** C3
Admiral Wk, W9 . . . . . . **53** D3
Adolphus St, SE8 . . . . **176** B1
Adpar St, W2 . . . . **54** C2
Adrian Ms, SW10 . . . . **137** F4
Adriatic Bldg, E14 . . . . **95** E2
Adventurers Ct, E14
  off Newport Av **99** D3
Aegean Apts, E16
  off Western Gateway . **101** D3
Affleck St, N1 . . . . **38** B3
★ **Africa Cen**, WC2 . . . **87** E2
Agar Gro, NW1 . . . . **14** B4
Agar Gro Est, NW1 . . . **14** C4
Agar Pl, NW1 . . . . **14** B4
Agar St, WC2 . . . . **87** E3
Agate Cl, E16 . . . . **103** D1
Agate Rd, W6 . . . . **106** A3
Agatha Cl, E1 . . . . **93** F4
Agdon St, EC1 . . . . **61** E1
Agnes Cl, E6 . . . . **105** D1
Agnes St, E14 . . . . **68** B5
Agricola Ct, E3 . . . . **46** B1
Ailsa St, E14 . . . . **70** B3
Ainger Ms, NW3 . . . . . . **12** B4
Ainger Rd, NW3 . . . . . . **12** A4
Ainsdale Dr, SE1 . . . . **148** C3
Ainsley St, E2 . . . . **43** F5
Ainsty Est, SE16 . . . . . **122** C2
Ainsworth Cl, SE15 . . **171** F5
Ainsworth Rd, E9 . . . . . **22** A4
Ainsworth Way, NW8 . . **10** A5
Aintree Est, SW6 . . . . **159** F1
Aintree St, SW6 . . . . . **159** F2
Aird Ho, SE1
  off Rockingham St . . **118** A4
Airdrie Cl, N1 . . . . **16** A4
Airlie Gdns, W8 . . . . . . **80** C5
Airport Rbt, E16 . . . . . **102** C4
Air St, W1 . . . . **86** B3
Aisgill Av, W14 . . . . . . **136** B3
Aitken Cl, E8 . . . . **20** C5

Akerman Rd, SW9 . . . . **169** E4
Alamaro Lo, SE10
   off Renaissance Wk . **128** B3
Aland Ct, SE16 . . . . . . **123** F3
Alan Hocken Way, E15. **49** E3
Alaska Bldg, SE13
   off Deals Gateway . . **177** E4
Alaska St, SE1 . . . . **88** C5
Alban Highwalk, EC2
   off London Wall **62** B4
Albany, W1 . . . . **86** A3
Albany Ctyd, W1. . . . . . **86** B3
Albany Mans, SW11 . . **163** F2
Albany Ms, N1 . . . . **16** C3
  SE5 . . . . **146** B5
Albany Rd, SE5 . . . . . . **146** C5
  SE17 . . . . **146** C5
Albany St, NW1. . . . . . . **35** E2
Alba Pl, W11 . . . . **52** A5
Albatross Cl, E6 . . . . . . **76** B2
Albatross Way, SE16 . **122** C2
Albemarle St, W1 . . . . . **85** F3
Albemarle Way, EC1. . . **61** E2
Alberta Est, SE17 . . . . **145** F2
Alberta St, SE17 . . . . . **145** E2
Albert Av, SW8 . . . . . . **168** A2
Albert Barnes Ho, SE1. **118** A4
Albert Basin, E16 . . . . **105** F3
Albert Basin Way,
  E16 . . . . **105** F3
Albert Bigg Pt, E15. . . . **48** B1
Albert Br, SW3 . . . . . . **139** F5
  SW11 . . . . **139** F5
Albert Br Rd, SW11. . . **163** F4
Albert Cl, E9 . . . . **43** F1
Albert Ct, SW7. . . . . . . **110** C2
Albert Embk, SE1 . . . . **143** F3
Albert Gdns, E1 . . . . . . **94** C1
Albert Gate, SW1 . . . . **112** B1
Albert Hall Mans, SW7. **110** C2
Albert Mans, SW11. . . **164** A2
★ Albert Mem, SW7 . . **110** C1
Albert Ms, E14
   off Narrow St **95** E2
  W8 . . . . **110** A3
Albert Pl, W8. . . . . **109** F2
Albert Rd, E16. . . . . . . **103** F5
  NW6 . . . . **30** B3
Albert Sq, SW8 . . . . . . **168** A2
Albert St, NW1 . . . . **35** F1
Albert Ter, NW1 . . . . . . **12** C5
Albert Ter Ms, NW1 . . . **34** C1
Albert Way, SE15 . . . . **173** E1
Albion Av, SW8 . . . . . . **166** C5
Albion Cl, W2 . . . . **83** D1
Albion Dr, E8. . . . . **20** A4
Albion Est, SE16 . . . . . **122** C2
Albion Ms, N1 . . . . **16** C5
  NW6 . . . . **8** A3
  W2. . . . . **83** F1
Albion Pl, EC1 . . . . **61** E3
Sch Albion Prim Sch,
  SE16 . . . . **122** B2

Albion Riverside Bldg,
  SW11 . . . . **163** F1
Albion Sq, E8. . . . . **20** A4
Albion St, SE16 . . . . . . **122** B2
  W2 . . . . **83** F1
Albion Ter, E8 . . . . **20** A4
Albion Wk, N1. . . . . **37** F3
Albion Way, EC1 . . . . . . **62** A4
Albion Yd, N1 . . . . **37** F3
Albury St, SE8 . . . . **152** C5
Albyn Rd, SE8 . . . . **176** A4
Aldbridge St, SE17 . . . **147** F2
Aldburgh Ms, W1 . . . . . **57** D5
Aldebert Ter, SW8 . . . **167** F2
Aldeburgh Pl, SE10. . . **157** D1
Aldeburgh St, SE10 . . **156** C2
Aldenham St, NW1 . . . . **36** B3
Alder Cl, SE15 . . . . **148** B5
Alder Ho, NW3 . . . . **12** B1
Aldermanbury, EC2 . . . **62** B3
Aldermanbury Sq, EC2. **62** B4
Alderman's Wk, EC2 . . . **63** E4
Alderney Ho, N1
   off Arran Wk **18** B2
Alderney Ms, SE1 . . . . **118** C3
Alderney Rd, E1 . . . . . . **66** C1
Alderney St, SW1 . . . . **141** F2
Aldersgate St, EC1 . . . . **62** A5
Aldershot Rd, NW6. . . . . **8** B5
Alderson St, W10 . . . . . **51** F1
Alderville Rd, SW6 . . . **160** B5
Aldford St, W1. . . . . **84** C4
⊖ Aldgate. **92** A1
Aldgate, EC3. . . . . **92** A1
Aldgate Av, E1 . . . . **64** A5
Aldgate Barrs Shop Cen,
  E1 . . . . **64** B5
⊖ Aldgate East **64** B5
Aldgate High St, EC3 . . **92** A1
Aldine Ct, W12 . . . . . . **106** B1
Aldine Pl, W12 . . . . **78** B5
Aldine St, W12 . . . . . . **106** B1
Aldington Rd, SE18 . . **131** D4
Aldridge Rd Vil, W11 . . **52** B2
Aldsworth Cl, W9 . . . . . **53** E2
Aldworth Rd, E15 . . . . . **27** E4
Aldwych, WC2. . . . . **88** A2
Aldwych Underpass, WC2
   off Kingsway **88** A1
Alestan Beck Rd, E16. . **75** D5
Alexa Ct, W8 . . . . **109** E5
★ Alexander Fleming
  Laboratory Mus, W2. **55** D5
Alexander Ms, W2. . . . . **53** E5
Alexander Pl, SW7 . . . **111** E5
Alexander Sq, SW3 . . **111** E5
Alexander St, W2 . . . . . **53** D5
Alexandra Av, SW11. . **164** C3
Alexandra Cl, SE8 . . . . **152** A4
Alexandra Cotts,
  SE14 . . . . **176** B4
Alexandra Ct, W9 . . . . . **54** B1
Alexandra Pl, NW8 . . . . **10** B5
Alexandra Rd, NW8 . . . **10** B5
Alexandra St, E16. . . . . **72** C3
  SE14 . . . . **175** F1
Alexis St, SE16 . . . . . . **120** C5

Alford Pl, N1 . . . . **40** B3
Alfreda St, SW11. . . . . **165** E3
Alfred Ms, W1 . . . . **58** C3
Alfred Pl, WC1 . . . . **58** C3
Alfred Rd, W2 . . . . **53** D3
Sch Alfred Salter Prim Sch,
  SE16 . . . . **123** D2
Alfred St, E3 . . . . **46** B3
Algernon Rd, NW6 . . . . **30** C1
Alice Gilliatt Ct, W14 . **136** A4
Alice La, E3 . . . . **46** A1
Alice St, SE1 . . . . **119** E4
Alie St, E1 . . . . **92** B1
Alison Cl, E6 . . . . **105** D1
Allendale Cl, SE5. . . . . **170** C5
Sch Allendale Sch, W8 . **109** D3
Allen Edwards Dr,
  SW8 . . . . **167** E3
Sch Allen Edwards Prim Sch,
  SW4 . . . . **167** E3
Allen Rd, E3. . . . . **46** A2
Allensbury Pl, NW1 . . . **15** D4
Allen St, W8 . . . . **109** D3
Allestree Rd, SW6 . . . **159** E2
Allgood St, E2 . . . . **42** B3
Allhallows La, EC4 . . . . **90** C3
★ All Hallows-on-the-Wall
  C of E Ch, EC2 . . . . . . **63** D4
Allhallows Rd, E6 . . . . . **75** E4
Alliance Rd, E13 . . . . . . **74** A2
Allied Ct, N1 . . . . **19** F4
Allingham Ms, N1. . . . . **40** A2
Allingham St, N1 . . . . . **40** A2
Allington Rd, W10 . . . . **29** E4
Allington St, SW1 . . . . **114** A4
Allison Cl, SE10. . . . . . **178** B4
Allitsen Rd, NW8. . . . . . **33** E3
Alloa Rd, SE8. . . . . **151** D2
Allonby Ho, E14 . . . . . . **67** D4
Alloway Rd, E3 . . . . **45** F4
Allport Ms, E1 . . . . **66** B2
DLR All Saints **98** A2
All Saints Cl, SW8 . . . **167** E3
Sch All Saints C of E Prim
  Sch, SE3 . . . . **179** E5
  SW6. . . . . **159** E5
All Saints Dr, SE3 . . . . **179** F5
All Saints Rd, W11 . . . . **52** A4
All Saints St, N1 . . . . . . **38** A2
Allsop Pl, NW1 . . . . **56** B2
Sch All Souls C of E Prim
  Sch, W1. . . . . **58** A4
All Souls Pl, W1. . . . . . . **57** F4
Alma Gro, SE1. . . . . . . **148** B1
Sch Alma Prim Sch,
  SE16 . . . . **121** D5
Alma Sq, NW8 . . . . **32** B4
Alma St, E15 . . . . **26** C1
  NW5 . . . . **13** F1
Alma Ter, W8
   off Allen St **109** D4
Almeida St, N1 . . . . **17** E4
Almond Rd, SE16 . . . . **121** F5
Almorah Rd, N1 . . . . . . **18** C4
Alnwick Rd, E16 . . . . . **102** A1
Alperton St, W10 . . . . . **51** F1
Alphabet Sq, E3 . . . . . . **69** D3

Alpha Cl, NW1 . . . . **55** F1
Alpha Gro, E14 . . . . . . **125** D2
Alpha Pl, NW6 . . . . **31** D2
SW3 . . . . **139** F4
Alpha Rd, SE14 . . . . . . **176** B3
Alpine Gro, E9 . . . . **22** B4
Alpine Rd, SE16 . . . . . **150** B1
Alpine Way, E6 . . . . **76** C3
Alsace Rd, SE17 . . . . . **147** E2
Alscot Rd, SE1 . . . . **120** B5
Alscot Way, SE1 . . . . . **120** A5
Althorpe Gro, SW11 . . **163** D3
Althorpe Ms, SW11 . . . **163** D4
Alton Ho, E3
off Bromley High St . . **47** F4
Alton St, E14 . . . . **69** E4
Alverstone Rd, NW2 . . . . **6** A3
Alverton St, SE8 . . . . . **152** A3
Alvey Est, SE17 . . . . . . **147** E1
Alvey St, SE17 . . . . **147** E2
Alwyne La, N1 . . . . **17** F3
Alwyne Pl, N1 . . . . **18** A2
Alwyne Rd, N1 . . . . **17** F3
Alwyne Sq, N1 . . . . **18** A1
Alwyne Vil, N1 . . . . **17** F3
Alzette Ho, E2 . . . . **44** C4
Amazon St, E1 . . . . **93** E1
Ambassador Gdns, E6 . **76** A4
Ambassador's Ct, SW1. **86** B5
Ambassador Sq, E14 . **153** E1
Ambergate St, SE17 . . **145** F2
Amberley Rd, W9 . . . . . **53** D3
Amber St, E15 . . . . **27** D2
Amber Wf, E2 . . . . **42** A1
Ambleside Pt, SE15 . . **174** A1
Ambrosden Av, SW1 . . **114** B4
Ambrose Cl, E6 . . . . **76** A4
Ambrose St, SE16 . . . . **121** E5
Ambrose Wk, E3 . . . . . . **46** C3
Amelia St, SE17 . . . . . **145** F2
Amen Cor, EC4 . . . . **89** F1
Amen Ct, EC4 . . . . **61** F5
Sch American Sch in London,
The, NW8 . . . . **32** C2
America Sq, EC3 . . . . . . **92** A2
America St, SE1 . . . . **90** A5
Amersham Gro, SE14 . **176** A1
Amersham Rd, SE14 . . **176** A2
Amersham Vale, SE14 . **176** B1
Amesbury Twr, SW8 . . **166** A5
Amiel St, E1 . . . . **66** B1
Amina Way, SE16 . . . . **120** C4
Amor Rd, W6 . . . . **106** A4
Amoy Pl, E14 . . . . **96** C1
Ampthill Sq Est, NW1 . . **36** B3
Ampton Pl, WC1 . . . . . . **38** A5
Ampton St, WC1 . . . . . . **38** A5
Amsterdam Rd, E14 . . **126** B4
Amundsen Ct, E14
off Napier Av **153** D2
Amwell St, EC1 . . . . **38** C4
Amy Warne Cl, E6 . . . . . **75** F3
Anchorage Pt, E14 . . . **124** B1
Anchorage Pt Ind Est,
SE7 . . . . **130** A4
Anchor & Hope La,
SE7 . . . . **129** F4

Anchor Ms, N1 . . . . **19** F2
SW11
off Westbridge Rd . . **163** D4
Anchor Retail Pk, E1 . . **66** B2
Anchor St, SE16 . . . . . **121** E5
Anchor Ter, E1 . . . . **66** B2
Anchor Wf, E3
off Watts Gro **69** E3
Anchor Yd, EC1 . . . . **62** B1
Ancill Cl, W6 . . . . **135** D5
Anderson Rd, E9 . . . . . . **22** C1
Andersons Sq, N1 . . . . . **39** E1
Anderson St, SW3 . . . . **140** A2
Andover Av, E16 . . . . . **102** C1
Andover Pl, NW6 . . . . . **31** E2
Andrew Borde St,
WC2 . . . . **59** D5
Andrewes Gdns, E6 . . . **75** E5
Andrewes Ho, EC2 . . . . **62** B4
Andrew Pl, SW8 . . . . . **167** D3
Andrews Cl, E6 . . . . **75** E5
Andrews Crosse, WC2 . **88** C1
Andrew's Rd, E8 . . . . . . **43** E1
Andrew St, E14 . . . . **70** A5
Andrews Wk, SE17 . . . **145** F5
Anerley St, SW11 . . . . **164** B5
⊖ Angel **39** D2
Angel All, E1 . . . . **64** B5
Angel Ct, EC2 . . . . **63** D5
SW1 . . . . **86** B5
Angel Gate, EC1 . . . . . . **39** F4
Angelica Dr, E6 . . . . **77** D4
Angelis Apts, N1
off Graham St **39** F3
Angel La, E15 . . . . **27** D1
Angell Town Est, SW9. **168** C5
Angel Ms, E1 . . . . **93** F2
N1 . . . . **39** D3
Angel Pas, EC4 . . . . **90** C3
Angel Pl, SE1 . . . . **118** C1
Angel Southside, EC1 . . **39** D3
Angel Sq, EC1 . . . . **39** D3
Angel St, EC1 . . . . **62** A5
Angel Wk, W6 . . . . **134** A1
Angerstein La, SE3 . . . **180** B3
Angler's La, NW5 . . . . . **13** F2
Anglia Ho, E14 . . . . **95** F1
Anglo Rd, E3 . . . . **46** B2
Angrave Ct, E8 . . . . **20** B5
Angrave Pas, E8 . . . . . . **20** B5
Angus St, SE14 . . . . . . **175** F1
Anhalt Rd, SW11 . . . . **163** F1
Anley Rd, W14 . . . . . . **106** C2
Annabel Cl, E14 . . . . . . **97** E1
Anna Cl, E8 . . . . **20** B5
Annandale Rd, SE10 . . **156** A3
Anne Goodman Ho, E1
off Jubilee St **66** A5
Annesley Rd, SE3 . . . . **181** E3
Anne St, E13 . . . . **72** C1
Annette Cres, N1 . . . . . **18** B4
Annie Besant Cl, E3 . . . **46** B1
Anning St, EC2 . . . . **63** F1
Annis Rd, E9 . . . . **23** E2
Ann La, SW10 . . . . **162** C5
Ann Moss Way, SE16 . **122** A3
Ann's Cl, SW1 . . . . **112** B2

Alp - Arc **185**

Ann's Pl, E1 . . . . **64** A4
Ansdell Rd, SE15 . . . . . **174** A5
Ansdell St, W8 . . . . **109** F3
Ansdell Ter, W8 . . . . . . **109** F3
Anselm Rd, SW6 . . . . . **136** C5
Ansleigh Pl, W11 . . . . . **79** D3
Anson Ho, E1 . . . . **67** E2
Antelope Rd, SE18 . . . **132** A3
Anthony St, E1 . . . . **65** F5
Antill Rd, E3 . . . . **45** E4
Antill Ter, E1 . . . . **66** C5
Antonine Hts, SE1 . . . **119** E2
Antrim Gro, NW3 . . . . . **12** A1
Antrim Mans, NW3 . . . **11** F1
Antrim Rd, NW3 . . . . . . **12** A1
Apollo, E14 . . . . **124** C5
★ Apollo Hammersmith,
W6 . . . . **134** B2
Apollo Pl, SW10 . . . . . **162** C1
★ Apollo Thea, W1 . . . . **86** C2
★ Apollo Victoria Thea,
SW1 . . . . **114** A4
Apothecary St, EC4 . . . **89** E1
Apple Blossom Ct, SW8
off Pascal St. **167** D1
Appleby Rd, E8 . . . . **21** D3
E16 . . . . **100** B1
Appleby St, E2 . . . . **42** A2
Appleford Rd, W10 . . . . **51** F2
Applegarth Rd, W14. . **106** C4
Apple Tree Yd, SW1 . . . **86** B4
Applewood Dr, E13. . . . **73** E1
Appold St, EC2 . . . . **63** E3
Approach Rd, E2 . . . . . . **44** A3
★ Apsley Ho (Wellington
Mus), W1 . . . . **112** C1
Apsley Way, W1 . . . . . **113** D1
Aquila St, NW8 . . . . **33** D2
Aquinas St, SE1 . . . . . . **89** D4
Aragon Twr, SE8 . . . . . **152** A1
Aran Ms, N7
off Barnsbury Gro . . . **16** C3
Arbery Rd, E3 . . . . **45** E4
Arbour Sq, E1 . . . . **94** C1
Arbuthnot Rd, SE14 . . **174** C5
Arbutus St, E8 . . . . **20** A5
Arcade, The, EC2 . . . . . **63** E4
Arcadia St, E14 . . . . **69** D5
Archangel St, SE16 . . . **123** D2
Sch Archbishop Sumner
C of E Prim Sch,
SE11 . . . . **145** D1
Sch Archbishop Tenison's
Sch, SE11 . . . . **144** B5
Archel Rd, W14 . . . . . . **136** A4
Archer Ho, N1
off Phillipp St **41** F1
SW11 . . . . **162** C5
Archer Sq, SE14 . . . . . **151** E5
Archer St, W1 . . . . **86** C2
Archery Cl, W2 . . . . **83** F1
Archery Steps, W2
off St. Georges Flds . . **83** F2

Sch School   **Coll** College   **Uni** University   **H** Hospital   **DLR** Docklands Light Railway station

Arches, The, SW6 .... **160** A5
SW8 *off New Covent*
Gdn Mkt. **167** D1
WC2 .... **87** F4
Archibald Ms, W1 ..... **85** D3
Archibald St, E3 ...... **46** C1
Archie St, SE1 .... **119** F2
▨Architectural Assoc Sch
of Architecture, WC1 . **59** D4
Arch St, SE1 .... **118** A4
Archway Cl, W10 ..... **50** C4
Arden Cres, E14 ..... **125** D5
Arden Est, N1 .... **41** E3
Ardleigh Rd, N1 ...... **19** D2
Argon Ms, SW6 ...... **161** D2
▨Argyle Prim Sch,
WC1 .... **37** E4
Argyle Rd, E1 .... **66** C1
E16 .... **101** F1
Argyle Sq, WC1 ...... **37** E4
Argyle St, WC1 ...... **37** E4
Argyle Way, SE16 .... **149** D3
Argyll Rd, W8 .... **108** C2
Argyll St, W1 .... **86** A1
Aria Ho, WC2 .... **59** F5
Arica Ho, SE16 ...... **121** F3
Ariel Rd, NW6 .... **8** C2
Ariel Way, W12 ...... **78** B4
Arizona Bldg, SE13
off Deals Gateway .. **177** E4
Arklow Ho, SE17 ..... **146** C4
Arklow Rd, SE14 ..... **152** A5
Arlington Av, N1 ...... **40** B1
Arlington Bldg, E3 .... **47** D3
Arlington Pl, SE10 ... **178** A2
Arlington Rd, NW1 ... **35** F1
Arlington Sq, N1 ..... **40** B1
Arlington St, SW1 .... **86** A4
Arlington Way, EC1 ... **39** D4
Armada Ct, SE8 ...... **152** C5
Armadale Rd, SW6 ... **160** C1
Armagh Rd, E3 .... **46** B1
Armitage Rd, SE10 ... **156** A2
Armour Cl, N7 .... **16** A2
Armstrong Cl, E6 ..... **76** B5
Armstrong Rd, SW7 .. **110** C4
Arne Ho, SE11 ...... **144** A2
Arne St, WC2 .... **87** F1
Arneway St, SW1 .... **115** D4
Arnhem Pl, E14 ...... **124** C4
Arnhem Wf, E14
off Arnhem Pl **124** C4
▨Arnhem Wf Prim Sch,
E14 .... **124** C4
Arnold Circ, E2 ...... **42** A5
Arnold Est, SE1 ..... **120** B2
▨Arnold Ho Sch, NW8. **32** C4
Arnold Rd, E3 .... **46** C1
Arnside St, SE17 ..... **146** B4
Arran Wk, N1 .... **18** A3
Arrol Ho, SE1 ...... **118** B4
Arrow Rd, E3 .... **47** E4

Arrowsmith Ho, SE11. **144** A2
Arta Ho, E1 .... **94** B1
Artesian Rd, W2 ...... **80** C1
Arthingworth St, E15.. **27** E5
Arthur Ct, SW11 ..... **165** D4
W2 .... **53** E5
Arthur Henderson Ho,
SW6 .... **160** A5
Arthur St, EC4 .... **91** D3
Artichoke Hill, E1 .... **93** E3
Artichoke Pl, SE5 .... **170** C3
Artillery La, E1 ...... **63** F4
Artillery Mans, SW1 . **114** C4
Artillery Pas, E1 ..... **63** F4
Artillery Pl, SW1 .... **114** C4
Artillery Row, SW1 .. **114** C4
Artisan Cl, E6 .... **105** E2
Artizan St, E1 .... **63** F5
Arundel Gdns, W11 ... **80** A2
Arundel Gt Ct, WC2... **88** B2
Arundel Pl, N1 .... **16** C2
Arundel Sq, N7 ...... **16** C2
Arundel St, WC2 ..... **88** B2
Ascalon St, SW8 .... **166** A2
▨Ashbourne Indep 6th
Form Coll, W8..... **109** E1
Ashbridge St, NW8.... **55** E2
Ashburn Gdns, SW7 . **110** A5
Ashburnham Gro,
SE10 .... **177** F2
Ashburnham Pl, SE10. **177** F2
▨Ashburnham Prim Sch,
SW10 .... **162** C1
Ashburnham Retreat,
SE10 .... **177** F2
Ashburnham Rd,
NW10 .... **28** A4
SW10 .... **162** B2
Ashburnham Twr, SW10
off Blantyre St **162** C1
Ashburn Pl, SW7 ..... **110** A5
Ashburton Rd, E16.... **73** D5
Ashby Gro, N1 .... **18** B3
Ashby Ho, N1 .... **18** B3
Ashby St, EC1 .... **39** F5
Ashcroft Rd, E3 ...... **45** F4
Ashcroft Sq, W6 ..... **134** A1
Ashdene, SE15 ...... **173** E3
Ashdown Wk, E14 ... **125** D5
Ashen, E6 .... **76** C5
Ashenden, SE17 ..... **118** A5
Ashentree Ct, EC4.... **89** D1
Asher Way, E1 .... **93** D4
Ashfield St, E1 .... **65** E4
Ashfield Yd, E1 ...... **66** A4
Ashford St, N1 .... **41** E4
Ash Gro, E8 .... **43** F1
Ash Ho, SE1
off Longfield Est. ... **148** B1
Ashington Ho, E1
off Barnsley St **65** F1
Ashington Rd, SW6 .. **160** B5
Ashland Pl, W1 ...... **56** C3
Ashley Gdns, SW1 ... **114** B4
Ashley Pl, SW1 ..... **114** A4
▨Ashmead Prim Sch,
SE8 .... **176** C5

Ashmead Rd, SE8 ... **176** C5
Ashmill St, NW1 ..... **55** E3
Ashmole Pl, SW8 ... **144** B5
▨Ashmole Prim Sch,
SW8 .... **144** B5
Ashmole St, SW8 ... **144** B5
Ashmore Cl, SE15 ... **172** B2
Ashmore Rd, W9 .... **52** B1
Ashton St, E14 ...... **98** B2
Ashwell Cl, E6 ...... **75** F5
Ashwin St, E8 .... **20** A1
Ashworth Cl, SE5 ... **170** C5
Ashworth Rd, W9 .... **31** F4
Aske St, N1 .... **41** E4
Asland Rd, E15 ...... **49** E1
Asolando Dr, SE17 .. **146** B1
Aspect Ct, SW6 ..... **162** B5
Aspen Ho, NW3 ..... **12** B1
Aspenlea Rd, W6 ... **134** C4
Aspen Way, E14 ..... **97** D3
Aspinden Rd, SE16... **121** F5
Assam St, E1 .... **64** C5
Assata Ms, N1 .... **17** F1
Assembly Pas, E1..... **66** B3
Astbury Business Pk, SE15
off Station Pas **174** A3
Astbury Ho, SE11 ... **116** C3
Astbury Rd, SE15 ... **174** A3
Astell St, SW3 ...... **139** F2
Aste St, E14 .... **126** A2
Asteys Row, N1 ..... **17** F4
Astle St, SW11 ..... **164** C5
Astley Ho, SE1
off Rowcross St **148** B2
Aston Ho, SW8 ..... **166** C4
Aston St, E14 .... **67** E5
Astrop Ms, W6 ..... **106** A3
Astrop Ter, W6 ..... **106** A3
Astwood Ms, SW7... **110** A5
Asylum Rd, SE15 ... **173** F1
Atalanta St, SW6 ... **159** D3
Athelstane Gro, E3... **46** A3
Athelstan Gdns, NW6... **7** F4
Athena Ct, SE1
off Long La. **119** E2
Athens Gdns, W9 .... **52** C2
Atherstone Ct, W2 ... **53** F3
Atherstone Ms, SW7.. **110** B5
Atherton St, SW11 .. **163** F5
Athlone St, NW5 ..... **13** D1
Atholl Ho, W9 .... **32** A5
Athol Sq, E14 .... **98** B1
Atkinson Ho, SW11
off Austin Rd **164** C4
Atkinson Rd, E16 .... **74** B4
Atlanta Bldg, SE13
off Deals Gateway .. **177** E4
Atlas Gdns, SE7 .... **130** A5
Atlas Ms, E8 .... **20** B1
N7 .... **16** B2
Atley Rd, E3 .... **46** C1
Atterbury St, SW1.... **143** D1
Attneave St, WC1 ... **38** C5
Aubrey Beardsley Ho, SW1
off Vauxhall Br Rd .. **142** B1
Aubrey Moore Pt, E15 . **48** B2
Aubrey Pl, NW8 ..... **32** A3

Aubrey Rd, W8 . . . . **80** B4
Aubrey Wk, W8 . . . . **80** B5
Auburn Cl, SE14 . . . . **175** E2
Auckland St, SE11 . . **144** A3
Auden Pl, NW1 . . . . **12** C5
Audley Dr, E16 . . . . . . **101** E4
Audley Sq, W1 . . . . **85** D4
Audrey St, E2 . . . . **42** C2
Augusta St, E14 . . . . . . **69** C5
Augustine Rd, W14 . . **106** C4
Augustus Ct, SE1 . . . . **119** E5
Augustus Ho, NW1
    off Augustus St **36** A4
Augustus St, NW1 . . . . **35** F3
Aulton Pl, SE11 . . . . . . **145** D3
Auriol Rd, W14 . . . . . . **135** E1
Austen Ho, NW6 . . . . . . **30** C4
Austin Friars, EC2 . . . . . **63** D5
Austin Friars Pas, EC2 . **63** D5
Austin Friars Sq, EC2 . . **63** D5
Austin Rd, SW11 . . . . . **164** C4
Austin St, E2 . . . . **42** A5
Austral St, SE11 . . . . . . **117** C5
Autumn St, E3 . . . . **47** D1
Avalon Rd, SW6 . . . . . **161** E3
Avebury Ct, N1
    off Avebury St **40** C1
Avebury St, N1 . . . . **40** C1
Aveline St, SE11 . . . . . **144** C2
Ave Maria La, EC4 . . . . . **89** F1
Avenons Rd, E13 . . . . . . **72** C2
Avenue, The, NW6 . . . . . **7** E4
    SE10 . . . . **178** C1
Avenue Cl, NW8 . . . . . . **33** F1
Avenue Rd, NW3 . . . . . . **10** C3
    NW8 . . . . **11** D4
Averill St, W6 . . . . **134** C5
Avery Fm Row, SW1 . . **141** E1
Avery Row, W1 . . . . **85** E2
Aviary Cl, E16 . . . . **72** B4
Avington Ct, SE1
    off Old Kent Rd **147** F1
Avis Sq, E1 . . . . **67** D5
Avocet Cl, SE1 . . . . **148** C2
Avondale Ct, E16 . . . . . **71** F3
Avondale Ho, SE1
    off Avondale Sq **148** C3
Avondale Pk Gdns,
    W11 . . . . **79** E3
Sch Avondale Pk Prim Sch,
    W11 . . . . **79** E3
Avondale Pk Rd, W11 . . **79** E2
Avondale Rd, E16 . . . . . **71** F3
Avondale Sq, SE1 . . . . **148** C3
Avonley Rd, SE14 . . . . **174** B2
Avonmore Gdns, W14
    off Avonmore Rd . . . **136** A1
Avonmore Pl, W14 . . . **107** F5
Sch Avonmore Prim Sch,
    W14 . . . . **107** F5
Avonmore Rd, W14 . . . **108** A5
Avonmouth St, SE1 . . . **118** A3
Avon Pl, SE1 . . . . **118** B2
Axis Ct, SE10 . . . . **155** E4
    SE16 *off East La* **121** D1
Aybrook St, W1 . . . . **56** C4
Aylesbury Est, SE17 . . **147** D3

Aylesbury Rd, SE17 . . **147** D3
Aylesbury St, EC1 . . . . . **61** E2
Aylesford St, SW1 . . . . **142** C1
Aylesham Cen, SE15 . **172** C4
Aylestone Av, NW6 . . . . . **6** C5
Aylton Est, SE16 . . . . . **122** B2
Aylward St, E1 . . . . **66** A5
Aylwyn Est, SE1 . . . . . **119** F3
Aynhoe Rd, W14 . . . . . **107** D5
Ayres St, SE1 . . . . **118** B1
Ayrton Gould Ho, E2 . . **45** D4
Ayrton Rd, SW7 . . . . . **110** C3
Azania Ms, NW5 . . . . . . **13** E1
Azenby Rd, SE15 . . . . . **172** A5
Azof St, SE10 . . . . **155** F1

B

Babington Ct, WC1
    off Ormond Cl **59** F3
Babmaes St, SW1 . . . . . **86** C3
Bacchus Wk, N1 . . . . . . **41** E3
Baches St, N1 . . . . **41** D5
Back Ch La, E1 . . . . **92** C2
Back Hill, EC1 . . . . **60** C2
Backhouse Pl, SE17 . . **147** F1
Bacon Gro, SE1 . . . . . . **120** A4
Sch Bacon's Coll, SE16 . **123** E1
Bacon St, E1 . . . . **64** B1
    E2 . . . . **64** B1
Bacton St, E2 . . . . **44** B4
Baddow Wk, N1 . . . . . . **18** A5
Baden Pl, SE1 . . . . **118** C1
Badminton Ms, E16 . . **101** D4
Badsworth Rd, SE5 . . **170** A3
Baffin Way, E14 . . . . . . **98** B3
Bagley's La, SW6 . . . . **161** F4
Bagshot St, SE17 . . . . **147** F3
Baildon St, SE8 . . . . . **176** B2
Bainbridge St, WC1 . . . **59** D5
Baird St, EC1 . . . . **62** B1
Bakers Hall Ct, EC3 . . . . **91** F1
Baker's Ms, W1 . . . . **56** C5
Baker's Rents, E2 . . . . . **42** A5
Bakers Row, E15 . . . . . . **49** E2
Baker's Row, EC1 . . . . . **60** C2
→ Baker Street **56** B3
Baker St, NW1 . . . . **56** B2
    W1 . . . . **56** B3
Baker's Yd, EC1 . . . . . . **60** C2
Bakery Cl, SW9 . . . . . . **168** B3
Balaam St, E13 . . . . **73** D1
Balaclava Rd, SE1 . . . . **148** B1
Balcombe St, NW1 . . . . **56** A2
Balcorne St, E9 . . . . **22** B4
Balderton St, W1 . . . . . **85** D1
Baldock St, E3 . . . . **47** E3
Baldwin Cres, SE5 . . . **170** A3
Baldwin's Gdns, EC1 . . . **60** C3
Baldwin St, EC1 . . . . . . **40** C5
Baldwin Ter, N1 . . . . . . **40** A2
Balearic Apts, E16
    off Western Gateway . **101** D3
Bale Rd, E1 . . . . **67** E3
Coll Bales Coll, W10 . . . . **29** D5

Balfern St, SW11 . . . . . **163** F4
Balfe St, N1 . . . . **37** F3
Balfour Ho, W10 . . . . . . **51** D3
Balfour Ms, W1 . . . . **85** D4
Balfour Pl, W1 . . . . **85** D3
Balfour St, SE17 . . . . . **118** C5
Balfron Twr, E14 . . . . . . **70** A5
Balkan Wk, E1 . . . . **93** E3
Balladier Wk, E14 . . . . . **69** E4
Ballance Rd, E9 . . . . **23** D1
Ballast Quay, SE10 . . . **155** D2
Ball Ct, EC3
    off Castle Ct **91** D1
Ballinger Pt, E3 . . . . **47** E4
Balliol Rd, W10 . . . . **50** B5
Ballow Cl, SE5 . . . . **171** E2
Balls Pond Pl, N1 . . . . . **19** D1
Balls Pond Rd, N1 . . . . . **19** D1
Balmer Rd, E3 . . . . **46** A3
Balmes Rd, N1 . . . . **19** D5
Balmoral Apts, W2
    off Praed St **55** E4
Balmoral Gro, N7 . . . . . **16** A2
Balmore Cl, E14 . . . . . . **70** B5
Balniel Gate, SW1 . . . . **143** D2
Baltic Apts, E16
    off Western Gateway . **101** D3
Baltic Ct, SE16 . . . . . . **123** D1
Baltic Pl, N1 . . . . **41** E1
Baltic Quay, SE16 . . . . **123** F5
Baltic St E, EC1 . . . . **62** A2
Baltic St W, EC1 . . . . . . **62** A2
Balvaird Pl, SW1 . . . . . **143** D3
Bamber Rd, SE15 . . . . **172** A3
Bamborough Gdns,
    W12 . . . . **106** B2
Banbury Ct, WC2 . . . . . **87** E2
Banbury Rd, E9 . . . . **22** C4
Banbury St, SW11 . . . **163** F5
Banchory Rd, SE3 . . . . **181** E1
Bancroft Ct, SW8 . . . . **167** E3
Bancroft Rd, E1 . . . . **44** B5
Sch Bangabandhu Prim
    Sch, E2 . . . . **44** B5
Banister Ms, NW6 . . . . . **9** E3
Banister Rd, W10 . . . . . **29** D4
→ Bank **90** C1
DLR Bank **90** C1
Bank End, SE1 . . . . **90** B4
★ Bank of England,
    EC2 . . . . **90** C1
★ Bank of England Mus,
    EC2 . . . . **91** D1
Banks Ho, SE1 . . . . **118** A4
Bankside, SE1 . . . . **90** A3
★ Bankside Gall, SE1 . . **89** F3
Bankside Lofts, SE1 . . **89** F4
Riv Bankside Pier **90** A3
Bank St, E14 . . . . **97** D5
Bannerman Ho, SW8 . **144** A5
Banner St, EC1 . . . . **62** B2
Banning St, SE10 . . . . **155** E3
★ Banqueting Ho, SW1 . **87** E5

Bantry St, SE5.......**171** D2
Banyard Rd, SE16....**121** F4
Baptist Gdns, NW5....**12** C1
Barandon Wk, W11....**79** D2
Barbara Brosnan Ct,
NW8.............**32** C3
Barbara Castle Cl,
SW6.............**136** B5
Barbers Rd, E15......**47** E2
BARBICAN, EC2.......**62** A4
⇌Barbican..........**61** F3
⊖Barbican..........**61** F3
★ Barbican Arts &
Conf Cen, EC2......**62** B3
Barb Ms, W6........**106** B4
Barbon Cl, WC1......**59** F3
Barchester St, E14...**69** E4
Barclay Cl, SW6.....**160** C2
Barclay Rd, E13.....**74** A2
SW6.............**160** C2
Bard Rd, W10.......**78** C3
Bardsey Pl, E1.......**66** A2
Bardsey Wk, N1......**18** B2
Bardsley La, SE10....**154** A5
Barfett St, W10.....**52** A1
Barfleur La, SE8.....**152** A1
Barford St, N1.......**39** D1
Barge Ho Rd, E16....**105** E5
Barge Ho St, SE1....**89** D4
Barge La, E3........**45** F1
Baring St, N1.......**40** C1
Barkantine Shop Par,
The, E14........**124** C2
Barker Dr, NW1.....**14** B4
Barker St, SW10....**138** A4
Barkham Ter, SE1...**117** D3
Barking Rd, E16.....**72** A4
Bark Pl, W2.........**81** E2
Barkston Gdns, SW5..**137** E2
Barkworth Rd, SE16..**149** F3
Barlborough St, SE14.**174** B1
Barlby Gdns, W10.....**50** C2
Barlby Prim Sch,
W10.............**51** D2
Barlby Rd, W10.......**50** C3
Barleycorn Way, E14..**96** A2
Barley Mow Pas, EC1..**61** F4
Barley Shotts Business Pk,
W10 off Acklam Rd..**52** A3
Barlow Ho, SE16
off Rennie Est.....**149** F1
Barlow Pl, W1........**85** F3
Barlow Rd, NW6.....**8** B1
Barlow St, SE17.....**119** D5
Barnaby Pl, SW7....**138** C1
Barnard Cl, SE18....**133** D5
Barnardo Gdns, E1...**94** C2
Barnardo St, E1......**94** C1
Barnard's Inn, EC1...**61** D5
Barnby Sq, E15......**27** E5
Barnby St, E15......**27** E5
NW1.............**36** B3
Barnes Ct, E16......**74** B3
Barnes St, E14.......**95** E1
Barnes Ter, SE8......**152** B3
Barnet Gro, E2.......**42** C4
Barnett St, E1.......**65** E5
Barnfield Pl, E14.....**153** D1
Barnham St, SE1.....**119** F1
BARNSBURY, N1......**16** B3
Barnsbury Est, N1....**38** B1
Barnsbury Gro, N7....**16** B2
Barnsbury Pk, N1.....**16** C3
Barnsbury Rd, N1.....**38** C2
Barnsbury Sq, N1.....**16** C4
Barnsbury St, N1.....**16** C4
Barnsbury Ter, N1....**16** B4
Barnsdale Av, E14...**125** D5
Barnsdale Rd, W9.....**52** B1
Barnsley St, E1......**65** F1
Barnston Wk, N1.....**18** A5
Barnwood Cl, W9.....**53** E2
Baroness Rd, E2......**42** B4
⊖Barons Court......**135** E2
Barons Ct Rd, W14...**135** E2
Barons Keep, W14...**135** E2
Barons Pl, SE1......**117** D2
Baron St, N1........**38** C2
Baron Wk, E16......**72** A3
Barque Ms, SE8......**152** C4
Barrett St, W1.......**85** D1
Barriedale, SE14.....**175** F5
Barrie Est, W2.......**82** C2
Barrier App, SE7....**130** C4
Barrier Pt Rd, E16...**102** A5
Barrier Pt Twr, E16
off Barrier Pt Rd....**130** A1
Barrow Hill Est, NW8..**33** E3
Barrow Hill Jun Sch,
NW8.............**33** E3
Barrow Hill Rd, NW8..**33** E3
Barry Ho, SE16
off Rennie Est.....**149** F2
Barry Rd, E6........**75** F5
Barter St, WC1......**59** F4
Bartholomew Cl, EC1..**62** A4
Bartholomew Ct, E14
off Newport Av....**99** D3
Bartholomew La, EC2..**91** D1
Bartholomew Pl, EC1..**62** A4
Bartholomew Rd, NW5..**14** C2
Bartholomew Sq, E1...**65** F1
EC1.............**62** B1
Bartholomew St, SE1..**118** C4
Bartholomew Vil, NW5..**14** A2
Bartle Rd, W11......**79** D1
Bartlett Cl, E14......**69** D5
Bartlett Ct, EC4.....**61** D5
Bartletts Pas, EC4...**61** D5
Barton Cl, E6.......**76** B5
Barton Ho, E3
off Bow Rd.......**47** E4
N1.............**17** F3
Barton Rd, W14.....**135** E3
Barton St, SW1.....**115** E3
Bartonway, NW8.....**32** C1
Baseing Cl, E6.......**105** D2
Basevi Way, SE8.....**153** E4
Basil St, SW3.......**112** A3
Basin App, E14......**95** F1
Basing Ct, SE15.....**172** B4
Basinghall Av, EC2....**62** C4
Basinghall St, EC2....**62** C5
Basing Ho Yd, E2.....**41** F4
Basing Pl, E2.........**41** F4
Basing St, W11......**52** A5
Basire St, N1........**18** A5
Basque Ct, SE16.....**122** C1
Bassett Rd, W10......**51** D5
Bassishaw Highwalk, EC2
off Aldermanbury Sq.**62** B4
Bastion Highwalk, EC2.**62** A4
Bastion Ho, EC2
off London Wall.....**62** A4
Bastwick St, EC1.....**62** A1
Basuto Rd, SW6.....**160** C4
Batavia Ms, SE14....**175** F2
Batavia Rd, SE14....**175** F2
Batchelor St, N1......**38** C2
Bateman Ho, SE17...**145** E5
Bateman's Bldgs, W1..**86** C1
Bateman's Row, EC2..**63** F1
Bateman St, W1......**86** C1
Bate St, E14........**96** B2
Bath Cl, SE15.......**173** F2
Bath Ct, EC1........**60** C2
EC1 off St. Luke's Est..**40** C5
Bath Ho, SE1
off Bath Ter.......**118** B3
Bath Pl, EC2........**41** E5
Bath St, EC1........**40** B5
Bath Ter, SE1.......**118** A4
Bathurst Ms, W2......**82** C2
Bathurst St, W2......**82** C2
Bathway, SE18......**133** D5
Batoum Gdns, W6...**106** B3
Batson Ho, E1
off Fairclough St....**93** D1
Batten Cl, E6.......**104** B1
BATTERSEA, SW11...**164** B3
Battersea Br, SW3...**163** D1
SW11...........**163** D1
Battersea Br Rd,
SW11...........**163** E2
Battersea Ch Rd,
SW11...........**163** D3
★ Battersea Dogs Home,
SW8............**165** F2
Battersea High St,
SW11...........**163** D4
★ Battersea Park,
SW11...........**164** B1
⇌Battersea Park....**165** E3
Battersea Pk Rd, SW8.**165** E3
Battersea Sq, SW11
off Battersea High St.**163** D4
Battersea Tech Coll,
SW11...........**164** B4
Battishill Gdns, N1
off Waterloo Ter.....**17** E4
Battishill St, N1......**17** E4
Battlebridge Ct, N1...**37** F2
Battle Br La, SE1.....**91** E5
Battle Br Rd, NW1....**37** E3
Batty St, E1.........**65** D5
Batwa Ho, SE16.....**149** F3
Bawtree Rd, SE14....**175** E1

Baxendale St, E2......**42** C4
Baxter Ho, E3
  off Bromley High St..**47** E4
Baxter Rd, E16.......**74** B5
  N1................**19** D2
Bayford Ms, E8........**21** F4
Bayford Rd, NW10....**28** C5
Bayford St, E8........**21** F4
Bayham Pl, NW1......**36** A2
Bayham St, NW1......**36** A1
Bayley St, WC1.......**58** C4
Baylis Rd, SE1.......**116** C2
Bayne Cl, E6.......**104** B1
Baynes Ms, NW3......**11** D1
Baynes St, NW1......**14** B4
Bayonne Rd, W6.....**135** E5
BAYSWATER, W2......**81** F1
Bayswater.........**81** E2
Bayswater Rd, W2....**83** D2
Baythorne St, E3....**68** B3
Baytree Ms, SE17....**118** C5
Bazely St, E14.......**98** A2
Beachy Rd, E3........**24** C4
Beacons Cl, E6......**75** F4
Beaconsfield Cl, SE3..**156** C4
Beaconsfield Rd, E16..**72** A2
  SE3..............**156** B5
  SE17.............**147** D3
Beaconsfield Ter Rd,
  W14.............**107** E4
Beaconsfield Wk, E6..**105** D1
  SW6.............**160** B4
Beadon Rd, W6......**134** A1
Beak St, W1.........**86** B2
Beale Pl, E3..........**46** A2
Beale Rd, E3..........**46** A1
Beaminster Ho, SW8
  off Dorset Rd......**168** A1
Beamish Ho, SE16
  off Rennie St......**150** A1
Beanacre Cl, E9......**24** B1
Bear All, EC4.........**61** E5
Bear Gdns, SE1.......**90** A4
Bear La, SE1.........**89** F4
Bear St, WC2.........**87** D2
Beaton Cl, SE15.....**172** B3
Beatrice Cl, E13......**72** C1
Beatrice Pl, W8......**109** E4
Beatrice Rd, SE1.....**149** D1
SchBeatrice Tate Sch,
  E2...............**43** F4
Beatson Wk, SE16.....**95** E4
Beatty St, NW1.......**36** A2
Beauchamp Pl, SW3..**111** F3
Beauchamp St, EC1...**60** C4
Beaufort, E6.........**77** D5
Beaufort Ct, SW6....**136** C4
Beaufort Gdns, SW3..**111** F3
Beaufort Ms, SW6....**136** B4
Beaufort St, SW3.....**139** D5
Beaufoy Wk, SE11...**144** B1
Beaulieu Av, E16....**101** E4
Beaumont Av, W14..**136** A2
Beaumont Cres, W14..**136** A2
Beaumont Gro, E1...**66** C2
Beaumont Ms, W1....**57** D3
Beaumont Pl, W1....**58** B1

Beaumont Sq, E1.....**66** C3
Beaumont St, W1....**57** D3
Beaumont Wk, NW3...**12** B3
Beccles St, E14.......**96** B2
Beck Cl, SE13.......**177** E4
Becket St, SE1......**118** C3
Beckford Cl, W14....**136** B1
Beckford Pl, SE17....**146** B3
Beck Rd, E8.........**21** E5
BECKTON, E6........**77** D4
DLRBeckton..........**76** C4
DLRBeckton Park.....**104** B2
Beckton Pk Rbt, E16.**104** A2
Beckton Retail Pk, E6..**76** C3
Beckton Rd, E16......**72** B3
Beckton Triangle
  Retail Pk, E6.......**77** D1
Beckway St, SE17....**147** D1
Becquerel Ct, SE10...**128** B4
Bedale St, SE1........**90** C5
Bedford Av, WC1......**59** D4
Bedfordbury, WC2....**87** E2
Bedford Ct, WC2......**87** E3
Bedford Gdns, W8....**80** C5
Bedford Pas, SW6....**159** F1
Bedford Pl, WC1......**59** E3
Bedford Row, WC1....**60** B3
Bedford Sq, WC1......**59** D4
Bedford St, WC2......**87** E2
Bedford Way, WC1....**59** D2
Bedlam Ms, SE11....**116** B5
Bedser Cl, SE11......**144** B4
Beeby Rd, E16.......**73** E4
Beech Cl, SE8.......**152** B5
Beech Gdns, EC2
  off White Lyon Ct....**62** A3
Beech Ho, NW3
  off Maitland Pk Vil...**12** B1
Beechmore Rd, SW11.**164** B4
Beech St, EC2........**62** A3
Beech Tree Cl, N1....**16** C3
Beechwood Rd, E8...**20** A1
Beehive Cl, E8........**20** A3
Beehive Pas, EC3....**91** E1
Beeston Pl, SW1....**113** F4
Beethoven St, W10...**29** F4
Begonia Cl, E6.......**75** F3
Bekesbourne St, E14..**95** E1
Belfort Rd, SE15.....**174** B5
Belfry Cl, SE16......**149** F2
Belgrave Ct, E14.....**96** B3
Belgrave Gdns, NW8..**31** F1
Belgrave Ms N, SW1..**112** C2
Belgrave Ms S, SW1..**113** D3
Belgrave Ms W, SW1..**112** C3
Belgrave Pl, SW1....**113** D3
Belgrave Rd, E13.....**73** F1
  SW1..............**142** A1
Belgrave Sq, SW1....**112** C3
Belgrave St, E1......**95** D1
Belgrave Yd, SW1....**113** E4
BELGRAVIA, SW1....**112** C4
Belgrove St, WC1.....**37** E4
Belham Wk, SE5.....**171** D3
Belitha Vil, N1.......**16** B3
Bellamy Cl, E14.....**124** C1
  W14..............**136** B3

Bellenden Rd, SE15..**172** B5
CollBellerbys Coll, SE8.**153** D5
Bellevue Pl, E1......**66** A2
Bellfield Cl, SE3.....**181** D1
Bellflower Cl, E6.....**75** E3
Bell Inn Yd, EC3......**91** D1
Bell La, E1..........**64** A4
  E16...............**100** C4
Bellmaker Ct, E3......**68** C3
Bellot Gdns, SE10....**155** F2
Bellot St, SE10......**155** F2
Bells Gdn Est, SE15..**172** C2
Bell St, NW1.........**55** F3
Bell Water Gate, SE18.**133** D3
Bell Wf La, EC4......**90** B3
Bell Yd, WC2.........**60** C5
Bell Yd Ms, SE1.....**119** F2
Belmont St, NW1....**13** D3
Belmore St, SW8....**166** C3
Belsham St, E9.......**22** A1
Belsize Av, NW3......**11** D1
Belsize Gro, NW3....**11** F1
Belsize La, NW3......**10** C2
Belsize Ms, NW3......**11** D1
BELSIZE PARK, NW3..**11** E2
Belsize Pk, NW3......**10** C2
Belsize Pk Gdns, NW3.**11** D1
Belsize Pk Ms, NW3..**11** D1
Belsize Pl, NW3......**11** D1
Belsize Rd, NW6......**10** B4
Belsize Sq, NW3......**11** D1
Belsize Ter, NW3.....**11** D1
Belson Rd, SE18.....**132** A5
Belton Way, E3.......**68** C3
Belvedere, The, SW10.**162** B4
Belvedere Bldgs, SE1.**117** F2
Belvedere Ct, N1......**19** E5
Belvedere Ms, SE3...**181** D2
Belvedere Pl, SE1....**117** F2
Belvedere Rd, SE1...**116** B1
Belvoir Ho, SW1
  off Vauxhall Br Rd..**114** B5
Bembridge Cl, NW6...**7** E3
Bemerton Est, N1....**15** F4
Bemerton St, N1.....**16** A5
Benbow St, SE8......**153** D4
Bendall Ms, NW1....**55** F3
Bengal Ct, EC3
  off Birchin La.....**91** D1
Benhill Rd, SE5.....**171** D2
Benjamin Cl, E8.....**43** D1
Benjamin St, EC1....**61** E3
Ben Jonson Ho, EC2
  off The Barbican...**62** B3
SchBen Jonson Prim Sch,
  E1...............**67** F2
Ben Jonson Rd, E1....**67** D4
Benledi Rd, E14......**70** C5
Bennet's Hill, EC4....**89** F2
Bennet St, SW1......**86** A4
Bennett Gro, SE13..**177** F4
Bennett Ho, SW1
  off Page St.......**115** D5

Bennett Rd, E13 . . . . . . **74** A2
Bennetts Yd, SW1 . . . . . **115** D4
Benn St, E9 . . . . **23** F1
Ben Smith Way, SE16. **121** D3
Benson Ct, SW8
  off Hartington Rd . . **167** E3
Benson Quay, E1 . . . . . **94** A3
Bentham St, N1 . . . . . . **18** A4
Bentham Ho, SE1
  off Falmouth Rd . . .**118** C3
Bentham Rd, E9 . . . . . . **22** C2
Ben Tillett Cl, E16. . . . **104** A5
Bentinck Cl, NW8
  off Prince Albert Rd . .**33** F3
Bentinck Ms, W1 . . . . . .**57** D5
Bentinck St, W1 . . . . . . **57** D5
Bentley Rd, N1 . . . . **19** F2
Benville Ho, SW8 . . . **168** B2
Benwick Cl, SE16 . . . . **121** F5
Benworth St, E3 . . . . . . **46** B4
Benyon Rd, N1 . . . . **19** D5
Benyon Wf, E8 . . . . **19** F5
Sch Beormund Sch, SE1. **119** D2
Berber Pl, E14 . . . . **96** C2
Berenger Twr, SW10
  off Blantyre St **162** C1
Berenger Wk, SW10
  off Blantyre St **162** C1
Berens Rd, NW10 . . . . . **28** C5
Beresford Sq, SE18 . . . **133** E5
Beresford St, SE18 . . . **133** E4
Bere St, E1 . . . . **95** D2
Bergen Sq, SE16 . . . . . **123** F3
Sch Berger Prim Sch, E9. **22** C1
Berger Rd, E9 . . . . **22** C1
Berghem Ms, W14 . . . **107** D4
Bergholt Ms, NW1 . . . . **14** B4
Berglen Ct, E14 . . . . **95** E1
Bering Sq, E14 . . . . . . **153** D2
Bering Wk, E16 . . . . . . **102** C1
Berkeley Gdns, W8 . . . . **81** D5
Berkeley Ho, E3 . . . . . . **46** B5
Berkeley Ms, W1 . . . . . . **56** B5
Berkeley Sq, W1 . . . . . . **85** F3
Berkeley St, W1 . . . . . . **85** F3
Berkeley Twr, E14 . . . . **96** B4
Berkley Gro, NW1 . . . . **12** B4
Berkley Rd, NW1 . . . . . **12** B4
Berkshire Rd, E9 . . . . . . **24** B1
BERMONDSEY, SE1. . . **120** A4
❸ Bermondsey **121** D3
Bermondsey Sq, SE1 . **119** F3
Bermondsey St, SE1. . . **91** E5
Bermondsey Wall E,
  SE16 . . . . **121** D2
Bermondsey Wall W,
  SE16 . . . . **120** C1
Bernard Ashley Dr,
  SE7 . . . . **157** E3
Bernard Cassidy St,
  E16 . . . . **72** B3
Bernard St, WC1 . . . . . . **59** E2
Berners Ms, W1. . . . . . . **58** B4

Berners Pl, W1 . . . . **58** B5
Berners Rd, N1 . . . . **39** D2
Berners St, W1 . . . . **58** B4
Bernhardt Cres, NW8 . . **55** E1
Berryfield Rd, SE17 . .**145** F2
Berry Pl, EC1 . . . . **39** F5
Berry St, EC1 . . . . **61** F5
Berthon St, SE8. . . . . . **177** D1
Berwick Rd, E16 . . . . . **102** A1
Berwick St, W1 . . . . **86** C1
Beryl Av, E6. . . . . **75** F3
Beryl Rd, W6 . . . . **134** C3
Bessborough Gdns,
  SW1. . . . . **143** D2
Bessborough Pl, SW1.**142** C2
Bessborough St, SW1.**142** C2
Bessie Lansbury Cl,
  E6 . . . . **104** C1
Besson St, SE14 . . . . . **174** B3
Bessy St, E2 . . . . **44** B4
Bestwood St, SE8 . . . **151** D1
Bethell Av, E16 . . . . **72** A1
BETHNAL GREEN, E2 . . **43** E4
🚉 Bethnal Green **65** E1
❸ Bethnal Green **44** A5
Bethnal Grn Est, E2 . . . **44** A5
Bethnal Grn Rd, E1. . . . **64** A1
  E2 . . . . **64** A1
Sch Bethnal Grn Tech Coll,
  E2 . . . . **42** B5
Coll Bethnal Grn Training
  Cen, E1 . . . . **64** C3
Bethwin Rd, SE5 . . . . . **169** F1
Betterton St, WC2. . . . . **87** E1
Bettons Pk, E15 . . . . . . **49** F1
Betts St, E1 . . . . **93** E3
Bevan St, N1 . . . . **40** B1
Bevenden St, N1 . . . . . . **41** D4
Beverly, NW8 . . . . **33** E5
Beverston Ms, W1. . . . . **56** A4
Bevin Cl, SE16 . . . . **95** E4
Bevin Ct, WC1 . . . . **38** B4
Bevington Path, SE1
  off Tanner St **120** A2
Sch Bevington Prim Sch,
  W10. . . . . **51** F3
Bevington Rd, W10 . . . **51** F3
Bevington St, SE16. . .**121** D2
Bevin Way, WC1 . . . . . . **38** C4
Bevis Marks, EC3 . . . . . **63** F5
Bewdley St, N1 . . . . **16** C3
Bewick Ms, SE15. . . . .**173** E2
Bewley St, E1 . . . . **93** F2
Bexhill Wk, E15 . . . . . . **49** F1
Bianca Rd, SE15 . . . . .**148** C5
Bibury Cl, SE15 . . . . . .**147** F5
Bickenhall St, W1 . . . . . **56** B3
Bidborough St, WC1. . . **37** E5
Bidder St, E16. . . . . **71** E3
Biddulph Rd, W9. . . . . . **31** E5
Bidwell St, SE15 . . . . .**173** F4
★ Big Ben (St. Stephens
  Twr), SW1 . . . . **115** F2
Biggerstaff Rd, E15 . . . **26** A5
Sch Bigland Grn Prim Sch,
  E1 . . . . **93** E1
Bigland St, E1 . . . . **93** E1

Bill Faust Ho, E1
  off Tarling St **94** A1
Billing Pl, SW10 . . . . .**161** F1
Billing Rd, SW10. . . . .**161** F1
★ Billingsgate Mkt,
  E14 . . . . **97** F4
Billing St, SW10 . . . . .**161** F1
Billington Rd, SE14 . .**174** C2
Billiter Sq, EC3 . . . . **91** F2
Billiter St, EC3. . . . . **91** F1
Billson St, E14 . . . . . . **154** B1
Bilton Twrs, W1 *off Great
  Cumberland Pl* **84** B1
Bina Gdns, SW5 . . . . .**138** A1
Binfield Rd, SW4. . . . .**167** F4
Bingfield St, N1. . . . . . . **15** F5
Bingham Ct, N1 . . . . . . **17** F3
Bingham Pl, W1 . . . . . . **56** C3
Bingham St, N1 . . . . . . **18** C1
Bingley Rd, E16 . . . . . . **74** A5
Binne Ho, SE1
  off Bath Ter **118** A4
Binney St, W1 . . . . **85** D2
Birch Cl, E16 . . . . **71** F3
Birchdown Ho, E3. . . . . **47** E5
Birches, The, SE7 . . . . **157** F4
Birchfield St, E14 . . . . . **96** C2
Birchington Rd, NW6 . . . **9** D5
Birchin La, EC3 . . . . **91** D1
Birdcage Wk, SW1 . . . **114** B2
Bird in Bush Rd, SE15.**173** D1
Birdsfield La, E3 . . . . . . **24** A5
Bird St, W1 . . . . **85** D1
Uni Birkbeck Coll, Main Bldg,
  WC1 . . . . **59** D2
  Clore Management Cen,
  WC1 . . . . **59** D2
  Gordon Ho & Ingold
  Laboratories, WC1 . . . **58** C1
  Gordon Sq, WC1 . . . . . **59** D1
  Russell Sq, WC1 . . . . . **59** D3
Birkbeck St, E2 . . . . **43** F5
Birkdale Cl, SE16 . . . .**149** E3
Birkenhead St, WC1 . . . **37** F4
Biscayne Av, E14 . . . . . **98** B3
Biscay Rd, W6 . . . .**134** C3
Sch Bishop Challoner Cath
  Collegiate Sch, E1 . .**94** B1
Bishop Kings Rd, W14.**107** F5
Bishop's Av, SW6 . . . .**159** D5
Bishops Br, W2 . . . . **54** B5
Bishops Br Rd, W2 . . . . **81** F1
Bishop's Ct, EC4 . . . . . . **61** E5
  WC2 . . . . **60** C5
Bishopsgate, EC2 . . . . . **91** E1
Bishopsgate Arc, EC2. . **63** F4
Bishopsgate Chyd, EC2.**63** E4
Coll Bishopsgate Inst,
  EC2 . . . . **63** F4
Bishops Ho, SW8 *off South
  Lambeth Rd* **167** F2
Bishopsmead, SE5
  off Camberwell Rd . .**170** B2
Bishop's Pk, SW6 . . . .**158** C5
Bishop's Pk Rd, SW6 .**159** D5
Bishops Rd, SW6. . . . .**160** A2
Bishop's Rd, SW11. . .**163** F1

Bishops Sq, E1 . . . . 63 F3
Bishops Ter, SE11. . . . 117 D5
Bishop St, N1 . . . . 18 A5
Bishops Way, E2. . . . . . 43 F2
Bishop Wilfred Wd Cl,
    SE15 . . . . 173 D5
Bisson Rd, E15 . . . . 48 B2
Bittern St, SE1. . . . . . . 118 A2
Blackall St, EC2. . . . . . . 63 C1
Blackbird Yd, E2 . . . . . . 42 B4
Black Bull Yd, EC1
    off Hatton Wall 60 C3
Blackburne's Ms, W1 . . 84 C2
Blackburn Rd, NW6 . . . . 9 E2
⇌ Blackfriars 89 F2
◉ Blackfriars 89 F2
Blackfriars Br, EC4 . . . 89 E2
    SE1 . . . . 89 E2
Blackfriars Ct, EC4 . . . . 89 E2
Black Friars La, EC4 . . . 89 E2
Riv Blackfriars Millennium
    Pier 89 D2
Blackfriars Pas, EC4 . . . 89 E2
Blackfriars Rd, SE1. . . 117 E2
BLACKHEATH, SE3 . . . 179 F4
★ Blackheath, SE3. . . 180 B4
Blackheath Av, SE10 . 179 F4
Sch Blackheath Bluecoat
    C of E Sch, SE3 . . . . 181 F1
Sch Blackheath High Sch,
    Sen Dept, SE3 . . . . . 180 C1
Blackheath Hill, SE10. 177 F4
Sch Blackheath Nurs &
    Prep Sch, SE3 . . . . . 180 C3
Blackheath Rd, SE10 . 177 E3
Blackheath Vale, SE3 . 179 F5
Black Horse Ct, SE1 . . 119 D3
Blackhorse Rd, SE8. . . 151 F4
Blacklands Ter, SW3 . 140 A1
Black Prince Rd, SE1 . 144 A1
    SE11 . . . . 144 B1
Blacks Rd, W6. . . . . . . 134 A1
Blackstone Est, E8 . . . . 21 D4
Blackstone Ho, SW1
    off Churchill Gdns . . 142 A3
Black Swan Yd, SE1 . . 119 E1
Blackthorn St, E3 . . . . . 69 D2
DLR Blackwall 98 B3
Blackwall La, SE10 . . . 155 F2
Blackwall Pier, E14. . . . 99 E3
Blackwall Trd Est, E14 . 71 D4
Blackwall Tunnel, E14 . 98 C3
Blackwall Tunnel App,
    SE10 . . . . 127 E2
Blackwall Tunnel
    Northern App, E3. . . 47 D2
    E14 . . . . 48 A4
Blackwall Way, E14 . . . 98 B3
Blackwood St, SE17 . . 146 C2
Blagrove Rd, W10. . . . . 51 F4
Blair Cl, N1 . . . . 18 B1
Blair Ho, SW9 . . . . 168 A5
Blair St, E14 . . . . 98 B1
Blake Cl, W10 . . . . 50 B3
Blake Gdns, SW6. . . . . 161 E3
Blakeney Cl, NW1. . . . . 14 C4
Blake Rd, E16 . . . . 72 A2

Blaker Rd, E15 . . . . 48 A1
Blakes Rd, SE15 . . . . . 171 F1
Blake St, SE8 . . . . 152 C4
Blanchard Way, E8. . . . 21 D2
Blanch Cl, SE15. . . . . . 174 A2
Blanche St, E16. . . . . . . 72 A2
Blandford Sq, NW1. . . . 55 F2
Blandford St, W1. . . . . . 56 B5
Blantyre St, SW10 . . . 162 C1
Blantyre Twr, SW10 . . 162 C1
Blantyre Wk, SW10
    off Blantyre St 162 C1
Blashford, NW3. . . . . . . 12 A3
Blasker Wk, E14 . . . . . 153 D2
Blechynden St, W10. . . 79 D2
Bledlow Cl, NW8. . . . . . 55 D2
Bleeding Heart Yd, EC1. 61 D4
Blemundsbury, WC1
    off Dombey St 60 A3
Blenheim Cres, W11. . . 79 E2
Blenheim Gdns, NW2. . . 6 B1
Blenheim Pas, NW8 . . . 32 A2
Blenheim Rd, NW8 . . . . 32 A2
Blenheim St, W1. . . . . . 85 E1
Blenheim Ter, NW8. . . . 32 A2
Sch Blessed Sacrament
    RC Prim Sch, N1. . . . 38 A1
Bletchley Ct, N1 . . . . . . 40 C3
Bletchley St, N1 . . . . . . 40 B3
Bletsoe Wk, N1. . . . . . . 40 B2
Bliss Cres, SE13 . . . . . 177 F5
Blissett St, SE10 . . . . . 178 A3
Bliss Ms, W10 . . . . 29 F4
Blithfield St, W8 . . . . . 109 E4
Blomfield Ct, SW11. . . 163 D3
Blomfield Ms, W2 . . . . . 54 A4
Blomfield Rd, W9 . . . . . 54 A3
Blomfield St, EC2 . . . . . 63 D4
Blomfield Vil, W2 . . . . . 53 F4
Blondel St, SW11 . . . . 164 C5
Blondin St, E3 . . . . 46 C2
Bloomburg St, SW1 . . 142 B1
Bloomfield Pl, W1. . . . . 85 F2
Bloomfield Ter, SW1. . 141 D2
Bloom Pk Rd, SW6 . . . 160 A2
BLOOMSBURY, WC1 . . 59 D4
Bloomsbury Ct, WC1 . . 59 F4
Bloomsbury Pl, WC1. . . 59 F3
Bloomsbury Sq, WC1 . . 59 F4
Bloomsbury St, WC1 . . 59 D4
Bloomsbury Way, WC1. 59 E5
Blore Cl, SW8. . . . . 166 C4
Blore Ct, W1 . . . . 86 C1
Blossom St, E1 . . . . 63 F3
Blount St, E14. . . . . 67 F5
Blucher Rd, SE5 . . . . . 170 B2
Blue Anchor La, SE16. 121 D5
Blue Anchor Yd, E1. . . . 92 C2
Blue Ball Yd, SW1 . . . . . 86 A5
Bluebell Cl, E9. . . . . 22 A5
Sch Blue Gate Flds Inf &
    Jun Schs, E1. . . . . . . 94 A2
Bluelion Pl, SE1. . . . . . 119 E3
Blundell St, N7 . . . . 15 F3
Blyth Cl, E14. . . . . 126 C5
Blythe Ms, W14 . . . . . 107 D3
Blythe Rd, W14. . . . . . 107 E5

Blythe St, E2 . . . . 43 E4
Blyth's Wf, E14. . . . . . . 95 F3
Boadicea St, N1 . . . . . . 38 A1
Boardwalk Pl, E14 . . . . 98 A4
Boathouse Wk, SE15 . 172 B1
Boat Lifter Way, SE16. 123 F5
Bocking St, E8. . . . . 21 E5
Bohemia Pl, E8 . . . . 21 F1
Bohn Rd, E1 . . . . 67 E3
Bolden St, SE8. . . . . . . 177 E5
Bolina Rd, SE16 . . . . . 150 B2
Bolingbroke Rd, W14. 107 D3
Bolingbroke Wk,
    SW11. . . . . 163 D2
Bolney Gate, SW7. . . . 111 E2
Bolney St, SW8 . . . . . . 168 A2
Bolsover St, W1 . . . . . . 57 F2
Bolt Ct, EC4 . . . . 89 D1
Bolton Cres, SE5 . . . . . 145 D5
Bolton Gdns, NW10 . . . 28 C3
    SW5. . . . . 137 E2
Bolton Gdns Ms,
    SW10. . . . . 138 A2
Bolton Rd, NW8 . . . . . . 31 F1
Boltons, The, SW10 . . 138 A2
Boltons Pl, SW5 . . . . . 138 A2
Bolton St, W1 . . . . 85 F4
Bombay St, SE16 . . . . 121 E5
Bomore Rd, W11. . . . . . 79 D2
Bonar Rd, SE15. . . . . . 172 C2
Bonchurch Rd, W10 . . . 51 E3
Bond Ct, EC4 . . . . 90 C1
Bondfield Rd, E6. . . . . . 75 F4
Bonding Yd Wk, SE16. 123 F2
◉ Bond Street 85 D1
Bondway, SW8 . . . . . . 143 F5
Boneta Rd, SE18. . . . . 132 A4
Bonhill St, EC2 . . . . 63 D2
Sch Bonner Prim Sch, E2. 44 B3
Bonner Rd, E2. . . . . 44 A2
Bonner St, E2 . . . . 44 B3
Bonnington Ho, N1
    off Killick St 38 A3
Bonnington Sq, SW8 . 144 A4
Bonny St, NW1 . . . . 14 A4
Bonsor St, SE5 . . . . . . 171 E2
Booker Cl, E14. . . . . 68 B4
Book Ms, WC2. . . . . 87 D1
Boord St, SE10 . . . . . . 127 F3
Booth Cl, E9 . . . . 43 F1
Booth La, EC4 . . . . 90 A2
Booth's Pl, W1 . . . . 58 B4
Boot St, N1 . . . . 41 E5
Boreas Wk, N1 . . . . 39 F3
Boreham Av, E16 . . . . 100 C1
Borgard Rd, SE18 . . . . 132 A5
◉ Borough 118 B2
BOROUGH, THE, SE1 . 118 A2
Borough High St, SE1. 118 A2
★ Borough Mkt, SE1 . . 90 C5
Borough Rd, SE1. . . . . 117 E3
Borough Sq, SE1. . . . . 118 A2
Borrett Cl, SE17 . . . . . 146 A3

Borthwick St, SE8 .... **152** C3
Boscobel Pl, SW1 .... **113** D5
Boscobel St, NW8 ..... **55** D2
Boss Ho, SE1 .... **120** A1
Boss St, SE1 .... **120** A1
Boston Pl, NW1 .... **56** A2
Bosun Cl, E14 .... **125** D1
Boswell St, WC1 ...... **59** F3
Boswell St, WC1 ...... **59** F3
Bosworth Rd, W10 .... **51** F2
Botha Rd, E13 .... **73** F3
Bothwell Cl, E16 ...... **72** B4
Bothwell St, W6 ..... **135** D5
Botolph All, EC3 ...... **91** E2
Botolph La, EC3 ...... **91** D3
Botts Ms, W2 .... **81** D1
Botts Pas, W2 .... **81** D1
Boulcott St, E1 .... **95** D1
Boulevard, The, SW6 . **162** B4
Boultwood Rd, E6 .... **103** F1
Boundary La, SE17 ... **146** B5
Boundary Pas, E2 ..... **64** A1
Boundary Rd, NW8 .... **31** F1
Boundary Row, SE1 .. **117** E1
Boundary St, E2 ...... **42** A5
Bourchier St, W1 ...... **86** C2
Bourdon Pl, W1 .... **85** F2
Bourdon St, W1 .... **85** F2
Bourlet Cl, W1 .... **58** A4
Bourne Est, EC1 ...... **60** D1
Bourne St, SW1 ...... **140** C1
Bourne Ter, W2 .... **53** E3
Sch Bousfield Prim Sch,
   SW5 .... **138** A2
Sch Boutcher C of E Prim
   Sch, SE1 .... **120** A5
Bouton Pl, N1
   off Waterloo Ter **17** E4
Bouverie Pl, W2 .... **55** D5
Bouverie St, EC4 ...... **89** D1
Bovingdon Rd, SW6 . **161** E4
BOW, E3 .... **45** F3
Bowater Pl, SE3 ..... **181** F1
Bowater Rd, SE18 ... **131** D4
Bow Back Rivers Wk,
   E15 .... **25** F3
Bow Br Est, E3 .... **47** E4
DLR Bow Church **47** D4
Bow Chyd, EC4 .... **90** B1
Bow Common La, E3 .. **68** A2
Bowden St, SE11 .... **145** D1
Bowditch, SE8 .... **152** A2
Bowen St, E14 .... **69** F5
Bower Av, SE10 ..... **179** E3
Bowerdean St, SW6 . **161** E4
Bowerman Av, SE14 .. **151** F5
Bower St, E1 .... **94** C1
Bowers Wk, E6 .... **75** D5
Bowfell Rd, W6 ..... **134** B5
Bowhill Cl, SW9 ..... **169** D1
Bow Ind Est, E15 .... **25** D3
Bowland Yd, SW1 .... **112** B2
Bow La, EC4 .... **90** B1

Bowl Ct, EC2 .... **63** F2
Bowling Grn La, EC1 .. **61** D1
Bowling Grn Pl, SE1 .. **118** C1
Bowling Grn Row,
   SE18 .... **132** A4
Bowling Grn St, SE11 . **144** C4
Bowling Grn Wk, N1 .. **41** E4
Bowman Av, E16 .... **100** B2
Bowmans Ms, E1 ..... **92** C2
Bowmore Wk, NW1 .. **15** D3
Bowness Cl, E8 .... **20** A2
⊖ Bow Road **46** B4
Bow Rd, E3 .... **46** B5
Sch Bow Sch, E3 .... **47** D3
Bowsprit Pt, E14 .... **124** C3
Bow St, WC2 .... **87** F1
Bow Triangle Business
   Cen, E3 .... **47** D5
Bowyer Cl, E6 .... **76** B3
Bowyer Pl, SE5 ..... **170** B1
Bowyer St, SE5 ..... **170** A1
Boxley St, E16 ...... **101** E5
Boxworth Gro, N1 ..... **16** B5
Boyce St, SE1 .... **88** B5
Boyce Way, E13 ...... **72** C1
Boydell Ct, NW8 ...... **10** C4
Boyd St, E1 .... **92** C1
Boyfield St, SE1 .... **117** F2
Boyle St, W1 .... **86** A2
Boyne Ter Ms, W11 ... **80** A4
Boyson Rd, SE17 .... **146** A4
Boyton Cl, E1 .... **66** B1
Brabant St, EC3 ...... **91** E2
Brabazon St, E14 ..... **69** E5
Bracer Ho, N1
   off Nuttall St **41** F2
Bracewell Rd, W10 .... **50** A4
Bracken Cl, E6 .... **76** A4
Brackley St, EC1 ..... **62** A3
Bracklyn Cl, N1 ...... **40** C2
Bracklyn Ct, N1 ...... **40** C2
Bracklyn St, N1 ...... **40** C2
Bradbourne St, SW6 . **161** D5
Braddyll St, SE10 ... **155** E3
Bradenham Cl, SE17 . **146** C4
Braden St, W9 .... **53** E2
Bradfield Ho, SW8
   off Wandsworth Rd . **166** C5
Bradfield Rd, E16 .... **129** D1
Bradiston Rd, W9 ..... **30** B4
Bradley Cl, N1 .... **39** D2
   N7 .... **15** F2
Bradley Ho, E3
   off Bromley High St .. **47** F3
Bradley Lynch Ct, E2
   off Morpeth St **44** C4
Bradley Stone Rd, E6 .. **76** A4
Bradmead, SW8 ..... **165** F2
Bradstock Rd, E9 ..... **23** D2
Brad St, SE1 .... **89** D5
Bradwell St, E1 .... **45** D5
Bradymead, E6 .... **77** D5
Brady St, E1 .... **65** E2
Braemar Cl, SE16 .... **149** E2
Braemar Rd, E13 ..... **72** B2
Braemer Ho, W9 ...... **32** A5
Braes St, N1 .... **17** F3

Braganza St, SE17 ... **145** E2
Braham St, E1 .... **92** B1
Braidwood Pas, EC1
   off Cloth St **62** A3
Braidwood St, SE1 .... **91** E5
Braintree St, E2 ...... **66** A1
Braithwaite Ho, EC1 .. **62** B1
Braithwaite Twr, W2 .. **54** C3
Bramah Grn, SW9 ... **169** D3
★ Bramah Mus, SE1 ... **90** B5
Bramber Rd, W14 ... **136** A4
Bramcote Gro, SE16 . **150** A2
Bramerton St, SW3 .. **139** E4
Bramham Gdns, SW5 . **137** E2
Bramhope La, SE7 ... **157** F4
Bramley Cres, SW8 .. **167** D1
Bramley Ho, W10 ..... **79** D1
Bramley Rd, W10 ..... **79** D2
Sch Brampton Manor Sch,
   E6 .... **75** D1
Brampton Rd, E6 ..... **75** D1
Bramshaw Rd, E9 ..... **23** D2
Bramshot Av, SE7 ... **157** D3
Bramwell Ho, SE1
   off Harper Rd **118** B4
   SW1 .... **142** A3
Bramwell Ms, N1 ..... **16** B5
Branch Pl, N1 .... **19** D5
Branch Rd, E14 .... **95** E2
Branch St, SE15 .... **171** F2
Brandon Est, SE17 .. **145** F5
Brandon Ms, EC2
   off The Barbican **62** C4
Brandon Rd, N7 ...... **15** E3
Brandon St, SE17 ... **146** A1
Brandreth Rd, E6 ..... **76** B5
Brand St, SE10 ..... **178** A2
Brangton Rd, SE11 .. **144** B3
Branksea St, SW6 ... **159** E2
Bransdale Cl, NW6 .... **9** D5
Brasenose Dr, SW13 . **134** A5
Brassett Pt, E15 ..... **49** F1
Brassey Rd, NW6 ...... **8** B1
Brass Tally All, SE16 . **123** D2
Bratley St, E1 .... **64** C2
Bravington Pl, W9 .... **52** A1
Bravington Rd, W9 ... **52** A1
Bravingtons Wk, N1 .. **37** F3
Brawne Ho, SE17 ... **145** F5
Bray, NW3 .... **11** F3
Bray Cres, SE16 .... **122** C1
Bray Dr, E16 .... **100** B2
Brayfield Ter, N1 ..... **16** C4
Brayford Sq, E1 ...... **66** B2
Bray Pas, E16 .... **100** C2
Bray Pl, SW3 .... **140** A1
Bread St, EC4 .... **90** B1
Bream's Bldgs, EC4 .. **60** C5
Bream St, E3 .... **25** D4
Brechin Pl, SW7 .... **138** B1
Sch Brecknock Prim Sch,
   NW1 .... **15** D1
Brecon Rd, W6 ..... **135** F5
Breezers Hill, E1 ..... **93** D3
Bremner Rd, SW7 ... **110** B2
Brendon St, W1 ...... **55** F5
Brenthouse Rd, E9 ... **22** A3

Brenton St, E14.......**67** F5
Brent Rd, E16.......**73** D5
Bressenden Pl, SW1 ..**113** F3
Breton Ho, EC2
   off The Barbican **62** B3
Brettell St, SE17 .....**147** D3
Brewer's Grn, SW1 ...**114** C3
Brewers Hall Gdns, EC2.**62** B4
Brewer St, W1.........**86** B2
★ **Brewery, The**, EC1 ..**62** B3
Brewery Rd, N7 ......**15** E3
Brewery Sq, EC1 .....**61** E1
  SE1 ....**92** A5
Brewhouse La, E1....**93** F5
Brewhouse Rd, SE18 .**132** B5
Brewhouse Wk, SE16 ..**95** E5
Brewhouse Yd, EC1 ...**61** F1
Brewster Gdns, W10 ..**50** A3
Brewster Ho, E14.....**96** A2
Briant Est, SE1 ......**116** C4
Briant Ho, SE1.......**116** B4
Briant St, SE14 ......**174** C3
Briar Wk, W10.......**51** E1
Briary Cl, NW3 ......**11** E3
Briary Ct, E16.......**100** B1
Brick Ct, EC4 ....**88** C1
Brick La, E1 ....**64** B1
  E2 ....**42** B5
Bricklayer's Arms
  Distribution Cen,
  SE1 ....**147** F1
Bricklayer's Arms Rbt,
  SE1 ....**118** C5
Brick St, W1........**85** E5
Brideale Cl, SE15 ....**148** B5
Bride Ct, EC4........**89** E1
Bride La, EC4........**89** E1
Bridel Ms, N1 ....**39** E1
Brides Pl, N1.........**19** E4
Bride St, N7.........**16** B2
Bridewain St, SE1....**120** A3
Bridewell Pl, E1 .....**93** F5
  EC4 ....**89** E1
Bridford Ms, W1 .....**57** F3
Bridge, The, SW8 ....**165** E2
Bridge App, NW1 ....**12** C3
Bridge Cl, W10 ....**79** D1
Bridge Ct, E14
  off Newport Av......**99** D2
Bridgefoot, SE1......**143** E3
Bridge Ho, NW3
  off Adelaide Rd **12** C3
  SW8
  off St. George Wf...**143** E3
Bridge Ho Quay, E14 ..**98** B5
Bridgeland Rd, E16 ..**101** D2
Bridge La, SW11 .....**163** F4
Bridgeman Rd, N1 ....**16** A4
Bridgeman St, NW8 ...**33** E3
Bridge Meadows,
  SE14 ....**150** C4
Bridge Pl, SW1 ......**113** F5
Bridgeport Pl, E1 ....**93** D4
Bridge Rd, E15 ....**27** D4
Sch Bridge Sch, The,
  Prim Dept, N7 .....**15** D1
Bridges Pl, SW6 .....**160** B3

Bridge St, SW1 ......**115** E2
Bridge Ter, E15......**27** D4
Bridge Vw, W6 ......**134** A2
Bridgewater Sq, EC2 ..**62** A3
Bridgewater St, EC2..**62** A3
Bridgeway St, NW1 ..**36** B3
Bridge Yd, SE1.......**91** D4
Bridgwater Rd, E15 ..**48** A1
Bridle La, W1........**86** B2
Bridport Pl, N1 ......**41** D2
Bridport Ter, SW8 ....**166** C4
Bridstow Pl, W2 ......**53** D5
Brief St, SE5.........**169** E5
Brierly Gdns, E2 ......**44** B3
Brightlingsea Pl, E14 ..**96** A2
Brighton Gro, SE14...**175** E5
Bright St, E14 ....**69** F5
Brig Ms, SE8 ....**152** C5
Brill Pl, NW1 ....**37** D3
Brimstone Ho, E15
  off Victoria St.......**27** E3
Brindley St, SE14 ....**176** A4
Brinklow Ho, W2......**53** D3
Brinkworth Way, E9...**24** B1
Brinsley Ho, E1
  off Tarling St **94** A1
Brinton Wk, SE1 .....**89** E5
Brion Pl, E14........**70** A4
Brisbane St, SE5 .....**170** C2
Briset St, EC1 ....**61** E3
Bristol Gdns, W9.....**53** F2
Bristol Ho, SE11
  off Lambeth Wk....**116** C4
Bristol Ms, W9........**53** F2
★ **Britain at War**
  Experience, SE1 ....**91** E5
Britannia Bldg, N1
  off Ebenezer St......**40** C4
Britannia Gate, E16 ..**101** D4
Britannia Rd, E14....**153** D1
  SW6..............**161** E2
Britannia Row, N1 ...**17** F5
Britannia St, WC1 ....**38** A4
Sch Britannia Village
  Prim Sch, E16......**101** E5
Britannia Wk, N1 ....**40** C4
Britannia Way, SW6...**161** F2
★ **British Dental Assoc**
  Mus, W1 ....**57** E4
★ **British Lib**, NW1 ....**37** D4
★ **British Med Assoc**,
  WC1 ....**59** D1
★ **British Mus, The**,
  WC1 ....**59** D4
★ **British Red Cross Mus &**
  Archives, SW1......**62** C3
Coll British Sch of Osteopathy,
  SE1 ....**118** B2
British St, E3..........**46** B5
Brittany Pt, SE11 ....**144** C1
Britten St, SW3 ......**139** E3
Britton St, EC1 ......**61** E2
Brixham St, E16 .....**104** B5
Brixton Rd, SW9 .....**168** C2
Broadbent St, W1.....**85** E2
Broadbridge Cl, SE3 ..**180** C1
Broad Ct, WC2........**87** F1

Broadfield La, NW1....**15** E3
BROADGATE, EC2 .....**63** D3
Broadgate Circle, EC2 .**63** E3
Broadgate Rd, E16 ....**74** C5
Broadhurst Cl, NW6 ...**10** A2
Broadhurst Gdns, NW6 .**9** E2
Broad La, EC2 ....**63** E3
Broadley St, NW8 ....**55** D3
Broadley Ter, NW1 ...**55** F2
Broadmayne, SE17...**146** B2
Broad Sanctuary,
  SW1..............**115** D2
Broadstone Pl, W1 ....**56** C4
Broad St Av, EC2......**63** E4
Broad St Pl, EC2 .....**63** D4
Broad Wk, NW1.......**35** E5
  W1..............**84** C4
Broad Wk, The, W8....**81** F3
Broadwalk Ct, W8.....**81** D4
Broadwall, SE1 ....**89** D4
Broadway, E15 ....**27** D4
  SW1..............**114** C3
Broadway Mkt, E8 ....**43** D1
Broadway Mkt Ms, E8 .**43** D1
Broadway Shop Cen,
  W6..............**134** B1
Broadway Wk, E14...**125** D3
Broadwick St, W1 .....**86** B2
Broadwood Ter, W8
  off Pembroke Rd ...**108** B5
Broad Yd, EC1........**61** E2
Brocas Cl, NW3......**11** F3
Brockham St, SE1 ....**118** B3
Brocklebank Rd, SE7 .**157** E1
Brocklehurst St, SE14.**175** D1
Brockley Gdns, SE4 ..**176** A5
Brock Pl, E3.........**69** E2
Brock Rd, E13 ....**73** F3
Brockweir, E2 ....**44** A3
Brodick Ho, E3 ....**46** A2
Brodie Ho, SE1
  off Coopers Rd **148** B2
Brodie St, SE1 ....**148** B2
Brodlove La, E1.......**94** C2
Broken Wf, EC4.......**90** A2
Brokesley St, E3 .....**46** A5
Broke Wk, E8........**20** B5
Bromehead Rd, E1 ...**66** A5
Bromehead St, E1.....**66** A5
Bromfield St, N1......**39** D2
BROMLEY, E3 ....**69** F2
⊖ Bromley-by-Bow...**69** F1
Bromley Hall Rd, E14..**70** A3
Bromley High St, E3...**47** E4
Bromley Pl, W1.......**58** A3
Bromley St, E1 ....**67** D4
BROMPTON, SW3 ....**111** E4
Brompton Arc, SW3 ..**112** A2
★ **Brompton Oratory**,
  SW7..............**111** E4
Brompton Pk Cres,
  SW6..............**137** E5
Brompton Pl, SW3 ...**111** F3

Brompton Rd, SW1 . . . **111** F3
  SW3 . . . . **111** E5
  SW7 . . . . **111** F3
Brompton Sq, SW3 . . . **111** E3
Bromyard Ho, SE15 . . . **113** E3
BRONDESBURY, NW2 . . **7** E3
⟳ Brondesbury **8** A3
Brondesbury Ct, NW2 . . **6** C2
Brondesbury Ms, NW6 . . **8** C4
BRONDESBURY PARK,
  NW6 . . . . **6** B4
⟳ Brondesbury Park . . . **7** E5
Brondesbury Pk, NW6 . . **7** E4
Brondesbury Rd, NW6 . **30** A2
Brondesbury Vil, NW6 . **30** B2
Bronsart Rd, SW6 . . . . **159** E2
Bronte Ho, NW6 . . . . . . **31** D4
Bronti Cl, SE17 . . . . . . **146** B3
Bronze St, SE8 . . . . **177** D1
Brook Dr, SE11 . . . . . . **117** D4
Brooke Ct, W10 . . . . . . **29** F3
Brooke's Ct, EC1 . . . . . . **60** C3
Brookes Mkt, EC1 . . . . . **61** D3
Brooke St, EC1 . . . . **60** C4
Brookfield Rd, E9 . . . . . **23** F2
Brook Gate, W1 . . . . **84** B3
Brook Grn, W6 . . . . **107** D5
Brooklands Pas, SW8 . **166** C3
Brook La, SE3 . . . . **181** F5
Brooklyn Pas, W12 . . . **106** A2
Brookmarsh Ind Est,
  SE10 . . . . **177** E1
Brook Ms N, W2 . . . . . . **82** B2
Brookmill Rd, SE8 . . . . **177** D3
Brooks Av, E6 . . . . **76** A1
Brooksbank St, E9 . . . . **22** C2
Brooksby Ms, N1 . . . . . **17** D3
Brooksby St, N1 . . . . . . **17** D4
Brook's Ms, W1 . . . . **85** E2
Brook St, W1 . . . . **85** D2
  W2 . . . . **83** D2
Brooksville Av, NW6 . . . **29** F1
Brookville Rd, SW6 . . . **160** A2
Broome Way, SE5 . . . . **170** C2
Broomfield St, E14 . . . . **69** D4
Broomhouse Rd, SW6 . **160** C5
Brougham Rd, E8 . . . . . **20** C5
Brougham St, SW11 . . **164** B5
Brough Cl, SW8 . . . . . . **167** F2
Broughton Rd, SW6 . . **161** E4
Broughton Rd App,
  SW6 . . . . **161** E5
Broughton St, SW8 . . . **165** E5
Brownfield St, E14 . . . . **97** F1
Brown Hart Gdns, W1 . **85** D2
Browning Cl, W9 . . . . . . **54** B2
Browning Ms, W1 . . . . . **57** E4
Browning St, SE17 . . . **146** B3
Brownlow Ms, WC1 . . . . **60** B2
Brownlow Rd, E8 . . . . . . **20** B5
Brownlow St, WC1 . . . . **60** B4
Brown's Bldgs, EC3 . . . **91** F1
Brown St, W1 . . . . **56** A5

Broxwood Way, NW8 . . **33** F1
Bruce Cl, W10 . . . . **51** D2
Bruce Rd, E3 . . . . **47** E5
Bruckner St, W10 . . . . . **29** F5
Bruford Ct, SE8 . . . . . . **153** D5
Bruges Pl, NW1 . . . . **14** B4
★ Brunei Gall, WC1 . . . **59** D3
★ Brunel Engine Ho,
  SE16 . . . . **122** A1
Brunel Est, W2 . . . . **52** C4
Brunel Ms, W10 . . . . . . **29** D4
Brunel Rd, SE16 . . . . . **122** A2
Brunel St, E16 . . . . **100** A1
Brune St, E1 . . . . **64** A4
Brunlees Ho, SE1
  off Bath Ter **118** A4
Brunswick Ct, EC1
  off Tompion St **39** E5
  SE1 . . . . **119** F2
  SW1 *off Regency St* . . **143** D1
Brunswick Gdns, W8 . . **81** D5
Brunswick Ms, W1 . . . . **56** B5
Brunswick Pk, SE5 . . . **171** D3
Sch Brunswick Pk Prim Sch,
  SE5 . . . . **171** D2
Brunswick Pl, N1 . . . . . **41** D5
  NW1 . . . . **57** D1
Brunswick Quay,
  SE16 . . . . **123** D4
Brunswick Rd, E14
  off Blackwall Tunnel
  Northern App. **98** B1
Brunswick Shop Cen,
  WC1 . . . . **59** E1
Brunswick Sq, WC1 . . . **59** F2
Brunswick Vil, SE5 . . . **171** E3
Brunton Pl, E14 . . . . . . **95** F1
Brushfield St, E1 . . . . . . **63** F3
Brushwood Cl, E14 . . . . **69** F3
Bruton La, W1 . . . . **85** F3
Bruton Pl, W1 . . . . **85** F3
Bruton St, W1 . . . . **85** F3
Bryan Rd, SE16 . . . . . . **124** A1
Bryan's All, SW6 . . . . . **161** E5
Bryanston Ms E, W1 . . **56** A4
Bryanston Ms W, W1 . . **56** A4
Bryanston Pl, W1 . . . . . **56** A4
Bryanston Sq, W1 . . . . **56** A4
Bryanston St, W1 . . . . . **84** A1
Bryant Ct, E2 . . . . **42** A2
Bryant St, E15 . . . . **27** D4
Brydale Ho, SE16 . . . . **122** C5
Brydges Pl, WC2 . . . . . . **87** E3
Brydon Wk, N1 . . . . **15** F5
Bryer Ct, EC2
  off Bridgewater St . . . **62** A3
Brymay Cl, E3 . . . . **47** D3
Brynmaer Rd, SW11 . . **164** A4
Buckfast St, E2 . . . . **43** D5
Buck Hill Wk, W2 . . . . . **83** D3
Buckhurst St, E1 . . . . . . **65** F2
Buckingham Arc, WC2 . **87** F3
Buckingham Chambers, SW1
  off Greencoat Pl **114** B5
Buckingham Gate,
  SW1 . . . . **114** A2
Buckingham Ms, N1 . . . **19** F2

Buckingham Ms, SW1 . **114** A3
★ Buckingham Palace,
  SW1 . . . . **113** F2
Buckingham Palace Rd,
  SW1 . . . . **141** E1
Buckingham Pl, SW1 . **114** A3
Buckingham Rd, N1 . . . **19** E2
Buckingham St, WC2 . . **87** F3
Buckland Cres, NW3 . . **10** C3
Buckland St, N1 . . . . . . **41** D3
Bucklebury, NW1 . . . . . **58** A1
Bucklers All, SW6 . . . . **136** B5
Bucklersbury, EC4 . . . . **90** C1
Bucklersbury Pas,
  EC4 . . . . **90** C1
Buckle St, E1 . . . . **64** B5
Buckley Rd, NW6 . . . . . . **8** B4
Buckley St, SE1 . . . . **88** C5
Bucknall St, WC2 . . . . . **59** D5
Buck St, NW1 . . . . **13** F4
Buckters Rents, SE16 . . **95** E5
Budge Row, EC4 . . . . . . **90** C2
Budge's Wk, W2 . . . . . . **82** A4
Bugsby's Way, SE7 . . **157** D1
  SE10 . . . . **128** A5
Building 22, SE18
  off Carriage St **133** F4
Building 45, SE18
  off Hopton Rd **133** F3
Coll Building Crafts Coll,
  E15 . . . . **26** C4
Bulinga St, SW1 . . . . . **143** D1
Bullace Row, SE5 . . . . **170** C2
Bullards Pl, E2 . . . . **44** C4
Bullen Ho, E1 . . . . **65** F2
Bullen St, SW11 . . . . . **163** E5
Buller Cl, SE15 . . . . . . **172** C2
Buller Rd, NW10 . . . . . . **29** D5
Bullied Way, SW1 . . . . **141** F1
Bull Inn Ct, WC2 . . . . . . **87** F3
Bullivant St, E14 . . . . . . **98** A1
Bulls Gdns, SW3 . . . . . **111** F5
Bull's Head Pas, EC3 . . **91** E1
Bull Yd, SE15 . . . . **173** D4
Bulmer Ms, W11 . . . . . . **80** C4
Bulmer Pl, W11 . . . . **80** C4
Bulow Est, SW6 . . . . . . **161** F4
Bulstrode Pl, W1 . . . . . . **57** D4
Bulstrode St, W1 . . . . . . **57** D5
Bulwer St, W12 . . . . **78** B5
Bunhill Row, EC1 . . . . . . **62** C1
Bunhouse Pl, SW1 . . . **140** C2
Bunning Way, N7 . . . . . **15** F3
Bunsen St, E3 . . . . **45** E2
Bunton St, SE18 . . . . . **133** D4
Bunyan Ct, EC2
  off The Barbican **62** A3
Buonaparte Ms, SW1 . **142** C2
Burbage Cl, SE1 . . . . . **118** C4
Sch Burbage Prim Sch,
  N1 . . . . **41** E2
Burcham St, E14 . . . . . . **69** F5
Burchell Rd, SE15 . . . **173** F4
Burcher Gale Gro,
  SE15 . . . . **171** F1
Burder Cl, N1 . . . . **19** F1
Burder Rd, N1 . . . . **19** F1

★ Place of interest   ⇌ Railway station   ⟳ London Overground station   ⊖ London Underground station

Sch Burdett Coutts C of E
Prim Sch, SW1 ....114 C4
Burdett Ms, NW3 .....11 D1
W2...............53 E5
Burdett Rd, E3 ....67 F1
E14................67 F1
Burdett St, SE1 ....116 C3
Burford Rd, E15 ......26 C4
Burford Wk, SW6......161 F2
Burford Wf Apts, E15 ..26 C5
Burgess Business Pk,
SE5 ....171 D1
Burgess St, E14.......68 C4
Burge St, SE1 ....119 D4
Burgh St, N1 ....39 F2
Burgon St, EC4 ....89 F1
Burgos Gro, SE10 ....177 E3
Burke St, E16 ....72 B4
Burleigh Ho, W10 .....51 D3
Burleigh St, WC2......88 A2
Burley Rd, E16 ....74 A4
Burlington Arc, W1...86 A3
Burlington Cl, E6 .....75 F5
W9................52 B2
Burlington Gdns, W1 ..86 A3
Burlington Rd, SW6 ..159 F5
Burnaby St, SW10 ....162 A2
Burne Jones Ho, W14.136 A1
Burnell Wk, SE1 .....148 B2
Burness Cl, N7 ....16 A1
Burne St, NW1.......55 E3
Burney St, SE10 .....178 B1
Burnfoot Av, SW6....159 F4
Burnham, NW3 ......11 E3
Burnham Cl, SE1.....148 B1
Burnham St, E2.......44 A4
Burnhill Cl, SE15......173 F1
Burnley Rd, SW9.....168 A5
Burnsall St, SW3.....139 F2
Burnside Cl, SE16.....95 D4
Burnthwaite Rd, SW6.160 B2
Buross St, E1.........93 F1
Burrard Rd, E16......73 E5
Burr Cl, E1...........92 C4
Burrell St, SE1........89 E4
Burrells Wf Sq, E14....153 E2
Burrows Ms, SE1......117 E1
Burrows Rd, NW10....28 A4
Burslem St, E1 ....93 D1
Burton Cl, SW3
off Franklin's Row ...140 B2
Burton Gro, SE17 ....146 C3
Burton La, SW9.......169 D5
Burton Ms, SW1 .....141 D1
Burton Pl, WC1 ....37 D5
Burton Rd, NW6 ....8 B4
SW9...............169 E5
Burton St, WC1 ....37 D5
Burwash Ho, SE1 ....119 D2
Burwell Cl, E1 ....93 F1
Burwell Wk, E3 ....69 D1
Burwood Pl, W2 ......55 F5
Bury Cl, SE16.........95 D4
Bury Ct, EC3 ....63 F5
Bury Pl, WC1 ....59 E4
Bury St, EC3 ....91 F1

Bury St, SW1 ....86 B4
Bury Wk, SW3 ....139 E1
Busbridge Ho, E14 ....69 D5
Busby Ms, NW5
off Busby Pl 14 C1
Busby Pl, NW5 ....14 C1
Busby St, E2 ....64 B1
Bushbaby Cl, SE1 ....119 E4
Bushberry Rd, E9 .....23 F1
Bush Ct, W12 ....107 D3
Bushell St, E1 ....93 D5
Bushey Hill Rd, SE5 ..171 F4
Bush La, EC4 ....90 C2
Bush Rd, E8...........43 E1
SE8 ....123 D5
Bushwood Dr, SE1 ...148 B1
★ Business Design Cen,
N1 ....39 D1
Butcher Row, E1......95 D2
E14...............95 D2
Butchers Rd, E16 .....73 D5
Bute Gdns, W6 ......134 C1
Sch Bute Ho Prep Sch for
Girls, W6 ....106 C5
Bute St, SW7........110 C5
Bute Wk, N1 ....18 C2
Butler Pl, SW1.......114 C3
Butlers & Colonial Wf,
SE1 ....120 B1
Butler St, E2 ....44 B4
Butlers Wf, SE1 ....92 A5
Butterfield Cl, SE16 ..121 E2
Butterfield Sq, E6 ....104 A1
Butterfly Wk, SE5 ....170 C4
Buttermere Cl, SE1...148 A1
Buttermere Wk, E8...20 B2
Butterwick, W6......134 B1
Buttesland St, N1......41 D4
Buxhall Cres, E9 ......24 A1
Buxted Rd, E8 ....20 A3
Buxton Ct, N1.........40 B4
Buxton Ms, SW4 .....167 D5
Buxton St, E1 ....64 B2
Byfield Cl, SE16......123 F1
Byford Cl, E15........27 F4
Sch Bygrove Prim Sch,
E14...............97 E1
Bygrove St, E14.......97 E1
Bylands Cl, SE16......95 D4
Byng Pl, WC1 ....58 C2
Byng St, E14.........124 C1
Byron Cl, E8 ....20 C5
Byron Ct, W9.........53 D1
Byron Ms, W9 ....53 D1
Byron St, E14.........70 A5
Byward St, EC3.......91 F3
Bywater Pl, SE16......95 F4
Bywater St, SW3.....140 A2
Bywell Pl, W1 ....58 A4

C

Cabbell St, NW1 ......55 E4
Cable Pl, SE10.......178 B3
Cable St, E1..........92 C2

Cabot Pl, E14 ....97 D4
Cabot Sq, E14........97 D4
Cactus Cl, SE15......171 F5
Cadbury Way, SE16 ..120 B4
Cadell Cl, E2 ....42 B3
Cade Rd, SE10.......178 C3
Cadet Dr, SE1 ....148 B2
Cadet Pl, SE10.......155 E2
Cadiz St, SE17.......146 B3
Cadman Cl, SW9
off Langton Rd.....169 E2
Cadogan Cl, E9 ....24 B3
Cadogan Gdns, SW3..112 B5
Cadogan Gate, SW1 ..112 B5
Cadogan La, SW1 ....112 C4
Riv Cadogan Pier.....139 F5
Cadogan Pl, SW1 ....112 B3
Cadogan Rd, SE18 ...133 F3
Cadogan Sq, SW1 ...112 B4
Cadogan St, SW3 ...140 A1
Cadogan Ter, E9 .....24 A2
Cahill St, EC1.........62 B2
Cahir St, E14.........153 E1
Caird St, W10 ....29 F5
Caithness Rd, W14...106 C5
Calabria Rd, N5.......17 E1
Calais Gate, SE5 .....169 E3
Calais St, SE5 ....169 F3
Caldecot Rd, SE5 ....170 B5
Calderon Pl, W10 .....50 A4
Calderwood St, SE18 .133 D5
Caldwell Gdns Est,
SW9..............168 C3
Caldwell St, SW9.....168 B2
Caldy Wk, N1 ....18 A3
Caleb St, SE1........118 A1
☉ Caledonian Road ...15 F1
Caledonian Rd, N1 ...37 F3
N7................16 A1
☉ Caledonian Road &
Barnsbury 16 B3
Caledonian Sq, NW1...14 C1
Caledonian Wf, E14 ..154 C1
Caledonia St, N1......37 F3
Cale St, SW3 ....139 E2
Caletock Way, SE10 ..156 A2
California Bldg, SE13
off Deals Gateway ..177 E3
Callaby Ter, N1 ......19 D2
Callcott Rd, NW6......8 A4
Callcott St, W8 ....80 C4
Callendar Rd, SW7 ...110 C3
Callingham Cl, E14....68 B4
Callisons Pl, SE10....155 F2
Callow St, SW3 .....138 C2
Calmington Rd, SE5 ..147 F3
Calshot St, N1........38 A2
Calthorpe St, WC1....60 B1
Calvert Av, E2........41 F5
Calverton, SE5 ......147 D4
Sch Calverton Prim Sch,
E16..............103 D1
Calvert Rd, SE10.....156 A3

Calvert's Bldgs, SE1 . . . **90** C5
Calvert St, NW1 . . . . **12** C1
Calvin St, E1 . . . . **64** A2
Calydon Rd, SE7 . . . . . **157** F3
Calypso Cres, SE15 . . . **172** A1
Calypso Way, SE16 . . . **124** A4
CAMBERWELL, SE5 . . . **170** B2
Camberwell Business Cen,
  SE5 . . . . **170** C2
Camberwell Ch St,
  SE5 . . . . **170** C4
Uni Camberwell Coll of Arts,
  Peckham Rd, SE5. . . . **171** F3
  Wilson Rd, SE5 . . . . . **171** E4
Camberwell Glebe,
  SE5 . . . . **171** E4
Camberwell Grn, SE5 . **170** C3
Camberwell Gro, SE5 . **171** D4
Camberwell New Rd,
  SE5 . . . . **144** C5
Camberwell Pas, SE5 . **170** B3
Camberwell Rd, SE5 . . **146** B5
Camberwell Sta Rd,
  SE5 . . . . **170** A4
Camborne Ms, W11 . . . **79** E1
Cambria St, SW6 . . . . . **161** F2
Cambridge Av, NW6 . . . **31** D2
Cambridge Circ, WC2 . . **87** D1
Cambridge Cres, E2 . . . **43** E3
Cambridge Gdns, NW6. **31** D2
  W10 . . . . **51** F5
Cambridge Gate, NW1 . **35** F5
Cambridge Gate Ms,
  NW1 . . . . **35** F5
≈ Cambridge Heath . . **43** E2
Cambridge Heath Rd,
  E1 . . . . **65** F3
  E2 . . . . **65** F3
Cambridge Mans,
  SW11 . . . . **164** A4
Cambridge Pl, W8 . . . . **109** F2
Cambridge Rd, NW6 . . . **30** C4
  SW11 . . . . **164** A4
Coll Cambridge Sch of
  English, The, WC2 . . **59** F5
Cambridge Sq, W2 . . . . **55** E5
Cambridge St, SW1 . . . **141** F1
Cambridge Ter, NW1 . . **35** F5
Cambridge Ter Ms,
  NW1 . . . . **35** F5
Cambus Rd, E16 . . . . . . **73** D3
Camden Gdns, NW1 . . . **13** F4
Camden High St, NW1 . **13** F5
Camdenhurst St, E14 . . **67** F5
★ Camden Lock Mkt &
  Waterbuses, NW1 . . **13** E4
Camden Lock Pl, NW1 . **13** E4
Camden Ms, NW1 . . . . . **14** B3
Camden Pk Rd, NW1 . . **14** C2
Camden Pas, N1 . . . . . . **39** E2
⟳ Camden Road **14** A4
Camden Rd, N7 . . . . **14** A4
  NW1 . . . . **14** C1

Sch Camden Sch for Girls,
  NW5 . . . . **14** B2
Camden Sq, NW1 . . . . . **14** C3
  SE15 . . . . **172** A3
Camden St, NW1 . . . . . . **14** A5
Camden Ter, NW1 . . . . . **14** C2
CAMDEN TOWN, NW1 . **36** A4
⊖ Camden Town **13** F5
Camden Wk, N1 . . . . **39** E1
Camelford Wk, W11 . . . **79** E1
Camellia St, SW8 . . . . **167** D2
Camel Ho, NW1 . . . . **15** D1
Sch Camelot Prim Sch,
  SE15 . . . . **149** E5
Camelot St, SE15 . . . . **149** E5
Camel Rd, E16 . . . . **103** D4
Camera Pl, SW10 . . . . . **138** C5
Sch Cameron Ho, SW3 . . **139** D4
  SE5 off Comber Gro . . **170** A2
Cameron Pl, E1 . . . . **65** C5
Camerton Cl, E8 . . . . . . **20** B2
Camilla Rd, SE16 . . . . **149** E1
Camlet St, E2 . . . . **64** A1
Camley St, NW1 . . . . . . **37** D2
★ Camley St Natural Pk,
  NW1 . . . . **37** D2
Camomile St, EC3 . . . . **63** E5
Campana Rd, SW6 . . . **160** C5
Campbell Rd, E3 . . . . . . **47** D4
Campbell Wk, N1 . . . . . **15** F5
Campden Gro, W8 . . . **109** D1
Campden Hill, W8. . . . **108** C1
Campden Hill Ct, W8 . **109** D1
Campden Hill Gdns,
  W8 . . . . **80** B4
Campden Hill Gate,
  W8 . . . . **108** C1
Campden Hill Pl, W11 . **80** B4
Campden Hill Rd, W8 . **109** D2
Campden Hill Sq, W8 . **80** B4
Campden Hill Twrs,
  W11 . . . . **80** C4
Campden Ho Cl, W8 . . **108** C1
Campden St, W8 . . . . . . **80** C5
Camperdown St, E1 . . **92** B1
Campion Cl, E6 . . . . . . **104** B2
Camplin St, SE14 . . . . **175** D1
Cam Rd, E15 . . . . **26** C5
Canada Est, SE16 . . . . **122** B3
Canada Sq, E14 . . . . **97** E4
Canada St, SE16 . . . . . **122** C2
⊖ Canada Water **122** B2
Canal App, SE8 . . . . . . **151** E3
Canal Boul, NW1 . . . . . **14** C1
Canal Cl, E1 . . . . **67** L1
  W10 . . . . **51** D1
Canal Gro, SE15 . . . . . **149** D4
Canal Path, E2 . . . . **42** A1
Canal St, SE5 . . . . **146** C5
Canal Wk, N1 . . . . **19** D5
  NW1 . . . . **33** F4
  NW8 . . . . **33** E5
  W2 . . . . **53** F3
  W9 . . . . **52** B3
  W10 . . . . **52** B3
Canal Way Wk, W10 . . . **50** C1

⊖ Canary Wharf **97** E5
DLR Canary Wharf **97** D4
Riv Canary Wharf Pier . . **96** B4
Cancell Rd, SW9 . . . . . **169** D3
Candover St, W1 . . . . . . **58** A4
Candy St, E3 . . . . **24** B5
Canfield Gdns, NW6 . . . **10** A3
Canfield Pl, NW6 . . . . . . **10** A2
Canning Pas, W8 . . . . **110** A3
Canning Pl, W8 . . . . . . **110** A3
Canning Pl Ms, W8 . . . **110** A2
Canning Rd, E15 . . . . . . **49** E3
CANNING TOWN, E16 . . **72** C5
⊖ Canning Town **71** F5
DLR Canning Town **71** F5
Canning Town, E16 . . . **71** F4
Cannon Ct, EC1
  off Brewhouse Yd **61** F1
Cannon Dr, E14 . . . . **96** C3
≈ Cannon Street **90** C3
⊖ Cannon Street **90** C3
Cannon St, EC4 . . . . **90** A1
Cannon St Rd, E1 . . . . . **65** E5
Cannon Wf Business Cen,
  SE8 . . . . **151** E1
Cannon Workshops,
  E14 . . . . **96** C3
Canon All, EC4
  off St. Paul's Chyd . . . **89** F1
Sch Canon Barnett Prim
  Sch, E1 . . . . **64** B5
Canon Beck Rd, SE16 . **122** B1
CANONBURY, N1 . . . . . **17** F2
Canonbury Cres, N1 . . . **18** A3
Canonbury Gro, N1 . . . **18** A3
Canonbury La, N1 . . . . . **17** E3
Canonbury Pk N, N1 . . . **18** A2
Canonbury Pk S, N1 . . . **18** A2
Canonbury Pl, N1 . . . . . **17** lF2
Sch Canonbury Prim Sch,
  N1 . . . . **17** F2
Canonbury Rd, N1 . . . . . **17** E2
Canonbury Sq, N1 . . . . **17** F3
Canonbury St, N1 . . . . . **18** A3
Canonbury Vil, N1 . . . . **17** F3
Canonbury Yd, N1 . . . . **18** B5
Canonbury Yd W, N1 . . **17** F2
Canon Row, SW1 . . . . **115** C2
Canon St, N1 . . . . **40** A1
Canrobert St, E2 . . . . . . **43** E4
Cantelowes Rd, NW1 . . **15** D2
Canterbury Cl, E6 . . . . . **76** A5
Canterbury Ho, E3
  off Bow Rd **47** E4
  SE1 . . . . **116** B3
Canterbury Pl, SE17 . . **145** F1
Canterbury Rd, NW6 . . **30** C3
Canterbury Ter, NW6 . . **30** C2
Cantium Retail Pk,
  SE1 . . . . **148** C4
Canton St, E14 . . . . **96** C1
Cantrell Rd, E3 . . . . **68** B2
Canute Gdns, SE16 . . **122** C5
Canvey St, SE1 . . . . **89** F4
Capel Ct, EC2 . . . . **91** D1
Coll Capel Manor Coll,
  NW1 . . . . **35** D5

Capener's Cl, SW1 ... **112** C2
Cape Yd, E1 .... **93** D4
H Capio Nightingale Hosp,
NW1 .... **55** F3
Coll Capital Coll, SE15 .. **173** F1
Coll Capital Coll (CIFE)
London Sch of Insurance,
WC1 .... **60** A3
Capital E Apts, E16
off Western Gateway. **101** D3
Capland St, NW8...... **55** D1
Capper St, WC1 .... **58** B2
Capstan Rd, SE8 ..... **124** A5
Capstan Sq, E14 ..... **126** B2
Capstan Way, SE16 ... **95** F5
Capulet Ms, E16 ..... **101** D4
Capulet Sq, E3 ...... **47** F5
Caradoc Cl, W2 .... **52** C5
Caradoc St, SE10 .... **155** E2
Caravel Cl, E14 ..... **124** C3
Caravel Ms, SE8 ..... **152** C4
Caraway Cl, E13 ..... **73** E3
Carbis Rd, E14 ...... **68** A5
Carburton St, W1 .... **57** F3
Cardale St, E14...... **126** A2
Cardigan Rd, E3 ..... **46** B2
Cardigan St, SE11... **144** C2
Cardigan Wk, N1
off Ashby Gro....... **18** B3
Cardinal Bourne St,
SE1 .... **119** D4
Cardinal Cap All, SE1
off New Globe Wk ... **90** A3
Sch Cardinal Pole RC Sch,
Annexe, E9........ **23** D4
Sch Cardinal Vaughan Mem
Sch, W14.......... **107** E1
Cardinal Wk, SW1
off Palace St **114** A3
Cardine Ms, SE15 .... **173** E1
Cardington St, NW1 .. **36** A4
Sch Cardwell Prim Sch,
SE18 .... **132** A5
Carew St, SE5 ...... **169** F5
Carey Gdns, SW8 .... **166** C4
Carey La, EC2 .... **62** A5
Carey Pl, SW1 ...... **142** C1
Carey St, WC2 .... **88** B1
Carfree Cl, N1 ...... **17** D3
Carisbrooke Gdns,
SE15 .... **172** B1
Carlile Cl, E3 .... **46** B3
Carlisle Av, EC3...... **91** F1
Carlisle La, SE1 ..... **116** B4
Carlisle Ms, NW8..... **55** D3
Carlisle Pl, SW1...... **114** A4
Carlisle Rd, NW6...... **7** E5
Carlisle St, W1...... **86** C1
Carlisle Wk, E8 ...... **20** A2
Carlos Pl, W1........ **85** D3
Carlow St, NW1 ...... **36** A2
Carlton Ct, SW9..... **169** E3
Carlton Gdns, SW1 .. **86** C5
Carlton Gro, SE15 ... **173** E3
Carlton Hill, NW8 ... **32** A1
Carlton Ho Ter, SW1 .. **86** C5
Carlton Sq, E1....... **66** C1

Carlton St, SW1...... **86** C3
Carlton Twr Pl, SW1 .. **112** B3
Carlton Vale, NW6 ... **31** D3
Sch Carlton Vale Inf Sch,
NW6 .... **30** B4
Carlyle Ct, SW10
off Chelsea Harbour. **162** B3
Carlyle Ms, E1........ **67** D1
★ Carlyle's Ho, SW3 . **139** E5
Carlyle Sq, SW3..... **139** D3
Carly Ms, E2 .... **42** C5
Carmarthen Pl, SE1 .. **119** E1
Carmel Ct, W8....... **109** E1
Carmelite St, EC4 ... **89** D2
Carmen St, E14...... **69** E5
Carnaby St, W1...... **86** A1
Carnegie St, N1...... **38** A1
Carnoustie Dr, N1.... **16** A4
Caroline Cl, W2...... **81** F3
Caroline Gdns, SE15.. **173** E1
Caroline Pl, W2...... **81** F2
Caroline Pl Ms, W2... **81** F3
Caroline St, E1 ..... **95** D1
Caroline Ter, SW1... **140** C1
Caroline Wk, W6..... **135** E5
Carol St, NW1 ...... **14** A5
Carpenters Business Pk,
E15 .... **25** D3
Sch Carpenters Prim Sch,
E15 .... **26** B5
Carpenters Rd, E15 .. **25** D2
Carpenter St, W1 .... **85** E3
Carre Ms, SE5 ...... **169** F4
Carr Gro, SE18...... **131** F5
Carriage Dr E, SW11.. **164** C1
Carriage Dr N, SW11.. **141** D5
Carriage Dr S, SW11.. **164** A3
Carriage Dr W, SW11.. **164** A2
Carriage St, SE18 ... **133** F4
Carrick Ms, SE8 .... **152** C4
Carrington St, W1.... **85** E5
Carron Cl, E14....... **69** F5
Carroun Rd, SW8.... **168** A1
Carr St, E14........ **67** F4
Carson Rd, E16...... **73** D2
Carteret St, SW1 ... **114** C2
Carteret Way, SE8 .. **151** F1
Carter La, EC4 ...... **89** F1
Carter Pl, SE17 ..... **146** B3
Carter St, SE17 ..... **146** A4
Carthusian St, EC1 ... **62** A3
Cartier Circle, E14... **97** F5
Carting La, WC2 ..... **87** F3
Cartmel, NW1 ...... **36** A4
Carton St, W1 ...... **56** B5
Cartridge Pl, SE18 ... **133** F4
Cartwright Gdns, WC1 . **37** E5
Cartwright St, E1 ... **92** B2
Casby Ho, SE16...... **120** C3
Cascades Twr, E14 ... **96** B5
Casella Rd, SE14..... **174** C2
Casey Cl, NW8....... **33** E5
Caspian St, SE5...... **170** C1
Caspian Wk, E16..... **102** C1
Caspian Wf, E3
off Violet Rd........ **69** E3
Cassidy Rd, SW6..... **160** C2

Cassilis Rd, E14 ..... **125** D2
Cassland Rd, E9 ...... **22** B3
Casson St, E1 .... **64** C4
Castalia Sq, E14 ..... **126** A2
Castalia St, E14
off Plevna St....... **126** A2
Castellain Rd, W9..... **54** A2
Casterbridge, NW6..... **9** F5
Casterton St, E8 ..... **21** F2
Castile Rd, SE18 ..... **133** D5
Castle Baynard St,
EC4 .... **89** F2
Castlebrook Cl, SE11 . **117** E5
Castle Ct, EC3 .... **91** D1
Castlehaven Rd, NW1 . **13** E4
Castle La, SW1 ...... **114** B3
Castlemaine Twr,
SW11............. **164** B5
Castlemain St, E1..... **65** E3
Castlemead, SE5..... **170** B2
Castle Ms, NW1...... **13** E2
Castle Pl, NW1 ...... **13** F2
Castlereagh St, W1... **55** F5
Castle Rd, NW1 ...... **13** E2
Castletown Rd, W14 . **135** F3
Castle Yd, SE1....... **89** F4
Castor La, E14........ **97** E3
Catesby St, SE17 .... **147** D1
Cathay St, SE16 ..... **121** F2
Cathcart Rd, SW10 .. **137** E4
Cathcart St, NW5 .... **13** E1
Cathedral Piazza, SW1. **114** A4
Sch Cathedral Sch of
St. Saviour & St. Mary
Overie, The, SE1... **118** B1
Cathedral St, SE1 .... **90** C4
Cathedral Wk, SW1... **114** A3
Catherine Griffiths Ct,
EC1 .... **61** D1
Catherine Gro, SE10.. **177** E3
Catherine Ho, N1
off Phillipp St....... **41** F1
Catherine Pl, SW1.... **114** A3
Catherine St, WC2.... **88** A2
Catherine Wheel All,
E1 .... **63** F4
Catherine Wheel Yd,
SW1 .... **86** A5
Catherwood Ct, N1
off Murray Gro...... **40** C3
Catlin St, SE16 ..... **149** D3
Cator St, SE15 ...... **148** A5
Cato St, W1 .... **55** F4
Catton St, WC1 ..... **60** A4
Caughley Ho, SE11
off Lambeth Wk.... **116** C4
Caulfield Rd, SE15 .. **173** F5
Causton St, SW1.... **143** D1
Cavaye Pl, SW10..... **138** B3
Cavell St, E1 .... **65** F3
Cavendish Av, NW8 .. **33** D3
Cavendish Cl, NW6... **8** A2
NW8 .... **33** D4

Coll Cavendish Coll, WC1 . 58   C3
Cavendish Ct, EC3 63   F5
Cavendish Ms N, W1 . . 57   F3
Cavendish Ms S, W1 . . . 57   F4
Cavendish Pl, NW2 7   D2
   W1 57   F5
Cavendish Rd, NW6 7   F4
Sch Cavendish Sch, The,
   NW1 13   F5
Cavendish Sq, W1 57   F5
Cavendish St, N1 40   C3
Caversham Flats,
   SW3 140   A4
Caversham Rd, NW5 . . 14   A1
Caversham St, SW3 . . 140   A4
Caverswall St, W12 . . 50   A5
Caxton Gro, E3 46   C4
Caxton Rd, W12 106   C1
Caxton St, SW1 114   B3
Caxton St N, E16 100   A4
Cayenne Ct, SE1 92   B5
Sch Cayley Prim Sch,
   E14 67   E5
Cayton Pl, EC1 40   C5
Cayton St, EC1 40   C5
Cecil St, WC2 87   D3
★ Cecilia Coleman Gall,
   NW8 33   D2
★ Cecil Sharp Ho, NW1 . 13   D5
Cedar Cl, E3 24   B5
Cedar Ct, N1 18   B3
Cedarne Rd, SW6 161   E2
Cedars Rd, E15 27   F1
Cedar Way, NW1 14   C4
Celandine Cl, E14 68   C4
Celandine Dr, E8 20   B3
Celandine Way, E15 . . . 49   F4
Celbridge Ms, W2 53   F5
Celtic St, E14 69   F3
★ Cenotaph, The,
   SW1 115   E1
Central Av, SW11 . . . 164   A2
★ Central Criminal Ct
   (Old Bailey), EC4 . . . 61   F5
Sch Central Foundation Boys'
   Sch, EC2 63   D1
Sch Central Foundation Girls'
   Sch, Lwr Sch, E3 45   F4
   Upr Sch, E3 46   B5
Central Ho, E15
   off Marshgate La 48   A2
Uni Central St. Martins Coll
   of Art & Design, WC1 . . 60   A4
   Back Hill Site, EC1 . . . 61   D2
   Catton St Site, WC1 . . 60   A4
   Charing Cross Rd Site,
   WC2 87   D1
Coll Central Sch of Ballet,
   EC1 61   D2
Uni Central Sch of Speech &
   Drama, NW3 10   C4
Central St, EC1 40   A5

Centre Av, W10 28   B5
Centre Pt, SE1 148   C2
Centrepoint, WC1 59   D5
Centre St, E2 43   E3
Centric Cl, NW1 13   E5
Centurion Bldg, SW8 . 141   E5
Centurion Cl, N7 16   A3
Centurion La, E3 46   B2
Cephas Av, E1 66   B5
Cephas St, E1 66   A2
Cerise Rd, SE15 173   D4
Cerney Ms, W2 82   C2
Cervantes Ct, W2 81   F1
Cester St, E2 42   C1
Ceylon Rd, W14 107   D4
Chadbourn St, E14 . . . 69   F4
Chadwell St, EC1 39   D4
Chadwick St, SW1 115   D4
Chadwin Rd, E13 73   E3
Chagford St, NW1 56   A2
Chalbury Wk, N1 38   B2
Chalcot Cres, NW1 12   B5
Chalcot Gdns, NW3 . . 12   A2
Chalcot Rd, NW1 12   C4
Sch Chalcot Sch, NW1 . . 13   E3
Chalcot Sq, NW1 12   C4
Chaldon Rd, SW6 159   E1
⊖ Chalk Farm 12   B3
Chalk Fm Rd, NW1 . . . 12   C3
Chalk Hill Rd, W6 . . . 134   C1
Chalk Rd, E13 73   F3
Challoner Cres, W14 . . 136   A3
Challoner St, W14 . . . 136   A2
Chalmers Wk, SE17 . . 145   F5
Chaloner Ct, SE1 118   C1
Chalton St, NW1 37   D4
Chamberlain Cotts,
   SE5 171   D4
Chamberlain St, NW1 . . 12   B4
Chamberlayne Rd,
   NW10 28   C4
Chambers St, SE16 . . . 120   C1
Chamber St, E1 92   B2
Chambord St, E2 42   B5
Chancellor Pas, E14 . . 97   D5
Chancellors Ct, WC1
   off Orde Hall St 60   A3
Chancellors Rd, W6 . . 134   A3
Chancellors St, W6 . . 134   A3
Chancellors Wf, W6 . . 134   A3
Chancel St, SE1 89   E4
⊖ Chancery Lane 60   C4
Chancery La, WC2 60   C5
Chance St, E1 64   A1
   E2 64   A1
Chandler Av, E16 72   C3
Chandlers Ms, E14 . . . 124   C1
Chandler St, E1 93   F4
Chandler Way, SE15 . . 147   F5
Chandos Pl, WC2 87   E3
Chandos St, W1 57   F4
Change All, EC3 91   D1
Channel Ho, E14 67   E4
Channel Islands Est, N1 . 18   B2
Channelsea Ho Business
   Cen, E15 49   D3
Channelsea Rd, E15 . . . 26   C5

Chantry Cl, W9 52   B2
Chantry Sq, W8
   off St. Mary's Pl 109   E4
Chantry St, N1 39   F1
Chant Sq, E15 27   D4
Chant St, E15 27   D4
Chapel Ct, SE1 118   C1
Chapel Ho St, E14 153   F2
Chapel Mkt, N1 38   C2
Chapel Pl, EC2 41   E5
   N1 39   D2
   W1 85   E1
Chapel Side, W2 81   E2
Chapel St, NW1 55   E4
   SW1 113   D3
Chaplin Cl, SE1 117   D1
Chaplin Rd, E15 49   F2
Chapman Rd, E9 24   B2
Chapman St, E1 93   E2
Chapone Pl, W1 86   C1
Chapter Chambers, SW1
   off Chapter St 142   C1
Chapter Ho Ct, EC4 . . . 90   A1
Chapter Rd, SE17 145   F3
Chapter St, SW1 142   C1
Chardwell Cl, E6 76   A5
Charecroft Way, W12 . 106   C2
   W14 106   C2
Charfield Ct, W9 53   E2
Charford Rd, E16 73   D4
Chargeable La, E13 . . . 72   B1
Chargeable St, E16 . . . 72   B1
Chargrove Cl, SE16 . . . 123   D1
⇌ Charing Cross 87   E4
⊖ Charing Cross 87   E4
Charing Cross, SW1 . . . 87   D4
H Charing Cross Hosp,
   W6 134   C4
Charing Cross Rd, WC2 . 59   D5
Chariot Cl, E3 46   C1
Charlbert St, NW8 33   E2
Charlemont Rd, E6 . . . 76   B1
Charles Coveney Rd,
   SE15 172   A3
Charles Dickens Ho, E2 . 43   E5
★ Charles Dickens Mus,
   WC1 60   B1
Sch Charles Dickens Prim
   Sch, SE1 118   A2
Sch Charles Edward Brooke
   C of E Girls' Sch, Lwr Sch,
   SE5 169   E4
   Upr Sch, SW9 169   F3
Charles Flemwell Ms,
   E16 101   D5
Charles Gardner Ct, N1 . 41   D4
Charles Grinling Wk,
   SE18 132   C5
Charles La, NW8 33   D3
Charles Mackenzie Ho,
   SE16 off Linsey St . . 120   C5
Charles Pl, NW1 36   B5
Charles Rowan Ho,
   WC1 38   C5
Charles II Pl, SW3
   off King's Rd 140   A3
Charles II St, SW1 86   C4

Charles Sq, N1 .... 41 D5
Charles Sq Est, N1 .... 41 D5
Charles St, W1......... 85 E4
Charleston St, SE17 .. 146 B1
Charles Townsend Ho,
  EC1 .... 61 D1
Charles Whincup Rd,
  E16 .... 101 E4
Charleville Rd, W14 .. 135 F3
Charlie Chaplin Wk, SE1
  off Waterloo Br 88 B5
Charlotte Despard Av,
  SW11............. 165 D4
Charlotte Ms, W1 ..... 58 B3
  W10 .... 78 C1
  W14 .... 107 E5
Charlotte Pl, SW1 .... 142 A1
  W1................ 58 B4
Charlotte Rd, EC2 .... 63 E1
Sch Charlotte Sharman
  Prim Sch, SE11....117 E4
Charlotte St, W1 ...... 58 B3
Charlotte Ter, N1 ..... 88 B1
Sch Charlotte Turner Prim
  Sch, SE8 .... 153 D4
Charlton, SE7 .... 157 F2
Charlton Pl, N1 .... 39 D2
Charlton Rd, SE3..... 181 E1
  SE7 .... 181 E1
Sch Charlton Sch, Royal Hill,
  SE10 .... 178 B2
Charlton Way, SE3 ... 179 E4
Charlwood Ho, SW1
  off Vauxhall Br Rd .. 142 C1
Charlwood Pl, SW1... 142 B1
Charlwood St, SW1... 142 B1
Charmouth Ho, SW8
  off Dorset Rd 168 A1
Charnwood Gdns, E14. 125 D5
Charrington St, NW1 .. 36 C2
★ Charterhouse, EC1.. 61 F3
Charterhouse Bldgs,
  EC1 .... 61 F2
Charterhouse Ms, EC1 . 61 F3
Charterhouse Sq, EC1.. 61 F3
Sch Charterhouse Sq Sch,
  EC1 .... 62 A3
Charterhouse St, EC1.. 61 D4
Charteris Rd, NW6 .... 30 B1
Chart St, N1.......... 41 D4
Chaseley St, E14...... 95 E1
Chater Ho, E2
  off Roman Rd....... 44 C4
Chatham Cl, SE18.... 133 F3
Chatham Pl, E9....... 22 A1
Chatham St, SE17.... 118 C5
Chatsworth Ct, W8... 108 C5
Chatsworth Rd, NW2 ... 7 E2
Chaucer Dr, SE1 ..... 148 B1
Chaucer Ho, SW1 .... 142 A3
Chauntler Cl, E16 .... 101 F2
Cheapside, EC2 ...... 90 B1
Chearsley, SE17
  off Deacon Way.... 118 B5
Chedworth Cl, E16 ... 72 A5
Cheesemans Ter, W14. 136 A3
Chelmsford Cl, E6.... 104 A1

Chelmsford Cl, W6 ... 135 D4
Chelmsford Sq, NW10 . 28 A1
CHELSEA, SW3 .... 138 C4
H Chelsea & Westminster
  Hosp, SW10 ...... 138 B5
★ Chelsea Antique Mkt,
  SW3............. 139 D4
Chelsea Br, SW1 ..... 141 E4
  SW8............. 141 E4
Chelsea Br Rd, SW1 .. 140 C2
Chelsea Cloisters,
  SW3............. 139 F1
Uni Chelsea Coll of Art &
  Design, SW1...... 143 E2
Chelsea Cres, SW10 .. 162 B4
Chelsea Embk, SW3 .. 139 F5
★ Chelsea FC, SW6 .. 161 E1
Chelsea Gdns, SW1
  off Chelsea Br Rd... 141 D3
Chelsea Harbour,
  SW10............ 162 B4
Chelsea Harbour Dr,
  SW10............ 162 B3
Riv Chelsea Harbour
  Pier 162 C4
Chelsea Manor Ct,
  SW3............. 139 F4
Chelsea Manor Gdns,
  SW3............. 139 E4
Chelsea Manor St,
  SW3............. 139 E3
Chelsea Pk Gdns, SW3. 138 C4
★ Chelsea Physic Gdn,
  SW3............. 140 A4
Chelsea Reach Twr,
  SW10............ 162 C1
Chelsea Sq, SW3 ..... 139 D2
Chelsea Twrs, SW3
  off Chelsea Manor
  Gdns 139 F3
Chelsea Vista, SW6 .. 162 B4
Chelsea Wf, SW10.... 162 C2
Cheltenham Ter, SW3. 140 B2
Chenies Ms, WC1 ..... 58 C2
Chenies Pl, NW1 ...... 36 C2
Chenies St, WC1 ...... 58 C3
Cheniston Gdns, W8.. 109 E3
Chepstow Cres, W11 .. 80 C2
Chepstow Pl, W2 ..... 81 D2
Chepstow Rd, W2..... 53 D5
Chepstow Vil, W11.... 80 B2
Chequer St, EC1 ...... 62 B2
Cherbury Ct, N1 ...... 41 D3
Cherbury St, N1 ...... 41 D3
Sch Cherry Gdn Sch,
  SE16 .... 121 D5
Cherry Gdn St, SE16.. 121 E2
Cherry Tree Cl, E9..... 22 B5
Sch Cherry Trees Sch,
  The, E3 .... 47 D5
Cherry Tree Wk, EC1... 62 B2
Cherry Tree Way, E13 . 74 C1
Cherrywood Cl, E3 ... 45 F4
Cherwell Ho, NW8
  off Church St Est 55 D2
Cheryls Cl, SW6...... 161 F3
Chesham Cl, SW1 .... 112 C4

Chesham Ms, SW1 ... 112 C3
Chesham Pl, SW1 .... 112 C4
Chesham St, SW1 .... 112 C4
Cheshire Cl, SE4 ..... 176 A5
Cheshire Ct, EC4 ..... 89 D1
Cheshire St, E2 .... 64 B1
Chesil Ct, E2 .... 44 A2
Chesilton Rd, SW6 ... 160 A3
Chesney St, SW11 ... 164 C4
Chesson Rd, W14 .... 136 A4
Chester Cl, SW1 ..... 113 D2
Chester Cl N, NW1 .... 35 F4
Chester Cl S, NW1..... 35 F5
Chester Cotts, SW1... 140 C1
Chester Ct, NW1
  off Albany St 35 F5
  SE5 .... 170 C2
Chesterfield Gdns,
  SE10 .... 178 C2
  W1 .... 85 E4
Chesterfield Hill, W1 .. 85 E3
Chesterfield St, W1.... 85 E4
Chesterfield Wk, SE10. 179 D3
Chesterfield Way,
  SE15 .... 174 A2
Chester Gate, NW1.... 35 E5
Chester Ms, SW1 .... 113 E3
Chester Pl, NW1 ...... 35 E4
Chester Rd, E16 ...... 71 F2
  NW1 .... 35 D5
Chester Row, SW1 ... 140 C1
Chester Sq, SW1 .... 113 E5
Chester Sq Ms, SW1 .. 113 E4
Chester St, E2 .... 65 D1
  SW1............. 113 D3
Chester Ter, NW1 ..... 35 E4
Sch Chesterton Prim Sch,
  SW11............ 164 C4
Chesterton Rd, W10... 51 D4
Chesterton Sq, W8 ... 108 B5
Chester Way, SE11... 145 D1
Chestnut All, SW6.... 136 B5
Chestnut Cl, SE14.... 176 A3
Chestnut Ct, SW6 .... 136 B5
Chestnut Ho, NW3
  off Maitland Pk Vil... 12 B1
Chettle Cl, SE1 ...... 118 C3
Chetwood Wk, E6 ..... 75 F4
Cheval Pl, SW7 ...... 111 F3
Cheval St, E14....... 124 C3
Chevening Rd, NW6 ... 29 E1
  SE10 .... 156 B3
Chevron Cl, E16 ...... 73 D5
Cheyne Cl, SW3 ..... 140 A4
Cheyne Gdns, SW3... 139 F4
Cheyne Ms, SW3..... 139 F4
Cheyne Pl, SW3...... 140 A4
Cheyne Row, SW3 ... 139 E5
Cheyne Wk, SW3..... 139 F5
  SW10 .... 162 C1
Chicheley St, SE1 .... 116 B1
Chichester Cl, E6 .... 103 F1
Chichester Ct, NW1 ... 14 A3

Chichester Rents, WC2. **60** C5
Chichester Rd, NW6 . . . **30** C3
W2. . . . . **53** F3
Chichester St, SW1 . . . **142** B3
Chichester Way, E14 . **126** C5
Chicksand St, E1. . . . . . **64** B4
Chiddingstone St,
SW6. . . . . **161** D5
Chigwell Hill, E1. . . . . **93** E3
Chilcot Cl, E14. . . . . . . **97** F1
Sch Childeric Prim Sch,
SE14 . . . . **175** F2
Childeric Rd, SE14 . . . **175** F2
Childerley St, SW6 . . . **159** E3
Childers St, SE8. . . . . **151** F4
Child La, SE10. . . . . . **128** B4
Child's Ms, SW5
off Child's Pl. **137** E1
Child's Pl, SW5 . . . . . **137** D1
Child's St, SW5 . . . . . **137** D1
Child's Wk, SW5 . . . . **137** D1
Chiltern Rd, E3 . . . . . . **69** D2
Chiltern St, W1 . . . . . . **56** C3
Chilton Gro, SE8 . . . . **151** D1
Chilton St, E2 . . . . **64** B1
Chilver St, SE10 . . . . **156** B2
Chilworth Ms, W2. . . . **82** B1
Chilworth St, W2. . . . . **82** B1
China Hall Ms, SE16 . . **122** B4
★ Chinatown, W1
off Gerrard St. **86** C2
Ching Ct, WC2 . . . . **87** E1
Chipka St, E14 . . . . . . **126** A2
Chipley St, SE14 . . . . **151** E5
Chippendale Ho, SW1. **141** F3
Chippenham Gdns,
NW6 . . . . **30** C5
Chippenham Ms, W9 . . **52** C2
Chippenham Rd, W9 . . **52** C2
Chipstead St, SW6 . . . **161** D4
Sch Chisenhale Prim Sch,
E3 . . . . **45** E2
Chisenhale Rd, E3 . . . . **45** E2
Chisledon Wk, E9 . . . . **24** B1
Chiswell Sq, SE3 . . . . . **181** F5
Chiswell St, EC1 . . . . . **62** B3
SE5 . . . . **171** D1
Chitty St, W1. . . . . **58** B3
Choppins Ct, E1 . . . . . . **93** F4
Chopwell Cl, E15. . . . . **27** D4
Chrisp St, E14 . . . . **69** C4
Christchurch Av, NW6 . . **7** F3
Sch Christ Ch Bentinck
C of E Prim Sch,
NW1 . . . . **55** F3
Sch Christchurch (Brixton)
C of E Prim Sch,
SW9. . . . . **169** D3
Sch Christ Ch Brondesbury
C of E Prim Sch, NW6. **8** A4
Sch Christ Ch C of E Prim
Sch, NW1. . . . . **35** F4
SW3. . . . . **140** A4

Sch Christ Ch C of E Sch,
E1 . . . . **64** B3
Christchurch Ct, NW6 . . . **7** E3
Christ Ch Pas, EC1 . . . . **61** F5
Sch Christ Ch Prim Sch,
SE10 . . . . **155** F2
Christchurch Sq, E9 . . **44** A1
Christchurch St, SW3 . **140** A4
Christchurch Ter, SW3. **140** A4
Christchurch Way,
SE10 . . . . **155** F1
Christian Ct, SE16. . . . . **96** A5
Christian St, E1. . . . . . . **65** D5
Christie Rd, E9 . . . . **23** E2
Coll Christie's Ed, W1 . . . **57** F3
Christina St, EC2 . . . . . **63** C1
Christopher Cl, SE16 . **122** C1
Sch Christopher Hatton
Prim Sch, EC1 . . . . . . **60** C2
Christopher Pl, NW1. . . **37** D5
Christopher's Ms, W11. **79** F4
Christopher St, EC2 . . . **63** D2
Chryssell Rd, SW9 . . . **169** C2
Chubworthy St, SE14. **151** E5
Chudleigh Rd, NW6 . . . . **6** B4
Chudleigh St, E1. . . . . . **66** C5
Chumleigh St, SE5 . . . **147** E4
Church Av, NW1 . . . . . . **13** F2
Church Cl, W8 . . . . **109** E1
Church Cres, E9. . . . . . . **22** C3
Church Entry, EC4. . . . . **89** F1
Churchfields, SE10 . . . **178** A1
Church Hill, SE18 . . . . **132** B4
Churchill Gdns, SW1. . **142** A3
Sch Churchill Gdns Prim
Sch, SW1 . . . . **142** B3
Churchill Gdns Rd,
SW1. . . . . **141** F3
★ Churchill Mus & Cabinet
War Rooms, SW1 . . **115** D1
Churchill Pl, E14. . . . . . **97** F4
Churchill Rd, E16 . . . . . **74** B5
Church Manor Est,
SW9. . . . . **169** D2
Churchmead, SE5
off Camberwell Rd . . **170** B2
Church Pas, EC2
off Gresham St. **62** B5
Church Pl, SW1 . . . . **86** B3
Church Rd, N1. . . . . **18** B2
Church St, E15 . . . . **27** F5
E16 . . . . **105** E5
NW8 . . . . **55** D3
W2. . . . . **55** D3
Church St Est, NW8 . . . **55** D2
Church St N, E15. . . . . . **27** F5
Church St Pas, E15 . . . . **27** F5
Church Ter, SW8 . . . . . **167** D5
Churchward Ho, W14
off Ivatt Pl **136** B3
Churchway, NW1 . . . . . **37** D4
Churchwell Path, E9. . . **22** A1
Churchyard Row,
SE11 . . . . **117** F5
Church Yd Wk, W2 . . . . **54** C3
Churton Pl, SW1 . . . . . **142** B1
Churton St, SW1 . . . . . **142** B1

Chusan Pl, E14 . . . . **96** B1
Cicely Rd, SE15. . . . . . **173** D4
Cinnabar Wf, E1 . . . . . . **93** D5
Cinnamon Cl, SE15. . . **172** A1
Cinnamon St, E1. . . . . . **93** F5
Circle, The, SE1. . . . . . **120** A1
Circus Lo, NW8 . . . . . . **32** C4
Circus Ms, W1 . . . . **56** A3
Circus Pl, EC2 . . . . **63** D2
Circus Rd, NW8 . . . . . . **32** C4
Coll Circus Space, N1 . . . **41** E5
Circus St, SE10 . . . . . . **178** A2
Cirencester St, W2 . . . . **53** E3
Coll Citadel Pl, SE11 . . . . **144** A2
Coll City & Guilds of London
Art Sch, SE11 . . . . . **145** D3
Coll City & Islington Coll,
Cen for Applied Sciences,
EC1 . . . . **39** E4
Dalby Ho, EC4. . . . . . **39** E3
Coll City & Islington
6th Form Coll, EC1 . . **39** E4
City Business Cen, SE16
off Lower Rd **122** A2
Coll City Business Coll,
EC1 . . . . **39** F5
Coll City Coll, The, N1. . . **40** C4
City Cross Business Pk,
SE10 . . . . **127** F5
City Forum, EC1 . . . . . . **40** A4
City Gdn Row, N1. . . . . **39** F3
Coll City Learning Cen,
NW10 . . . . **28** C1
Coll City Lit, Keeley Ho,
WC2. . . . . **88** A1
Stukeley St, WC2. . . . **59** F5
City Mill River Towpath,
E15 . . . . **25** E3
Sch City of London Acad
(Southwark), The,
SE1 . . . . **149** D2
Sch City of London Sch,
EC4 . . . . **90** A2
Sch City of London Sch for
Girls, EC2 . . . . **62** B3
★ City of Westminster
Archives Cen, SW1. **115** D3
Coll City of Westminster Coll,
Cockpit Thea, NW8 . . **55** E2
Cosway St Cen, NW1. . **55** F3
Maida Vale Cen, W9 . . **31** E5
Paddington Grn Cen,
W2. . . . . **54** C3
Queens Pk Cen, W9. . . **30** C5
City Pt, EC2. . . . . **62** C3
City Rd, EC1 . . . . **39** E3
⇌ City Thameslink. . . . **89** E1
City Twr, E14 . . . . **125** F3
Uni City Uni, Cass Business
Sch, EC1. . . . . **62** C2
Halls of Res & Saddlers
Sports Cen, EC1 . . . . . **62** A1
Northampton Sq Campus,
EC1 . . . . **39** E5
Walmsley Bldg, EC1 . . **61** E1
Walter Sickert Hall of Res,
N1 . . . . **40** A4

Uni City Uni - Inns of Ct Sch of Law, Atkin Bldg, WC1 . . . . **60** B3
Gray's Inn Pl, WC1 . . **60** B4
Princeton St, WC1 . . . . **60** B3
Uni City Uni - St. Bartholomew Sch of Nursing & Midwifery, E1 . . . . **65** F4
City Vw Apts, N1 . . . . . **18** A4
City Wk, SE1 . . . . **119** E2
Clabon Ms, SW1 . . . . . **112** A4
Clack St, SE16 . . . . **122** B2
Claire Pl, E14 . . . . **125** D3
Clandon St, SE8 . . . . . **177** D5
Clanricarde Gdns, W2 . **81** D3
Clapham Rd, SW9 . . . . **168** A3
Claps Gate La, E6 . . . . . **77** E1
Sch Clara Grant Sch, E3 . **69** D2
Clara Pl, SE18 . . . . **133** D5
Claredale St, E2 . . . . . . **43** D3
Clare Gdns, W11 . . . . . . **79** F1
Clare Ho, E3 . . . . **24** A5
Clare La, N1 . . . . **18** B4
Clare Mkt, WC2 . . . . . . **88** A1
Clare Ms, SW6 . . . . . . **161** E2
Claremont Cl, E16 . . . **105** D5
N1 . . . . **39** D3
Claremont Rd, W9 . . . **29** F3
Claremont Sq, N1 . . . . . **38** C3
Claremont St, E16 . . . **105** D5
SE10 . . . . **177** F1
Clarence Gdns, NW1 . . . **35** F5
Clarence Gate Gdns, NW1
off Glentworth St **56** B2
★ Clarence Ho, SW1 . . **114** B1
Clarence Ms, SE16 . . . . **94** C5
Clarence Rd, E16 . . . . . **71** F2
NW6 . . . . **8** A4
SE8 . . . . **153** E5
Clarence Ter, NW1 . . . . **56** B1
Clarence Wk, SW4 . . . . **167** E5
Clarence Way, NW1 . . . **13** E3
Clarence Way Est, NW1 . **13** E3
Clarendon Cl, E9 . . . . . . **22** B4
W2 . . . . **83** E2
Clarendon Cross, W11 . **79** F3
Clarendon Gdns, W9 . . **54** B2
Clarendon Gro, NW1 . . **36** C4
Clarendon Ms, W2 . . . . **83** E1
Clarendon Pl, W2 . . . . . **83** E2
Clarendon Rd, W11 . . . **79** E2
Clarendon St, SW1 . . . **141** F3
Clarendon Ter, W9 . . . . **54** B1
Clarendon Wk, W11 . . . **79** E1
Clare Rd, SE14 . . . . . . **176** A4
Clare St, E2 . . . . **43** F3
Clareville Gro, SW7 . . . **138** B1
Clareville St, SW7 . . . . **138** B1
Clarges Ms, W1 . . . . **85** E4
Clarges St, W1 . . . . **85** F4
Claribel Rd, SW9 . . . . . **169** E5
Clarissa St, E8 . . . . **42** A1
Clarke's Ms, W1 . . . . . . **57** D3
Clarkson Rd, E16 . . . . . **72** A5
Clarkson Row, NW1 . . . **36** A3
Clarkson St, E2 . . . . **43** E4
Clarks Pl, EC2 . . . . **63** E5

Clark St, E1 . . . . **65** F4
Claude St, E14 . . . . . . **124** C5
Clavell St, SE10 . . . . . **154** A4
Claverton St, SW1 . . . . **142** B3
Clave St, E1 . . . . **94** A5
Claxton Gro, W6 . . . . **135** D3
Claybrook Rd, W6 . . . . **135** D4
Claydon, SE17
off Deacon Way **118** A5
Claylands Pl, SW8 . . . . **168** C1
Claylands Rd, SW8 . . . **144** B5
Claypole Rd, E15 . . . . . **48** B2
Clay St, W1 . . . . **56** B4
Clayton Cl, E6 . . . . **76** B5
Clayton Cres, N1 . . . . . **37** F1
Clayton Dr, SE8 . . . . . **151** E2
Clayton Ms, SE10 . . . . **178** C3
Clayton Rd, SE15 . . . . **173** D4
Clayton St, SE11 . . . . . **144** C4
Clearbrook Way, E1 . . . **66** B5
Clearwater Ter, W11 . . **107** D1
Clearwell Dr, W9 . . . . . . **53** E2
Cleaver Sq, SE11 . . . . . **145** D2
Cleaver St, SE11 . . . . . **145** D2
Clegg St, E1 . . . . **93** F4
Clem Attlee Ct, SW6 . . **136** A5
Clem Attlee Par, SW6
off North End Rd . . . **136** B5
Clemence St, E14 . . . . . **68** A4
Clement Cl, NW6 . . . . **6** B4
Clements Av, E16 . . . . **100** C2
Clement's Inn, WC2 . . . **88** B1
Clement's Inn Pas, WC2 . . . . **88** B1
Clements La, EC4 . . . . . **91** D2
Clements Rd, SE16 . . . **121** D4
Clennam St, SE1 . . . . . **118** B1
Clenston Ms, W1 . . . . . . **56** A5
★ Cleopatra's Needle, WC2 . . . . **88** A4
Clephane Rd, N1 . . . . . . **18** C2
Clere St, EC2 . . . . **63** D1
CLERKENWELL, EC1 . . . **61** E2
Clerkenwell Cl, EC1 . . . **61** D1
Clerkenwell Grn, EC1 . . **61** D2
Sch Clerkenwell Parochial C of E Prim Sch, EC1 . **38** C4
Clerkenwell Rd, EC1 . . . **60** C2
Clermont Rd, E9 . . . . . . **22** A5
Cleveland Gdns, W2 . . . **82** A1
Cleveland Gro, E1 . . . . . **66** A2
Cleveland Ms, W1 . . . . . **58** A3
Cleveland Pl, SW1 . . . . . **86** B4
Cleveland Rd, N1 . . . . . . **19** D4
Cleveland Row, SW1 . . . **86** A5
Cleveland Sq, W2 . . . . . **82** A1
Cleveland St, W1 . . . . . . **58** A2
Cleveland Ter, W2 . . . . . **54** B5
Cleveland Way, E1 . . . . . **66** A2
Cleveley Cl, SE7 . . . . . **131** D5
Cleve Rd, NW6 . . . . **9** D3
Clichy Est, E1 . . . . **66** B4
Clifford Gdns, NW10 . . **28** A3
Clifford Rd, E16 . . . . **72** A2
Clifford's Inn Pas, EC4 . **88** C1
Clifford St, W1 . . . . **86** A3
Cliff Rd, NW1 . . . . **15** D1

Cliff Ter, SE8 . . . . **177** D5
Cliff Vil, NW1 . . . . **15** D1
Cliff Wk, E16 . . . . **72** B3
Clifton Ct, NW8 . . . . **54** C1
Clifton Cres, SE15 . . . . **173** F2
Clifton Est, SE15 . . . . . **173** D4
Clifton Gdns, W9 . . . . . . **54** A2
Clifton Gro, E8 . . . . **20** C1
Clifton Hill, NW8 . . . . . . **32** A1
Clifton Pl, SE16 . . . . . . **122** B1
W2 . . . . **83** D2
Clifton Ri, SE14 . . . . . . **175** F2
Clifton Rd, E16 . . . . **71** F3
N1 . . . . **18** B2
W9 . . . . **54** B1
Clifton St, EC2 . . . . **63** E3
Clifton Vil, W9 . . . . **53** F3
Clifton Wk, E6 . . . . **75** F5
Clifton Way, SE15 . . . . **173** F2
Clinch Ct, E16 . . . . **73** D4
Clinger Ct, N1 . . . . **41** E1
★ Clink Prison Mus, SE1 . . . . **90** C4
Clink St, SE1 . . . . **90** B4
Clinton Rd, E3 . . . . **45** E5
Clipper Cl, SE16 . . . . . **122** C1
Clipstone Ms, W1 . . . . . **58** A2
Clipstone St, W1 . . . . . . **57** F3
Clive Ct, W9 . . . . **54** B1
Cliveden Pl, SW1 . . . . . **112** C5
Cloak La, EC4 . . . . **90** B2
★ Clockmakers Company Collection, The (Guildhall Lib), EC2 . . **62** B5
Clock Twr Ms, N1 . . . . . **40** B1
Clock Twr Pl, N7 . . . . . . **15** E1
Cloisters Business Cen, SW8 off Battersea Pk Rd **165** F2
Cloncurry St, SW6 . . . . **159** D5
Clonmel Rd, SW6 . . . . **160** B2
Cloth Ct, EC1 . . . . **61** F4
Cloth Fair, EC1 . . . . **61** F4
Clothier St, E1 . . . . **63** F5
Cloth St, EC1 . . . . **62** A3
Cloudesley Pl, N1 . . . . . **38** C1
Cloudesley Rd, N1 . . . . **16** C5
Cloudesley Sq, N1 . . . . **38** C1
Cloudesley St, N1 . . . . . **39** D1
Clove Cres, E14 . . . . **98** B2
Clovelly Way, E1 . . . . . . **66** B5
Clover Ms, SW3 . . . . . **140** A4
Clove St, E13 . . . . **72** C2
Cloysters Grn, E1 . . . . . **92** C4
Club Row, E1 . . . . **64** A1
E2 . . . . **64** A1
Clunbury St, N1 . . . . . . **41** D3
Cluny Est, SE1 . . . . **119** E3
Cluny Ms, SW5 . . . . . . **136** C1
Cluny Pl, SE1 . . . . **119** E3
Cluse Ct, N1 . . . . **40** C2
Clutton St, E14 . . . . **69** F4
Clydesdale Rd, W11 . . . **52** A5

Clyde St, SE8........**152** B5
Clyston St, SW8 .....**166** C5
Coach & Horses Yd, W1.**85** F2
Coach Ho Ms, SE14...**174** C5
Coalport Ho, SE11
　　off Walnut Tree Wk .**116** C5
Coate St, E2..........**43** D3
Cobbett St, SW8 .....**168** B2
Cobble La, N1 ....**17** E3
Cobb's Ct, EC4
　　off Pilgrim St **89** F1
Cobb St, E1 ....**64** A4
Cobham Ms, NW1 .....**14** C3
Coborn Rd, E3 ....**46** A3
Coborn St, E3 ....**46** B4
SchCobourg Prim Sch,
　　SE5 ....**148** A4
Cobourg Rd, SE5.....**148** A4
Cobourg St, NW1 .....**36** B5
Coburg Cl, SW1 ......**114** B5
Cochrane Ms, NW8 ....**33** D3
Cochrane St, NW8.....**33** D3
Cockayne Way, SE8 ..**151** D1
Cock Hill, E1 ....**63** F4
Cock La, EC1 ....**61** E4
Cockpit Steps, SW1...**115** D2
Cockpit Yd, WC1 .....**60** B3
Cockspur Ct, SW1 .....**87** D4
Cockspur St, SW1 .....**87** D4
Coda Cen, The, SW6..**159** E2
Code St, E1 ....**64** B2
Codling Cl, E1 ....**93** D4
Codrington Ms, W11...**79** F1
Cody Rd, E16..........**71** D3
Cody Rd Business Cen,
　　E16 ....**71** D2
Coffey St, SE8 ....**177** D1
Coin St, SE1 ....**88** C4
Coity Rd, NW5.........**13** D1
Coke Rd, E1 ....**64** C5
Colas Ms, NW6 ....**9** D5
Colbeck Ms, SW7.....**137** F1
Colchester St, E1 .....**64** B5
Coldbath Sq, EC1 .....**60** C1
Coldbath St, SE13....**177** F4
Cold Blow La, SE14...**151** D5
Cold Harbour, E14 ....**98** B5
Coldharbour Pl, SE5 ..**170** C5
Colebeck Ms, N1 .....**17** F2
Colebert Av, E1 ......**66** A1
Colebrooke Pl, N1.....**39** F1
Colebrooke Row, N1...**39** E3
Colebrook Ho, E14 ....**69** E5
Coleby Path, SE5 ....**171** D2
Colechurch Ho, SE1
　　off Avondale Sq **148** C3
Colegrove Rd, SE15 ..**148** B5
Coleherne Ct, SW5 ...**137** F3
Coleherne Ms, SW10 .**137** E3
Coleherne Rd, SW10..**137** E3
Colehill Gdns, SW6 ..**159** E4
Colehill La, SW6 .....**159** E4
Coleman Flds, N1 .....**18** B5

Coleman Rd, SE5 ....**171** E1
Coleman St, EC2 ......**62** C5
Coleraine Rd, SE3....**156** A5
Coleridge Gdns, NW6..**10** A4
　　SW10 ....**161** F1
Coleridge Ho, SW1 ...**142** A3
Coleridge Sq, SW10 ..**162** A1
Coleshill Flats, SW1
　　off Pimlico Rd **141** D1
Colestown St, SW11..**163** F5
Cole St, SE1 ....**118** B2
Colet Gdns, W14.....**135** D2
Coley St, WC1 ....**60** B2
Colinsdale, N1........**39** E1
Collard Pl, NW1......**13** E3
College App, SE10 ...**154** B5
College Cres, NW3 ...**10** C2
College Cross, N1 ....**17** D4
College Gro, NW1 ....**36** C1
College Hill, EC4 .....**90** B2
College Ms, SW1 .....**115** E3
★ College of Arms, EC4.**89** F2
CollCollege of Law, The,
　　Bloomsbury Cen, WC1.**58** C3
　　Bream's Bldgs, EC4...**60** C5
　　Moorgate Cen, EC1 ..**62** C2
CollCollege of N W London,
　　Kilburn Cen, NW6....**8** C5
SchCollege Pk Sch, W2 .**81** E1
College Pl, NW1 ......**36** B1
　　SW10 ....**162** A1
College Rd, NW10.....**28** A3
College St, EC4 ......**90** B2
College Ter, E3 ......**46** A4
Collent St, E9 ....**22** B2
Collett Rd, SE16 .....**121** D4
Collier Cl, E6 ....**105** E2
Collier St, N1.........**38** A3
Collingham Gdns,
　　SW5.............**137** F1
Collingham Pl, SW5 ..**137** E1
Collingham Rd, SW5..**109** F5
SchCollingham Sch,
　　SW5.............**137** F1
Collington St, SE10...**155** D3
Collingwood St, E1....**65** F1
Collinson St, SE1.....**118** A2
Collinson Wk, SE1....**118** A2
Collin's Yd, N1 ....**39** E1
Colls Rd, SE15.......**174** A3
Collyer Pl, SE15 .....**172** C4
Colman Rd, E16......**74** A4
Colmar Cl, E1 ....**66** C1
Colmore Ms, SE15....**173** F4
Colnbrook St, SE1....**117** E4
Colombo St, SE1 .....**89** E5
Colomb St, SE10.....**155** F3
Colonnade, WC1 .....**59** E2
Colonnade Wk, SW1..**141** E1
Colorado Bldg, SE13
　　off Deals Gateway..**177** E4
Colosseum Ter, NW1
　　off Albany St **57** F1
Coltman St, E14......**67** F4
Columbia Pt, SE16...**122** B3
SchColumbia Prim Sch,
　　E2 ....**42** B4

Columbia Rd, E2......**42** A4
　　E13 ....**72** B3
Columbine Av, E6.....**75** E4
Columbus Ct, SE16
　　off Rotherhithe St ...**94** B5
Columbus Ctyd, E14...**96** C4
Colville Est, N1 ......**41** E1
Colville Gdns, W11....**80** B1
Colville Hos, W11 .....**52** A5
Colville Ms, W11......**80** B1
Colville Pl, W1........**58** B4
SchColville Prim Sch,
　　W11..............**80** B1
Colville Rd, W11 .....**80** B1
Colville Sq, W11 .....**80** A1
Colville Ter, W11......**80** A1
Colwith Rd, W6......**134** B5
Colworth Gro, SE17 ..**146** B1
Colwyn Ho, SE1
　　off Briant Est **116** C4
Colyer Cl, N1.........**38** B2
Combe, The, NW1.....**35** F5
Combe Av, SE3 ......**180** B1
Combedale Rd, SE10 .**156** C2
Combe Ms, SE3 .....**180** A1
Comber Gro, SE5.....**170** A3
SchComber Gro Prim Sch,
　　SE5 ....**170** A2
Comber Ho, SE5
　　off Comber Gro **170** B2
Comeragh Ms, W14 ..**135** F2
Comeragh Rd, W14 ..**135** E3
Comet Pl, SE8 ....**176** C2
Comet St, SE8 ....**176** C2
Comfort St, SE15....**147** E5
Commercial Rd, E1....**64** C5
　　E14 ....**95** D2
Commercial St, E1 ...**64** A2
Commercial Way,
　　SE15.............**172** A2
Commerell St, SE10 ..**155** F2
Commodity Quay, E1..**92** B3
Commodore St, E1 ...**67** E2
Common, The, E15....**27** F1
CollCommunity Coll Hackney,
　　London Flds, E8.....**21** F4
　　Shoreditch Campus,
　　N1 ....**41** F4
CollCommunity Ed Lewisham,
　　Mornington Cen,
　　SE8 ....**176** B2
Compayne Gdns, NW6..**9** E3
Compton Av, N1......**17** E2
Compton Cl, E3.......**69** D3
　　NW1 ....**35** F5
　　SE15 ....**172** C2
Compton Ho, SW11
　　off Parkham St.....**163** E3
Compton Pas, EC1 ...**61** F1
Compton Pl, WC1 ....**59** E1
Compton Rd, N1......**17** F2
　　NW10 ....**28** C5
Compton St, EC1.....**61** E1
Compton Ter, N1 ....**17** E2
Comus Pl, SE17......**147** E1
Comyns Cl, E16......**72** A3
Conant Ms, E1........**92** C2

Concert Hall App,
SE1 . . . .**88** B5
Concorde Dr, E6 . . . . . .**76** A3
Concorde Way, SE16 .**150** C1
Condell Rd, SW8 . . . . .**166** B4
Conder St, E14 . . . .**67** E5
Condray Pl, SW11 . . . .**163** E2
Conduit Av, SE10 . . . .**179** D3
Conduit Ct, WC2 . . . . . .**87** C2
Conduit Ms, W2 . . . . . .**82** C1
Conduit Pas, W2 . . . . . .**82** C1
Conduit Pl, W2 . . . .**82** C1
Conduit St, W1 . . . .**85** F2
Coney Way, SW8 . . . .**144** B5
Congreve St, SE17 . . . .**119** E5
Congreve Wk, E16 . . . .**74** C4
Coniger Rd, SW6 . . . . .**160** C5
Conington Rd, SE13 . .**177** F5
Conistone Way, N7 . . .**15** F3
Coniston Ho, SE5 . . . .**170** A1
Conlan St, W10 . . . .**51** E1
Conley St, SE10 . . . . . .**155** F2
Connaught Br, E16 . . .**102** C5
Connaught Cl, W2 . . . . .**83** E1
Sch Connaught Ho Sch,
W2 . . . .**84** A1
Connaught Pl, W2 . . . .**84** A2
Connaught Rd, E16 . .**103** D4
Connaught Rbt, E16 . .**102** C2
Connaught Sq, W2 . . . .**84** A1
Connaught St, W2 . . . .**83** E1
Connor Ct, SW11
off Alfreda St **165** E4
Connor St, E9 . . . .**22** C5
Consort Rd, SE15 . . . .**173** E5
Cons St, SE1 . . . .**117** D1
Constable Av, E16 . . .**101** E4
Constable Ho, E14
off Cassilis Rd **125** D2
NW3 . . . .**12** B3
Constance St, E16 . . .**103** E5
Constitution Hill, SW1 .**113** E1
Content St, SE17 . . . . .**146** B1
Convent Gdns, W11 . . .**79** F1
Sch Convent of Jesus &
Mary RC Inf Sch, NW2 .**6** A2
Conway Ms, W1 . . . . . .**58** A1
Conway St, E13 . . . .**72** C2
W1 . . . .**58** A2
Conybeare, NW3 . . . . . .**11** F3
Conyer St, E3 . . . .**45** E3
Cook Ct, SE16
off Rotherhithe St . . .**94** B5
Cookham Cres, SE16 .**122** C1
Cooks Cl, E14
off Cabot Sq **97** D4
Cook's Rd, E15 . . . .**47** E2
Cooks Rd, SE17 . . . . . .**145** E4
Coolfin Rd, E16 . . . . . .**101** D1
Coomassie Rd, W9 . . . .**52** A1
Coombs St, N1 . . . .**39** F3
Coomer Ms, SW6 . . . . .**136** B5
Coomer Pl, SW6 . . . . .**136** B5
Coomer Rd, SW6 . . . . .**136** B5
Cooper Cl, SE1 . . . .**117** D2
Coopers Cl, E1 . . . .**66** A2
Coopers La, NW1 . . . . .**37** D2

Coopers Rd, SE1 . . . . .**148** B3
Cooper's Row, EC3 . . . .**92** A2
Cooper St, E16 . . . .**72** B4
Coopers Yd, N1 . . . .**17** E3
Copeland Dr, E14 . . . .**125** D5
Copeland Rd, SE11 . . .**116** B4
Copenhagen Pl, E14 . .**96** A1
Sch Copenhagen Prim Sch,
N1 . . . .**38** A1
Copenhagen St, N1 . . .**37** F1
Cope Pl, W8 . . . .**108** C4
Cope St, SE16 . . . .**122** C5
Copford Wk, N1 . . . . . .**18** A5
Copley Cl, SE17 . . . . . .**145** F5
Copley St, E1 . . . .**66** C4
Copperas Rd, SE8 . . . .**153** E5
Copperfield Rd, E3 . . . .**67** F2
Copperfield St, SE1 . . .**117** F1
Copper Row, SE1 . . . . .**92** A5
Copse Cl, SE7 . . . .**157** F5
Copthall Av, EC2 . . . . . .**63** D5
Copthall Bldgs, EC2 . . .**62** C5
Copthall Cl, EC2 . . . . . .**62** C5
Copthall Ct, EC2 . . . . . .**62** C5
Coptic St, WC1 . . . .**59** E4
Coral Apts, E16 off Western
Gateway **101** D3
Coral St, SE1 . . . .**117** D2
★ Coram's Flds, WC1 . .**59** F1
Coram St, WC1 . . . .**59** E2
Corbden Cl, SE15 . . . .**172** B3
Corbet Ct, EC3 . . . .**91** D1
Corbet Pl, E1 . . . .**64** A3
Corbetts La, SE16 . . . .**150** A1
Corbetts Pas, SE16 . . .**150** A1
Corbidge Ct, SE8 . . . . .**153** E4
Corbiere Ho, N1 . . . . . .**19** E5
Corbin Ho, E3 . . . .**47** F4
Corbridge Cres, E2 . . .**43** E2
Corby Way, E3 . . . .**68** C2
Cordelia St, E14 . . . . . .**69** E5
Cording St, E14 . . . .**69** F4
Uni Cordwainers at London
Coll of Fashion, EC1 .**62** A2
Cord Way, E14 . . . . . .**125** D3
Corfe Ho, SW8
off Dorset Rd **168** A1
Corfield St, E2 . . . .**43** F5
Coriander Av, E14. . . . .**98** C1
Cork Sq, E1 . . . .**93** E4
Cork St, W1 . . . .**86** A3
Cork St Ms, W1 . . . .**86** A3
Corlett St, NW1 . . . .**55** E3
Cormont Rd, SE5. . . . . .**169** E4
Cornelia St, N7 . . . .**16** B2
Corner Ho St, WC2 . . . .**87** E4
Cornhill, EC3 . . . .**91** D1
Cornish Ho, SE17 . . . .**145** E5
Cornwall Av, E2 . . . . . .**44** A5
Cornwall Cres, W11 . . .**79** E2
Cornwall Gdns, SW7 . .**109** F4
Cornwall Gdns Wk,
SW7. . . . .**109** F4
Cornwallis St, SW8 . . .**167** E3
Cornwall Ms S, SW7 . .**110** A4
Cornwall Ms W, SW7 .**109** F4
Cornwall Rd, SE1 . . . . .**88** C4

Cornwall Sq, SE11 . . .**145** D2
Cornwall St, E1 . . . .**93** F2
Cornwall Ter, NW1 . . . .**56** B2
Cornwall Ter Ms, NW1 .**56** B2
Cornwood Dr, E1. . . . . .**66** A5
Coronet St, N1 . . . .**41** E5
Corporation Row, EC1 .**61** D1
Corporation St, E15 . . .**49** F3
Corsham St, N1. . . . . . .**41** D5
Corsica St, N5 . . . .**17** E1
Cortayne Rd, SW6 . . .**160** B5
Corunna Rd, SW8 . . . .**166** B3
Corunna Ter, SW8 . . . .**166** A3
Corvette Sq, SE10. . . .**155** D4
Coryton Path, W9 . . . . .**52** B1
Cosmo Pl, WC1 . . . .**59** F3
Cossall Wk, SE15 . . . .**173** E5
Cosser St, SE1 . . . .**116** C3
Cosway St, NW1 . . . . . .**55** F3
Cotall St, E14 . . . .**69** D5
Cotham St, SE17 . . . . .**146** B1
Cotleigh Rd, NW6 . . . . . .**8** C3
Cotswold Ct, EC1 . . . . .**62** A1
Cotswold Ms, SW11 . .**163** D4
Cottage Grn, SE5 . . . .**171** D1
Cottage Pl, SW3 . . . . .**111** E3
Cottage St, E14. . . . . . .**97** F2
Cottesbrook St, SE14 .**175** E1
Cottesloe Ms, SE1. . . .**117** D3
Cottesmore Gdns, W8 .**109** F3
Cottingham Rd, SW8 .**144** B5
Cottington St, SE11 . . .**145** D2
Cottle Way, SE16 . . . .**121** F2
Cottons Gdns, E2 . . . . .**41** F4
Cottons La, SE1. . . . . . .**91** D4
Cotton St, E14. . . . .**98** A2
Cottrell Ct, SE10
off Greenroof Way . .**128** B5
Cottrill Gdns, E8 . . . . . .**21** E1
Coulson St, SW3 . . . . .**140** A2
Councillor St, SE5 . . . .**170** A2
Counter Ct, SE1
off Borough High St . .**90** C5
Counter St, SE1 . . . . . .**91** E4
County Gro, SE5 . . . . .**170** A3
★ County Hall, SE1 . .**116** A1
County Rd, E6. . . . .**77** E4
County St, SE1 . . . . . .**118** B4
Courland Gro, SW8 . . .**167** D4
Courland Gro Hall,
SW8. . . . .**167** D5
Courland St, SW8 . . . .**167** D4
★ Courtauld Inst of Art,
WC2. . . . .**88** A2
Courtenay Sq, SE11 . .**144** C3
Courtenay St, SE11 . .**144** C2
Courtfield Gdns, SW5 .**109** F5
Courtfield Ms, SW5 . . .**138** A1
Courtfield Rd, SW7 . . .**137** F1
Court Gdns, N7 . . . .**17** D2
Courtnell St, W2 . . . . . .**52** C5
Court St, E1. . . . .**65** E3
Courtyard, The, N1. . . .**16** B3

Courtyard Ho, SW6
  off Lensbury Av **162** B5
Cousin La, EC4 . . . . **90** C3
Couthurst Rd, SE3 . . . **157** F5
Covelees Wall, E6 . . . . . **77** D5
Covell Ct, SE8
  off Reginald Sq **177** D2
★ Covent Garden,
  WC2 . . . . **87** F2
⊖ Covent Garden **87** E2
Covent Gdn Mkt, WC2 . **87** F2
Coventry Cl, E6 . . . . . . **104** A1
  NW6 . . . . **31** D1
Coventry Rd, E1 . . . . . . **65** F1
  E2 . . . . **65** F1
Coventry St, W1 . . . . . . **86** C3
Coverdale Rd, NW2 . . . . . **7** D3
Coverley Cl, E1 . . . . . . **65** D3
Cowan Cl, E6 . . . . **75** F4
Cowcross St, EC1 . . . . . **61** E3
Cowdenbeath Path, N1.**16** A5
Cowdry Rd, E9
  off East Cross Route . **24** A2
Cow Leaze, E6 . . . . **77** D5
Cowley Est, SW9 . . . . . **168** C3
Cowley Rd, SW9 . . . . . . **169** D4
Cowley St, SW1 . . . . . . **115** E3
Cowling Cl, W11 . . . . . . **79** E3
Cowpers Ct, EC3
  off Birchin La **91** D1
Cowper St, EC2 . . . . . . **63** D1
Cowper Ter, W10 . . . . . **50** C4
Cowthorpe Rd, SW8 . . **167** D3
Coxson Way, SE1 . . . . . **120** A2
Crabtree Cl, E2 . . . . **42** A2
Crabtree La, SW6 . . . . . **158** C1
Craddock St, NW5 . . . . **12** C2
Craigerne Rd, SE3 . . . . **181** E1
Craigs Ct, SW1 . . . . **87** E4
Craik Ct, NW6 . . . . **30** B3
Crail Row, SE17 . . . . . . **147** D1
Cramer St, W1 . . . . **57** D4
Crammond Cl, W6 . . . **135** E4
Sch Crampton Prim Sch,
  SE17 . . . . **145** F2
Crampton St, SE17 . . . **146** A1
Cranberry La, E16 . . . . . **71** E2
Cranbourn All, WC2
  off Cranbourn St **87** D2
Cranbourne Pas, SE16. **121** D2
Cranbourn St, WC2 . . . **87** D2
Cranbrook Rd, SE8 . . . **177** D4
Cranbrook St, E2 . . . . . **45** D3
Cranbury Rd, SW6 . . . **161** F5
Crane Ct, EC4 . . . . **89** D1
Crane Gro, N7 . . . . **17** D1
Crane Ho, E5 . . . . **172** A4
Crane St, SE10 . . . . . . **154** C3
  SE15 . . . . **172** A3
Cranfield Row, SE1 . . . **117** D3
Cranford Cotts, E1
  off Cranford St **95** D2
Cranford St, E1 . . . . . . **95** D2

Cranhurst Rd, NW2 . . . . . **6** B1
Cranleigh St, NW1 . . . . **36** B3
Cranley Gdns, SW7 . . . **138** B2
Cranley Ms, SW7 . . . . **138** B2
Cranley Pl, SW7 . . . . . **138** C1
Cranley Rd, E13 . . . . . . **73** E3
Cranmer Ct, SW3 . . . . **139** F1
Cranmer Ho, SW11
  off Surrey La **163** E3
Cranmer Rd, SW9 . . . . **169** D1
Cranston Est, N1 . . . . . **41** D3
Cranswick Rd, SE16 . . **149** F2
Cranwell Cl, E3 . . . . . . **69** E2
Cranwood St, EC1 . . . . . **40** C5
Cranworth Gdns, SW9. **168** C4
Craven Hill, W2 . . . . **82** B3
Craven Hill Gdns, W2 . . **82** A2
Craven Hill Ms, W2 . . . **82** B2
Craven Pas, WC2 . . . . . **87** E4
Craven Rd, W2 . . . . **82** B2
Craven St, WC2 . . . . . . **87** E4
Craven Ter, W2 . . . . **82** B2
Crawford Est, SE5 . . . . **170** B5
Crawford Ms, W1 . . . . . **56** A4
Crawford Pas, EC1 . . . . **60** C2
Crawford Pl, W1 . . . . . . **55** F5
Sch Crawford Prim Sch,
  SE5 . . . . **170** B4
Crawford Rd, SE5 . . . . **170** B4
Crawford St, W1 . . . . . . **56** A4
Crawshay Ct, SW9 . . . . **169** D3
Crayford Cl, E6 . . . . **75** E5
Creasy Est, SE1 . . . . . . **119** E4
Crediton Rd, E16 . . . . . **72** C5
  NW10 . . . . **28** C1
Credon Rd, SE16 . . . . . **149** F2
Creechurch La, EC3 . . . . **91** F1
Creechurch Pl, EC3 . . . . **91** F1
Creed Ct, EC4
  off Ludgate Sq **89** F1
Creed La, EC4 . . . . **89** F1
Creek Rd, SE8 . . . . **152** C5
  SE10 . . . . **152** C5
Creekside, SE8 . . . . . . **177** E2
Crefeld Cl, W6 . . . . **135** D5
Creighton Rd, NW6 . . . . **29** D2
Cremer St, E2 . . . . **42** A3
Cremorne Est, SW10 . . **162** C1
Cremorne Rd, SW10 . . **162** B2
Crescent, EC3 . . . . **92** A2
Crescent Arc, SE10 . . . **154** A5
Crescent Ho, SE13
  off Ravensbourne Pl. **177** E5
Crescent Pl, SW3 . . . . **111** E5
Crescent Row, EC1 . . . . **62** A2
Crescent St, N1 . . . . **16** B3
Cresford Rd, SW6 . . . . **161** E4
Cresset Rd, E9 . . . . **22** B2
Cresset St, SW4 . . . . . **171** F4
Cressfield Cl, NW5 . . . . **11** D2
Cresswell Gdns, SW5 . **138** A2
Cresswell Pl, SW10 . . . **138** A2
Cressy Ct, E1 . . . . **66** B3
  W6 . . . . **134** A3
Cressy Ho, E1
  off Hannibal Rd **66** B3
Cressy Pl, E1 . . . . **66** B3
Crestfield St, WC1 . . . . **37** F4
Creswick Wk, E3 . . . . . . **46** C4
Creton St, SE18 . . . . . . **133** D4

Crewdson Rd, SW9 . . . **168** C2
Crews St, E14 . . . . **124** C5
Crichton St, SW8 . . . . . **166** A5
Cricketers Ct, SE11 . . . **145** E1
Crimscott St, SE1 . . . . **119** F4
Crimsworth Rd, SW8 . **167** D3
Crinan St, N1 . . . . **37** F2
Cringle St, SW8 . . . . . **166** A1
Cripplegate St, EC2 . . . . **62** A3
Crispin Pl, E1 . . . . **64** A3
Crispin St, E1 . . . . **64** A4
Crisp Rd, W6 . . . . **134** A3
Cristowe Rd, SW6 . . . . **160** B5
Crofters Ct, SE8
  off Croft St **151** E1
Crofters Way, NW1 . . . . **14** C5
Crofton Rd, E13 . . . . . . **73** E1
  SE5 . . . . **171** F4
Crofts St, E1 . . . . **92** C3
Croft St, SE8 . . . . **151** E1
Crogsland Rd, NW1 . . . **12** C3
Cromer St, WC1 . . . . . . **37** F5
Crompton St, W2 . . . . . **54** C2
Cromwell Cres, SW5 . . **108** C5
Cromwell Gdns, SW7 . **111** D4
Cromwell Gro, W6 . . . **106** B3
Cromwell Highwalk, EC2
  off Silk St **62** B3
H Cromwell Hosp, The,
  SW5 . . . . **109** E5
Cromwell Ms, SW7 . . . **111** D5
Cromwell Pl, SW7 . . . . **111** D5
Cromwell Rd, SW5 . . . **109** D5
  SW7 . . . . **110** C5
  SW9 . . . . **169** E3
Cromwell Twr, EC2 . . . . **62** B3
Crondace Rd, SW6 . . . **161** D4
Crondall Ct, N1 . . . . **41** E3
Crondall St, N1 . . . . **41** D3
Cronin St, SE15 . . . . . . **172** A2
Crooked Billet Yd, E2 . . **41** F4
Crooke Rd, SE8 . . . . . . **151** E2
Crookham Rd, SW6 . . . **160** A4
Croombs Rd, E16 . . . . . **74** A4
Crooms Hill, SE10 . . . . **178** B1
Crooms Hill Gro, SE10. **178** B1
Cropley Ct, N1 . . . . **40** C2
Cropley St, N1 . . . . **40** C2
Cropthorne Ct, W9 . . . . **32** B5
Crosby Ct, SE1 . . . . . . **118** C1
Crosby Row, SE1 . . . . . **118** C2
Crosby Sq, EC3 . . . . . . **91** E1
Crosby Wk, E8 . . . . **20** A2
Cross Av, SE10 . . . . . . **155** D5
Cross Cl, SE15 . . . . . . **173** E5
Crossfield Rd, NW3 . . . **11** D2
Crossfield St, SE8 . . . . **176** C1
DLR Crossharbour **125** F3
Cross Keys Cl, W1 . . . . **57** D4
Cross Keys Sq, EC1 . . . . **62** A4
Cross La, EC3 . . . . **91** E3
Crosslet St, SE17 . . . . . **119** D5
Crosslet Vale, SE10 . . . **177** E4
Crossley St, N7 . . . . **16** C1
Crossmount Ho, SE5 . **170** A1
Cross Rd, SE5 . . . . **171** F5
Cross St, N1 . . . . **17** E5

Crosstrees Ho, E14
  off Cassilis Rd 125 D3
Crosswall, EC3 ....92 A2
Croston St, E8 ....21 D5
Crowder St, E1 ....93 E2
Crowhurst Cl, SW9 ...169 D5
Crowland Ter, N1 .....18 C3
Crowline Wk, N1
  off Clephane Rd 18 B1
Crown Cl, E3 ....24 C5
  NW6 ....9 E1
Crown Ct, EC2 ....90 B1
  WC2..............87 F1
Crowndale Rd, NW1 ...36 A2
Crowngate Ho, E3 ....46 B3
Crown Office Row,
  EC4 ....88 C2
Crown Pas, SW1 ......86 B5
Crown Pl, EC2 ....63 E3
  NW5 ....13 F1
  SE16 ....149 F3
Crown Reach, SW1 ...143 D3
Crown St, SE5 ....170 B1
Crown Wks, E2 ....43 E3
Crows Rd, E15........49 D4
Crowther Cl, SW6 ...136 B5
Crowthorne Rd, W10 ..78 C1
Croxley Rd, W9 ....30 B5
Croxteth Ho, SW8 ....166 C5
Croydon Rd, E13......72 B2
Crucifix La, SE1 .....119 E1
Cruden Ho, SE17.....145 E5
Cruden St, N1 ....39 F1
Cruikshank St, WC1 ..38 C4
Crutched Friars, EC3...91 F2
Crystal Wf, N1........39 F3
Cuba St, E14 ....124 C1
Cubitt Bldg, SW1 ....141 E3
Cubitt Steps, E14 .....97 D4
Cubitt St, WC1........38 C4
Cubitts Yd, WC2 ......87 F2
CUBITT TOWN, E14 ..126 B3
Sch Cubitt Town Inf &
  Jun Schs, E14 ......126 B4
Cuddington, SE17.....118 A5
Cudworth St, E1 ......65 F1
Cuff Pt, E2 ....42 A4
Culford Gdns, SW3 ...140 B1
Culford Gro, N1.......19 E2
Culford Ms, N1 ....19 E1
Culford Rd, N1 ....19 E3
Culling Rd, SE16......122 A3
Culloden Cl, SE16 ....149 D3
Sch Culloden Prim Sch,
  E14 ....98 B1
Culloden St, E14......70 B5
Cullum St, EC3 ....91 E2
Culmore Rd, SE15....173 E2
Culross St, W1........84 C3
Culvert Rd, SW11 ....164 B4
Culworth St, NW8....33 E3
Cumberland Cl, E8 ...20 A2
Cumberland Cres,
  W14..............107 F5
Cumberland Gdns,
  WC1..............38 B4
Cumberland Gate, W1 .84 A2

Cumberland Mkt,
  NW1 ....35 F4
Cumberland Mkt Est,
  NW1 ....35 F4
Cumberland Ms, SE11.145 D3
Cumberland Mills Sq,
  E14 ....154 C2
Cumberland Pl, NW1 ..35 E4
Cumberland Rd, E13 ..73 E3
Sch Cumberland Sch,
  E13 ....74 A1
Cumberland St, SW1 .141 F2
Cumberland Ter, NW1 .35 E3
Cumberland Ter Ms,
  NW1 ....35 E3
★ Cuming Mus, SE17.146 A1
Cumming St, N1......38 A3
Cunard Pl, EC3 ....91 F1
Cunard Wk, SE16 ....123 D5
Cundy Rd, E16 ......102 A1
Cundy St, SW1 ......141 D1
Cundy St Est, SW1 ...141 D1
Cunningham Pl, NW8..54 C1
Cupar Rd, SW11 .....165 D3
Cureton St, SW1 .....143 D1
Curlew St, SE1.......120 A1
Curnock Est, NW1....36 A1
Cursitor St, EC4......60 C5
Curtain Pl, EC2 ....63 F1
Curtain Rd, EC2......63 E2
Curtis St, SE1 ....120 A5
Curtis Way, SE1 .....120 A5
Curzon Gate, W1......84 C5
Curzon Sq, W1.......85 D5
Curzon St, W1 ....85 D5
CUSTOM HOUSE, E16...75 D5
DLR Custom House for
  ExCeL 101 F2
Custom Ho Reach,
  SE16 ....124 A2
Custom Ho Wk, EC3 ...91 E3
Cut, The, SE1........117 D1
Cuthbert St, W2 ......54 C3
Cuthill Wk, SE5 ......170 C4
Cutlers Gdns, E1......63 F5
Cutlers Gdns Arc, EC2
  off Devonshire Sq....63 F5
Cutlers Sq, E14......153 D1
Cutlers Ter, N1 ....19 E1
Cutler St, E1 ....63 F5
★ Cutty Sark, SE10 ..154 A4
DLR Cutty Sark for Maritime
  Greenwich 154 A5
Cutty Sark Gdns, SE10.154 A4
Cyclops Ms, E14......124 C5
Cygnet St, E1 ....64 B1
Cynthia St, N1 ....38 B3
Cyntra Pl, E8 ....21 F4
Cypress Pl, W1 ....58 B2
DLR Cyprus 105 D2
Cyprus Pl, E2........44 B3
  E6 ....105 D2
Cyprus Rbt, E16 .....105 D2
Cyprus St, E2 ....44 A3
Sch Cyril Jackson Prim Sch,
  N Bldg, E14 ....96 B2
  S Bldg, E14 ....96 B3

Cyril Mans, SW11 ....164 B4
Cyrus St, EC1.........61 F1
Czar St, SE8 ....152 C4

D

Dabin Cres, SE10 ....178 A3
Dacca St, SE8 ....152 B4
Dace Rd, E3..........24 C4
Dacre St, SW1.......114 C3
Dagmar Gdns, NW10 ..28 C3
Dagmar Pas, N1 ......17 F5
Dagmar Rd, SE5 .....171 E4
Dagmar Ter, N1 ......17 F5
Dagnall St, SW11 ....164 B5
Daintry Way, E9 ......24 A1
Dairy Fm Pl, SE15....174 A4
Daisy Rd, E16 ....71 E1
Dakin Pl, E1..........67 E4
Dakota Bldg, SE13
  off Deals Gateway...177 D4
Dakota Gdns, E6.....75 F2
Dalby St, NW5........13 E2
Daleham Ms, NW3 ....11 D1
Dalehead, NW1.......36 A3
Dalemain Ms, E16 ...101 D4
Dale Rd, SE17 ....145 F5
Dale Row, W11 ....79 F1
Daley St, E9..........23 D1
Dalgarno Gdns, W10 ..50 A3
Dalgarno Way, W10...50 A2
Dalgleish St, E14 .....95 F1
Daling Way, E3.......45 F1
Sch Dallington Sch, EC1.61 F1
Dallington Sq, EC1
  off Dallington St 61 F1
Dallington St, EC1 ....61 F1
DALSTON, E8.........20 C3
↺ Dalston Kingsland..19 F1
Dalston La, E8........20 A1
Dalwood St, SE5 .....171 E4
Damask Cres, E16 ....71 F1
Damer Ter, SW10 ....162 B2
Dame St, N1 ....40 A2
Damien St, E1........65 F5
Danbury St, N1.......39 F2
Dancer Rd, SW6 .....160 A4
Dandridge Cl, SE10...156 B2
Danehurst St, SW6 ...159 E3
Dane Pl, E3..........46 A2
Danesdale Rd, E9 ....23 E2
Danesfield, SE5......147 E4
Dane St, WC1........60 A4
Daneville Rd, SE5 ....170 C4
Daniel Bolt Cl, E14 ....69 F3
Daniel Gdns, SE15 ...172 A1
Dan Leno Wk, SW6 ..161 E2
Dansey Pl, W1........86 C2
Dante Pl, SE11 ......117 F5
Dante Rd, SE11......117 E5
Danube St, SW3 .....139 F2

Danvers St, SW3 . . . . . **139** D5
Daplyn St, E1 . . . . **64** C3
D'Arblay St, W1 . . . . . . **86** B1
Darcy Ho, E8 . . . . **21** E5
Darfield Wlk, W10 . . . . **78** C2
Dark Ho Wk, EC3
  off Grant's Quay Wf . . **91** D3
Darlan Rd, SW6 . . . . . **160** B2
Darling Row, E1 . . . . . . **65** F2
Darnaway Pl, E14 . . . . . **70** B4
Darnley Ho, E14 . . . . . . **67** F5
Darnley Rd, E9 . . . . **21** F2
Darnley Ter, W11 . . . . . **79** D4
Darsley Dr, SW8 . . . . . **167** D3
Dartford Ho, SE1
  off Longfield Est **148** B1
Dartford St, SE17 . . . . **146** B4
Dartmoor Wk, E14 . . . **125** D5
Dartmouth Cl, W11 . . . . **52** B5
Dartmouth Gro, SE10 . **178** B4
Dartmouth Hill, SE10 . **178** B4
Dartmouth Rd, E16 . . . **72** C5
  NW2 . . . . **6** C1
Dartmouth Row, SE10 . **178** B5
Dartmouth St, SW1 . . **114** C2
Dartmouth Ter, SE10 . **178** C4
Dartrey Twr, SW10
  off Blantyre St **162** C1
Dartrey Wlk, SW10
  off Blantyre St **162** C1
Dart St, W10 . . . . **29** F4
Darwen Pl, E2 . . . . **43** E1
Darwin Ct, SE17 . . . . . **147** D5
Darwin St, SE17 . . . . . **119** D5
Datchelor Pl, SE5 . . . . **171** D4
Date St, SE17 . . . . **146** C3
Daubeney Twr, SE8 . . . **152** A1
Davenant St, E1 . . . . . . **65** D4
Davenport Ho, SE11
  off Walnut Tree Wk . **116** C5
Daventry St, NW1 . . . . . **55** E3
Davern Cl, SE10 . . . . . **156** A1
Davey Rd, N7 . . . . **16** B2
Davey Rd, E9 . . . . **24** C3
Davey St, SE15 . . . . . . **148** B5
Davidge St, SE1 . . . . . **117** E2
David Lee Pt, E15 . . . . . **49** F1
David Ms, W1 . . . . **56** B3
Davidson Gdns, SW8 . **167** E2
David St, E15 . . . . **27** D1
Coll Davies Laing & Dick
  Indep Coll, W1 . . . . . **57** D5
Davies Ms, W1 . . . . **85** E2
Davies St, W1 . . . . **85** E2
Dawes Ho, SE17 . . . . . **146** C1
Dawes Rd, SW6 . . . . . . **159** E1
Dawes St, SE17 . . . . . . **147** D2
Dawlish Rd, NW2 . . . . . . **7** D1
Dawn Cres, E15 . . . . . . **27** D5
Dawson Pl, W2 . . . . **80** C2
Dawson St, E2 . . . . **42** B3
Dayton Gro, SE15 . . . . **174** A3
Deacon Ms, N1 . . . . **19** D4

Deacon Way, SE17 . . . **118** A5
Deal Porters Way,
  SE16 . . . . **122** B3
Deals Gateway, SE13 . **177** D3
Deal St, E1 . . . . **64** C3
Deal Wk, SW9 . . . . **168** C2
Dean Bradley St, SW1 . **115** E4
Dean Cl, SE16 . . . . **95** D5
Dean Ct, SW8
  off Thorncroft St . . . **167** E2
Deancross St, E1 . . . . . . **94** A1
Deanery Ms, W1 . . . . . . **85** D4
Deanery Rd, E15 . . . . . . **27** E2
Deanery St, W1 . . . . **85** D4
Dean Farrar St, SW1 . . **114** C3
Dean Ho, E1
  off Tarling St **94** A1
Dean Rd, NW2 . . . . **6** A2
Dean Ryle St, SW1 . . . **115** E5
Deans Bldgs, SE17 . . . **146** C1
Deans Ct, EC4 . . . . **89** F1
Deans Ms, W1 . . . . **57** F5
Dean Stanley St, SW1 . **115** E4
Dean St, W1 . . . . **58** C3
Dean's Yd, SW1 . . . . . **115** D3
Dean Trench St, SW1 . **115** E4
Deason St, E15 . . . . **48** B1
De Beauvoir Cres, N1 . . **19** E5
De Beauvoir Est, N1 . . . **19** D5
Sch De Beauvoir Prim Sch,
  N1 . . . . **19** F2
De Beauvoir Rd, N1 . . . **19** E3
De Beauvoir Sq, N1 . . . **19** F4
DE BEAUVOIR TOWN,
  N1 . . . . **19** D5
Debnams Rd, SE16 . . . **150** A1
Decima St, SE1 . . . . . . **119** E3
Deck Cl, SE16 . . . . **123** D1
De Crespigny Pk, SE5 . **170** C5
Deeley Rd, SW8 . . . . . **166** C3
Deerhurst Rd, NW2 . . . . . **7** D2
Dee St, E14 . . . . **70** B5
Defiance Wk, SE18 . . . **132** A4
Defoe Cl, SE16 . . . . **124** A2
Defoe Ho, EC2
  off The Barbican **62** A3
Defoe Pl, EC2
  off The Barbican **62** B3
De Gama Pl, E14
  off Maritime Quay . . **153** D2
Delacourt Rd, SE3 . . . . **181** E2
Delafield Ho, E1 . . . . . . **93** D1
Delafield Rd, SE7 . . . . **157** F2
Delaford Rd, SE16 . . . **149** F2
Delaford St, SW6 . . . . **159** F1
Delamere St, W2 . . . . . **54** A3
Delamere Ter, W2 . . . . . **53** F3
Delancey Pas, NW1 . . . **35** F1
Delancey St, NW1 . . . . **35** E1
De Laune St, SE17 . . . **145** E3
Delaware Rd, W9 . . . . . **53** E1
Delhi St, N1 . . . . **37** F1
Delius Gro, E15 . . . . **48** C2
Dell Cl, E15 . . . . **27** D5
Dellow St, E1 . . . . **93** F2
Dell's Ms, SW1 . . . . . . **142** B1
Delme Cres, SE3 . . . . . **181** F5

Deloraine St, SE8 . . . . **176** C4
Delorme St, W6 . . . . . . **134** C5
Delta St, E2 . . . . **42** C4
Delverton Rd, SE17 . . **145** F3
Delvino Rd, SW6 . . . . . **160** C4
Denbigh Cl, W11 . . . . . . **80** B2
Denbigh Ms, SW1 . . . . **142** A1
Denbigh Pl, SW1 . . . . . **142** A2
Denbigh Rd, W11 . . . . . **80** B2
Denbigh St, SW1 . . . . . **142** A1
Denbigh Ter, W11 . . . . . **80** B2
Denford St, SE10 . . . . **156** A2
Dengie Wk, N1 . . . . **18** A5
Denham St, SE10 . . . . **156** C2
Denholme Rd, W9 . . . . . **30** B4
Denman Pl, W1
  off Great Windmill St . **86** C3
Denman Rd, SE15 . . . . **172** A4
Denman St, W1 . . . . **86** C3
Denmark Gro, N1 . . . . . **38** C2
Denmark Hill, SE5 . . . . **170** C4
Denmark Pl, E3 . . . . **47** D4
  WC2 . . . . **59** D5
Denmark Rd, NW6 . . . . . **30** B3
  SE5 . . . . **170** A4
Denmark St, E13 . . . . . . **73** E3
  WC2 . . . . **87** D1
Denne Ter, E8 . . . . **42** B1
Dennetts Gro, SE14 . . **174** C5
Dennetts Rd, SE14 . . . **174** B4
Denning Cl, NW8 . . . . . **32** B4
Denning Pt, E1 . . . . **64** A5
Dennington Pk Rd,
  NW6 . . . . **9** D1
Dennison Pt, E15 . . . . . **26** B4
Denny Cl, E6 . . . . **75** E4
Denny Cres, SE11 . . . . **145** D1
Denny St, SE11 . . . . . . **145** D2
Densham Rd, E15 . . . . . **27** F5
Denton, NW1
  off Malden Cres **13** D2
Denyer St, SW3 . . . . . . **139** F1
★ Department for
  Constitutional Affairs
  (DCA), SW1 . . . . **114** B3
★ Department for
  Environment, Food &
  Rural Affairs (D.E.F.R.A.),
  SW1 . . . . **87** E4
★ Department for Transport
  (DfT), SW1 . . . . **115** D5
★ Department of Health &
  Dept for Work & Pensions
  (D.W.P.), SW1 . . . . . . **115** D1
Depot Rd, W12 . . . . **78** B2
DEPTFORD, SE8 . . . . . **152** B3
⚆Deptford **176** C1
DLR Deptford Bridge . . . **177** D3
Deptford Br, SE8 . . . . . **177** D3
Deptford Bdy, SE8 . . . **176** C3
Deptford Ch St, SE8 . . **153** D5
Deptford Ferry Rd,
  E14 . . . . **153** D1
Deptford Grn, SE8 . . . **153** D5
Sch Deptford Grn Sch,
  SE14 . . . . **176** A1
  Lwr Sch, SE14 . . . . . **175** F1

★ Place of interest ⇌ Railway station ⚆ London Overground station ⊖ London Underground station

Deptford High St, SE8 . **152** C5
Sch Deptford Pk Prim Sch,
SE8 . . . . **151** F2
Deptford Strand, SE8 . . **152** B1
Deptford Wf, SE8 . . . . **124** A5
De Quincey Ho, SW1
off Lupus St **142** A3
De Quincey Ms, E16 . . **101** D4
Derby Gate, SW1 . . . . **115** E1
Derby Ho, SE11
off Walnut Tree Wk . **116** C5
Derby Rd, E9 . . . . **22** C5
Derbyshire St, E2 . . . . . **43** D5
Derby St, W1 . . . . **85** D5
Dereham Pl, EC2 . . . . . . **41** F5
Dericote St, E8 . . . . **21** D5
Derifall Cl, E6 . . . . **76** B3
Dering St, W1 . . . . **85** E1
Derrick Gdns, SE7 . . . **130** A4
Derry St, W8 . . . . **109** E2
Derwent St, SE10 . . . . **155** E2
Desborough Cl, W2 . . . . **53** F3
Desborough Ho, W14
off North End Rd . . **136** B4
Desborough St, W2 . . . **53** E3
Desford Ms, E16 . . . . . . **71** F2
Desford Rd, E16 . . . . . . **71** F2
★ Design Mus, SE1 . . **92** B5
Desmond St, SE14 . . . **151** F5
Devalls Cl, E6 . . . . **105** D2
Devas St, E3 . . . . **69** F1
De Vere Gdns, W8 . . . . **110** A2
Deverell St, SE1 . . . . . **118** C4
De Vere Ms, W8 . . . . . **110** A3
Devereux Ct, WC2 . . . . . **88** C1
Devizes St, N1 . . . . **41** D1
Devonia Rd, N1 . . . . **39** F2
Devon Mans, SE1
off Tooley St **120** A1
Devonport St, E1 . . . . . **94** C1
Devons Est, E3 . . . . **47** F5
Devonshire Cl, W1 . . . . **57** E3
Devonshire Dr, SE10 . **177** E2
Devonshire Gro, SE15 . **149** F5
Devonshire Ho, SE1
off Bath Ter **118** A3
Devonshire Ms, SW10
off Park Wk **138** C4
Devonshire Ms N, W1 . . **57** E3
Devonshire Ms S, W1 . . **57** E3
Devonshire Ms W, W1 . **57** E2
Devonshire Pl, W1 . . . . **57** D2
W8 . . . . **109** E4
Devonshire Pl Ms, W1 . **57** D2
Devonshire Rd, E16 . . . **73** F5
Devonshire Row, EC2 . . **63** F4
Devonshire Row Ms,
W1 . . . . **57** F2
Devonshire Sq, EC2 . . . **63** F5
Devonshire Ter, W1 . . . **57** D3
Devonshire Ter, W2 . . . **82** B1
DLR Devons Road **69** E1
Devons Rd, E3 . . . . **69** D3
Devon St, SE15 . . . . . . **149** F5
De Walden St, W1 . . . . . **57** D4
Dewberry Gdns, E6 . . . **75** E3
Dewberry St, E14 . . . . . **70** A4

Dewey Rd, N1 . . . . **38** C2
Dewhurst Rd, W14 . . . **106** C3
Dewsbury Ter, NW1 . . . **13** F5
D'Eynsford Rd, SE5 . . . **170** C3
Dhonan Ho, SE1
off Longfield Est **120** B5
Diadem Ct, W1 . . . . **86** C1
Dial Wk, The, W8 . . . . **109** F1
Diamond St, SE15 . . . . **171** F2
Diamond Ter, SE10 . . . **178** B3
Diamond Way, SE8 . . . **177** D1
Diana Cl, SE8 . . . . **152** B4
★ Diana Princess of Wales
Mem, W2 . . . . **83** D5
Dibden St, N1 . . . . **17** F5
Dibdin Ho, W9 . . . . **31** E2
Dickens Est, SE1 . . . . . **120** C1
SE16 . . . . **120** C2
Dickens Ho, NW6 . . . . . **30** C4
Dickens Ms, EC1 . . . . . . **61** E3
Dickens Sq, SE1 . . . . . **118** B3
Dickens St, SW8 . . . . . **165** F5
Dickinson Ct, EC1
off Brewhouse Yd . . . **61** F2
Dieppe Cl, W14 . . . . . . **136** B2
Digby St, E2 . . . . **44** B5
Diggon St, E1 . . . . **66** C4
Dighton Ct, SE5 . . . . . **146** A5
Dignum St, N1 . . . . **38** C2
Digswell St, N7 . . . . **17** D1
Dilke St, SW3 . . . . **140** B4
Dilston Gro, SE16 . . . . **122** A5
Dimson Cres, E3 . . . . . . **68** C1
Dingle Gdns, E14 . . . . . **97** D3
Dingley Pl, EC1 . . . . **40** B5
Dingley Rd, EC1 . . . . . . **40** A5
Dinmont St, E2 . . . . **43** E2
Dinsdale Rd, SE3 . . . . . **156** A4
Disbrowe Rd, W6 . . . . **135** E5
Discovery Business Pk, SE16
off St. James's Rd . . **121** D4
Discovery Wk, E1 . . . . . **93** E3
Disney Pl, SE1 . . . . **118** B1
Disney St, SE1 . . . . **118** B1
Diss St, E2 . . . . **42** A4
Distaff La, EC4 . . . . **90** A2
Distillery La, W6 . . . . . **134** B3
Distillery Rd, W6 . . . . . **134** B3
Distin St, SE11 . . . . . . **144** C1
Ditch All, SE10 . . . . . . **177** F4
Ditchburn St, E14 . . . . . **98** B3
Dixon Clark Ct, N1 . . . . **17** E2
Dixon Cl, E6 . . . . **76** B5
Dixon Ho, W10 . . . . **78** C1
Dixon Rd, SE14 . . . . . . **175** F3
Dixon's All, SE16 . . . . **121** E2
Dobson Cl, NW6 . . . . . . **10** C4
Doby Ct, EC4 . . . . **90** B2
Dockers Tanner Rd,
E14 . . . . **124** C4
Dockhead, SE1 . . . . . . **120** B2
Dock Hill Av, SE16 . . . **123** D1
Dockland St, E16 . . . . **104** C5
Dockley Rd, SE16 . . . . **120** C4
Dock Rd, E16 . . . . **100** B3
Dockside Rd, E16 . . . . **102** C3
Dock St, E1 . . . . **92** C2

★ Doctor Johnson's Ho,
EC4 . . . . **89** D1
Dodd Ho, SE16
off Rennie Est **149** F1
Doddington Gro, SE17 . **145** E4
Doddington Pl, SE17 . **145** E4
Dodson St, SE1 . . . . . . **117** D2
Dod St, E14 . . . . **68** B5
Doherty Rd, E13 . . . . . . **73** D1
Dolben St, SE1 . . . . **89** E5
Dolland St, SE11 . . . . **144** B3
Dolphin Cl, SE16 . . . . **122** C1
Dolphin La, E14 . . . . . . **97** E3
Dolphin Sq, SW1 . . . . **142** B3
Dolphin Twr, SE8 . . . . **152** B5
Dombey St, WC1 . . . . . . **60** A3
Domingo St, EC1 . . . . . . **62** A1
Dominion St, EC2 . . . . . **63** D3
★ Dominion Thea,
W1 . . . . **59** D5
Donaldson Rd, NW6 . . . **30** B1
Donato Dr, SE15 . . . . . **147** E5
Donegal St, N1 . . . . **38** B3
Doneraile St, SW6 . . . . **159** D5
Dongola Rd, E1 . . . . **67** E3
Donkin Ho, SE16
off Rennie Est **149** F1
Donne Pl, SW3 . . . . . . **111** F5
Donovan Ct, SW10
off Drayton Gdns . . **138** C3
Don Phelan Cl, SE5 . . **171** D3
Doon St, SE1 . . . . **88** C5
Doran Wk, E15 . . . . **26** B4
Dora St, E14 . . . . **68** A5
Doria Rd, SW6 . . . . **160** B5
Doric Way, NW1 . . . . . . **36** C4
Dorking Cl, SE8 . . . . . . **152** A4
Dorman Way, NW8 . . . . **10** C5
Dornberg Cl, SE3 . . . . **181** D1
Dornberg Rd, SE3 . . . . **181** E1
Dorncliffe Rd, SW6 . . . **159** F5
Dorney, NW3 . . . . **11** F3
Dorrington Pt, E3 . . . . . **47** E4
Dorrington St, EC1 . . . . **60** C1
Dorrit St, SE1 . . . . **118** B1
Dorset Bldgs, EC4 . . . . . **89** E1
Dorset Cl, NW1 . . . . **56** A3
Dorset Est, E2 . . . . **42** B4
Dorset Ms, SW1 . . . . . **113** E3
Dorset Pl, E15 . . . . **26** C1
Dorset Ri, EC4 . . . . **89** E1
Dorset Rd, SW8 . . . . . . **167** F1
Dorset Sq, NW1 . . . . **56** A2
Dorset St, W1 . . . . **56** B4
Dorton Cl, SE15 . . . . . **171** F2
Doughty Ms, WC1 . . . . . **60** A2
Doughty St, WC1 . . . . . . **60** A1
Douglas Path, E14 . . . . **154** C4
Douglas Rd, E16 . . . . . . **73** D4
N1 . . . . **18** A3
NW6 . . . . **8** A5
Douglas St, SW1 . . . . **142** C1
Douglas Way, SE8 . . . **176** B2

Doulton Ho, SE11
   off Lambeth Wk **116** B4
Doulton Ms, NW6 . . . . . . **9** F1
Douro Pl, W8 . . . . **109** F3
Douro St, E3 . . . . **46** C2
Douthwaite Sq, E1 . . . . **93** D4
Dove App, E6 . . . . **75** E4
Dove Ct, EC2 . . . . **90** C1
Dovehouse St, SW3 . . **139** E2
Dove Ms, SW5 . . . . **138** A1
Dovercourt Est, N1 . . . . **19** D2
Dover Flats, SE1 . . . . . . **147** F1
Dover Rd, N1 . . . . **18** C1
Dove Row, E2 . . . . **42** C1
Dover St, W1 . . . . **85** F3
Dover Yd, W1 . . . . **86** A4
Doves Yd, N1 . . . . **39** D1
Dovet Ct, SW8 . . . . . . **168** A3
Doveton St, E1 . . . . **66** A1
Dove Wk, SW1 . . . . . . **140** C2
Dowgate Hill, EC4 . . . . . **90** C2
Dowland St, W10 . . . . . **29** F4
Dowlas Est, SE5 . . . . . **171** E1
Dowlas St, SE5 . . . . . . **171** E1
Downfield Cl, W9 . . . . . **53** E2
Downham Rd, N1 . . . . . **18** C4
Downings, E6 . . . . **77** D5
Downing St, SW1 . . . . **115** E1
Down St, W1 . . . . **85** E5
Down St Ms, W1 . . . . . . **85** E5
Downtown Rd, SE16 . . **123** F1
Dowrey St, N1 . . . . **16** C5
Doyce St, SE1 . . . . **118** A1
D'Oyley St, SW1 . . . . . **112** C5
Draco St, SE17 . . . . . . **146** A4
Dragon Rd, SE15 . . . . . **147** E5
Dragoon Rd, SE8 . . . . . **152** A3
Drake Cl, SE16 . . . . . . **123** D1
Drake Ct, W12 . . . . . . **106** A2
Drake Ho, SW8
   off St. George Wf . . . **143** E3
Drakes Ctyd, NW6 . . . . . **8** B3
Drake St, WC1 . . . . **60** A4
Draper Ho, SE1 . . . . . **117** F5
Draper Pl, N1
   off Dagmar Ter **17** F5
Drappers Way, SE16 . . **121** D5
Drawdock Rd, SE10 . . . **99** D5
Draycott Av, SW3 . . . . **111** F5
Draycott Cl, SE5 . . . . . **170** C2
Draycott Ms, SW6 . . . . **160** B5
Draycott Pl, SW3 . . . . **140** A1
Draycott Ter, SW3 . . . **112** B5
Drayford Cl, W9 . . . . . . **52** B1
Drayson Ms, W8 . . . . . **109** D2
Drayton Gdns, SW10 . **138** B2
Dresden Cl, NW6 . . . . . . **9** F1
Dresden Ho, SE11
   off Lambeth Wk **116** B5
Sch Drew Prim Sch,
   E16 . . . . **103** E5
Drew Rd, E16 . . . . **103** E5
Driffield Rd, E3 . . . . . . **45** F2

Drive, The, SW6 . . . . . **159** F5
Droop St, W10 . . . . **51** E1
Drovers Pl, SE15 . . . . . **173** E1
Druid St, SE1 . . . . **119** F1
Drummond Cres, NW1 . **36** C4
Drummond Gate, SW1 . **143** D2
Drummond Rd, SE16 . **121** E3
Drummond St, NW1 . . . **58** A1
Drum St, E1 . . . . **64** B5
Drury La, WC2 . . . . **87** F1
Dryden Ct, SE11 . . . . . **145** D1
Dryden St, WC2 . . . . . . **87** F1
Dryfield Wk, SE8 . . . . . **152** C4
Drysdale Pl, N1 . . . . . . **41** F5
Drysdale St, N1 . . . . . . **41** F5
Dublin Av, E8 . . . . **21** D5
Ducal St, E2 . . . . **42** B5
Du Cane Cl, W12 . . . . . **78** A1
Duchess Ms, W1 . . . . . **57** F4
Duchess of Bedford's Wk,
   W8 . . . . **108** C2
Duchess St, W1 . . . . . . **57** F4
Duchy St, SE1 . . . . **89** D4
Duckett St, E1 . . . . **67** E3
Duck La, W1 . . . . **86** C1
Dudley Ho, W2
   off North Wf Rd **54** C4
Dudley Rd, NW6 . . . . . . **30** A2
Dudley St, W2 . . . . **54** C4
Dudmaston Ms, SW3 . **139** D2
Duffell Ho, SE11 . . . . . **144** B1
Dufferin Av, EC1 . . . . . . **62** C2
Dufferin St, EC1 . . . . . . **62** B2
Duff St, E14 . . . . **97** E1
Dufour's Pl, W1 . . . . . . **86** B1
Dugard Way, SE11 . . . **117** E5
Duke Humphrey Rd,
   SE3 . . . . **179** F3
Duke of Wellington Av,
   SE18 . . . . **133** F4
Duke of Wellington Pl,
   SW1 . . . . **113** D1
Duke of York Sq, SW3 . **140** B1
Duke of York St, SW1 . . **86** B4
Duke Shore Pl, E14 . . . **96** A3
Duke Shore Wf, E14 . . . **96** A3
Dukes La, W8 . . . . **109** D1
Duke's Ms, W1 . . . . **57** D5
Dukes Pl, EC3 . . . . **91** F1
Duke's Rd, WC1 . . . . . . **37** D5
Duke St, SW1 . . . . **86** B4
   W1 . . . . **57** D5
Duke St Hill, SE1 . . . . . **91** D4
Duke's Yd, W1 . . . . **85** D2
Dulford St, W11 . . . . . . **79** E2
Dumpton Pl, NW1 . . . . **12** C4
Dunbridge St, E2 . . . . . **65** D1
Duncannon St, WC2 . . **87** E3
Duncan Rd, E8 . . . . **21** E5
Duncan St, N1 . . . . **39** E2
Duncan Ter, N1 . . . . . . **39** E3
Dunch St, E1 . . . . **93** F1
Dundas Rd, SE15 . . . . **174** A5
Dundee Ho, W9 . . . . . . **32** A4
Dundee St, E1 . . . . **93** E5
Dundonald Cl, E6 . . . . . **75** F5
Dundonald Rd, NW10 . . **28** C1

Dunedin Ho, E16
   off Manwood St **104** B5
Dunelm St, E1 . . . . **66** C5
Dunloe St, E2 . . . . **42** A3
Dunlop Pl, SE16 . . . . . **120** B4
Dunmore Pt, E2 . . . . . . **42** A5
Dunmore Rd, NW6 . . . . **29** E1
Dunmow Wk, N1 . . . . . **18** A5
Dunnage Cres, SE16 . . **123** F5
Dunnock Rd, E6 . . . . . . **75** F5
Dunns Pas, WC1 . . . . . **59** F5
Dunraven St, W1 . . . . . **84** B2
Dunsany Rd, W14 . . . . **106** C4
Dunstable Ms, W1 . . . . **57** D3
Dunstan Ho, E1
   off Stepney Grn **66** B3
Dunster Ct, EC3 . . . . . . **91** E2
Dunster Gdns, NW6 . . . . **8** B3
Dunsterville Way, SE1 . **119** D2
Dunston Rd, E8 . . . . . . **42** A1
Dunston St, E8 . . . . . . **20** A5
Dunton Rd, SE1 . . . . . **148** A2
Dunworth Ms, W11 . . . **52** A5
Duplex Ride, SW1 . . . . **112** B2
Dupree Rd, SE7 . . . . . **157** E2
Durand Gdns, SW9 . . . **168** B3
Sch Durand Prim Sch,
   SW9 . . . . **168** B3
   Cowley Rd Annexe,
   SW9 . . . . **169** D4
Durands Wk, SE16 . . . **123** F1
Durant St, E2 . . . . **42** C4
Durban Rd, E15 . . . . . . **49** E4
Durfey Pl, SE5 . . . . . . **171** D1
Durham Ho St, WC2 . . . **87** F3
Durham Pl, SW3 . . . . . **140** A3
Durham Rd, E16 . . . . . . **71** F2
Durham Row, E1 . . . . . . **67** D4
Durham St, SE11 . . . . **144** A3
Durham Ter, W2 . . . . . . **53** E5
Durham Yd, E2 . . . . **43** E4
Durnford St, SE10 . . . . **154** B5
Durrell Rd, SW6 . . . . . **160** A4
Durrington Twr, SW8 . **166** B5
Durward St, E1 . . . . **65** E3
Durweston Ms, W1 . . . . **56** B3
Durweston St, W1 . . . . **56** B3
Dutton St, SE10 . . . . . **178** A3
Dwight Ct, SW6 . . . . . **159** F5
Dye Ho La, E3 . . . . **47** D1
Dyer's Bldgs, EC1 . . . . **60** C4
Dyne Rd, NW6 . . . . **7** F1
Dynham Rd, NW6 . . . . . **8** C3
Dyott St, WC1 . . . . **59** E5
Dysart St, EC2 . . . . **63** D2

E

Eagle Cl, SE16 . . . . . . **150** A3
Eagle Ct, EC1 . . . . **61** E3
Eagle Ms, N1 . . . . **19** E2
Eagle Pl, SW1 . . . . **86** B3
   SW7 . . . . **138** B2
Eagle St, WC1 . . . . **60** A4
Eagle Wf Rd, N1 . . . . . . **40** B2

Eagling Cl, E3 .... 47 D5
Eamont St, NW8 ...... 33 E2
Eardley Cres, SW5 .. 137 D3
Earlham St, WC2 ..... 87 D1
EARLS COURT, SW5 .. 136 B2
⊖ Earls Court 137 D1
★ Earls Court Exhib Cen, SW5 ... 136 C2
Earls Ct Gdns, SW5 .. 137 E1
Earls Ct Rd, SW5 .... 109 D5
  W8 .... 109 D5
Earls Ct Sq, SW5 .... 137 E2
Earlsferry Way, N1 ... 15 F4
Earlsmead Rd, NW10 .. 28 A4
Earls Ter, W8 .... 108 B4
Earlstoke St, EC1 .... 39 E4
Earlston Gro, E9 ..... 43 F1
Earl St, EC2 .... 63 E3
Earls Wk, W8 .... 108 C4
Earlswood St, SE10 .. 155 F3
Early Ms, NW1 .... 13 F5
Earnshaw St, WC2 .... 59 D5
Earsby St, W14 ...... 107 F5
Easley's Ms, W1 ..... 57 D5
East Arbour St, E1 ... 66 C5
Eastbourne Ms, W2 ... 54 B5
Eastbourne Rd, E15 .. 49 F1
Eastbourne Ter, W2 .. 54 B5
Eastbrook Rd, SE3 ... 181 F2
Eastbury Rd, E6 ...... 76 C2
Eastbury Ter, E1 ..... 66 C2
Eastcastle St, W1 .... 58 A5
Eastcheap, EC3 ...... 91 D2
Eastcombe Av, SE7 .. 157 E4
East Cross Cen, E15 .. 25 D2
East Cross Route, E3 . 24 B3
  E9 .... 23 F2
Eastern Gateway, E16. 102 B3
Eastern Quay Apts, E16
  off Rayleigh Rd 101 F4
East Ferry Rd, E14 .. 125 F5
Eastfield St, E14 ..... 67 F4
East Ham Ind Est, E6 .. 75 E2
East Ham Manor Way, E6 ... 76 C5
★ East Ham Nature Reserve & Visitor Cen, E6 ... 76 B1
East Harding St, EC4 .. 61 D5
🚉 East India 99 D2
East India Dock Rd, E14 ... 96 B1
Eastlake Ho, NW8
  off Frampton St 55 D2
East La, SE16 .... 120 C2
🏫 Eastlea Comm Sch, E16 ... 71 F1
Eastlea Ms, E16 ..... 71 F2
🏥 Eastman Dental Hosp, WC1 ... 38 A5
Eastmoor Pl, SE7 .... 130 C4
Eastmoor St, SE7 .... 130 C4
East Mt St, E1 .... 65 F4
Eastney St, SE10 .... 154 C3
Easton St, WC1 ...... 38 C4
East Parkside, SE10 .. 128 A2
East Pas, EC1 .... 61 F3
East Pier, E1 .... 93 E5

East Pt, SE1 .... 148 C2
East Poultry Av, EC1 .. 61 E4
East Rd, N1 .... 40 C5
  SW3 .... 140 C3
East Row, W10 .... 51 E2
East Smithfield, E1... 92 B3
East St, SE17 .... 146 B2
East Surrey Gro, SE15. 172 A2
East Tenter St, E1.... 92 B1
Eastway, E9 .... 24 A1
Eaton Cl, SW1 .... 140 C1
Eaton Gate, SW1..... 112 C5
Eaton Ho, E14
  off Westferry Circ ... 96 B3
Eaton La, SW1 .... 113 F4
Eaton Ms N, SW1 .... 112 C5
Eaton Ms S, SW1 .... 113 D5
Eaton Ms W, SW1 ... 113 D5
Eaton Pl, SW1 .... 112 C4
Eaton Row, SW1 ..... 113 E3
Eaton Sq, SW1 ...... 113 E3
Eaton Ter, SW1 ...... 112 C5
Eaton Ter Ms, SW1 .. 112 C5
Ebbisham Dr, SW8 .. 144 A4
Ebenezer Ho, SE11 ... 145 D1
Ebenezer St, N1 ...... 40 C4
Ebley Cl, SE15 ...... 148 A5
Ebor St, E1 .... 64 A1
Ebury Br, SW1 .... 141 E2
Ebury Br Est, SW1 ... 141 E2
Ebury Br Rd, SW1 ... 141 D3
Ebury Ms, SW1 ...... 113 D5
Ebury Ms E, SW1 .... 113 E5
Ebury Sq, SW1 ...... 141 D1
Ebury St, SW1 .... 113 E5
Ecclesbourne Rd, N1 . 18 B4
Eccleston Br, SW1 ... 113 F5
Eccleston Ms, SW1 .. 113 D4
Eccleston Pl, SW1 .... 113 E5
Eccleston Sq, SW1 .. 141 F1
Eccleston Sq Ms, SW1. 142 A1
Eccleston St, SW1 ... 113 E4
Eckford St, N1 .... 38 C2
Eclipse Rd, E13 ...... 73 E3
🏫 Ecole Française de Londres, W6 ... 107 D5
Edbrooke Rd, W9 ..... 52 C1
Eddiscombe Rd, SW6 . 160 B5
Eddystone Twr, SE8 .. 151 F1
Edenbridge Cl, SE16.. 149 F3
Edenbridge Rd, E9 ... 23 D4
Eden Cl, W8 .... 109 D3
Edenham Way, W10.. 52 A3
Eden Way, E3
  off Old Ford Rd 46 B1
Edgarley Ter, SW6 ... 159 E4
Edgar Rd, E3 .... 47 F4
Edgar Wallace Cl, SE15 ... 171 F1
Edge St, W8 .... 81 D4
Edgson Ho, SW1
  off Ebury Br Rd 141 E2
⊖ Edgware Road 55 E4
Edgware Rd, W2 ..... 55 F5
Edgware Rd Sub, W2
  off Edgware Rd 55 E4
Edinburgh Cl, E2 ..... 44 A3

Edinburgh Gate, SW1. 112 A1
Edinburgh Ho, W9 .... 31 F4
Edison Ct, SE10 ..... 128 B5
Edis St, NW1 .... 12 C5
Edith Gro, SW10 ..... 138 A5
🏫 Edith Neville Prim Sch, NW1 ... 36 C3
Edith Rd, W14 .... 135 E1
Edith Row, SW6 ..... 161 F3
Edith St, E2 .... 42 C2
Edith Summerskill Ho, SW6 ... 136 B5
Edith Ter, SW10 ..... 162 A1
Edith Vil, W14 .... 136 A1
Edith Yd, SW10 ..... 162 B1
Edmeston Cl, E9 ..... 23 F1
Edmund Halley Way, SE10 ... 127 E2
Edmund Hurst Dr, E6.. 77 E4
Edmund St, SE5 ..... 170 C1
🏫 Edmund Waller Prim Sch, SE14 ... 174 C5
Edna St, SW11 ...... 163 E4
Edrich Ho, SW4 ..... 167 E4
Edric Ho, SW1
  off Page St 115 D5
Edric Rd, SE14 ...... 174 C1
Edward Ct, E16 ...... 72 C3
Edwardes St, W8..... 108 B4
Edwardes Sq, W8 ... 108 B4
Edward Ms, NW1 .... 35 F3
Edward Pl, SE8 ...... 152 B5
Edwards Cotts, N1 ... 17 E2
Edwards Ms, N1 ..... 17 D3
  W1 .... 84 C1
Edward Sq, N1 ...... 38 A1
  SE16 .... 95 F1
Edward St, E16 ...... 72 C2
  SE8 .... 176 A1
  SE14 .... 175 F1
🏫 Edward Wilson Prim Sch, W2 ... 53 E3
Edwin St, E1 .... 66 B1
  E16 .... 72 C4
Eel Brook Cl, SW6 ... 161 E3
Eel Brook Studios, SW6 ... 161 D2
Effie Pl, SW6 .... 161 D2
Effie Rd, SW6 .... 161 D2
Egbert St, NW1 ...... 12 C5
Egeremont Rd, SE13 . 177 F5
Egerton Cres, SW3 .. 111 F5
Egerton Dr, SE10 .... 177 E3
Egerton Gdns, NW10 . 28 A1
  SW3 .... 111 E4
Egerton Gdns Ms, SW3. 111 F4
Egerton Pl, SW3 ..... 111 F4
Egerton Ter, SW3 .... 111 F4
Egham Rd, E13 ...... 73 F3
Eglington Ct, SE17 .. 146 A4
Eglon Ms, NW1 ...... 12 B4
Egmont St, SE14 .... 175 D2
Egremont Ho, SE13 .. 177 F5

Eisenhower Dr, E6 . . . . **75** F4
Elam St, SE5 . . . . **169** F5
Elba Pl, SE17. . . . . **118** B5
Elbe St, SW6 . . . . **162** A5
Elbury Dr, E16. . . . . . . **101** D1
Elcho St, SW11 . . . . . . **163** E5
Elcot Av, SE15. . . . . . . **173** E1
Elderflower Way,
  E15 . . . . **27** E3
Elder St, E1 . . . . **64** A3
Elder Wk, N1 . . . . **17** F5
Eldon Rd, W8 . . . . **109** F4
Eldon St, EC2. . . . . **63** D4
Eleanor Cl, SE16 . . . . . **122** C1
Eleanor Rd, E8 . . . . **21** E2
Eleanor St, E3 . . . . **46** C5
Electra Business Pk,
  E16 . . . . **71** D3
Elektron Ho, E14. . . . . . **99** D2
⚞Elephant & Castle . . **118** A5
⊖Elephant & Castle . . **118** A5
Elephant & Castle,
  SE1 . . . . **117** F4
Elephant & Castle
  Shop Cen, SE1
  off Elephant & Castle. **118** A5
Elephant La, SE16. . . . **122** A1
Elephant Rd, SE17 . . . **118** A5
Elf Row, E1 . . . . **94** B2
Elgar Cl, SE8 . . . . **176** C2
Elgar St, SE16 . . . . **123** F3
Elgin Av, W9 . . . . **31** E5
Elgin Cres, W11. . . . . . . **80** A1
Elgin Ms, W11 . . . . **79** F1
Elgin Ms N, W9 . . . . **31** F4
Elgin Ms S, W9 . . . . **31** F4
Elgood Cl, W11 . . . . **79** E3
Elia Ms, N1 . . . . **39** E3
Elias Pl, SW8 . . . . **144** C5
Elia St, N1 . . . . **39** E3
Elim Est, SE1. . . . . **119** E3
Elim St, SE1. . . . . **119** D3
Eliot Ms, NW8 . . . . **32** B3
Elizabeth Av, N1. . . . . . . **18** B5
Elizabeth Br, SW1 . . . . **141** E1
Elizabeth Cl, E14. . . . . . **97** E1
  W9. . . . . **54** B1
Elizabeth Ct, SW1 . . . . **115** D4
Elizabeth Est, SE17. . . **146** C4
Elizabeth Fry Rd, E8. . . **21** F4
SchElizabeth Garrett
  Anderson Language
  Coll, N1 . . . . **38** B2
Elizabeth Ms, NW3 . . . . **11** F2
SchElizabeth Selby Inf Sch,
  E2 . . . . **43** D4
Elizabeth Sq, SE16 . . . . **95** E3
Elizabeth St, SW1 . . . . **113** D5
Elkington Pt, SE11 . . . **144** C1
Elkington Rd, E13. . . . . **73** E2
Elkstone Rd, W10. . . . . . **52** A3
Ellaline Rd, W6 . . . . . . **134** C5
Ellen St, E1 . . . . **93** D1

Ellen Wilkinson Ho, E2
  off Usk St. **44** C4
SchEllen Wilkinson Prim Sch,
  E6 . . . . **75** E4
Ellerby St, SW6 . . . . . . **159** D4
Ellesmere Rd, E3. . . . . . **45** C2
Ellesmere St, E14. . . . . . **69** E5
Ellingfort Rd, E8 . . . . . . **21** F3
Ellington Ho, SE1 . . . . . **118** B3
Ellington St, N7 . . . . **16** C2
Elliot Cl, E15 . . . . **27** E4
Elliott Rd, SW9 . . . . . . **169** E2
Elliott's Pl, N1. . . . . **39** F1
Elliott Sq, NW3 . . . . **11** F3
Elliotts Row, SE11 . . . **117** E5
Ellison Ho, SE13 . . . . . **178** A5
Ellis St, SW1 . . . . **112** B5
Ellsworth St, E2 . . . . **43** E4
Ellwood Ct, W9 . . . . **53** E2
Elmbridge Wk, E8. . . . . . **21** D3
Elm Ct, EC4 . . . . **88** C2
Elmfield Way, W9. . . . . . **52** C3
Elm Friars Wk, NW1 . . . **15** D4
Elmgreen Cl, E15. . . . . . **27** F5
Elm Gro, SE15 . . . . **172** B5
Elmington Est, SE5. . . **171** D1
Elmington Rd, SE5 . . . **170** C3
Elmley Cl, E6. . . . . **75** F4
Elmore St, N1 . . . . **18** B3
Elm Pk Gdns, SW10 . . **138** C3
Elm Pk La, SW3. . . . . . **138** C3
Elm Pk Mans, SW10 . . **138** B4
Elm Pk Rd, SW3. . . . . . **138** C4
Elm Pl, SW7. . . . . **138** C2
Elm Quay Ct, SW8. . . . **142** C4
Elmslie Pt, E3 . . . . **68** B4
Elms Ms, W2 . . . . **82** C2
Elmstone Rd, SW6 . . . **160** C3
Elm St, WC1. . . . . **60** B2
Elm Tree Cl, NW8 . . . . . **32** C4
Elm Tree Rd, NW8. . . . . **32** C4
Elmwood Ct, SW11. . . **165** E3
Elnathan Ms, W9 . . . . . **53** F2
Elrington Rd, E8 . . . . . . **20** C2
Elsa St, E1 . . . . **67** E4
Elsdale St, E9 . . . . **22** B2
Elsden Ms, E2 . . . . **44** B3
Elsham Rd, W14. . . . . . **107** E2
Elsham Ter, W14. . . . . . **107** E2
Elsted St, SE17 . . . . . . **147** D1
Elswick St, SW6. . . . . . **162** A5
Elsworthy Ri, NW3 . . . . **11** F3
Elsworthy Rd, NW3 . . . **11** F4
Elsworthy Ter, NW3 . . . **11** F4
Elthiron Rd, SW6. . . . . **161** D4
Elton Ho, E3 . . . . **24** B5
Elvaston Ms, SW7. . . . **110** B3
Elvaston Pl, SW7. . . . . **110** A4
Elver Gdns, E2. . . . . **43** D4
Elverson Rd, SE8. . . . . **177** F5
Elverton St, SW1 . . . . **114** C5
Elvis Rd, NW2 . . . . **6** A1
Elwin St, E2 . . . . **42** C4
Ely Ct, EC1 . . . . **61** D4
Ely Pl, EC1 . . . . **61** D4
Elysium Bldg, The,
  SE8 . . . . **151** D2

Elystan Pl, SW3. . . . . . **139** F2
Elystan St, SW3 . . . . . . **139** E1
Elystan Wk, N1. . . . . **38** C1
⊖Embankment **87** F4
Embankment Gdns,
  SW3. . . . . **140** B4
RivEmbankment Pier . . **88** A4
Embankment Pl, WC2 . **87** F4
Emba St, SE16. . . . . . . **121** D2
Emberton, SE5 . . . . . . **147** E4
Emberton Ct, EC1
  off Tompion St. **39** E5
Emden St, SW6. . . . . . **161** F3
Emerald Cl, E16 . . . . . . **103** E1
Emerald St, WC1. . . . . . **60** A3
Emerson St, SE1 . . . . . . **90** A4
Emery Hill St, SW1 . . . **114** B4
Emery St, SE1 . . . . **117** D3
Emma St, E2 . . . . **43** E2
Emmott Cl, E1. . . . . **67** F2
Emperor's Gate, SW7. **109** F4
Empire Sq, SE1 . . . . . . **118** C2
Empire Sq E, SE1
  off Empire Sq. **118** C2
Empire Sq S, SE1
  off Empire Sq. **118** C2
Empire Sq W, SE1
  off Empire Sq. **118** C2
Empire Wf Rd, E14 . . . **154** C1
Empress App, SW6 . . . **136** C3
Empress Ms, SE5 . . . . **170** A5
Empress Pl, SW6. . . . . **136** C3
Empress St, SE17 . . . . **146** B4
Empson St, E3. . . . . **69** F1
Enbrook St, W10. . . . . . **29** F5
Endell St, WC2. . . . . **59** E5
Enderby St, SE10 . . . . **155** D3
Endsleigh Gdns, WC1. . **58** C1
Endsleigh Pl, WC1. . . . . **59** D1
Endsleigh St, WC1 . . . . **58** C1
Enfield Rd, N1. . . . . **19** D3
Enford St, W1 . . . . **56** A3
Englands La, NW3 . . . . **12** A2
Englefield Rd, N1 . . . . . **18** C2
English Grds, SE1 . . . . . **91** E5
SchEnglish Martyrs' Cath
  Prim Sch, SE17 . . . . **147** D1
SchEnglish Martyrs RC
  Prim Sch, E1. . . . . . . **92** B1
English St, E3 . . . . **68** A1
Enid St, SE16. . . . . **120** B3
Ennerdale Ho, E3. . . . . . **68** A1
Ennismore Gdns, SW7. **111** E2
Ennismore Gdns Ms,
  SW7. . . . . **111** E3
Ennismore Ms, SW7 . . **111** E3
Ennismore St, SW7. . . **111** E3
Ensign Ho, SW8
  off St. George Wf . . . **143** E4
Ensign St, E1. . . . . **92** C2
Ensor Ms, SW7 . . . . . . **138** C2
Enterprise Ind Est,
  SE16 . . . . **150** A2
Enterprize Way, SE8. . **124** A5
Epirus Ms, SW6 . . . . . . **160** C1
Epirus Rd, SW6 . . . . . . **160** B1
Epping Cl, E14 . . . . . . **125** D5

Epping Pl, N1 .... 17 D2
Epple Rd, SW6....... 160 B3
Epworth St, EC2 ..... 63 D2
Equana Apts, SE8.... 151 E2
Equity Sq, E2......... 42 B5
Erasmus St, SW1.... 143 D1
Eresby Pl, NW6....... 8 C4
Eric Clarke La, Bark.
  IG11............. 77 F1
Eric Fletches Ct, N1
  off Essex Rd 18 B3
Eric St, E3 .... 68 A1
Erin Ct, NW2........ 6 B1
Erlanger Rd, SE14.... 175 D5
Ermine Ms, E2....... 42 A1
Ernest St, E1 .... 67 D2
★ Eros, W1......... 86 C3
Errington Rd, W9.... 52 B1
Errol St, EC1 .... 62 B2
Erskine Ms, NW3.... 12 B4
Erskine Rd, NW3..... 12 B4
Escreet Gro, SE18.... 132 C5
Eskdale, NW1 .... 36 A3
Esk Rd, E13 .... 73 D1
Esmeralda Rd, SE1.. 149 D1
Esmond Rd, NW6.... 30 B1
Sch Essendine Prim Sch,
  W9.............. 31 D5
Essendine Rd, W9.... 53 D1
Essex Ct, EC4........ 88 C1
Essex Ho, E14....... 69 E5
⇌ Essex Road....... 18 A4
Essex Rd, N1....... 18 A4
Essex St, WC2 ..... 88 C2
Essex Vil, W8 ...... 108 C2
Essian St, E1 ...... 67 E4
Estcourt Rd, SW6 ... 160 A1
Esterbrooke St, SW1.. 142 C1
★ Estorick Collection of
  Modern Italian Art,
  N1............. 17 F2
Eternit Wk, SW6 .... 158 B3
Ethelburga St, SW11. 163 F3
Ethelburga Twr, SW11.163 F3
Ethel Rd, E16...... 101 E1
Ethel St, SE17 ..... 146 A1
Ethnard Rd, SE15.... 149 E5
Eton Av, NW3 ..... 11 E3
Eton Coll Rd, NW3 ... 12 B2
Eton Ct, NW3....... 11 D3
Eton Garages, NW3... 11 F2
Eton Hall, NW3...... 12 B2
Eton Pl, NW3........ 12 C3
Eton Ri, NW3........ 12 B2
Eton Rd, NW3....... 12 A3
Eton Vil, NW3 ...... 12 B2
Etta St, SE8 .... 151 F4
Ettrick St, E14...... 70 B5
Eugenia Rd, SE16.... 150 B1
Coll Eurocentres,
  London Cen, SW1 .. 141 F1
Europa Pl, EC1 ..... 40 A5
Europe Rd, SE18..... 132 B4
Eustace Bldg, SW8... 141 E5
Eustace Pl, SE18..... 132 A5
Eustace Rd, SW6..... 160 C1
⇌ Euston 36 B4

↻ Euston 36 B4
⊖ Euston 36 B4
Euston Cen, NW1
  off Triton Sq....... 58 A1
Euston Gro, NW1 ... 36 C5
Euston Rd, N1...... 37 E4
  NW1 .... 57 F2
⊖ Euston Square 58 B1
Euston Sq, NW1 .... 36 C5
Euston Sta Colonnade,
  NW1 .... 36 C5
Euston St, NW1..... 58 B1
Euston Twr, NW1.... 58 A1
Evan Cook Cl, SE15.. 174 A4
Evandale Rd, SW9 ... 169 D5
Evans Cl, E8........ 20 B2
H Evelina Children's Hosp,
  SE1 .... 116 A3
Eveline Lowe Est,
  SE16 .... 120 C4
Sch Eveline Lowe Prim Sch,
  SE1........... 149 D3
Evelyn Ct, N1....... 40 C3
Evelyn Denington Rd,
  E6 .... 75 F2
Evelyn Fox Ct, W10 .. 50 B4
Evelyn Gdns, SW7 ... 138 C3
Evelyn Rd, E16..... 101 E4
Evelyn St, SE8...... 151 E1
Evelyn Wk, N1...... 40 C3
Evelyn Yd, W1...... 58 C5
Everest Pl, E14...... 70 A3
Evergreen Sq, E8 .... 20 A3
Everilda St, N1...... 38 B1
Everington St, W6 ... 135 D4
Eve Rd, E15........ 49 F3
Eversholt St, NW1... 36 B2
Eversley Rd, SE7..... 157 E4
Everton Bldgs, NW1.. 36 A5
Evesham St, W11.... 78 C3
Evesham Wk, SE5.... 170 C5
  SW9........... 168 C4
Ewart Pl, E3......... 46 A2
Ewe Cl, N7......... 15 F1
Ewer St, SE1 .... 90 A5
Ewhurst Cl, E1...... 66 B4
Excel Ct, WC2 ...... 87 D3
★ ExCeL London, E16. 101 F3
ExCeL Marina, E16 ... 101 E3
ExCeL Waterfront,
  E16........... 101 F3
Exchange, The, E1
  off Commercial St ... 64 A2
Exchange Arc, EC2 ... 63 E3
Exchange Ct, WC2.... 87 F3
Exchange Pl, EC2 .... 63 E3
Exchange Sq, EC2.... 63 E3
Exeter Cl, E6........ 76 A5
Exeter Ms, NW6....... 9 E2
  SW6........... 160 C1
Exeter Rd, E16 ...... 73 D4
  NW2 .... 7 F2
Exeter St, WC2 ..... 87 F2
Exeter Way, SE14.... 176 A2
Exhibition Cl, W12... 78 A3
Exhibition Rd, SW7... 111 D2
Exmoor St, W10 ..... 51 D2

Exmouth Mkt, EC1 ... 60 C1
Exmouth Ms, NW1 ... 36 B5
Exmouth Pl, E8...... 21 E4
Exmouth St, E1...... 66 B5
Exning Rd, E16..... 72 A2
Exon St, SE17 ...... 147 E1
Exton St, SE1........ 88 C5
Eynham Rd, W12.... 50 A4
Eyre Ct, NW8....... 32 C2
Eyre St Hill, EC1 ..... 60 C2
Eythorne Rd, SW9.... 169 D3
Ezra St, E2.......... 42 B4

F

Fabian Rd, SW6 .... 160 B1
Fabian St, E6........ 75 F2
Factory Rd, E16 ... 103 E5
Fairbairn Grn, SW9.. 169 D3
Fairbank Est, N1..... 41 D3
Fairburn Ho, W14
  off Ivatt Pl 136 B3
Fairby Ho, SE1 ..... 120 B5
Faircharm Trd Est,
  SE8........... 177 E1
Fairchild Pl, EC2 ..... 63 F2
Fairchild St, EC2 .... 63 F2
Fairclough St, E1 .... 93 D1
Fairfax Ms, E16..... 101 E4
Fairfax Pl, NW6...... 10 B4
  W14.......... 107 F3
Fairfax Rd, NW6 ..... 10 B4
Fairfield Rd, E3...... 46 C2
Fairfoot Rd, E3...... 68 C2
Fairford Ho, SE11 ... 145 D1
Fairhazel Gdns, NW6 ... 9 F2
Fairholme Rd, W14... 135 F3
Fairholt St, SW7 .... 111 F3
Fairlead Ho, E14
  off Cassilis Rd 125 D3
Fairlie Ct, E3
  off Stroudley Wk 47 E4
Fairmont Av, E14 .... 98 C4
Fairstead Wk, N1 .... 18 A5
Fair St, SE1 .... 119 F1
Fairthorn Rd, SE7 ... 157 D2
Fakruddin St, E1..... 65 D2
Falconberg Ct, W1 ... 59 D5
Falconberg Ms, W1.. 58 C5
Falcon Ct, EC4....... 88 C1
Falcon St, E13...... 72 C1
Falcon Way, E14.... 125 F5
Falkirk Ho, W9...... 31 F4
Falkirk St, N1 ...... 41 F3
Sch Falkner Ho Sch,
  SW7........... 138 B1
Fallow Ct, SE16..... 149 D3
Falmouth Rd, SE1.... 118 B3
Fane St, W14....... 136 D1
★ Fan Mus, SE10 .... 178 B1
Fann St, EC1 .... 62 A2

Fann St, EC2 . . . . **62** A2
Fanshaw St, N1 . . . . . . **41** E4
Faraday Cl, N7 . . . . **16** B2
Faraday Lo, SE10
   off Renaissance Wk . **128** B3
★ **Faraday Mus**, W1 . . . **86** A3
Faraday Rd, W10 . . . . . **51** E3
Faraday Way, SE18 . . **130** C4
Fareham St, W1 . . . . . . **58** C5
Faringford Rd, E15 . . . . **27** E4
Farm Cl, SW6 . . . . **161** D1
Farmdale Rd, SE10 . . **155** D2
Farmers Rd, SE5 . . . . . **169** F1
Farmer St, W8 . . . . **80** C4
Farm La, SW6 . . . . **137** D5
Farm La Trd Cen, SW6 . **136** C5
Farm Pl, W8 . . . . **80** C4
Farm St, W1 . . . . **85** E3
Farncombe St, SE16 . . **121** D2
Farnell Ms, SW5 . . . . . **137** E2
Farnham Pl, SE1 . . . . . . **89** F5
Farnham Royal, SE11 . **144** B3
Farnsworth Ct, SE10
   off West Parkside . . . **128** B4
Faroe Rd, W14 . . . . **107** D4
Farrance St, E14 . . . . . . **96** B1
Farrell Ho, E1 . . . . **94** B1
Farrier St, NW1 . . . . **13** F3
Farrier Wk, SW10 . . . . **138** A4
⇌Farringdon **61** D3
⊖Farringdon **61** D3
Farringdon La, EC1 . . . **61** D2
Farringdon Rd, EC1 . . **60** C1
Farringdon St, EC4 . . . **61** E5
Farrins Rents, SE16 . . . **95** E5
Farrow La, SE14 . . . . . **174** B1
Farrow Pl, SE16 . . . . . **123** E2
Farthingale Wk, E15 . . **26** C4
Farthing All, SE1 . . . . . **120** C2
Farthing Flds, E1 . . . . . **93** F2
Fashion St, E1 . . . . **64** A4
Fassett Rd, E8 . . . . **21** D1
Fassett Sq, E8 . . . . **20** C1
Faulkner's All, EC1 . . . . **61** E3
Faulkner St, SE14 . . . . **174** B3
Faunce St, SE17 . . . . . **145** E4
Favart Rd, SW6 . . . . . . **161** D3
Fawcett St, SW10 . . . . **138** A4
Fawe St, E14 . . . . **69** F4
Fawkham Ho, SE1
   off Longfield Est . . . **148** B1
Fearon St, SE10 . . . . . **156** C2
Feathers Pl, SE10 . . . . **155** D4
Featherstone St, EC1 . . **62** C1
Felden St, SW6 . . . . . . **160** A3
Felixstowe Ct, E16 . . . **105** F5
Fellbrigg St, E1 . . . . **65** F2
Fellmongers Path,
   SE1 . . . . **119** F2
Fellows Ct, E2 . . . . **42** A3
Fellows Rd, NW3 . . . . . **11** D3
Felltram Ms, SE7 . . . . . **157** D2
Felltram Way, SE7 . . . **157** D2

Felstead Gdns, E14 . . **154** A3
Felstead St, E9 . . . . **24** B2
Felsted Rd, E16 . . . . . . **102** C1
Felton St, N1 . . . . **41** D1
Fenchurch Av, EC3 . . . **91** E1
Fenchurch Bldgs, EC3 . **91** F1
⇌Fenchurch Street . . . **91** F2
Fenchurch Pl, EC3 . . . . . **91** F2
Fenchurch St, EC3 . . . . **91** E2
Fen Ct, EC3 . . . . **91** E1
Fendall St, SE1 . . . . . . **119** F4
Fendt Cl, E16 . . . . **100** B1
Fenelon Pl, W14 . . . . . **136** B1
Fenham Rd, SE15 . . . . **173** D2
Fennel Cl, E16 . . . . **71** F1
Fenner Cl, SE16 . . . . . . **121** F5
Fenning St, SE1 . . . . . . **119** E1
Fen St, E16 . . . . **100** B2
Fentiman Rd, SW8 . . . **143** F5
Fenton Cl, E8 . . . . **20** B1
   SW9 . . . . **168** A5
Ferdinand Pl, NW1 . . . **13** D3
Ferdinand St, NW1 . . . **13** D2
Ferguson Cl, E14 . . . . . **152** C1
Fermoy Rd, W9 . . . . **52** A2
Fern Cl, N1 . . . . **41** E2
Ferndale Ct, SE3 . . . . . **180** A1
Ferndale St, E6 . . . . . . **105** E2
Fernhead Rd, W9 . . . . . **30** B4
Fernhill St, E16 . . . . . . **104** B5
Fernhurst Rd, SW6 . . . **159** F3
Fernleigh Cl, W9 . . . . . . **30** B4
Fernsbury St, WC1 . . . . **38** C5
Fernshaw Rd, SW10 . . **138** A5
Fern St, E3 . . . . **69** D2
Fern Wk, SE16 . . . . **149** D3
Ferranti Cl, SE18 . . . . . **131** D4
Ferriby Cl, N1 . . . . **16** C3
Ferrier Pt, E16 . . . . **72** C4
Ferrybridge Ho, SE11 . **116** B4
Ferry Pl, SE18 . . . . **133** D4
Ferry St, E14 . . . . **154** A2
🎬Festival Pier **88** A4
Festoon Way, E16 . . . . **102** C2
Fetter La, EC4 . . . . **89** D1
Ffinch St, SE8 . . . . **176** C1
Field Ct, WC1 . . . . **60** B4
Fieldgate St, E1 . . . . **65** F2
Fielding Ho, NW6 . . . . . **31** D4
Fielding Rd, W14 . . . . . **107** D3
Fielding St, SE17 . . . . . **146** A4
Field Rd, W6 . . . . **135** E3
Fields Est, E8 . . . . **21** D4
Field St, WC1 . . . . **38** A4
Fife Rd, E16 . . . . **72** C4
Fife Ter, N1 . . . . **38** B2
Fifth Av, W10 . . . . **29** E5
Filigree Ct, SE16 . . . . . . **95** F5
Filmer Rd, SW6 . . . . . . **160** A3
Finborough Rd, SW10 . **137** E4
Finch La, EC3 . . . . **91** D1
Finchley Pl, NW8 . . . . . **32** C2
⊖Finchley Road **10** A1
Finchley Rd, NW3 . . . . . **10** A1
   NW8 . . . . **32** C1
Finch Ms, SE15 . . . . . . **172** A3
Findhorn St, E14 . . . . . . **70** B5

Fingal St, SE10 . . . . . . **156** B2
Finland Quay, SE16 . . **123** F4
Finland St, SE16 . . . . . **123** F3
Finlay St, SW6 . . . . **158** C4
Finnis St, E2 . . . . **43** F5
FINSBURY, EC1 . . . . . . **39** D4
Finsbury Av, EC2 . . . . . **63** D4
Finsbury Av Sq, EC2 . . **63** D4
Finsbury Circ, EC2 . . . . **63** D4
Finsbury Est, EC1 . . . . . **39** D5
Finsbury Mkt, EC2 . . . . **63** E2
Finsbury Pavement,
   EC2 . . . . **63** D3
Finsbury Sq, EC2 . . . . . **63** D3
Finsbury St, EC2 . . . . . **62** C3
Finsbury Twr, EC1 . . . . **62** C2
Finstock Rd, W10 . . . . . **50** C5
Firbank Cl, E16 . . . . **74** C3
Firbank Rd, SE15 . . . . . **173** F5
Firefly Gdns, E6 . . . . . . **75** D2
★ **Firepower**, SE18 . . . **133** F3
Fir Gro Rd, SW9 . . . . . . **169** D5
First Av, W10 . . . . **52** A1
First St, SW3 . . . . **111** F5
Firth Gdns, SW6 . . . . . **159** E4
Fir Trees Cl, SE16 . . . . . **95** F5
Fishermans Dr, SE16 . **123** D1
Fisherman's Wk, E14 . . **96** C4
Fishers Ct, SE14 . . . . . **174** C3
Fisher St, E16 . . . . **72** C3
   WC1 . . . . **59** F4
Fisherton St, NW8 . . . . **54** C2
Fishguard Way, E16 . . **133** F1
Fish St Hill, EC3 . . . . **91** D2
Fitzalan St, SE11 . . . . . **116** C5
Fitzgeorge Av, W14 . . **135** E1
Fitzgerald Ho, E14 . . . . **97** F1
Fitzhardinge St, W1 . . . **56** C5
Fitzjames Av, W14 . . . **135** F1
Fitzmaurice Ho, SE16
   off Rennie Est **149** F1
Fitzmaurice Pl, W1 . . . . **85** F4
Fitzroy Ct, W1 . . . . **58** B2
Fitzroy Ms, W1 . . . . **58** A2
Fitzroy Rd, NW1 . . . . . . **12** B5
Fitzroy Sq, W1 . . . . **58** A2
Fitzroy St, W1 . . . . **58** A2
Fitzroy Yd, NW1 . . . . . . **12** C5
Fitzwilliam Ms, E16 . . **100** C4
Five Bell All, E14 . . . . . . **96** B1
Fives Ct, SE11 . . . . **117** E5
Fiveways Rd, SW9 . . . **169** D5
Flagstaff Ho, SW8
   off St. George Wf . . . **143** E4
Flamborough St, E14 . . **67** E5
Flamborough Wk, E14 . **95** E1
Flanders Way, E9 . . . . . **22** C1
Flank St, E1 . . . . **92** C2
Flat Iron Sq, SE1
   off Union St **90** B5
Flavell Ms, SE10 . . . . . **155** F2
Flaxman Ct, W1 . . . . . . **86** C1
Flaxman Ter, WC1 . . . . . **37** D5
Fleece Wk, N7 . . . . **15** F1
Fleet Pl, EC4
   off Limeburner La . . . **61** E5
Fleet Sq, WC1 . . . . **38** B5

★ Place of interest ⇌ Railway station ⊖ London Overground station ⊖ London Underground station

Fleet St, EC4 . . . . **88** C1
Fleet St Hill, E1 . . . . . . **64** C2
Fleetwood Cl, E16 . . . . **74** C3
Fleetwood Ct, E6 . . . . . **76** A3
Fleming Cl, W9 . . . . **52** C2
Fleming Ct, W2 . . . . **54** C3
Fleming Rd, SE17 . . . . **145** F4
Fletcher Cl, E6 . . . . **105** E2
Fletcher Path, SE8 . . . . **177** D2
Fletcher St, E1 . . . . **93** D2
Fleur de Lis St, E1 . . . . . **63** F2
Flinton St, SE17 . . . . . **147** F2
Flint St, SE17 . . . . **147** D1
Flitcroft St, WC2 . . . . . **59** D5
Flockton St, SE16 . . . . **120** C2
Flodden Rd, SE5 . . . . . **170** A4
Flood Pas, SE18 . . . . . **132** A4
Flood St, SW3 . . . . **139** F3
Flood Wk, SW3 . . . . . . **139** F4
Flora Cl, E14 . . . . **97** E1
Flora Ho, E3
    off Garrison Rd **46** C1
Floral St, WC2 . . . . **87** E2
Florence Ct, W9
    off Maida Vale **32** B5
Florence Nightingale Ho,
    N1 off Nightingale Rd. **18** B2
★ Florence Nightingale
    Mus, SE1 . . . . **116** A2
Florence Rd, SE14 . . . . **176** B4
Florence St, E16 . . . . . . **72** B1
    N1 . . . . **17** E4
Florence Ter, SE14 . . . **176** B3
Florfield Pas, E8 . . . . . . **21** F2
Florfield Rd, E8 . . . . **21** F2
Florida St, E2 . . . . **42** C5
Florin Ct, SE1
    off Tanner St **120** A2
Flower & Dean Wk, E1 . **64** B4
Flower Wk, The, SW7 . **110** A2
Foley Ho, E1
    off Tarling St **94** A1
Foley St, W1 . . . . **58** A4
Folgate St, E1 . . . . **63** F3
Foliot Ho, N1
    off Priory Grn Est **38** A2
Follett St, E14 . . . . **98** A1
Folly Ms, W11 . . . . **80** A1
Folly Wall, E14 . . . . . . **126** B2
Fontenelle, SE5 . . . . . . **171** E3
Forbes St, E1 . . . . **93** D1
Ford Cl, E3 . . . . **45** F2
Fordham St, E1 . . . . **65** D5
Fordingley Rd, W9 . . . . **30** B5
Ford Rd, E3 . . . . **46** A2
Fords Pk Rd, E16 . . . . . . **72** C5
Ford Sq, E1 . . . . **65** F4
Ford St, E3 . . . . **45** F1
    E16 . . . . **72** A5
★ Foreign & Commonwealth
    Office, SW1 . . . . **115** D1
Foreign St, SE5 . . . . . . **169** F5
Foreshore, SE8 . . . . . . **152** B1
Forest Cl, NW6 . . . . **7** E4
Forest Gro, E8 . . . . **20** A2
Forest La, E15 . . . . **27** F1
Fore St, EC2 . . . . **62** B4

Fore St Av, EC2 . . . . **62** C4
Forest Rd, E8 . . . . **20** A2
Forfar Rd, SW11 . . . . . **165** D3
Forge Pl, NW1 . . . . **13** D2
Formation, The, E16 . **133** E1
Formosa St, W9 . . . . . . **54** A2
Formunt Cl, E16 . . . . . . **72** B4
Forset St, W1 . . . . **55** F5
Forston St, N1 . . . . **40** C2
Forsyth Gdns, SE17 . . **145** F4
Forsyth Ho, SW1
    off Tachbrook St . . . **142** B2
Fortescue Av, E8 . . . . . . **21** F4
Fortis Cl, E16 . . . . **102** A1
★ Fortnum & Mason,
    W1 . . . . **86** A4
Fort Rd, SE1 . . . . **148** B1
Fortrose Cl, E14 . . . . . . **71** D5
Fort St, E1 . . . . **63** F4
    E16 . . . . **101** F5
Fortuna Cl, N7 . . . . **16** B1
Fortune Pl, SE1 . . . . . . **148** B3
Fortune St, EC1 . . . . **62** B2
Forty Acre La, E16 . . . . **72** C4
Forum Cl, E3 . . . . **46** C1
Forum Magnum Sq,
    SE1 . . . . **116** A1
Fosbury Ms, W2 . . . . . . **81** F3
Foscote Ms, W9 . . . . **53** D2
Fossdene Prim Sch,
    SE7 . . . . **157** F3
Fossdene Rd, SE7 . . . . **157** F3
Foster La, EC2 . . . . **62** A5
Foster Rd, E13 . . . . **72** C1
Foubert's Pl, W1 . . . . . . **86** A1
Foulis Ter, SW7 . . . . . . **139** D2
Founder Cl, E6 . . . . **105** E1
Founders Ct, EC2 . . . . . . **62** C5
★ Foundling Mus, WC1. **59** F1
Foundry Cl, SE16 . . . . . **95** E4
Foundry Ms, NW1 . . . . . **58** B1
Foundry Pl, E1 . . . . **66** A3
Fountain Ct, EC4 . . . . . . **88** C2
Fountain Grn Sq,
    SE16 . . . . **121** D2
Fountain Ho, SW6
    off The Boulevard . . **162** B5
    SW8
    off St. George Wf . . . **143** F3
Fountain Ms, NW3 . . . . **12** A1
Fountain Pl, SW9 . . . . **169** D4
Fountain Sq, SW1 . . . . **113** E5
Fount St, SW8 . . . . **167** D2
Fournier St, E1 . . . . **64** A3
Four Seasons Cl, E3 . . . **46** C2
Fourth Av, W10 . . . . **29** E5
Fowey Cl, E1 . . . . **93** E4
Fowler Rd, N1 . . . . **17** F4
Fox & Knot St, EC1 . . . . **61** F3
Fox Cl, E1 . . . . **66** B1
    E16 . . . . **72** C4
Foxcote, SE5 . . . . **147** F3
Foxley Ho, E3
    off Bromley High St . . **47** F4
Foxley Rd, SW9 . . . . . . **169** D1
Foxley Sq, SW9 . . . . . . **169** E3
Foxmore St, SW11 . . . **164** A4

Sch Fox Prim Sch, W8 . . . **80** C4
Fox Rd, E16 . . . . **72** A4
Foyle Rd, SE3 . . . . **156** A5
Frampton Pk Est, E9 . . **22** A3
Frampton Pk Rd, E9 . . . **22** A2
Frampton St, NW8 . . . . **54** C2
Coll Frances King Sch of English,
    South Kensington,
    SW7 . . . . **110** B5
    Victoria, SW1 . . . . . . **113** F3
Frances St, SE18 . . . . . **132** A5
Francis Chichester Way,
    SW11 . . . . **165** D4
Francis Cl, E14 . . . . . . **126** C5
Sch Francis Holland Sch,
    NW1 . . . . **56** A1
    SW1 . . . . **141** D1
Francis St, SW1 . . . . . . **114** A5
Francis Wk, N1 . . . . **16** A5
Sch Frank Barnes Sch for
    Deaf Children, NW3 . **11** D4
Frank Burton Cl, SE7 . **157** F3
Frankham St, SE8 . . . . **176** C2
Frankland Cl, SE16 . . . **121** F4
Frankland Rd, SW7 . . . **110** C4
Franklin Cl, SE13 . . . . . **177** E4
Franklin Pl, SE13 . . . . . **177** E4
Franklin Sq, W14 . . . . **136** B3
Franklin's Row, SW3 . **140** B2
Franklin St, E3 . . . . **47** F4
Frank St, E13 . . . . **73** D2
Fraser Cl, E6 . . . . **75** E5
Frazier St, SE1 . . . . **116** C2
Frean St, SE16 . . . . **120** C3
Freda Corbett Cl,
    SE15 . . . . **172** C1
Frederica St, N7 . . . . . . **16** A3
Frederick Cl, W2 . . . . . . **83** F2
Frederick Cres, SW9 . . **169** E2
Frederick Rd, SE17 . . . **145** F4
Frederick's Pl, EC2 . . . . **90** C1
Frederick Sq, SE16 . . . **95** E3
Frederick's Row, EC1 . **39** E4
Frederick St, WC1 . . . . . **38** A5
Frederick Ter, E8 . . . . . . **20** A4
Frederic Ms, SW1 . . . . **112** B2
Fred White Wk, N7 . . . . **15** F1
Freedom St, SW11 . . . **164** B5
Freeling St, N1 . . . . **16** A4
Freemantle St, SE17 . . **147** E2
★ Freemason's Hall
    (United Grand Lo of
    England), WC2 . . . . . . **59** F5
Freemasons Rd, E16 . . **73** E4
Free Trade Wf, E1 . . . . . **94** C2
★ Freightliners Fm, N7. **16** B1
Fremont St, E9 . . . . **22** A5
French Ordinary Ct,
    EC3 . . . . **91** F2
French Pl, E1 . . . . **63** F1
Frensham St, SE15 . . . **149** D5
Frere St, SW11 . . . . **163** F5
Freshfield Av, E8 . . . . . . **20** A4

Sch School   Coll College   Riv Thames ferry landing stage   DLR Docklands Light Railway station

Freston Rd, W10......**78** C2
W11 ....**79** D3
★ Freud Mus, NW3....**10** B1
Friars Cl, SE1.........**89** E5
Friars Mead, E14 ....**126** A4
Sch Friars Prim Sch,
SE1 ....**117** F1
Friar St, EC4 ....**89** F1
Friary Ct, SW1........**86** B5
Friary Est, SE15 .....**149** D5
Friary Rd, SE15......**149** D5
Friday St, EC4 ....**90** A1
Friendly Pl, SE13 ....**177** F4
Friendly St, SE8 ......**176** C5
Friendly St Ms, SE8
off Friendly St.....**176** C5
Friendship Way, E15 .. **26** B5
Friend St, EC1 ....**39** E4
Frigate Ms, SE8......**152** C4
Frimley Way, E1 ......**66** C1
Frinstead Ho, W10 ....**78** C2
Frith St, W1..........**86** C1
Frithville Gdns, W12...**78** A4
Frobisher Cres, EC2
off The Barbican **62** B3
Frobisher Pas, E14 ....**97** D4
Frobisher Pl, SE15 ...**174** A4
Frobisher Rd, E6......**76** B4
Frobisher St, SE10 ...**155** F4
Frognal, NW3 ....**10** A1
Frognal Ct, NW3 .....**10** B1
Frognal Par, NW3
off Frognal Ct.......**10** B1
Frome St, N1.........**40** A2
Frostic Wk, E1........**64** B4
Fruiterers Pas, EC4
off Southwark Br **90** B3
Frying Pan All, E1.....**64** A4
Fulbourne St, E1......**65** E3
Fulford St, SE16 .....**121** F2
FULHAM, SW6.......**159** E5
⊖ Fulham Broadway, **161** D1
Fulham Bdy, SW6....**161** D1
Fulham Bdy Retail Cen,
SW6 off Fulham Bdy. **161** D1
Fulham Ct, SW6 .....**160** C3
Sch Fulham Cross Sec Sch,
SW6..............**159** E1
★ Fulham FC, SW6...**158** C4
Fulham Palace Rd,
SW6.............**159** D1
W6 ....**134** B2
Fulham Pk Rd, SW6 .. **160** A5
Sch Fulham Prep Sch,
Upr Sch, W14......**135** F4
Sch Fulham Prim Sch,
SW6.............**136** C5
Fulham Rd, SW3 .....**138** C3
SW6..............**161** F1
SW10 ....**138** C3
Fuller Cl, E2..........**64** C1
Fullwoods Ms, N1....**41** D4
Fulmead St, SW6 ....**161** F4

Fulmer Rd, E16 ......**74** C4
Fulthorp Rd, SE3.....**180** B5
Fulton Ms, W2........**82** A2
Fulwood Pl, WC1......**60** B4
Furley Rd, SE15 .....**173** D2
Furlong Rd, N7.......**17** D1
Furness Rd, SW6.....**161** F5
Furnival St, EC4 ......**60** C5
Furzefield Rd, SE3....**157** E5
Furze St, E3..........**69** D3
Fynes St, SW1.......**114** C5

G

Gables Cl, SE5.......**171** E3
Gabrielle Ct, NW3.....**11** D2
Gabriel's Wf, SE1 .....**88** C4
Gadwall Cl, E16.......**73** E5
Gage Rd, E16 ....**71** F4
Gage St, WC1 ....**59** F3
Gainford St, N1.......**16** C5
Sch Gainsborough Comm
Sch, E9 ....**24** C1
Gainsborough Ct,
W12...........**106** A2
Gainsborough Ho,
E14 ....**125** D2
Sch Gainsborough Prim
Sch, E15 ....**49** F5
Gainsborough Rd, E15. **49** E5
Gainsborough St, E9 .. **24** B2
Gainsborough Studios,
N1.............**40** C1
Gainsford St, SE1 ....**120** A1
Gairloch Rd, SE5.....**171** F5
Gaisford St, NW5 .....**14** A1
Gaitskell Ct, SW11 ...**163** D5
Gaitskell Way, SE1
off Weller St.......**118** A1
Galaxy, E14
off Crews St.......**124** C5
Galbraith St, E14 ....**126** A3
Galen Pl, WC1 ....**59** F4
Gales Gdns, E2 ......**43** F5
Gale St, E3...........**69** D3
Galleon Cl, SE16 .....**122** B1
Galleon Ho, SW8
off St. George Wf ...**143** E4
Galleywall Rd, SE16..**149** E1
Sch Gallions Prim Sch,
E6 ....**77** E5
DLR Gallions Reach....**105** F1
Gallions Rd, SE7 .....**157** F1
Gallions Rbt, E16 ....**105** E2
Galsworthy Av, E14 ...**67** F4
Galton St, W10 ....**51** E1
Galway Cl, SE16 .....**149** F3
Galway Ho, EC1 ......**40** B5
Galway St, EC1 ......**40** B5
Gambia St, SE1 ......**89** F5
Gambier Ho, EC1 .....**40** B4
Gandolfi St, SE15 ....**147** E5
Ganton St, W1........**86** A2
Garbutt Pl, W1 ......**57** D3
Garden Ct, EC4 ......**88** C2

Sch Garden Ho Sch,
SW3.............**140** B2
Garden Ms, W2 ....**81** D3
Garden Pl, E8 ....**20** B5
Garden Rd, NW8 .....**32** B4
Garden Row, SE1 ....**117** E4
Garden St, E1 ....**67** D4
Garden Ter, SW1 ....**142** C2
Garden Wk, EC2 ......**41** E5
Gardner Ct, EC1
off Brewery Sq **61** E1
Gardner Rd, E13......**73** E1
Gardners La, EC4 .....**90** A2
Gard St, EC1 ....**39** E4
Garfield Rd, E13......**72** B2
Garford St, E14 ......**96** C3
Garland Ct, SE17
off Wansey St **146** B1
Garlick Hill, EC4 .....**90** B2
Garlinge Rd, NW2.....**8** A2
Garnault Ms, EC1 .....**39** D5
Garnault Pl, EC1 .....**39** D5
Garner St, E2.........**43** D3
Garnet St, E1.........**94** A3
Garnet Wk, E6........**75** F3
Garnies Cl, SE15 .....**172** A1
Garrett St, EC1 ......**62** B3
Garrick St, WC2 ......**87** E2
Garrison Rd, E3.......**46** B1
Garter Way, SE16 ....**122** C2
Garvary Rd, E16 .....**101** F5
Garway Rd, W2.......**81** E1
Gascoigne Pl, E2......**42** A5
Gascony Av, NW6......**8** C4
Gascoyne Rd, E9......**23** D3
Gaselee St, E14.......**98** B3
Gaskell St, SW4.....**167** E5
Gaskin St, N1 ....**17** E5
Gaspar Cl, SW5 .....**109** F5
Gaspar Ms, SW5 ....**109** F5
Gastein Rd, W6......**135** D4
★ Gasworks Gall,
SE11 ....**144** B4
Gataker St, SE16.....**121** F3
Gatcombe Rd, E16 ...**101** D4
Gateforth St, NW8 ...**55** E2
Sch Gatehouse Sch, E2.. **44** C2
Gate Ho Sq, SE1 .....**90** B4
Gate Ms, SW7 ....**111** F2
Gatesborough St, EC2 . **63** E1
Gate St, WC2 ....**60** A5
Gateway, SE17 ......**146** B4
Sch Gateway Prim Sch,
NW8 ....**55** D1
Gateway Retail Pk, E6. **77** F2
Gateways, The, SW3 . **139** F1
Gathorne St, E2 ......**45** D3
Gatliff Cl, SW1
off Ebury Br Rd **141** E3
Gatliff Rd, SW1 ......**141** D3
Gatonby St, SE15 ....**172** B3
Gaumont Ter, W12
off Lime Gro......**106** A1
Gaunt St, SE1 ....**117** F3
Gautrey Rd, SE15 ....**174** B5
Gautrey Sq, E6 ......**104** B1
Gavel St, SE17.......**119** D5

Gaverick Ms, E14 ....**124** C5
Gawber St, E2 ....**44** B4
Gawthorne Ct, E3
  off Mostyn Gro......**46** C3
Gaydon Ho, W2.......**53** F3
Gayfere St, SW1 .....**115** E4
Gayhurst, SE17 ......**147** D4
SchGayhurst Comm Sch,
  E8 ....**21** D3
Gayhurst Rd, E8 ......**20** C3
Gay Rd, E15 ....**48** C2
Gayton Ho, E3........**69** D2
Gaywood Est, SE1 ....**117** E4
Gaywood St, SE1 .....**117** F4
Gaza St, SE17 ....**145** E3
Gazelle Ho, E15........**27** E1
Gedling Pl, SE1 ......**120** B3
Gees Ct, W1..........**85** D1
Gee St, EC1 ....**62** A1
Geffrye Ct, N1 ....**41** F3
Geffrye Est, N1 ....**41** F3
★ Geffrye Mus, E2 .....**41** F3
Geffrye St, E2 ....**42** A2
Geldart Rd, SE15......**173** E2
Gellatly Rd, SE14 ....**174** B5
Gemini Ho, E3
  off Garrison Rd......**46** C1
Gemini Project, SE14 .**151** D3
General Gordon Pl,
  SE18 ....**133** E5
General Wolfe Rd,
  SE10 ....**179** D3
Gentian Row, SE13...**178** A4
Gentry Gdns, E13 ....**73** D1
SchGeoffrey Chaucer
  Tech Coll, SE1.....**118** C4
George Beard Rd, SE8.**152** A1
George Belt Ho, E2....**44** C4
George Ct, WC2.......**87** F3
George Eliot Ho, SW1
  off Vauxhall Br Rd ..**142** B1
SchGeorge Eliot Inf Sch,
  NW8 ....**10** C5
SchGeorge Eliot Jun Sch,
  NW8 ....**10** C5
George Elliston Ho, SE1
  off Old Kent Rd **148** C3
SchGeorge Green's Sch,
  E14 ....**154** B2
★ George Inn, SE1 ....**90** C5
George Inn Yd, SE1....**90** C5
George Loveless Ho, E2.**42** B4
George Lowe Ct, W2...**53** E3
George Mathers Rd,
  SE11 ....**117** E5
George Ms, NW1......**36** A5
George Row, SE16 ...**120** C2
Georges Sq, SW6.....**136** B4
George St, E16 ......**100** A1
  W1................**56** B5
Georgette Pl, SE10 ..**178** B2
George Yd, EC3.......**91** D1
  W1................**85** D2
Georgiana St, NW1....**14** A5
Georgina Gdns, E2...**42** B4
Geraldine St, SE11 ..**117** E4
Gerald Ms, SW1......**113** D5

Gerald Rd, E16 ....**72** A1
  SW1.............**113** D5
Gerard Pl, E9.........**22** C3
Gerards Cl, SE16.....**150** A3
Germander Way, E15...**49** F5
Gernon Rd, E3........**45** E3
Gerrard Ho, SE14 ....**174** B2
Gerrard Pl, W1 ....**87** D2
Gerrard Rd, N1 ....**39** F2
Gerrard St, W1 ....**86** C2
Gerridge St, SE1 .....**117** D2
Gerry Raffles Sq, E15..**27** D2
Gertrude St, SW10 ...**138** B5
Gervase St, SE15 ....**173** F1
Ghent Way, E8 ....**20** B1
Gibbins Rd, E15 .....**26** B4
Gibbons Rents, SE1
  off Magdalen St.....**91** E5
Gibbs Grn, W14......**136** B2
SchGibbs Grn Sch,
  W14.............**136** B2
Gibraltar Wk, E2 .....**42** B5
Gibson Cl, E1........**66** B1
Gibson Rd, SE11 ....**144** B1
Gibson Sq, N1........**17** D5
Gibson St, SE10 .....**155** E3
Giffin St, SE8 ....**176** C1
Gifford St, N1 ....**15** F4
Gilbert Ho, EC2
  off The Barbican **62** B3
  SE8 ....**153** D4
  SW1.............**141** F3
Gilbert Pl, WC1 ....**59** E4
Gilbert Rd, SE11 ....**145** D1
Gilbert St, W1 ....**85** D1
Gilbeys Yd, NW1......**13** D4
Gildea St, W1 ....**57** F4
Gill Av, E16 ....**101** D1
Gillender St, E3.......**70** A1
  E14 ....**70** A1
Gillfoot, NW1........**36** A3
Gilling Ct, NW3 ....**11** F1
Gillingham Row, SW1.**114** A5
Gillingham St, SW1 ..**113** F5
Gillison Wk, SE16
  off Tranton Rd **121** D3
Gill St, E14...........**96** B2
Gilpin Cl, W2.........**54** C3
Gilstead Rd, SW6 ....**161** F5
Gilston Rd, SW10 ....**138** B3
Giltspur St, EC1.......**61** F5
Giralda Cl, E16 ....**74** C4
Giraud St, E14........**69** E5
Girdlers Rd, W14 ....**107** D5
Gironde Rd, SW6.....**160** B2
Girton Vil, W10.......**51** D5
Gissing Wk, N1 ....**17** D4
Gladstone Ct, SW1
  off Regency St.....**143** D1
  SW8 off Havelock Ter.**165** F3
Gladstone Ms, NW6 ....**8** B2
Gladstone Pl, E3......**46** B2
Gladstone St, SE1....**117** E3
Gladys Rd, NW6 ......**9** D3
Glaisher St, SE8 ....**153** D4
Glamis Pl, E1.........**94** B2
Glamis Rd, E1 ....**94** B2

Glasgow Ho, W9......**31** F3
Glasgow Ter, SW1....**142** A3
Glasier Ct, E15 ......**27** F3
Glaskin Ms, E9 ......**23** F2
Glasshill St, SE1 .....**117** F1
Glasshouse Flds, E1...**94** C2
Glasshouse St, W1 ...**86** B3
Glasshouse Wk, SE11.**143** F5
Glasshouse Yd, EC1 ...**62** A2
Glass St, E2..........**65** F1
Glass Yd, SE18 .....**133** D3
Glastonbury Ho, SW1.**141** E2
Glastonbury Pl, E1....**94** A1
Glaucus St, E3........**69** E3
Glazbury Rd, W14....**135** F1
Glebe Pl, SW3 ....**139** E4
Glebe Rd, E8 ....**20** A4
Gledhow Gdns, SW5..**138** A1
Gledstanes Rd, W14..**135** F3
Glenaffric Av, E14....**154** B1
Glenalvon Way, SE18.**131** E5
Glenavon Rd, E15.....**27** F3
Glencairne Cl, E16 ...**74** C3
Glendower Pl, SW7...**110** C5
SchGlendower Sch,
  SW7.............**110** C5
Gleneagles Cl, SE16..**149** E3
Glenfinlas Way, SE5..**169** F1
Glenforth St, SE10 ..**156** B2
Glengall Causeway,
  E14 ....**124** C3
Glengall Gro, E14....**126** A3
Glengall Rd, NW6 .....**30** B1
  SE15 ....**148** B4
Glengall Ter, SE15 ..**148** B4
Glengarnock Av, E14.**154** B1
Glenilla Rd, NW3......**11** E1
Glenister Rd, SE10 ..**156** A2
Glenister St, E16.....**105** D5
Glenkerry Ho, E14 ....**70** A5
Glenloch Rd, NW3.....**11** E1
Glenluce Rd, SE3.....**156** C5
Glenmore Rd, NW3....**11** E1
Glen Rd, E13 ....**74** A1
Glenrosa St, SW6 ...**162** A5
Glenroy St, W12 .....**50** A5
Glen Ter, E14.........**126** A1
Glenthorne Rd, W6...**106** A5
Glentworth St, NW1 ..**56** B2
Glenville Gro, SE8....**176** B2
Glenworth Av, E14....**154** C1
Gliddon Rd, W14.....**135** E1
Global App, E3 ....**47** F3
Globe Pond Rd, SE16..**95** E5
SchGlobe Prim Sch, E2 ..**44** B4
Globe Rd, E1 ....**44** B4
  E2 ....**44** A3
Globe Rope Wk, E14..**154** A1
Globe St, SE1.........**118** B3
Globe Ter, E2.........**44** A4
Globe Town, E2.......**44** C3
Globe Wf, SE16 ......**95** D3
Globe Yd, W1.........**85** E1

Gloucester Arc, SW7 . . 110 A5
Gloucester Av, NW1 . . . . 13 D5
Gloucester Circ, SE10 . 178 B1
Gloucester Cres, NW1 . 13 E5
Gloucester Gdns, W2 . . 53 F5
Gloucester Gate, NW1 . 35 E2
Gloucester Gate Ms,
  NW1 . . . . 35 E2
Gloucester Ho, NW6 . . 31 D3
Gloucester Ms, W2 . . . . 82 B1
Gloucester Ms W, W2 . . 82 A1
Gloucester Pk, SW7 . . 110 A5
Gloucester Pl, NW1 . . . 56 A1
  W1 . . . . 56 B3
Gloucester Pl Ms, W1 . . 56 B4
Sch Gloucester Prim Sch,
  SE15 . . . . 172 A1
⊖ Gloucester Road . . 110 B5
Gloucester Rd, SW7 . . 110 A3
Gloucester Sq, E2 . . . . . 42 A3
  W2 . . . . 83 D1
Gloucester St, SW1 . . . 142 A3
Gloucester Ter, W2 . . . . 54 A5
Gloucester Wk, W8 . . . 109 D1
Gloucester Way, EC1 . . 39 D5
Glynde Ms, SW3 . . . . . 111 F4
Glyn St, SE11 . . . . 144 A3
Goaters All, SW6 . . . . . 160 A2
Godalming Rd, E14 . . . 69 E4
Godbold Rd, E15 . . . . . 49 E5
Godfrey Ho, EC1 . . . . . . 40 C5
Godfrey St, E15 . . . . . . 48 B2
  SW3 . . . . 139 F2
Goding St, SE11 . . . . . 143 F3
Godley Cl, SE14 . . . . . 174 B4
Godliman St, EC4 . . . . . 90 A1
Godson St, N1 . . . . 38 C2
Godwin Cl, N1 . . . . 40 B2
Godwin Ct, NW1 . . . . . . 36 B2
Godwin Ho, NW6
  off Tollgate Gdns 31 E2
Col Goethe Institut,
  SW7 . . . . 111 D3
Goffers Rd, SE3 . . . . . 179 E5
Golborne Gdns, W10 . . 51 F2
Golborne Ms, W10 . . . . 51 E4
Golborne Rd, W10 . . . . 51 F4
Goldcrest Cl, E16 . . . . . 74 C3
Golden Cross Ms, W11 . 52 A5
★ Golden Hinde, SE1 . . 90 C4
Golden Jubilee Br, SE1 . 88 A5
  WC2 . . . . 87 F4
Golden La, EC1 . . . . . . 62 A2
Golden La Est, EC1 . . . . 62 A2
Golden Plover Cl, E16 . . 73 E5
Golden Sq, W1 . . . . 86 B2
⊖ Goldhawk Road . . . 106 A2
Goldhurst Ter, NW6 . . . 10 A4
Golding St, E1 . . . . 93 D1
Golding Ter, SW11
  off Longhedge St . . . 165 D5
Goldington Cres, NW1 . 36 C2
Goldington St, NW1 . . . 36 C2

Goldman Cl, E2 . . . . . . 64 C1
Goldney Rd, W9 . . . . . . 52 C2
Goldsboro Rd, SW8 . . . 167 D3
Goldsmith Rd, SE15 . . . 172 C3
Uni Goldsmiths Coll,
  SE14 . . . . 175 F3
★ Goldsmiths' Hall,
  EC2 . . . . 62 A5
Goldsmith's Pl, NW6 . . 31 E1
Goldsmith's Row, E2 . . 42 C3
Goldsmith's Sq, E2 . . . . 43 D2
Goldsmith St, EC2 . . . . 62 B5
Goldsworthy Gdns,
  SE16 . . . . 150 B1
Goldwin Cl, SE14 . . . . 174 B3
Goldwing Cl, E16 . . . . . 101 D1
Gomm Rd, SE16 . . . . . 122 A4
Gonson St, SE8 . . . . . . 153 E5
Goodge Pl, W1 . . . . 58 B4
⊖ Goodge Street 58 B3
Goodge St, W1 . . . . 58 B4
Goodhart Pl, E14 . . . . . 95 F2
Goodinge Cl, N7 . . . . . . 15 E1
Goodmans Ct, E1 . . . . . 92 A2
Goodman's Stile, E1 . . . 64 C5
Goodmans Yd, E1 . . . . . 92 A2
Goods Way, NW1 . . . . . 37 E2
Goodway Gdns, E14 . . . 70 C5
Goodwin Cl, SE16 . . . . 120 B4
Goodwins Ct, WC2 . . . . 87 E2
Goodwood Rd, SE14 . . . 175 E2
Goose Sq, E6 . . . . 104 A1
Gophir La, EC4 . . . . 90 C2
Gopsall St, N1 . . . . 41 D1
H Gordon Hosp, SW1 . 142 C1
Gordon Ho, E1 . . . . 94 A2
Gordon Pl, W8 . . . . . . 109 D1
Gordon Rd, SE15 . . . . . 173 E4
Gordon Sq, WC1 . . . . . . 59 D2
Gordon St, WC1 . . . . . . 58 C1
Gorefield Pl, NW6 . . . . 30 C2
Gore Rd, E9 . . . . 44 B1
Gore St, SW7 . . . . 110 B3
Gorham Pl, W11 . . . . . . 79 E3
Goring St, EC3 . . . . 63 F5
Gorleston St, W14 . . . 107 F5
Gorman Rd, SE18 . . . . . 132 B5
Gorse Cl, E16 . . . . 100 C1
Gorsuch Pl, E2 . . . . 42 A4
Gorsuch St, E2 . . . . 42 A4
Gosfield St, W1 . . . . 58 A3
Goslett Yd, WC2 . . . . . . 87 D1
Gosling Way, SW9 . . . 169 D4
Gosset St, E2 . . . . 42 B4
Gosterwood St, SE8 . . 151 E4
Goswell Rd, EC1 . . . . . . 62 A2
Gough Sq, EC4 . . . . 61 D5
Gough St, WC1 . . . . 60 B1
Gough Wk, E14 . . . . 96 C1
Goulden Ho App,
  SW11 . . . . 163 E5
Goulston St, E1 . . . . 64 A5
Govan St, E2 . . . . 43 D1
Govier Cl, E15 . . . . 27 F4
Gowan Av, SW6 . . . . . . 159 E4
Gower Ct, WC1 . . . . 58 C1
Gower Ms, WC1 . . . . 58 C4

Gower Pl, WC1 . . . . 58 B1
Gower St, WC1 . . . . 58 B1
Gower's Wk, E1 . . . . 64 C5
Gracechurch St, EC3 . . . 91 D2
Grace Jones Cl, E8 . . . . 20 C2
Grace Pl, E3 . . . . 47 F5
Grace's All, E1 . . . . 92 C2
Graces Ms, SE5 . . . . . 171 D5
Graces Rd, SE5 . . . . . 171 E5
Grace St, E3 . . . . 47 F5
Graduate Pl, SE1
  off Long La 119 E3
Grafton Cres, NW1 . . . . 13 E2
Grafton Ho, E3 . . . . 46 C5
Grafton Ms, W1 . . . . 58 A2
Grafton Pl, NW1 . . . . . . 36 C5
Grafton Rd, NW5 . . . . . 13 E1
Grafton St, W1 . . . . 85 F3
Grafton Way, W1 . . . . . . 58 A2
  WC1 . . . . 58 A2
Grafton Yd, NW5 . . . . . 13 F2
Graham Rd, E8 . . . . 20 C1
  E13 . . . . 72 C1
Graham St, N1 . . . . 39 F3
Graham Ter, SW1 . . . . 140 C1
Granary Rd, E1 . . . . 65 E2
Granary Sq, N1 . . . . 17 D2
Granary St, NW1 . . . . . 36 C1
Granby Pl, SE1 . . . . . . 116 C2
Granby St, E2 . . . . 64 B1
Granby Ter, NW1 . . . . . 36 A3
Grand Av, EC1 . . . . 61 F3
Grand Junct Wf, N1 . . . 40 A3
Grand Union Cl, W9 . . . 52 B3
Grand Union Cres, E8 . . 21 D4
Grand Union Wk, NW1 . 13 F4
Grand Wk, E1 . . . . 67 F1
Granfield St, SW11 . . . 163 D4
Grange, The, SE1 . . . . 120 A3
  W14 off Lisgar Ter . . 136 A1
Grange Ct, WC2 . . . . . . 88 B1
Grange Gro, N1 . . . . 17 F1
Grange Pl, NW6 . . . . 8 C4
Sch Grange Prim Sch,
  SE1 . . . . 119 E4
Grange Rd, SE1 . . . . . . 119 F3
Grange St, N1 . . . . 41 D1
Grange Wk, SE1 . . . . . 119 F3
Grange Wk Ms, SE1 . . 119 F4
Grangeway, NW6 . . . . . . 8 C4
Grange Yd, SE1 . . . . . . 120 A4
Granite Apts, E15 . . . . . 27 D1
Gransden Av, E8 . . . . . . 21 F4
Grantbridge St, N1 . . . . 39 F2
Grantham Pl, W1 . . . . . 85 E5
Grantley St, E1 . . . . 44 C5
Grant's Quay Wf, EC3 . . 91 D3
Grant St, N1 . . . . 38 C2
Grantully Rd, W9 . . . . . 31 E5
Granville Ct, N1 . . . . . . 19 D5
Granville Pl, SW6 . . . . 161 E2
  W1 . . . . 84 C1
Granville Rd, NW6 . . . . 30 C3
Granville Sq, SE15 . . . 171 F1
  WC1 . . . . 38 B5
Granville St, WC1 . . . . . 38 B5
Grape St, WC2 . . . . 59 E5

Graphite Sq, SE11....144 A2
Grasmere Pt, SE15...174 A1
Gratton Rd, W14.....107 E4
Gravel La, E1.........64 A5
Grayling Cl, E16 ......71 F1
Grayling Sq, E2.......43 D4
★ Gray's Inn, WC1 .....60 B3
Gray's Inn Pl, WC1...60 B4
Gray's Inn Rd, WC1 ...38 A5
Gray's Inn Sq, WC1...60 C3
Grayson Ho, EC1......40 B5
Gray St, SE1 ....117 D2
Gray's Yd, W1 ....85 D1
Great Arthur Ho, EC1 .62 A2
Great Bell All, EC2....62 C5
Great Castle St, W1 ...57 F5
Great Cen St, NW1 ...56 A3
Great Chapel St, W1...58 C5
Great Ch La, W6 .....135 D2
Great Coll St, SW1 ...115 D3
Great Cross Av, SE10 .179 E2
Great Cumberland Ms,
  W1................84 A1
Great Cumberland Pl,
  W1................56 A5
Great Dover St, SE1 ..118 B2
Great Eastern Enterprise
  Cen, E14..........125 E2
Great Eastern Rd, E15 .26 C3
Great Eastern St, EC2..41 E5
Great Eastern Wk, EC2.63 F4
Greatfield Av, E6......76 A1
Great George St, SW1.115 D2
Great Guildford St, SE1 .90 A4
Great James St, WC1 ..60 A2
Great Marlborough St,
  W1................86 A1
Great Maze Pond, SE1.119 D1
Great Newport St, WC2
  off Charing Cross Rd .87 D2
Great New St, EC4 ....61 D5
Greatorex St, E1 ......64 C3
Great Ormond St, WC1.59 F3
🄷 Great Ormond St Hosp
  for Children, The,
  WC1...............59 F2
Great Percy St, WC1...38 B4
Great Peter St, SW1 ..114 C4
⊖Great Portland
  Street 57 F2
Great Portland St, W1 .57 F3
Great Pulteney St, W1 .86 B2
Great Queen St, WC2 ..87 F1
Great Russell St, WC1 .59 D5
Great St. Helens, EC3..63 E5
Great St. Thomas Apostle,
  EC4 ....90 B2
Great Scotland Yd, SW1.87 E5
Great Smith St, SW1...115 D3
Great Suffolk St, SE1...89 F5
Great Sutton St, EC1 ..61 D4
Great Swan All, EC2 ..62 C5
Great Titchfield St, W1.58 A5
Great Twr St, EC3 .....91 E2
Great Trinity La, EC4 ..90 B2
Great Turnstile, WC1 ..60 B4
Great Western Rd, W2 .52 C4

Great Western Rd, W9 .52 B2
  W11 ....52 C4
Great Winchester St,
  EC2................63 D5
Great Windmill St,
  W1................86 C2
Great Yd, SE1 ....119 F1
Greaves Twr, SW10 ..162 B1
Greek Ct, W1 ....87 D1
★ Greek Orthodox Cath of
  the Divine Wisdom
  (St. Sophia), W2 ....81 E2
Greek St, W1 ....87 D1
Greek Yd, WC2 ....87 E2
Green, The, E15 ......27 F2
Greenacre Sq, SE16 ..123 D1
Green Arbour Ct, EC1 ..61 E5
Green Bk, E1 ....93 E5
Greenberry St, NW8 ...33 E3
Greencoat Pl, SW1 ...114 B5
Greencoat Row, SW1 .114 B4
Greencroft Cl, E6......75 E4
Greencroft Gdns, NW6 ..9 A4
Green Dragon Ct, SE1..90 C4
Green Dragon Yd, E1 ..64 C4
Greenfell Mans, SE8 ..153 E4
Greenfield Rd, E1 .....65 D4
Greenham Cl, SE1....116 C2
Greenheath Business Cen,
  E2 off Three Colts La .65 F1
Greenhill's Rents, EC1 .61 E3
Greenhills Ter, N1.....19 D2
Green Hundred Rd,
  SE15 ....149 D5
Greenland Ms, SE8 ..151 D3
🅁Greenland Pier....124 A4
Greenland Pl, NW1 ...13 F5
Greenland Quay,
  SE16 ....123 D5
Greenland Rd, NW1 ...13 F5
Greenland St, NW1...13 F5
Greenlaw St, SE18 ...132 C4
Greenman St, N1 .....18 A4
⊖ Green Park 86 A5
★ Green Park, The,
  SW1 ....85 F5
Green Pl, SE10 ......127 E1
Green Pt, E15 ....27 F2
Greenroof Way, SE10.128 B4
Green's Ct, W1 ....86 C2
Green's End, SE18 ...133 E5
Greenshields Ind Est,
  E16 ....101 D5
Green St, W1 ....84 B2
Green Ter, EC1 ....39 D5
Green Wk, SE1.......119 E4
Greenwell St, W1 .....57 F2
GREENWICH, SE10 ...178 C1
⇌Greenwich 177 F1
🅓🅛🅡Greenwich 177 F1
Greenwich Cen Business
  Pk, SE10 ....177 F1
Greenwich Ch St, SE10.154 B4
Greenwich Cres, E6 ...75 E4
Greenwich Foot Tunnel,
  E14 ....154 B3
  SE10 ....154 B3

Greenwich High Rd,
  SE10 ....177 E3
Greenwich Ind Est,
  SE7 ....157 E1
Greenwich Mkt, SE10.154 B5
★ Greenwich Park,
  SE10 ....179 E1
Greenwich Pk St,
  SE10 ....155 D3
🅁Greenwich Pier ...154 A4
Greenwich Quay, SE8.153 E5
🅒🅞🅛🅛Greenwich Sch of
  Management, SE10.178 A1
Greenwich Shop Pk,
  SE7 ....157 D1
Greenwich S St, SE10.177 F3
Greenwich Vw Pl, E14.125 E4
Greenwood Ct, SW1 ..142 A2
Greenwood Rd, E8 ....21 D2
Greet St, SE1 ....89 D5
Gregor Ms, SE3 ......181 D2
Gregory Pl, W8 ......109 E1
Greig Ter, SE17 ......145 F4
Grenade St, E14 ......96 B2
Grenadier St, E16 ....104 C5
Grenard Ct, SE15.....172 C2
Grendon Ho, N1
  off Priory Grn Est....38 A3
Grendon St, NW8 .....55 E1
Grenfell Ho, SE5
  off Comber Gro 170 A2
Grenfell Rd, W11......79 D2
Grenfell Twr, W11.....79 D2
Grenfell Wk, W11 .....79 D2
Grenville Pl, SW7 ....110 A4
Grenville St, WC1 .....59 F2
Gresham Rd, E16 ....101 F1
Gresham St, EC2......62 A5
Gresse St, W1 ....58 C4
Greswell St, SW6 ....158 C4
Greville Hall, NW6 ....31 E2
Greville Ms, NW6 .....31 E1
Greville Pl, NW6 ......31 F2
Greville Rd, NW6 .....31 E2
Greville St, EC1 ....61 D4
Greycoat Gdns, SW1
  off Greycoat St 114 C4
🅒🅗Grey Coat Hosp Sch,
  Lwr Sch, SW1......114 C4
  Upr Sch, SW1 .....142 C1
Greycoat Pl, SW1 ....114 C4
Greycoat St, SW1 ....114 C4
Grey Eagle St, E1 .....64 A3
Greyfriars Pas, EC1...61 F5
Greyhound Rd, W6...135 D4
  W14 ....135 D4
Greyladies Gdns,
  SE10 ....178 B4
Greystoke Pl, EC4.....60 C5
Griggs Pl, SE1 ....119 F4
Grimsby Gro, E16.....133 F1
Grimsby St, E2 ....64 B2
Grimsel Path, SE5....169 F1

Grimthorpe Ho, EC1 ... **61** E1
Grindal St, SE1 ..... **116** C2
SchGrinling Gibbons
  Prim Sch, SE8 ..... **152** B5
Grinling Pl, SE8....... **152** C5
Grinstead Rd, SE8..... **151** E3
Grittleton Rd, W9 ..... **52** C1
Grocer's Hall Ct, EC2 .. **90** C1
Groombridge Rd, E9... **22** C4
Groom Pl, SW1 .... **113** D3
Grosvenor Cotts, SW1. **112** C5
Grosvenor Ct, NW6.... **7** D5
Grosvenor Cres, SW1 . **113** D2
Grosvenor Cres Ms,
  SW1............. **112** C2
Grosvenor Est, SW1 .. **115** D5
Grosvenor Gdns, SW1. **113** E3
Grosvenor Gdns Ms E,
  SW1............. **113** F3
Grosvenor Gdns Ms N,
  SW1............. **113** E4
Grosvenor Gdns Ms S,
  SW1............. **113** F4
Grosvenor Gate, W1... **84** B3
Grosvenor Hill, W1 .... **85** E2
Grosvenor Pk, SE5 ... **146** A5
Grosvenor Pl, SW1 ... **113** D2
Grosvenor Rd, SW1... **141** E4
Grosvenor Sq, W1 .... **85** D2
Grosvenor St, W1 .... **85** E2
Grosvenor Ter, SE5... **169** F1
Grosvenor Wf Rd, E14. **154** C1
Grotto Pas, W1 .... **57** D3
Grove, The, E15 ...... **27** E1
Grove Cotts, SW3 .... **139** F4
Grove Cres Rd, E15.... **27** D2
Grove Dws, E1........ **66** A3
Grove End Gdns, NW8
  off Grove End Rd **32** C3
Grove End Rd, NW8 ... **32** C3
Grove Gdns, NW8..... **33** F5
Grove Hall Ct, NW8.... **32** B4
Groveland Ct, EC4..... **90** B1
Grove La, SE5 .... **170** C4
Grove Ms, W6 .... **106** A3
  W11 .... **80** A1
Grove Pas, E2 .... **43** E2
Grove Rd, E3 .... **45** D2
  NW2 .... **6** A1
Grove St, SE8 ...... **124** A5
Grove Vil, E14....... **97** F2
Groveway, SW9 ..... **168** B4
Grummant Rd, SE15.. **172** A3
Grundy St, E14...... **97** E1
SchGuardian Angels RC
  Prim Sch, E3....... **67** F1
★ Guards Mus, SW1.. **114** B2
Guerin Sq, E3 .... **46** A4
Guernsey Ho, N1 ..... **18** B2
Guildford Gro, SE10 .. **177** F3
Guildford Rd, E6 .... **104** A1
  SW8.............. **167** F3
★ Guildhall, The, EC2 . **62** C5

★ Guildhall Art Gall
  (Guildhall Lib), EC2.. **62** B5
Guildhall Bldgs, EC2... **62** C5
CollGuildhall Sch of Music &
  Drama, EC2........ **62** B3
  Hall of Res, EC1...... **62** C3
Guildhall Yd, EC2 ..... **62** B5
Guildhouse St, SW1 .. **114** A5
Guilford Pl, WC1 ...... **60** A2
Guilford St, WC1 ..... **59** F2
Guinness Cl, E9....... **23** E4
Guinness Ct, E1 ...... **92** B1
Guinness Sq, SE1 .... **119** E5
Guinness Trust Bldgs, SE1
  off Snowsfields..... **119** E1
  SE11 .... **145** E2
  SW3.............. **140** A1
  W6 off Fulham
  Palace Rd......... **134** B2
Guion Rd, SW6 ...... **160** B5
Gulland Wk, N1
  off Nightingale Rd ... **18** B2
Gulliver St, SE16...... **124** A3
Gulston Wk, SW3 .... **140** B1
Gunmakers La, E3 .... **45** F1
Gunpowder Sq, EC4 ... **61** D5
Gun St, E1 .... **64** A4
Gunter Gro, SW10... **138** A5
Gunterstone Rd, W14. **135** E1
Gunthorpe St, E1 .... **64** B4
Gunwhale Cl, SE16... **95** D5
Gurdon Rd, SE7...... **157** D3
Guthrie St, SW3 ..... **139** E2
Gutter La, EC2....... **62** B5
HGuy's Hosp, SE1... **119** D1
Guy St, SE1 .... **119** D1
Gwendwr Rd, W14... **135** F2
Gwyn Cl, SW6 ...... **162** A2
Gwynne Pl, WC1 ..... **38** B5
Gwynne Rd, SW11 ... **162** C5

H

Haarlem Rd, W14.... **106** C4
Haberdasher Est, N1
  off Haberdasher St... **41** D4
Haberdasher Pl, N1 ... **41** D4
SchHaberdashers' Aske's
  Hatcham Coll, SE14. **175** E3
Haberdasher St, N1 ... **41** D4
Hackford Rd, SW9.... **168** C2
Hackford Wk, SW9 ... **168** B4
HACKNEY, E8 .... **21** E2
⊖Hackney Central ... **21** E1
★ Hackney City Fm,
  E2 .... **42** C3
⇌Hackney Downs.... **21** E1
SchHackney Free & Parochial
  C of E Sch, E9 ...... **22** A2
Hackney Gro, E8
  off Reading La **21** F2
★ Hackney Mus, E8... **21** F2
Hackney Rd, E2 ...... **42** A5
HACKNEY WICK, E9 .. **24** C1
⊖Hackney Wick **24** C2

Hackworth Pt, E3 ..... **47** D5
Hacon Sq, E8......... **21** F3
Haddo Ho, SE10
  off Haddo St **153** F5
Haddonfield, SE8 .... **151** D1
Haddo St, SE10 ..... **154** A5
Hadleigh Cl, E1...... **66** A1
Hadleigh St, E2...... **44** B5
Hadleigh Wk, E6 ..... **75** F5
Hadley St, NW1...... **13** E2
Hadrian Cl, E3....... **46** C1
Hadrian Est, E2...... **43** D3
Hadrian Ms, N7...... **16** B3
Hadrian St, SE10.... **155** E2
HAGGERSTON, E2..... **42** B2
Haggerston Rd, E8 .... **20** A4
SchHaggerston Sch, E2 . **42** B2
Haggerston Studios, E8
  off Kingsland Rd ... **20** A5
SchHague Prim Sch, E2 . **65** F1
Hague St, E2......... **43** D5
Haines Cl, N1 .... **19** E4
Hainton Cl, E1....... **93** F1
Halcomb St, N1...... **41** F1
Halcrow St, E1 ...... **65** F4
Haldane Rd, SW6 .... **160** B1
Hale Rd, E6 .... **75** F2
Hales Prior, N1
  off Calshot St...... **38** A3
Hales St, SE8 ...... **176** C2
Hale St, E14........ **97** E2
Half Moon Ct, EC1.... **62** A4
Half Moon Cres, N1 .. **38** B2
Half Moon Pas, E1 ... **92** B1
Half Moon St, W1 .... **85** F4
Halford Rd, SW6 .... **137** D5
Haliday Wk, N1....... **19** D1
Halkin Arc, SW1 .... **112** C3
Halkin Ms, SW1..... **112** C3
Halkin Pl, SW1 ..... **112** C3
Halkin St, SW1 ..... **113** D2
Hallam Ms, W1 ...... **57** F3
Hallam St, W1....... **57** F2
SchHalley Prim Sch,
  E14 .... **67** F4
Halley St, E14....... **67** E4
Hallfield Est, W2..... **54** A5
SchHallfield Inf & Jun Schs,
  W2 .... **81** F1
Hall Gate, NW8...... **32** B4
Halliday Ho, E1
  off Christian St..... **93** D1
Halliford St, N1...... **18** B3
Hallings Wf Studios,
  E15 .... **26** C5
Hall Oak Wk, NW6..... **8** B1
Hall Pl, W2.......... **54** C2
Hall Rd, NW8........ **32** B5
SchHallsville Prim Sch,
  E16 .... **100** C1
Hallsville Rd, E16..... **100** A1
Hall Twr, W2........ **55** D3
Hallywell Cres, E6 .... **76** B4
Halpin Pl, SE17...... **147** D1

Halsey Ms, SW3 . . . . . 112 A5
Halsey St, SW3 . . . . . . 112 A5
Halsmere Rd, SE5 . . . . 169 F3
Halstead Ct, N1 . . . . . . 40 C3
Sch Halstow Prim Sch,
    SE10 . . . . 156 C3
Halstow Rd, NW10 . . . . 28 C5
    SE10 . . . . 156 C2
Halton Cross St, N1 . . 17 F5
Halton Pl, N1 . . . . 18 A3
Halton Rd, N1 . . . . 17 F3
Hambley Ho, SE16
    off Manor Est 149 E1
Hamelin St, E14 . . . . . . 98 A1
Hameway, E6 . . . . 76 C1
Hamilton Cl, NW8 . . . . . 32 C5
    SE16 . . . . 123 F2
Hamilton Ct, W9 . . . . . . 32 A4
Hamilton Gdns, NW8 . . 32 B4
Hamilton Ho, SW8
    off St. George Wf . . 143 E4
Hamilton Ms, W1 . . . . 113 E1
Hamilton Pl, W1 . . . . . . 85 D5
Hamilton Rd, E15 . . . . . 49 F5
Coll Hamilton Rd Cen,
    E15 . . . . 49 F5
Hamilton Sq, SE1 . . . . 119 D1
Hamilton St, SE8 . . . . 176 C1
Hamilton Ter, NW8 . . . . 32 B4
Hamlets Way, E3 . . . . . 68 A1
Hamlet Way, SE1 . . . . 119 D1
★ Hamleys, W1 . . . . . . 86 A2
Hammelton Grn, SW9 . 169 E3
HAMMERSMITH, W6 . . 134 B2
✪ Hammersmith 134 B1
Coll Hammersmith & W
    London Coll . . . 135 E2
Hammersmith Br Rd,
    W6 . . . . 134 A3
Hammersmith Bdy,
    W6 . . . . 134 B1
Hammersmith Flyover,
    W6 . . . . 134 B2
Hammersmith Gro,
    W6 . . . . 106 A4
Hammersmith Rd, W6 . 134 C1
    W14 . . . . 134 C1
Hammett St, EC3 . . . . 92 A2
Hammond Ho, SE14
    off Lubbock St 174 B2
Hammond St, NW5 . . . . 14 A1
Hamond Sq, N1 . . . . . . 41 E2
Hampden Cl, NW1 . . . . 37 D3
Sch Hampden Gurney C of E
    Prim Sch, W1 . . . . 55 F5
Hampden Gurney St,
    W1 . . . . 84 A1
Sch Hampshire Sch, The,
    Pre-Prep Sch, SW7 . . 111 E2
    Prep Sch, W2 . . . . 82 A2
Hampshire St, NW5 . . . 14 A3
Hampson Way, SW8 . . 168 A3
Hampstead Rd, NW1 . . 36 A2
Hampstead Wk, E3
    off Waterside Cl 24 B5
Hampton Cl, NW6 . . . . 30 C5
Hampton Ct, N1 . . . . . . 17 E2

Hampton St, SE1 . . . . 145 F1
    SE17 . . . . 145 F1
Ham Yd, W1 . . . . 86 C2
Hanameel St, E16 . . . . 101 D4
Hanbury Ms, N1 . . . . . . 40 B1
Hanbury St, E1 . . . . 64 A3
Hancock Rd, E3 . . . . . . 48 A5
Handa Wk, N1 . . . . 18 B1
Hand Ct, WC1 . . . . 60 B4
Handel St, WC1 . . . . . . 59 E1
Handforth Rd, SW9 . . 168 C1
Handley Rd, E9 . . . . 22 B5
Hands Wk, E16 . . . . 73 D5
Hanging Sword All,
    EC4 . . . . 89 D1
Hankey Pl, SE1 . . . . . 119 D2
Hannah Mary Way,
    SE1 . . . . 149 D1
Hannell Rd, SW6 . . . . . 159 E1
Hannibal Rd, E1 . . . . . . 66 B3
Hanover Av, E16 . . . . . 100 C4
Hanover Gdns, SE11 . . 144 C5
Hanover Gate, NW1 . . . 33 F5
Hanover Gate Mans,
    NW1 . . . . 55 F1
Hanover Pk, SE15 . . . . 172 C4
Hanover Pl, E3 . . . . 46 A5
    WC2 . . . . 87 F1
Sch Hanover Prim Sch,
    N1 . . . . 39 F2
Hanover Rd, NW10 . . . . 6 B5
Hanover Sq, W1 . . . . . . 85 F1
Hanover Steps, W2
    off St. Georges Flds . . 83 F1
Hanover St, W1 . . . . . . 85 F1
Hanover Ter, NW1 . . . . 33 F5
Hanover Ter Ms, NW1 . 33 F5
Hanover Yd, N1 . . . . 39 F2
Hansard Ms, W14 . . . . 107 D1
Hans Cres, SW1 . . . . . 112 A3
Hanson St, W1 . . . . 58 A3
Hans Pl, SW1 . . . . 112 B3
Hans Rd, SW3 . . . . 112 A3
Hans St, SW1 . . . . 112 B4
Hanway Pl, W1 . . . . 58 C5
Hanway St, W1 . . . . 58 C5
Harads Pl, E1 . . . . 93 D3
Harben Rd, NW6 . . . . . . 10 B3
Harbet Rd, W2 . . . . 55 D4
Sch Harbinger Prim Sch,
    E14 . . . . 153 E1
Harbinger Rd, E14 . . . 153 E1
Harbledown Rd, SW6 . 160 C3
Harbord Cl, SE5 . . . . . 170 C5
Harbord St, SW6 . . . . . 158 C3
Harbour Av, SW10 . . . 162 B3
Harbour Ex Sq, E14 . . 125 F2
Harbour Reach, SW6
    off The Boulevard . . 162 B4
Harbour Yd, SW10 . . . 162 B4
Harcourt St, W1 . . . . . . 55 F4
Harcourt Ter, SW10 . . 137 F3
Hardens Manorway,
    SE7 . . . . 130 C4
Harders Rd, SE15 . . . . 173 E5
Harding Cl, SE17 . . . . 146 A4
Hardinge St, E1 . . . . . . 94 B1

Hardman Rd, SE7 . . . . 157 E2
Hardwicke Ho, E3
    off Bromley High St . . 47 E4
Hardwicke Ms, WC1 . . . 38 B5
Hardwick St, EC1 . . . . . 39 D5
Hardwidge St, SE1 . . . 119 E1
Hardy Av, E16 . . . . 101 D4
Hardy Cl, SE16 . . . . . . 123 D2
Hardy Rd, SE3 . . . . 156 B5
Hare & Billet Rd, SE3 . 178 C4
Harebell Dr, E6 . . . . 77 D4
Hare Ct, EC4 . . . . 88 C1
Harecourt Rd, N1 . . . . . 18 A1
Hare Marsh, E2 . . . . 64 C1
Hare Pl, EC4 . . . . 89 D1
Hare Row, E2 . . . . 43 F2
Hare St, SE18 . . . . 133 D4
Hare Wk, N1 . . . . 41 F3
Harewood Av, NW1 . . . 55 F2
Harewood Pl, W1 . . . . . 85 F1
Harewood Row, NW1 . . 55 F3
Harford St, E1 . . . . 67 E2
Harkness Ho, E1
    off Christian St 93 D1
Harleyford Rd, SE11 . . 144 A4
Harleyford St, SE11 . . 144 C5
Harley Gdns, SW10 . . 138 B3
Harley Gro, E3 . . . . 46 B4
Harley Pl, W1 . . . . 57 E4
Harley Rd, NW3 . . . . . . 11 D4
Harley St, W1 . . . . 57 E4
H Harley St Clinic, The,
    W1 . . . . 57 E3
Harling Ct, SW11 . . . . 164 A5
Harlinger St, SE18 . . . 131 E3
Harman Cl, SE1
    off Avondale Sq 148 C3
Harmony Pl, SE1 . . . . . 148 B2
Harmood Gro, NW1 . . . 13 E3
Harmood Pl, NW1 . . . . 13 E3
Harmood St, NW1 . . . . 13 E2
Harmsworth Ms, SE11 . 117 E4
Harmsworth St, SE17 . 145 E2
Harold Est, SE1 . . . . . 119 F4
Harold Laski Ho, EC1 . 39 E5
Harold Pl, SE11
    off Kennington La . . 144 C3
Harp All, EC4 . . . . 61 E5
Harper Rd, E6 . . . . 104 A1
    SE1 . . . . 118 A3
Harp La, EC3 . . . . 91 E3
Sch Harpley Sch, E1 . . . . 66 C1
Harpley Sq, E1 . . . . 44 B5
Harpsden St, SW11 . . 164 C4
Harpur Ms, WC1 . . . . . 60 A3
Harpur St, WC1 . . . . . . 60 A3
Harrap St, E14 . . . . 98 B2
Harrier Way, E6 . . . . . . 76 B4
Harriet Cl, E8 . . . . 20 C5
Harriet St, SW1 . . . . . 112 B2
Harriet Wk, SW1 . . . . . 112 B2
Harrington Ct, W10
    off Dart St 30 A4

Harrington Gdns, SW7. **137** F1
Harrington Ho, NW1... **36** A4
Harrington Rd, SW7 .. **110** B5
Harrington Sq, NW1 ... **36** A3
Harrington St, NW1 ... **36** A4
Harrington Way, SE18. **131** D3
Harriott Cl, SE10..... **156** A1
SchHarris Acad Bermondsey,
    SE16 .... **120** B5
Harrison St, WC1 ..... **37** F5
Harris St, SE5 .... **171** D2
★ Harrods, SW1 ...... **112** A3
Harrowby St, W1 ..... **55** F5
Harrowgate Rd, E9 .... **23** E2
Harrow La, E14 .... **98** A3
Harrow Pl, E1 .... **63** F5
Harrow Rd, NW10 ..... **28** C5
    W2 .... **53** E4
    W9 .... **52** C2
    W10 .... **51** F1
SchHarry Gosling Prim Sch,
    E1 .... **93** D1
Hartfield Ter, E3 ..... **47** D3
Hartington Rd, E16 .. **101** E1
    SW8 .... **167** E2
Hartismere Rd, SW6.. **160** B1
Hartlake Rd, E9 ...... **23** D2
Hartland Rd, NW1 .... **13** E3
    NW6 .... **30** A2
Hartlepool Ct, E16 ... **105** F5
Hartley Ho, SE1
    off Longfield Est.... **120** B5
Hartley St, E2 .... **44** B4
Hartmann Rd, E16 ... **103** D4
Harton St, SE8....... **176** C3
Hartopp Pt, SW6
    off Pellant Rd...... **159** F1
Hartshorn All, EC3 .... **91** F1
Hartshorn Gdns, E6 ... **76** C1
Harts La, SE14....... **175** E2
Hart St, EC3......... **91** F2
Hartwell St, E8 ...... **20** A1
Harvey Rd, SE5...... **170** C3
Harvey St, N1 .... **41** D1
Harvington Wk, E8 .... **21** D3
Harvist Rd, NW6 ..... **29** D4
Harwood Rd, SW6.... **161** D2
Harwood Ter, SW6 ... **161** E3
Hascombe Ter, SE5... **170** C5
Hasker St, SW3 ...... **111** F5
Haslam Cl, N1....... **17** D3
Haslam St, SE15..... **172** B2
Hassard St, E2 .... **42** B3
Hassendean Rd, SE3 . **157** E5
Hassett Rd, E9 .... **23** D1
Hastings Cl, SE15 .... **172** C2
Hastings St, WC1 .... **37** E5
Hat & Mitre Ct, EC1 .. **61** F2
Hatcham Ms Business
    Cen, SE14 .... **175** D3
Hatcham Pk Ms, SE14. **175** D3
Hatcham Pk Rd, SE14. **175** D3
Hatcham Rd, SE15 ... **150** A5

Hatchers Ms, SE1 .... **119** F2
Hatcliffe St, SE10 .... **156** A2
Hatfield Cl, SE14..... **174** C2
Hatfields, SE1 .... **89** D4
Hatherley Gdns, E6 ... **75** D1
Hatherley Gro, W2 .... **53** E5
Hatherley St, SW1 ... **142** B1
Hathorne Cl, SE15 ... **173** F5
Hatteraick St, SE16 .. **122** B1
Hatton Gdn, EC1...... **61** D3
Hatton Ho, E1........ **93** D2
Hatton Pl, EC1....... **61** D2
Hatton Row, NW8..... **55** D2
Hatton St, NW8...... **55** D2
Hatton Wall, EC1 ..... **60** C3
Haul Rd, NW1 .... **37** E2
Haunch of Venison Yd,
    W1 .... **85** E1
Havannah St, E14.... **125** D2
Havelock St, N1 ...... **15** F5
Havelock Ter, SW8 ... **165** E1
Haven Ms, N1 .... **17** D4
Haven St, NW1 .... **13** E4
Haverfield Rd, E3 ..... **45** E4
Havering St, E1....... **94** C1
Haverstock Pl, N1
    off Haverstock St **39** F4
SchHaverstock Sch,
    NW3 .... **12** C2
Haverstock St, N1..... **39** F3
Havil St, SE5 .... **171** D4
Hawes St, N1 .... **17** F4
Hawgood St, E3 ...... **69** D4
Hawke Pl, SE16...... **123** D1
Hawke Twr, SE14 .... **151** E5
Hawkridge, NW5...... **13** D1
Hawkshead, NW1..... **36** A4
Hawks Ms, SE10 .... **178** B2
Hawksmoor Cl, E6 ... **75** E5
Hawksmoor Ms, E1... **93** E2
Hawksmoor St, W6... **135** D5
Hawkstone Est, SE16. **150** B1
Hawkstone Rd, SE16 . **150** B1
Hawkwell Wk, N1 ..... **18** B5
Hawley Cres, NW1 .... **13** F4
SchHawley Inf Sch,
    NW1 .... **13** F4
Hawley Ms, NW1 ..... **13** E3
Hawley Rd, NW1..... **13** F3
Hawley St, NW1 ...... **13** E4
Hawthorn Av, E3 ..... **24** A5
Hawthorne Cl, N1..... **19** E5
Hawthorn Wk, W10 ... **51** E1
Hawtrey Rd, NW3..... **11** E4
Hay Cl, E15 .... **27** F3
Hay Currie St, E14.... **69** F5
Hayday Rd, E16 ...... **72** C3
Haydens Pl, W11 ..... **52** A5
Haydon St, EC3...... **92** A2
Haydon Wk, E1....... **92** B1
Hayes Pl, NW1 .... **55** F2
Hayfield Pas, E1...... **66** B2
Hayfield Yd, E1....... **66** B2
Hay Hill, W1 .... **85** F3
Hayles St, SE11...... **117** E5
Hayman St, N1....... **17** F4
Haymarket, SW1...... **86** C3

Haymarket Arc, SW1 .. **86** C3
Haymerle Rd, SE15 .. **148** C5
SchHaymerle Sch,
    SE15............ **148** C5
Hayne St, EC1........ **61** F3
★ Hay's Galleria, SE1 . **91** E5
Hay's La, SE1 .... **91** E5
Hay's Ms, W1 .... **85** E3
Hay St, E2 .... **43** D1
Hayton Cl, E8 .... **20** B2
★ Hayward Gall, SE1.. **88** B4
Hayward's Pl, EC1 .... **61** E2
Hazel Ho, NW3
    off Maitland Pk Rd... **12** B1
Hazelmere Rd, NW6 .... **8** B5
Hazel Rd, NW10 ...... **28** A4
Hazel Way, SE1...... **120** A5
Hazlebury Rd, SW6... **161** E5
Hazlewood Cres, W10 . **51** F2
Hazlewood Twr, W10 . **51** F2
Hazlitt Ms, W14 ..... **107** E4
Hazlitt Rd, W14 ..... **107** E4
Headfort Pl, SW1 .... **113** D2
Headlam St, E1....... **65** F2
Head's Ms, W11 ...... **80** C1
Head St, E1 .... **94** C1
Heald St, SE14 ...... **176** C3
Healey St, NW1...... **13** E2
Hearn's Bldgs, SE17.. **147** D1
Hearnshaw St, E14.... **67** E4
Hearn St, EC2 .... **63** F2
H Heart Hosp, The, W1. **57** D4
Heathcock Ct, WC2
    off Exchange Ct **87** F3
Heathcote Pt, E9 ..... **22** C2
Heathcote St, WC1 .... **60** A1
Heather Cl, E6........ **105** E1
CollHeatherley's Sch of
    Fine Art, SW10 .... **162** B2
Heather Wk, W10 ..... **51** F1
Heathfield Cl, E16.... **74** C3
Heathfield Pk, NW2 .... **6** A2
Heathfield St, W11 .... **79** E3
Heathmans Rd, SW6 . **160** B4
Heathway, SE3....... **180** C2
Hebden Ct, E2........ **42** A1
Heckfield Pl, SW6 ... **160** C2
Heckford St, E1....... **95** D2
Heddon St, W1 .... **86** A2
Hedgers Gro, E9 ..... **23** E2
Hedger St, SE11...... **117** E5
Hedingham Cl, N1 .... **18** A4
Heiron St, SE17...... **145** F5
Helena Pl, E9........ **43** F1
Helena Sq, SE16 ..... **95** E3
Helen's Pl, E2........ **44** A4
Helen St, SE18 ...... **133** F5
Hellings St, E1 .... **93** D5
Helmet Row, EC1 ..... **62** B1
Helmsley Pl, E8....... **21** E4
Helsinki Sq, SE16 ... **123** F3
Hemans St, SW8..... **167** D1
Hemingford Rd, N1 ... **38** B1
Hemming St, E1 ...... **65** D2
Hemp Wk, SE17 ..... **119** D5
Hemstal Rd, NW6 ..... **8** C3
Hemsworth Ct, N1 .... **41** E1

Hemsworth St, N1 .... **41** E2
Hemus Pl, SW3 .... **139** F3
Hen & Chicken Ct, EC4 . **88** C1
Henderson Dr, NW8 ... **54** C1
Hendre Rd, SE1...... **147** F1
Heneage La, EC3...... **91** F1
Heneage St, E1....... **64** B3
Henley Cl, SE16 off St.
   Marychurch St..... **122** A1
Henley Dr, SE1 ...... **120** B5
Henley Prior, N1
   off Collier St........ **38** A3
Henley Rd, E16...... **132** B1
   NW10 .... **6** B5
Henley St, SW11..... **165** D5
Henniker Ms, SW3 ... **138** C4
Henning St, SW11.... **163** E4
Henrietta Cl, SE8 .... **153** D4
Henrietta Ms, WC1 ... **59** F1
Henrietta Pl, W1..... **85** E1
Henrietta St, WC2.... **87** F2
Henriques St, E1...... **65** D5
Henry Addlington Cl,
   E6 .... **77** E4
SchHenry Compton
   Sec Sch, SW6 ..... **159** E3
Henry Dickens Ct, W11. **79** D4
SchHenry Fawcett Prim Sch,
   SE11 .... **144** C4
Henry Wise Ho, SW1
   off Vauxhall Br Rd . . **142** B1
Henshall Pt, E3....... **47** E4
Henshall St, N1....... **19** D2
Henshaw St, SE17 ... **118** C5
Hensley Pt, E9 .... **23** D2
Henstridge Pl, NW8 ... **33** E2
Henty Cl, SW11...... **163** F2
Hepscott Rd, E9 ..... **24** C2
Hepworth Ct, SW1 ... **141** D3
Herald's Pl, SE11 .... **117** E5
Herald St, E2........ **65** F1
Herbal Hill, EC1....... **61** D2
Herbert Cres, SW1 ... **112** B3
Herbert Morrison Ho,
   SW6............. **136** A5
SchHerbert Morrison
   Prim Sch, SW8 .... **167** E2
Herbert St, NW5..... **12** C1
Herbrand St, WC1..... **59** E1
Hercules Rd, SE1 .... **116** B4
Hereford Ho, NW6.... **31** D3
Hereford Ms, W2...... **81** D1
Hereford Pl, SE14 .... **176** A1
Hereford Retreat,
   SE15 .... **148** C5
Hereford Rd, E3 ...... **46** B3
   W2................ **53** D5
Hereford Sq, SW7 ... **138** B1
Hereford St, E2....... **64** C1
SchHereward Ho Sch,
   NW3 .... **11** E3
Hermes Cl, W9 ...... **52** C2
Hermes St, N1........ **38** C3
SchHermitage Prim Sch,
   E1 .... **93** D5
Hermitage St, W2.... **54** C4
Hermitage Wall, E1 ... **93** D5

Hermitage Waterside,
   E1 .... **92** C4
Hermit Pl, NW6...... **31** E1
Hermit Rd, E16...... **72** A3
Hermit St, EC1....... **39** E4
Heron Pl, SE16 ...... **95** F4
Heron Quay, E14 .... **96** C5
DLRHeron Quays **97** D5
Herrick St, SW1..... **115** D5
Herries St, W10..... **29** F3
Herringham Rd, SE7. . **130** B4
Hertford Pl, W1...... **58** A2
Hertford Rd, N1 ..... **19** F5
Hertford St, W1...... **85** E4
Hertsmere Rd, E14.... **96** C3
Hervey Rd, SE3...... **181** F3
Hesketh Pl, W11..... **79** E3
Hesper Ms, SW5 .... **137** E2
Hesperus Cres, E14 .. **153** E1
Hessel St, E1........ **93** D1
Hestercombe Av, SW6. **159** F5
Hester Rd, SW11..... **163** E2
Hestia Ho, SE1
   off Royal Oak Yd . . . **119** E2
Heston St, SE14 ..... **176** C3
Hevelius Cl, SE10 .... **156** A2
Hewer St, W10 ...... **51** D3
Hewett St, EC2 ...... **63** F2
Hewison St, E3...... **46** B2
Hewlett Rd, E3 ...... **45** F2
Heyford Av, SW8..... **167** E5
Heyford Ter, SW8
   off Heyford Av **167** F1
Heygate St, SE17 ... **146** A1
Heylyn Sq, E3 .... **46** B4
UniHeythrop Coll, W8 . **109** E3
Hickin St, E14....... **126** A3
Hickman Cl, E16..... **74** C4
Hicks St, SE8........ **151** E2
Hide, E6 .... **77** D5
Hide Pl, SW1 .... **142** C1
Hides St, N7 .... **16** B1
Hide Twr, SW1...... **142** C1
High Br, SE10 .... **155** D3
High Br Wf, SE10 .... **154** C3
⟳Highbury &
   Islington.......... **17** D2
⟴Highbury &
   Islington.......... **17** D2
Highbury Cor, N5..... **17** E1
Highbury Gro, N5..... **17** F1
Highbury New Pk, N5 . **17** F1
Highbury Pl, N5 ..... **17** E1
Highbury Sta Rd, N1 . . **17** D2
Highcombe, SE7 ..... **157** F4
Highfield Ms, NW6 ... **9** E3
High Holborn, WC1... **59** F5
Highlever Rd, W10 ... **50** B4
High Meads Rd, E16.. **74** C5
Highmore Rd, SE3 ... **179** F1
Highshore Rd, SE15 . **172** B5
SchHighshore Sch,
   SE15 .... **172** B4
High St, E15 .... **48** A2
⟴High Street
   Kensington........ **109** E2
High Timber St, EC4. . **90** A2

Highway, The, E1..... **93** D3
   E14 .... **93** D3
Hilary Cl, SW6....... **161** E1
Hilda Rd, E16 .... **71** F2
Hilda Ter, SW9 ...... **169** D5
Hildyard Rd, SW6 ... **137** D4
Hiley Rd, NW10 ..... **28** A3
Hilgrove Rd, NW6.... **10** B4
Hillbeck Cl, SE15.... **174** A1
Hillcroft Rd, E6 ..... **77** E3
Hillery Cl, SE17...... **147** D1
Hill Fm Rd, W10 ..... **50** B3
Hillgate Pl, W8 ...... **80** C4
Hillgate St, W8 ...... **80** C4
SchHill Ho Int Jun Sch,
   SW1............. **112** B4
Hilliards Ct, E1 ...... **93** F4
Hillingdon St, SE17... **145** F5
Hillman Dr, W10..... **50** B2
Hillman St, E8....... **21** F2
Hill Rd, NW8 .... **32** B3
Hillside Cl, NW8 ..... **31** F2
Hillsleigh Rd, W8 ... **80** B4
Hills Pl, W1 .... **86** A1
Hill St, W1 .... **85** D4
Hilltop Rd, NW6 ..... **9** D3
Hillyard St, SW9 .... **168** B4
RivHilton Docklands
   Nelson Dock Pier . . . **96** A4
Hind Ct, EC4........ **89** D1
Hinde Ms, W1
   off Marylebone La . . . **57** D5
Hinde St, W1........ **57** D5
Hind Gro, E14....... **96** C1
Hindmarsh Cl, E1..... **93** D2
Hindon Ct, SW1...... **114** A5
Hippodrome Ms, W11 . **79** E3
Hippodrome Pl, W11 . **79** F3
Hirst Ct, SW1....... **141** E3
Hitchin Sq, E3....... **45** F2
Hithe Gro, SE16 .... **122** B4
★ H.M.S. Belfast, SE1 . **91** F4
★ H.M.S. President,
   EC4 .... **89** D3
★ H.M. Treasury, SW1. **115** E1
Hobart Pl, SW1 ..... **113** E3
Hobbs Pl Est, N1...... **41** E5
Hobday St, E14...... **69** E5
Hobsons Pl, E1 ...... **64** C3
Hobury St, SW10 ... **138** B5
Hocker St, E2........ **42** A5
Hockett Cl, SE8 .... **123** F5
Hodister Cl, SE5 .... **170** B2
Hodnet Gro, SE16... **122** C5
Hoffman Sq, N1
   off Chart St **41** D4
Hofland Rd, W14 .... **107** D3
Hogan Ms, W2....... **54** C3
Hogarth Cl, E16 ..... **74** C3
Hogarth Ct, EC3 ..... **91** F2
Hogarth Pl, SW5 .... **137** E1
Hogarth Rd, SW5 ... **137** E1
Hogshead Pas, E1 .... **93** F3

Holbeck Row, SE15...**173** D2
Holbein Ms, SW1.....**140** C2
Holbein Pl, SW1......**140** C1
HOLBORN, WC2.......**60** A5
◆Holborn...........**59** F4
Holborn, EC1........**60** C4
Holborn Circ, EC1 .....**61** D4
🏛Holborn Coll, SE7..**131** D5
Holborn Pl, WC1......**60** A4
Holborn Rd, E13......**73** E2
Holborn Viaduct, EC1..**61** D4
Holcroft Rd, E9 ......**22** B3
Holden Pt, E15.......**27** D1
Holegate St, SE7.....**130** C4
Holford Ho, SE16
  off Manor Est......**149** E1
Holford Ms, WC1......**38** C3
Holford Pl, WC1......**38** B4
Holford St, WC1......**38** C4
Holford Yd, WC1......**38** B3
Holland Gdns, W14 ..**107** F3
Holland Gro, SW9....**169** D2
★ Holland Pk, W8 ...**108** A1
◆Holland Park **80** A5
Holland Pk, W11......**79** F5
Holland Pk Av, W11 ...**107** F5
🏫Holland Pk Comm Sch,
  W8...............**108** B1
Holland Pk Gdns, W14..**79** E5
Holland Pk Ms, W11...**79** F5
Holland Pk Rd, W14...**108** A4
Holland Pk Rbt, W11..**107** D1
Holland Pas, N1 ......**18** A5
Holland Pl, W8 ....**109** E1
Holland Ri Ho, SW9 ...**168** B2
Holland Rd, E15 .....**49** F4
  W14 ....**107** D1
Holland St, SE1 ......**89** F4
  W8 ....**109** D2
Holland Town Est, SW9
  off Mandela St....**169** D2
Holland Vil Rd, W14...**107** E1
Holland Wk, W8 ......**80** B5
Hollen St, W1 ....**58** C5
Holles St, W1.........**57** F5
Holloway Rd, N7 .....**17** D1
Hollybush Gdns, E2 ...**43** F4
Hollybush Pl, E2......**43** F4
Holly Ct, SE10.......**128** B4
Hollydale Rd, SE15...**174** A4
Hollydene, SE15......**173** E3
Holly Gro, SE15......**172** B5
Holly Ms, SW10.....**138** B3
Hollymount Cl, SE10 .**178** A3
Holly St, E8 ....**20** B3
Hollywood Ms, SW10.**138** A4
Hollywood Rd, SW10.**138** A3
Holman Ho, E2
  off Roman Rd......**44** C4
Holmead Rd, SW6....**161** F2
Holmefield Ct, NW3 ...**11** F1
Holmes Pl, SW10 ....**138** B4
Holmes Rd, NW5......**13** E1

Holmes Ter, SE1 .....**116** C1
Holms St, E2 ....**42** C2
Holmwood Vil, SE7...**157** D2
Holsworthy Sq, WC1...**60** B2
Holton St, E1.........**66** C1
Holt Rd, E16 ....**103** F5
🏫Holy Cross RC Prim Sch,
  SW6.............**160** C3
🏫Holy Family RC Prim
  Sch, E14 ....**97** C3
Holyhead Cl, E3 ......**47** D5
  E6 ....**76** A3
Holyoake Ct, SE16 ...**123** F1
Holyoak Rd, SE11....**117** E5
Holyport Rd, SW6....**158** B1
Holyrood Ms, E16....**101** D4
Holyrood St, SE1......**91** D3
🏫Holy Trinity & St. Silas
  C of E Prim Sch,
  NW1 ....**13** E3
🏫Holy Trinity C of E
  Prim Sch, E8......**20** A2
  NW3 ....**10** B2
  Jun, SW1........**112** C5
  Inf, SW3..........**112** B5
Holywell Cl, SE3 ....**157** D4
  SE16 ....**149** F2
Holywell La, EC2......**63** F1
Holywell Row, EC2....**63** E2
Homefield St, N1 .....**41** E3
★ Home Office, SW1 .**115** D4
Homer Dr, E14 ......**152** C1
Home Rd, SW11 ....**163** E5
Homer Rd, E9 ....**23** F2
Homer Row, W1 .....**55** F4
Homer St, W1 ....**55** F4
◈Homerton........**22** C1
Homerton Ter, E9......**22** B1
Homestead Rd, SW6..**160** A2
Honduras St, EC1 .....**62** A1
Honey La, EC2........**90** B1
Honeyman Cl, NW6 ....**6** C3
Honiton Rd, NW6 .....**30** A2
Hood Ct, EC4.........**89** D1
Hooks Cl, SE15 .....**173** F4
Hooper Rd, E16......**101** D1
Hooper's Ct, SW3 ...**112** A2
Hooper St, E1 ....**92** C2
Hope Cl, N1 ....**18** B1
Hopedale Rd, SE7....**157** E5
Hopefield Av, NW6.....**29** F2
Hopetown St, E1......**64** B3
Hopewell St, SE5 ...**171** D2
Hopewell Yd, SE5....**171** D2
Hope Wf, SE16 *off St.*
  Marychurch St...**122** A1
Hop Gdns, WC2......**87** E3
Hopgood St, W12....**106** B1
Hopkinsons Pl, NW1...**12** B5
Hopkins St, W1.......**86** B1
Hopping La, N1.......**17** F2
Hop St, SE10........**128** B5
Hopton Rd, SE18 ....**133** F3
Hopton's Gdns, SE1 ...**89** F4
Hopton St, SE1 ......**89** F4
Hopwood Rd, SE17..**147** D4
Hopwood Wk, E8 .....**21** D3

Horace Bldg, SW8
  off Queenstown Rd .**165** E1
Horatio Ct, SE16
  off Rotherhithe St ...**94** B5
Horatio Pl, E14......**126** B1
Horatio St, E2 ....**42** C3
Horbury Cres, W11....**80** C3
Horbury Ms, W11 ....**80** B3
Horder Rd, SW6 .....**159** F4
Horizon Way, SE7...**157** F1
Horle Wk, SE5 ......**169** E5
Hormead Rd, W9 .....**52** A2
Hornbeam Cl, SE11...**116** C5
Hornbeam Ho, NW3 ...**12** B1
Hornbeam Sq, E3 .....**24** A5
Hornblower Cl, SE16 .**123** E5
Hornby Cl, NW3 ......**11** D3
Horn La, SE10 ....**156** C1
Horn Link Way, SE10 .**128** C5
Hornshay St, SE15 ...**150** B5
Hornton Pl, W8......**109** D2
Hornton St, W8......**109** D1
Horse & Dolphin Yd,
  W1..............**87** D2
Horseferry Pl, SE10 ..**154** A5
Horseferry Rd, E14....**95** E2
  SW1.............**114** C4
★ Horse Guards Av, SW1. **87** E5
★ Horse Guards Par,
  SW1.............**87** D5
Horse Guards Rd, SW1. **87** D5
Horse Leaze, E6 .....**77** D5
Horselydown La, SE1 .**120** A1
Horsemongers Ms,
  SE1.............**118** B2
Horse Ride, SW1.....**86** B5
Horseshoe Cl, E14 ...**154** A2
Horse Shoe Ct, EC1
  off Brewhouse Yd....**61** F1
Horse Yd, N1.........**17** F5
Horsleydown Old Stairs,
  SE1 ....**92** A5
Horsley St, SE17.....**146** C4
Hortensia Rd, SW10..**138** A5
Horton Ho, SW8 .....**168** A1
Horton Rd, E8 ....**21** E1
Hosier La, EC1........**61** E4
Hoskins Cl, E16......**74** B5
Hoskins St, SE10.....**155** D3
🏥 Hospital of St. John &
  St. Elizabeth, NW8...**32** C3
Hotham St, E15 .....**27** E5
Hothfield Pl, SE16....**122** B4
Hotspur St, SE11.....**144** C2
Houghton Cl, E8 .....**20** B2
Houghton St, WC2 ....**88** B1
Houndsditch, EC3.....**63** F5
Houseman Way, SE5 .**171** D2
★ Houses of Parliament,
  SW1.............**115** F2
Howard Bldg, SW8 ...**141** E5
Howell Wk, SE1......**145** F1
Howick Pl, SW1......**114** B4
Howie St, SW11 ....**163** E2
Howitt Cl, NW3 ......**11** F1
Howitt Rd, NW3......**11** E1
Howland Est, SE16...**122** B3

Howland Ms E, W1 . . . . 58 B3
Howland St, W1 . . . . . . 58 A3
Howland Way, SE16. . . 123 F2
Howley Pl, W2 . . . . 54 B3
Hows St, E2. . . . . 42 A2
HOXTON, N1 . . . . 41 E3
Hoxton Mkt, N1 . . . . . . 41 E5
Hoxton Sq, N1. . . . . . . 41 E5
Hoxton St, N1 . . . . 41 F5
Hoyland Cl, SE15 . . . . 173 E1
Hoy St, E16 . . . . 100 A1
★ H.Q.S. Wellington,
    Master Mariners' Hall,
    WC2 . . . . 88 C2
Hubbard St, E15 . . . . . . 49 E1
Huddart St, E3 . . . . 68 B3
Huddleston Cl, E2. . . . . 44 A2
Hudson Ct, E14
    off Maritime Quay . . 153 D2
Hudson's Pl, SW1 . . . . 113 F5
Huggin Ct, EC4 . . . . . . 90 B2
Huggin Hill, EC4 . . . . . 90 B2
Hugh Dalton Av, SW6. 136 A5
Hugh Gaitskell Cl,
    SW6 . . . . 136 A5
Hugh Ms, SW1. . . . . . 141 F1
Sch Hugh Myddelton
    Prim Sch, EC1 . . . . 39 D5
Hugh St, SW1 . . . . 141 F1
Huguenot Pl, E1 . . . . . . 64 B3
Hullbridge Ms, N1 . . . . 18 C5
Hull Cl, SE16 . . . . 123 D1
Hull St, EC1 . . . . 40 A5
Hulme Pl, SE1 . . . . 118 B2
Humber Dr, W10. . . . . . 50 C2
Humber Rd, SE3 . . . . . 156 A4
Humbolt Rd, W6. . . . . 135 E5
Hume Ter, E16 . . . . 74 A4
Humphrey St, SE1 . . . 148 A2
Hungerford Br, SE1. . . . 87 F4
    WC2. . . . . 87 F4
Sch Hungerford Prim Sch,
    N7 . . . . 15 D1
Hungerford Rd, N7. . . . 15 D1
Hungerford St, E1. . . . . 65 F5
Hunsdon Rd, SE14 . . . 174 C1
Hunslett St, E2 . . . . . . 44 B3
Hunt Cl, W11 . . . . 79 D4
Hunter Cl, SE1 . . . . . . 119 D4
Hunter St, WC1 . . . . . . 59 F1
Huntingdon St, E16 . . 100 B1
    N1 . . . . 16 A4
Huntley St, WC1 . . . . . 58 B2
Hunton St, E1 . . . . 64 C2
Hunt's Cl, SE3 . . . . 181 D5
Hunt's Ct, WC2 . . . . . . 87 D3
Hunts La, E15 . . . . 48 A3
Huntsman St, SE17 . . 147 D1
Huntsworth Ms, NW1. . 56 A2
Hurdwick Pl, NW1
    off Harrington Sq . . 36 A2
Hurley Cres, SE16. . . . 123 D1
Hurley Ho, SE11 . . . . . 145 D1
Uni Huron Uni USA in
    London, WC1 . . . . . 59 E3
Hurry Cl, E15. . . . . 27 F4

Hurstway Wk, W11. . . . 79 D2
Huson Cl, NW3 . . . . 11 E3
Hutchings St, E14. . . . 124 C2
Hutchins Cl, E15. . . . . . 26 B4
Hutton St, EC4 . . . . 89 D1
Huxley St, W10. . . . . . . 29 E5
Hyde La, SW11 . . . . . . 163 E3
★ Hyde Park, W2 . . . . . 83 E4
Hyde Pk, SW7 . . . . 83 E4
    W1. . . . . 83 E4
✆ Hyde Park Corner . 112 C1
Hyde Pk Cor, W1. . . . . 113 D1
Hyde Pk Cres, W2. . . . 83 E1
Hyde Pk Gdns, W2 . . 83 D2
Hyde Pk Gdns Ms, W2 . 83 D2
Hyde Pk Gate, SW7 . . 110 B2
Hyde Pk Gate Ms,
    SW7 . . . . 110 B2
Hyde Pk Pl, W2 . . . . . . 83 F2
Hyde Pk Sq, W2 . . . . . 83 E1
Hyde Pk Sq Ms, W2 . . 83 E1
Hyde Pk St, W2. . . . . . 83 E1
Hyderabad Way, E15. . 27 E3
Hyde Rd, N1 . . . . 41 D1
Hydes Pl, N1. . . . . 17 E3
Hyde St, SE8 . . . . 152 C5
Hyde Vale, SE10 . . . . . 178 B2
Hyndman St, SE15 . . . 149 E5
Hyperion Ho, E3 . . . . . . 45 E3
Hyson Rd, SE16 . . . . . 149 F2

Uni Imperial Coll London,
    St. Mary's Campus,
    W2 . . . . 55 D5
    South Kensington Campus,
    SW7 . . . . 110 C3
Imperial Coll Rd, SW7. 110 C4
Imperial Ct, NW8 . . . . . 33 F2
Imperial Cres, SW6. . . 162 A5
Imperial Rd, SW6 . . . . 161 F3
Imperial Sq, SW6 . . . . 161 F3
Imperial St, E3 . . . . 48 A5
★ Imperial War Mus,
    SE1 . . . . 117 D4
Imperial Wf, SW6 . . . . 162 A5
Coll Inchbald Sch of Design,
    Garden Design Faculty,
    SW1 . . . . 141 F1
    Interior Design Faculty,
    SW1 . . . . 112 C5
Indescon Ct, E14 . . . . 125 D2
Indiana Bldg, SE13
    off Deals Gateway. . 177 D4
India Pl, WC2. . . . . 88 A2
India St, EC3 . . . . 92 A1
Indigo Ms, E14 . . . . 98 B1
Ingal Rd, E13. . . . . 72 C2
Ingate Pl, SW8 . . . . . . 165 F4
Ingestre Ct, W1
    off Ingestre Pl 86 B2
Ingestre Pl, W1. . . . . . . 86 B1
Inglebert St, EC1. . . . . . 38 C4
Ingleborough St, SW9. 168 C5
Ingle Ms, EC1 . . . . 38 C4
Inglesham Wk, E9. . . . . 24 B1
Ingleside Gro, SE3 . . . 156 B5
Inglethorpe St, SW6 . . 158 C3
Ingleton St, SW9. . . . . 168 C5
Inglewood Cl, E14 . . . 125 D5
Inglis St, SE5. . . . . 169 F4
Ingram Cl, SE11 . . . . . 116 B5
Ingram Ho, E3. . . . . 45 E2
Inigo Pl, WC2. . . . . 87 E2
Inkerman Rd, NW5 . . . . 13 E1
Inkerman Ter, W8
    off Allen St. 109 D4
Inner Circle, NW1 . . . . 34 C5
Inner Temple La, EC4 . . 88 C1
Innes St, SE15 . . . . . . 171 F1
Insley Ho, E3 off Bow Rd. 47 E4
★ Institute of Contemporary
    Arts (I.C.A.), SW1 . . 87 D2
Uni Institute of Ed, WC1. 59 D2
Sch International Comm
    Sch, NW1. . . . . 57 D2
Inver Ct, W2 . . . . 81 F1
Inverine Rd, SE7 . . . . . 157 F3
Inverness Gdns, W8 . . 81 E5
Inverness Ms, W2 . . . . 81 F2
Inverness Pl, W2. . . . . . 81 F2
Inverness St, NW1 . . . . 13 E5
Inverness Ter, W2. . . . . 81 F2
Invicta Cl, E3. . . . . 69 D4
Invicta Plaza, SE1 . . . . 89 E4

I

Sch Ian Mikardo High Sch,
    E3 . . . . 47 F5
Ibbotson Av, E16 . . . . . 72 B5
Ibbott St, E1 . . . . 66 B1
Ibex Ho, E15 . . . . 27 F1
Iceland Rd, E3. . . . . 47 D1
Iceland Wf, SE16. . . . . 123 E5
Iceni Ct, E3 . . . . 46 B1
Ice Wf, N1 . . . . 37 F2
Ice Wf Marina, N1
    off New Wf Rd 37 F2
Idaho Bldg, SE13
    off Deals Gateway. . 177 E4
Ida St, E14. . . . . 98 A1
Idol La, EC3 . . . . 91 E3
Idonia St, SE8 . . . . 176 B1
Ifield Rd, SW10 . . . . . . 137 F4
Ifor Evans Pl, E1 . . . . . . 67 D2
Ilbert St, W10 . . . . 29 D5
Ilchester Gdns, W2. . . . 81 E2
Ilchester Pl, W14 . . . . 108 A3
Sch Ilderton Prim Sch,
    SE16 . . . . 150 A3
Ilderton Rd, SE15 . . . . 150 A4
    SE16 . . . . 149 F2
Iliffe St, SE17. . . . . 145 F2
Iliffe Yd, SE17. . . . . 145 F2
Ilkley Rd, E16 . . . . 74 A4
Imber St, N1 . . . . 40 C1
Uni Imperial Coll London,
    Charing Cross Campus,
    W6. . . . . 134 C3

Ivy St, N1............**41** E2
Ixworth Pl, SW3 .....**139** E2

J

Jacaranda Gro, E8 ....**20** B4
Jack Clow Rd, E15 ....**49** F3
Jack Dash Way, E6....**75** E2
Jackman St, E8 ....**43** E1
Jackson Cl, E9........**22** B4
Sch Jack Taylor Sch,
  NW8 ....**10** A5
Jacob St, SE1........**120** B1
Jacob's Well Ms, W1...**57** D5
Jade Cl, E16.........**103** D1
Jago Wk, SE5........**170** C2
Sch Jamahiriya Sch,
  SW3...............**139** E4
Jamaica Rd, SE1......**120** B2
  SE16 ....**121** E3
Jamaica St, E1 ....**66** B5
James Clavell Sq,
  SE18 ....**133** F3
James Collins Cl, W9 ..**52** A3
James Ct, N1.........**18** B4
James Hammett Ho, E2.**42** B3
Jameson Ct, E2.......**44** A3
Jameson Ho, SE11
  off Glasshouse Wk..**144** A2
Jameson St, W8 ....**81** D4
James Riley Pt, E15....**26** B5
James St, W1 ....**57** D5
  WC2..............**87** F2
Jamestown Rd, NW1 ...**13** E5
Jamestown Way, E14...**99** D3
Sch James Wolfe Prim Sch,
  SE10 ....**178** A1
Jamuna Cl, E14.......**67** F4
Jane St, E1..........**65** E5
Janet St, E14........**125** D3
Janeway Pl, SE16.....**121** E2
Janeway St, SE16.....**121** D2
Jardine Rd, E1........**95** D2
Jarman Ho, E1 ....**66** A4
Jarrow Rd, SE16......**150** A1
Jasmine Sq, E3 ....**46** A1
Jason Ct, W1
  off Marylebone La ...**57** D5
Jasper Rd, E16 ......**103** D1
Jasper Wk, N1........**40** C4
Jay Ms, SW7 ....**110** B2
Jebb St, E3..........**47** D3
Jeffreys Pl, NW1 .....**14** A3
Jeffreys Rd, SW4....**167** E5
Jeffreys St, NW1 .....**13** F3
Jeffreys Wk, SW4....**167** E5
Coll Jeff Wooller Coll,
  WC1..............**59** F3
Jeger Av, E2 ....**42** A1
Jellicoe Ho, SW8
  off St. George Wf ...**143** E4
Jellicoe Rd, E13.......**73** D2
Jenkinson Ho, E2
  off Usk St..........**44** C4
Jenkins Rd, E13 ......**73** F2

Ivy Ct, SE16.........**149** D3
Ivy Rd, E16 ....**72** C5

Sch Invicta Prim Sch,
  SE3 ....**157** D5
Invicta Rd, SE3 .....**181** D1
Inville Rd, SE17......**147** D3
Inwen Ct, SE8 ....**151** F3
Inworth St, SW11 ....**163** A5
Inworth Wk, N1.......**18** A5
Ionian Bldg, E14.....**95** E2
Ion Sq, E2 ....**42** C3
Ireland Cl, E6........**76** A4
Ireland Yd, EC4.......**89** F1
Irene Rd, SW6 ....**160** C4
Ireton St, E3 ....**68** C1
Iris Cl, E6 ....**75** F3
Ironmonger La, EC2 ...**90** C1
Ironmonger Pas, EC1 ..**62** B5
Ironmonger Row, EC1 .**40** B5
Ironmongers Pl, E14 ..**153** D1
Ironside Cl, SE16......**122** C1
Iron Wks, E3 ....**24** C5
Irvine Cl, E14........**69** F3
Irving Ms, N1 ....**18** A2
Irving Rd, W14 ......**107** D3
Irving St, WC2 ....**87** D3
Irwell Est, SE16
  off Neptune St **122** A2
Isaac Way, SE1 ......**118** B1
Isabella Ms, N1.......**19** E1
Isabella St, SE1 ......**89** E5
Isabel St, SW9 ......**168** B3
Isambard Ms, E14 ...**126** B4
Isambard Pl, SE16 ....**94** B5
Sch Islamia Prim Sch,
  NW6...............**7** F5
DLR Island Gardens ...**154** A1
Island Rd, SE16......**150** C1
Island Row, E14 ......**96** A1
Islay Wk, N1 ....**18** B2
ISLINGTON, N1 ......**38** C1
Islington Grn, N1 .....**39** E1
Sch Islington Grn Sch,
  N1 ....**40** A1
Islington High St, N1 ..**39** D3
Islington Pk Ms, N1 ...**17** E3
Islington Pk St, N1 ...**17** D3
★ Ismaili Cen, SW7 ..**111** D5
Sch Italia Conti Acad of
  Thea Arts, EC1 ....**62** A2
Ivatt Pl, W14........**136** B3
Iveagh Cl, E9........**23** D5
Iverna Ct, W8 ....**109** D3
Iverna Gdns, W8.....**109** D3
Iverson Rd, NW6......**8** B2
Ives Rd, E16 ....**71** E4
Ives St, SW3 ....**111** F5
Ivimey St, E2........**43** D4
Ivor Pl, NW1 ....**56** A2
Ivor St, NW1 ....**14** A4
Ivybridge La, WC2 ....**87** F3
Ivychurch La, SE17...**148** A2
Ivy Cotts, E14........**97** F2

Jephson St, SE5 .....**170** C4
Jepson Ho, SW6
  off Pearscroft Rd ...**161** F4
Jerdan Pl, SW6 ......**161** D1
Jeremiah St, E14......**97** E1
Jermyn St, SW1......**86** A4
Jerningham Rd, SE14.**175** E3
Jerome Cres, NW8 ....**55** E1
Jerome St, E1 ....**64** A3
Jerrard St, N1 ....**41** F3
Jersey Ho, N1 ....**18** B2
Jersey Rd, E16 ......**74** A5
Jersey St, E2 ....**43** F5
Jerusalem Pas, EC1 ...**61** C2
Jervis Ct, W1 ....**85** F1
Jervis Rd, SW6 ......**136** B5
Jessel Ho, SW1
  off Page St........**115** D5
Jessop Sq, E14 ......**96** C5
Jethou Ho, N1
  off Nightingale Rd ...**18** B2
★ Jewel Twr (Houses of
  Parliament), SW1...**115** E3
★ Jewish Mus, NW1...**35** E1
Jewry St, EC3 ....**92** A1
Jigger Mast Ho, SE18.**132** B3
Jim Bradley Cl, SE18 .**133** D5
Jim Griffiths Ho, SW6
  off Clem Attlee Ct ..**136** B5
Joan St, SE1.........**89** E5
Jocelyn St, SE15 ....**172** C3
Jockey's Flds, WC1....**60** B3
Jodane St, SE8 ......**152** A1
Jodrell Rd, E3 ....**24** B5
Sch Johanna Prim Sch,
  SE1 ....**116** C2
Johanna St, SE1 .....**116** C2
John Adam St, WC2 ...**87** F4
John Aird Ct, W2 ....**54** B3
John Carpenter St, EC4.**89** E2
Sch John Donne Prim Sch,
  SE15 ....**173** E4
John Fearon Wk, W10 .**29** F4
John Felton Rd, SE16 .**120** C2
John Fisher St, E1.....**92** C2
Sch John F. Kennedy
  Post 16 (Beckton)
  Annexe, E16......**74** C3
Sch John F. Kennedy Sch,
  E15 ....**27** D5
John Harrison Ho, E1
  off Philpot St **65** F5
John Harrison Way,
  SE10 ....**128** A4
John Horner Ms, N1 ...**40** A2
John Islip St, SW1....**143** E1
John Kennedy Ho,
  SE16 ....**122** B5
John Maurice Cl, SE17.**118** C5
John McKenna Wk,
  SE16 ....**121** D3
John Penn St, SE13 ..**177** F4
John Princes St, W1...**57** F5
John Rennie Wk, E1 ...**93** F4
Sch John Roan Sch, The,
  SE3 ....**179** F1
John Roll Way, SE16 .**121** D3

Sch John Ruskin Prim Sch,
  SE5 . . . . **146** A5
John Ruskin St, SE5 . . **169** E1
Sch John Scurr Prim Sch,
  E1 . . . . **66** A2
John Silkin La, SE8 . . **151** D1
John's Ms, WC1 . . . . **60** B2
John Smith Av, SW6 . . **160** A1
John Smith Ms, E14 . . . **98** C2
Johnson Cl, E8 . . . . **20** C5
Johnson Ho, E2 . . . . **43** D4
Johnson's Ct, EC4
  off Fleet St **89** D1
Johnson's Pl, SW1 . . . **142** A3
Johnson St, E1 . . . . **94** B1
John Spencer Sq, N1 . . **17** F2
John's Pl, E1 . . . . **65** F5
Johnston Cl, SW9 . . . . **168** B4
John St, WC1 . . . . **60** B2
John Trundle Ct, EC2
  off The Barbican **62** A3
John Williams Cl,
  SE14 . . . . **150** C5
John Wilson St, SE18 . **132** C4
Joiner's Arms Yd, SE5 . **170** C4
Joiner St, SE1 . . . . **91** D5
Joiners Yd, N1
  off Caledonia St **37** F3
Jolles Ho, E3
  off Bromley High St . . **47** F4
Jonathan St, SE11 . . . **144** A2
Jones Rd, E13 . . . . **73** F2
Jones St, W1 . . . . **85** E3
Joseph Conrad Ho, SW1
  off Tachbrook St . . . **142** B1
Joseph Hardcastle Cl,
  SE14 . . . . **175** D1
Sch Joseph Lancaster
  Prim Sch, SE1 . . . . . **118** C4
Joseph St, E3 . . . . **68** B2
Joseph Trotter Cl, EC1
  off Myddelton St **39** D5
Joshua St, E14 . . . . **70** A5
Joubert St, SW11 . . . . **164** A5
Jowett St, SE15 . . . . . . **172** B2
Jubilee Cres, E14 . . . . **126** B4
★ Jubilee Gdns, SE1 . . . **88** A5
Jubilee Mkt Hall, WC2 . **87** F2
Jubilee Pl, SW3 . . . . . . **139** F2
Jubilee St, E1 . . . . **66** A5
Jubilee Trust, SE10
  off Egerton Dr **177** F2
Judd St, WC1 . . . . **37** E5
Jude St, E16 . . . . **100** A1
Juer St, SW11 . . . . **163** F2
Julia Garfield Ms, E16. **101** F4
Julian Pl, E14 . . . . **153** F2
Julius Nyerere Cl, N1 . . **38** A1
Junction Av, W10 . . . . . **28** B5
Junction Ms, W2 . . . . . . **55** E5
Junction Pl, W2 . . . . . . **55** D5
Juniper Cres, NW1 . . . . **13** D4
Juniper La, E6 . . . . **75** F4
Juniper St, E1 . . . . **94** A2
Juno Ho, E3
  off Garrison Rd **46** C1
Juno Way, SE14 . . . . . **151** D4

Jupiter Way, N7 . . . . . . **16** B1
Jupp Rd, E15 . . . . **26** C4
Jupp Rd W, E15 . . . . . . **26** B5
Justice Wk, SW3 . . . . . **139** E5
Justines Pl, E2 . . . . **45** D4
Jutland Rd, E13 . . . . . . **73** D2
Juxon St, SE11 . . . . . . **116** B5

K

Sch Kaizen Prim Sch,
  E13 . . . . **73** E2
Kassala Rd, SW11 . . . . **164** B4
Katherine Cl, SE16 . . . **94** C5
Katherine Sq, W11 . . . . **79** E4
Kay St, E2 . . . . **43** D2
Kay Way, SE10 . . . . **177** F1
Kean St, WC2 . . . . **88** A1
Keats Av, E16 . . . . **101** E4
Keats Cl, SE1 . . . . **148** A1
Keats Ho, SW1 . . . . . . **142** B4
Keats Pl, EC2 . . . . **62** C4
Kedleston Wk, E2 . . . . . **43** F4
Keel Cl, SE16 . . . . **95** D5
Keel Ct, E14
  off Newport Av **99** D2
Keeley St, WC2 . . . . **88** A1
Keeling Ho, E2 . . . . **43** E3
Sch Keen Students Sch,
  E1 . . . . **65** D3
Keens Yd, N1 . . . . **17** F2
Keetons Rd, SE16 . . . . **121** E3
Keir Hardie Ho, W6 . . . **134** B4
Sch Keir Hardie Prim Sch,
  E16 . . . . **72** C4
Kelfield Gdns, W10 . . . **50** B5
Kelfield Ms, W10 . . . . . **50** C4
Kelland Rd, E13 . . . . . . **73** D1
Kell St, SE1 . . . . **117** F3
Kelly Av, SE15 . . . . **172** A2
Kelly Ms, W9 . . . . **52** B2
Kelly St, NW1 . . . . **13** F2
Kelsall Cl, SE3 . . . . **181** F5
Kelsey St, E2 . . . . **65** D1
Kelson Ho, E14 . . . . . . **126** B3
Kelso Pl, W8 . . . . **109** F3
Kelvedon Ho, SW8 . . . . **167** F3
Kelvedon Rd, SW6 . . . . **160** B2
Kember St, N1 . . . . **16** A4
Kemble St, WC2 . . . . . . **88** A1
Kemp Ct, SW8 . . . . **167** E2
Kempe Rd, NW6 . . . . . . **28** C3
Kemp Ho, W1
  off Berwick St **86** C2
Kemp's Ct, W1 . . . . **86** B1
Kemps Dr, E14 . . . . **97** D2
Kempsford Gdns, SW5. **137** D3
Kempsford Rd, SE11 . . **145** D1
Kempson Rd, SW6 . . . . **161** D3
Kempthorne Rd, SE8 . **123** F5
Kempton Ct, E1 . . . . **65** E3
Kemsing Rd, SE10 . . . . **156** C2
Kenbury Gdns, SE5 . . . **170** A5
Kenbury St, SE5 . . . . . **170** A5
Kenchester Cl, SW8 . . **167** F2

Kendal Cl, SW9 . . . . . . **169** E1
Kendal Ho, N1 . . . . **38** B2
Kendall Pl, W1 . . . . **56** C4
Kendal Steps, W2
  off St. Georges Flds . . **83** F1
Kendal St, W2 . . . . **83** F1
Sch Kender Prim Sch,
  SE14 . . . . **174** B3
Kender St, SE14 . . . . . **174** B2
Kendrick Ms, SW7 . . . . **110** C5
Kendrick Pl, SW7 . . . . . **138** C1
Kenilworth Rd, E3 . . . . . **45** E2
  NW6 . . . . **8** B5
Kenley Wk, W11 . . . . . . **79** E3
Kennacraig Cl, E16 . . . **101** D5
Kennard Rd, E15 . . . . . **26** C4
Kennard St, E16 . . . . . **104** A5
  SW11 . . . . **164** C4
Kennedy Ho, SE11
  off Vauxhall Wk **144** A2
Kennedy Wk, SE17
  off Flint St **147** D1
Kennet Ho, NW8 . . . . . . **55** D3
Kennet Rd, W9 . . . . **52** B1
Kennet St, E1 . . . . **93** D4
Kennet Wf La, EC4 . . . **90** B2
Kenning St, SE16 . . . . **122** B1
Kennings Way, SE11 . **145** E2
Kenning Ter, N1 . . . . . . **19** E5
KENNINGTON, SE11 . . **144** C5
⊕ Kennington **145** E2
Kennington Grn, SE11. **144** C3
Kennington La, SE11 . **145** D2
Kennington Oval,
  SE11 . . . . **144** B4
Kennington Pk, SW9 . **169** D1
Kennington Pk Est,
  SE11 . . . . **144** C5
Kennington Pk Gdns,
  SE11 . . . . **145** E4
Kennington Pk Pl,
  SE11 . . . . **145** D3
Kennington Pk Rd,
  SE11 . . . . **145** D4
Kennington Rd, SE1 . . **116** C3
  SE11 . . . . **116** C4
Kenrick Pl, W1 . . . . **56** C3
KENSAL GREEN, NW10. **28** B4
↻ Kensal Green **28** B4
⊕ Kensal Green **28** B4
★ Kensal Green Cem,
  W10 . . . . **28** A5
KENSAL RISE, NW6 . . . **28** C3
↻ Kensal Rise **28** B3
Sch Kensal Ri Prim Sch,
  NW6 . . . . **51** C3
Kensal Rd, W10 . . . . **51** F1
KENSAL TOWN, W10 . . **51** D1
Kensal Wf, W10 . . . . . . **51** D1
KENSINGTON, W8 . . . . . **80** B5
Coll Kensington & Chelsea
  Coll, Hortensia Cen,
  SW10 . . . . **162** A1

Coll Kensington & Chelsea
Coll, Marlborough Cen,
  SW3 . . . . **139** F1
  Wornington Cen, W10 . **51** F3
Kensington Ch Ct, W8 . **109** E2
Kensington Ch St, W8 . **81** D4
Kensington Ch Wk,
  W8 . . . . **109** E1
Coll Kensington Coll of
  Business, WC2 . . . . . **60** A5
Kensington Ct, W8 . . . . **109** F2
Kensington Ct Gdns, W8
  off Kensington Ct Pl . **109** F3
Kensington Ct Ms, W8 . **109** F2
Kensington Ct Pl, W8 . **109** F3
★ Kensington Gdns,
  W2 . . . . **82** B5
Kensington Gdns Sq,
  W2 . . . . **81** E1
Kensington Gate, W8 . **110** A3
Kensington Gore,
  SW7 . . . . **110** C2
Kensington Grn, W8 . **109** E4
Kensington Hall Gdns,
  W14 . . . . **136** A2
Kensington High St,
  W8 . . . . **108** C3
  W14 . . . . **108** A4
Kensington Mall, W8 . . **81** D4
⟳ Kensington
  (Olympia) **107** E3
⊖ Kensington
  (Olympia) **107** E3
★ Kensington Palace,
  W8 . . . . **81** F5
Kensington Palace Gdns,
  W8 . . . . **81** E4
Kensington Pk Gdns,
  W11 . . . . **80** A3
Kensington Pk Ms,
  W11 . . . . **80** A1
Kensington Pk Rd,
  W11 . . . . **80** A2
Kensington Pl, W8 . . . . **80** C5
Kensington Rd, SW7 . . **111** D2
  W8 . . . . **109** F2
Kensington Sq, W8 . . **109** E2
Kensington Village,
  W14 . . . . **136** B1
Kentish Bldgs, SE1 . . . **90** C5
KENTISH TOWN, NW5 . . **14** A4
Kentish Town Rd, NW1 . **13** F4
  NW5 . . . . **13** F4
⟳ Kentish Town West . **13** D2
Kenton Ct, W14 . . . . . **108** A4
Kenton Rd, E9 . . . . **22** C2
Kenton St, WC1 . . . . . . **59** E1
Kent Pas, NW1 . . . . . . **56** C2
Kent St, E2 . . . . **42** B2
Kent Ter, NW1 . . . . **33** F5
Kent Yd, SW7 . . . . . . **111** F2
Kenway Rd, SW5 . . . . **137** E1
Kenwood Av, SE14 . . . **174** B3

Kenyon St, SW6 . . . . . **158** C3
Keogh Rd, E15 . . . . **27** F1
Keppel Row, SE1 . . . . . . **90** A5
Keppel St, WC1 . . . . **59** D3
Kerbela St, E2 . . . . **64** C1
Kerbey St, E14 . . . . **69** D3
Kerfield Cres, SE5 . . . . **170** C4
Kerfield Pl, SE5 . . . . . **170** C4
Kerridge Ct, N1 . . . . **19** F5
Kerrison Rd, E15 . . . . . . **26** C1
Kerry Cl, E16 . . . . **101** E1
Kerry Ho, E1
  off Sidney St **66** A5
Kerry Path, SE14 . . . . **152** A5
Kerry Rd, SE14 . . . . . **152** A5
Kersley Ms, SW11 . . . . **164** A4
Kersley St, SW11 . . . . **164** A5
Kerwick Cl, N7 . . . . **15** F3
Keslake Rd, NW6 . . . . . **28** C3
Kestrel Av, E6 . . . . **75** C4
Kestrel Ho, EC1 . . . . **40** A4
  SW8
  off St. George Wf . . . **143** E4
Kestrel Pl, SE14
  off Milton Ct Rd **151** F5
Kevan Ho, SE5 . . . . **170** A2
Key Cl, E1 . . . . **65** F2
Keyham Ho, W2 . . . . . . **52** C4
Keyse Rd, SE1 . . . . **120** A4
Keystone Cres, N1 . . . . . **37** F3
Keyworth Pl, SE1 . . . . **117** F3
Sch Keyworth Prim Sch,
  SE17 . . . . **145** E3
Keyworth St, SE1 . . . . **117** F3
Kezia Ms, SE8 . . . . **151** E2
Kezia St, SE8 . . . . **151** E3
Kibworth St, SW8 . . . . **168** A2
Kidbrooke Gdns, SE3 . **180** C5
Kidbrooke Gro, SE3 . . **181** D3
Kidbrooke Pk Cl, SE3 . **181** E4
Kidbrooke Pk Rd, SE3 . **181** D4
Kiffen St, EC2 . . . . **63** D1
KILBURN, NW6 . . . . **30** C2
⊖ Kilburn **7** F2
Kilburn Br, NW6 . . . . . . **31** D1
Kilburn Gate, NW6 . . . . **31** E2
⟳ Kilburn High Road . . **31** D1
Kilburn High Rd, NW6 . . **8** B3
Kilburn La, W9 . . . . **29** D5
  W10 . . . . **29** D5
⊖ Kilburn Park **30** C2
Sch Kilburn Pk Jun Sch,
  NW6 . . . . **30** B3
Kilburn Pk Rd, NW6 . . . **30** C5
Kilburn Pl, NW6 . . . . . . **31** D1
Kilburn Priory, NW6 . . . **31** E1
Kilburn Sq, NW6 . . . . . . **8** C5
Kilburn Vale, NW6 . . . . **31** E1
Kilby Ct, SE10
  off Child La **128** B4
Kildare Gdns, W2 . . . . . **53** D5
Kildare Rd, E16 . . . . **72** C3
Kildare Ter, W2 . . . . **53** D5
Kildare Wk, E14 . . . . . . **96** C1
Killick St, N1 . . . . **38** A2
Killip Cl, E16 . . . . **72** B5
Killowen Rd, E9 . . . . **22** C2

Killyon Rd, SW8 . . . . . **166** B5
Kilmaine Rd, SW6 . . . . **159** F2
Kilmarsh Rd, W6 . . . . . **106** A5
Kilner St, E14 . . . . **68** C4
Kilravock St, W10 . . . . . **29** E5
Kimbell Gdns, SW6 . . . **159** E4
Kimberley Rd, E16 . . . . **72** A1
  NW6 . . . . **7** F5
Kimbolton Row, SW3 . **139** E1
Kimpton Rd, SE5 . . . . . **170** C3
Kinburn St, SE16 . . . . **122** C1
Kincaid Rd, SE15 . . . . **170** E2
Kincardine Gdns, W9 . . **52** C3
Kinder St, E1 . . . . **93** E1
Kinefold Ho, N7 . . . . . . **15** E1
King & Queen St,
  SE17 . . . . **146** B1
King & Queen Wf, SE16 . **94** C4
King Arthur Cl, SE15 . . **174** A2
King Charles St, SW1 . **115** D1
King Charles Ter, E1
  off Sovereign Cl **93** F3
King David La, E1 . . . . . **94** A2
Kingdon Rd, NW6 . . . . . . **9** D1
⊞ King Edward VII's Hosp
  for Officers, W1 . . . . . **57** D3
King Edwards Rd, E9 . . **21** F5
King Edward St, EC1 . . **62** A5
King Edward III Ms,
  SE16 . . . . **121** F2
King Edward Wk, SE1 . **117** D3
Kingfield St, E14 . . . . . **154** B1
Kingfisher Sq, SE8 . . . **152** B5
Kingfisher St, E6 . . . . . **75** F3
King Frederik IX Twr,
  SE16 . . . . **124** A3
King George Av, E16 . . **74** C5
DLR King George V **105** D5
King George V Dock,
  E16 . . . . **104** A4
King George St, SE10 **178** B2
Kingham Cl, W11 . . . . **107** E1
King Henry's Reach,
  W6 . . . . **134** B4
King Henry's Rd,
  NW3 . . . . **11** F4
King Henry's Wk, N1 . . **19** E1
King Henry Ter, E1 . . . . **93** F3
Kinghorn St, EC1 . . . . . **62** A4
King James Ct, SE1 . . **117** F2
King James St, SE1 . . **117** F2
King John Ct, EC2 . . . . **63** F1
King John St, E1 . . . . . . **67** D4
Kinglake Est, SE17 . . . **147** F2
Kinglake St, SE17 . . . . **147** E3
Kingly Ct, W1 . . . . **86** A2
Kingly St, W1 . . . . **86** A1
Kings Arms Ct, E1 . . . . **64** C4
Kings Arms Yd, EC2 . . **62** C5
Kings Bench St, SE1 . . **117** F1
Kings Bench Wk, EC4 . **89** D1
Kingsbridge Ct, E14
  off Dockers
  Tanner Rd **125** D4
Kingsbridge Rd, W10 . **50** B5
Kingsbury Rd, N1 . . . . . **19** F1
Kingsbury Ter, N1 . . . . **19** F1

★ Place of interest ≷ Railway station ⟳ London Overground station ⊖ London Underground station

Uni King's Coll,
Guy's Campus, SE1 . **118** C3
Maughan Lib & Information
Services Cen, WC2 ... **60** C5
Strand Campus, WC2 . **88** B2
Waterloo Campus, SE1. **88** C5
Kings Coll Rd, NW3.... **11** E3
Kingscote St, EC4 ..... **89** E2
Kings Ct S, SW3 *off Chelsea
Manor Gdns*....... **139** F3
Kingscroft Rd, NW2 ... **7** F1
KING'S CROSS, N1 ..... **15** D5
⇌King's Cross **37** E3
King's Cross Br, N1 ... **37** F4
King's Cross Rd, WC1.. **38** B4
⊖King's Cross
St. Pancras........ **37** E3
⇌King's Cross
Thameslink **37** F3
Kingsdale Gdns, W11..**79** D5
Kingsdown Cl, SE16 .. **149** F3
W10 .... **79** D1
Sch Kingsford Comm Sch,
E6 .... **76** A5
Kingsford Way, E6 .... **76** B4
Kings Gdns, NW6 ..... **9** D4
Kingsgate Est, N1..... **19** F2
Kingsgate Pl, NW6 ..... **8** C4
Sch Kingsgate Prim Sch,
NW6............... **8** C3
Kingsgate Rd, NW6 .... **8** C3
Kings Gro, SE15 ..... **173** F2
Kings Head Yd, SE1 ... **90** C5
Kingshill, SE17 ...... **146** B1
Kingshold Est, E9 .... **22** A5
Kingshold Rd, E9 .... **22** B4
King's Ho, SW8 ...... **167** F1
Kingside, SE18 ...... **131** E4
KINGSLAND, N1 ...... **19** E2
Kingsland, NW8 ...... **33** F1
Kingsland Basin, N1... **19** F5
Kingsland Grn, E8..... **19** F1
Kingsland High St,
E8 .... **20** A1
Kingsland Pas, E8..... **19** F1
Kingsland Rd, E2 ..... **41** F4
E8 .... **19** F5
Kingsland Shop Cen,
E8 .... **20** A1
Kingsley Flats, SE1... **119** E5
Kingsley Ms, E1 ...... **93** F3
W8 .... **109** F4
Kingsley Rd, NW6..... **8** B5
Kings Mall, W6 ..... **134** A1
Kingsman Par, SE18.. **132** B4
Kingsman St, SE18... **132** B4
King's Ms, WC1...... **60** B2
Kingsmill Ter, NW8... **33** D2
Sch King Solomon Acad,
NW1 .... **55** E3
Kings Pl, SE1....... **118** A2
King Sq, EC1 ...... **40** A5
King's Quay, SW10... **162** B3
King's Reach Twr,
SE1 .... **89** D4
King's Rd, SW1 ..... **139** F2
SW3.............. **139** F2

King's Rd, SW6 ..... **161** F2
SW10 .... **161** F2
King's Scholars' Pas,
SW1............. **114** A4
King Stairs Cl, SE16 .. **121** F1
King's Ter, NW1 ..... **36** A1
Kingstown St, NW1 ... **12** C5
King St, E13......... **72** C2
EC2 .... **90** B1
SW1.............. **86** B5
WC2.............. **87** E2
Kings Wk Shop Mall, SW3
off King's Rd **140** A2
Kingswater Pl, SW11
off Battersea Ch Rd . **163** E2
Kingsway, WC2...... **60** A5
Kingsway Pl, EC1 ..... **61** D3
Kings Wf, E8 .... **19** F5
Kingswood Av, NW6.. **29** E1
Kingswood Cl, SW8... **167** F2
King William La, SE10.**155** E3
King William St, EC4.. **91** D3
King William Wk,
SE10 .... **154** B4
Coll Kingwood City Learning
Cen, The, SW6 .... **159** E3
Kingwood Rd, SW6.. **159** D3
Kinnerton Pl N, SW1..**112** B2
Kinnerton Pl S, SW1 .. **112** B2
Kinnerton St, SW1 ... **112** C2
Kinnerton Yd, SW1 .. **112** B2
Kinnoul Rd, W6...... **135** E4
Kintore Way, SE1 .... **120** A5
Kipling Est, SE1...... **119** D2
Kipling St, SE1 ...... **119** D2
Kirby Est, SE16...... **121** E3
Kirby Gro, SE1....... **119** E1
Kirby St, EC1 .... **61** D3
Kirkham Rd, E6....... **75** F5
Kirkland Wk, E8 ...... **20** A2
Kirkman Pl, W1...... **58** C4
Kirkmichael Rd, E14...**70** B5
Kirkside Rd, SE3 ..... **156** C4
Kirk St, WC1........ **60** A2
Kirkwall Pl, E2........ **44** B4
Kirkwood Rd, SE15... **173** F5
Kirtling St, SW8...... **166** A1
Kirton Gdns, E2....... **42** B5
Kirwyn Way, SE5 .... **169** F1
Kitcat Ter, E3 .... **47** D4
Kite Pl, E2 .... **43** D4
Kite Yd, SW11 ...... **164** A4
Kitson Rd, SE5 ...... **170** B1
Kleine Wf, N1 .... **41** F1
Knapp Rd, E3 .... **68** C2
Knaresborough Pl,
SW5.............. **109** E5
Knatchbull Rd, SE5...**170** A4
Knighten St, E1....... **93** E5
Knighthead Pt, E14 .. **124** C3
Knightrider Ct, EC4
off Knightrider St **90** A2
Knightrider St, EC4... **90** A2
Knights Arc, SW1 .... **112** A2
⊖Knightsbridge **112** A2
Knightsbridge, SW1 .. **112** B2
SW7.............. **111** F2

Knightsbridge Apts, The,
SW7
off Knightsbridge ... **112** A2
Knightsbridge Grn,
SW1.............. **112** A2
Knights Rd, E16 ..... **129** D1
Knights Wk, SE11 .... **145** E1
Knivet Rd, SW6...... **136** C5
Knobs Hill Rd, E15 .... **25** E5
Knottisford St, E2..... **44** B4
Knox St, W1.......... **56** A3
Knoyle St, SE14 ..... **151** E5
Sch Kobi Nazrul Prim Sch,
E1 .... **65** D5
Kossuth St, SE10 .... **155** E2
Kotree Way, SE1 .... **149** D1
Kramer Ms, SW5 ..... **137** D3
Kylemore Rd, NW6..... **8** C3
Kynance Ms, SW7.... **110** A4
Kynance Pl, SW7..... **110** A4

L

Laburnum Cl, SE15... **174** A2
Laburnum Ct, E2...... **42** A1
Laburnum St, E2...... **42** A1
Lacey Ms, E3 .... **46** C2
Lackington St, EC2 ... **63** D3
Ladbroke Cres, W11 ... **79** F1
Ladbroke Gdns, W11 .. **80** A2
⊖Ladbroke Grove **51** F5
Ladbroke Gro, W10... **51** D1
W11 .... **79** F1
Ladbroke Ms, W11 ... **79** F5
Ladbroke Rd, W11 ... **79** F4
Ladbroke Sq, W11.... **80** A3
Ladbroke Ter, W11 ... **80** B3
Ladbroke Wk, W11 ... **80** B4
Lady Dock Path, SE16.**123** E2
Sch Lady Eden's Sch,
W8............... **110** A3
Sch Lady Margaret Sec Sch,
SW6.............. **160** C4
Lafone St, SE1....... **120** A1
Lagado Ms, SE16...... **95** D5
Laing Ho, SE5
off Comber Gro **170** A2
Laird Ho, SE5........ **170** A2
Lairs Cl, N7 .... **15** F1
Lakanal, SE5
off Sceaux Gdns.... **171** F3
Lakeside Rd, W14....**106** C3
Lakeview Est, E3...... **45** D2
Lalor St, SW6........ **159** E5
Lambert Jones Ms, EC2
off The Barbican **62** A3
Lambert Rd, E16...... **73** E5
Lambert St, N1 ...... **16** C4
LAMBETH, SE1 ...... **116** A3
Lambeth Br, SE1 ..... **115** F5
SW1.............. **115** F5

Coll Lambeth Coll,
Vauxhall Cen, SW8 . **167** D3
Lambeth High St, SE1. **144** A1
Lambeth Hill, EC4..... **90** A2
⊖ Lambeth North ... **116** C2
★ Lambeth Palace,
SE1 .... **116** A4
Lambeth Palace Rd,
SE1 .... **116** A4
Lambeth Pier, SE1 ... **115** F4
Lambeth Rd, SE1 .... **116** B4
SE11 .... **116** B4
Lambeth Twrs, SE11. **116** C4
Lambeth Wk, SE1 .... **116** B5
SE11 .... **116** B5
Lambfold Ho, N7..... **15** E1
Lamb La, E8.......... **21** E4
Lambolle Pl, NW3..... **11** F2
Lambolle Rd, NW3 .... **11** F2
Lambourne Gro, SE16. **150** C1
Lambourne Pl, SE3 ... **181** E3
Lambrook Ter, SW6 . **159** E3
Lamb's Bldgs, EC1 ... **62** C2
Lambs Conduit Pas,
WC1 .... **60** A3
Lamb's Conduit St,
WC1 .... **60** A2
Lambs Ms, N1 .... **39** E1
Lamb's Pas, EC1 ..... **62** C3
Lamb St, E1 .... **64** A3
Lambton Pl, W11 ..... **80** B2
Lamb Wk, SE1 .... **119** E2
Lamerton St, SE8 ... **152** C5
Lamlash St, SE11 ... **117** E5
Lammas Rd, E9....... **23** D4
Lamont Rd, SW10..... **138** B5
Lamont Rd Pas, SW10
off Lamont Rd **138** C5
Lampern Sq, E2....... **43** D4
Lampeter Sq, W6 ... **135** E5
Lamplighter Cl, E1 .. **66** A4
Lamp Office Ct, WC1.. **60** A2
Lamport Cl, SE18 ... **132** B5
Lanark Ms, W9 .... **32** A5
Lanark Pl, W9 .... **54** B1
Lanark Rd, W9........ **32** A5
Lanark Sq, E14 ..... **125** F3
Lancashire Ct, W1... **85** F2
Lancaster Cl, N1 ..... **19** F4
Lancaster Ct, SW6 .. **160** C2
W2................ **82** B3
Lancaster Dr, E14..... **98** B5
NW3 .... **11** E2
⊖ Lancaster Gate..... **82** C2
Lancaster Gate, W2 ... **82** B3
Lancaster Gro, NW3 ... **11** D2
★ Lancaster Ho, SW1. **114** A1
Lancaster Ms, W2..... **82** B2
Lancaster Pl, WC2..... **88** A2
Lancaster Rd, W11 ... **79** E1
Lancaster St, SE1 ... **117** F2
Lancaster Ter, W2..... **82** C2
Lancaster Wk, W2... **110** C1

Lancaster W, W11
off Grenfell Rd **79** D2
Lancefield St, W10 .... **30** A4
Lancelot Pl, SW7..... **112** A2
Lancer Sq, W8....... **109** E1
Lancey Cl, SE7....... **131** D5
Lanchester Way, SE14. **174** B3
Lancing St, NW1 ...... **36** C5
Lancresse Ct, N1...... **19** E5
Landmann Ho, SE16.. **149** F1
Landmann Way, SE14. **151** D4
Landon Pl, SW1...... **112** A3
Landons Cl, E14 ...... **98** B4
Landon Wk, E14 ...... **97** F2
Landridge Rd, SW6... **159** F5
Lane, The, NW8....... **32** A2
Lanesborough Pl,
SW1............. **113** D1
Lanfranc Rd, E3....... **45** E3
Lanfrey Pl, W14 .... **136** A3
Langbourne Pl, E14.. **153** E2
Langdale, NW1 .... **36** A4
Langdale Cl, SE17.... **146** A4
Langdale Rd, SE10... **178** A2
Langdale St, E1....... **93** E1
DLR Langdon Park..... **69** F4
Sch Langdon Pk Sch,
E14.............. **69** F5
Langdon Way, SE1... **149** D1
Langford Cl, NW8 .... **32** B2
Langford Ct, NW8 .... **32** A3
Langford Ms, N1...... **17** D3
Langford Pl, NW8 .... **32** B3
Sch Langford Prim Sch,
SW6............. **161** F5
Langford Rd, SW6.... **161** F5
Langham Pl, W1 ...... **57** F4
Langham St, W1 ...... **57** F4
Langler Rd, NW10..... **28** B3
Langley Ct, WC2...... **87** E2
Langley La, SW8 .... **143** F4
Langley St, WC2...... **87** E1
Lang St, E1 .... **66** A1
Langthorn Ct, EC2.... **62** C5
Langthorne St, SW6. **158** C2
Langton Cl, WC1 ..... **38** B5
Langton Rd, SW9 .... **169** F2
Langton St, SW10... **138** B5
Langton Way, SE3 ... **180** B3
Langtry Pl, SW6 .... **137** D4
Langtry Rd, NW8 ..... **31** E1
Langtry Wk, NW8 ..... **10** A5
Lanhill Rd, W9........ **52** C1
Lannoy Pt, SW6
off Pellant Rd...... **159** F1
Lanrick Rd, E14....... **71** D5
Lansbury Est, E14..... **69** E5
Lansbury Gdns, E14... **70** C5
Sch Lansbury Lawrence
Prim Sch, E14...... **97** E1
Lanscombe Wk, SW8 . **167** E3
Coll Lansdowne Coll, W2. **81** E3
Lansdowne Cres, W11 . **79** F3
Lansdowne Dr, E8..... **21** D2
Lansdowne Gdns,
SW8............. **167** E3
Lansdowne Grn, SW8. **167** D2

Lansdowne Ms, W11 ..**80** A4
Lansdowne Pl, SE1...**119** D3
Lansdowne Ri, W11...**79** F3
Lansdowne Rd, W11...**79** F2
Lansdowne Row, W1..**85** F4
Lansdowne Ter, WC1 . **59** F2
Lansdowne Wk, W11 . **79** F4
Lansdowne Way, SW8.**167** D3
Lanterns Ct, E14.....**125** D2
Lant St, SE1........**118** A1
Lanvanor Rd, SE15...**174** A5
Lapford Cl, W9.......**52** B1
Lapwing Twr, SE8...**152** A4
Larch Cl, E13........**74** A1
SE8 ....**152** B5
Larcom St, SE17 ....**146** B1
Larissa St, SE17 ....**147** D2
Lark Row, E2.........**44** A1
Larkspur Cl, E6 ......**75** E3
Sch Larmenier & Sacred Heart
Prim Sch, W6 ....**135** D1
Larnach Rd, W6 .....**134** C5
Lassell St, SE10......**155** D3
Lasseter Pl, SE3 ....**155** F4
Latchmere Rd, SW11 .**164** A5
Latchmere St, SW11.**164** A5
Latham Cl, E6 ....**75** F5
Latham Ho, E1 ....**67** D5
Latimer, SE17 ....**147** E3
Latimer Pl, W10 .....**50** B5
⊖ Latimer Road......**79** D2
Latimer Rd, W10 .....**50** A4
Latona Rd, SE15 ....**148** C5
Latymer Ct, W6......**135** D1
Lauderdale Pl, EC2
off The Barbican **62** A3
Lauderdale Rd, W9...**31** E5
Lauderdale Twr, EC2 . **62** A3
Laud St, SE11 ......**144** A2
Laugan Wk, SE17
off East St **146** B2
Launcelot St, SE1 ...**116** C2
Launceston Pl, W8 ...**110** A3
Launch St, E14 ......**126** A3
Laundry La, N1.......**18** A4
Laundry Rd, W6 .....**135** E5
Laurel Aps, SE17
off Townsend St....**119** E5
Laurel Bk Gdns, SW6 .**160** B5
Laurel St, E8 ....**20** B2
Laurence Pountney Hill,
EC4.............**90** C2
Laurence Pountney La,
EC4.............**90** C2
Laurie Gro, SE14.....**175** F3
Sch Lauriston Prim Sch,
E9 ....**22** C5
Lauriston Rd, E9......**22** C5
Lausanne Rd, SE15...**174** B4
Lavender Cl, SW3 ...**139** D5
Lavender Gro, E8 ....**20** B4
Lavender Rd, SE16 ...**95** E4
Lavender St, E15......**27** E1
Laverton Ms, SW5...**137** F1
Laverton Pl, SW5 ...**137** F1
Lavina Gro, N1.......**38** A2
Lavington Cl, E9 ......**24** A1

Lavington St, SE1 . . . . . 89 F5
Sch Lawdale Jun Sch, E2. 43 D4
Lawford Rd, N1 . . . . 19 E4
  NW5 . . . . 14 A2
Lawless St, E14 . . . . . . 97 F2
Lawn Ho Cl, E14 . . . . . 126 A1
Lawn La, SW8 . . . . . . 143 F4
Lawrence Cl, E3 . . . . . . 46 C3
Lawrence Hall, E13 . . . 73 E1
Lawrence La, EC2 . . . . . 90 B1
Lawrence Pl, N1 . . . . . . 15 F5
Lawrence St, E16 . . . . . 72 B4
  SW3 . . . . 139 E5
Lawson Cl, E16 . . . . . . 74 B4
Lawson Est, SE1 . . . . . 118 C4
Law St, SE1 . . . . 119 D3
Lawton Rd, E3 . . . . 45 F5
Laxley Cl, SE5 . . . . . . 169 F1
Laxton Pl, NW1 . . . . . . 57 F1
Layard Rd, SE16 . . . . . 121 F5
Layard Sq, SE16 . . . . . 121 F5
Sch Laycock Prim Sch,
  N1 . . . . 17 E2
Laycock St, N1 . . . . . . 17 D2
Laystall St, EC1 . . . . . . 60 C2
Laytons Bldgs, SE1 . . 118 B1
Lazenby Ct, WC2 . . . . . 87 E2
Leabank Sq, E9 . . . . . . 24 C1
★ Leadenhall Mkt, EC3 . 91 E1
Leadenhall Pl, EC3 . . . 91 E1
Leadenhall St, EC3 . . . 91 E1
Leadenham Ct, E3 . . . . 68 C2
Leake St, SE1 . . . . 116 B1
Leamington Rd Vil,
  W11 . . . . 52 B4
Leamouth Rd, E6 . . . 75 E5
  E14 . . . . 99 D1
Leander Ct, SE8 . . . . . 176 C4
Learoyd Gdns, E6 . . . 104 C2
Lea Sq, E3 . . . . 46 B1
Leatherdale St, E1 . . . 44 C5
Leather Gdns, E15 . . . 49 F1
Leather La, EC1 . . . . . . 61 D4
Leather Mkt, The, SE1 . 119 E2
Leathermarket Ct, SE1 . 119 E2
Leathermarket St, SE1 . 119 E2
Leather Rd, SE16 . . . 150 C1
Leathwell Rd, SE8 . . . 177 F5
Lea Valley Wk, E3 . . . 48 A3
  E14 . . . . 68 C5
  E15 . . . . 25 D5
Lecky St, SW7 . . . . . . 138 C2
Leda Rd, SE18 . . . . . . 132 A4
Ledbury Est, SE15 . . . 173 E1
Ledbury Ms N, W11 . . 80 C2
Ledbury Ms W, W11 . . 80 C2
Ledbury Rd, W11 . . . . 52 B5
Ledbury St, SE15 . . . 173 D1
Leeke St, WC1 . . . . . . 38 A4
Leerdam Dr, E14 . . . . 126 B4
Leeside Ct, SE16 . . . . 94 C4
Lees Pl, W1 . . . . 84 C2
Lee St, E8 . . . . 20 A5
Leeway, SE8 . . . . 152 A2
Lefevre Wk, E3 . . . . . . 46 C2
Leggatt Rd, E15 . . . . . 48 B2
Legion Cl, N1 . . . . 17 D2

Legion Ter, E3 . . . . 46 B1
Leicester Ct, WC2 . . . . 87 D2
Leicester Pl, WC2 . . . . 87 D2
⊖ Leicester Square . . 87 D2
Leicester Sq, WC2 . . . 87 D3
Leicester St, WC2 . . . . 87 D2
Leigh Ct, SE4
  off Lewisham Way . . 176 C5
Leigh Gdns, NW10 . . . 28 A3
Leigh Hunt St, SE1 . . . 118 A1
Leigh Pl, EC1 . . . . 60 C3
Leigh St, WC1 . . . . 59 E1
★ Leighton Ho Mus,
  W14 . . . . 108 B3
Leinster Gdns, W2 . . . 82 A1
Leinster Ms, W2 . . . . . 82 A2
Leinster Pl, W2 . . . . . . 82 A1
Leinster Sq, W2 . . . . . 81 D2
Leinster Ter, W2 . . . . . 82 A2
Leith Yd, NW6 . . . . 8 C5
Lelitia Cl, E8 . . . . 42 C1
Leman St, E1 . . . . 92 B1
Lemmon Rd, SE10 . . . 155 E4
Lena Gdns, W6 . . . . . 106 B4
Sch Lena Gdns Prim Sch,
  W6 . . . . 106 B3
Lenanton Steps, E14 . 125 D1
Len Freeman Pl, SW6 . 136 A5
Lennox Gdns, SW1 . . 112 A4
Lennox Gdns Ms, SW1 . 112 A4
Lensbury Av, SW6 . . . 162 B5
Lenthall Ho, SW1 . . . 142 B3
Lenthall Rd, E8 . . . . . . 20 B3
Lenthorp Rd, SE10 . . . 156 A2
Leonard St, E16 . . . . . 103 F5
  EC2 . . . . 63 D1
Leontine Cl, SE15 . . . 173 D2
Leopards Ct, EC1 . . . . 60 C3
Leopold Ms, E9 . . . . . 22 A5
Leopold St, E3 . . . . . . 68 B3
Leo St, SE15 . . . . 173 F1
Leo Yd, EC1 . . . . 61 F2
Leroy St, SE1 . . . . 119 E5
Lerry Cl, W14 . . . . 136 B4
Leslie Rd, E16 . . . . . . 101 E1
Lester Av, E15 . . . . 49 F5
Lethbridge Cl, SE13 . . 178 A4
Letterstone Rd, SW6 . 160 A2
Lettice St, SW6 . . . . . 160 A4
Lett Rd, E15 . . . . 26 C4
Lettsom St, SE5 . . . . . 171 E5
Levehurst Way, SW4 . 167 F5
Leven Rd, E14 . . . . 70 B4
Leverett St, SW3 . . . . 111 F5
Lever St, EC1 . . . . 39 F5
Lewey Ho, E3 . . . . 68 B2
Coll Lewisham Coll, Deptford
  Campus, SE8 . . . . . . 177 D3
Lewisham Rd, SE13 . . 177 F4
Lewisham St, SW1 . . . 115 D2
Lewisham Way, SE4 . . 176 A3
  SE14 . . . . 176 A3
Lewis St, NW1 . . . . . . 13 F2
Lexham Gdns, W8 . . . 109 E5
Lexham Gdns Ms, W8 . 109 F4
Lexham Ms, W8 . . . . . 109 D5
Lexham Wk, W8 . . . . . 109 F4

Lexington Apts, EC1 . . . 62 C1
Lexington Bldg, E3
  off Fairfield Rd 47 D3
Lexington St, W1 . . . . . 86 B1
Leybourne Rd, NW1 . . . 13 F4
Leybourne St, NW1 . . . 13 E4
Leyden St, E1 . . . . 64 A4
Leydon Cl, SE16 . . . . . 95 D5
Leyland Rd, SE14 . . . . 175 D1
Leywick St, E15 . . . . . . 49 E2
Liardet St, SE14 . . . . . 151 F5
Liberia Rd, N5 . . . . 17 F1
★ Liberty, W1 . . . . 86 A1
Liberty St, SW9 . . . . . 168 B4
Libra Rd, E3 . . . . 46 B1
Library Pl, E1 . . . . 93 F2
Library St, SE1 . . . . . . 117 E2
Lichfield Rd, E3 . . . . . . 45 F4
Lickey Ho, W14
  off North End Rd . . . 136 B4
Liddell Gdns, NW10 . . . 28 A2
Liddell Rd, NW6 . . . . . . 8 C1
Lidgate Rd, SE15 . . . . 172 A2
Lidlington Pl, NW1 . . . . 36 A3
Coll Lifelong Learning,
  The Shadwell Cen, E1 . 94 C2
Lighter Cl, SE16 . . . . . 123 F5
Lighterman Ms, E1 . . . 67 D5
Lightermans Rd, E14 . 125 D2
Ligonier St, E2 . . . . 64 A1
Lilac Pl, SE11 . . . . 144 A1
Lilestone St, NW8 . . . . 55 E1
Lilford Rd, SE5 . . . . . . 169 E5
Sch Lilian Baylis Tech Sch,
  SE11 . . . . 144 B3
Lilley Cl, E1 . . . . 93 D5
Lillie Rd, SW6 . . . . . . 135 D5
Lillie Yd, SW6 . . . . . . 136 C4
Lillington Gdns Est,
  SW1 . . . . 142 B1
Lily Cl, W14 . . . . 135 E1
Lily Pl, EC1 . . . . 61 D3
Lilyville Rd, SW6 . . . . 160 A3
Limeburner La, EC4 . . . 89 E1
Lime Cl, E1 . . . . 93 D4
Lime Gro, W12 . . . . . . 106 A1
Limeharbour, E14 . . . 125 F2
LIMEHOUSE, E14 . . . . . 95 F2
≋ Limehouse 95 E1
DLR Limehouse 95 E1
Limehouse Causeway,
  E14 . . . . 96 B2
Limehouse Link, E14 . . 96 B3
Limekiln Dr, SE7 . . . . 157 F4
Limerston St, SW10 . . 138 B4
Limes, The, W2 . . . . . . 81 D3
Lime St, EC3 . . . . 91 E2
Lime St Pas, EC3 . . . . 91 E1
Lime Wk, E15 . . . . 27 F5
Linacre Ct, W6 . . . . . . 135 D2
Linale Ho, N1
  off Murray Gro 40 C3
Linberry Wk, SE8 . . . . 151 F1

Lincoln Ms, NW6 . . . . **8** A5
Lincoln Rd, E13 . . . . **73** B2
★ Lincoln's Inn, WC2 . . **60** B5
Lincoln's Inn Flds, WC2 . **60** A5
Lincoln St, SW3 . . . . . . **140** A1
Linden Av, NW10 . . . . . **28** C3
Linden Ct, W12 . . . . **78** A4
Linden Gdns, W2 . . . . . . **81** D3
Linden Ms, W2 . . . . **81** D3
Lindfield St, E14 . . . . . . **68** B1
Lindley Est, SE15 . . . . **172** C1
Lindley St, E1 . . . . **66** A3
Lindrop St, SW6 . . . . . **162** A5
Lindsay Ct, SW11 . . . . **163** D4
Lindsay Sq, SW1 . . . . . **143** D2
Lindsell St, SE10 . . . . . **178** A3
Lindsey Ms, N1 . . . . **18** B3
Lindsey St, EC1 . . . . . . **61** F3
Lind St, SE8 . . . . **177** D5
Lindwood Cl, E6 . . . . . . **75** F4
Linford St, SW8 . . . . . **166** A3
Lingham St, SW9 . . . . **167** F5
Ling Rd, E16 . . . . **73** D3
Linhope St, NW1 . . . . . **56** A1
Link St, E9 . . . . **22** B1
Links Yd, E1 . . . . **64** C3
Linkwood Wk, NW1 . . . **15** D3
★ Linley Sambourne Ho,
　W8 . . . . **109** D2
Linnell Rd, SE5 . . . . . **171** F5
Linsey St, SE16 . . . . . **120** C1
Linstead St, NW6 . . . . . . **8** C3
Lintaine Cl, W6 . . . . . . **135** F5
Linton Gdns, E6 . . . . . . **75** E5
Linton St, N1 . . . . **40** B1
Linver Rd, SW6 . . . . . **160** B5
Lionel Ms, W10 . . . . . . **51** E3
Lion Mills, E2 . . . . **43** D3
Lion Plaza, EC2
　off Lothbury **62** C5
Lion Rd, E6 . . . . **76** B4
Lipton Rd, E1 . . . . **94** C1
Lisford St, SE15 . . . . . **172** B3
Lisgar Ter, W14 . . . . . **108** A5
Liskeard Gdns, SE3 . . . **181** D4
Lisle St, WC2 . . . . **87** D2
Lismore Wk, N1 . . . . . . **19** F3
Lisson Grn Est, NW8 . . **33** E5
LISSON GROVE, NW8 . . **55** D1
Lisson Gro, NW1 . . . . . **55** E1
　NW8 . . . . **33** D5
Lisson St, NW1 . . . . . . **55** E3
🄷 Lister Hosp, The,
　SW1 . . . . **141** E3
Listowel Cl, SW9 . . . . **169** D1
Litchfield Av, E15 . . . . . **27** E2
Litchfield St, WC2 . . . . **87** D2
Lithos Rd, NW3 . . . . **9** F1
Little Albany St, NW1 . . **57** F1
Little Argyll St, W1 . . . **86** A1
Little Boltons, The,
　SW5 . . . . **137** F2
　SW10 . . . . **137** F2

Little Britain, EC1 . . . . . **62** A5
Little Chester St, SW1 . **113** D3
Little Cloisters, SW1
　off College Ms **115** E3
Little Coll La, EC4
　off College St **90** C2
Little Coll St, SW1 . . . **115** E3
Littlecombe, SE7 . . . . . **157** F4
Little Cottage Pl, SE10 . **177** F1
Little Dean's Yd, SW1 . **115** E3
Little Dorrit Ct, SE1 . . **118** B1
Little Edward St, NW1 . **35** F4
Little Essex St, WC2 . . . **88** C2
Little George St, SW1 . **115** E2
Little London Ct, SE1
　off Mill St **120** B2
Little Marlborough St, W1
　off Foubert's Pl **86** A1
Little Newport St, WC2 . **87** D2
Little New St, EC4 . . . . . **61** D5
Little Portland St, W1 . . **58** A3
Little Russell St, WC1 . . **59** E4
Little St. James's St,
　SW1 . . . . **86** A5
Little Sanctuary, SW1 . **115** D2
Little Smith St, SW1 . . **115** D3
Little Somerset St, E1 . . **92** A1
Little Titchfield St, W1 . **58** A4
Littleton Ho, SW1
　off Lupus St **142** A3
Little Trinity La, EC4 . . . **90** B2
Little Turnstile, WC1 . . . **60** A5
★ Little Venice
　(Waterbuses), W2 . . **54** A3
Livermere Rd, E8 . . . . . **20** A5
Liverpool Gro, SE17 . . **146** B3
Liverpool Rd, E16 . . . . . **71** F3
　N1 . . . . **17** D4
　N7 . . . . **16** C1
⇌Liverpool Street **63** E4
⊖ Liverpool Street **63** E4
Liverpool St, EC2 . . . . . **63** E4
★ Livesey Mus for
　Children, SE15 . . . . **149** E5
Livesey Pl, SE15 . . . . . **149** D4
Livingstone Pl, E14 . . **154** A3
Livingstone Rd, E15 . . . **48** B1
Livonia St, W1 . . . . **86** B1
Lizard St, EC1 . . . . **40** B5
Lizban St, SE3 . . . . **181** E1
Llewellyn St, SE16 . . . **121** D2
Lloyd Baker St, WC1 . . . **38** B5
Lloyd's Av, EC3 . . . . **91** F1
★ Lloyd's of London,
　EC3 . . . . **91** E1
Lloyd Sq, WC1 . . . . **38** C4
Lloyd's Row, EC1 . . . . . **39** D5
Lloyd St, WC1 . . . . **38** C4
Lloyd Vil, SE4 . . . . **176** C5
🄢Lloyd Williamson Sch,
　W10 . . . . **51** E3
Loanda Cl, E8 . . . . **20** A5
Lobelia Cl, E6 . . . . **75** E3
Lochaline St, W6 . . . . . **134** B4
Lochnagar St, E14 . . . . **70** B4
Lock Bldg, The, E15 . . . **48** A2
Lockesfield Pl, E14 . . . **153** F2

Lockhart Cl, N7 . . . . **16** A1
Lockhart St, E3 . . . . **68** B2
Lockington Rd, SW8 . . **165** F3
Lock Ms, NW1 . . . . **14** C1
Locksley Est, E14 . . . . . **68** A5
Locksley St, E14 . . . . . . **68** A4
Locksons Cl, E14 . . . . . **69** D3
Lockton St, W10 . . . . . . **78** C2
Lockwood Sq, SE16 . . **121** E3
Lockyer Est, SE1 . . . . . **119** D1
Lockyer St, SE1 . . . . . . **119** D2
Locton Grn, E3 . . . . **24** B5
Loddiges Rd, E9 . . . . . . **22** A3
Loder St, SE15 . . . . . . **174** A3
Lodge Rd, NW8 . . . . . . **33** D5
Lodore St, E14 . . . . **98** A1
Loftie St, SE16 . . . . . . **121** D2
Lofting Rd, N1 . . . . **16** C4
Logan Ms, W8 . . . . . . **108** C5
Logan Pl, W8 . . . . **108** C5
Lolesworth Cl, E1 . . . . . **64** A4
Lollard St, SE11 . . . . . **116** B5
Loman St, SE1 . . . . . . **117** F1
Lomas Dr, E8 . . . . **20** B3
Lomas St, E1 . . . . **65** D3
Lombard Ct, EC3 . . . . . **91** D2
Lombard La, EC4 . . . . . **89** D1
Lombard St, EC3 . . . . . **91** D1
Lombard Wall, SE7 . . . **129** E4
Lombardy Pl, W2 . . . . . **81** E3
Lomond Gro, SE5 . . . . **170** C1
Loncroft Rd, SE5 . . . . . **147** F4
Londinium Twr, E1
　off Mansell St **92** B2
🄒London Acad of Music &
　Dramatic Art,
　W14 . . . . **135** D2
★ London Aquarium,
　SE1 . . . . **116** A1
★ London Brass Rubbing
　Cen (St. Martin-in-the-
　Fields Ch), WC2 . . . . **87** E3
⇌London Bridge **91** E5
⊖ London Bridge **91** E5
London Br, EC4 . . . . . . **91** D4
　SE1 . . . . **91** D4
🄡London Bridge City
　Pier **91** E4
🄷 London Br Hosp,
　SE1 . . . . **91** D4
London Br St, SE1 . . . . **90** C5
🄒London Business Sch,
　NW1 . . . . **56** A1
★ London Canal Mus, The,
　N1 off New Wf Rd . . . **37** F2
★ London Cen Mkts
　(Smithfield Mkt), EC1 . **61** E3
★ London Cen Mosque,
　NW8 . . . . **33** F4
🄷 London Chest Hosp,
　E2 . . . . **44** B2
★ London City Airport,
　E16 . . . . **103** E4
🄓London City
　Airport **103** E4
🄒London City Coll,
　SE1 . . . . **88** C5

H London Clinic, The, W1 . . . . **57** D2
★ London Coliseum, WC2 . . . . **87** E3
Coll London Coll of Beauty Therapy, W1 . . . . **86** A1
Uni London Coll of Communication, SE1 . . . . **117** F4
Uni London Coll of Fashion, Barrett St, W1 . . . . . . **85** D1
Curtain Rd, EC2 . . . . . . **63** F1
John Princes St, W1 . . . **57** F5
Lime Gro, W12 . . . . . **106** A1
Mare St, E8 . . . . **21** F3
★ London Dungeon, SE1 . . . . **91** D5
Coll London Electronics Coll, SW5 . . . . **137** E2
★ London Eye, SE1 . . **116** F1
⇌ London Fields **21** E4
London Flds, E8 . . . . . . **21** E3
London Flds E Side, E8 . . **21** E4
Sch London Flds Prim Sch, E8 . . . . **21** E5
London Flds W Side, E8 . **21** D3
★ London Fire Brigade Mus, SE1 . . . . **118** A1
London Fruit Ex, E1 off Brushfield St **64** A4
H London Indep Hosp, E1 . . . . **66** C3
London Ind Est, E6 . . . . **77** D3
London La, E8 . . . . **21** F3
★ London Met Archives, EC1 . . . . **61** D1
Uni London Met Uni - London City Campus, Calcutta Ho, E1 . . . . . **64** B5
Central Ho, E1 . . . . **64** C5
Commercial Rd, E1 . . . **65** D5
Goulston St, E1 . . . . . . **64** A5
Jewry St, EC3 . . . . **92** A1
Moorgate, EC2 . . . . . . **63** D4
Students Union, E1 . . . **64** B5
Tower Hill, EC3 . . . . . . **92** A2
Whitechapel High St, E1 . . . . **64** B5
Uni London Met Uni - London N Campus, Dept of Architecture, N7 . . . . **17** D1
James Leicester Hall of Res, N7 . . . . **15** F1
London Ms, W2 . . . . . . **83** D1
Sch London Nautical Sch, SE1 . . . . **89** D4
Sch London Oratory Sec Sch, The, SW6 . . . . **161** E1
★ London Palladium, W1 . . . . **86** A1
London Pav, The, W1 . . **86** C3
★ London Peace Pagoda, SW11 . . . . **164** B1
★ London Regatta Cen, E16 . . . . **103** D3
London Rd, SE1 . . . . . . **117** E3

Uni London Sch of Economics & Political Science, WC2 . . . . **88** B1
Uni London Sch of Hygiene & Tropical Med, WC1 . . **59** D3
★ London Silver Vaults, WC2 . . . . **60** C4
Uni London S Bk Uni, SE1 . . . . **117** F3
Caxton Ho, SE1 . . . . . **117** E3
★ London Stone, EC4 . . **90** C2
London St, EC3 . . . . **91** F2
W2 . . . . **82** C1
Coll London Studio Cen, N1 . . . . **37** F2
★ London Television Cen, SE1 . . . . **88** C4
London Ter, E2 . . . . **42** C3
★ London Transport Mus, WC2 . . . . **87** F2
★ London Trocadero, The, W1 . . . . **86** C3
London Wall, EC2 . . . . . **45** C2
London Wall Bldgs, EC2 . **63** D4
★ London Zoo, NW1 . . . **34** C2
Long Acre, WC2 . . . . . . **87** C2
Longfellow Way, SE1 . **148** B1
Longfield Est, SE1 . . . . **148** B1
Longford Ho, E1 off Jubilee St **66** A5
Longford St, NW1 . . . . . **57** F1
Longhedge St, SW11 . **165** D5
Longhope Cl, SE15 . . . **148** A5
Longland Ct, SE1 . . . . **148** C2
Longlands Ct, W11 . . . . **80** B2
Long La, EC1 . . . . **61** F3
SE1 . . . . **118** C2
Longleat Ho, SW1 off Rampayne St . . . **142** C2
Longley Ct, SW8 . . . . . **167** E3
Longley St, SE1 . . . . . . **148** C1
Long Mark Rd, E16 . . . . **74** C4
Longmoore St, SW1 . . **142** A1
Longnor Rd, E1 . . . . **45** D5
Long Pond Rd, SE3 . . . **179** F4
Longridge Ho, SE1 . . . **118** B4
Longridge Rd, SW5 . . . **136** C1
Long's Ct, WC2 . . . . **86** C2
Longshore, SE8 . . . . . . **152** A1
Longstone Ct, SE1 . . . **118** B2
Long St, E2 . . . . **42** A4
Longton Ho, SE11 off Lambeth Wk **116** B5
Longville Rd, SE11 . . . **117** E5
Long Wk, SE1 . . . . **119** F3
Long Yd, WC1 . . . . **60** A2
Lonsdale Cl, E6 . . . . **75** E1
Lonsdale Ms, W11 . . . . **80** B1
Lonsdale Pl, N1 . . . . **17** D4
Lonsdale Rd, NW6 . . . . **30** A2
W11 . . . . **80** B1
Lonsdale Sq, N1 . . . . . . **17** D4
Lord Amory Way, E14 . **126** A1
Lorden Wk, E2 . . . . **42** C5
Lord Hills Br, W2 . . . . . . **53** F4
Lord Hills Rd, W2 . . . . . **53** F3
Lord Holland La, SW9 . **169** D5

Lord N St, SW1 . . . . . . **115** E4
Lord Roberts Ms, SW6 . **161** E2
★ Lord's (Marylebone CC & Mus, Middlesex CCC), NW8 . . . . **33** D4
Lordship Pl, SW3 . . . . **139** E5
Lord St, E16 . . . . **103** F5
Lord's Vw, NW8 . . . . . . **33** D5
Lord Warwick St, SE18 . **132** A4
Lorenzo St, WC1 . . . . . . **38** A4
Loring Rd, SE14 . . . . . **175** F3
Loris Rd, W6 . . . . **106** B4
Lorn Ct, SW9 . . . . **168** C5
Lorne Cl, NW8 . . . . **33** F5
Lorne Gdns, W11 . . . . **107** D1
Lorn Rd, SW9 . . . . **168** B5
Lorrimore Rd, SE17 . . . **145** F4
Lorrimore Sq, SE17 . . . **145** F4
Lothbury, EC2 . . . . **62** C5
Lothian Rd, SW9 . . . . . **169** F3
Lothrop St, W10 . . . . . . **29** E4
Lots Rd, SW10 . . . . . . **162** A2
Loudoun Rd, NW8 . . . . **32** B2
Loughborough Rd, SW9 . . . . **168** C5
Loughborough St, SE11 . . . . **144** B2
Lough Rd, N7 . . . . **16** B1
Louisa Cl, E9 . . . . **23** D5
Louisa Gdns, E1 . . . . . . **66** C2
Louisa St, E1 . . . . **66** C2
Louise Rd, E15 . . . . **27** F1
Lovage App, E6 . . . . **75** F4
Lovat La, EC3 . . . . **91** E3
Lovegrove St, SE1 . . . **149** D3
Lovegrove Wk, E14 . . . **98** A5
Love La, EC2 . . . . **62** B5
Lovelinch Cl, SE15 . . . **150** B5
Lovell Ho, E8 . . . . **20** C5
Lovell Pl, SE16 . . . . . . **123** F3
Loveridge Ms, NW6 . . . . **8** B2
Loveridge Rd, NW6 . . . . **8** B2
Lovers Wk, SE10 . . . . . **155** E5
Lover's Wk, W1 . . . . . . **84** C4
Love Wk, SE5 . . . . **170** C5
Lowe Av, E16 . . . . **73** D4
Lowell St, E14 . . . . **95** F1
Lower Addison Gdns, W14 . . . . **107** D2
Lower Belgrave St, SW1 . . . . **113** E4
Lower Clarendon Wk, W11 off Lancaster Rd **79** E1
Lower Grosvenor Pl, SW1 . . . . **113** E3
Lower James St, W1 . . **86** B2
Lower John St, W1 . . . . **86** B2
Lower Lea Crossing, E14 . . . . **99** E2
E16 . . . . **99** E2
Lower Marsh, SE1 . . . . **116** C2
Lower Mast Ho, SE18 . **132** B3
Lower Merton Ri, NW3 . **11** F3

Lower Rd, SE1 . . . . **116** C1
SE8 . . . . **122** A3
SE16 . . . . **122** C5
Lower Robert St, WC2
off John Adam St **87** F3
Lower Sloane St, SW1 . **140** C1
Lower Thames St,
EC3 . . . . **91** D3
Lowestoft Ms, E16 . . . **133** F1
Lowfield Rd, NW6 . . . . . . **8** C3
Lowndes Cl, SW1 . . . . **113** D4
Lowndes Ct, W1 . . . . . . **86** A1
Lowndes Pl, SW1 . . . . **112** C4
Lowndes Sq, SW1 . . . . **112** B2
Lowndes St, SW1 . . . . **112** B3
Lowood St, E1 . . . . **93** F2
Lowry Ho, E14
off Cassilis Rd **125** D2
Lowther Gdns, SW7 . . **110** C3
Lowth Rd, SE5 . . . . **170** A4
Loxham St, WC1 . . . . . . **37** F5
Sch L.S.O. St. Luke's,
EC1 . . . . **62** B1
Lubbock St, SE14 . . . . **174** B2
Lucan Pl, SW3 . . . . **139** E1
Lucas Ct, SW11 . . . . . . **165** D4
Lucas St, SE8 . . . . **176** C5
Sch Lucas Vale Prim Sch,
SE8 . . . . **176** C4
Lucerne Ms, W8 . . . . . . **81** D4
Lucey Rd, SE16 . . . . . . **120** C4
Lucey Way, SE16 . . . . **121** D4
Ludgate Bdy, EC4 . . . . . **89** E1
Ludgate Circ, EC4 . . . . . **89** E1
Ludgate Hill, EC4 . . . . . **89** E1
Ludgate Sq, EC4 . . . . . . **89** F1
Ludlow St, EC1 . . . . **62** A1
Ludwick Ms, SE14 . . . . **175** F1
Lugard Rd, SE15 . . . . . **173** F5
Luke Ho, E1 . . . . **93** E1
Luke St, EC2 . . . . **63** E1
Lukin St, E1 . . . . **94** B1
Lulworth, NW1 . . . . **14** B4
SE17 . . . . **146** C2
Lulworth Ho, SW8 . . . . **168** A1
Lulworth Rd, SE15 . . . **173** F5
Lumley Ct, WC2 . . . . . . **87** F3
Lumley Flats, SW1
off Holbein Pl **140** C2
Lumley St, W1 . . . . **85** D1
Luna Ho, SE16 . . . . **121** D1
Lund Pt, E15 . . . . **26** A5
Lundy Wk, N1 . . . . **18** B2
Lupino Ct, SE11 . . . . . . **144** B1
Lupin Pt, SE1 . . . . **120** B2
Lupus St, SW1 . . . . **142** B3
Luralda Gdns, E14 . . . . **154** B2
Lurgan Av, W6 . . . . **135** D4
Lurline Gdns, SW11 . . **165** D3
Luscombe Way, SW8 . **167** E1
Luton Pl, SE10 . . . . **178** B2
Luton Rd, E13 . . . . **72** C2
Luton St, NW8 . . . . **55** D2

Lutyens Ho, SW1
off Churchill Gdns . . **142** A3
Luxborough St, W1 . . . . **56** C3
Luxborough Twr, W1
off Luxborough St . . . **56** C3
Luxemburg Gdns, W6 . **106** C1
Luxford St, SE16 . . . . . **150** C1
Luxmore St, SE4 . . . . . **176** B4
Lyall Ms, SW1 . . . . **112** C4
Lyall Ms W, SW1 . . . . . **112** C4
Lyall St, SW1 . . . . **112** C4
Lyal Rd, E3 . . . . **45** F3
Lycée, The, SE11 . . . . . **145** D3
Sch Lycée Français Charles
de Gaulle, SW7 . . . . **110** C5
Lydford Rd, NW2 . . . . **6** B2
W9 . . . . **52** B1
Lygon Ho, SW6 . . . . . . **159** E3
Lygon Pl, SW1 . . . . **113** E4
Lyme Gro, E9 . . . . **22** A3
Lyme St, NW1 . . . . **14** A4
Lyme Ter, NW1 . . . . **14** A4
Lymington Cl, E6 . . . . . . **76** A3
Lymington Rd, NW6 . . . . **9** E1
Lympstone Gdns,
SE15 . . . . **173** D1
Lynbrook Gro, SE15 . . **171** F1
Lynch Wk, SE8 . . . . **152** B4
Lyndale Cl, SE3 . . . . . . **156** A5
Lyndhurst Gro, SE15 . **171** F5
Sch Lyndhurst Prim Sch,
SE5 . . . . **171** D5
Lyndhurst Sq, SE15 . . **172** B4
Lyndhurst Way, SE15 . **172** B3
Lyn Ms, E3 . . . . **46** A5
Lynton Est, SE1 . . . . . . **148** C1
Lynton Rd, NW6 . . . . . . **30** B1
SE1 . . . . **148** B1
Lynx Way, E16 . . . . **102** C2
Lyons Pl, NW8 . . . . **54** C1
Lyon St, N1 . . . . **16** A4
Lyons Wk, W14 . . . . . . **107** E5
★ Lyric Hammersmith,
W6 . . . . **134** A1
Lysander Ho, E2 . . . . . . **43** E3
Lysia St, SW6 . . . . **158** C2
Lyte St, E2 . . . . **44** A2
Lytham St, SE17 . . . . . **146** C3
Lyttelton Cl, NW3 . . . . . **11** E4
Lyveden Rd, SE3 . . . . . **181** E1

M

Mabledon Pl, WC1 . . . . **37** D5
Mablethorpe Rd, SW6 . **159** E2
Mabley St, E9 . . . . **23** E1
McAuley Cl, SE1 . . . . . . **116** C3
Macauley Ms, SE13 . . **178** B4
Macbean St, SE18 . . . . **133** D4
McCall Cl, SW4 . . . . . . **167** E5
Macclesfield Br, NW1 . . **33** F2
Macclesfield Rd, EC1 . . **40** A4
Macclesfield St, W1 . . . **87** D2
McCoid Way, SE1 . . . . . **118** A2
McCrone Ms, NW3 . . . . **11** D1

McCullum Rd, E3 . . . . . **46** A1
McDowall Cl, E16 . . . . . **72** B4
McDowall Rd, SE5 . . . . **170** A4
Macduff Rd, SW11 . . . . **165** D3
Mace Cl, E1 . . . . **93** E4
Mace St, E2 . . . . **44** C3
McEwen Way, E15 . . . . **27** D5
Macey Ho, SW11
off Surrey La **163** F4
Macfarland Gro, SE15 . **171** F1
Macfarlane Rd, W12 . . . **78** A4
Macfarren Pl, NW1 . . . . **57** D2
Macgregor Rd, E16 . . . . **74** B3
McGregor Rd, W11 . . . . **52** A5
Mackennal St, NW8 . . . **33** F3
Mackenzie Rd, N7 . . . . . **16** A1
Mackenzie Wk, E14 . . . . **97** D5
McKerrell Rd, SE15 . . . **173** D4
Macklin St, WC2 . . . . . . **59** F5
Mackrow Wk, E14 . . . . . **98** A2
Macks Rd, SE16 . . . . . . **121** D5
Mackworth St, NW1 . . . **36** A4
McLeod's Ms, SW7 . . . **109** F4
Macleod St, SE17 . . . . **146** B3
Maclise Rd, W14 . . . . . **107** E4
McMillan St, SE8 . . . . . **153** D5
McMillan Student Village,
SE8 . . . . **153** D5
Maconochies Rd, E14 . **153** E2
Macquarie Way, E14 . . **153** F1
Macroom Rd, W9 . . . . . **30** B4
Mac's Pl, EC4 . . . . **61** D5
★ Madame Tussauds,
NW1 . . . . **56** C2
Sch Madani Girls Sch, E1. **65** E5
Maddams St, E3 . . . . . . **69** E2
Maddock Way, SE17 . . **145** F5
Maddox St, W1 . . . . **85** F2
Madison Bldg, SE10
off Blackheath Rd . . **177** E3
Madras Pl, N7 . . . . **16** C1
Madrigal La, SE5 . . . . . **169** F2
Madron St, SE17 . . . . . **147** F2
Mafeking Rd, E16 . . . . . **72** A1
Magdalene Gdns, E6 . . **76** C1
Magdalen Ms, NW3 . . . **10** A1
Magdalen Pas, E1 . . . . . **92** B2
Magdalen St, SE1 . . . . . **91** E5
Magee St, SE11 . . . . . . **144** C4
Magellan Pl, E14
off Maritime Quay . . **153** D1
Maggie Blakes Causeway,
SE1 *off Shad Thames* . **92** A5
Magnin Cl, E8 . . . . **21** D5
Magpie All, EC4 . . . . **89** D1
Magpie Pl, SE14
off Milton Ct Rd **151** F5
Magri Wk, E1 . . . . **66** A4
Maguire St, SE1 . . . . . . **120** B1
Mahogany Cl, SE16 . . . **95** F5
Maida Av, W2 . . . . **54** B3
MAIDA HILL, W9 . . . . . . **52** C1
MAIDA VALE, W9 . . . . . . **53** F1
⊖ Maida Vale **31** F4
Maida Vale, W9 . . . . **32** A5
Maiden La, NW1 . . . . . . **15** D3
SE1 . . . . **90** B4

Maiden La, WC2	87	F3
Maiden Rd, E15	27	F3
Maidenstone Hill,		
SE10	178	A3
Maidstone Bldgs Ms,		
SE1	90	B5
Maidstone Ho, E14	69	E5
Maismore St, SE15	149	D5
Maitland Cl Est, SE10	177	F2
Maitland Pk Est, NW3	12	B1
Maitland Pk Rd, NW3	12	B2
Maitland Pk Vil, NW3	12	B1
Major Rd, SE16	121	D3
Makins St, SW3	139	F1
Malabar St, E14	124	C2
Malam Gdns, E14	97	E2
Malcolm Pl, E2	66	A1
Malcolm Rd, E1	66	A1
Malden Cres, NW1	13	D2
Maldon Cl, N1	18	A5
Malet Pl, WC1	58	C2
Malet St, WC1	58	C2
Mall, The, SW1	114	B4
Mallard Cl, E9	24	B1
NW6	31	D1
Mallard Pt, E3	47	E5
Mall Chambers,		
off Kensington Mall	81	D4
★ Mall Galleries, SW1	87	D4
Mallord St, SW3	139	D4
Mallory Cl, E14	69	F3
Mallory St, NW8	55	F1
Mallow St, EC1	62	C1
Malmesbury, E2	44	A3
Sch Malmesbury Prim Sch,		
E3	46	B4
Malmesbury Rd, E3	46	A4
E16	71	F3
Malmesbury Ter, E16	72	A3
Sch Malorees Inf & Jun Sch,		
NW6	7	D4
Malpas Rd, E8	21	E1
Malta St, EC1	61	F1
Maltby St, SE1	120	A2
Malting Ho, E14	96	A2
Maltings Cl, E3	48	A5
Maltings Pl, SE1	119	F2
SW6	161	F4
Malton Ms, W10		
off Malton Rd	51	E5
Malton Rd, W10	51	E5
Maltravers St, WC2	88	B2
Malt St, SE1	148	C4
Malvern Cl, W10	52	A4
Malvern Cl, SE14	174	B1
SW7	139	D1
Malvern Gdns, NW6	30	B3
Malvern Ms, NW6	30	C5
Malvern Pl, NW6	30	B4
Malvern Rd, E8	20	C4
NW6	30	C4
Malvern Ter, N1	16	C5
Managers St, E14	98	B5
Manbey Gro, E15	27	E1
Manbey Pk Rd, E15	27	E1
Manbey Rd, E15	27	E1
Manbey St, E15	27	E2

Manbre Rd, W6	134	B4
Manchester Ct, E16	101	F1
Manchester Dr, W10	51	E2
Manchester Gro, E14	154	A2
Manchester Ms, W1	56	C4
Manchester Rd, E14	154	A2
Manchester Sq, W1	56	C5
Manchester St, W1	56	C4
Manciple St, SE1	118	C2
Mandarin St, E14	96	C2
Mandela Rd, E16	101	D1
Mandela St, NW1	14	B5
SW9	168	C2
Mandela Way, SE1	119	F5
Coll Mander Portman		
Woodward 6th Form		
Tutorial Coll, SW7	138	C1
Mandeville Cl, SE3	180	B2
Mandeville Ho, SE1	148	B2
Mandeville Pl, W1	57	D5
Mandrake Way, E15	27	E3
Manette St, W1	87	D1
Manger Rd, N7	15	F1
Manhattan Bldg, E3	47	D2
Manhattan Wf, E16	128	C1
Manilla St, E14	124	C1
Manitoba Ct, SE16	122	B2
Manley St, NW1	12	C5
Manneby Prior, N1		
off Cumming St	38	B3
Manningford Cl, EC1	39	E4
Manningtree St, E1	64	C5
Manor Ct, SW6	161	F4
Manor Est, SE16	149	E1
Sch Manorfield Prim Sch,		
E14	69	F3
Manor Gro, SE15	150	A5
Manor Ho Dr, NW6	7	D4
Manor Ms, NW6	31	D2
SE4	176	B5
Manor Pl, SE17	145	F3
Sch Manor Prim Sch,		
E15	49	E2
Manor Rd, E15	49	E3
E16	71	E1
Sch Manor Sch, NW10	28	B1
Manresa Rd, SW3	139	E3
Mansell St, E1	92	B3
Mansfield Ms, W1	57	E4
Mansfield St, W1	57	E4
Mansford St, E2	43	D3
Mansion Cl, SW9	169	D3
★ Mansion Ho, EC4	90	C1
⊖ Mansion House	90	B2
Mansion Ho Pl, EC4	90	C1
Mansion Ho St, EC4	90	C1
Mansions, The, SW5		
off Earls Ct Rd	137	E2
Manson Ms, SW7	138	B1
Manson Pl, SW7	138	C1
Mantle Way, E15	27	E3
Mantus Cl, E1	66	B1
Mantus Rd, E1	66	A1
Manwood St, E16	104	B5
Mapesbury Rd, NW2	7	D1
Mapeshill Pl, NW2	6	B2
Mape St, E2	65	E1

Maplecroft Cl, E6	75	E5
Mapledene Est, E8	20	C3
Mapledene Rd, E8	20	B3
Maple Ho, NW3		
off Maitland Pk Vil	12	B1
Maple Leaf Sq, SE16	123	D1
Maple Ms, NW6	31	E2
Maple Pl, W1	58	B2
Maples Pl, E1	65	F3
Maple St, E2	43	D3
W1	58	A3
Maple Wk, W10	51	D1
Maplin Rd, E16	73	E5
Maplin St, E3	46	A5
Marathon Ho, NW1	56	A3
Marban Rd, W9	30	A4
★ Marble Arch, W1	84	B2
⊖ Marble Arch	84	B2
Marble Arch Apts, W1		
off Harrowby St	55	F5
Marble Quay, E1	92	C4
Marchant St, SE14	151	E5
Marchbank Rd, W14	136	B4
Marchmont St, WC1	59	E1
Marchwood Cl, SE5	171	F2
Marcia Rd, SE1	147	F1
Marcus Ct, E15	27	F5
Marcus St, E15	27	F5
Marden Sq, SE16	121	E4
Mardyke Ho, SE17		
off Crosslet St	119	D5
Mare St, E8	43	F1
Margaret Ct, W1	58	A5
Margaret Ingram Cl,		
SW6	136	A5
Margaret St, W1	57	F5
Margaretta Ter, SW3	139	E4
Margery St, WC1	38	C5
Margravine Gdns, W6	135	D2
Margravine Rd, W6	135	D3
Maria Cl, SE1	121	D5
Sch Maria Fidelis Conv Sch,		
Lwr Sch, NW1	36	B5
Upr Sch, NW1	36	C4
Marian Pl, E2	43	E2
Marian Sq, E2	43	D2
Marian St, E2	43	E2
Maria Ter, E1	66	C3
Marie Curie, SE5		
off Sceaux Gdns	171	F3
Marie Lloyd Ho, N1	40	C3
Marie Lloyd Wk, E8	20	B2
Marigold All, SE1	89	E3
Marigold St, SE16	121	E2
Marinefield Rd, SW6	161	F5
Mariners Ms, E14	126	C5
Marine St, SE16	120	C3
Marine Twr, SE8	152	A4
Sch Marion Richardson		
Prim Sch, E1	94	C1
Maritime Ho, SE18	133	E5
Maritime Quay, E14	153	D2
Maritime St, E3	68	B2

Marjorie Ms, E1.......**94** C1
Market App, W12....**106** A1
Market Ct, W1.........**58** A5
Market Est, N7 ....**15** E1
Market Hill, SE18....**133** D4
Market La, W12....**106** A4
Market Ms, W1 ....**85** E5
Market Pl, SE16 ....**121** D5
W1.............**58** A5
Market Rd, N7.......**15** E2
Market Sq, E14 ....**97** F1
Market St, E1.........**64** A3
SE18 ....**133** D5
Market Way, E14 .....**97** F1
Market Yd Ms, SE1 ...**119** E3
Markham Pl, SW3 ....**140** A2
Markham Sq, SW3 ...**140** A2
Markham Ho, SW3....**139** F2
Markland Ho, W10 ....**78** C2
Mark La, EC3 ....**91** F3
Mark Sq, EC2 ....**63** E1
Mark St, E15 ....**27** E4
EC2 ....**63** E1
Marlborough, SW3 ...**111** F5
Marlborough Av, E8 ...**42** C1
Marlborough Cl, SE17.**145** F4
Marlborough Ct, W1...**86** A1
W8 ....**108** C5
Marlborough Gate Ho,
W2..............**82** C2
Marlborough Gro, SE1.**148** C3
Marlborough Hill, NW8.**32** B1
★ Marlborough Ho,
SW1.............**86** B5
Marlborough Pl, NW8..**32** A3
Sch Marlborough Prim Sch,
SW3.............**139** F1
Marlborough Rd,
SE18 ....**133** F3
SW1.............**86** B3
Marlborough St, SW3.**139** E1
Marley St, SE16......**150** C1
Marloes Rd, W8 ....**109** E4
Marlow Ct, NW6 ......**7** D3
Marlowe Path, SE8...**153** E4
Marlowes, The, NW8 ..**32** C1
Marlow Way, SE16 ...**122** C1
Marlton St, SE10....**156** B2
Marmara Apts, E16
off Western
Gateway **101** D3
Marmont Rd, SE15 ...**173** D3
Sch Marner Prim Sch, E3.**69** F1
Marne St, W10 ....**29** E4
Maroon St, E14......**67** E4
Marquess Est, N1 .....**18** B1
Marquess Rd, N1 .....**18** C2
Marquis Rd, NW1 .....**15** D2
Marriott Rd, E15......**27** E5
Marryat Sq, SW6.....**159** E3
Marsden St, NW5 ....**12** C2
Marshall, W2
off Hermitage St **54** C4

Marshall's Gro, SE18 .**131** F5
Marshalls Pl, SE16....**120** B4
Marshall St, W1........**86** B1
Marshalsea Rd, SE1 ..**118** B1
Marsham St, SW1....**115** D4
Marshfield St, E14 ...**126** A3
Marshgate La, E15 ....**25** E4
Marshgate Sidings,
E15 ....**47** E1
Marsh St, E14 ....**153** E1
Marsh Wall, E14 .....**96** C5
Marsland Cl, SE17....**145** F3
Marston, SE17
off Deacon Way....**118** B5
Marston Cl, NW6......**10** B3
Marsworth Ho, E2.....**42** C1
Martara Ms, SE17....**146** A3
Martello St, E8 ....**21** E3
Martello Ter, E8 ......**21** E3
Martel Pl, E8 ....**20** B1
Martha Ct, E2 ....**43** F2
Martha Rd, E15.......**27** F1
Martha's Bldgs, EC1...**62** C1
Martha St, E1 ....**93** F1
Martindale Av, E16...**101** D2
Martineau St, E1......**94** A1
Martin Ho, SE1 .....**118** B4
Martin La, EC4.......**91** D2
Martlett Ct, WC2......**87** F1
Marville Rd, SW6 ....**160** A2
Marvin St, E8.........**21** F1
Mary Ann Gdns, SE8..**152** C5
Marybank, SE18 .....**132** A5
Mary Datchelor Cl,
SE5..............**171** D3
Mary Grn, NW8.......**31** F1
⇌ Maryland...........**27** E1
Maryland Pt, E15
off The Grove **27** E1
Marylands Rd, W9 ....**53** D2
Maryland Wk, N1 .....**18** A5
Mary Lawrenson Pl,
SE3 ....**180** C2
MARYLEBONE, NW1 ...**56** A5
⇌ Marylebone **56** A2
⊖ Marylebone **56** A2
Marylebone Flyover,
NW1 ....**55** D4
W2 ....**55** D4
Marylebone High St,
W1..............**57** D3
Marylebone La, W1 ...**85** E1
Marylebone Ms, W1 ...**57** E4
Marylebone Pas, W1 ..**58** B5
Marylebone Rd, NW1..**55** F3
Marylebone St, W1...**57** D4
Marylee Way, SE11 ..**144** B2
Mary Macarthur Ho, E2.**44** C4
W6 ....**135** E4
Maryon Rd, SE7 .....**131** E5
SE18 ....**131** E5
Mary Pl, W11........**79** E3
Mary Rose Mall, E6....**76** B4
Mary Seacole Cl, E8 ...**20** A5
Mary St, E16 ....**72** A3
N1 ....**40** B1
Mary Ter, NW1 ....**35** F1

Coll Mary Ward Adult Ed
Cen, The, WC1 .....**59** F3
Masbro Rd, W14....**107** D4
Masefield Gdns, E6....**76** C5
Maskelyne Cl, SW11..**163** F3
Mason Cl, E16.......**100** C3
SE16 ....**149** D2
Masons Arms Ms, W1..**85** F1
Masons Av, EC2 ......**62** C5
Masons Pl, EC1 ......**39** F4
Mason St, SE17.....**147** D1
Masons Yd, EC1 ......**39** F4
Mason's Yd, SW1 .....**86** B4
Massie Rd, E8 ....**20** C2
Massinger St, SE17...**147** E1
Massingham St, E1....**66** C1
Masterman Ho, SE5 ..**170** B5
Masters Dr, SE16....**149** E3
Masters St, E1........**67** D3
Riv Masthouse Terrace.**153** D2
Mast Ho Ter, E14 ...**153** D1
Mast Leisure Pk, SE16.**123** D4
Mastmaker Rd, E14 ..**125** D2
Mast Quay, SE18
off Woolwich Ch St..**132** B3
Matheson Rd, W14...**136** A1
Matilda Gdns, E3 .....**46** C3
Matilda St, N1........**38** B1
Matlock St, E14......**67** E5
Matson Ho, SE16 ....**121** F3
Matthew Cl, W10 .....**50** C2
Matthew Parker St,
SW1.............**115** D2
Matthews St, SW11 ..**164** A5
Matthews Yd, WC2....**87** E1
Mattingley Way, SE15.**172** A1
Maud Cashmore Way,
SE18 ....**132** B4
Maude Rd, SE5 ......**171** E4
Maudlin's Grn, E1....**92** C4
H Maudsley Hosp,
SE5 ....**171** D5
Maud St, E16.........**72** A4
Maunsel St, SW1....**114** C5
Maurer Ct, SE10 ....**128** B3
Mauritius Rd, SE10...**155** F1
Maverton Rd, E3.....**46** C1
Mavis Wk, E6.........**75** E4
Mawbey Est, SE1 ...**148** C3
Mawbey Ho, SE1
off Old Kent Rd **148** B3
Mawbey Pl, SE1 ....**148** B3
Mawbey Rd, SE1.....**148** B3
Mawbey St, SW8.....**167** E2
Maxilla Gdns, W10 ....**51** D5
Maxilla Wk, W10......**79** D1
Maxwell Rd, SW6 ....**161** E2
Maya Cl, SE15.......**173** E5
Maybury Rd, E13 .....**74** A2
Maydew Ho, SE16 ...**122** A5
MAYFAIR, W1........**85** E3
Mayfair Ms, NW1 ....**12** B4
Mayfair Pl, W1 ....**85** F4
Mayfield Cl, E8 ....**20** A2
Mayfield Rd, E8......**20** A4
E13 ....**72** B2
Mayflower Cl, SE16 ..**123** D5

Mayflower Ct, SE16 *off St.*
  Marychurch St **122** A2
Sch Mayflower Prim Sch,
  E14 . . . . **97** E1
Mayflower St, SE16 . . **122** A2
Maygood St, N1 . . . . . . **38** D2
Maygrove Rd, NW6 . . . . . **8** A2
Mayhill Rd, SE7 . . . . . . **157** E5
Maynard Cl, SW6 . . . . **161** F2
Maynards Quay, E1 . . . **94** A3
May's Bldgs Ms, SE10. **178** B2
Mays Ct, WC2 . . . . **87** E3
Mayston Ms, SE10
  off Westcombe Hill . **157** D3
May St, W14 . . . . **136** B3
⇌ Maze Hill **155** E4
Maze Hill, SE3 . . . . . . **180** B3
  SE10 . . . . **155** E4
Mazenod Av, NW6 . . . . . . **9** D4
Mead Cl, NW1 . . . . **13** D3
Meadcroft Rd, SE11 . . **145** E5
Meadowbank, NW3 . . . **12** A4
Meadowbank Cl, SW6. **158** B2
Meadow Ms, SW8 . . . . **144** A5
Meadow Pl, SW8 . . . . . **167** F1
Meadow Rd, SW8 . . . . **168** A1
Meadow Row, SE1 . . . **118** A4
Meadowsweet Cl, E16 . **74** C4
Mead Pl, E9 . . . . **22** B2
Mead Row, SE1 . . . . . . **116** C3
Meakin Est, SE1 . . . . . **119** E3
Meard St, W1 . . . . **86** C1
Meath Cres, E2 . . . . **44** C5
Meath St, SW11 . . . . . **165** E3
Mecklenburgh Pl, WC1. **60** A1
Mecklenburgh Sq, WC1. **60** A1
Mecklenburgh St, WC1. **60** A1
Medburn St, NW1 . . . . . **36** C2
Medhurst Cl, E3 . . . . . . **45** F3
★ Medici Galleries, W1. **85** F1
Medland Ho, E14 . . . . . . **95** E2
Medlar St, SE5 . . . . **170** B3
Medley Rd, NW6 . . . . **9** D2
Medway Bldgs, E3 . . . . **45** F3
Medway Ms, E3 . . . . **45** F3
Medway Rd, E3 . . . . **45** F3
Medway St, SW1 . . . . . **115** D4
Meecham Ct, SW11 . . **163** D5
Meeting Fld Path, E9 . . **22** B1
Meeting Ho All, E1 . . . . **93** F4
Meeting Ho La, SE15 . **173** E3
Mehetabel Rd, E9 . . . . . **22** A1
Melba Way, SE13 . . . . **177** F4
Melbourne Ms, SW9 . . **168** C4
Melbourne Pl, WC2 . . . . **88** B2
Melbourne Sq, SW9 . . **168** C4
Melbourne Ter, SW6
  off Moore Pk Rd **161** E2
Melbury Cl, W8 . . . . . . **108** B3
Melbury Dr, SE5 . . . . . **171** E2
Melbury Rd, W14 . . . . **108** A3
Melcombe Ho, SW8
  off Dorset Rd **168** A2
Melcombe Pl, NW1 . . . . **56** A3
Sch Melcombe Prim Sch,
  W6 . . . . **134** C4
Melcombe St, NW1 . . . . **56** B2

Meldon Cl, SW6 . . . . . . **161** F4
Melford Rd, E6 . . . . **76** A1
Melina Pl, NW8 . . . . **32** C5
Melior Pl, SE1 . . . . **119** E1
Melior St, SE1 . . . . **119** D1
Mellish Ind Est, SE18 . **131** D3
Mellish St, E14 . . . . . . **124** C3
Mell St, SE10 . . . . **155** E3
Melon Pl, W8 . . . . **109** E1
Melon Rd, SE15 . . . . . . **172** C3
Melrose Gdns, W6 . . . . **106** B3
Melrose Ter, W6 . . . . . . **106** B2
Melton Ct, SW7 . . . . . . **139** D1
Melton St, NW1 . . . . **36** B5
Melville Pl, N1 . . . . **18** A4
Memel Ct, EC1 . . . . **62** A2
Memel St, EC1 . . . . **62** A2
Memorial Av, E15 . . . . . **49** E4
Menai Pl, E3 . . . . **46** C2
Mendip Hos, E2 . . . . **44** B4
Mendora Rd, SW6 . . . . **159** F1
Menotti St, E2 . . . . **65** D1
Mentmore Ter, E8 . . . . . **21** F4
Mepham St, SE1 . . . . . . **88** B5
Merceron Hos, E2
  off Globe Rd **44** A4
Merceron St, E1 . . . . . . **65** E2
Mercers Cl, SE10 . . . . . **156** A1
Mercers Pl, W6 . . . . . . **106** B5
Mercer St, WC2 . . . . **87** E1
Merchants Ho, SE10
  off Collington St **155** D3
Merchants Row, SE10
  off Hoskins St **155** D3
Merchant St, E3 . . . . . . **46** B5
Mercury Ho, E3
  off Garrison Rd **46** C1
Mercury Way, SE14 . . **150** C4
Meredith St, EC1 . . . . . . **39** E5
Mereton Mans, SE8 . . **177** D3
Meridian Ct, SE16
  off East La **120** C1
Meridian Gate, E14 . . **126** A1
Meridian Pl, E14 . . . . . **125** F1
Sch Meridian Prim Sch,
  SE10 . . . . **155** D3
Meridian Sq, E15 . . . . . **26** C3
Meridian Trd Est, SE7. **129** F5
Merlin St, WC1 . . . . **38** C5
Mermaid Ct, SE1 . . . . . **118** C1
  SE16 . . . . **96** A5
Mermaid Twr, SE8 . . . **152** A5
Merriam Av, E9 . . . . **24** B1
Merrick Sq, SE1 . . . . . . **118** B3
Merrington Rd, SW6. . **137** D4
Merrow St, SE17 . . . . . **146** C4
Merrow Wk, SE17 . . . . **147** D2
Merton Ri, NW3 . . . . . . **11** F4
Messina Av, NW6 . . . . . . **8** C4
Methley St, SE11 . . . . . **145** D3
★ Methodist Cen Hall,
  SW1 . . . . **115** D2
Methwold Rd, W10 . . . . **50** C3
Metro Cen Hts, SE1 . . . **118** A4
Metropolitan Cl, E14 . . **69** D4
Mews, The, N1 . . . . **18** B5

Mews Deck, E1 . . . . **93** F3
Mews St, E1 . . . . **92** C4
Meymott St, SE1 . . . . . . **89** E5
Meynell Cres, E9 . . . . . . **22** C3
Meynell Gdns, E9 . . . . . **22** C3
Meynell Rd, E9 . . . . **22** C3
★ MI5 (Security Service)
  Thames Ho, SW1 . . **115** E5
Miah Ter, E1 . . . . **93** D5
Micawber St, N1 . . . . . . **40** B4
Michael Cliffe Ho, EC1 . **39** D5
Michael Faraday Ho,
  SE17 . . . . **147** D3
Sch Michael Faraday
  Prim Sch, SE17 . . . . **147** D4
Michael Rd, SW6 . . . . . **161** F3
Michael Stewart Ho, SW6
  off Clem Attlee Ct . . **136** B5
Sch Michael Tippett Sch,
  Kennington, SE11 . . **117** D5
Michigan Bldg, E14 . . . **98** B3
Micklethwaite Rd,
  SW6 . . . . **137** D5
Middle Dartrey Wk, SW10
  off Blantyre St **162** C1
Middle Fld, NW8 . . . . . . **10** C5
Middle Row, W10 . . . . . **51** E2
Sch Middle Row Prim Sch,
  W10 . . . . **51** E1
Middlesex Pas, EC1 . . . **61** F4
Middlesex St, E1 . . . . . . **63** F4
Middle St, EC1 . . . . **62** A3
Middle Temple, EC4 . . . **88** C2
Middle Temple La, EC4. **88** C1
Middleton Dr, SE16 . . **123** D2
Middleton Pl, W1 . . . . . . **58** A4
Middleton Rd, E8 . . . . . **20** B4
Middleton St, E2 . . . . . . **43** E4
Middle Yd, SE1 . . . . **91** E4
Midford Pl, W1 . . . . **58** B2
Midhope St, WC1 . . . . . **37** F5
Midland Cres, NW3. . . . **10** A1
Midland Pl, E14 . . . . . . **154** A2
Midland Rd, NW1 . . . . . **37** D3
Midlothian Rd, E3. . . . . **68** A2
Midship Cl, SE16 . . . . . . **95** D5
Midship Pt, E14 . . . . . . **124** C2
Milborne Gro, SW10 . . **138** B3
Milborne St, E9 . . . . **22** B2
Milcote St, SE1 . . . . **117** E2
Mildmay Av, N1 . . . . **19** D1
Mildmay St, N1 . . . . **19** D1
MILE END, E1 . . . . **45** E5
⊖ Mile End **68** A1
H Mile End Hosp, E1 . . **67** D1
Mile End Pl, E1 . . . . **66** C1
Mile End Rd, E1 . . . . . . **65** F3
  E3 . . . . **65** F3
Sch Miles Coverdale
  Prim Sch, W12 . . . . **106** A1
Miles Pl, NW1 . . . . **55** D3
Miles St, SW8 . . . . **143** E5
Milford La, WC2 . . . . . . **88** B2

Milk St, E16 . . . . **105** E5
  EC2 . . . . **90** B4
Milkwell Yd, SE5 . . . . **170** B4
Milk Yd, E1 . . . . **94** A3
Millbank, SW1 . . . . . . **115** E4
Millbank Ct, SW1 . . . . **115** E5
Riv Millbank Millennium
  Pier **143** F1
Sch Millbank Prim Sch,
  SW1 . . . . **143** D1
Millbank Twr, SW1 . . . **143** E1
Millbrook Pl, NW1
  off Hampstead Rd . . . **36** A2
Millender Wk, SE16 . . . **150** B1
Millennium Br, EC4 . . . . **90** A2
  SE1 . . . . **90** A2
Millennium Cl, E16 . . . . **73** D5
Millennium Dr, E14 . . **126** C5
Millennium Harbour,
  E14 . . . . **124** B1
Millennium Pl, E2 . . . . . **43** F3
Sch Millennium Prim Sch,
  SE10 . . . . **128** A4
Millennium Sq, SE1 . . **120** A1
Millennium Way,
  SE10 . . . . **127** E1
Miller St, NW1 . . . . **36** A2
Millers Way, W6 . . . . . **106** B2
Miller Wk, SE1 . . . . **89** D5
Millgrove St, SW11 . . . **164** C5
Millharbour, E14 . . . . . **125** E3
Milligan St, E14 . . . . **96** B3
Millman Ms, WC1 . . . . . **60** A2
Millman Pl, WC1
  off Millman St **60** A2
Millman St, WC1 . . . . . . **60** A2
Mill Pl, E14 . . . . **95** F1
Mill Pond Cl, SW8 . . . . **167** D2
Millpond Est, SE16 . . . **121** E2
Mill Rd, E16 . . . . **101** F4
Mill Row, N1 . . . . **41** F1
Mills Ct, EC2 . . . . **41** F5
Mills Gro, E14 . . . . **70** A4
Millshott Cl, SW6 . . . . **158** B3
Millstream Rd, SE1 . . . **120** A2
Mill St, SE1 . . . . **120** B2
  W1 . . . . **85** F2
MILLWALL, E14 . . . . . . **125** E5
Millwall Dock Rd, E14 . **124** C3
★ Millwall FC, SE16 . . **150** B3
Millwood St, W10 . . . . . **51** E4
Mill Yd, E1 . . . . **92** C2
Milman Rd, NW6 . . . . . . **29** D2
Milman's St, SW10 . . . **138** C5
Milner Pl, N1 . . . . **17** D5
Milner Rd, E15 . . . . **49** E5
Milner Sq, N1 . . . . **17** E4
Milner St, SW3 . . . . **112** A5
Milroy Wk, SE1 . . . . **89** E4
Milson Rd, W14 . . . . . . **107** D3
Milton Cl, SE1 . . . . **148** A1
Milton Ct, EC2 . . . . **62** C3
Milton Ct Rd, SE14 . . . **151** F5

Milton St, EC2 . . . . **62** C3
Milverton Rd, NW6 . . . . . **6** B4
Milverton St, SE11 . . . **145** D2
Milward St, E1 . . . . **65** F4
Mimosa St, SW6 . . . . . **160** A4
Mina Rd, SE17 . . . . **147** F3
Mincing La, EC3 . . . . . . **91** E2
Minera Ms, SW1 . . . . . **113** D5
Minerva Cl, SW9 . . . . . **169** D2
Minerva St, E2 . . . . **43** E3
Minet Rd, SW9 . . . . . . **169** E5
Minford Gdns, W14 . . . **106** C2
Ming St, E14 . . . . **97** D2
★ Ministry of Defence,
  SW1 . . . . **87** E5
Miniver Pl, EC4
  off Garlick Hill **90** B2
Minnow St, SE17 . . . . . **147** F1
Minnow Wk, SE17
  off Minnow St **147** F1
Minories, EC3 . . . . **92** A2
Minshull St, SW8 . . . . . **166** C4
Minson Rd, E9 . . . . **23** D5
Minster Ct, EC3 . . . . **91** E2
Minster Pavement, EC3
  off Mincing La **91** E2
Mint Business Pk, E16 . **73** D4
Mintern St, N1 . . . . **41** D2
Minton Ho, SE11
  off Walnut Tree Wk . **116** C5
Minton Ms, NW6 . . . . **9** F1
Mint St, SE1 . . . . **118** A1
Mirabel Rd, SW6 . . . . . **160** B1
Miranda Cl, E1 . . . . **66** A4
Mirfield St, SE7 . . . . . . **130** C5
Mission Pl, SE15 . . . . . **173** D3
Mistral, SE5
  off Sceaux Gdns . . . **171** F3
Mitali Pas, E1 . . . . **92** C1
Mitchell St, EC1 . . . . **62** A1
Mitchell Wk, E6 . . . . **75** E4
Mitchison Rd, N1 . . . . . . **18** C2
Mitre, The, E14 . . . . **96** A2
Mitre Ct, EC2 . . . . **62** B5
Mitre Rd, E15 . . . . **49** E2
  SE1 . . . . **117** D1
Mitre Sq, EC3 . . . . **91** F1
Mitre St, EC3 . . . . **91** F1
Mizzen Mast Ho, SE18 . **132** C3
Modbury Gdns, NW5 . . **12** B2
Modling Ho, E2 . . . . **44** C3
Moffat Ho, SE5
  off Comber Gro **170** A2
Molesford Rd, SW6 . . . **160** C4
Molyneux St, W1 . . . . . . **55** F4
Monarch Dr, E16 . . . . . . **74** C4
Mona Rd, SE15 . . . . . . **174** B5
Mona St, E16 . . . . **72** B3
Monck St, SW1 . . . . . . **115** D4
Moncorvo Cl, SW7 . . . . **111** E2
Moncrieff Cl, E6 . . . . **75** E5
Moncrieff Pl, SE15 . . . **172** C5
Moncrieff St, SE15 . . . **173** D5
Monier Rd, E3 . . . . **24** C4
Monk Dr, E16 . . . . **100** C1
Monk Pas, E16 . . . . **100** C2
Monk St, SE18 . . . . **133** D5

Monkton St, SE11 . . . . **117** D5
Monkwell Sq, EC2 . . . . . **62** B4
Monmouth Ho, NW5 . . . **13** F1
Monmouth Pl, W2 . . . . . **81** D1
Monmouth Rd, W2 . . . . **81** D1
Monmouth St, WC2 . . . . **87** E1
Monnow Rd, SE1 . . . . . **148** C2
Sch Monson Prim Sch,
  SE14 . . . . **174** C1
Monson Rd, SE14 . . . . **174** C2
Montague Cl, SE1 . . . . . **90** C4
Montague Pl, WC1 . . . . **59** D3
Montague Sq, SE15 . . . **174** B2
Montague St, EC1 . . . . . **62** A4
  WC1 . . . . **59** E3
Montagu Mans, W1 . . . . **56** B3
Montagu Ms N, W1 . . . . **56** B4
Montagu Ms S, W1 . . . . **56** B5
Montagu Ms W, W1 . . . . **56** B5
Montagu Pl, W1 . . . . **56** A4
Montagu Row, W1 . . . . . **56** B4
Montagu Sq, W1 . . . . . . **56** B4
Montagu St, W1 . . . . **56** B5
Montaigne Cl, SW1 . . . **143** D1
Montana Bldg, SE13
  off Deals Gateway . . **177** E3
Montclare St, E2 . . . . . . **42** A5
Montevetro, SW11 . . . . **162** C3
Montford Pl, SE11 . . . . **144** C3
Montgomery Ct, W2
  off Harrow Rd **54** C4
Montgomery St, E14 . . . **97** F5
Monthope Rd, E1 . . . . . . **64** C4
Montpelier Ms, SW7 . . **111** F3
Montpelier Pl, E1 . . . . . . **94** A1
  SW7 . . . . **111** F3
Montpelier Rd, SE15 . . **173** F3
Montpelier Sq, SW7 . . **111** F2
Montpelier St, SW7 . . . **111** F2
Montpelier Ter, SW7 . . **111** F2
Montpelier Wk, SW7 . . **111** F3
Montreal Pl, WC2 . . . . . **88** A2
Montrose Av, NW6 . . . . **29** F2
Montrose Ct, SW7 . . . . **111** E2
Montrose Pl, SW1 . . . . **113** D2
⊖ Monument **91** D2
★ Monument, The,
  EC3 . . . . **91** D3
Monument St, EC3 . . . . **91** D3
Monza St, E1 . . . . **94** A3
Moodkee St, SE16 . . . . **122** A3
Moody Rd, SE15 . . . . . **172** A2
Moody St, E1 . . . . **45** D5
Moon St, N1 . . . . **17** E5
Moore Ho, E14 . . . . **125** D2
Moore Pk Rd, SW6 . . . . **161** E2
Moore St, SW3 . . . . **112** A5
Moorfields, EC2 . . . . **62** C4
H Moorfields Eye Hosp,
  EC1 . . . . **40** C5
Moorfields Highwalk,
  EC2 . . . . **62** C4
⇌ Moorgate **62** C4
⊖ Moorgate **62** C4
Moorgate, EC2 . . . . **62** C5
Moorgate Pl, EC2 . . . . . **62** C5
Moorhouse Rd, W2 . . . . **52** C5

Moorings, The, E16
   off Prince Regent La . 74 A4
Moor La, EC2 ....62 C4
Moor Pl, EC2 ....62 C4
Moor St, W1..........87 D1
Morant St, E14 ....97 D2
Mora St, EC1 ....40 B5
Morat St, SW9 ......168 B3
Moravian Pl, SW10 ...139 D5
Moravian St, E2 ......44 A3
Morden Hill, SE13....178 A5
Morden La, SE13.....178 B4
Sch Morden Mt Prim Sch,
   SE13 ....177 F5
Morden Rd, SE3 .....180 C5
Morden St, SE13.....177 F4
Morden Wf Rd, SE10..127 E4
Morecambe Cl, E1.....66 C3
Morecambe St, SE17 .146 B3
More Cl, E16 ....72 B5
   W14 ....135 D1
Sch More Ho Sch, SW1 .112 B4
Sch Moreland Prim Sch,
   EC1 ....39 F4
Moreland St, EC1 .....39 F4
More London Pl, SE1 ..91 E5
More London Riverside,
   SE1 ....91 F5
Moreton Cl, SW1.....142 B3
Moreton Ho, SE16....121 F3
Moreton Pl, SW1.....142 B2
Moreton St, SW1.....142 B2
Moreton Ter, SW1....142 B2
Moreton Ter Ms N,
   SW1.............142 B2
Moreton Ter Ms S,
   SW1.............142 B2
Morgan Ct, SW11
   off Battersea
   High St..........163 D4
Morgan Ho, SW1
   off Vauxhall Br Rd ..142 B1
Morgan Rd, W10......52 A3
Morgans La, SE1 ......91 E5
Morgan St, E3 ....45 F5
   E16 ....72 B3
Morland Est, E8 ......21 D3
Morland Ms, N1 ......17 D4
Coll Morley Coll, SE1...117 D3
Morley St, SE1......117 D3
Morna Rd, SE5 ......170 B5
Morning La, E9 ....22 A1
Sch Morningside Prim Sch,
   E9 ....22 B1
Mornington Av, W14 .136 A1
◆ Mornington
   Crescent.........36 A2
Mornington Cres, NW1.36 A2
Mornington Gro, E3 ...46 C5
Mornington Ms, SE5...170 A3
Mornington Pl, NW1...35 F2
Mornington Rd, SE8 ..176 B2
Mornington St, NW1...35 F2
Mornington Ter, NW1...35 F1
Morocco St, SE1 ....119 E2
Morpeth Gro, E9 .....22 C5
Morpeth Rd, E9.......44 B1

Sch Morpeth Sch, E2....44 B5
   Annexe, E2 ....44 A5
Morpeth St, E2 ....44 C4
Morpeth Ter, SW1....114 A4
Morrells Yd, SE11....145 D2
Morris Rd, E14 ....69 E3
Morris St, E1.........93 F1
Morshead Rd, W9 .....31 D5
Mortham St, E15......49 E1
Mortimer Ho, W11
   off St. Anns Rd......79 D4
Mortimer Cres, NW6...31 E1
Mortimer Est, NW6....31 E1
Mortimer Mkt, WC1 ...58 B2
Mortimer Pl, NW6.....31 E1
Mortimer Rd, N1......19 F4
   NW10 ....28 A4
Mortimer Sq, W11.....79 D3
Mortimer St, W1......58 A5
Mortlake Rd, E16 .....73 F5
Mortlock Cl, SE15 ...173 E4
Morton Cl, E1 ....94 A1
Morton Ms, SW5 ....137 E1
Morton Pl, SE1......116 C4
Morton Rd, N1 ....18 B4
Morville St, E3........46 C2
Morwell St, WC1 .....59 D4
Moscow Pl, W2 ....81 E2
Moscow Rd, W2 ......81 E2
Moseley Row, SE10 ..128 B5
Moss Cl, E1 ....65 D3
Mossford St, E3......68 A1
Mossington Gdns,
   SE16 ....150 A1
Mossop St, SW3 ....111 F5
Mostyn Gdns, NW10 ..28 C4
Mostyn Gro, E3.......46 B3
Mostyn Rd, SW9.....168 C4
Motcomb St, SW1 ...112 B3
Motley Av, EC2 ....63 E1
Motley St, SW8 .....166 A5
Moulins Rd, E9 ....22 B4
Mountague Pl, E14....98 A2
Mountain Ho, SE11...144 A2
Mountbatten Ct, SE16
   off Rotherhithe St ...94 B5
Mountfort Cres, N1....16 C3
Mountfort Ter, N1.....16 C4
Mountjoy Ho, EC2
   off The Barbican 62 B4
Mount Mills, EC1......39 F5
Mount Pleasant, WC1..60 B2
Mount Pleasant Rd,
   NW10 ....6 B4
Mount Row, W1 ......85 E3
Mounts Pond Rd, SE3.178 C5
Mount St, W1 ....85 D3
Mount St Ms, W1 .....85 E3
Mount Ter, E1 ....65 E4
Mowbray Rd, NW6 ....7 E3
Sch Mowlem Prim Sch,
   E2 ....44 A2
Mowlem St, E2 ....43 F2
Mowll St, SW9......168 C2
Moxon St, W1 ....56 C4
Moye Cl, E2..........43 D2
Moylan Rd, W6 ......135 F5

Mozart St, W10 ....30 A5
Mozart Ter, SW1 .....141 D1
DLR Mudchute........125 F5
Mudlarks Boul, SE10 off John
   Harrison Way......128 B3
Muirfield Cl, SE16....149 F3
Muirfield Cres, E14...125 E3
Muir St, E16 ....104 A5
Mulberry Business Cen,
   SE16 ....123 D2
Mulberry Cl, SW3
   off Beaufort St....139 D5
Mulberry Ct, EC1
   off Tompion St....39 F5
Mulberry Ms, SE14...176 A3
Mulberry Rd, E8 .....20 A3
Sch Mulberry Sch for Girls,
   E1 ....93 E1
Coll Mulberry Sch for Girls -
   St. George's, E1 ....93 E2
Mulberry St, E1.......64 C5
Mulberry Wk, SW3 ...139 D4
Mulgrave Rd, SW6 ...136 A4
Sch Mulgrave Sch & Early
   Years Cen, SE18 ...133 E4
Mullet Gdns, E2 ......43 D4
Mull Wk, N1..........18 B2
Mulready St, NW8 ....55 E2
Mulvaney Way, SE1 ..119 D2
Mumford Mills, SE10 .177 E3
Munday Rd, E16.....100 C1
Munden Ho, E3
   off Bromley High St ..47 F4
Munden St, W14.....107 E5
Mund St, W14 ......136 B3
Mundy St, N1 ....41 E4
Munkenbeck, W2
   off Hermitage St 54 C4
Munro Ms, W10.......51 F3
Munro Ter, SW10 ....138 C5
Munster Ms, SW6 ...159 E1
Munster Rd, SW6 ...159 E1
Munster Sq, NW1 ....35 F5
Munton Rd, SE17 ...118 B5
Murdock Cl, E16 .....72 B5
Murdock St, SE15 ...149 E5
Muriel St, N1.........38 B2
Murphy St, SE1......116 C2
Murray Gro, N1.......40 B3
Murray Ms, NW1......14 C3
Murray Sq, E16......101 D1
Murray St, NW1......14 B3
Murrays Yd, SE18....133 E5
Mursell Est, SW8....168 A4
Musard Rd, W6......135 F4
   W14 ....135 F4
Musbury St, E1.......66 A5
Muscal, W6 ....135 E4
Muscatel Pl, SE5.....171 F2
Muscovy St, EC3......91 F3
★ Museum in Docklands,
   E14 ....97 D3
Museum La, SW7 ....111 D4

★ Museum of Childhood at
 Bethnal Green, E2 .. **43** F4
★ Museum of Gdn History,
 SE1 .... **116** A4
★ Museum of Instruments
 (Royal College of Music),
 SW7 .... **110** C3
★ Museum of London,
 EC2 .... **62** A4
Museum Pas, E2...... **44** A4
Museum St, WC1..... **59** E4
Musgrave Cres, SW6.. **161** D2
Musgrove Rd, SE14 .. **175** D4
Mustow Pl, SW6 ..... **160** B5
Mutrix Rd, NW6....... **9** D5
Mutton Pl, NW1 ..... **13** D2
🔲Myatt Gdn Prim Sch,
 SE4 .... **176** B5
Myatt Rd, SW9 ...... **169** E4
Myatts Flds S, SW9 off St.
 Lawrence Way **169** D5
Myatts N, SW9
 off Fairbairn Grn ... **169** D3
Mycenae Rd, SE3 .... **180** C1
Myddelton Pas, EC1.. **39** D4
Myddelton Sq, EC1... **39** D4
Myddelton St, EC1 ... **39** D5
Myers La, SE14 ...... **150** C4
Mylius Cl, SE14...... **174** B3
Mylne St, EC1 .... **38** C4
Myrdle St, E1......... **65** D4
Myrtleberry Cl, E8 .... **20** A2
Myrtle Wk, N1........ **41** E3

N

N1 Shop Cen, N1...... **39** D2
Nag's Head Ct, EC1 ... **62** A2
Nairn St, E14......... **70** B4
Nankin St, E14 .... **97** D1
Nantes Pas, E1 ...... **64** A3
Nant St, E2 .... **43** A4
Naoroji St, WC1...... **38** C5
Napier Av, E14 ...... **153** D2
Napier Cl, SE8 ...... **176** B1
 W14 .... **108** A3
Napier Gro, N1 ...... **40** B3
Napier Pl, W14 ...... **108** A4
Napier Rd, E15 ...... **49** F3
 W14 .... **108** A4
Napier Ter, N1....... **17** E4
Narrow St, E14 ...... **95** E2
Nascot St, W12....... **50** A5
Naseby Cl, NW6 .... **10** B3
Nash Ho, SW1 ...... **141** F3
Nash St, NW1 ...... **35** F5
Nassau St, W1........ **58** A4
Nathaniel Cl, E1 ..... **64** B4
★ National Army Mus,
 SW3............. **140** B4
★ National Gall, WC2.. **87** D3

🅷 National Hosp for Neurology
 & Neurosurgery, The,
 WC1............... **59** F2
★ National Maritime Mus,
 SE10 .... **154** C5
★ National Portrait Gall,
 WC2............... **87** D3
🔲National Sch of Govt,
 SW1............. **142** A1
National Ter, SE16
 off Bermondsey
 Wall E **121** E2
★ National Thea, SE1 . **88** B4
★ Natural History Mus,
 SW7............. **110** C4
Naval Row, E14 ...... **98** B2
Navarino Gro, E8 .... **21** D1
Navarino Rd, E8 ..... **21** D1
Navarre St, E2........ **64** A1
Navenby Wk, E3...... **69** D1
Naxos Bldg, E14..... **124** C2
Naylor Rd, SE15 ..... **173** E1
Nazareth Gdns, SE15 . **173** E5
Nazrul St, E2........ **42** A4
Neal St, WC2 .... **87** E1
Neal's Yd, WC2...... **87** E1
Neate St, SE5 ...... **148** A4
Neathouse Pl, SW1... **114** A5
Neatscourt Rd, E6 .... **75** D4
Nebraska Bldg, SE13
 off Deals Gateway .. **177** E4
Nebraska St, SE1 .... **118** C2
Neckinger, SE16 ..... **120** B3
Neckinger Est, SE16.. **120** B3
Neckinger St, SE1.... **120** B2
Nectarine Way, SE13 . **177** F5
Needham Rd, W11 ... **80** C1
Needleman St, SE16.. **122** C4
Nella Rd, W6........ **134** C5
Nelldale Rd, SE16... **122** A5
Nelson Cl, NW6..... **30** A4
Nelson Ct, SE16
 off Brunel Rd **94** B5
Nelson Gdns, E2...... **43** D4
Nelson Pas, EC1..... **40** B5
Nelson Pl, N1 .... **39** F3
Nelson Rd, SE10 .... **154** B5
★ Nelson's Column,
 WC2.............. **87** E4
Nelson Sq, SE1 ..... **117** E1
Nelson St, E1......... **65** E5
 E16 .... **100** A2
Nelsons Yd, NW1 .... **36** A2
Nelson Ter, N1 ...... **39** F3
Nelson Wk, SE16..... **95** F5
Neptune Ho, E3
 off Garrison Rd...... **46** C1
Neptune St, SE16... **122** A3
Nesham St, E1 ...... **92** C4
Ness St, SE16 ...... **120** C3
Netherhall Gdns, NW3 . **10** B1
Netherton Gro, SW10. **138** B5
Netherwood Pl, W14 . **106** C3
Netherwood Rd, W14. **106** C3
Netherwood St, NW6 .. **8** B3
🔲Netley Prim Sch,
 NW1 .... **36** A5

Netley St, NW1 .... **36** A5
Nettleton Rd, SE14... **175** D3
Nevada Bldg, SE10
 off Blackheath Rd .. **177** E3
Nevada St, SE10 .... **178** B1
Nevern Pl, SW5 ..... **137** D1
Nevern Rd, SW5 .... **136** C1
Nevern Sq, SW5 .... **137** D1
Neville Cl, NW1 ...... **37** D3
 NW6 .... **30** B3
 SE15 .... **172** C2
Neville Rd, NW6 .... **30** B3
Neville St, SW7 ..... **138** C2
Neville Ter, SW7 .... **138** C2
Newall Ho, SE1 ..... **118** B3
Newark Knok, E6 .... **76** C5
Newark St, E1....... **65** E4
New Atlas Wf, E14 .. **124** B4
New Barn St, E13 .... **73** D1
New Bond St, W1 .... **85** E1
New Br St, EC4 ...... **89** E1
New Broad St, EC2 ... **63** E4
Newburgh St, W1 .... **86** A1
New Burlington Ms,
 W1............... **86** A2
New Burlington Pl, W1. **86** A2
New Burlington St, W1. **86** A2
Newburn St, SE11.... **144** B3
Newbury Ms, NW5 .... **13** D2
Newbury St, EC1..... **62** A4
New Butt La, SE8 ... **177** D2
New Butt La N, SE8 .. **177** D2
Newby Pl, E14 .... **98** A2
New Caledonian Wf,
 SE16 .... **124** A3
Newcastle Cl, EC4..... **61** E5
Newcastle Pl, W2 .... **55** D4
Newcastle Row, EC1... **61** D1
New Cavendish St, W1. **57** F3
New Change, EC4..... **90** A1
New Charles St, EC1... **39** F4
NEW CHARLTON, SE7. **130** A5
New Ch Rd, SE5 ..... **170** B1
New Coll Ct, NW3
 off Finchley Rd...... **10** B2
New Coll Ms, N1 ..... **17** D3
New Coll Par, NW3
 off Finchley Rd...... **10** C2
Newcombe St, W8 .... **81** D4
Newcomen St, SE1... **118** C1
New Compton St, WC2. **87** D1
New Concordia Wf,
 SE1 .... **120** B1
New Ct, EC4......... **88** C2
Newcourt St, NW8 ... **33** E3
★ New Covent Garden
 Flower Mkt, SW8 .. **143** D5
★ New Covent Garden
 Mkt, SW8......... **166** C2
New Crane Pl, E1 .... **94** A4
NEW CROSS, SE14 ... **175** E3
⇌New Cross **176** B2
⊕New Cross **176** B2
New Cross, SE14..... **176** A2
NEW CROSS GATE,
 SE14 .... **174** C3
⇌New Cross Gate... **175** E2

◆New Cross Gate . . . **175** E2
New Cross Rd, SE14 . . **174** D1
Newell St, E14 . . . . **96** A1
Newent Cl, SE15 . . . . . **171** E1
New Ferry App, SE18 . **132** C3
New Fetter La, EC4 . . . . **61** D5
Newgate St, EC1 . . . . . . **61** F5
New Globe Wk, SE1 . . . **90** A4
New Goulston St, E1 . . **64** A5
◫ **Newham Cen for Mental**
   Health, E13 . . . . **74** C2
◫ **Newham Coll of Further**
   Ed, SE1 . . . . **119** F1
   Stratford Campus, E15 . **27** F4
◫ **Newham 6th Form Coll**,
   Main Site, E13 . . . . **73** F1
   Stratford Site, E15 . . . . **27** D4
Newhams Row, SE1 . . **119** F2
◫ **Newham Uni Hosp**,
   E13 . . . . **74** B1
   Gateway Surgical Cen,
   E13 . . . . **74** C2
Newham Way, E16 . . . . **72** C4
Newhaven La, E16 . . . **72** B2
NEWINGTON, SE1 . . . . **118** A5
Newington Butts, SE1 . **145** F1
   SE11 . . . . **145** F1
Newington Causeway,
   SE1 . . . . **117** F4
New Inn Bdy, EC2 . . . . . **63** F1
New Inn Pas, WC2 . . . . **88** B1
New Inn Sq, EC2 . . . . . . **63** F1
New Inn St, EC2 . . . . . . **63** F1
New Inn Yd, EC2 . . . . . . **63** F1
New Kent Rd, SE1 . . . . **118** A4
◫ **New King's Prim Sch**,
   SW6 . . . . **160** B5
New King St, SE8 . . . . **152** C4
Newland Ct, EC1
   off St. Luke's Est **62** C1
Newlands Quay, E1 . . . **94** A3
Newlands Ter, SW8
   off Queenstown Rd . **165** E5
Newland St, E16 . . . . . **103** F5
Newling Cl, E6 . . . . **76** B5
New London St, EC3 . . **91** F2
New Lydenburg Commercial
   Est, SE7 off New
   Lydenburg St **130** B4
New Lydenburg St,
   SE7 . . . . **130** B4
Newman Pas, W1 . . . . . **58** B4
Newman's Ct, EC3 . . . . **91** D1
Newman's Row, WC2 . . **60** B4
Newman St, W1 . . . . . . **58** B4
Newman Yd, W1 . . . . . . **58** B5
New Mt St, E15 . . . . **27** D5
Newnham Ter, SE1 . . **116** C3
◫ **New North Comm Sch**,
   N1 . . . . **18** A5
New N Pl, EC2 . . . . **63** E2
New N Rd, N1 . . . . **41** D3
New N St, WC1 . . . . **60** A3
New Oxford St, WC1 . . **59** D5
New Pl Sq, SE16 . . . . . **121** E3
New Plaistow Rd, E15 . **27** F5
Newport Av, E13 . . . . . . **73** F2

Newport Av, E14 . . . . . . **99** D3
Newport Ct, WC2 . . . . . **87** D2
Newport Pl, WC2 . . . . . **87** D2
Newport St, SE11 . . . . **144** A1
New Priory Ct, NW6 . . . . . **9** D4
New Providence Wf,
   E14 . . . . **98** C4
New Quebec St, W1 . . . **84** B1
New Ride, SW7 . . . . . . **112** A1
New River Head, EC1 . . **39** D4
New River Wk, N1 . . . . . **18** A2
New Rd, E1 . . . . **65** E4
New Row, WC2 . . . . **87** E2
★ **New Scotland Yd**,
   SW1 . . . . **114** C3
New Spring Gdns Wk,
   SE11 . . . . **143** F3
New Sq, WC2 . . . . **60** B5
New St, EC2 . . . . **63** F4
New St Sq, EC4 . . . . **61** D5
◫ **Newton Prep Sch**,
   SW8 . . . . **165** F3
Newton Rd, W2 . . . . **81** D1
Newton St, WC2 . . . . . . **59** F5
Newtown St, SW11 . . **165** E3
New Turnstile, WC1 . . . **60** A4
New Union Cl, E14 . . . **126** B3
New Union St, EC2 . . . . **62** C4
New Wf Rd, N1 . . . . **37** F2
Niagara Cl, N1
   off Cropley St **40** B2
Nicholas La, EC4 . . . . . . **91** D2
Nicholas Pas, EC4 . . . . . **91** D2
Nicholas Rd, E1 . . . . **66** B1
Nicholl St, E2 . . . . **42** C1
Nichols Ct, E2 . . . . **42** A3
Nicholson St, SE1 . . . . . **89** E5
Nightingale Ho, E1
   off Thomas More St . . **92** C4
Nightingale Ms, E3 . . . . **45** E2
   SE11 . . . . **117** D5
Nightingale Pl, SW10 . **138** B4
Nightingale Rd, N1 . . . . **18** B2
Nightingale Way, E6 . . **75** F3
Nile St, N1 . . . . **40** B4
Nile Ter, SE15 . . . . **148** A3
Nimrod Pas, N1 . . . . **19** F2
Nina Mackay Cl, E15 . . **27** E5
NINE ELMS, SW8 . . . . . **166** B1
Nine Elms La, SW8 . . . **142** B5
Niton St, SW6 . . . . **158** C1
No. 1 St, SE18 . . . . **133** F4
Noble St, EC2 . . . . **62** A5
Noel Coward Ho, SW1
   off Vauxhall Br Rd . . **142** B1
Noel Rd, E6 . . . . **75** E2
   N1 . . . . **39** E2
Noel St, W1 . . . . **86** B1
Noko, W10 . . . . **29** D4
Norbiton Rd, E14 . . . . . **68** A5
Norburn St, W10 . . . . . **51** E4
Norfolk Cres, W2 . . . . . . **55** F5
Norfolk Ho, SE3 . . . . . . **155** F4
   SW1 off Regency St . . **115** D5
Norfolk Ms, W10 . . . . . . **51** F4
Norfolk Pl, W2 . . . . **55** D5

New - Nor   **239**

Norfolk Rd, NW8 . . . . . . **33** D1
Norfolk Row, SE1 . . . . **116** A5
Norfolk Sq, W2 . . . . **83** D1
Norfolk Sq Ms, W2 . . . . **83** D1
Norfolk Ter, W6 . . . . . . **135** E3
Norland Ho, W11 . . . . . **79** D5
Norland Pl, W11 . . . . . . **79** F5
◫ **Norland Pl Sch**, W11 . **79** E5
Norland Rd, W11 . . . . . **79** D5
Norland Sq, W11 . . . . . **79** F5
◫ **Normand Cft Comm Sch**
   for Early Years & Prim Ed,
   W14 . . . . **136** B4
Normand Gdns, W14
   off Greyhound Rd . . **135** F4
Normand Ms, W14 . . . **135** F4
Normand Rd, W14 . . . **136** A4
Normandy Rd, SW9 . . **168** C4
Normandy Ter, E16 . . . **101** E1
Norman Gro, E3 . . . . . . **45** F3
Norman Rd, E6 . . . . **76** B1
   SE10 . . . . **177** F1
Norman St, EC1 . . . . **40** A5
Norris St, SW1 . . . . **86** C3
Northampton Pk, N1 . . **18** B1
Northampton Rd, EC1 . **61** D1
Northampton Row,
   EC1 . . . . **39** D5
Northampton Sq, EC1 . **39** E5
Northampton St, N1 . . **18** A3
North Audley St, W1 . . **84** C1
North Bk, NW8 . . . . **33** D5
NORTH BECKTON, E6 . . **75** F2
◫ **North Beckton Prim Sch**,
   E6 . . . . **76** B3
North Branch Av, W10 . **28** B5
◫ **North Br Ho Sen Sch**,
   NW1 . . . . **35** E1
Northburgh St, EC1 . . . **61** F1
North Carriage Dr, W2 . **83** E2
Northchurch, SE17 . . . **147** D2
Northchurch Rd, N1 . . . **18** C3
Northchurch Ter, N1 . . . **19** E4
North Colonnade, The,
   E14 . . . . **97** D4
North Cres, E16 . . . . **71** D2
   WC1 . . . . **58** C3
Northdown St, N1 . . . . . **37** F2
North End Cres, W14 . **136** A1
North End Ho, W14 . . . **135** F1
North End Par, W14 . . . **135** F1
North End Rd, SW6 . . . **136** B4
   W14 . . . . **136** A2
Northey St, E14 . . . . **95** F2
North Flockton St,
   SE16 . . . . **120** C1
North Gdn, E14
   off Westferry Circ **96** B4
North Gate, NW8 . . . . . **33** E3
North Gower St, NW1 . . **36** B5
◆ **North Greenwich** . . . **127** E1
Northiam St, E9 . . . . **43** F1
Northington St, WC1 . . **60** A2

NORTH KENSINGTON,
  W10..............51 D4
North Ms, WC1 ....60 B2
Northpoint Sq, NW1 ...14 C1
North Pole Rd, W10 ...50 A4
Northport St, N1.......41 D1
North Ride, W2 ....83 E3
North Ri, W2
  off St. Georges Flds ..83 F1
North Rd, N7.........15 D1
North Row, W1 ....84 B2
North Several, SE3
  off Orchard Dr 179 D5
North Tenter St, E1....92 B1
North Ter, SW3 ....111 E4
Northumberland All,
  EC3 ....91 F1
Northumberland Av,
  WC2..............87 E4
Northumberland Pl,
  W2................52 C5
Northumberland Rd,
  E6 ....75 F5
Northumberland St,
  WC2..............87 E4
Northumbria St, E14 ..69 D5
North Vil, NW1 ....14 C2
North Wk, W2 ....82 A3
Northways Par, NW3
  off Finchley Rd......10 C3
Sch North W London Jewish
  Prim Sch, NW6 ......7 E3
Northwest Pl, N1 .....39 D2
North Wf Rd, W2......54 C4
Northwick Cl, NW8 ....54 C1
Northwick Ter, NW8....54 C1
NORTH WOOLWICH,
  E16 ....131 F1
★ North Woolwich
  Old Sta Mus, E16 ..133 D1
North Woolwich Rd,
  E16 ....100 B4
North Woolwich Rbt,
  E16 ....102 C5
Norton Folgate, E1....63 F3
Norway Gate, SE16 ...123 F3
Norway Pl, E14.......96 A1
Norway St, SE10.....153 F5
Norwich Ho, E14......69 F5
Norwich St, EC4 ......60 C5
Notley St, SE5.......170 C1
Sch Notre Dame Sch,
  SE1 ....117 E3
Notting Barn Rd, W10 .50 C2
Nottingdale Sq, W11 ..79 E3
Nottingham Av, E16...74 A4
Nottingham Ct, WC2 ..87 E1
Nottingham Pl, W1....56 C2
Nottingham St, W1....56 C3
Nottingham Ter, NW1 ..56 C2
NOTTING HILL, W11....79 F2
⊖ Notting Hill Gate ...80 C3
Notting Hill Gate, W11.80 C4

Nova, E14 ....124 C5
Novello St, SW6 .....160 C4
Nugent Ter, NW8 .....32 B3
Nun Ct, EC2 ....62 C5
Nursery La, E2 ....42 A1
  W10 ....50 A4
Nursery Rd, E9 ....22 A1
Nursery Row, SE17...146 C1
Nutbourne St, W10....29 C4
Nutcroft Rd, SE15....173 E2
Nutford Pl, W1 ....55 F5
Nutley Ter, NW3 ......10 B1
Nutmeg Cl, E16......71 F1
Nutmeg La, E14 ......98 C1
Nuttall St, N1 ....41 F2
Nutt St, SE15........172 B1
Nynehead St, SE14...175 E1

O

★ O2, The, SE10......99 E5
O2 Shop Cen, NW3 ....10 A1
Oak Cres, E16 ....71 F4
Oakdene, SE15 ......173 E3
Oakden St, SE11......117 D5
Oakes Cl, E6 ....104 B1
Oakey La, SE1.......116 C3
Oakfield St, SW10....138 A4
Oak Ho, NW3
  off Maitland Pk Vil...12 B1
Oakington Rd, W9 .....53 D1
Sch Oaklands Sch, E2...43 E4
Oak La, E14..........96 A2
Oakley Cl, E6........75 F5
Oakley Cres, EC1......39 F3
Oakley Gdns, SW3 ...139 F4
Oakley Pl, SE1.......148 A3
Oakley Rd, N1........18 C3
Oakley Sq, NW1 ......36 B3
Oakley St, SW3 ......139 E4
Oakley Wk, W6 ......135 D4
Oakley Yd, E2 ....64 B1
Oak Tree Rd, NW8.....33 D5
Oakwood Ct, W14....108 A3
Oakwood La, W14....108 A3
Oakworth Rd, W10....50 B3
Oat La, EC2 ....62 A5
Oban Cl, E13 ....74 A2
Oban Ho, E14 ....71 D5
Oban St, E14.........71 D5
O'Brien Ho, E2 ....45 D4
Observatory Gdns,
  W8..............108 C1
Observatory Ms, E14 .126 C5
Occupation Rd, SE17 .146 A2
Ocean Est, E1 ....67 D2
Ocean St, E1 ....67 D3
Ocean Wf, E14.......124 C2
Ockenden Ms, N1.....18 C2
Ockendon Rd, N1.....18 C2
Octagon Arc, EC2 .....63 E4
Octavia Ms, W9.......52 A1
Octavia St, SW11....163 E4
Octavius St, SE8 .....176 C1
Odessa St, SE16 .....124 A2

Odger St, SW11......164 B5
Odhams Wk, WC2.....87 F1
Offenbach Ho, E2 .....44 C3
Offley Rd, SW9 .....168 C1
Offord Rd, N1 ....16 A3
Offord St, N1.........16 A3
Ogle St, W1 ....58 A3
Ohio Bldg, SE13
  off Deals Gateway ..177 E4
Ohio Rd, E13.........72 B2
Okehampton Rd,
  NW10 ....28 B1
Olaf St, W11 ....79 D3
★ Old Admiralty Bldg
  (M.o.D.), SW1.......87 D5
Old Bailey, EC4 ......89 F1
Old Barge Ho All, SE1
  off Upper Grd......89 D4
Old Barrack Yd, SW1 .112 C1
Old Barrowfield, E15 ..49 F1
Old Bellgate Pl, E14 ..124 C4
Old Bethnal Grn Rd, E2. 42 C4
Old Billingsgate Wk, EC3
  off Lower Thames St .91 E3
Old Bond St, W1 ......86 A3
Old Brewers Yd, WC2 ..87 E1
Old Broad St, EC2 ....91 D1
Old Brompton Rd,
  SW5..............137 D3
  SW7..............137 D3
Old Bldgs, WC2 ......60 C5
Old Burlington St, W1 .86 A2
Oldbury Pl, W1 ....57 D3
Old Canal Ms, SE15 ..148 B3
Old Castle St, E1......64 A4
Old Cavendish St, W1..57 E5
Old Change Ct, EC4
  off Carter La 90 A1
Old Chelsea Ms, SW3 .139 D5
Old Ch Rd, E1 ....94 C1
Old Ch St, SW3 .....139 D3
Old Compton St, W1...86 C2
Old Ct Pl, W8........109 E1
★ Old Curiosity Shop,
  WC2..............60 A5
Old Dover Rd, SE3 ...181 D1
Oldfield Gro, SE16 ...150 C1
Old Fish St Hill, EC4 ...90 A2
Old Fleet La, EC4......61 E5
OLD FORD, E3 ....24 A4
Sch Old Ford Prim Sch,
  E3 ....46 A2
Old Ford Rd, E2.......43 F4
  E3 ....45 D2
Old Gloucester St, WC1. 59 F3
Old Jamaica Rd, SE16. 120 C3
Old Jewry, EC2 ....90 C1
Old Kent Rd, SE1.....119 D4
  SE15 ....149 D4
Old Manor Yd, SW5...137 D2
Old Mkt Sq, E2 ....42 A4
Old Marylebone Rd,
  NW1 ....55 F4
Old Mitre Ct, EC4 .....89 D1
Old Montague St, E1 ..64 C4
Old Nichol St, E2......64 A1
Old N St, WC1 ....60 A3

★ Old Operating Thea Mus
& Herb Garret, SE1 . . **91** D5
Sch Old Palace Prim Sch,
E3 . . . . **47** F4
Old Palace Yd, SW1 . . **115** C3
Old Paradise St, SE11 . **116** A5
Old Pk La, W1 . . . . **85** D5
Old Pearson St, SE10 . **177** F1
Old Pye St, SW1 . . . . . . **114** C3
Old Quebec St, W1 . . . . **84** B1
Old Queen St, SW1 . . . **115** D2
Old River Lea Towpath,
E15 . . . . **25** D5
Old Royal Free Pl, N1
  off Old Royal Free Sq . **39** D1
Old Royal Free Sq, N1 . **39** D1
Old Sch Cl, SE10 . . . . . **127** F4
Old Sch Sq, E14 . . . . **96** C1
Old Seacoal La, EC4 . . . **61** E5
Old S Lambeth Rd,
SW8 . . . . **167** F1
★ Old Spitalfields Mkt,
E1 . . . . **64** A3
Old Sq, WC2 . . . . **60** B5
⇌ Old Street **40** C5
⊖ Old Street **40** C5
Old St, EC1 . . . . **62** A1
Old Thea Ct, SE1
  off Porter St **90** B4
Old Woolwich Rd,
SE10 . . . . **155** D4
O'Leary Sq, E1 . . . . **66** A3
Sch Olga Prim Sch, E3 . . **45** F3
Olga St, E3 . . . . **45** F3
Oliphant St, W10 . . . . . **29** D4
Oliver Gdns, E6 . . . . **75** F5
Oliver-Goldsmith Est,
SE15 . . . . **173** D3
Sch Oliver Goldsmith
Prim Sch, SE5 . . . . . **172** A3
Oliver Ms, SE15 . . . . . . **172** C5
Olivers Yd, EC1 . . . . **63** D1
Ollerton Grn, E3 . . . . . . **24** B5
Olliffe St, E14 . . . . **126** B4
Olmar St, SE1 . . . . **148** C4
Olney Rd, SE17 . . . . . . **146** A4
★ Olympia, W14 . . . . **107** F4
Olympia Ms, W2 . . . . . . **81** F3
Olympia Way, W14 . . **107** F4
O'Meara St, SE1 . . . . . . **90** B5
Omega Cl, E14 . . . . **125** E3
Omega Pl, N1 . . . . **37** F3
Omega St, SE14 . . . . . **176** B3
Omega Wks, E3 . . . . **25** D3
Ommaney Rd, SE14 . . **175** E4
Onega Gate, SE16 . . . . **123** E3
Ongar Rd, SW6 . . . . . . **136** C4
Onslow Cl, W10 . . . . **30** A4
Onslow Cres, SW7 . . . **139** D1
Onslow Gdns, SW7 . . **138** C1
Onslow Ms E, SW7 . . . **138** C1
Onslow Ms W, SW7 . . **138** C1
Onslow Sq, SW7 . . . . . **111** D5
Onslow St, EC1 . . . . **61** D2
Ontario St, SE1 . . . . . . **117** F4
Ontario Twr, E14 . . . . . . **98** B3
Ontario Way, E14 . . . . . **96** C3

Onyx Ms, E15
  off Vicarage La **27** F2
Opal Cl, E16 . . . . **103** D1
Opal Ms, NW6 . . . . **8** B5
Opal St, SE11 . . . . **145** E1
Uni Open Uni in London,
The, NW1 . . . . **13** F3
Ophir Ter, SE15 . . . . . . **172** C4
Oppenheim Rd, SE13 . **178** A5
Oppidans Ms, NW3 . . . . **12** A4
Oppidans Rd, NW3 . . . . **12** A4
Orange Ct, E1
  off Hermitage Wall . . **93** D5
Orange Pl, SE16 . . . . . **122** B4
Orange Sq, SW1 . . . . . **141** D1
Orange St, WC2 . . . . **86** C3
Orange Yd, W1 . . . . **87** D1
Oransay Rd, N1 . . . . . . **18** B2
Oransay Wk, N1
  off Oransay Rd **18** B2
Oratory La, SW3 . . . . . **139** D2
Sch Oratory RC Prim Sch,
SW3 . . . . **139** E2
Orbain Rd, SW6 . . . . . . **159** F2
Orbel St, SW11 . . . . . . **163** E4
Orb St, SE17 . . . . **146** C1
Orchard, The, SE3 . . . . **179** D5
Orchard Cl, N1 . . . . **18** B4
W10 . . . . **51** F3
Orchard Dr, SE3 . . . . . . **179** D5
Orchard Hill, SE13 . . . **177** F5
Orchard Ms, N1 . . . . **19** D4
Orchard Pl, E14 . . . . **99** E2
Sch Orchard Prim Sch,
E9 . . . . **22** B4
Orchard Rd, SE3 . . . . . **179** E5
Orchardson Ho, NW8
  off Orchardson St **55** D1
Orchardson St, NW8 . . . **54** C2
Orchard Sq, W14 . . . . . **136** A3
Orchard St, W1 . . . . **84** C1
Orchid Cl, E6 . . . . **75** E3
Orde Hall St, WC1 . . . . . **60** A2
Ordell Rd, E3 . . . . **46** B3
Ordnance Cres, SE10 . **127** D1
Ordnance Hill, NW8 . . . **33** D1
Ordnance Ms, NW8 . . . . **33** D2
Ordnance Rd, E16 . . . . . **72** A3
Oregano Dr, E14 . . . . . . **99** D1
Oregon Bldg, SE13
  off Deals Gateway . . **177** E3
Oriel Rd, E9 . . . . **23** D1
Oriental Rd, E16 . . . . . **103** D4
Oriental St, E14 . . . . **97** D2
Orient St, SE11 . . . . . . **117** E5
Orion Ho, E1 . . . . **65** F2
Orion Pt, E14 . . . . **124** C5
Orkney St, SW11 . . . . . **164** C5
Orleston Ms, N7 . . . . . . **17** D1
Orleston Rd, N7 . . . . . . **17** D1
Orlop St, SE10 . . . . **155** E3
Orme Ct, W2 . . . . **81** E3
Orme Ct Ms, W2 . . . . . . **81** F3
Orme La, W2 . . . . **81** E3
Orme Sq, W2 . . . . **81** E3
Ormiston Rd, SE10 . . . **156** C3
Ormond Cl, WC1 . . . . . . **59** F3

Ormonde Gate, SW3 . . **140** B3
Ormonde Pl, SW1 . . . . **140** C1
Ormonde Ter, NW8 . . . . **34** A1
Ormond Ms, WC1 . . . . . **59** F2
Ormond Yd, SW1 . . . . . . **86** B4
Ormsby St, E2 . . . . **42** A2
Ormside St, SE15 . . . . **150** A5
Orpheus St, SE5 . . . . . **170** C4
Orsett St, SE11 . . . . . . **144** B2
Orsett Ter, W2 . . . . **53** F5
Orsman Rd, N1 . . . . **41** E1
Orton St, E1 . . . . **92** C5
Orville Rd, SW11 . . . . . **163** D5
Osbert St, SW1 . . . . . . **142** C1
Osborn Cl, E8 . . . . **20** C5
Osborne Rd, E9 . . . . **24** B1
Osborn St, E1 . . . . **64** B4
Oscar Faber Pl, N1 . . . . **19** F4
Oscar St, SE8 . . . . **176** C5
Oseney Cres, NW5 . . . . **14** B1
Osier La, SE10 . . . . **128** B4
Osier St, E1 . . . . **66** B2
Oslo Ct, NW8 . . . . **33** E3
Oslo Sq, SE16 . . . . **123** F3
Sch Osmani Prim Sch,
E1 . . . . **65** D3
Osman Rd, W6 . . . . **106** B3
Osmington Ho, SW8 . . **168** A2
Osnaburgh St, NW1 . . . **57** F2
NW1 (north section) . . **35** F5
Osnaburgh Ter, NW1 . . **57** F1
Osprey Cl, E6 . . . . **75** E4
Osram Ct, W6 . . . . **106** C3
Osric Path, N1 . . . . **41** E3
Ossington Bldgs, W1 . . **56** C3
Ossington Cl, W2 . . . . . **81** D3
Ossington St, W2 . . . . . **81** D3
Ossory Rd, SE1 . . . . . . **148** C3
Ossulston St, NW1 . . . . **36** C3
Osten Ms, SW7 . . . . . . **109** F4
Osterley Ho, E14 . . . . . . **69** E5
Oswald Bldg, SW8 . . . **141** E5
Oswell Ho, E1 . . . . **93** F4
Oswin St, SE11 . . . . . . **117** F5
Oswyth Rd, SE5 . . . . . **171** F5
Othello Cl, SE11 . . . . . **145** E2
Otis St, E3 . . . . **48** A4
Otley Rd, E16 . . . . **74** A5
Otterburn Ho, SE5 . . . **170** A1
Otter Cl, E15 . . . . **48** A1
Otto St, SE17 . . . . **145** E5
Sch Our Lady & St. Joseph
RC Prim Sch, N1 . . . . **19** E2
Sch Our Lady of Dolours
RC Prim Sch, W2 . . . . **53** E3
Sch Our Lady of Grace
RC Prim Sch, SE7 . . **157** F5
Sch Our Lady of Victories
RC Prim Sch, SW7 . **138** B1
Sch Our Lady's Prim Sch,
E14 . . . . **96** B1
Sch Our Lady's RC Prim Sch,
NW1 . . . . **14** A5

Outer Circle, NW1 . . . . . 56 C2
Outram Pl, N1 . . . . 15 F5
Outwich St, EC3 . . . . . . 63 F5
⊖ Oval 144 C5
★ Oval, The (Surrey CCC),
   SE11 . . . . 144 B4
Oval, The, E2 . . . . 43 E2
Oval Pl, SW8 . . . . 168 A1
Oval Rd, NW1 . . . . 13 E4
Oval Way, SE11 . . . . . 144 B3
Oversley Ho, W2 . . . . . . 52 C3
Overstone Rd, W6 . . . 106 A4
Ovex Cl, E14 . . . . 126 B2
Ovington Gdns, SW3 . 111 F4
Ovington Ms, SW3 . . . 111 F4
Ovington Sq, SW3 . . . . 111 F4
Ovington St, SW3 . . . . 111 F4
Owen's Row, EC1 . . . . . 39 E4
Owen St, EC1 . . . . 39 E3
Owgan Cl, SE5 . . . . 171 D2
Oxberry Av, SW6 . . . . . 159 F5
Oxendon St, SW1 . . . . . 86 C3
Oxenholme, NW1 . . . . . 36 B3
Oxestalls Rd, SE8 . . . . 151 F2
⊖ Oxford Circus 58 A5
Oxford Circ Av, W1 . . . 86 A5
Oxford Ct, EC4 . . . . 90 C2
Oxford Dr, SE1 . . . . 91 E5
Oxford Gdns, W10 . . . . 51 F4
Sch Oxford Gdns Prim Sch,
   W10 . . . . 50 C5
Oxford Gate, W6 . . . . 107 D5
Oxford Rd, E15 . . . . 27 D2
   NW6 . . . . 31 D3
Oxford Sq, W2 . . . . 83 F1
Oxford St, W1 . . . . 58 B5
Oxleas, E6 . . . . 77 E5
Oxley Cl, SE1 . . . . 148 B2
Oxo Twr Wf, SE1 . . . . . 89 D3
Oyster Catchers Cl, E16. 73 E5
Oystergate Wk, EC4
   off Swan La 90 C3
Oyster Row, E1 . . . . 94 B1
Oyster Wf, SW11 . . . . . 162 C5
Ozolins Way, E16 . . . . . 72 C5

P

Pace Pl, E1 . . . . 93 F1
Pacific Rd, E16 . . . . 72 C5
Pacific Wf, SE16
   off Rotherhithe St . . . 94 C5
Packington Sq, N1 . . . . 40 A1
Packington St, N1 . . . . 17 F5
Padbury, SE17 . . . . . . 147 E3
Padbury Ct, E2 . . . . 42 B5
PADDINGTON, W2 . . . . 54 A4
⇌ Paddington 54 C5
⊖ Paddington 54 C5
Sch Paddington Acad,
   W9 . . . . 53 D2
Paddington Grn, W2 . . . 55 D3
Sch Paddington Grn
   Prim Sch, W2 . . . . . . 54 C2
Paddington St, W1 . . . . 56 C3
Pagden St, SW8 . . . . . 165 F3
Pageant Cres, SE16 . . . 95 F4
Pageantmaster Ct, EC4. 89 E1
Page St, SW1 . . . . 115 D5
Pages Wk, SE1 . . . . . . 119 E5
Paget St, EC1 . . . . 39 E4
Pagnell St, SE14 . . . . 176 A1
Painters Ms, SE16
   off Macks Rd 121 D5
Pakenham St, WC1 . . . . 38 B5
Palace Av, W8 . . . . 81 F5
Palace Ct, W2 . . . . 81 E2
Palace Gdns Ms, W8 . . 81 D4
Palace Gdns Ter, W8 . . 81 D4
Palace Gate, W8 . . . . . 110 A2
Palace Grn, W8 . . . . . . 109 F1
Palace Ms, SW1 . . . . . 141 D1
   SW6 . . . . 160 B2
Palace Pl, SW1 . . . . . . 114 A3
Palace St, SW1 . . . . . . 114 A3
Palemead Cl, SW6 . . . 158 C3
Palfrey Pl, SW8 . . . . . . 168 B1
Palgrave Gdns, NW1 . . 55 F1
Palissy St, E2 . . . . 42 A5
Palliser Rd, W14 . . . . . 135 E2
Pall Mall, SW1 . . . . 86 B5
Pall Mall E, SW1 . . . . . 87 D4
Palmer Ho, SE14
   off Lubbock St 174 C2
Palmer Rd, E13 . . . . . . 73 F2
Palmers Rd, E2 . . . . 45 D3
Palmerston Ho, SW11
   off Strasburg Rd 165 D4
   W8 . . . . 80 C5
Palmerston Rd, NW6 . . . 8 C3
Palmerston Way, SW8. 165 F5
Palmer St, SW1 . . . . . . 114 C2
Pamela Wk, E8 . . . . 20 C5
Pancras La, EC4 . . . . . . 90 B1
Pancras Rd, NW1 . . . . . 36 C2
Pancras Way, E3 . . . . . . 46 C2
Pandian Way, NW1 . . . 14 C1
Pandora Rd, NW6 . . . . . 8 C1
Pangbourne Av, W10 . . 50 B3
Pankhurst Av, E16 . . . 101 F4
Pankhurst Cl, SE14 . . . 174 C2
Panton St, SW1 . . . . . . 86 C3
Panyer All, EC4 . . . . . . 90 A1
Parade, The, SW11 . . . 164 B1
Paradise Rd, SW4 . . . . 167 E5
Paradise Row, E2 . . . . . 43 F4
Paradise St, SE16 . . . . 121 E2
Paradise Wk, SW3 . . . . 140 A4
Paragon, The, SE3 . . . 180 B5
Paragon Cl, E16 . . . . . . 72 C5
Paragon Ms, SE1 . . . . . 119 D5
Paragon Pl, SE3 . . . . . 180 B5
Paragon Rd, E9 . . . . 21 F2
Pardoner St, SE1 . . . . . 119 D3
Pardon St, EC1 . . . . 61 F1
Parfett St, E1 . . . . 65 D4
Parfrey St, W6 . . . . 134 B4
Paris Gdn, SE1 . . . . 89 E4
Parish Wf, SE18 . . . . . 131 F5
Park Av, E15 . . . . 27 E2
Park Cen Bldg, E3
   off Fairfield Rd 47 D2
Park Cl, E9 . . . . 22 B5
   SW1 . . . . 112 A2
   W14 . . . . 108 B3
Park Ct, SW11 . . . . . . 165 E3
Park Cres, W1 . . . . 57 E2
Park Cres Ms E, W1 . . . 57 F2
Park Cres Ms W, W1 . . . 57 E3
Park E Bldg, E3
   off Fairfield Rd 47 D2
Parker Cl, E16 . . . . 103 E5
Parker Ms, WC2 . . . . . . 59 F5
Parkers Row, SE1 . . . . 120 B2
Parker St, E16 . . . . 103 E5
   WC2 . . . . 59 F5
Parkfield Rd, SE14 . . . 176 A3
Parkfield St, N1 . . . . . . 39 D2
Parkgate Rd, SW11 . . . 163 E2
Parkham St, SW11 . . . 163 D4
Parkhill Rd, NW3 . . . . . 12 B1
Parkholme Rd, E8 . . . . . 20 B1
Parkhouse St, SE5 . . . 171 D1
Parkinson Ho, SW1
   off Tachbrook St 142 C2
Park La, E15 . . . . 26 C5
   W1 . . . . 85 D5
Park Mans, SW1
   off Knightsbridge . . . 112 A2
   SW8 . . . . 143 F4
Park Ms, SE10 . . . . . . 156 B3
Park Pl, E14 . . . . 96 C4
   N1 . . . . 19 D5
   SW1 . . . . 86 A5
Park Pl Vil, W2 . . . . 54 B3
Park Rd, NW1 . . . . 33 E4
   NW8 . . . . 33 E4
Park Row, SE10 . . . . . . 154 C4
Parkside, SE3 . . . . 180 A1
Parkside Business Est,
   SE8 . . . . 151 F4
Parkside Est, E9 . . . . . . 22 C5
Parkside Rd, SW11 . . . 164 C4
Parkside Wk, SE10 . . . 127 E4
Park S, SW11 . . . . 164 C4
Park Sq E, NW1 . . . . . . 57 E1
Park Sq Ms, NW1 . . . . . 57 E2
Park Sq W, NW1 . . . . . . 57 E1
Park Steps, W2
   off St. Georges Flds . . 83 F2
Park St, SE1 . . . . 90 A4
   W1 . . . . 84 C2
Park Twrs, W1
   off Brick St 85 E5
Park Vw Est, E2 . . . . . . 44 B2
Park Vw Ms, SW9 . . . . 168 B5
Park Village E, NW1 . . . 35 E1
Park Village W, NW1 . . 35 E2
Parkville Rd, SW6 . . . . 160 A2
Park Vista, SE10 . . . . . 155 D5
Park Wk, SE10 . . . . . . 178 C2
   SW10 . . . . 138 B4
Sch Park Wk Prim Sch,
   SW10 . . . . 138 C5
Parkway, NW1 . . . . 35 E1

Park W, W2 . . . . 83 F1
Park W Bldg, E3
  off Fairfield Rd 47 D2
Park W Pl, W2 . . . . 55 F5
Parliament Ct, E1 . . . . . . 63 F4
Parliament Sq, SW1 . . 115 E2
Parliament St, SW1 . . 115 E2
Parliament Vw Apts,
  SE1 . . . . 116 A5
Parmiter St, E2 . . . . 43 F2
Parmoor Ct, EC1 . . . . . . 62 A1
Parnell Rd, E3 . . . . 46 B1
Parnham St, E14 . . . . . . 67 F5
Parr Ct, N1 . . . . 40 C2
Parr St, N1 . . . . 40 C2
Parry Av, E6 . . . . 104 A1
Parry Pl, SE18 . . . . 133 F5
Parry Rd, W10 . . . . 29 F4
Parry St, SW8 . . . . 143 E4
Parsonage St, E14 . . . . 154 B1
PARSONS GREEN,
  SW6 . . . . 160 C3
⊖ Parsons Green, SW6 . 160 B4
Parsons Grn, SW6 . . . . 160 C4
Parsons Grn La, SW6 . 160 C3
Parson's Ho, W2 . . . . . . 54 C2
Parthenia Rd, SW6 . . . 161 D4
Partridge Cl, E16 . . . . . 74 C4
Partridge Sq, E6 . . . . . . 75 F3
Parvin St, SW8 . . . . . . 166 C3
Pascal St, SW8 . . . . . . 167 D1
Pasley Cl, SE17 . . . . . . 146 A3
Passfield Dr, E14 . . . . . 69 F3
Passing All, EC1 . . . . . . 61 F2
Passmore St, SW1 . . . 140 C1
★ Passport Office,
  SW1 . . . . 113 F5
Pastor St, SE11 . . . . . . 117 F5
Patcham Ter, SW8 . . . 165 F3
Paternoster La, EC4
  off Warwick La 89 F1
Paternoster Row, EC4 . 90 A1
Paternoster Sq, EC4 . . 89 F1
Paterson Ct, EC1
  off St. Luke's Est 40 C5
Pater St, W8 . . . . 108 C4
Patmore Est, SW8 . . . 166 A3
Patmore St, SW8 . . . . 166 B3
Patmos Rd, SW9 . . . . . 169 E2
Paton Cl, E3 . . . . 47 D4
Paton St, EC1 . . . . 40 A5
Patrick Connolly Gdns,
  E3 . . . . 47 F5
Patriot Sq, E2 . . . . 43 F3
Patshull Pl, NW5 . . . . . 14 A2
Patshull Rd, NW5 . . . . 13 F1
Patterdale Rd, SE15 . . 174 A1
Pattina Wk, SE16 . . . . . 95 F5
Paul Cl, E15 . . . . 27 E4
Paulet Rd, SE5 . . . . . . 169 F5
Pauline Ho, E1 . . . . 65 D3
Paul Julius Cl, E14 . . . . 98 C3
Paul St, E15 . . . . 27 E5
  EC2 . . . . 63 D2
Paul's Wk, EC4 . . . . 89 F2
Paultons Sq, SW3 . . . . 139 D4
Paultons St, SW3 . . . . 139 D5

Paveley Dr, SW11 . . . . 163 E2
Paveley Ho, N1
  off Priory Grn Est 38 A3
Paveley St, NW8 . . . . . . 55 F1
Pavilion Par, W12 . . . . . 50 A5
Pavilion Rd, SW1 . . . . . 112 B4
Pavilion St, SW1 . . . . . 112 B4
Pavilion Ter, W12 . . . . . 50 A5
Paxton Ter, SW1 . . . . . 141 F4
Payne Rd, E3 . . . . 47 E3
Payne St, SE8 . . . . 152 B5
Paynes Wk, W6 . . . . . . 135 E5
Peabody Av, SW1 . . . . 141 E2
Peabody Cl, SE10 . . . . 177 F3
  SW1 . . . . 141 F4
Peabody Dws, WC1 . . 59 E1
Peabody Est, EC1
  (Clerkenwell)
  off Farringdon La 61 D2
  EC1 (St. Luke's) 62 B2
  N1 (Islington) 18 A4
  SE1 . . . . 89 D5
  SE17 . . . . 146 C1
  SW1 . . . . 114 A5
  SW3 . . . . 139 F4
  SW6 . . . . 136 C4
  W6 . . . . 134 B3
  W10 . . . . 50 B3
Peabody Sq, SE1 . . . . . 117 E2
Peabody Twr, EC1
  off Golden La 62 B2
Peabody Trust, SE1 . . 90 A5
Peabody Trust Camberwell
  Grn Est, SE5 . . . . . . 170 C3
Peabody Trust
  Old Pye St Est,
  SW1 off Old Pye St . 114 C4
Peabody Yd, N1 . . . . . . 18 A5
Peach Rd, W10 . . . . 29 D4
Peachum Rd, SE3 . . . . 156 B4
Peachwalk Ms, E3 . . . . . 45 D2
Peacock St, SE17 . . . . 145 F1
Peacock Wk, E16 . . . . . . 73 F5
Peacock Yd, SE17 . . . . 145 F1
Pear Cl, SE14 . . . . 175 E1
Pearl Cl, E6 . . . . 76 C5
Pearl St, E1 . . . . 93 F4
Pearman St, SE1 . . . . . 117 D3
Pear Pl, SE1 . . . . 116 C1
Pearscroft Ct, SW6 . . . 161 F4
Pearscroft Rd, SW6 . . . 161 E5
Pearse St, SE15 . . . . . . 147 F5
Pearson Cl, SE5 . . . . . . 170 B3
Pearsons Av, SE14 . . . . 176 C3
Pearson St, E2 . . . . 41 F2
Pear Tree Cl, E2 . . . . . . 42 A1
Pear Tree Ct, EC1 . . . . . 61 D2
Peartree La, E1 . . . . 94 B3
Pear Tree St, EC1 . . . . . 61 F1
Peartree Way, SE10 . . 128 C5
Peary Pl, E2 . . . . 44 B4
PECKHAM, SE15 . . . . . 172 A5
Peckham Gro, SE15 . . 171 F1
Peckham High St,
  SE15 . . . . 172 C4
Peckham Hill St, SE15. 172 C1
Peckham Pk Rd, SE15. 172 C1

Sch Peckham Pk Sch,
  SE15 . . . . 173 D2
Peckham Rd, SE5 . . . . 171 E4
  SE15 . . . . 171 E4
⇌ Peckham Rye 172 C5
Pecks Yd, E1 . . . . 64 A3
Pedlars Wk, N7 . . . . 15 F1
Pedley St, E1 . . . . 64 B2
Pedworth Gdns, SE16. 150 A1
Peel Gro, E2 . . . . 44 A3
Peel Pas, W8 . . . . 80 C5
Peel Prec, NW6 . . . . 30 C3
Peel Rd, NW6 . . . . 30 B4
Peel St, W8 . . . . 80 C5
Peerless St, EC1 . . . . . . 40 C5
Pegasus Pl, SE11 . . . . 144 C4
  SW6 off Ackmar Rd . . 160 C4
Pekin Cl, E14 . . . . 97 D1
Pekin St, E14 . . . . 97 D1
Peldon Wk, N1 . . . . 17 F5
Pelham Cres, SW7 . . . 139 E1
Pelham Ho, W14 . . . . . 136 A1
Pelham Pl, SW7 . . . . . . 139 E1
Pelham St, SW7 . . . . . 111 D5
Pelican Est, SE15 . . . . 172 A4
Pelican Ho, SE5
  off Peckham Rd 172 A4
Pelican Pas, E1 . . . . 66 A1
Pelier St, SE17 . . . . 146 B4
Pellant Rd, SW6 . . . . . 135 F5
Pelling St, E14 . . . . 68 C5
Pelter St, E2 . . . . 42 A4
Pelton Rd, SE10 . . . . . 155 E2
Pember Rd, NW10 . . . . 28 C5
Pemberton Pl, E8 . . . . . 21 F4
Pemberton Row, EC4 . . 61 D5
Pembridge Cres, W11 . 80 C2
Pembridge Gdns, W2 . . 80 C3
Coll Pembridge Hall, W2. 81 D3
Sch Pembridge Hall Sch,
  W2 . . . . 81 D3
Pembridge Ms, W11 . . . 80 C2
Pembridge Pl, W2 . . . . . 81 D2
Pembridge Rd, W11 . . . 80 C3
Pembridge Sq, W2 . . . . 80 C3
Pembridge Vil, W2 . . . . 80 C2
  W11 . . . . 80 C2
Pembroke Av, N1 . . . . . 15 F5
Pembroke Cl, SW1 . . . 113 D2
Pembroke Cotts, W8
  off Pembroke Sq 108 C4
Pembroke Gdns, W8 . . 108 B5
Pembroke Gdns Cl,
  W8 . . . . 108 B4
Pembroke Ms, E3 . . . . . 45 F4
  W8 . . . . 108 C4
Pembroke Pl, W8 . . . . 108 C4
Pembroke Rd, E6 . . . . . 76 A3
  W8 . . . . 108 C5
Pembroke Sq, W8 . . . . 108 C4
Pembroke St, N1 . . . . . 15 F4
Pembroke Studios,
  W8 . . . . 108 B4

Pembroke Vil, W8 . . . . **108** C5
Pembroke Wk, W8 . . . **108** C5
Pembry Cl, SW9 . . . . . **168** C4
Pemell Cl, E1 . . . . **66** B1
Penally Pl, N1 . . . . **19** D5
Penang St, E1 . . . . **93** F3
Penarth St, SE15 . . . . . **150** A4
Pencombe Ms, W11 . . . **80** B2
Pencraig Way, SE15 . . **149** E5
Penfields Ho, N7 . . . . . . **15** E2
Penfold Pl, NW1 . . . . . **55** D3
Penfold St, NW1 . . . . . **55** D2
    NW8 . . . . **55** D2
Penford St, SE5 . . . . . . **169** E5
Penhall Rd, SE7 . . . . . **130** C5
Penhurst Pl, SE1 . . . . . **116** B4
Peninsula Apts, W2
    off Praed St **55** E4
Peninsula Hts, SE1 . . . **143** F2
Peninsular Pk Rd, SE7 . **157** D1
Pennack Rd, SE15 . . . . **148** B5
Pennant Ms, W8 . . . . . **109** C5
Pennard Rd, W12 . . . . **106** A1
Pennethorne Cl, E9 . . . . **44** A1
Pennethorne Rd,
    SE15 . . . . **173** E2
Pennington St, E1 . . . . **93** D3
Penn St, N1 . . . . **41** D1
Pennyfields, E14 . . . . . . **96** C2
Pennymoor Wk, W9 . . . **52** B1
Pennyroyal Av, E6 . . . **104** C1
Penpoll Rd, E8 . . . . **21** E1
Penrose Gro, SE17 . . . . **146** A3
Penrose Ho, SE17 . . . . **146** A3
Penrose St, SE17 . . . . **146** A3
Penryn St, NW1 . . . . . . **36** C2
Penry St, SE1 . . . . **147** E2
Pensbury Pl, SW8 . . . . **166** B5
Pensbury St, SW8 . . . . **166** B5
Penshurst Rd, E9 . . . . . **22** C4
Pentland Rd, NW6 . . . . **30** C4
Penton Gro, N1 . . . . **38** C3
Penton Pl, SE17 . . . . . **145** F2
Penton Ri, WC1 . . . . . . **38** B4
Penton St, N1 . . . . **38** C2
PENTONVILLE, N1 . . . . **38** C3
Pentonville Rd, N1 . . . . **38** A3
Pentridge St, SE15 . . . **172** A1
Penywern Rd, SW5 . . . **137** D2
Penzance Pl, W11 . . . . . **79** E4
Penzance St, W11 . . . . . **79** E4
Pepler Ms, SE5 . . . . . . **148** A4
Peploe Rd, NW6 . . . . . . **29** D2
Pepper Cl, E6 . . . . **76** B3
Pepper St, E14 . . . . . . **125** E3
    SE1 . . . . **118** A1
Pepys Cres, E16 . . . . . **101** D4
Pepys Rd, SE14 . . . . . **175** D4
Pepys St, EC3 . . . . **91** F2
★ Percival David Foundation
    of Chinese Art, WC1 . **59** D1
Percival St, EC1 . . . . . . **61** E1
Percy Circ, WC1 . . . . . . **38** B4

Percy Ms, W1 . . . . **58** C4
Percy Pas, W1 . . . . **58** B4
Percy Rd, E16 . . . . **71** F3
Percy St, W1 . . . . **58** C4
Percy Yd, WC1 . . . . **38** B4
Peregrine Ho, EC1 . . . . **39** F1
Perham Rd, W14 . . . . . **135** F3
Peridot St, E6 . . . . **75** F3
Perkin's Rents, SW1 . . **114** C3
Perkins Sq, SE1 . . . . . . **90** B4
Perren St, NW5 . . . . . . **13** E1
Perry Ct, E14
    off Maritime Quay . . **153** D2
Perrymead St, SW6 . . **161** D4
Perryn Rd, SE16 . . . . . **121** E3
Perrys Pl, W1 . . . . **58** C5
Perseverance Pl, SW9 . **169** D2
Peterboat Cl, SE10 . . . **127** F5
Peterborough Ms,
    SW6 . . . . **160** C5
Peterborough Rd,
    SW6 . . . . **160** C5
Peterborough Vil,
    SW6 . . . . **161** E3
Peterchurch Ho, SE15 . **173** E1
Peter Heathfield Ho, E15
    off Wise Rd **26** C5
Sch Peter Hills with St. Mary's
    & St. Paul's C of E
    Prim Sch, SE16 . . . . . **95** D4
Peterhouse Gdns,
    SW6 . . . . **161** F4
Peterley Business Cen,
    E2 . . . . **43** E3
★ Peter Pan Statue,
    W2 . . . . **82** C4
Petersham La, SW7 . . **110** A3
Petersham Ms, SW7 . . **110** A4
Petersham Pl, SW7 . . **110** A3
Peters Hill, EC4 . . . . . . **90** A2
Peter's La, EC1 . . . . . . **61** F3
Peter St, W1 . . . . **86** B2
Petiver Cl, E9 . . . . **22** B3
Petley Rd, W6 . . . . **134** B5
Peto Pl, NW1 . . . . **57** F1
Peto St N, E16 . . . . . . **100** A1
Petrie Cl, NW2 . . . . **7** F1
★ Petrie Mus of Egyptian
    Archaeology, WC1
    off Malet Pl **58** C2
★ Petticoat Lane Mkt,
    E1 . . . . **63** F4
Petticoat Sq, E1 . . . . . . **64** A5
Petticoat Twr, E1 . . . . . **64** A5
Pett St, SE18 . . . . **131** E5
Petty France, SW1 . . . **114** B3
Petty Wales, EC3 . . . . . **91** F3
Petworth St, SW11 . . . **163** F3
Petyt Pl, SW3 . . . . **139** E5
Petyward, SW3 . . . . . . **139** F1
Peverel, E6 . . . . **76** C5
Peyton Pl, SE10 . . . . . . **178** A1
Pheasant Cl, E16 . . . . . **73** D5
Phelp St, SE17 . . . . . . **146** C4
Phene St, SW3 . . . . . . **139** F4
Philbeach Gdns, SW5 . **136** B2
Philchurch Pl, E1 . . . . . **93** D1

Philip St, E13 . . . . **72** C1
Phillimore Gdns, NW10 . **6** A5
    W8 . . . . **108** C2
Phillimore Gdns Cl,
    W8 . . . . **108** C3
Phillimore Pl, W8 . . . . **108** C2
Phillimore Wk, W8 . . . **108** C3
Phillipp St, N1 . . . . **41** E1
Philpot La, EC3 . . . . **91** E2
Philpot St, E1 . . . . **65** F5
Phipp's Ms, SW1 . . . . **113** F4
Phipp St, EC2 . . . . **63** E1
Phoenix Cl, E8 . . . . **20** A5
Phoenix Pl, WC1 . . . . . . **60** B1
Phoenix Rd, NW1 . . . . **36** C4
Sch Phoenix Sch, E3 . . **46** B4
Sch Phoenix Sch, The,
    NW3 . . . . **10** B2
Phoenix St, WC2 . . . . . **87** D1
Phoenix Wf, SE10 . . . **128** A1
Phoenix Wf Rd, SE1 . . **120** B2
Phoenix Yd, WC1 . . . . . **38** B5
★ Photographers' Gall,
    WC2 . . . . **87** D2
★ Physical Energy Statue,
    W2 . . . . **82** B5
Physic Pl, SW3 . . . . . . **140** A4
Piccadilly, W1 . . . . **85** F5
Piccadilly Arc, SW1 . . . . **86** A4
⊖ Piccadilly Circus . . . **86** B3
Piccadilly Circ, W1 . . . . **86** C3
Piccadilly Ct, N7 . . . . . . **16** A1
Piccadilly Pl, W1 . . . . . . **86** B3
Pickard St, EC1 . . . . . . **39** F4
Pickering Cl, E9 . . . . . . **22** C3
Pickering Ms, W2 . . . . . **53** F5
Pickering Pl, SW1 . . . . . **86** B5
Pickering St, N1 . . . . . . **17** F5
Pickfords Wf, N1 . . . . . **40** A3
Pickwick St, SE1 . . . . . **118** A2
Pickworth Cl, SW8 . . . **167** F2
Picton Pl, W1 . . . . **85** D1
Picton St, SE5 . . . . . . **170** C2
Pied Bull Yd, N1
    off Theberton St **17** E5
Pier Head, E1 . . . . **93** E5
Pier Par, E16 . . . . **104** C5
Pierrepoint Arc, N1 . . . **39** E2
Pierrepoint Row, N1 . . **39** E2
Pier Rd, E16 . . . . **132** C2
Pier St, E14 . . . . **126** B5
Pigott St, E14 . . . . **96** C1
Pilgrimage St, SE1 . . . **118** C2
Pilgrims Ct, SE3 . . . . . **181** D3
Pilgrims Ms, E14 . . . . . **99** D2
Pilgrim St, EC4 . . . . **89** E1
Sch Pilgrims' Way Prim Sch,
    SE15 . . . . **150** A5
Pilot Busway, SE10 . . **127** F2
Pilot Cl, SE8 . . . . **152** A4
Pilton Pl, SE17 . . . . . . **146** B2
PIMLICO, SW1 . . . . . . **142** A2
⊖ Pimlico **142** C2
Pimlico Rd, SW1 . . . . . **140** C2
Sch Pimlico Sch, SW1 . **142** B3
Pimlico Wk, N1 . . . . . . **41** E4
Pinchin St, E1 . . . . **93** D2

Pindar St, EC2 . . . . **63** E3
Pindock Ms, W9 . . . . . . **53** F2
Pineapple Ct, SW1 . . . **114** A3
Pinedene, SE15 . . . . . . **173** E3
Pinefield Cl, E14 . . . . . . **96** C2
Pinelands Cl, SE3 . . . . **180** B2
Pine Ms, NW10 . . . . . . **28** C2
Pine St, EC1 . . . . **60** C1
Pintail Cl, E6 . . . . **75** E4
Pioneer Cl, E14 . . . . **69** E4
Pioneer St, SE15 . . . . . **172** C3
Pirie St, E16 . . . . **101** F5
Pitchford St, E15 . . . . . . **27** D4
Pitfield Est, N1 . . . . **41** D4
Pitfield St, N1 . . . . **41** E5
Pitman Ho, SE8
    off Tanners Hill . . . **176** C3
Pitman St, SE5 . . . . . . **170** A1
Pitmaston Ho, SE13 . . **178** A5
Pitmaston Rd, SE13 . . **178** A5
Pitsea Pl, E1 . . . . **95** D1
Pitsea St, E1 . . . . **95** D1
Pitt's Head Ms, W1 . . . . **85** D5
Pitt St, W8 . . . . **109** E4
Pixley St, E14 . . . . **68** B5
Plantain Pl, SE1 . . . . . **118** C1
Plantation La, EC3
    off Rood La **91** E2
Platina St, EC2 . . . . **63** D1
Platt St, NW1 . . . . **36** C2
Playfair St, W6 . . . . . . **134** B3
Playhouse Ct, SE1
    off Southwark Br Rd. **118** A1
Playhouse Yd, EC4 . . . . **89** E1
Plaza Par, NW6
    off Kilburn High Rd . . **31** E2
Plaza Shop Cen, The,
    W1 . . . . **58** B5
Pleasant Pl, N1 . . . . **17** F4
Pleasant Row, NW1 . . . **35** F1
Plender St, NW1 . . . . . . **36** A1
Plevna St, E14 . . . . **126** A3
Pleydell Ct, EC4 . . . . . . **89** D1
Pleydell Est, EC1
    off Radnor St **40** B5
Pleydell St, EC4 . . . . **89** D1
Plimley Pl, W12 . . . . . **106** C1
Plimsoll Cl, E14 . . . . **97** E1
Plough Ct, EC3 . . . . **91** D2
Ploughmans Cl, NW1 . . **14** C5
Plough Pl, EC4 . . . . **61** D5
Plough St, E1 . . . . **64** C5
Plough Way, SE16 . . . . **123** D5
Plough Yd, EC2 . . . . **63** F2
Plover Way, SE16 . . . . **123** E3
Plowden Bldgs, EC4
    off Middle Temple La . **88** C2
Plumbers Row, E1 . . . . **64** C4
Plumbridge St, SE10 . **178** A3
Plumstead Rd, SE18. . **133** F5
Plumtree Ct, EC4 . . . . . **61** D5
Plymouth Rd, E16 . . . . **72** C4
Plymouth Wf, E14 . . . **126** C5
Plympton Av, NW6 . . . . . **8** A4
Plympton Pl, NW8 . . . . **55** E2
Plympton Rd, NW6 . . . . . **8** A4
Plympton St, NW8 . . . . **55** E2

Pocock St, SE1 . . . . . . **117** E1
Podium, The, E2 . . . . . . **44** B4
Point Cl, SE10 . . . . **178** B3
Sch Pointer Sch, The,
    SE3 . . . . **180** C2
Pointers Cl, E14 . . . . . **153** E2
Point Hill, SE10 . . . . . . **178** B2
Point of Thomas Path,
    E1 . . . . **94** B3
Point W, SW7 . . . . **109** F5
Poland Ho, E15 . . . . **26** C5
Poland St, W1 . . . . **86** B1
Polesworth Ho, W2 . . . **53** D3
★ Polish Inst & Sikorski Mus,
    SW7 *off Princes Gate*. **111** D2
Pollard Cl, E16 . . . . . . **100** C2
Pollard Row, E2 . . . . . . **43** D4
Pollard St, E2 . . . . **43** D4
Pollen St, W1 . . . . **85** F1
Pollitt Dr, NW8 . . . . **54** C1
★ Pollock's Toy Mus,
    W1 . . . . **58** B3
Polperro Ms, SE11 . . . **117** D5
Polygon Rd, NW1 . . . . . **36** C3
Polytechnic St, SE18 . **133** D5
Pomell Way, E1 . . . . . . **64** B5
Pomeroy St, SE14 . . . . **174** B2
Ponder St, N7 . . . . **16** A3
Ponsford St, E9 . . . . . . **22** B1
Ponsonby Pl, SW1 . . . **143** D2
Ponsonby Ter, SW1 . . **143** D2
Ponton Rd, SW8 . . . . . **143** D5
DLR Pontoon Dock **102** A5
Pont St, SW1 . . . . **112** A4
Pont St Ms, SW1 . . . . . **112** A4
Pontypool Pl, SE1 . . . . **117** E1
Poole Ho, SE11
    off Lambeth Wk **116** B4
Poole Rd, E9 . . . . **22** C2
Pooles Bldgs, EC1. . . . . **60** C2
Pooles La, SW10 . . . . . **162** A2
Poole St, N1 . . . . **40** C1
Poolmans St, SE16 . . . **122** C1
Poonah St, E1 . . . . **94** B1
Pope Ho, SE16 . . . . . . **149** E1
Pope's Head All, EC3
    off Cornhill **91** D1
Pope St, SE1 . . . . **119** F2
Popham Rd, N1 . . . . . . **40** A1
Popham St, N1 . . . . **17** F5
POPLAR, E14 . . . . **97** E4
DLR Poplar **97** E3
Poplar Bath St, E14 . . . **97** F2
Poplar Business Pk,
    E14 . . . . **98** A3
Poplar Gro, W6 . . . . . . **106** B2
Poplar High St, E14 . . . **97** E2
Poplar Pl, W2 . . . . **81** E2
Poplars Av, NW10 . . . . . . **6** A2
Poppins Ct, EC4 . . . . . . **89** E1
Porchester Gdns, W2 . . **81** E2
Porchester Gdns Ms,
    W2 . . . . **81** F1

Porchester Gate, W2
    off Bayswater Rd **82** A3
Porchester Ms, W2 . . . . **53** F5
Porchester Pl, W2 . . . . . **83** F1
Porchester Rd, W2 . . . . **53** E5
Porchester Sq, W2 . . . . **53** F5
Porchester Sq Ms, W2 . **53** F5
Porchester Ter, W2 . . . . **82** A1
Porchester Ter N, W2 . . **53** F5
Porlock St, SE1 . . . . . . **118** C1
Portbury Cl, SE15 . . . . **173** D4
Port Cres, E13 . . . . **73** E2
★ Portcullis Ho, SW1
    off Bridge St. **115** E2
Portelet Ct, N1 . . . . **19** D5
Portelet Rd, E1 . . . . **44** C5
Porten Rd, W14 . . . . . **107** E4
Porter Rd, E6 . . . . **76** B5
Porter St, SE1 . . . . **90** B4
    W1 . . . . **56** B3
Porters Wk, E1 . . . . **93** F3
Porteus Rd, W2 . . . . **54** B4
Portgate Cl, W9 . . . . **52** B1
Portia Way, E3 . . . . **68** A2
Portland Ct, SE1
    off Falmouth Rd . . . **118** C3
Portland Gro, SW8 . . . **168** A3
H Portland Hosp for
    Women & Children,
    The, W1 . . . . **57** F2
Portland Ms, W1 . . . . . . **86** B1
Portland Pl, W1 . . . . **57** F4
Sch Portland Pl Sch, W1. **57** F3
Portland Rd, W11 . . . . . **79** F4
Portland Sq, E1 . . . . **93** E4
Portland St, SE17 . . . . **146** C2
Portland Wk, SE17 . . . **147** D4
Portman Cl, W1 . . . . **56** B5
Portman Gate, NW1 . . . **55** F2
Portman Ms S, W1 . . . . **84** C1
Portman Pl, E2 . . . . **44** B5
Portman Sq, W1 . . . . . . **56** B5
Portman St, W1 . . . . . . **84** C1
Portnall Rd, W9 . . . . **52** A1
Portobello Ct, W11 . . . . **80** B1
Portobello Ms, W11 . . . **80** C3
Portobello Rd, W10 . . . **52** A5
    W11 . . . . **80** B2
Portpool La, EC1 . . . . . . **60** C3
Portree St, E14 . . . . **71** D5
Portsea Ms, W2. . . . . . . **83** F1
Portsea Pl, W2 . . . . **83** F1
Portslade Rd, SW8 . . . **166** A5
Portsmouth Ms, E16 . **101** F4
Portsmouth St, WC2 . . **88** A1
Portsoken St, E1 . . . . . . **92** A2
Portugal St, WC2 . . . . . **88** A1
Post Office Ct, EC3 . . . . **91** D1
Post Office Way, SW8. **166** C1
Potier St, SE1 . . . . **119** D4
Potters Cl, SE15 . . . . . **171** F1
Potters Flds, SE1. . . . . . **91** F5
Pottery La, W11 . . . . . . **79** E3

Pottery St, SE16 . . . . . **121** E2
Pott St, E2 . . . . **43** F5
Poulton Cl, E8 . . . . **21** E1
Poultry, EC2 . . . . **90** C1
Powis Gdns, W11 . . . . **52** B5
Powis Ms, W11 . . . . . . **52** B5
Powis Pl, WC1 . . . . . . **59** F2
Powis Rd, E3 . . . . **47** F5
Powis Sq, W11 . . . . . . **52** B5
Powis St, SE18 . . . . . **132** C4
Powis Ter, W11 . . . . . **52** B5
Powlett Pl, NW1 . . . . . **13** D3
Pownall Rd, E8 . . . . . . **42** B1
Poynter Ho, W11 . . . . **79** D4
Poyser St, E2 . . . . **43** F3
Praed Ms, W2 . . . . **55** D5
Praed St, W2 . . . . **55** D5
Pratt Ms, NW1 . . . . **36** A1
Pratt St, NW1 . . . . **36** A1
Pratt Wk, SE11 . . . . . **116** B5
Prebend St, N1 . . . . . . **40** A1
Premier Cnr, W9 . . . . . **30** A3
Premiere Pl, E14 . . . . . **96** C3
Prescot St, E1 . . . . **92** B2
Prescott Ho, SE17 . . . . **145** F5
President Dr, E1 . . . . . . **93** E4
President St, EC1 . . . . . **40** A4
Press Ct, SE1 . . . . **148** C2
Prestage Way, E14 . . . . **98** B2
Preston Cl, SE1 . . . . . . **119** E5
Prestons Rd, E14 . . . . **126** B1
Prestwood St, N1 . . . . **40** B3
Pretoria Rd, E16 . . . . . **72** A4
Prices Ms, N1 . . . . **16** B5
Price's St, SE1 . . . . **89** F5
Prideaux Pl, WC1 . . . . **38** B4
Priest Ct, EC2 . . . . **62** A5
Priestman Pt, E3 . . . . . **47** E5
Prima Rd, SW9 . . . . . . **168** C1
Primrose Cl, E3 . . . . . . **46** E3
Primrose Gdns, NW3 . . **11** F1
PRIMROSE HILL, NW8 . . **12** A5
Primrose Hill, EC4 . . . . **89** D1
Primrose Hill Ct, NW3 . **12** A4
[Sch]Primrose Hill Prim Sch,
    NW1 . . . . **13** D5
Primrose Hill Rd,
    NW3 . . . . **12** A3
Primrose Hill Studios,
    NW1 . . . . **12** C5
Primrose Ms, NW1 . . . . **12** B4
    SE3 . . . . **181** E2
Primrose Sq, E9 . . . . . . **22** B4
Primrose St, EC2 . . . . . **63** E3
Primrose Wk, SE14 . . . **175** F1
Prince Albert Rd, NW1 . **33** F3
    NW8 . . . . **33** F3
Prince Charles Rd,
    SE3 . . . . **180** A3
Prince Consort Rd,
    SW7 . . . . **110** B3
Princedale Rd, W11 . . . **79** F4
Prince Edward Rd, E9 . . **24** B2

★ Prince Henry's Room,
    EC4 . . . . **88** C1
Princelet St, E1 . . . . . . **64** B3
Prince of Orange La,
    SE10 . . . . **178** A1
Prince of Wales Dr,
    SW8 . . . . **165** F2
    SW11 . . . . **164** A4
Prince of Wales Gate,
    SW7 . . . . **111** E1
Prince of Wales Pas,
    NW1 . . . . **36** A5
Prince of Wales Rd,
    NW5 . . . . **13** D2
    SE3 . . . . **180** B4
Prince of Wales Ter,
    W8 . . . . **109** F2
[DLR]Prince Regent **102** A2
Prince Regent La, E13 . **74** A4
    E16 . . . . **74** A4
Prince Regent Ms, NW1 . **36** A5
Prince's Arc, SW1 . . . . **86** B4
Princes Ct, SE16 . . . . . **121** E4
    SW3 off Brompton Rd . **112** A3
Princes Ct Business Cen,
    E1 . . . . **93** F3
[Coll]Prince's Foundation,
    The, EC2 . . . . **63** E1
Princes Gdns, SW7 . . . **111** D3
Princes Gate, SW7 . . . **111** E2
Princes Gate Ct, SW7 . **111** D2
Princes Gate Ms, SW7 . **111** D3
Princes Ms, W2 . . . . . . **81** E2
Princes Pl, SW1 . . . . . . **86** B4
    W11 . . . . **79** E4
Princes Ri, SE13 . . . . . **178** B5
Princes Riverside Rd,
    SE16 . . . . **94** C4
[Sch]Princess Frederica C of E
    Prim Sch, NW10 . . . . **28** A3
[H]Princess Grace Hosp,
    The, W1 . . . . **56** C2
Princess Louise Cl, W2 . **55** D3
[H]Princess Louise Hosp,
    W10 . . . . **50** C4
Princess Ms, NW3 . . . . **11** D1
Princes Sq, W2 . . . . . . **81** E2
Princess Rd, NW1 . . . . **12** C5
    NW6 . . . . **30** C3
Princess St, SE1 . . . . . **117** F4
Princes St, EC2 . . . . . . **62** C5
    W1 . . . . **85** F1
Prince St, SE8 . . . . **152** B4
Princes Yd, W11 . . . . . **79** F5
Princethorpe Ho, W2 . **53** D3
Princeton St, WC1 . . . . **60** A3
Printers Inn Ct, EC4 . . . **60** C5
Printers Ms, E3 . . . . . . **45** F1
Printer St, EC4 . . . . . . **61** D5
Printing Ho Yd, E2 . . . . **41** F4
Prior Bolton St, N1 . . . . **17** F2
Prioress Ho, E3
    off Bromley High St . . **47** F4
Prioress St, SE1 . . . . . **119** D4
Prior St, SE10 . . . . **178** A2
[Sch]Prior Weston Prim Sch,
    EC1 . . . . **62** B2

Priory Ct, EC4 . . . . **89** F1
    off Carter La **167** D4
    SW8 . . . . **167** D4
Priory Grn Est, N1 . . . . **38** A2
Priory Gro, SW8 . . . . . **167** E5
Priory Hts, N1 . . . . **38** A2
Priory Ms, SW8 . . . . . . **167** E4
Priory Pk Rd, NW6 . . . . **8** B5
Priory Rd, NW6 . . . . . . **9** E5
Priory St, E3 . . . . **47** F4
Priory Ter, NW6 . . . . . . **9** E5
Priory Wk, SW10 . . . . . **138** B3
Pritchard's Rd, E2 . . . . **43** D1
Priter Rd, SE16 . . . . . . **121** D4
Probyn Ho, SW1
    off Page St **115** D5
Procter Ho, SE1 . . . . . **148** C2
Procter St, WC1 . . . . . . **60** A4
Prospect Pl, E1 . . . . . . **94** A4
Prospect St, SE16 . . . . **121** F3
Prospect Vale, SE18 . . **131** E5
Protea Cl, E16 . . . . **72** A1
Prothero Rd, SW6 . . . . **159** F1
Provence St, N1 . . . . . . **40** A2
Providence Cl, E9 . . . . . **23** D5
Providence Ct, W1 . . . **85** D2
Providence Pl, N1 . . . . **17** E5
Providence Row, N1
    off Pentonville Rd . . . **38** A3
Providence Row Cl, E2
    off Ainsley St **43** F5
Providence Sq, SE1
    off Jacob St **120** C1
Providence Yd, E2 . . . . **42** C4
Provost Est, N1 . . . . . . **40** C4
Provost Rd, NW3 . . . . . **12** B3
Provost St, N1 . . . . **40** C5
Prowse Pl, NW1 . . . . . . **14** A3
Prudent Pas, EC2 . . . . . **62** B5
Prusom St, E1 . . . . **93** F5
★ P.S. Tattershall Castle,
    SW1 . . . . **87** F5
Pudding La, EC3 . . . . . . **91** D3
[DLR]Pudding Mill Lane . . **47** C2
Pudding Mill La, E15 . . **25** E5
Puddle Dock, EC4 . . . . **89** F2
Pulham Ho, SW8
    off Dorset Rd **168** A2
Pulteney Cl, E3 . . . . . . **46** A1
Pulteney Ter, N1 . . . . . **38** B1
Pulton Pl, SW6 . . . . . . **160** C2
Puma Ct, E1 . . . . **64** A3
Pump Ct, EC4 . . . . **88** C1
Pump Ho Cl, SE16 . . . . **122** B2
★ Pumphouse Ed Mus,
    Rotherhithe, SE16 . . **95** F4
Pump Ho Ms, E1 . . . . . **92** C2
Pump La, SE14 . . . . . . **174** B1
Pundersons Gdns, E2 . . **43** F4
Purbeck Ho, SW8
    off Bolney St **168** A2
Purbrook Est, SE1 . . . . **119** F2
Purbrook St, SE1 . . . . . **119** F3
Purcell Cres, SW6 . . . . **159** E1
Purcell St, N1 . . . . **41** C2
Purchese St, NW1 . . . . **37** D2
Purdy St, E3 . . . . **69** E1

Purley Pl, N1.........17 E3
Purser's Cross Rd,
  SW6............160 B3
Purves Rd, NW10.....28 A3
Puteaux Ho, E2.......44 C3
Pynfolds, SE16......121 F2

Q

Quadrangle, The,
  SW10............162 B3
  W2..............55 E5
Quadrangle Cl, SE1...119 E5
Quadrangle Ho, E15...27 F2
Quadrant Arc, W1......86 B3
Quaker Ct, E1........64 A2
  EC1..............62 C1
Quaker St, E1........64 A2
Quality Ct, WC2......60 C5
Quarrendon St, SW6..161 D4
Quarterdeck, The,
  E14............124 C2
Quebec Ms, W1.......84 B1
Quebec Way, SE16....123 D2
Queen Anne Ms, W1...57 F4
Queen Anne Rd, E9...22 B4
Queen Anne's Gate,
  SW1............114 C2
Queen Anne St, W1...57 E5
Queen Anne's Wk, WC1
  off Queen Sq.......59 F2
Queen Anne Ter, E1
  off Sovereign Cl.....93 F3
Queen Caroline Est,
  W6.............134 A3
Queen Caroline St,
  W6.............134 B1
★ Queen Elizabeth Hall &
  Purcell Room, SE1..88 A4
Queen Elizabeth's Coll,
  SE10...........178 A1
★ Queen Elizabeth II
  Conf Cen, SW1...115 D2
Sch Queen Elizabeth II
  Jubilee Sch, W9....52 B1
Queen Elizabeth St,
  SE1............119 F1
Queenhithe, EC4......90 B2
Uni Queen Mary - Barts & The
  London Sch of Med &
  Dentistry, Royal London
  Hosp, E1..........65 E4
  EC1..............61 F2
Uni Queen Mary,
  Mile End Campus, E1.67 E1
Queen Marys Bldgs, SW1
  off Stillington St....114 B5
★ Queen Mary's Gdns,
  NW1.............34 C5
Queen of Denmark Ct,
  SE16...........124 A3
Queensberry Ms W,
  SW7............110 C5
Queensberry Pl,
  SW7............110 C5

Queensberry Way,
  SW7............110 C5
Queensborough Ms,
  W2..............82 A2
Queensborough Pas,
  W2..............82 A2
Queensborough Studios,
  W2..............82 A2
Queensborough Ter,
  W2..............81 F2
Sch Queensbridge Prim Sch,
  E8..............20 B4
Queensbridge Rd, E2..20 B5
  E8..............20 B2
Queensbury St, N1....18 B4
Queen's Circ, SW8...165 E2
  SW11...........165 E2
★ Queens Club (Tennis Cen),
  W14............135 E3
Queens Club Gdns,
  W14............135 F4
Sch Queen's Coll, W1...57 E4
Queen's Cres, NW5....12 C2
Queensdale Cres, W11.79 D4
Queensdale Pl, W11...79 E4
Queensdale Rd, W11...79 D5
Queensdale Wk, W11...79 E5
Queens Elm Par, SW3
  off Old Ch St......139 D2
Queen's Elm Sq, SW3.139 D3
★ Queen's Gall, The,
  SW1............113 F2
Queens Gdns, W2.....82 A2
Queen's Gate, SW7...110 B2
Queen's Gate Gdns,
  SW7............110 B4
Queensgate Ho, E3
  off Hereford Rd.....46 B3
Queen's Gate Ms,
  SW7............110 B2
Queensgate Pl, NW6...8 C4
Queen's Gate Pl, SW7.110 B4
Queen's Gate Pl Ms,
  SW7............110 B4
Sch Queen's Gate Sch,
  SW7............110 C5
Queen's Gate Ter,
  SW7............110 A3
Queen's Gro, NW8....32 C1
Queen's Gro Ms, NW8.32 C1
Queen's Head Pas, EC4.62 A5
Queen's Head St, N1...39 F1
Queens Head Yd, SE1..90 C5
★ Queen's Ice & Bowl,
  W2..............81 F3
Queensland Ho, E16
  off Rymill St.......104 C5
Sch Queen's Manor
  Prim Sch, SW6....158 C2
Queensmead, NW8.....11 D5
Queens Ms, W2.......81 F2
Queensmill Rd, SW6..158 C2
↻ Queen's Park......29 F3
⊖ Queen's Park......29 F3
Sch Queens Pk Comm Sch,
  NW6..............6 C5
Queens Pk Ct, W10...29 D5

Sch Queen's Pk Prim Sch,
  W10.............51 F1
Queen Sq, WC1.......59 F2
Queen Sq Pl, WC1.....59 F2
Queens Rd, SE14....173 E3
  SE15...........173 E3
⇌ Queens Road
  Peckham........173 F3
Queen's Row, SE17...146 C4
Queen's Ter, NW8.....32 C2
★ Queen's Twr, SW7.110 C3
Queenstown Ms, SW8.165 E4
Queenstown Rd, SW8.141 E5
⇌ Queenstown Road
  (Battersea).......165 F3
Queen St, EC4........90 B2
  W1..............85 E4
Queen St Pl, EC4......90 B3
Queen's Wk, SW1.....86 A5
Queen's Wk, The, SE1.88 A5
⊖ Queensway.......81 F3
Queensway, W2......81 F1
Queens Yd, WC1......58 B2
★ Queen Victoria Mem,
  SW1............114 A1
Queen Victoria St, EC4.89 F2
Queen Victoria Ter, E1
  off Sovereign Cl.....93 F3
Quex Ms, NW6..........9 D5
Quex Rd, NW6..........9 D5
Quick St, N1.........39 F3
Quick St Ms, N1......39 E3
Quickswood, NW3....11 F3
Quilp St, SE1.......118 A1
Quilter St, E2........42 C4
Quilting Ct, SE16
  off Poolmans St....122 C1
Quince Rd, SE13.....177 F5
Sch Quintin Kynaston Sch,
  NW8.............32 C1
Quixley St, E14......98 C2

R

Rabbit Row, W8......81 D4
Raby St, E14.........67 E5
Racton Rd, SW6.....136 C5
Radcliffe Rd, SE1....119 F3
Radcot St, SE11.....145 D3
Raddington Rd, W10..51 F4
Radipole Rd, SW6....160 A3
Radland Rd, E16......100 B1
Radlett Pl, NW8......11 E5
Radley Ct, SE16.....123 D1
Radley Ms, W8......109 D4
Radnor Ms, W2........83 D1
Radnor Pl, W2........83 E1
Radnor Rd, NW6......29 E1
  SE15...........172 C1
Radnor St, EC1.......40 B5
Radnor Ter, W14.....108 A5

Radnor Wk, E14 . . . . . **125** D5
SW3 . . . . **139** F3
Radstock St, SW11 . . **163** A4
★ Ragged Sch Mus, E3. **67** F3
Raglan St, NW5 . . . . **13** F1
Rahere Ho, EC1 . . . . **40** A4
Railway App, SE1 . . . . . **91** D4
Railway Arches, W12. **106** A2
Railway Av, SE16 . . . . . . **122** B1
Railway Ms, E3 . . . . **46** C5
W10 . . . . **51** F5
Railway St, N1 . . . . **37** F3
Rainbow Av, E14 . . . . . **153** C2
Rainbow Quay, SE16. **123** F4
Rainbow St, SE5 . . . . . **171** E2
Sch Raine's Foundation Sch,
Lwr Sch, E2 . . . . **43** F4
Upr Sch, E2 . . . . **44** B3
Raine St, E1 . . . . **93** F4
Rainham Rd, NW10 . . . **28** B5
Rainhill Way, E3 . . . . . . **47** D4
Rainsborough Av, SE8. **151** E1
Rainsford St, W2 . . . . . . **55** E5
Rainton Rd, SE7 . . . . . **157** D2
Rainville Rd, W6 . . . . . **134** B5
Raleana Rd, E14 . . . . . **98** B4
Raleigh Ms, N1
off Queen's Head St . . **39** F1
Raleigh St, N1 . . . . **39** F1
Ralph Ct, W2 . . . . **53** F5
Ralston St, SW3 . . . . . **140** A3
Ramac Way, SE7 . . . . . **157** E1
Ramillies Pl, W1 . . . . . . **86** A1
Ramillies St, W1 . . . . . . **86** A1
Rampart St, E1 . . . . **93** E1
Rampayne St, SW1 . . . **142** C2
Ram Pl, E9 . . . . **22** B4
Ramsay Ms, SW3 . . . . **139** E4
Ramsey St, E2 . . . . **65** D1
Ramsey Wk, N1 . . . . **18** C2
Ramsfort Ho, SE16
off Manor Est **149** E1
Ramsgate Cl, E16 . . . . **101** E5
Ramsgate St, E8 . . . . . . **20** B1
Sch Randal Cremer
Prim Sch, E2 . . . . . . **42** A2
Randall Cl, SW11 . . . . **163** E3
Randall Pl, SE10 . . . . **178** A4
Randall Rd, SE11 . . . . **144** A2
Randall Row, SE11 . . . **144** A1
Randell's Rd, N1 . . . . . . **15** F5
Randolph App, E16 . . **102** B1
Randolph Av, W9 . . . . . **54** B1
Randolph Cres, W9 . . . . **54** A2
Randolph Gdns, NW6. . **31** E3
Randolph Ms, W9 . . . . . **54** B2
Randolph Rd, W9 . . . . . **54** A2
Randolph St, NW1 . . . . **14** A4
Ranelagh Br, W2
off Gloucester Ter **53** F4
★ Ranelagh Gdns,
SW3 . . . . **140** C3
Ranelagh Gro, SW1 . . **141** D2

Sch Ranelagh Prim Sch,
E15 . . . . **49** F2
Ranelagh Rd, E15 . . . . . **49** F1
SW1 . . . . **142** B3
Rangers Sq, SE10 . . . . **178** C3
Rangoon St, EC3 . . . . . . **92** A1
Rankine Ho, SE1
off Bath Ter **118** A4
Rannoch Rd, W6 . . . . . **134** B4
Ransome's Dock Business
Cen, SW11 . . . . **163** F4
Ranston St, NW1 . . . . . **55** E3
Ranwell Cl, E3 . . . . **46** A1
Ranwell St, E3 . . . . **46** A1
Raphael St, SW7 . . . . . **112** A2
Ratcliffe Cross St, E1 . . **95** D1
Ratcliffe La, E14 . . . . . . **95** C1
Ratcliffe Orchard, E1 . . **95** D2
Coll Rathbone Ed Cen,
The, E16 . . . . **72** B3
Rathbone Mkt, E16. . . . **72** A4
Rathbone Pl, W1 . . . . . . **58** C5
Rathbone St, E16 . . . . . **72** A4
W1 . . . . **58** B4
Rathmore Rd, SE7 . . . **157** E2
Raul Rd, SE15 . . . . **173** D5
Ravenet St, SW11 . . . . **165** E4
Raven Row, E1 . . . . **65** F3
Ravensbourne Pl,
SE13 . . . . **177** F5
Ravenscroft Cl, E16 . . . **72** C3
Ravenscroft Pt, E9 . . . . **22** C2
Sch Ravenscroft Prim Sch,
E16 . . . . **73** D2
Ravenscroft Rd, E16. . . **73** D3
Ravenscroft St, E2 . . . . **42** B3
Ravensdon St, SE11 . . **145** D3
Ravenstone, SE17 . . . . **147** F3
Ravey St, EC2 . . . . **63** E1
Rawlings St, SW3 . . . . **112** A5
Rawreth Wk, N1 . . . . . . **18** B5
Rawson Ct, SW11
off Strasburg Rd **165** E4
Rawson St, SW11 . . . . **165** D4
Rawsthorne Cl, E16 . . **104** A5
Rawstorne Pl, EC1 . . . . **39** E4
Rawstorne St, EC1 . . . . **39** E4
Rayleigh Rd, E16 . . . . **101** F4
Raymond Bldgs, WC1 . **60** B3
Raymouth Rd, SE16. . **121** F5
Raynham, W2 . . . . **83** E1
Raynor Pl, N1 . . . . **18** B4
Ray St, EC1 . . . . **61** D2
Ray St Br, EC1 . . . . **61** D2
Reachview Cl, NW1 . . . **14** B4
Reading La, E8 . . . . **21** E2
Reapers Cl, NW1 . . . . . . **14** C5
Reardon Path, E1 . . . . . **93** F5
Reardon St, E1 . . . . **93** E4
Reaston St, SE14 . . . . **174** B1
Sch Reay Prim Sch,
SW9 . . . . **168** B2
Record St, SE15 . . . . . **150** A4
Rector St, N1 . . . . **40** A1
Rectory Pl, SE18 . . . . **132** C4
Rectory Sq, E1 . . . . **67** D3
Reculver Rd, SE16 . . . **150** C2

Red Anchor Cl, SW3 . . **139** E5
Redan Pl, W2 . . . . **81** E1
Redan St, W14 . . . . . . **107** D3
Redan Ter, SE5 . . . . . . **169** E5
Redbridge Gdns, SE5 . **171** F2
Redburn St, SW3 . . . . **140** A4
Redcar St, SE5 . . . . . . **170** A2
Redcastle Cl, E1 . . . . . . **94** A2
Redchurch St, E2 . . . . . **64** A1
Redcliffe Cl, SW5
off Old Brompton Rd. **137** E3
Redcliffe Gdns, SW5 . . **137** F3
SW10 . . . . **137** F3
Redcliffe Ms, SW10 . . **137** F3
Redcliffe Pl, SW10 . . . **138** A5
Redcliffe Rd, SW10 . . **138** A3
Sch Redcliffe Sch,
SW10 . . . . **138** A4
Redcliffe Sq, SW10 . . **137** F3
Redcliffe St, SW10 . . **137** F4
Redcross Way, SE1 . . **118** B1
Reddington Ho, N1 . . . **38** B2
Reddins Rd, SE15 . . . . **148** C5
Rede Pl, W2 . . . . **81** D5
Redesdale St, SW3 . . . **139** F4
Redfield La, SW5 . . . . **109** D5
Redfield Ms, SW5 . . . . **109** D5
Redford Wk, N1 . . . . . . **17** F5
Redhill St, NW1 . . . . . . **35** F4
Red Ho Sq, N1 . . . . **18** B2
Sch Redlands Prim Sch,
E1 . . . . **66** B3
Red Lion Cl, SE17 . . . . **146** B4
Red Lion Ct, EC4 . . . . . **61** D5
Red Lion Row, SE17 . . **146** B4
Red Lion Sq, WC1 . . . . . **60** A4
Red Lion St, WC1 . . . . . **60** A3
Red Lion Yd, W1 . . . . . . **85** D4
Redman's Rd, E1 . . . . . **66** A3
Redmead La, E1 . . . . . . **92** C5
Red Path, E9 . . . . **23** F1
Red Pl, W1 . . . . **84** C2
Redriff Est, SE16 . . . . **124** A3
Sch Redriff Prim Sch,
SE16 . . . . **123** F1
Redriff Rd, SE16 . . . . . **123** D4
Redruth Rd, E9 . . . . . . **22** B5
Redstart Cl, E6 . . . . **75** E3
SE14 . . . . **175** E1
Redvers St, N1 . . . . **41** F4
Redwood Cl, E3 . . . . . . **46** C2
SE16 . . . . **95** F5
Redwood Ct, NW6 . . . . . **7** E4
Reece Ms, SW7 . . . . . **110** C5
Reed Cl, E16 . . . . **72** C4
Reeds Pl, NW1 . . . . . . **14** A3
Reedworth St, SE11 . . **145** D1
Rees St, N1 . . . . **40** B1
Reeves Ms, W1 . . . . . . **84** C3
Reeves Rd, E3 . . . . **69** E1
Reflection, The, E16 . . **133** E1
Reform St, SW11 . . . . . **164** A5
Regal Cl, E1 . . . . **65** D3
Regal Ho, SW6
off Lensbury Av **162** B5
Regal La, NW1 . . . . **35** D1
Regal Pl, E3 . . . . **46** B5

Regal Pl, SW6 . . . . 161 F2
Regal Row, SE15. . . . . 174 A3
Regan Way, N1. . . . . . . 41 E3
Regency Ho, SW6
  off The Boulevard . . 162 B4
Regency Ms, SW9. . . . . 169 F2
Regency Pl, SW1. . . . . . 115 D5
Regency St, SW1 . . . . 114 C5
Regency Ter, SW7
  off Fulham Rd 138 C2
Regeneration Rd,
  SE16 . . . . 150 C1
Regent Pl, W1 . . . . 86 B2
Regents Br Gdns,
  SW8 . . . . 167 F1
Coll Regent's Coll, NW1 . 56 C1
Regents Ms, NW8 . . . . . 32 B2
REGENT'S PARK, NW1 . 35 D3
⊖ Regent's Park 57 E2
★ Regent's Park, The,
  NW1 . . . . 34 B3
Regent's Pk Est, NW1 . 35 F5
Regents Pk Rd, NW1 . . 12 B5
Regents Pk Ter, NW1 . . 13 B5
Regent's Pl, SE3 . . . . . 180 C5
Regent Sq, E3 . . . . 47 E5
  WC1. . . . . 37 F5
Regents Row, E8 . . . . . . 42 C1
Regent St, NW10 . . . . . 29 D5
  SW1. . . . . 86 C3
  W1. . . . . 57 F5
Regents Wf, N1. . . . . . . 38 A2
Reginald Rd, SE8 . . . . 176 C2
Reginald Sq, SE8. . . . . 176 C2
Regina Pt, SE16 . . . . . 122 B3
Regnart Bldgs, NW1. . . 58 B1
Relay Rd, W12 . . . . 78 B3
Reliance Sq, EC2. . . . . . 63 F1
Relton Ms, SW7. . . . . . 111 F3
Rembrandt Cl, E14. . . . 126 C4
  SW1. . . . . 140 C1
Remington Rd, E6 . . . . . 75 E5
Remington St, N1. . . . . 39 F3
Remnant St, WC2 . . . . . 60 A5
Remus Rd, E3 . . . . 24 C4
Renaissance Wk,
  SE10 . . . . 128 B3
Renforth St, SE16 . . . . 122 B2
Renfrew Cl, E6 . . . . . . 104 C1
Renfrew Rd, SE11. . . . 117 E5
Rennie Ct, SE1
  off Upper Grd 89 E4
Rennie Est, SE16. . . . . 149 F1
Rennie Ho, SE1
  off Bath Ter 118 A4
Rennie St, SE1. . . . . 89 E4
Renovation, The, E16. 133 E1
Rephidim St, SE1 . . . . 119 E4
Reporton Rd, SW6 . . . . 159 F2
Repton St, E14 . . . . 67 F5
Resolution Wk, SE18 . 132 A3
Resolution Way, SE8 . 176 C1
Restell Cl, SE3. . . . . . . 155 F4
Reston Pl, SW7 . . . . . . 110 A2
Restoration Sq, SW11. 163 D4
Retford St, N1. . . . . 41 F3
Retreat Pl, E9 . . . . 22 B2

Reunion Row, E1
  off Tobacco Dock 93 F3
Reuters Plaza, E14. . . . 97 D5
Reveley Sq, SE16 . . . . 123 F2
Reverdy Rd, SE1 . . . . . 148 C1
Rewell St, SW6 . . . . . . 162 A2
Rex Pl, W1. . . . . 85 D3
Reynard Pl, SE14
  off Milton Ct Rd 151 F5
Reynolah Gdns, SE7. . 157 F2
Reynolds Pl, SE3. . . . . 181 F1
Rheidol Ms, N1 . . . . 40 A2
Rheidol Ter, N1. . . . . . . 39 F2
Rhoda St, E2 . . . . 64 B1
Rhodeswell Rd, E14. . . 67 F3
Rhondda Gro, E3 . . . . . 45 F1
Sch Rhyl Prim Sch, NW5. 13 D1
Rhyl St, NW5. . . . . 13 D1
Ribbon Dance Ms,
  SE5 . . . . 171 D4
Ricardo St, E14. . . . . . . 97 E1
Sch Richard Cloudesley
  Sch, EC1 . . . . 62 A2
Sch Richard Cobden
  Prim Sch, NW1 . . . . . 36 B2
Richard Ho Dr, E16. . . 103 D1
Richard Robert Res, The,
  E15 *off Salway Pl* . . 27 D2
Richardson Cl, E8 . . . . . 20 A5
Richardson Rd, E15 . . . 49 E2
Richardson's Ms, W1 . . 58 A2
Richards Pl, SW3 . . . . 111 F5
Richard St, E1 . . . . 93 E1
Richbell Pl, WC1 . . . . . . 60 A3
Richborne Ter, SW8 . . 168 B1
Richbourne Ct, W1
  off Harrowby St 55 F5
Richford Gate, W6 . . . 106 A3
Richford St, W6. . . . . . 106 A2
Rich Ind Est, SE1. . . . . 119 F4
Rich La, SW5 . . . . 137 E3
Richmond Av, N1 . . . . . 16 A5
  NW10 . . . . 6 A2
Richmond Bldgs, W1 . . 86 C1
Richmond Cres, N1. . . . 16 B5
Richmond Gro, N1 . . . . 17 E4
Richmond Ho, NW1
  off Park Village E 35 F3
Richmond Ms, W1. . . . . 86 C1
Richmond Rd, E8 . . . . . 20 A3
Richmond Ter, SW1 . . 115 E1
Uni Richmond Uni - The
  American Int Uni In
  London, Kensington
  Campus, W8 . . . . . . 109 F3
Richmond Way, W12 . 107 D2
  W14 . . . . 107 D3
Rich St, E14. . . . . 96 B2
Rickett St, SW6 . . . . . 137 D4
Rickman St, E1 . . . . 66 B1
Rick Roberts Way, E15. 48 B1
Ridgdale St, E3. . . . . . . 47 D3
Ridgewell Cl, N1 . . . . . . 18 B5
Ridgmount Gdns, WC1. 58 C2
Ridgmount Pl, WC1 . . . 58 C3
Ridgmount St, WC1 . . . 58 C3
Ridgwell Rd, E16 . . . . . 74 B3

Riding Ho St, W1 . . . . . 58 A4
Rifle Ct, SE11 . . . . 145 D4
Rifle St, E14. . . . . 69 F4
Riga Ms, E1
  off Commercial Rd . . . 64 C5
Rigden St, E14 . . . . 97 E1
Riley Rd, SE1. . . . . 119 F3
Riley St, SW10 . . . . . . 162 C1
Ring, The, W2 . . . . 83 E2
Ringlet Cl, E16 . . . . 73 E4
Ringmer Av, SW6 . . . . 159 F4
Ring Rd, W12 . . . . 78 A3
Ringwood Gdns, E14. 125 D5
Ripley Rd, E16 . . . . 74 A5
Ripplevale Gro, N1. . . . 16 B4
Risborough, SE17
  off Deacon Way 118 A5
Risborough St, SE1. . . 117 F1
Risdon St, SE16. . . . . . 122 B2
Risinghill St, N1 . . . . . . 38 B2
Rising Sun Ct, EC1 . . . . 61 F4
Rita Rd, SW8 . . . . 143 F5
Ritchie St, N1 . . . . 39 D2
Ritson Rd, E8 . . . . 20 B1
Rivaz Pl, E9 . . . . 22 B1
River Barge Cl, E14 . . 126 B2
River Ct, SE1 . . . . 89 E3
Rivermill, SW1 . . . . . . 143 D3
River Pl, N1. . . . . 18 A4
Riverside, SE7. . . . . . . 129 E4
Riverside Ct, SW8. . . . 143 D4
Riverside Mans, E1. . . . 94 A3
Sch Riverside Prim Sch,
  SE16 . . . . 121 D2
Riverside Rd, E15 . . . . . 48 B3
Riverside Twr, SW6 . . 162 B5
Riverside Wk, E14
  off Ferry St. 154 A3
River St, EC1 . . . . 38 C4
River Ter, W6 . . . . 134 A3
Riverton Cl, W9. . . . . . . 30 B5
River Vw Hts, SE16. . . 120 C1
River Way, SE10 . . . . . 128 A3
Rivet Ho, SE1 . . . . 148 B2
Rivington Pl, EC2 . . . . . 41 F5
Rivington St, EC2 . . . . . 41 E5
Rivington Wk, E8 . . . . . 21 D5
Roach Rd, E3. . . . . 24 C3
Roan St, SE10 . . . . 154 A5
Robert Adam St, W1. . . 56 C5
Roberta St, E2. . . . . 42 C4
Sch Robert Blair Prim Sch,
  N7 . . . . 15 F2
Sch Robert Browning
  Prim Sch, SE17 . . . . 146 C2
Robert Cl, W9 . . . . 54 B2
Robert Dashwood Way,
  SE17 . . . . 146 A1
Robert Keen Cl, SE15 . 173 D4
Robert Lowe Cl, SE14. 175 D1
Robert Owen Ho, SW6. 159 D3
Roberts Cl, SE16. . . . . 123 D2
Roberts Ms, SW1. . . . . 112 C4

Robertson Rd, E15 . . . . . **26** B5
Robert's Pl, EC1 . . . . . . **61** D1
Robert St, E16 . . . . **105** D5
  NW1 . . . . **35** F5
  WC2 . . . . **87** F3
Robert Sutton Ho, E1
  off Tarling St **94** A1
Robeson St, E3 . . . . **68** B3
Robin Ct, SE16 . . . . . . **120** C5
Robin Cres, E6 . . . . **75** D3
Robin Hood Gdns, E14 . **98** B2
Robin Hood La, E14 . . . **98** B2
Robin Ho, NW8
  off Newcourt St **33** E3
Robinscroft Ms, SE10 . **177** F4
Sch Robinsfield Inf Sch,
  NW8 . . . . **33** E2
Robinson Ho, W10 . . . . **79** D1
Robinson Rd, E2 . . . . . . **44** A3
Robinson St, SW3 . . . . **140** A4
Robsart St, SW9 . . . . . **168** B5
Robson Cl, E6 . . . . **75** E5
Rochdale Way, SE8 . . **176** C1
Rochelle St, E2 . . . . **42** A5
Rochemont Wk, E8 . . . . **42** B1
Rochester Ms, NW1 . . . . **14** A3
Rochester Pl, NW1 . . . . **14** B3
Rochester Rd, NW1 . . . . **14** A2
Rochester Row, SW1 . **114** B5
Rochester Sq, NW1 . . . . **14** B3
Rochester St, SW1 . . . **114** C4
Rochester Ter, NW1 . . . . **14** A2
Rochester Wk, SE1 . . . . **90** C4
Rochester Way, SE3 . . **181** E3
Rochester Way Relief Rd,
  SE3 . . . . **181** F4
Rochford Wk, E8 . . . . . . **21** D3
Rock Gro Way, SE16 . . **121** D5
Rockingham Est, SE1 . **118** A4
Rockingham St, SE1 . . **118** A4
Rockley Rd, W14 . . . . **106** C2
Rockwood Pl, W12 . . **106** B1
Rocliffe St, N1 . . . . **39** F3
Roding Ms, E1 . . . . **93** D4
Roding Rd, E6 . . . . **77** D3
Rodmarton St, W1 . . . . **56** B4
Rodmere St, SE10 . . . . **155** F3
Rodney Ct, W9 . . . . **54** B1
Rodney Pl, SE17 . . . . . **118** B5
Rodney Rd, SE17 . . . . **118** B5
Rodney St, N1 . . . . **38** B2
Roebourne Way, E16 . **132** C1
Roffey St, E14 . . . . **126** A2
Roger Dowley Ct, E2 . . **44** A2
Rogers Est, E2
  off Globe Rd **44** B5
Rogers Ho, SW1
  off Page St **115** D5
Rogers Rd, E16 . . . . . . **100** B1
Roger St, WC1 . . . . **60** B2
Rokeby Rd, SE4 . . . . . **176** A5
Sch Rokeby Sch, E15 . . . **27** D5
Rokeby St, E15 . . . . **27** D5

Roland Gdns, SW7 . . . **138** B2
Roland Ms, E1 . . . . **66** C3
Roland Way, SE17 . . . **147** D3
  SW7 . . . . **138** B2
Rollins St, SE15 . . . . . . **150** B4
Rolls Bldgs, EC4 . . . . . . **60** C5
Rolls Pas, EC4 . . . . **60** C5
Rolls Rd, SE1 . . . . **148** B2
Rolt St, SE8 . . . . **151** E4
Roman Rd, E2 . . . . **44** A5
  E3 . . . . **45** E3
  E6 . . . . **75** D2
Sch Roman Rd Prim Sch,
  E6 . . . . **75** D1
Roman Way, N7 . . . . . . **16** B2
  SE15 . . . . **174** A2
Roman Way Ind Est,
  N1 . . . . **16** A3
Romford Rd, E15 . . . . . . **27** E3
Romford St, E1 . . . . **65** D4
Romilly St, W1 . . . . **86** C2
Romney Cl, SE14 . . . . **174** B2
Romney Ms, W1 . . . . . . **56** C3
Romney Rd, SE10 . . . . **154** B5
Romney St, SW1 . . . . . **115** D4
Ronald Av, E15 . . . . **49** F5
Ronald St, E1 . . . . **94** B1
Rona Wk, N1 . . . . **18** C2
Rood La, EC3 . . . . **91** E2
Rooke Way, SE10 . . . . **156** A2
Rook Wk, E6 . . . . **75** E5
★ Roosevelt Mem, W1 . **85** D2
Rootes Dr, W10 . . . . **50** C2
Ropemaker Rd, SE16 . **123** E2
Ropemakers Flds, E14 . **96** A3
Ropemaker St, EC2 . . . . **62** C3
Roper La, SE1 . . . . **119** F1
Ropers Orchard, SW3 . **139** D5
Ropery St, E3 . . . . **68** A2
Rope St, SE16 . . . . **123** F4
Ropewalk Gdns, E1 . . . **93** D1
Ropewalk Ms, E8 . . . . . **20** C4
Rope Yd Rails, SE18 . . **133** E4
Ropley St, E2 . . . . **42** C3
Rosaline Rd, SW6 . . . . **159** F4
Rosary Gdns, SW7 . . . **138** A1
Rosaville Rd, SW6 . . . . **160** A2
Roscoe St, EC1 . . . . **62** B2
Rose All, EC2 *off New St* . **63** F4
  SE1 . . . . **90** B4
Rose & Crown Ct, EC2 . **62** A5
Rose & Crown Yd, SW1 . **86** B4
Rosebank Gdns, E3 . . . **45** F3
Rosebank Wk, NW1 . . . **15** D3
  SE18 . . . . **131** F5
Roseberry Pl, E8 . . . . . . **20** A2
Roseberry St, SE16 . . . **149** E1
Rosebery Av, EC1 . . . . . **60** C2
Rosebery Ct, EC1
  off Rosebery Av **60** C1
Rosebery Sq, EC1 . . . . . **60** C2
Rose Ct, E1 . . . . **64** A4
Rosedene, NW6 . . . . **7** D5
Rosedew Rd, W6 . . . . . **134** C5
Rosefield Gdns, E14 . . . **96** C2
Roseford Ct, W12 . . . . **106** C2
Rosegate Ho, E3 . . . . . . **46** B3

Rosehart Ms, W11 . . . . **80** C1
Rosemary Dr, E14 . . . . **98** C1
Rosemary Rd, SE15 . . **172** B1
Rosemary St, N1 . . . . . . **18** C5
Rosemont Rd, NW3 . . . **10** A1
Rosemoor St, SW3 . . . **140** A1
Rosenau Cres, SW11 . **163** F4
Rosenau Rd, SW11 . . **163** F3
Roserton St, E14 . . . . **126** A2
Rose Sq, SW3 . . . . **139** D2
Rose St, EC4 . . . . **61** F5
  WC2 . . . . **87** E2
Rosetta Cl, SW8 . . . . . **167** F2
Sch Rosetta Prim Sch,
  E16 . . . . **73** F4
Rosewood Gdns, SE13
  off Morden Hill **178** A5
Rosher Cl, E15 . . . . **26** C4
Rosmead Rd, W11 . . . . **79** F2
Rosoman Pl, EC1 . . . . . . **61** D1
Rosoman St, EC1 . . . . . **39** D5
Rosse Ms, SE3 . . . . **181** E3
Rossendale Way, NW1 . **14** B4
Rossetti Ms, NW8 . . . . . **33** D1
Rossetti Rd, SE16 . . . . **149** D2
Rossmore Ct, NW1 . . . . **56** A1
Rossmore Rd, NW1 . . . **55** F2
Rostrevor Ms, SW6 . . . **160** A4
Rostrevor Rd, SW6 . . . **160** A3
Rotary St, SE1 . . . . **117** E3
Rothbury Rd, E9 . . . . . . **24** B3
Sch Rotherfield Prim Sch,
  N1 . . . . **18** B5
Rotherfield St, N1 . . . . . **18** B4
Rotherham Wk, SE1 . . . **89** E5
ROTHERHITHE, SE16 . **122** C3
⊖ Rotherhithe **122** B1
Rotherhithe New Rd,
  SE16 . . . . **149** D3
Rotherhithe Old Rd,
  SE16 . . . . **122** C4
Sch Rotherhithe Prim Sch,
  SE16 . . . . **122** C5
Rotherhithe St, SE16 . **122** B1
Rotherhithe Tunnel, E1 . **94** C4
Rotherhithe Tunnel App,
  E14 . . . . **95** E2
  SE16 . . . . **122** A2
Rothery St, N1 . . . . **17** E5
Rothery Ter, SW9 . . . . **169** E2
Rothsay St, SE1 . . . . . . **119** E3
Rothsay Wk, E14 . . . . . **125** D5
Rothwell St, NW1 . . . . . **12** B5
Rotten Row, SW1 . . . . **112** C1
  SW7 . . . . **111** E1
Rotterdam Dr, E14 . . . **126** B4
Rouel Rd, SE16 . . . . . . **120** C4
Rounton Rd, E3 . . . . **69** D1
Roupell St, SE1 . . . . **89** D5
Rousden St, NW1 . . . . . **14** A4
Routh St, E6 . . . . **76** B4
Rover Ho, N1
  off Phillipp St **41** F1
Rowallan Rd, SW6 . . . **159** E2
Rowan Ho, NW3
  off Maitland Pk Rd . . . **12** B1
Rowan Rd, W6 . . . . . . **134** C1

Rowan Ter, W6 . . . . . . **134** C1
Rowan Wk, W10 . . . . . . **51** E1
Rowberry Cl, SW6 . . . . . **158** B2
Rowcross St, SE1 . . . . **148** A2
Rowditch La, SW11 . . . . **164** C5
Rowington Cl, W2 . . . . . **53** E3
Rowland Ct, E16 . . . . . . **72** A1
Rowley Way, NW8 . . . . . **9** F5
Rowntree Clifford Cl,
  E13 . . . . **73** E1
Rowntree Cl, NW6 . . . . . **9** D2
Rowse Cl, E15 . . . . **26** B5
Roxby Pl, SW6 . . . . . . **137** D4
★ Royal Acad of Arts,
  W1 . . . . **86** A3
Coll Royal Acad of Dance,
  SW11 . . . . **163** D4
★ Royal Acad of Dramatic
  Art (R.A.D.A.), WC1 . **59** D3
Uni Royal Acad of Music,
  NW1 . . . . **57** D2
DLR Royal Albert **103** E2
Royal Albert Dock,
  E16 . . . . **104** A3
★ Royal Albert Hall,
  SW7 . . . . **110** C2
Royal Albert Rbt,
  E16 . . . . **103** E2
Royal Albert Way,
  E16 . . . . **103** D2
Royal Arc, W1 . . . . **86** A3
Royal Av, SW3 . . . . **140** A2
Coll Royal Ballet Sch, The,
  Upr Sch, WC2 . . . . **87** F1
H Royal Brompton Hosp,
  SW3 . . . . **139** E2
  Annexe, SW3 . . . . **139** D2
Royal Cl, SE8 . . . . **152** A4
Coll Royal Coll of
  Anaesthetists, The,
  WC1 . . . . **60** A4
Uni Royal Coll of Art,
  SW7 . . . . **110** B2
Coll Royal Coll of Defence
  Studies, SW1 . . . . . . **113** D3
Coll Royal Coll of Music,
  SW7 . . . . **110** C3
Coll Royal Coll of Nursing,
  W1 . . . . **57** E5
Coll Royal Coll of Obstetricians
  & Gynaecologists,
  NW1 . . . . **56** A1
Coll Royal Coll of Physicians,
  NW1 . . . . **57** F1
★ Royal College of Surgeons
  of England, WC2 . . . . **60** B5
Royal Coll St, NW1 . . . . **14** A3
Royal Ct, EC3
  off Royal Ex Bldgs . . . **91** D1
  SE16 . . . . **124** A3
★ Royal Courts of Justice,
  WC2 . . . . **88** B1
Royal Cres, W11 . . . . . . **79** D5
Royal Cres Ms, W11 . . . **79** D5
Sch Royal Docks Comm Sch,
  The, E16 . . . . **102** B1
Royal Docks Rd, E6 . . **105** F2

★ Royal Dress Collection
  (Kensington Palace),
  W8 . . . . **81** F5
★ Royal Exchange,
  EC3 . . . . **91** D1
Royal Ex Av, EC3 . . . . . **91** D1
Royal Ex Bldgs, EC3 . . . **91** D1
★ Royal Festival Hall,
  SE1 . . . . **88** B5
★ Royal Geographical
  Society, SW7 . . . . . . **110** C2
Royal Hill, SE10 . . . . . **178** A1
★ Royal Horticultural Society
  (Lawrence Hall),
  SW1 . . . . **114** C4
★ Royal Horticultural Society
  (Lindley Hall), SW1 . **114** C4
★ Royal Hosp Chelsea &
  Mus, SW3 . . . . **140** C3
Royal Hosp Rd, SW3 . . **140** A4
H Royal London
  Homoeopathic Hosp,
  WC1 . . . . **59** F3
H Royal London Hosp, The,
  St. Clements, E3 . . . . . **46** B5
  Whitechapel, E1 . . . . . **65** E4
  Whitechapel - Dentistry
  Cen, E1 . . . . **65** E4
H Royal Marsden Hosp,
  The, SW3 . . . . **139** D2
★ Royal Mews, The,
  SW1 . . . . **113** F3
Royal Mint Ct, EC3 . . . . **92** B3
Royal Mint Pl, E1 . . . . . **92** B2
Royal Mint St, E1 . . . . . **92** B2
H Royal Nat Orthopaedic
  Hosp, W1 . . . . **57** F2
H Royal Nat Throat, Nose &
  Ear Hosp, WC1 . . . . . **38** A4
Royal Naval Pl, SE14 . **176** A1
⊖ Royal Oak **53** F4
Royal Oak Ct, N1 . . . . . **41** E4
Royal Oak Rd, E8 . . . . . **21** E1
Royal Oak Yd, SE1 . . . **119** E2
★ Royal Observatory
  Greenwich (Flamsteed Ho),
  SE10 . . . . **179** D1
Royal Opera Arc, SW1 . **86** C4
★ Royal Opera Ho,
  WC2 . . . . **87** F1
Royal Par, SW6
  off Dawes Rd **159** E1
Royal Pl, SE10 . . . . . . **178** B2
Royal Rd, E16 . . . . **102** C1
  SE17 . . . . **145** E4
Royals Business Pk, The,
  E16 . . . . **103** E3
Royal St, SE1 . . . . **116** B3
Royalty Ms, W1 . . . . . . **86** C1
Uni Royal Vet Coll -
  Camden Campus,
  Beaumont Animal's Hosp,
  NW1 . . . . **36** B1
  Royal Coll St, NW1 . . **36** C1
DLR Royal Victoria **100** C2
Royal Victoria Dock,
  E16 . . . . **101** E3

Royal Victoria Pl, E16 . **101** F4
Royal Victoria Sq, E16 . **101** E3
Royal Victor Pl, E3 . . . . **45** D3
Roydon Cl, SW11 . . . . **164** B5
Roydon St, SW11 . . . . **165** E1
Royle Bldg, N1 . . . . **40** A2
Roy Sq, E14 . . . . **95** F2
Royston St, E2 . . . . **44** B3
Rozel Ct, N1 . . . . **19** E5
Ruby St, SE15 . . . . **149** E4
Ruby Triangle, SE15 . . **149** E4
Rudgwick Ter, NW8 . . . **33** F1
Rudolf Pl, SW8 . . . . . . **143** F5
Rudolph Rd, NW6 . . . . . **31** D3
Rudstone Ho, E3
  off Bromley High St . . **47** E4
Rufford St, N1 . . . . **15** F5
Rufus St, N1 . . . . **41** E5
Rugby St, WC1 . . . . **60** A2
Rugg St, E14 . . . . **96** C2
Rumbold Rd, SW6 . . . . **161** F2
Rum Cl, E1 . . . . **94** A3
Rumford Ho, SE1
  off Bath Ter **118** A3
Runcorn Pl, W11 . . . . . . **79** E2
Rundell Twr, SW8 . . . . **168** A3
Rupack St, SE16 . . . . . **122** A2
Rupert Ct, W1 . . . . **86** C2
Rupert Rd, NW6 . . . . . . **30** B3
Rupert St, W1 . . . . **86** C2
Ruscoe Rd, E16 . . . . **72** A5
Rushmead, E2 . . . . **43** E5
Rushton St, N1 . . . . **41** D2
Rushworth St, SE1 . . . **117** F1
Russell Ct, SW1 . . . . . . **86** B5
Russell Gdns, W14 . . . **107** E3
Russell Gdns Ms, W14 . **107** E2
Russell Gro, SW9 . . . . **169** D2
Russell Lo, SE1
  off Spurgeon St **118** C3
Russell Pl, SE16 . . . . . **123** E4
Russell Rd, E16 . . . . **73** D5
  W14 . . . . **107** E3
⊖ Russell Square **59** E2
Russell Sq, WC1 . . . . . . **59** E2
Russell St, WC2 . . . . . . **87** F2
Russell's Wf Flats,
  W10 . . . . **52** A1
Russia Dock Rd, SE16 . **95** F5
Russia La, E2 . . . . **44** A2
Russia Row, EC2 . . . . . . **90** B1
Russia Wk, SE16 . . . . . **123** E2
Rustic Wk, E16 . . . . **73** E5
Ruston Ms, W11 . . . . . . **79** E1
Ruston Rd, SE18 . . . . . **131** E4
Ruston St, E3 . . . . **24** B5
Rust Sq, SE5 . . . . **170** C1
Rutherford St, SW1 . . . **114** C5
Ruthin Rd, SE3 . . . . . . **156** C4
Ruthven St, E9 . . . . **22** C5
Rutland Ct, SW7
  off Rutland Gdns . . . **111** F2
Rutland Gdns, SW7 . . **111** F2

Rutland Gdns Ms,
  SW7 . . . . **111** F2
Rutland Gate, SW7 . . . **111** F2
Rutland Gate Ms,
  SW7 . . . . **111** F2
Rutland Ms, NW8 . . . . . **31** F1
Rutland Ms E, SW7 . . . **111** E3
Rutland Ms S, SW7 . . . **111** E3
Rutland Ms W, SW7
  off Ennismore St . . . **111** E3
Rutland Pk, NW2 . . . . . . **6** B2
Rutland Pk Gdns, NW2
  off Rutland Pk **6** B2
Rutland Pk Mans, NW2
  off Rutland Pk **6** B2
Rutland Pl, EC1 . . . . **62** C2
Rutland Rd, E9 . . . . **22** B5
Rutland St, SW7 . . . . . **111** F3
Rutley Cl, SE17 . . . . . . **145** C4
Rutts Ter, SE14 . . . . . . **174** C4
Ryculff Sq, SE3 . . . . . . **180** B5
Ryder Ct, SW1 . . . . **86** B4
Ryder Dr, SE16 . . . . . . **149** E3
Ryders Ter, NW8 . . . . . . **32** A2
Ryder St, SW1 . . . . **86** B4
Ryder Yd, SW1 . . . . **86** B4
Rydon St, N1 . . . . **18** B5
Rydston Cl, N7 . . . . **15** F3
Ryecroft St, SW6 . . . . **161** E4
Ryegates, SE15 . . . . . . **173** F5
Rye La, SE15 . . . . **172** C4
Ryland Rd, NW5 . . . . . . **13** E1
Rylston Rd, SW6 . . . . . **136** A5
Rymill St, E16 . . . . **104** C5
Rysbrack St, SW3 . . . . **112** A3

S

★ Saatchi Gall, The,
  SW3 . . . . **140** B2
Sabbarton St, E16 . . . **100** A1
Sabella Ct, E3 . . . . **46** B3
Sable St, N1 . . . . **17** F3
Sackville St, W1 . . . . . . **86** B3
Sch Sacred Heart RC
  High Sch, W6 . . . . . . **134** B1
Sch Sacred Heart RC
  Sch, SE5 . . . . **170** A3
Saddlers Ms, SW8
  off Portland Gro **167** F3
Saddle Yd, W1 . . . . **85** E4
Sadler Ho, E3
  off Bromley High St . . **47** F4
★ Sadler's Wells Thea,
  EC1 . . . . **39** E4
Saffron Av, E14 . . . . **98** C2
Saffron Hill, EC1 . . . . . . **61** D2
Saffron St, EC1 . . . . **61** D3
Sage Cl, E6 . . . . **76** A4
Sage St, E1 . . . . **94** A2
Sage Way, WC1 . . . . **38** A5

Saigasso Cl, E16 . . . . . **102** C1
Sail Ct, E14
  off Newport Av **99** D2
Sail St, SE11 . . . . **116** B5
St. Agnes Cl, E9 . . . . . . **44** A1
St. Agnes Pl, SE11 . . . **145** E5
Sch St. Agnes RC Prim Sch,
  E3 . . . . **47** E4
St. Agnes Well, EC1
  off Old St **63** D1
Sch St. Alban's C of E
  Prim Sch, EC1 . . . . . . **60** C3
St. Albans Ct, EC2 . . . . **62** B5
St. Albans Gro, W8 . . . **109** F3
St. Alban's Pl, N1 . . . . . **39** E1
St. Albans St, SW1 . . . . **86** C3
St. Albans Ter, W6 . . . **135** E4
St. Alfege Pas, SE10 . . **154** A5
Sch St. Alfege with St. Peter's
  C of E Prim Sch,
  SE10 . . . . **154** A5
Sch St. Aloysius RC Inf Sch,
  NW1 . . . . **36** C4
Sch St. Aloysius RC Jun Sch,
  NW1 . . . . **36** B3
St. Alphage Gdns, EC2 . **62** B4
St. Alphage Highwalk,
  EC2 . . . . **62** C4
St. Andrews Cl, SE16 . **149** F3
Sch St. Andrew's C of E
  Prim Sch, N1 . . . . **16** B5
St. Andrew's Hill, EC4 . **89** F2
St. Andrews Ms, SE3 . **180** C1
St. Andrews Pl, NW1 . . **57** F1
St. Andrews Rd, W14 . **135** E4
St. Andrews Sq, W11 . . **79** E1
St. Andrew St, EC4 . . . . **61** D4
St. Andrews Way, E3 . . **69** E2
St. Anne's Ct, W1 . . . . . **86** C1
St. Annes Pas, E14 . . . . **96** A1
Sch St. Anne's Prim Sch,
  E1 . . . . **64** C2
Sch St. Anne's RC Prim Sch,
  SE11 . . . . **144** A4
St. Anne's Row, E14 . . . **96** B1
St. Anne St, E14 . . . . . . **96** B1
St. Ann's Gdns, NW5 . . **12** C1
St. Ann's La, SW1 . . . . **115** D3
St. Anns Rd, W11 . . . . . . **79** D3
St. Ann's St, SW1 . . . . **115** D3
St. Ann's Ter, NW8 . . . . **33** D2
St. Anns Vil, W11 . . . . . . **79** D5
St. Anselm's Pl, W1 . . . **85** E1
St. Anthonys Cl, E1 . . . **92** C4
St. Aubins Ct, N1
  off De Beauvoir Est . . **19** D5
Sch St. Augustine RC
  Prim Sch, W6 . . . . . . **135** F5
Sch St. Augustine's C of E
  High Sch, NW6 . . . . . . **31** D3
Sch St. Augustine's C of E
  Prim Sch, NW6 . . . . . . **31** D3
St. Augustines Ct,
  SE1 . . . . **149** E2
St. Augustines Rd,
  NW1 . . . . **14** C3
St. Austell Rd, SE13 . . **178** B5

Sch St. Barnabas & St. Philip
  C of E Prim Sch, W8. **108** C4
Sch St. Barnabas C of E
  Prim Sch, SW1 . . . . . **141** D2
St. Barnabas St, SW1 . **141** D2
St. Barnabas Vil, SW8. **167** F3
H St. Bartholomew's
  Hosp, EC1 . . . . **61** F4
★ St. Bartholomew-the-
  Great Ch, EC1 . . . . . . **61** F4
St. Benet's Pl, EC3 . . . . **91** D2
St. Botolph Row, EC3 . . **92** A1
St. Botolph St, EC3 . . . **92** A1
St. Brelades Ct, N1
  off Balmes Rd **19** D5
St. Brides Av, EC4 . . . . . **89** E1
★ St. Bride's Ch, EC4 . . **89** E1
St. Bride's Pas, EC4
  off Salisbury Ct **89** E1
St. Bride St, EC4 . . . . . . **61** E5
St. Catherine's Ms,
  SW3 . . . . **112** A5
St. Cecelia's Pl, SE3 . . **156** C3
St. Chad's Pl, WC1 . . . . **37** F4
St. Chad's St, WC1 . . . . **37** F4
Coll St. Charles Cath 6th
  Form Coll, W10 . . . . . **51** D4
H St. Charles Hosp,
  W10 . . . . **51** D3
St. Charles Pl, W10 . . . **51** E4
Sch St. Charles RC Prim Sch,
  W10 . . . . **51** D3
St. Charles Sq, W10 . . . **51** E3
Sch St. Christina's Sch,
  NW8 . . . . **33** F2
St. Christopher's Pl,
  W1 . . . . **57** D5
St. Clare St, EC3 . . . . . . **92** A1
★ St. Clement Danes Ch,
  WC2 . . . . **88** B1
Sch St. Clement Danes C of E
  Prim Sch, WC2 . . . . . . **88** B1
Sch St. Clements & St. James
  C of E Prim Sch, W11. **79** E4
St. Clements Ct, EC4
  off Clements La **91** D2
  N7 . . . . **16** C2
St. Clement's La, WC2 . **88** B1
St. Clements St, N7 . . . **16** C2
St. Cross St, EC1 . . . . . . **61** D3
St. Cuthberts Rd, NW2. . **8** A1
Sch St. Cuthbert with
  St. Matthias C of E
  Prim Sch, SW5 . . . . . **137** E2
St. Davids Cl, SE16 . . . **149** F3
St. Davids Ms, E3
  off Morgan St **45** F5
St. Davids Sq, E14 . . . **153** F2
St. Dionis Rd, SW6 . . . **160** B5
Sch St. Dominic's RC
  Prim Sch, E9 . . . . **23** E1
St. Donatts Rd, SE14 . **176** A4
St. Dunstan's All, EC3 . **91** E2
St. Dunstan's Ct, EC4
  off Fleet St **89** D1
St. Dunstan's Hill, EC3. **91** E3
St. Dunstan's La, EC3. . **91** E3

St. Dunstans Rd, W6 . **134** C3
St. Edmunds Cl, NW8 . . **34** A1
Sch St. Edmund's RC
　Prim Sch, E14. . . . . **125** D5
St. Edmunds Sq,
　SW13. . . . . **134** A5
St. Edmunds Ter, NW8. **33** F2
Sch St. Edward's RC
　Prim Sch, NW1 . . . . . **55** F2
Sch St. Elizabeth's Prim Sch,
　E2 . . . . **44** B2
St. Elmos Rd, SE16 . . . **123** E1
St. Ermin's Hill, SW1 . **114** C3
St. Ervans Rd, W10. . . . **51** F3
Sch St. Eugene de Mazenod
　RC Prim Sch, NW6 . . . **9** D4
Sch St. Francis Cath Prim Sch,
　SE15 . . . . **173** D1
Sch St. Francis of Assisi RC
　Prim Sch, W11 . . . . . . **79** D3
St. Frideswides Ms,
　E14 . . . . **98** A1
St. Gabriel's Cl, E14 . . . **69** E4
Sch St. Gabriel's C of E
　Prim Sch, SW1 . . . . **142** A3
Sch St. George's Cath RC
　Prim Sch, SE1 . . . . . **117** E3
Sch St. George's Cath School,
　Maida Vale, W9 . . . . **31** F3
St. Georges Circ, SE1 . **117** E3
St. George's Cl, SW8. . **166** B3
Sch St. George's C of E
　Prim Sch, SE5 . . . . . **171** E1
　SW8. . . . . **166** B2
St. Georges Ct, E6. . . . **76** A1
　EC4 . . . . **61** E5
　SW7. . . . . **110** A3
St. George's Dr, SW1 . **141** F1
St. Georges Flds, W2 . . **83** F1
Sch St. George's Hanover Sq
　Prim Sch, W1 . . . . . . **85** D3
St. Georges La, EC3
　off Pudding La **91** D2
St. Georges Ms, NW1 . . **12** B4
　SE1 . . . . **117** D3
　SE8 . . . . **124** A5
St. Georges Rd, SE1 . . **117** D3
St. Georges Sq, E14 . . . **95** E2
　SE8 . . . . **124** A5
St. George's Sq, SW1 . **142** C2
St. George's Sq Ms,
　SW1. . . . . **142** C3
St. Georges Ter, NW1 . . **12** B4
St. George St, W1 . . . . . **85** F1
St. Georges Way,
　SE15 . . . . **147** E5
Sch St. George the Martyr
　C of E Prim Sch, WC1. **60** A2
St. George Wf, SW8. . . **143** E3
St. German's Pl, SE3. . **180** C4
Coll St. Giles Coll, London Cen,
　WC1. . . . . **59** F3
St. Giles Ct, WC2
　off St. Giles High St . . **59** E5
St. Giles High St, WC2 . **59** D5
St. Giles Pas, WC2 . . . . **87** D1
St. Giles Rd, SE5 . . . . . **171** E2

St. Gilles Ho, E2 . . . . . . **44** C3
St. Helena Rd, SE16 . . **150** C1
St. Helena St, WC1 . . . . **38** C5
St. Helens Gdns, W10. . **50** C4
St. Helens Pl, EC3. . . . . **63** E5
Sch St. Helen's RC Prim Sch,
　E13 . . . . **72** C1
St. Hildas Cl, NW6. . . . . . **7** D4
Sch St. James' & St. Michael's
　C of E Prim Sch, W2 . **82** B2
St. James Cl, NW8
　off St. James's Ter . . . **34** A1
Sch St. James' C of E
　Prim Sch, SE16. . . . **120** C3
St. James Gate, NW1 . . **15** D4
St. James Gro, SW11 . **164** B5
Sch St. James Hatcham C of E
　Prim Sch, SE14. . . . **175** F3
Sch St. James Indep Schs for
　Jun Boys & Girls &
　Sen Girls, W14 . . . . **107** F5
St. James Ms, E14 . . . **126** B4
ST. JAMES'S, SW1 . . . . . **86** B5
St. James's, SE14 . . . . **175** F3
Coll St. James's & Lucie
　Clayton Coll, SW5 . **138** A1
St. James's Av, E2 . . . . . **44** B3
St. James's Ct, SW1 . . **114** B3
St. James's Gdns, W11. **79** E4
St. James's Mkt, SW1. . **86** C3
★ St. James's Palace,
　SW1. . . . . **114** B1
★ St. James's Park,
　SW1. . . . . **114** C1
⊖ St. James's Park . . **114** C3
St. James's Pas, EC3 . . **91** F1
St. James's Pl, SW1 . . . **86** A5
St. James's Rd, SE1 . . **149** D2
　SE16 . . . . **121** D3
St. James's Sq, SW1 . . **86** B4
St. James's St, SW1 . . . **86** A4
St. James's Ter, NW8 . . **34** A2
St. James's Ter Ms,
　NW8 . . . . **34** A1
St. James St, W6. . . . . **134** A3
St. James's Wk, EC1 . . **61** E1
Sch St. James the Gt Cath
　Prim Sch, SE15. . . . **172** B3
Sch St. Joachim's RC
　Prim Sch, E16. . . . . **102** A1
Sch St. John Evangelist RC
　Prim Sch, N1. . . . . . . **39** E2
Sch St. John of Jerusalem
　C of E Prim Sch, E9. . **22** B4
ST. JOHN'S, SE8. . . . . **176** C5
⇌ St. John's **177** D5
St. John's Cl, SW6. . . . **160** C1
Sch St. John's C of E
　Prim Sch, SW6 . . . . **159** F3
St. John's Est, N1 . . . . . **41** D3
　SE1 . . . . **120** A2
St. John's Gdns, W11. . **83** A3
★ St. John's Gate & Mus
　of the Order of St. John,
　EC1 . . . . **61** E2
St. John's La, EC1 . . . . . **61** E1
St. John's Ms, W11. . . . **80** C1

St. John's Pk, SE3 . . . . **180** B2
St. John's Path, EC1 . . . **61** E2
St. John's Pl, EC1 . . . . . **61** E2
Sch St. John's Prim Sch,
　E2 . . . . **44** A3
Sch St. John's RC Prim Sch,
　SE16 . . . . **123** E2
St. Johns Rd, E16 . . . . **72** C5
St. John's Sq, EC1 . . . . . **61** E2
St. Johns Ter, W10 . . . . **51** D1
St. John St, EC1. . . . . . . **61** F2
St. Johns Vale, SE8. . . **177** D5
St. John's Vil, W8 . . . . **109** F4
Sch St. John's Walworth C of E
　Prim Sch, SE17. . . . **146** B1
ST. JOHN'S WOOD,
　NW8 . . . . **32** C4
⊖ St. John's Wood. . . . **32** C2
St. John's Wd Ct, NW8 . **33** D5
St. John's Wd High St,
　NW8 . . . . **33** D3
St. John's Wd Pk, NW8. **33** D1
St. John's Wd Rd, NW8. **54** C1
St. John's Wd Ter, NW8. **33** E2
Sch St. John the Baptist
　C of E Prim Sch, N1 . **41** E3
Sch St. John the Divine C of E
　Prim Sch, SE5 . . . . . **169** E1
Sch St. Joseph's Cath Infants' &
　Jun Schs, SE5 . . . . . **170** A1
St. Josephs Cl, W10 . . . **51** F4
St. Joseph's Ct, SE7 . . **157** F5
Sch St. Joseph's Prim Sch,
　SE8 . . . . **176** C1
　SW3. . . . . **140** A1
Sch St. Joseph's R.C.
　Prim Sch, SE1 . . . . . **118** B1
　SE10 . . . . **155** F2
　Bermondsey, SE16 . . **120** C2
　Rotherhithe, SE16. . . **122** B4
　W9. . . . . **32** A5
　WC2. . . . . **59** F5
St. Josephs St, SW8 . . **165** F3
Sch St. Jude's & St. Paul's
　C of E Prim Sch, N1 . **19** E1
Sch St. Jude's C of E
　Prim Sch, SE1 . . . . . **117** E3
St. Jude's Rd, E2. . . . . . **43** F3
St. Julian's Rd, NW6. . . . **8** B4
★ St. Katharine Docks,
　E1 . . . . **92** B3
Riv St. Katharine's Pier . **92** A4
St. Katharines Prec,
　NW1 . . . . **35** E2
St. Katharine's Way,
　E1 . . . . **92** B4
St. Katherine's Row, EC3
　off Fenchurch St **91** F1
St. Katherine's Wk,
　W11. . . . . **79** D4
St. Laurence Cl, NW6 . . **29** D1
★ St. Lawrence Jewry Ch,
　EC2 . . . . **62** B5

St. Lawrence St, E14 . . **98** B4
St. Lawrence Ter, W10 . **51** E3
St. Lawrence Way,
  SW9 . . . . **169** D4
St. Leonards Ct, N1 . . . **41** D4
St. Leonards Rd, E14 . . **69** F4
St. Leonards Sq, NW5 . . **13** D2
St. Leonards St, E3 . . . . **47** F4
St. Leonard's Ter,
  SW3 . . . . **140** A3
St. Loo Av, SW3 . . . . . . **139** F4
ST. LUKE'S, EC1 . . . . . . **62** B1
St. Luke's Cl, EC1 . . . . **62** B1
Sch St. Luke's C of E
  Prim Sch, EC1 . . . . . . **40** B5
  W9 . . . . **30** A4
Sch St. Luke's C of E (VA)
  Prim Sch, E16 . . . . . . **72** B5
St. Luke's Est, EC1 . . . . **40** C5
H St. Luke's Hosp for the
  Clergy, W1 . . . . **58** A2
St. Lukes Ms, W11 . . . . **52** B5
Sch St. Luke's Prim Sch,
  E14 . . . . **154** C1
St. Lukes Rd, W11 . . . . . **52** B4
St. Lukes Sq, E16 . . . . **100** B1
St. Luke's St, SW3 . . . . **139** F2
St. Luke's Yd, W9 . . . . . **30** A3
St. Margarets Cl, EC2
  off Lothbury **62** C5
St. Margaret's Ct, SE1 . **90** B5
St. Margarets La, W8 . **109** E4
St. Margaret's Rd,
  NW10 . . . . **28** A3
St. Margaret's St, SW1 . **115** E2
St. Marks Cl, SE10 . . . . **178** A2
  SW6 . . . . **160** C4
  W11 . . . . **79** A3
Sch St. Mark's C of E
  Prim Sch, SE11 . . . . **144** B4
St. Marks Cres, NW1 . . . **13** D5
St. Mark's Gate, E9 . . . . **24** B4
St. Mark's Gro, SW10 . **137** F5
St. Marks Pl, W11 . . . . . **79** E1
St. Marks Rd, W10 . . . . **51** D5
  W11 . . . . **79** E1
St. Marks Sq, NW1 . . . . **12** C5
St. Mark St, E1 . . . . **92** B1
★ St. Martin-in-the-Fields
  Ch, WC2 . . . . **87** E3
St. Martins Cl, NW1 . . . **14** A5
Coll St. Martin's Coll,
  Tower Hamlets Professional
  Dev Cen, E3 . . . . **68** A2
St. Martin's Ct, WC2
  off St. Martin's La . . . **87** E2
St. Martin's La, WC2 . . **87** E2
St. Martin's-le-Grand,
  EC1 . . . . **62** A5
St. Martin's Ms, WC2 . . **87** E3
St. Martins Pl, WC2 . . . **87** E3
St. Martin's Rd, SW9 . **168** A5
St. Martin's St, WC2 . . . **87** D3

Sch St. Mary Abbots C of E
  Prim Sch, W8 . . . . . **109** E2
St. Mary Abbots Pl,
  W8 . . . . **108** B4
St. Mary Abbots Ter,
  W14 . . . . **108** B4
Sch St. Mary & St. Michael
  Prim Sch, E1 . . . . **94** A1
Sch St. Mary & St. Pancras
  C of E Prim Sch, NW1 . **36** C3
St. Mary at Hill, EC3 . . . **91** E3
★ St. Mary at Hill Ch,
  EC3 . . . . **91** E3
St. Mary Axe, EC3 . . . . . **91** E1
St. Marychurch St,
  SE16 . . . . **122** A2
St. Mary Graces Ct, E1 . **92** B2
Sch St. Marylebone C of E
  Sch, W1 . . . . **57** D3
★ St. Mary-le-Bow Ch,
  EC2 . . . . **90** B1
Sch St. Mary Magdalene
  Acad, N7 . . . . **16** C1
Sch St. Mary Magdalene
  C of E Prim Sch,
  SE18 . . . . **132** C5
Sch St. Mary Magdalene's
  C of E Prim Sch, W2 . **53** E3
St. Mary Newington Cl,
  SE17 off Surrey Sq . . **147** F2
Sch St. Mary of the Angels
  RC Prim Sch, W2 . . . **52** C5
Sch St. Mary's Bryanston Sq
  C of E Prim Sch, W1 . **56** A3
Sch St. Mary's C of E
  Prim Sch, N1 . . . . **17** F5
St. Marys Ct, E6 . . . . . . **76** A1
St. Marys Est, SE16 off St.
  Marychurch St **122** A2
St. Mary's Gdns, SE11 . **111** D5
St. Mary's Gate, W8 . . **109** E4
St. Mary's Gro, N1 . . . . **17** F2
H St. Mary's Hosp, W2 . **55** D5
Sch St. Mary's Kilburn C of E
  Prim Sch, NW6 . . . . . . **9** D5
St. Marys Mans, W2 . . . **54** C3
St. Mary's Ms, NW6 . . . . **9** F4
St. Marys Path, N1 . . . . **17** F5
St. Marys Pl, W8 . . . . **109** E4
Sch St. Mary's RC Prim Sch,
  NW6 . . . . **30** C2
  SW8 . . . . **165** F3
  W10 . . . . **51** E2
  W14 . . . . **107** D4
St. Mary's Rd, SE15 . . **174** A4
St. Marys Sq, W2 . . . . . **54** C3
St. Marys Ter, W2 . . . . . **54** C3
St. Mary's Twr, EC1
  off Fortune St **62** B2
St. Mary St, SE18 . . . . **132** B5
St. Mary's Wk, SE11 . . **111** D5
Sch St. Matthew's C of E
  Prim Sch, SW1 . . . . **115** D3
St. Matthew's Row, E2 . **42** C5
St. Matthew St, SW1 . **114** C4
Sch St. Matthias C of E
  Prim Sch, E2 . . . . **64** B1

St. Maur Rd, SW6 . . . . **160** B3
Sch St. Michael & All Angels
  C of E Acad, SE5 . . . **170** A2
St. Michael's All, EC3 . . **91** D1
Sch St. Michael's Camden
  Town C of E Prim Sch,
  NW1 . . . . **14** A5
St. Michaels Cl, E16 . . . **74** C4
St. Michaels Gdns,
  W10 . . . . **51** E4
St. Michael's Ms, SW1. **140** C1
Sch St. Michael's RC Sch,
  SE16 . . . . **120** C2
St. Michael's Rd, SW9. **168** A5
St. Michaels St, W2 . . . . **55** D5
St. Mildred's Ct, EC2
  off Poultry **90** C1
Sch St. Monica's RC
  Prim Sch, N1 . . . . **41** E4
Sch St. Nicholas Prep Sch,
  SW7 . . . . **111** D2
St. Nicholas St, SE8 . . **176** B4
St. Olaf's Rd, SW6 . . . **159** F2
St. Olaves Ct, EC2 . . . . **90** C1
St. Olave's Est, SE1 . . **119** F1
St. Olaves Gdns, SE11 . **116** C5
St. Olav's Sq, SE16 . . . **122** A3
St. Oswald's Pl, SE11 . **144** A3
St. Oswulf St, SW1 . . . **143** D1
ST. PANCRAS, WC1 . . . . **37** E5
H St. Pancras Hosp,
  NW1 . . . . **36** C1
⇌ St. Pancras
  International **37** E4
⊖ St. Pancras
  International **37** E4
St. Pancras Way, NW1 . **14** B5
Sch St. Patrick's Cath
  Prim Sch, NW5 . . . . . **13** F1
⊖ St. Paul's **62** A5
St. Paul's All, EC4
  off St. Paul's Chyd . . . **89** F1
St. Paul's Av, SE16 . . . . **95** D4
★ St. Paul's Cath, EC4 . **90** A1
Sch St. Paul's Cath Sch,
  EC4 . . . . **90** A1
St. Paul's Chyd, EC4 . . . **89** F1
Sch St. Paul's C of E
  Prim Sch, E1 . . . . **93** D2
  NW3 . . . . **12** A4
  SE17 . . . . **146** A3
  W6 . . . . **134** A2
St. Paul's Ct, W14 . . . . **135** D1
St. Pauls Ctyd, SE8
  off Mary Ann Gdns . **152** C5
St. Paul's Cres, NW1 . . . **15** D3
Sch St. Paul's Girls Sch,
  W6 . . . . **106** C5
St. Paul's Ms, NW1 . . . . **15** D3
St. Paul's Pl, N1 . . . . . . **18** C1
St. Paul's Rd, N1 . . . . . . **17** E2
St. Paul's Shrubbery,
  N1 . . . . **18** C1
St. Paul's Ter, SE17 . . **145** F4
St. Paul St, N1 . . . . **40** A1
St. Pauls Way, E3 . . . . . **68** A4
  E14 . . . . **68** A4

Sch St. Paul's Way Comm
  Sch, E3 . . . . **68** C3
Sch St. Paul's with St. Luke's
  Prim Sch, E3 . . . . **68** B3
Sch St. Paul's with
  St. Michael's C of E
  Prim Sch, E8 . . . . **21** D5
Sch St. Peter & St. Paul's
  RC Prim Sch, EC1 . . . **61** F1
St. Peter's All, EC3 . . . . **91** D1
St. Peter's Av, E2 . . . . . **43** D3
St. Petersburgh Ms, W2. **81** E2
St. Petersburgh Pl, W2. . **81** E2
St. Peter's Cl, E2. . . . . . **43** D3
Sch St. Peter's C of E
  Prim Sch, SE17. . . . **146** C3
  W9. . . . . **52** C2
Sch St. Peter's Eaton Sq
  C of E Prim Sch,
  SW1. . . . . **113** F4
St. Peter's Pl, W9 . . . . . **53** E2
Sch St. Peter's Prim Sch,
  E1 . . . . **94** A4
St. Peter's Sq, E2 . . . . . **43** D3
St. Peter's St Ms, N1 . . **39** F2
St. Peters St, N1 . . . . . . **39** F1
St. Peters Ter, SW6. . . **159** F2
St. Peter's Way, N1 . . . **19** F4
St. Philip Sq, SW8. . . . **165** E5
St. Philip's Rd, E8 . . . . . **20** C2
Sch St. Philip's Sch,
  SW7. . . . . **138** B1
St. Philip's Way, N1 . . . **18** B5
St. Quintin Av, W10 . . **50** B4
St. Quintin Gdns, W10 . **50** A4
St. Rule St, SW8 . . . . . **166** A5
Sch St. Saviour's & St. Olave's
  Sch, SE1 . . . . **119** D4
Sch St. Saviour's C of E
  Prim Sch, W9 . . . . . . **53** F2
St. Saviour's Est, SE1 . **120** A3
Sch St. Saviour's Prim Sch,
  E14 . . . . **69** E4
St. Silas Pl, NW5. . . . . . **12** C2
St. Silas St Est, NW5. . . **12** C1
St. Stephens Cl, NW8 . . **33** F1
Sch St. Stephen's C of E
  Prim Sch, SE8 . . . . . **177** D5
  SW8. . . . . **168** A1
  W2. . . . . **53** D4
  W12 . . . . **106** A1
St. Stephens Cres,
  W2. . . . . **53** D5
St. Stephens Gdn Est,
  W2. . . . . **52** C5
St. Stephens Gdns, W2. **53** D4
St. Stephens Ms, W2 . . **53** D4
St. Stephen's Rd, E3. . . **46** A2
St. Stephens Row, EC4. **90** C1
St. Stephens Ter, SW8. **168** A2
St. Stephen's Wk,
  SW7. . . . . **110** A5
St. Swithin's La, EC4 . . **90** C2
Sch St. Thomas C of E
  Prim Sch, W10 . . . . . **51** F2
H St. Thomas' Hosp,
  SE1 . . . . **116** A3

Coll St. Thomas' Med Sch &
  the Nightingale Sch,
  SE1 . . . . **116** A4
Sch St. Thomas More Sec Sch,
  SW3. . . . . **140** A1
Sch St. Thomas RC Prim Sch,
  SW6 . . . . **160** A1
St. Thomas Rd, E16 . . . **72** C5
St. Thomas's Gdns,
  NW5 . . . . **12** C1
St. Thomas's Pl, E9 . . . **22** A3
St. Thomas's Sq, E9 . . . **21** F3
St. Thomas St, SE1 . . . **90** C5
St. Thomas's Way,
  SW6 . . . . **160** A1
Sch St. Thomas the Apostle
  Coll, SE15 . . . . **174** A5
Sch St. Ursula's Conv Sch,
  SE10 . . . . **178** C2
Sch St. Vincent de Paul RC
  Prim Sch, SW1 . . . . **114** A4
Sch St. Vincent's RC
  Prim Sch, W1 . . . . . **57** D4
St. Vincent St, W1. . . . . **57** D4
Salamanca Pl, SE1 . . . **144** A1
Salamanca St, SE1 . . . **143** F1
Salem Rd, W2 . . . . **81** F2
Sale Pl, W2 . . . . **55** E4
Sch Salesian Coll,
  SW11. . . . . **163** E4
Sale St, E2 . . . . **64** C1
Salisbury Cl, SE17 . . . **118** C5
Salisbury Ct, EC4 . . . . . **89** E1
Salisbury Ho, E14. . . . . **69** E5
Salisbury Ms, SW6 . . . **160** A2
Salisbury Pl, SW9 . . . . **169** F2
  W1. . . . . **56** A3
Salisbury Sq, EC4 . . . . . **89** D1
Salisbury St, NW8. . . . . **55** D2
Salmon La, E14 . . . . **67** E5
Salmon St, E14 . . . . **96** A1
Salomons Rd, E13 . . . . **74** A3
Salter Rd, SE16 . . . . . . **94** C5
Salters Hall Ct, EC4. . . . **90** C2
Salters Rd, W10 . . . . . . **50** C2
Salter St, E14 . . . . **96** C2
Saltley Cl, E6. . . . . **75** F5
Saltram Cres, W9 . . . . . **30** B4
Saltwell St, E14. . . . . . . **97** D2
Saltwood Gro, SE17 . . **146** C3
Sch Salusbury Prim Sch,
  NW6 . . . . **30** A1
Salusbury Rd, NW6 . . . **30** A3
Salutation Rd, SE10 . . **127** F5
Salway Pl, E15 . . . . **27** D2
Salway Rd, E15. . . . . . . **27** D2
Samford Ho, N1 . . . . . . **38** C1
Samford St, NW8 . . . . . **55** D2
Sampson St, E1. . . . . . . **93** D5
Samuel Cl, E8 . . . . **20** B5
  SE14 . . . . **150** C5
  SE18 . . . . **131** A4
Samuel Lewis Trust Dws,
  N1 . . . . **17** D2
  SW3. . . . . **139** C1
  SW6. . . . . **161** D1
  W14 . . . . **107** F5

Samuel Lewis Trust Est,
  SE5 off Warner Rd . . **170** B4
Sch Samuel Rhodes Sch,
  N1 . . . . **16** C5
Samuel St, SE15 . . . . **172** A1
  SE18 . . . . **132** A5
Sancroft St, SE11 . . . . **144** B2
Sanctuary, The, SW1 . **115** D2
Sanctuary Ms, E8 . . . . . **20** B2
Sanctuary St, SE1. . . . **118** B2
Sandall Ho, E3 . . . . **45** F2
Sandall Rd, NW5. . . . . . **14** B2
Sandal St, E15. . . . . **27** E5
Sandalwood Cl, E1 . . . . **67** E2
Sandbourne Rd, SE4. . **175** E5
Sandell St, SE1 . . . . . . **116** C1
Sandford Cl, E6. . . . . . . **76** A1
Sandford St, SW6 . . . . **161** F2
Sandgate St, SE15 . . . **149** E4
Sandhills, The, SW10
  off Limerston St. . . . **138** B4
Sandilands Rd, SW6. . **161** E4
Sandland St, WC1. . . . . **60** B4
Sandpiper Cl, SE16. . . **124** A1
Sandringham Ct, W9 . . **32** B5
Sandringham Flats, WC2
  off Charing Cross Rd . **87** D2
SANDS END, SW6 . . . . **162** A4
Sand's End La, SW6 . . **161** F3
Sandstone La, E16 . . . **101** F2
Sandtoft Rd, SE7. . . . . **157** E4
Sandwell Cres, NW6. . . . **9** D1
Sandwich St, WC1. . . . . **37** E5
Sandy's Row, E1. . . . . . . **63** F4
Sanford St, SE14 . . . . **151** E5
Sanford Wk, SE14 . . . **151** E5
San Ho, E9. . . . . **23** D2
Sansom St, SE5. . . . . . **171** D2
Sans Wk, EC1. . . . . **61** D1
Saperton Wk, SE11. . . **116** B5
Sapperton Ct, EC1. . . . . **62** C1
Sapphire Cl, E6 . . . . **76** B5
Sapphire Rd, SE8 . . . . **151** F1
Saracen's Head Yd,
  EC3 . . . . **91** F1
Saracen St, E14. . . . . . . **97** D1
Sch Sarah Bonnell Sch,
  E15 . . . . **27** F2
Sardinia St, WC2. . . . . . **88** A1
Sark Ho, N1
  off Clifton Rd **18** B2
Sark Wk, E16. . . . . **73** F5
Sarnesfield Ho, SE15 . **149** E5
Sch Sarum Hall Sch,
  NW3 . . . . **11** E3
Sarum Ter, E3 . . . . **68** A2
Satanita Cl, E16 . . . . . . **74** C5
Satchwell Rd, E2. . . . . . **42** C5
Saturn Ho, E3
  off Garrison Rd. **46** C1
Saunders Cl, E14. . . . . . **96** B2
Saunders Ness Rd,
  E14 . . . . **154** B2

Saunders St, SE11 . . .**144** C1
Savage Gdns, E6. . . . .**104** B1
EC3 . . . .**91** F2
Savannah Cl, SE15 . . .**172** A2
Savile Row, W1. . . . . . .**86** A2
Saville Rd, E16 . . . .**103** F5
Savona Est, SW8. . . . .**166** A2
Savona St, SW8. . . . . .**166** A2
Savoy Bldgs, WC2. . . .**88** A3
Savoy Cl, E15 . . . .**27** E5
Savoy Ct, WC2. . . . . . .**87** F3
Savoy Hill, WC2 . . . . . .**88** A3
RivSavoy Pier **88** A3
Savoy Pl, WC2. . . . . . .**87** F3
Savoy Row, WC2. . . . . .**88** A2
Savoy Steps, WC2
  off Savoy Row **88** A3
Savoy St, WC2. . . . . . .**88** A2
Savoy Way, WC2. . . . . .**88** A3
Sawmill Yd, E3 . . . .**45** F1
Sawyer St, SE1 . . . . . .**118** A1
Saxon Rd, E3. . . . .**46** A3
  E6 . . . .**76** A2
Sayes Ct, SE8 . . . .**152** B4
Sayes Ct St, SE8 . . . . .**152** B4
Scala St, W1 . . . .**58** B3
Scampston Ms, W10. . .**51** D5
Scandrett St, E1 . . . . . .**93** E5
Scarba Wk, N1. . . . .**18** C2
Scarborough St, E1. . .**92** B5
Scarsdale Pl, W8. . . . .**109** E3
Scarsdale Vil, W8 . . . .**109** D4
Scawen Rd, SE8 . . . . .**151** E3
Scawfell St, E2 . . . .**42** B3
Sceaux Gdns, SE5. . . .**171** F3
Sceptre Rd, E2. . . . .**44** B5
UniSchiller Int Uni, SE1.**88** D3
Schofield Wk, SE3. . . .**181** E1
Schomberg Ho, SW1
  off Page St **115** D5
Schoolbank Rd, SE10.**128** A5
Schoolbell Ms, E3 . . . . .**45** F3
Schoolhouse La, E1 . . .**94** C2
CollSchool of Economic
  Science, W1 . . . .**57** D5
UniSchool of Oriental & African
  Studies, Russell Sq Campus,
  WC1. . . . .**59** D2
  Vernon Sq Campus,
  WC1. . . . .**38** B4
UniSchool of Pharmacy,
  WC1. . . . .**59** F1
SchSchool of the Islamic
  Republic of Iran, The,
  NW6 . . . .**30** C3
School Sq, SE10
  off Greenroof Way . .**128** B4
Schooner Cl, E14 . . . .**126** C4
  SE16 . . . .**122** C1
★ Science Mus, SW7 .**111** D4
Sclater St, E1. . . . .**64** A1
Scoresby St, SE1. . . . .**89** E5
Scotland Pl, SW1. . . . .**87** E4

Scotswood St, EC1 . . . .**61** D1
Scott Ellis Gdns, NW8. .**32** C5
Scott Lidgett Cres,
  SE16 . . . .**120** C2
Scott Russell Pl, E14 .**153** E2
Scotts Pas, SE18
  off Spray St **133** F5
Scott St, E1 . . . .**65** E2
SchScott Wilkie Prim Sch,
  E16 . . . .**74** C5
Scoulding Rd, E16 . . . .**72** B5
Scouler St, E14 . . . .**98** C3
Scovell Cres, SE1. . . . .**118** A2
Scovell Rd, SE1. . . . . .**118** A2
Scriven St, E8 . . . .**20** B5
Scrutton St, EC2 . . . . . .**63** E2
Seabright St, E2 . . . . . .**43** E5
Seacon Twr, E14. . . . .**124** B2
Seaford St, WC1 . . . . . .**37** F5
Seaforth Pl, SW1
  *off Buckingham
  Gate*. **114** B3
Seagrave Cl, E1. . . . . . .**66** C4
Seagrave Rd, SW6 . . .**137** D4
Seagull La, E16. . . . . .**101** D2
Searles Cl, SW11. . . . .**163** F2
Searles Dr, E6 . . . .**77** E4
Searles Rd, SE1. . . . . .**119** D5
Sears St, SE5 . . . .**170** C1
Seaton Cl, E13. . . . .**73** D2
  SE11 . . . .**145** D2
Sebastian St, EC1 . . . . .**39** F5
Sebbon St, N1 . . . .**17** F4
Sebright Pas, E2 . . . . . .**43** D3
SchSebright Prim Sch,
  E2 . . . .**42** C2
Secker St, SE1 . . . .**88** C5
Second Av, W10 . . . .**51** F1
Sedan Way, SE17 . . . .**147** E2
Sedding St, SW1. . . . . .**112** C5
Seddon Highwalk, EC2
  off The Barbican **62** A3
Seddon Ho, EC2
  off The Barbican **62** A3
Seddon St, WC1. . . . . . .**38** B5
Sedgmoor Pl, SE5. . . .**171** F2
Sedlescombe Rd, SW6.**136** B5
Sedley Pl, W1 . . . .**85** E1
Seething La, EC3. . . . . .**91** F3
Sekforde St, EC1 . . . . . .**61** E2
Selborne Rd, SE5 . . . .**170** C5
Selby Cl, E6. . . . .**75** E4
Selby Rd, E13 . . . .**73** F3
Selby Sq, W10. . . . .**29** F4
Selby St, E1. . . . .**65** D2
★ Selfridges, W1 . . . . .**85** D1
Selsdon Way, E14. . . . .**125** F4
Selsey St, E14. . . . .**68** C4
Selway Ho, SW8 *off South
  Lambeth Rd*. **167** F3
Selwood Pl, SW7. . . . .**138** C2
Selwood Ter, SW7. . . .**138** C2
Selworthy Ho, SW11 .**163** D3
Selwyn Rd, E3. . . . .**46** A3
Semley Pl, SW1. . . . . .**141** D1
Senior St, W2 . . . .**53** E3
Senrab St, E1. . . . .**66** C5

Sentinel Pt, SW8
  off St. George Wf . . .**143** E4
Serjeants Inn, EC4 . . . .**89** D1
Serle St, WC2. . . . .**60** B5
Sermon La, EC4. . . . . . .**90** A1
★ Serpentine, The, W2.**83** E5
★ Serpentine Gall, W2.**83** D5
Serpentine Rd, W2 . . . .**84** A5
SchServite RC Prim Sch,
  SW10. . . . .**138** A4
Setchell Rd, SE1 . . . . .**120** A5
Setchell Way, SE1. . . .**120** A5
Seth St, SE16. . . . .**122** B2
Settlers Ct, E14
  off Newport Av. **99** D2
Settles St, E1. . . . .**65** D4
SchSeven Mills Prim Sch,
  E14 . . . .**125** D2
Seven Stars Yd, E1 . . . .**64** B3
Severnake Cl, E14. . . .**125** D5
Severn Av, W10. . . . . . .**29** F4
Seville Ms, N1. . . . .**19** E4
Seville St, SW1 . . . . . .**112** B2
Sevington St, W9 . . . . .**53** E2
Sewardstone Rd, E2. . .**44** B2
Seward St, EC1 . . . .**61** F1
Sextant Av, E14 . . . . . .**126** C5
Sexton Ct, E14
  off Newport Av. **99** D2
Seymour Ms, W1. . . . . .**56** C5
Seymour Pl, W1 . . . .**56** A4
Seymour St, W1 . . . . . .**84** A1
  W2. . . . .**84** A1
Seymour Wk, SW10 . .**138** A4
Seyssel St, E14. . . . . .**126** B5
Shackleton Ct, E14
  off Maritime Quay. .**153** D2
Shacklewell St, E2 . . . .**64** B1
Shad Thames, SE1 . . . .**92** A5
SHADWELL, E1 . . . .**94** A3
⊖Shadwell. **93** F2
DLRShadwell. **93** F2
Shadwell Gdns Est, E1.**94** A2
Shadwell Pierhead, E1.**94** B3
Shadwell Pl, E1. . . . . . .**94** A2
Shaftesbury Av, W1 . . .**86** C2
  WC2. . . . .**86** C2
Shaftesbury Ct, N1. . . .**40** C3
  SE1 *off Alderney Ms* .**118** C3
Shaftesbury Ms, W8. .**109** D4
Shaftesbury Pl, W14 .**136** B1
Shaftesbury St, N1. . . .**40** B3
Shafto Ms, SW1. . . . . .**112** A4
Shafton Rd, E9 . . . .**23** D5
★ Shakespeare's Globe
  Thea, SE1 . . . .**90** A3
Shakespeare Twr, EC2 .**62** B3
Shalbourne Sq, E9 . . . .**24** A1
Shalcomb St, SW10 . .**138** B5
Shalfleet Dr, W10. . . . .**78** C2
Shand St, SE1 . . . .**119** E1
Shandy St, E1. . . . .**67** D2
Shannon Pl, NW8 . . . . .**33** F2
SchShapla Prim Sch,
  E1 . . . .**92** C2
Shardeloes Rd, SE14 .**176** A5
Sharnbrook Ho, W14 .**136** C4

Name	Page	Grid
Sharon Gdns, E9	22	A5
Sharpleshall St, NW1	12	B4
Sharratt St, SE15	150	B4
Sharsted St, SE17	145	E3
Shavers Pl, SW1	86	C3
Shaw Cres, E14	67	F4
Shawfield St, SW3	139	F3
Shearling Way, N7	15	F1
Shearsmith Ho, E1	93	D2
Sheba Pl, E1	64	B2
Sheen Gro, N1	16	C5
Sheep La, E8	43	E1
Sheerness Ms, E16	133	F1
Sheerwater Rd, E16	74	C3
Sheffield Sq, E3	46	B4
Sheffield St, WC2	88	A1
Sheffield Ter, W8	80	C5
Sheldon Ct, SW8		
off Thorncroft St	167	E2
Sheldon Pl, E2	43	D3
Sheldon Sq, W2	54	B4
Sheldrake Cl, E16	104	A5
Sheldrake Pl, W8	108	C1
★ Shell Cen, SE1	88	B5
Shelley Cl, SE15	173	F5
Shelley Ho, SW1	142	B4
Shelmerdine Cl, E3	68	C3
Shelton St, WC2	87	E1
Shenfield St, N1	41	F3
Shenley Rd, SE5	171	F4
Shepherdess Pl, N1	40	B4
Shepherdess Wk, N1	40	B2
Shepherd Mkt, W1	85	E4
SHEPHERD'S BUSH, W12	78	B4
↻ Shepherd's Bush	106	C1
⊖ Shepherd's Bush	106	C1
Shepherds Bush Grn, W12	106	B1
⊖ Shepherd's Bush Market	78	A5
Shepherds Bush Mkt, W12	106	A2
Shepherds Bush Pl, W12	106	C1
Shepherds Bush Rd, W6	134	B1
Shepherds Cl, W1		
off Lees Pl	84	C2
Shepherds Ct, W12	106	C1
Shepherds Ho, N7		
off York Way	15	E2
Shepherd's Pl, W1	84	C2
Shepherd St, W1	85	E5
Sheppard Dr, SE16	149	E2
Sheppard St, E16	72	B1
Shepperton Rd, N1	18	B5
Sheppey Wk, N1	18	B3
Shepton Hos, E2		
off Welwyn St	44	B4
Sheraton St, W1	86	C1
Sherborne Ho, SW8		
off Bolney St	168	A2
Sherborne La, EC4	90	C2
Sherborne St, N1	18	B5
Sherbrooke Rd, SW6	159	F2
Sheringham Rd, N7	16	B1
ⓈⓒⓗSherington Prim Sch, SE7	157	F5
Sherington Rd, SE7	157	E5
★ Sherlock Holmes Mus, NW1	56	B2
Sherlock Ms, W1	56	C3
Sherriff Rd, NW6	9	D2
Sherwin Rd, SE14	174	C4
Sherwood Gdns, E14	125	D5
SE16	149	D3
Sherwood St, W1	86	B2
Shetland Rd, E3	46	A3
Shillibeer Pl, W1	55	F3
Shillingford St, N1	17	F4
Shinfield St, W12	78	A1
Ship & Half Moon Pas, SE18	133	E3
Ship & Mermaid Row, SE1	119	D1
Shipman Rd, E16	101	F1
Ship St, SE8	176	C3
Ship Tavern Pas, EC3	91	E2
Shipton St, E2	42	B4
Shipwright Rd, SE16	123	E2
Shipwright Yd, SE1	91	E5
Ship Yd, E14	153	E2
Shirbutt St, E14	97	E2
Shirland Ms, W9	30	B5
Shirland Rd, W9	30	C5
Shirley Rd, E15	27	F3
Shirley St, E16	72	A5
Shoe La, EC4	61	D5
Shona Ho, E13	74	A3
Shooters Hill Rd, SE3	180	B3
SE10	178	B4
SHOREDITCH, E1	64	A2
Shoreditch High St, E1	63	F2
Shoreditch Ho, N1	41	D5
Shore Pl, E9	22	A4
Shore Rd, E9	22	A4
Shore Way, SW9	169	D5
Shorncliffe Rd, SE1	148	A2
Shorrolds Rd, SW6	160	B1
Shorter St, E1	92	B2
Shortlands, W6	134	C1
Shorts Gdns, WC2	87	E1
Short St, SE1	117	D1
Short Wall, E15	48	B4
Shottendane Rd, SW6	160	C3
Shoulder of Mutton All, E14	95	F2
Shouldham St, W1	55	F4
Shrewsbury Ct, EC1		
off Whitecross St	62	B2
Shrewsbury Ms, W2	52	C4
Shrewsbury Rd, W2	52	C5
Shrewsbury St, W10	50	B2
Shropshire Pl, WC1	58	B2
Shroton St, NW1	55	E3
Shrubbery Cl, N1	40	B1
Shrubland Rd, E8	20	B5
Shuna Wk, N1		
off St. Paul's Rd	18	C1
Shurland Gdns, SE15	172	B1
Shuters Sq, W14	136	A3
Shuttle St, E1	64	C2
Shuttleworth Rd, SW11	163	D5
Sicilian Av, WC1	59	F4
Sidbury St, SW6	159	E3
Siddons La, NW1	56	B2
Sidford Ho, SE1		
off Briant Est	116	B4
Sidford Pl, SE1	116	B4
Sidmouth Par, NW2		
off Sidmouth Rd	6	A4
Sidmouth Rd, NW2	6	B3
Sidmouth St, WC1	37	F5
Sidney Gro, EC1	39	E3
Sidney Sq, E1	66	A4
Sidney St, E1	66	A5
Sidney Webb Ho, SE1	119	D3
Sidworth St, E8	21	F4
Siebert Rd, SE3	157	D5
Siemens Rd, SE18	131	D4
Signmakers Yd, NW1	35	F1
Silbury St, N1	40	C4
Silchester Rd, W10	79	D1
Silesia Bldgs, E8	21	F3
Silex St, SE1	117	F2
Silkin Ms, SE15	173	D2
Silk Mills Pas, SE13	177	F5
Silk Mills Sq, E9	24	B1
Silk St, EC2	62	B3
Silsoe Ho, NW1		
off Park Village E	35	F3
Silver Birch Gdns, E6	76	A4
Silverbirch Wk, NW3	12	B2
Silver Cl, SE14	175	E1
Silverdale, NW1	36	A4
Silverland St, E16	104	B5
Silver Pl, W1	86	B2
Silver Rd, W12	78	C3
Silverthorne Rd, SW8	165	E5
Silverton Rd, W6	134	C5
SILVERTOWN, E16	130	A1
Silvertown Way, E16	71	F5
Silver Wk, SE16	96	A5
Silvester St, SE1	118	B2
Silvocea Way, E14	99	D1
Silwood Est, SE16		
off Concorde Way	150	C1
Silwood St, SE16	150	B1
Simla Ho, SE1	119	D2
Simms Rd, SE1	148	C1
Simon Cl, W11	80	B2
Simpsons Rd, E14	97	F3
Simpson St, SW11	163	E5
Sinclair Gdns, W14	107	D2
Sinclair Rd, W14	107	D2
Singer St, EC2	41	D5
ⓈⓒⓗSion Manning RC Sch, The, W10	51	E4
Sirdar Rd, W11	79	D3
ⓈⓒⓗSir Francis Drake Prim Sch, SE8	151	E3
Sirinham Pt, SW8	144	A5
ⓈⓒⓗSir James Barrie Prim Sch, SW8	166	B4

Sch Sir John Cass's Foundation
& Redcoat Sch, E1 . . 67 D4
Sch Sir John Cass's Foundation
C of E Prim Sch, EC3. 92 A1
Sir John Kirk Cl, SE5 . . 170 A1
Sch Sir John Lillie Prim Sch,
SW6 . . . . 135 F5
★ Sir John Soane's Mus,
WC2 off Lincoln's
Inn Flds 60 A5
Sir Martin Bowles Ho, SE18
off Calderwood St . . 133 D5
Sir Thomas More Est,
SW3 . . . . 139 D5
Sch Sir William Burrough
Prim Sch, E14 . . . . . . 67 F5
Sise La, EC4 . . . . 90 C1
Sister Mabel's Way,
SE15 . . . . 172 C1
Sivill Ho, E2 . . . . 42 B4
Six Bridges Trd Est,
SE1 . . . . 149 D3
Sixth Av, W10 . . . . 29 E5
Skelton Cl, E8 . . . . 20 B2
Skelwith Rd, W6 . . . . . 134 B5
Skenfrith Ho, SE15 . . . . 149 E5
Sketchley Gdns, SE16. 150 C2
Skiers St, E15 . . . . 49 E5
Skinner Ct, E2 . . . . 43 F2
Skinner Pl, SW1 . . . . . . 140 C1
★ Skinners' Hall, EC4
off Dowgate Hill. 90 C2
Skinners La, EC4 . . . . . 90 B2
Skinner St, EC1 . . . . . . 39 D5
Skipworth Rd, E9 . . . . . 22 B5
Skomer Wk, N1
off Ashby Gro. 18 B3
Skylines Village, E14 . 126 A2
Slade Wk, SE17 . . . . . . 145 F5
Slaidburn St, SW10 . . . 138 B5
Sleaford Ho, E3 . . . . 69 D2
Sleaford St, SW8 . . . . . 166 A1
Slingsby Pl, WC2 . . . . . . 87 E2
Slippers Pl, SE16 . . . . . 121 E4
Slippers Pl Est, SE16 . 121 F4
Sloane Av, SW3 . . . . . . 139 F1
Sloane Ct E, SW3. . . . . 140 C2
Sloane Ct W, SW3 . . . . 140 C2
Sloane Gdns, SW1 . . . . 140 C1
Ө Sloane Square 140 C1
Sloane Sq, SW1 . . . . . . 140 C1
Sloane St, SW1 . . . . . . 112 B3
Sloane Ter, SW1 . . . . . 112 B5
Sly St, E1 . . . . 93 E1
Smallbrook Ms, W2 . . . 82 C1
Smart's Pl, WC2 . . . . . . 59 F5
Smart St, E2 . . . . 44 C4
Smeaton Ct, SE1 . . . . . 118 A4
Smeaton St, E1 . . . . 93 E4
Smedley St, SW4 . . . . . 167 D5
SW8 . . . . 167 D5
Smeed Rd, E3 . . . . 24 C4
Smiles Pl, SE13 . . . . . . 178 A5

Smith Cl, SE16 . . . . 94 C5
Smithfield St, EC1 . . . . . 61 E4
Smith's Ct, W1 . . . . 86 B2
Smith Sq, SW1 . . . . . . 115 E2
Smith St, SW3 . . . . 140 A2
Smith Ter, SW3 . . . . . . 140 A3
Smithy St, E1 . . . . 66 A3
Sch Smithy St Prim Sch,
E1 . . . . 66 B3
Smokehouse Yd, EC1 . . 61 F3
Smyrks Rd, SE17 . . . . . 147 F3
Smyrna Rd, NW6 . . . . . . 8 C4
Smythe St, E14 . . . . 97 F2
Snarsgate St, W10 . . . . 50 A4
Snowden St, EC2 . . . . . . 63 E2
Snow Hill, EC1 . . . . 61 E4
Snow Hill Ct, EC1 . . . . . 61 F5
Snowman Ho, NW6 . . . . . 9 E5
Snowsfields, SE1 . . . . . 119 D1
Sch Snowsfields Prim Sch,
SE1 . . . . 119 E1
SOHO, W1 . . . . 86 C2
Sch Soho Parish Sch, W1. 86 C2
Soho Sq, W1 . . . . 58 C5
Soho St, W1 . . . . 58 C5
Sojourner Truth Cl, E8 . 21 F2
Solander Gdns, E1 . . . . 94 A2
Solebay St, E1 . . . . 67 C1
Soley Ms, WC1 . . . . 38 C4
Solway Cl, E8 . . . . 20 B2
Somerfield St, SE16 . . 150 C2
Somerford St, E1 . . . . . . 65 E2
Somerford Way, SE16 . 123 E2
Somers Cl, NW1 . . . . . . 36 C2
Somers Cres, W2 . . . . . . 83 E1
Somerset Est, SW11 . . 163 D3
★ Somerset Ho, WC2 . . 88 A2
Somerset Sq, W14 . . . . 107 F2
Somers Ms, W2 . . . . 83 E1
SOMERS TOWN, NW1 . . 37 D4
Somerville Cl, SW9 . . . 168 B3
Sondes St, SE17 . . . . . 146 C4
Sophia Cl, N7 . . . . 16 A1
Sophia Rd, E16 . . . . 73 E5
Sophia Sq, SE16 . . . . . . 95 E3
Sopwith Way, SW8 . . . 165 E1
Sorrel Gdns, E6 . . . . 75 E3
Sorrel La, E14 . . . . 99 D1
Sorrell Cl, SE14 . . . . . . 175 E1
Sotheran Cl, E8 . . . . 21 D5
Sotheron Rd, SW6 . . . . 161 F2
Soudan Rd, SW11 . . . . 164 A4
Souldern Rd, W14 . . . . 107 D4
Southall Pl, SE1 . . . . . . 118 C2
Southampton Bldgs,
WC2 . . . . 60 C5
Southampton Ms, E16. 101 E4
Southampton Pl, WC1 . 59 F4
Southampton Row,
WC1 . . . . 59 F3
Southampton St, WC2 . 87 F2
Southampton Way,
SE5 . . . . 171 D1
Southam St, W10 . . . . . 51 F2
South Audley St, W1 . . 85 D3
Southbank Business Cen,
SW8 . . . . 143 D5

Sch Southbank Int Sch,
W11 . . . . 80 C3
Hampstead Campus,
NW3 . . . . 10 B1
≷ South
Bermondsey 150 A2
South Bolton Gdns,
SW5 . . . . 137 F2
Southborough Rd, E9 . . 22 C5
Coll South Camden City
Learning Cen, NW1 . 36 C2
Sch South Camden Comm
Sch, NW1 . . . . 36 C2
South Carriage Dr,
SW1 . . . . 112 A1
SW7 . . . . 111 D2
South City Ct, SE15 . . 171 F1
South Colonnade, The,
E14 . . . . 97 D4
Southcombe St, W14 . 107 E5
Southcott Ms, NW8 . . . 33 E3
South Cres, E16 . . . . . . 70 C2
WC1 . . . . 58 C4
South Eaton Pl, SW1 . 113 D5
South Edwardes Sq,
W8 . . . . 108 B4
South End, W8 . . . . 109 F3
South End Row, W8 . . . 109 F3
Southerngate Way,
SE14 . . . . 175 E1
Southern Gro, E3 . . . . . 68 A1
Southern Row, W10 . . . 51 E2
Southern St, N1 . . . . . . 38 A2
Southern Way, SE10. . 128 B5
Southerton Rd, W6 . . . 106 A4
Southey Ms, E16 . . . . . 101 D4
Southey Rd, SW9 . . . . . 168 C3
Southgate Gro, N1 . . . . 19 D4
Southgate Rd, N1 . . . . . 19 D5
SOUTH HACKNEY, E9 . . 21 F4
SOUTH HAMPSTEAD,
NW6 . . . . 9 F3
Ꙩ South Hampstead . . 10 B4
Sch South Hampstead
High Sch, NW3 . . . . . 10 B2
Jun Dept, NW3 . . . . 10 B1
Southill St, E14 . . . . . . 69 F5
South Island Pl, SW9 . 168 B2
SOUTH KENSINGTON,
SW7 . . . . 138 A1
Ө South Kensington . 111 D5
South Kensington Sta Arc,
SW7 off Pelham St. . 111 D5
SOUTH LAMBETH,
SW8 . . . . 167 F3
South Lambeth Est, SW8
off Dorset Rd 168 A2
South Lambeth Pl,
SW8 . . . . 143 F4
South Lambeth Rd,
SW8 . . . . 143 F5
South Lo, NW8 . . . . 32 C4
SW7
off Knightsbridge . . 111 F2
★ South London Art Gall,
SE5 . . . . 171 F3
South Molton La, W1 . . 85 E1

South Molton Rd, E16 . **73** D5
South Molton St, W1 . . **85** E1
Southmoor Way, E9 . . . **24** B1
Southolm St, SW11. . . **165** E4
South Par, SW3. . . . . . **139** D2
South Pl, EC2. . . . . **63** D3
South Pl Ms, EC2. . . . . **63** D4
🚈South Quay **125** E1
South Quay Plaza,
  E14 . . . . **125** E1
South Quay Sq, E14 . . **125** E1
South Row, SE3 . . . . . **180** B5
South Sea St, SE16. . . . **124** A4
South Sq, WC1. . . . . . . **60** C4
South St, W1. . . . . **85** D4
South Tenter St, E1 . . . **92** B2
South Ter, SW7 . . . . . **111** E5
South Vil, NW1 . . . . . . **15** D2
Southville, SW8. . . . . . **167** D3
SOUTHWARK, SE1. . . . **89** F5
⊖Southwark **89** E5
Southwark Br, EC4 . . . . **90** B4
  SE1 . . . . **90** B4
Southwark Br Rd, SE1. **117** F3
★ Southwark Cath,
  SE1 . . . . **90** C4
🄲Southwark Coll,
  Bermondsey Cen,
  SE16 . . . . **121** E3
  Camberwell Cen, SE5. **171** C4
  Grange Cen, SE1 . . . **119** F4
  Waterloo Cen, SE1. . . **117** E1
Southwark Pk, SE16. . **121** F4
Southwark Pk Est,
  SE16 . . . . **121** F5
🄢Southwark Pk Prim Sch,
  SE16 . . . . **121** F4
Southwark Pk Rd,
  SE16 . . . . **120** B5
Southwark St, SE1 . . . . **89** F4
Southwater Cl, E14. . . . **68** A5
Southwell Gdns, SW7. **110** A5
South Wf Rd, W2. . . . . . **54** C5
Southwick Ms, W2 . . . . **55** D5
Southwick Pl, W2 . . . . . **83** E1
Southwick St, W2 . . . . . **55** E5
Southwood Smith St,
  N1. . . . . **39** E1
Sovereign Cl, E1 . . . . . . **93** F3
Sovereign Cres, SE16 . . **95** E3
Sovereign Ms, E2 . . . . . **42** A2
Spafield St, EC1. . . . . . . **60** C1
Spa Grn Est, EC1. . . . . . **39** D4
Spanby Rd, E3 . . . . **69** D2
Spanish Pl, W1 . . . . **57** D5
Sparke Ter, E16. . . . . . . **72** A5
Sparkford Ho, SW11. . **163** D3
Spa Rd, SE16. . . . . **120** A4
Sparta St, SE10. . . . . . **177** F4
🄢Spa Sch, SE1. . . . . . **148** C1
★ Speaker's Cor, W2 . . **84** B2
Spear Ms, SW5 . . . . . . **137** D1
Speed Highwalk, EC2
  off Silk St **62** B3
Speed Ho, EC2. . . . . . . **62** C3
Speedwell St, SE8. . . . **176** C4
Speedy Pl, WC1. . . . . . . **37** E5

Speldhurst Rd, E9. . . . . **22** C4
Spellbrook Wk, N1 . . . . **18** B5
Spelman St, E1 . . . . **64** C3
Spence Cl, SE16 . . . . . **124** A2
★ Spencer Ho, SW1 . . . **86** A5
Spencer Ms, SW8 . . . . **168** A4
  W6 . . . . **135** E4
Spencer Pas, E2 . . . . . . **43** E2
Spencer Pl, N1 . . . . **17** E3
Spencer St, EC1. . . . . . . **39** E5
Spenser St, SW1 . . . . . **114** B3
Spert St, E14 . . . . **95** E2
Spey St, E14 . . . . **70** A4
Sphere, The, E16 . . . . **100** A1
Spice Quay Hts, SE1. . . **92** B5
Spicer Cl, SW9. . . . . . . **169** F5
Spindle Cl, SE18 . . . . . **131** F4
Spindrift Av, E14. . . . . **125** E5
Spire Ho, W2 . . . . **82** B2
Spirit Quay, E1 . . . . **93** D4
★ Spitalfields City Fm,
  E1 . . . . **64** C2
Spital Sq, E1. . . . . **63** F3
Spital St, E1. . . . . **64** C3
Spital Yd, E1. . . . . **63** F3
Spode Ho, SE11
  off Lambeth Wk. . . . **116** C4
Sportsman Ms, E2 . . . . **42** C1
Spray St, SE18 . . . . . . **133** F5
Sprimont Pl, SW3 . . . . **140** A2
Springall St, SE15. . . . **173** F2
Springbank Wk, NW1 . . **15** D3
Springfield La, NW6 . . . **31** E1
Springfield Rd, E15. . . . **49** F4
  NW8 . . . . **32** A1
Springfield Wk, NW6 . . **31** E1
Spring Gdns, SW1. . . . . **87** D4
Spring Ms, W1. . . . . **56** B3
Spring St, W2 . . . . **82** C1
Spring Tide Cl, SE15. . **173** D3
Springvale Est, W14. . **107** D4
Springvale Ter, W14. . **107** D4
Spring Wk, E1 . . . . **65** D3
Springwood Cl, E3 . . . . **46** C2
Spurgeon St, SE1 . . . . **118** C4
Spur Rd, SE1 . . . . **116** C1
  SW1. . . . . **114** C2
Square, The, W6. . . . . **134** B3
Squire Gdns, NW8. . . . . **32** C5
Squirries St, E2. . . . . . . **43** D4
Stable Ms, NW5 . . . . . . **13** E1
Stables Way, SE11. . . . **144** C2
Stable Way, W10 . . . . . **78** B1
Stable Yd, SW1 . . . . . . **114** A1
Stable Yd Rd, SW1 . . . . **86** A5
Stacey St, WC2 . . . . **87** D1
Stackhouse St, SW3 . . **112** A3
Stacy Path, SE5 . . . . . **171** E2
Stadium St, SW10. . . . **162** B2
Stafford Cl, NW6 . . . . . . **30** C5
Stafford Ct, SW8
  off Allen Edwards Dr. **167** E2
  W8 . . . . **108** C3
Stafford Cripps Ho, E2 . **44** B5
  SW6 off Clem
  Attlee Ct **136** B5
Stafford Pl, SW1 . . . . . **114** A3

Stafford Rd, E3 . . . . **46** A3
  NW6 . . . . **30** C4
Staffordshire St, SE15. **173** D3
Stafford St, W1 . . . . **86** A4
Stafford Ter, W8 . . . . . **108** C3
Staff St, EC1. . . . . **41** D5
Stainer St, SE1 . . . . **91** D5
Staining La, EC2 . . . . . . **62** B5
Stainsbury St, E2 . . . . . **44** B3
Stainsby Rd, E14 . . . . . **68** C5
Stalbridge St, NW1. . . . **55** F3
Stalham St, SE16 . . . . **121** F4
Stamford Cotts, SW10. **161** F1
Stamford Rd, N1. . . . . . **19** F3
Stamford St, SE1. . . . . . **88** C5
Stamp Pl, E2 . . . . **42** A4
Stanborough Pas, E8 . . **20** A1
Stanbury Rd, SE15 . . . **173** F4
Standard Ind Est, E16. **132** A1
Standard Pl, EC2. . . . . . **41** F5
Stanfield Ho, NW8
  off Frampton St **55** D1
Stanfield Rd, E3 . . . . . . **45** F3
Stanford Ct, SW6 . . . . **161** F4
Stanford Pl, SE17 . . . . **147** E1
Stanford Rd, W8 . . . . . **109** F3
Stanford St, SW1. . . . . **142** C1
Stangate, SE1 . . . . **116** A3
Stanhope Cl, SE16 . . . **123** D1
Stanhope Gdns, SW7 . **110** B5
Stanhope Gate, W1 . . . **85** D4
Stanhope Ms E, SW7. . **110** B5
Stanhope Ms S, SW7. . **138** B1
Stanhope Ms W, SW7 . **110** B5
Stanhope Par, NW1
  off Stanhope St **36** A4
Stanhope Pl, W2. . . . . . **84** A1
Stanhope Row, W1. . . . **85** E5
Stanhope St, NW1 . . . . **36** A5
Stanhope Ter, W2. . . . . **83** D2
Stanier Cl, W14. . . . . . **136** B3
Stanlake Ms, W12. . . . . **78** A5
Stanlake Vil, W12. . . . . **78** A5
Stanley Cl, SW8 . . . . . **144** A5
Stanley Cres, W11 . . . . **80** A2
Stanley Gdns, W11. . . . **80** A2
Stanley Gdns Ms, W11. **80** B2
Stanley Rd, E15 . . . . . . **48** C1
Stanley St, SE8 . . . . . . **176** B2
Stanliff Ho, E14. . . . . . **125** D3
Stanmer St, SW11. . . . **163** F4
Stanmore St, N1. . . . . . **16** A5
Stannard Ms, E8 . . . . . . **20** C1
Stannard Rd, E8 . . . . . . **20** C1
Stannary St, SE11. . . . **145** D4
Stansbury Sq, W10. . . . **29** F4
Stansfeld Rd, E6 . . . . . . **75** D4
  E16 . . . . **75** D4
Stansfield Ho, SE1 . . . **148** B1
Stanswood Gdns, SE5. **171** F2
Stanton Ho, SE16 . . . . **124** A1
Stanway Ct, N1. . . . . . . **41** F3
Stanway St, N1. . . . . . . **41** F2

Stanwick Rd, W14 ...**136** A1
Stanworth St, SE1...**120** A2
Staple Inn, WC1 ......**60** C4
Staple Inn Bldgs, WC1 .**60** C4
Staples Cl, SE16 ......**95** E4
Staple St, SE1 ......**119** D2
Star All, EC3 ....**91** F2
Starboard Way, E14..**125** D3
Starcross St, NW1....**36** B5
Star La, E16.........**71** E2
Star Pl, E1 ....**92** B3
Sch Star Prim Sch, E16..**71** F2
Star Rd, W14 ....**136** A4
Star St, E16 ....**72** B3
W2............**55** D5
Star Yd, WC2 ....**60** C5
Staten Bldg, E3
off Fairfield Rd **47** D2
Station App, SE1 ......**88** B3
Station Ct, SW6......**162** A4
Station Cres, SE3 ....**156** C3
Stationers Hall Ct, EC4
off Ludgate Hill **89** F1
Station Ms Ter, SE3
off Halstow Rd.....**156** C3
Station Par, NW2 ......**6** B1
Station Pas, SE15 ...**174** A3
Station Path, E8 ......**21** F1
Station St, E15 ......**26** C3
E16 ....**105** E5
Station Ter, NW10 ....**28** C3
SE5 ....**170** B3
Staunton St, SE8.....**152** B4
★ Stave Hill Ecological Pk,
SE16 ....**123** E1
Staveley Cl, SE15 ....**173** F3
Staverton Rd, NW2.....**6** A3
Stave Yd Rd, SE16 ....**95** E5
Stayner's Rd, E1......**66** C1
Stead St, SE17.......**146** C1
Stean St, E8.........**20** A5
Stebbing Ho, W11.....**79** D4
Stebondale St, E14...**154** B2
Sch Stebon Prim Sch,
E14 ....**68** C4
Stedham Pl, WC1 .....**59** E5
Steedman St, SE17...**146** A1
Steeles Ms N, NW3 ....**12** B2
Steeles Ms S, NW3 ....**12** B2
Steeles Rd, NW3 .....**12** A2
Steel's La, E1........**94** B1
Steelyard Pas, EC4 ....**90** C3
Steeple Ct, E1
off Coventry Rd **65** F1
Steeple Wk, N1 ......**18** B5
Steers Way, SE16 ...**123** F2
Stephan Cl, E8........**21** D5
Stephendale Rd, SW6.**161** F5
Sch Stephen Hawking Sch,
E14 ....**95** F1
Stephen Ms, W1 ......**58** C4
Stephenson Ho, SE1
off Bath Ter **118** A3

Stephenson St, E16 ...**71** E2
Stephenson Way, NW1.**58** B1
Stephen's Rd, E15 ....**49** F1
Stephen St, W1.......**58** C4
STEPNEY, E1 ....**66** C4
Stepney Causeway, E1.**95** D1
⊖ Stepney Green......**66** C2
Stepney Grn, E1 ......**66** B3
Sch Stepney Greencoat
C of E Prim Sch, E14.**68** A5
Sch Stepney Grn Sch, E1.**67** D4
Stepney High St, E1...**67** D4
Stepney Way, E1 ......**66** C4
Sterling Gdns, SE14 ..**151** E5
Sterling St, SW7 .....**111** F3
Sterndale Rd, W14....**106** C4
Sterne St, W12 ......**106** C1
Sterry St, SE1 ......**118** C2
Stevedore St, E1 ......**93** E4
Stevenage Rd, SW6 ..**158** C2
Stevens Av, E9 ....**22** B1
Stevenson Cres, SE16.**149** D2
Stevens St, SE1 ......**119** F3
Steward St, E1 ....**63** F4
Sch Stewart Headlam
Prim Sch, E1 ......**65** E1
Stewart's Gro, SW3 ..**139** D2
Stewart's Rd, SW8 ...**166** A2
Stewart St, E14......**126** B2
Stew La, EC4 ....**90** A2
Stillington St, SW1 ..**114** B5
★ Stock Exchange, EC4.**61** F5
Stockholm Ho, E1......**93** E2
Stockholm Rd, SE16..**150** B3
Stockholm Way, E1 ...**92** C4
Stockleigh Hall, NW8
off Prince Albert Rd ..**34** A2
Stocks Pl, E14.......**96** B2
Stockton Ho, E2
off Ellsworth St **43** E4
⊖ Stockwell **167** F5
Stockwell Gdns, SW9 .**168** A4
Stockwell Gdns Est,
SW9.............**167** F5
Stockwell Pk Cres,
SW9.............**168** B5
Stockwell Pk Rd, SW9.**168** A4
Sch Stockwell Pk Sch,
SW9.............**168** A4
Stockwell Rd, SW9 ...**168** A5
Stockwell St, SE10 ...**154** B5
Stockwell Ter, SW9...**168** A4
Stokenchurch St, SW6.**161** E4
Stokes Rd, E6 ....**75** E2
Stonebridge Common,
E8 ....**20** A4
Stone Bldgs, WC2.....**60** B4
Stonechat Sq, E6 .....**75** F3
Stonecutter St, EC4 ...**61** E5
Stonefield St, N1......**17** D5
Stone Hall Gdns, W8 .**109** E4
Stone Hall Pl, W8 ....**109** E4
Stone Ho Ct, EC3......**63** E5
Stone Lake Retail Pk,
SE7 ....**157** F1
Stoneleigh Ms, E3.....**45** F3
Stoneleigh Pl, W11....**79** D3

Stoneleigh St, W11....**79** D2
Stones End St, SE1 ..**118** A2
Stonewall, E6 ....**77** D4
Stoneyard La, E14 ....**97** E3
Stoney La, E1 ....**63** F5
Stoney St, SE1........**90** C4
Stonor Rd, W14......**136** A1
Stopes St, SE15......**172** B2
Stopford Rd, SE17....**145** F3
Store Rd, E16 ....**132** C3
Storers Quay, E14 ...**154** C1
Store St, WC1 ....**58** C4
Storey Ct, NW8
off St. John's Wd Rd..**32** C5
Storey's Gate, SW1...**115** D2
Storey St, E16.......**105** D5
Storks Rd, SE16 .....**121** D4
Story St, N1..........**16** A4
Stothard Pl, E1
off Spital Yd **63** F3
Stothard St, E1 ......**66** A1
Stoughton Cl, SE11...**144** B1
Stourcliffe St, W1 ....**84** A1
Stourhead Ho, SW1
off Tachbrook St ...**142** C2
Stour Rd, E3 ....**24** C4
Stowage, SE8 ....**153** D5
Strafford St, E14.....**124** C1
Strahan Rd, E3 ....**45** F4
Straightsmouth, SE10.**178** A1
Strait Rd, E6 ....**104** B2
STRAND, WC2 ....**87** E2
Strand, WC2 ....**87** E3
Strand La, WC2 ......**88** B2
Strangways Ter, W14.**108** A3
Stranraer Way, N1 ....**15** F4
Strasburg Rd, SW11..**165** D2
STRATFORD, E15 ....**26** B1
⟳ Stratford.........**26** B3
⊖ Stratford.........**26** B3
DLR Stratford.........**26** B3
Stratford Av, W8.....**109** D4
Stratford Cen, The, E15.**27** D3
⇌ Stratford
International **25** F2
Stratford Pl, W1 ......**85** E1
Stratford Rd, W8.....**109** D5
Stratford Vil, NW1 ....**14** B3
Strathearn Pl, W2.....**83** D2
Stratheden Par, SE3
off Stratheden Rd ..**181** D2
Stratheden Rd, SE3 ..**180** C3
Strathmore Gdns, W8..**81** D4
Strathnairn St, SE1...**149** D3
Strathray Gdns, NW3..**11** E2
Strattondale St, E14..**126** A3
Stratton St, W1.......**85** F4
Streatham St, WC1...**59** D5
Streatley Rd, NW6 ....**8** A4
Streimer Rd, E15......**48** B2
Stretton Mans, SE8...**153** D3
Strickland St, SE8....**177** D4
Strode Rd, SW6......**159** D1
Stroudley Wk, E3 .....**47** E4
Strouts Pl, E2 ....**24** A4
Strutton Grd, SW1 ...**114** C3
Strype St, E1.........**64** A4

Stuart Rd, NW6 . . . . **30** C5
Stuart Twr, W9 . . . . **32** B5
Stubbs Dr, SE16 . . . . **149** E2
Stubbs Pt, E13 . . . . **73** E2
Stucley Pl, NW1 . . . . . . **13** F4
Studd St, N1 . . . . **17** E5
Studholme St, SE15 . . **173** E4
Studio Pl, SW1 . . . . . . **112** B2
Studland, SE17 . . . . . . **146** C2
Studland Ho, E14 . . . . . **67** E5
Studley Ct, E14
    off Jamestown Way . . **99** D3
Studley Est, SW4 . . . . **167** E4
Studley Rd, SW4 . . . . . **167** E4
Stukeley St, WC1 . . . . . **59** F5
    WC2 . . . . **59** F5
Sturgeon Rd, SE17 . . . **146** A3
Sturge St, SE1 . . . . . . **118** A1
Sturry St, E14 . . . . **97** E1
Sturt St, N1 . . . . **40** B3
Stutfield St, E1 . . . . **93** D1
Stylus Ho, E1
    off Devonport St **94** B1
Sudbury, E6 . . . . **77** D5
Sudbury Ct, SW8
    off Allen Edwards Dr . **167** E3
Sudeley St, N1 . . . . **39** F3
Sudrey St, SE1 . . . . . . **118** A2
Suffolk La, EC4 . . . . **90** C2
Suffolk Pl, SW1 . . . . **87** D4
Suffolk St, SW1 . . . . **87** D4
Sugar Bakers Ct, EC3
    off Creechurch La . . . **91** F1
Sugar Ho La, E15 . . . . . **48** A2
Sugar Loaf Wk, E2 . . . . . **44** A4
Sugar Quay Wk, EC3 . . . **91** F3
Sulgrave Gdns, W6 . . . **106** B2
Sulgrave Rd, W6 . . . . . **106** B2
Sulkin Ho, E2
    off Knottisford St **44** C4
Sullivan Av, E16 . . . . . . **74** C3
Sullivan Ho, SW1
    off Churchill Gdns . . **141** F3
Sullivan Rd, SE11 . . . . **117** D5
Sultan St, SE5 . . . . **170** A1
Sumatra Rd, NW6 . . . . . . **9** D1
Summercourt Rd, E1 . . **66** B5
Summerfield Av, NW6 . **29** F2
Summers St, EC1 . . . . . **60** C2
Summit Ct, NW2 . . . . **7** F1
Sumner Av, SE15 . . . . **172** B3
Sumner Ct, SW8
    off Darsley Dr **167** E3
Sumner Pl, SW7 . . . . . **139** D1
Sumner Pl Ms, SW7 . . **139** D1
Sumner Rd, SE15 . . . . **148** B5
Sumner St, SE1 . . . . **89** F4
Sumpter Cl, NW3 . . . . . **10** B2
Sunbeam Cres, W10 . . . **50** B2
Sunbury La, SW11 . . . **163** D3
Sunbury St, SE18 . . . . **132** B4
Sunbury Workshops, E2
    off Swanfield St **42** A5
Sun Ct, EC3 . . . . **91** D1
Sunderland Ter, W2 . . . **53** E5
Sundra Wk, E1 . . . . **66** C2
Sunfields Pl, SE3 . . . . . **181** E1

Sun-In-The-Sands,
    SE3 . . . . **181** E2
Sun La, SE3 . . . . **181** F2
Sunlight Sq, E2 . . . . **43** F5
Sunningdale Cl, SE16 . **149** E3
Sunningdale Gdns,
    W8 . . . . **109** D4
Sun Pas, SE16 . . . . . . **120** C3
Sun Rd, W14 . . . . **136** A3
Sun St, EC2 . . . . **63** E4
Sun Wk, E1 . . . . **92** C3
Sunwell Cl, SE15 . . . . . **173** E4
Surma Cl, E1 . . . . **65** E2
Surrendale Pl, W9 . . . . . **53** D2
Surrey Canal Rd, SE14 . **150** B4
    SE15 . . . . **150** B4
★ Surrey Docks Fm,
    SE16 . . . . **124** A2
Surrey Gro, SE17 . . . . . **147** E3
Surrey La, SW11 . . . . . **163** E3
Surrey La Est, SW11 . . **163** E3
⊖ Surrey Quays **122** C5
Surrey Quays Rd,
    SE16 . . . . **122** B3
Surrey Quays Shop Cen,
    SE16 . . . . **122** C4
Surrey Row, SE1 . . . . . **117** E1
Surrey Sq, SE17 . . . . . **147** E2
Sch Surrey Sq Inf & Jun
    Schs, SE17 . . . . **147** E2
Surrey St, WC2 . . . . **88** B2
Surrey Ter, SE17 . . . . . **147** F1
Surrey Water Rd, SE16 . **95** D5
Susan Constant Ct, E14
    off Newport Av **99** D2
Susannah St, E14 . . . . . **97** F1
Sussex Gdns, W2 . . . . . **82** C2
Sch Sussex Ho Prep Sch,
    SW1 . . . . **112** A5
Sussex Ms E, W2 . . . . . **83** D1
Sussex Ms W, W2 . . . . **83** D2
Sussex Pl, NW1 . . . . **34** A5
    W2 . . . . **83** D1
    W6 . . . . **134** A2
Sussex Sq, W2 . . . . **83** D2
Sussex St, SW1 . . . . . . **141** F3
Sutherland Av, W9 . . . . **32** A5
Sutherland Pl, W2 . . . . . **52** C5
Sutherland Row, SW1 . **141** F2
Sutherland Sq, SE17 . . **146** A3
Sutherland St, SW1 . . **141** F2
Sutherland Wk, SE17 . **146** B3
Sutterton St, N7 . . . . . . **16** A2
Sutton Est, SW3 . . . . . **139** F2
    W10 . . . . **50** A3
Sutton Est, The, N1 . . . **17** E3
Sutton La, EC1 . . . . **61** F2
Sutton Rd, E13 . . . . **72** B2
Sutton Row, W1 . . . . . . **59** D5
Sutton St, E1 . . . . **94** A2
Sutton's Way, EC1 . . . . **62** B2
Sutton Wk, SE1 . . . . . . **88** B5
Sutton Way, W10 . . . . . **50** A2
Swain St, NW8 . . . . **55** E1
Swallow Cl, SE14 . . . . **174** B4
Swallowfield, NW1
    off Munster Sq **35** F5

Swallowfield Rd, SE7 . **157** F3
Swallow Ho, NW8
    off Allitsen Rd **33** E2
Swallow Pas, W1
    off Swallow Pl **85** F1
Swallow Pl, W1 . . . . **85** F1
Swallow St, E6 . . . . **75** F4
    W1 . . . . **86** B3
Swanage Ho, SW8 . . . **168** A1
Swan App, E6 . . . . **75** E4
Swanbourne, SE17 . . . **146** A1
Swan Ct, SW3 . . . . **139** F3
Swanfield St, E2 . . . . . . **42** A5
Swan La, EC4 . . . . **90** C3
Sch Swanlea Sch, E1 . . . . **65** E3
Swan Mead, SE1 . . . . . **119** E4
Swan Ms, SW6
    off Purser's Cross Rd . **160** C3
Swan Pas, E1
    off Cartwright St **92** B3
Swan Rd, SE16 . . . . . . **122** B1
    SE18 . . . . **131** D4
Swanscombe Ho, W11
    off St. Anns Rd **79** D4
Swanscombe Rd, W11 . **79** D5
Swansea Ct, E16 . . . . . **105** F5
Swan St, SE1 . . . . **118** B3
Swan Wk, SW3 . . . . . . **140** A4
Swan Yd, N1 . . . . **17** E2
Swaton Rd, E3 . . . . **69** D2
Swedenborg Gdns, E1 . **93** D2
Sweden Gate, SE16 . . **123** E4
Sweeney Cres, SE1 . . **120** B2
Swift St, SW6 . . . . **159** F3
Swinbrook Rd, W10 . . . **51** F3
Swinton Pl, WC1 . . . . . . **38** A4
Swinton St, WC1 . . . . . . **38** A4
⊖ Swiss Cottage **10** C3
Sch Swiss Cottage Sch,
    NW8 . . . . **11** D4
Swiss Ct, W1 . . . . **87** D3
Swiss Ter, NW6 . . . . **10** C3
Switch Ho, E14 . . . . **99** D2
Sybil Phoenix Cl, SE8 . **151** D2
Sycamore Av, E3 . . . . . **24** A5
Sycamore Cl, E16 . . . . . **71** E2
Sycamore Ho, NW3
    off Maitland Pk Vil . . **12** B1
Sycamore St, EC1 . . . . **62** A2
Sycamore Wk, W10 . . . **51** E1
Sydney Cl, SW3 . . . . . **139** D1
Sydney Ms, SW3 . . . . . **139** D1
Sydney Pl, SW7 . . . . . **139** D1
Sydney St, SW3 . . . . . **139** E2
Sylvan Gro, SE15 . . . . **173** D1
Sylvester Path, E8 . . . . **21** F1
Sylvester Rd, E8 . . . . . . **21** F1
Sch Sylvia Young Thea Sch,
    NW1 . . . . **55** F2
Symes Ms, NW1 . . . . . . **36** A2
Symington Ho, SE1 . . **118** C4
Symister Ms, N1 . . . . . . **41** E5
Symons St, SW3 . . . . . **140** B1

Symphony Ms, W10 .... **29** F4
🎓Syracuse Uni - London
Program, WC1 ..... **80** A3

T

Tabard Cen, SE1
off Prioress St **119** D4
Tabard Gdns Est, SE1.**119** D2
Tabard St, SE1.........**118** C2
Tabernacle Av, E13..**72** C2
Tabernacle St, EC2 ....**63** D2
Tachbrook Est, SW1 ..**143** D1
Tachbrook Ms, SW1 ..**114** A5
Tachbrook St, SW1 ...**142** B1
Tadema Ho, NW8 .....**55** D2
Tadema Rd, SW10 ....**162** B1
Tadmor St, W12 ......**78** C5
Taeping St, E14 .....**125** E5
Taft Way, E3 ....**47** F4
Tailworth St, E1 ....**64** C4
Tait Ct, SW8
off Darsley Dr **167** D3
Tait St, E1 ....**93** E1
Talacre Rd, NW5 ....**13** D1
Talbot Ct, EC3 ....**91** D2
Talbot Ho, E14 ......**69** E5
Talbot Pl, SE3 ....**179** D1
Talbot Rd, W2 ....**53** D5
W11 ....**52** B5
Talbot Sq, W2 ....**83** D1
Talbot Wk, W11.......**79** E1
Talbot Yd, SE1........**90** C5
Talfourd Pl, SE15 ...**172** A4
Talfourd Rd, SE15...**172** A4
Talgarth Rd, W6 ....**134** B2
W14 ....**135** D2
Tallis Cl, E16 ....**101** E1
Tallis Gro, SE7.......**157** F4
Tallis St, EC4 ....**89** D2
Talwin St, E3 ....**47** F5
Tamar Cl, E3 ....**46** B1
Tamar St, SE7 ....**131** E5
Tamarind Yd, E1 .....**93** D4
Tamworth St, SW6 ..**136** C5
Tankerton St, WC1 ....**37** F5
Tanners Hill, SE8 ....**176** B4
Tanners Ms, SE8 ....**176** B4
Tanner St, SE1........**119** F2
Tanners Yd, E2 ....**43** E3
Tanswell Est, SE1 ...**116** C2
Tanswell St, SE1 ....**116** C2
Tansy Cl, E6 ....**105** D1
Tant Av, E16 ....**72** A5
Taplow, NW3.........**11** D4
SE17 ....**147** D2
Taplow St, N1 ....**40** B3
Tapp St, E1 ....**65** E1
Taransay Wk, N1 ....**18** C1
Tarbert Wk, E1 ......**94** A2
Tariff Cres, SE8 .....**124** A5

Tarling Rd, E16......**100** B1
Tarling St, E1 ....**94** A1
Tarling St Est, E1 ...**94** A1
Tarn St, SE1.........**118** A4
Tarragon Cl, SE14....**175** E1
Tarrant Pl, W1 ....**56** A4
Tarver Rd, SE17 .....**145** F3
Tarves Way, SE10....**177** F1
Tasman Ct, E14
off Westferry Rd ...**153** E1
Tasman Wk, E16.....**102** C1
Tasso Rd, W6 ....**135** E4
Tate & Lyle Jetty,
E16 ....**131** E2
★ Tate Britain, SW1..**143** E1
★ Tate Modern, SE1..**89** F4
Tate Rd, E16 ....**104** A5
Tatham Pl, NW8 ....**33** D2
Tatum St, SE17 .....**147** D1
Taunton Ms, NW1....**56** A2
Taunton Pl, NW1.....**56** A1
Taverners Cl, W11 ...**79** E5
Tavern La, SW9 .....**169** D5
Tavistock Ct, WC2
off Tavistock St **87** F2
Tavistock Cres, W11..**52** B4
Tavistock Pl, WC1 ...**59** D1
Tavistock Rd, W11 ...**52** A5
Tavistock Sq, WC1 ...**59** D1
Tavistock St, WC2....**87** F2
Tavistock Twr, SE16..**123** E4
Taviton St, WC1 .....**58** C1
Tavy Cl, SE11 ....**145** D2
Tawny Way, SE16....**123** D5
Tayburn Cl, E14 .....**70** A5
Taylor Cl, SE8 ......**152** A4
Taylors Bldgs, SE18..**133** F5
Tayport Cl, N1........**15** F4
Teak Cl, SE16.........**95** F5
Teal Cl, E16 ....**74** C4
Teale St, E2 ....**43** D2
Teal St, SE10........**128** B3
Teasel Way, E15......**49** F4
Tedworth Gdns, SW3.**140** A3
Tedworth Sq, SW3 ...**140** A3
Teesdale Cl, E2 ......**43** D3
Teesdale St, E2 ......**43** E3
Teesdale Yd, E2 ......**43** D2
★ Telecom Twr, W1 ...**58** A3
Telegraph Pl, E14....**125** E5
Telegraph St, EC2....**62** C5
Telephone Pl, SW6 ...**136** B4
Telford Ho, SE1 .....**118** A4
Telford Rd, W10 .....**51** E3
Telfords Yd, E1 ......**93** D3
Telford Ter, SW1 ....**142** A4
Temair Ho, SE10
off Tarves Way.....**177** F1
Temeraire St, SE16...**122** B2
Templar Ct, NW8
off St. John's Wd Rd..**32** C5
Templar Ho, NW2 ....**8** A1
Templar St, SE5 .....**169** F4
⊖ Temple **88** B2
★ Temple, The, EC4..**88** C2
Temple Av, EC4......**89** D2
★ Temple Bar, EC4....**89** F1

★ Temple Bar Mem,
EC4 ....**88** C1
Templecombe Rd, E9 ..**22** A5
Temple Ct, E1
off Rectory Sq **66** C3
SW8 *off Thorncroft St*.**167** E2
Temple Dws, E2
off Temple Yd.......**43** E3
Temple La, EC4 ......**89** D1
★ Temple of Mithras, EC4
off Queen Victoria St.**90** C1
Temple Pl, WC2.......**88** B2
Temple St, E2 ....**43** E3
Templeton Pl, SW5...**137** D1
Temple W Ms, SE11 ..**117** E4
Temple Yd, E2........**43** E3
Tench St, E1 ....**93** E5
Tenda Rd, SE16......**149** E1
Tenison Ct, W1 ......**86** A2
Tenison Way, SE1....**88** C5
Tenniel Cl, W2 ......**82** A1
Tennis St, SE1 ......**118** C4
Tennyson Rd, E15 ...**27** E3
NW6 ....**8** A5
Tenterden St, W1 ...**85** F1
Tenter Grd, E1........**64** A4
Tenter Pas, E1.......**92** B1
Tent St, E1 ....**65** E1
Tequila Wf, E14
off Commercial Rd...**95** F1
Teredo St, SE16......**123** D4
Terling Wk, N1 ......**18** A5
Terminus Pl, SW1 ...**113** F4
Terrace, The, NW6 ...**8** C5
Terrace Rd, E9........**22** B3
Terretts Pl, N1.......**17** E4
Testerton Wk, W11...**79** D2
Tetbury Pl, N1 ......**39** E1
Tetcott Rd, SW10 ...**162** A1
Teversham La, SW8 ..**167** F3
Teviot St, E14 ......**70** A3
Thackeray St, W8....**109** F2
Thalia Cl, SE10 .....**155** D4
Thame Rd, SE16 ....**123** D1
Thames Av, SW10....**162** B3
★ Thames Barrier
Information & Learning
Cen, SE18 ....**131** D3
Thames Circle, E14...**125** D5
Thameside Ind Est,
E16 ....**131** D1
Thames Link, SE16 ...**94** C5
Thames Pt, SW6 .....**162** B4
Thames Quay, SW10 .**162** B4
Thames Rd, E16 ....**102** C5
Thames St, SE10.....**153** F4
Thames Tunnel Mills, SE16
off Rotherhithe St ..**122** A1
Thames Wf, E16 ....**100** A4
Thanet St, WC1 ......**37** E5
Thavies Inn, EC1.....**61** D5
Thaxted Ct, N1 .....**40** C3
Thaxton Rd, W14 ....**136** B4
Thayer St, W1 ......**57** D4
★ Theatre Royal, WC2.**87** F1
Theatre Sq, E15 .....**27** D2
Theberton St, N1 ....**17** D5

★ Place of interest ⇌ Railway station ⊖ London Overground station ⊖ London Underground station

Theed St, SE1 . . . . **88** C5
Theobald's Rd, WC1 . . . **60** A3
Theobald St, SE1. . . . . **118** C4
Thermopylae Gate,
E14 . . . . **153** F1
Theseus Wk, N1 . . . . . . **39** F3
Thessaly Rd, SW8. . . . **166** A2
Third Av, W10 . . . . **51** F1
Thirleby Rd, SW1 . . . . **114** B4
Thistle Gro, SW10. . . . **138** B2
Thistley Ct, SE8
off Glaisher St **153** E4
Sch Thomas Buxton Inf &
Jun Schs, E1 . . . . **65** D2
Thomas Cribb Ms, E6 . . **76** B5
Thomas Darby Ct, W11. **79** E1
Thomas Doyle St, SE1. **117** E3
Sch Thomas Fairchild
Comm Sch, N1 . . . . . **40** B2
Thomas Hollywood Ho,
E2 . . . . **44** A3
Sch Thomas Jones Prim Sch,
W11. . . . . **79** E1
Thomas More Ho, EC2
off The Barbican **62** A4
Thomas More St, E1 . . . **92** C3
Thomas N Ter, E16
off Barking Rd **72** A4
Thomas Pl, W8 . . . . . . **109** E4
Thomas Rd, E14 . . . . . . **68** B5
Sch Thomas's Prep Sch,
Battersea, SW11 . . . **163** D4
Kensington, W8. . . . . **109** F3
Thomas St, SE18. . . . . **133** D5
Thompsons Av, SE5 . . **170** A1
Thorburn Sq, SE1 . . . . **148** C1
Thoresby St, N1 . . . . . . **40** B4
Thorncroft St, SW8. . . **167** E2
Thorndike Cl, SW10 . . **162** A1
Thorndike Ho, SW1
off Vauxhall Br Rd . . **142** C2
Thorndike Rd, N1 . . . . . **18** B2
Thorndike St, SW1 . . . **142** C1
Thorne Cl, E16 . . . . **72** C5
Thorne Rd, SW8 . . . . . **167** E2
Thorne St, E16 . . . . **72** B5
Thorney Cres, SW11. . **163** D2
Thorney St, SW1. . . . . **115** E5
Thorngate Rd, W9 . . . . **53** D1
Thornham St, SE10. . . **153** F5
Thornhaugh Ms, WC1. . **59** D2
Thornhaugh St, WC1 . . **59** D3
Thornhill Br Wf, N1 . . . . **38** A1
Thornhill Cres, N1 . . . . **16** A4
Thornhill Gro, N1 . . . . . **16** B4
Sch Thornhill Prim Sch,
N1 . . . . **16** C4
Thornhill Rd, N1 . . . . . . **16** C3
Thornhill Sq, N1 . . . . . . **16** B4
Thornley Pl, SE10. . . . **155** E3
Thornton Ho, SE17 . . . **147** D1
Thornton Pl, W1 . . . . . . **56** B3
Thornton St, SW9 . . . . **168** C5
Thornville St, SE8 . . . **176** C4
Thornwood Gdns, W8. **108** C1
Thorparch Rd, SW8. . . **167** D3
Thorpe Cl, W10 . . . . **51** F5

Thoydon Rd, E3 . . . . . . **45** E3
Thrale St, SE1 . . . . **90** B5
Thrasher Cl, E8 . . . . **20** A5
Thrawl St, E1. . . . . **64** B4
Threadneedle St, EC2. . **91** D1
Three Barrels Wk, EC4 . **90** B3
Three Colts Cor, E2. . . . **64** C1
Three Colts La, E2. . . . . **65** E1
Three Colt St, E14. . . . . **96** B1
Three Cranes Wk, EC4
off Bell Wf La **90** B3
Three Cups Yd, WC1 . . . **60** B4
Three Kings Yd, W1 . . . **85** E2
Three Mill La, E3. . . . . . **48** A4
Three Oak La, SE1. . . . **100** B4
Three Quays Wk, EC3. . **91** F3
Threshers Pl, W11 . . . . . **79** E2
Throckmorton Rd, E16. **101** F1
Throgmorton Av, EC2. . **63** D5
Throgmorton St, EC2 . . **63** D5
Thrush St, SE17 . . . . . **146** A2
Thurland Ho, SE16
off Manor Est. **149** E1
Thurland Rd, SE16 . . . **120** C3
Thurloe Cl, SW7 . . . . . **111** E5
Thurloe Pl, SW7 . . . . . **111** D5
Thurloe Pl Ms, SW7 . . **111** D5
Thurloe Sq, SW7 . . . . . **111** E5
Thurloe St, SW7 . . . . . **111** D5
Thurlow St, SE17 . . . . **147** D2
Thurso Ho, NW6 . . . . . . **31** E3
Thurtle Rd, E2. . . . . **42** B1
Tibbatts Rd, E3. . . . . . . **69** E1
Tibberton Sq, N1 . . . . . **18** A4
Tiber Cl, E3 . . . . **46** C1
Tiber Gdns, N1 . . . . **37** F1
Tidal Basin Rd, E16 . . **100** B3
Sch Tidemill Prim Sch,
SE8 . . . . **177** D2
Tideway Ind Est,
SW8. . . . . **142** B5
Tideway Wk, SW8. . . . **142** A5
Tidey St, E3. . . . . **69** D3
Tidworth Rd, E3 . . . . . . **68** C1
Tilbury Cl, SE15 . . . . . **172** B1
Tile Yd, E14 . . . . **96** B1
Tileyard Rd, N7. . . . . . . **15** E3
Tiller Rd, E14 . . . . **124** C3
Tillett Sq, SE16 . . . . . **123** F2
Tillett Way, E2 . . . . **42** C4
Tillings Cl, SE5 . . . . . . **170** B4
Tillman St, E1 . . . . **93** F1
Tilloch St, N1. . . . . **16** A4
Tillotson Ct, SW8
off Wandsworth Rd . **167** E2
Tilney Ct, EC1 . . . . **62** B1
Tilney Gdns, N1 . . . . . . **19** D2
Tilney St, W1. . . . . **85** D4
Tilson Cl, SE5 . . . . **171** E1
Tilton St, SW6 . . . . **135** F5
Timberland Cl, SE15. . **172** C2
Timberland Rd, E1 . . . . **93** F1
Timber Pond Rd, SE16. **95** D5
Timber St, EC1 . . . . **62** A1
Timber Wf, E2. . . . . **42** A1
Timbrell Pl, SE16 . . . . . **96** A5
Tindal St, SW9. . . . . . . **169** E3

Tinsley Rd, E1. . . . . **66** B3
Tinto Rd, E16 . . . . **73** D2
Tinworth St, SE11. . . . **143** F2
Tisbury Ct, W1
off Rupert St **86** C2
Tisdall Pl, SE17. . . . . . **147** D1
Tissington Ct, SE16
off Rotherhithe
New Rd **150** C1
Titchborne Row, W2. . . **83** F1
Titchfield Rd, NW8 . . . . **33** F1
Tite St, SW3. . . . . **140** A3
Tiverton Rd, NW10. . . . **28** C1
Tiverton St, SE1 . . . . . **118** A4
Tivoli Ct, SE16. . . . . . . **124** A1
Tivoli Gdns, SE18 . . . . **131** E5
Tobacco Dock, E1 . . . . . **93** E3
Tobacco Quay, E1. . . . . **93** E3
Tobago St, E14 . . . . . . **124** C1
Tobin Cl, NW3 . . . . **11** F3
Toby La, E1 . . . . **67** E2
Tokenhouse Yd, EC2. . . **62** C5
Tolhurst Dr, W10 . . . . . . **29** F4
Tollbridge Cl, W10 . . . . **51** F1
Tollet St, E1. . . . . **66** C1
Tollgate Gdns, NW6 . . . **31** E2
Tollgate Ho, NW6 . . . . . **31** E2
Sch Tollgate Prim Sch,
E13 . . . . **74** B1
Tollgate Rd, E6 . . . . **74** C4
E16 . . . . **74** A3
Tolmers Sq, NW1 . . . . . **58** B1
Tolpuddle St, N1. . . . . . **38** C2
Tom Jenkinson Rd,
E16 . . . . **101** D4
Tomlins Gro, E3 . . . . . . **47** D4
Tomlinson Cl, E2. . . . . . **42** B5
Tomlins Ter, E14. . . . . . **67** F5
Tom Nolan Cl, E15 . . . . **49** F3
Tompion Ho, EC1
off Percival St. **61** F1
Tompion St, EC1 . . . . . . **39** E5
Tom Smith Cl, SE10 . . **155** E4
Tom Thumbs Arch, E3
off Malmesbury Rd . . **46** C3
Tom Williams Ho, SW6
off Clem Attlee Ct . . **136** A5
Tonbridge St, WC1 . . . . **37** E4
Tonbridge Wk, WC1
off Bidborough St. . . **37** E4
Tony Cannell Ms, E3. . . **46** A5
Took's Ct, EC4 . . . . **60** C5
Tooley St, SE1 . . . . **91** D4
Topham St, EC1. . . . . . . **60** C1
Topmast Pt, E14. . . . . **124** C2
Torbay Rd, NW6 . . . . **8** A4
Torbay St, NW1. . . . . . . **13** F4
Tor Gdns, W8 . . . . **108** C1
Tornay Ho, N1
off Priory Grn Est. . . **38** A2
Torquay St, W2. . . . . . . **53** E4
Torrens Sq, E15. . . . . . . **27** F1
Torrens St, EC1 . . . . **39** D3

Torres Sq, E14
off Maritime Quay . . 153 D2
Torrey Dr, SW9 . . . . . . 169 D5
SchTorriano Inf Sch,
NW5 . . . . 14 C1
Torridon Ho, NW6 . . . . . 31 E3
Torrington Pl, E1 . . . . . 93 D4
WC1 . . . . 58 B3
Torrington Sq, WC1 . . . 59 D2
Tothill Ho, SW1
off Page St 115 D5
Tothill St, SW1 . . . . . . 114 C2
Tottan Ter, E1 . . . . 67 D5
⊖Tottenham Court
Road 58 C5
Tottenham Ct Rd, W1 . . 58 B2
Tottenham Ms, W1 . . . . 58 B3
Tottenham Rd, N1 . . . . 19 E2
Tottenham St, W1 . . . . 58 B4
Toulmin St, SE1 . . . . . . 118 A2
Toulon St, SE5 . . . . 170 A1
Tournay Rd, SW6 . . . . . 160 B1
Toussaint Wk, SE16 . . 121 D3
Tovy Ho, SE1 . . . . 148 C3
Towcester Rd, E3 . . . . . 69 F2
Tower 42, EC2 . . . . 63 E5
Tower Br, E1 . . . . 92 A5
SE1 . . . . 92 A5
Tower Br App, E1 . . . . . 92 A4
★ Tower Br Exhib, SE1 . 92 A5
Tower Br Piazza, SE1 . . 92 A5
SchTower Br Prim Sch,
SE1 . . . . 120 A1
Tower Br Rd, SE1 . . . . 119 E4
Tower Br Wf, E1 . . . . . . 92 C5
Tower Bldgs, E1
off Brewhouse La 93 F5
Tower Ct, WC2 . . . . 87 E1
DLRTower Gateway 92 B2
CollTower Hamlets Coll,
Arbour Sq Cen, E1 . . 66 C5
Bethnal Grn Cen, E2 . . 42 C5
East India Dock Rd,
E14 . . . . 97 F1
Poplar Cen, E14 . . . . . 97 E3
⊖Tower Hill 91 F2
Tower Hill, EC3 . . . . . . 92 A3
Tower Hill Ter, EC3
off Byward St 91 F3
★ Tower Millennium Pier,
EC3 . . . . 91 F4
Tower Mill Rd, SE15 . . 147 E5
★ Tower of London,
EC3 . . . . 92 A3
Tower Pl E, EC3 . . . . . . 91 F3
Tower Pl W, EC3 . . . . . 91 F3
Tower Royal, EC4 . . . . . 90 B2
Tower St, WC2 . . . . 87 D1
Towing Path Wk, N1 . . 37 E2
Townley St, SE17 . . . . 146 C2
SchTownsend Prim Sch,
SE17 . . . . 119 E5
Townsend St, SE17 . . . 147 D1

Townshend Est, NW8 . . 33 E2
Townshend Rd, NW8 . . 33 E1
Toynbee St, E1 . . . . 64 A4
Trader Rd, E6 . . . . 105 E1
Tradescant Rd, SW8 . . 167 F2
Trafalgar Av, SE15 . . 148 B3
Trafalgar Cl, SE16 . . . 123 E5
Trafalgar Ct, E1 . . . . . . 94 B3
Trafalgar Gdns, E1 . . . 67 D3
W8 . . . . 109 E3
Trafalgar Gro, SE10 . . 155 D4
Trafalgar Ms, E9 . . . . . 24 A1
Trafalgar Rd, SE10 . . . 155 D4
Trafalgar Sq, SW1 . . . . 87 D4
WC2 . . . . 87 D4
Trafalgar St, SE17 . . . 146 C2
Trafalgar Way, E14 . . 98 A4
Trahorn Cl, E1 . . . . 65 E2
Tralee Ct, SE16 . . . . . . 149 E2
Tramway Av, E15 . . . . 27 E3
Transept St, NW1 . . . . 55 E4
Transom Cl, SE16 . . . 123 F5
Transom Sq, E14 . . . . 153 E1
Tranton Rd, SE16 . . . 121 D3
Trappes Ho, SE16
off Manor Est 149 E1
Treadgold St, W11 . . . 79 D2
Treadway St, E2 . . . . . 43 E3
Treaty St, N1 . . . . 38 A1
Trebeck St, W1 . . . . . . 85 E4
Trebovir Rd, SW5 . . . . 137 D2
Treby St, E3 . . . . 68 A2
Tredegar Ms, E3 . . . . . 46 A4
Tredegar Rd, E3 . . . . . 46 A3
Tredegar Sq, E3 . . . . . 46 A4
Tredegar Ter, E3 . . . . . 46 A4
Trederwen Rd, E8 . . . 21 D5
Tree Rd, E16 . . . . 74 A5
Trego Rd, E9 . . . . 24 C3
Tregunter Rd, SW10 . . 138 A4
Treherne Ct, SW9 . . . . 169 D3
Trelawney Est, E9 . . . . 22 A2
Trellick Twr, W10 . . . . 52 A2
Trellis Sq, E3 . . . . 46 B4
Trenchard St, SE10 . . 155 D3
Trenchold St, SW8 . . 143 E5
Tresham Cres, NW8 . . 55 E1
Tressell Cl, N1 . . . . 17 F4
Trevanion Rd, W14 . . . 135 F2
Trevelyan Gdns, NW10 . 28 A1
Trevelyan Ho, E2
off Morpeth St 44 C5
Treveris St, SE1 . . . . . . 89 E5
Treverton St, W10 . . . 51 D2
Trevithick Ho, SE16 . . 149 F1
Trevithick St, SE8 . . . 152 C4
Trevor Pl, SW7 . . . . . . 111 F2
Trevor Sq, SW7 . . . . . . 112 A2
Trevor St, SW7 . . . . . . 111 F2
Trevor Wk, SW7
off Trevor Sq 112 A2
Triangle, The, EC1 . . . 61 F1
Triangle Ct, E16 . . . . . 74 C3
Triangle Est, SE11 . . . 144 C3
Triangle Rd, E8 . . . . . . 21 E5
Trident St, SE16 . . . . . 123 D5
Trig La, EC4 . . . . 90 A2

Trigon Rd, SW8 . . . . . . 168 B1
Trim St, SE14 . . . . 152 A5
Trinidad St, E14 . . . . . 96 B2
Trinity Buoy Wf, E14 . 100 A3
Trinity Ch Sq, SE1 . . . 118 B3
Trinity Cl, E8 . . . . 20 B1
CollTrinity Coll of Music,
SE10 . . . . 154 B4
Trinity Ct, N1 . . . . 19 E5
Trinity Gdns, E16 . . . . 72 B3
Trinity Gro, SE10 . . . . 178 A3
★ Trinity Ho, EC3 . . . . 91 F2
Trinity Ho, SE1
off Bath Ter 118 B3
Trinity Ms, W10 . . . . . 51 D5
Trinity Pl, EC3 . . . . 92 A3
Trinity Sq, EC3 . . . . . . 91 F3
Trinity St, E16 . . . . 72 C4
SE1 . . . . 118 B2
Trinity Wk, NW3 . . . . . 10 B2
Trio Pl, SE1 . . . . 118 B2
Triton Sq, NW1 . . . . . . 58 A1
Triumph Rd, E6 . . . . . . 76 B5
Troon Cl, SE16 . . . . . . 149 F2
Troon St, E1 . . . . 67 E5
Trothy Rd, SE1 . . . . . . 121 D5
Trott St, SW11 . . . . . . 163 D4
Troughton Rd, SE7 . . . 157 E2
Troutbeck Rd, SE14 . . 175 E3
Trowbridge Est, E9 . . . 24 B1
Trowbridge Rd, E9 . . . 24 B2
Troy Ct, W8 . . . . 108 C3
Truesdale Rd, E6 . . . . 104 B1
Trump St, EC2 . . . . 90 B1
Trundle St, SE1 . . . . . . 118 A1
Trundleys Rd, SE8 . . . 151 D2
Trundleys Ter, SE8 . . . 151 D1
Truro St, NW5 . . . . 12 C2
Trussley Rd, W6 . . . . . 106 A4
Tryon Cres, E9 . . . . 22 A5
Tryon St, SW3 . . . . 140 A2
Tudor Gro, E9 . . . . 22 A4
Tudor Rd, E9 . . . . 21 F5
Tudor St, EC4 . . . . 89 D2
Tufton St, SW1 . . . . . . 115 D3
Tuilerie St, E2 . . . . 42 C2
SchTuke Sch, SE15 . . . . 173 E4
Tulip Cl, E6 . . . . 76 A4
Tunley Grn, E14
off Burdett Rd 68 B4
Tunnan Leys, E6 . . . . . 77 D5
Tunnel Av, SE10 . . . . . 127 D1
Tunnel Rd, SE16 . . . . . 122 A1
Turin St, E2 . . . . 42 C5
Turk's Head Yd, EC1 . . 61 E3
Turks Row, SW3 . . . . . 140 B2
Turley Cl, E15 . . . . 49 F1
Turnagain La, EC4 . . . 61 E5
Turnberry Cl, SE16 . . . 149 F3
Turnberry Quay,
E14 . . . . 125 F3
Turner Cl, SW9 . . . . . . 169 F3
Turner Ho, E14
off Cassilis Rd 125 D2
Turners Rd, E3 . . . . . . 68 A4
Turner St, E1 . . . . 65 E4
E16 . . . . 100 A1

Turneville Rd, W14 . . . **136** A4
Turnmill St, EC1 . . . . . . **61** D2
Turnpike Cl, SE8 . . . . . **176** B1
Turnpike Ho, EC1 . . . . . **39** F5
Turnpin La, SE10 . . . . . **154** B5
Turpentine La, SW1 . . **141** F2
Turpin Ho, SW11 . . . . . **165** E3
Turquand St, SE17 . . . **146** B1
Turville St, E2 . . . . **64** A1
Tuscan Ho, E2 . . . . **44** B4
Tuskar St, SE10 . . . . . . **155** E3
Tustin Est, SE15 . . . . . **150** A5
Tweezer's All, WC2 . . . . **88** C2
Twelvetrees Business Pk,
  E3 . . . . **70** C2
Twelvetrees Cres, E3 . . **70** A1
Twig Folly Cl, E2 . . . . . . **45** D3
Twine Ct, E1 . . . . **94** A2
Twine Ter, E3
  off Ropery St **68** A2
Twycross Ms, SE10 . . . **155** F1
Twyford Pl, WC2 . . . . . . **60** A5
Twyford St, N1 . . . . **16** A5
Tyas Rd, E16 . . . . **72** A2
Tyburn Way, W1 . . . . . . **84** B2
Tyers Est, SE1 . . . . **119** E1
Tyers Gate, SE1 . . . . . . **119** E1
Tyers St, SE11 . . . . **144** A2
Tyers Ter, SE11 . . . . . . **144** A3
Tyler Cl, E2 . . . . **42** A2
Tyler's Ct, W1 . . . . **86** C1
Tyler St, SE10 . . . . **155** F3
Tyndale Ct, E14 . . . . . . **153** E2
Tyndale La, N1 . . . . **17** E3
Tyndale Ter, N1 . . . . . . **17** E3
Tynemouth Cl, E6 . . . . **105** E1
Tynemouth St, SW6 . . **162** A5
Tyne St, E1
  off Old Castle St **64** B5
Type St, E2 . . . . **44** C3
Tyrawley Rd, SW6 . . . **161** E3
Tysoe St, EC1 . . . . **38** C5
Tyssen Pas, E8 . . . . **20** A1
Tyssen St, E8 . . . . **20** B1
  N1 . . . . **41** F2

U

Uamvar St, E14 . . . . **69** F3
Udall St, SW1 . . . . **142** B1
Ufford St, SE1 . . . . **117** D1
Ufton Gro, N1 . . . . **19** D3
Ufton Rd, N1 . . . . **19** D4
Ullin St, E14 . . . . **70** A4
Ulster Pl, NW1 . . . . **57** E2
Ulster Ter, NW1 . . . . . . **57** E2
Ulundi Rd, SE3 . . . . . . **155** F5
Umberston St, E1 . . . . . **65** E5
Underhill Pas, NW1 . . . **13** F5
Underhill St, NW1 . . . . **35** F1
Undershaft, EC3 . . . . . . **91** E1
Underwood Rd, E1 . . . . **64** C2
Underwood Row, N1 . . **40** B4
Underwood St, N1 . . . . **40** B4
Undine Rd, E14 . . . . . . **125** F5

Unicorn Pas, SE1
  off Tooley St **91** F5
Union Cotts, E15 . . . . . . **27** F3
Union Ct, EC2 . . . . **63** E5
Union Dr, E1 . . . . **67** F1
Union Jack Club,
  SE1 . . . . **116** C1
Union Pk, SE10 . . . . . **156** A3
Union Rd, SW4 . . . . . . **166** C5
  SW8 . . . . **166** C5
Union Sq, N1 . . . . **40** A1
Union St, E15 . . . . **48** C1
  SE1 . . . . **89** F5
Union Wk, E2 . . . . **41** F4
Union Wf, N1 . . . . **40** A3
Unity Ct, SE1
  off Mawbey Pl **148** B2
Unity Way, SE18 . . . . . **130** C3
Unity Wf, SE1 . . . . **120** B1
H University Coll Hosp,
  NW1 . . . . **58** B1
  Elizabeth Garrett Anderson
  Wing, NW1 . . . . **58** B1
  Hosp for Tropical Diseases,
  WC1 . . . . **58** B2
  Obstetric Hosp, WC1 . . **58** B2
  Private Wing, WC1 . . . **58** B2
Uni University Coll London,
  Main Site, WC1 . . . . . **58** C1
  Arthur Stanley Ho,
  W1 . . . . **58** B3
  Dorville & Doran Ho,
  W1 . . . . **58** A4
  Eastman Dental Inst,
  WC1 . . . . **38** A5
  Inst of Ophthalmology,
  EC1 . . . . **40** C5
  Ludwig Inst for Cancer
  Research, W1 . . . . **58** B3
  Prankerd Ho, NW1 . . . **58** B1
  Ramsay Hall of Res,
  W1 . . . . **58** A2
  Slade Research Cen,
  WC1 . . . . **59** D2
  The Inst of Neurology,
  WC1 . . . . **59** F2
  The Warburg Inst, WC1. **59** D2
  Windeyer Bldg, W1 . . . **58** B3
  Wolfson Ho, NW1 . . . . **36** B5
  Wolfson Inst for Biomedical
  Research, WC1 . . . . . . **58** B2
Uni University of E London -
  London Docklands
  Campus, E16 . . . . . . **105** D2
Uni University of E London -
  Stratford Campus,
  Clinical Ed Cen, E15 . . **27** F1
  Duncan Ho, E15 . . . . . **26** C5
  Ed Bldg, E15 . . . . **27** F1
  Edwards Bldg, E15 . . . **27** F1
  Lecture Thea & Student
  Services, E15 . . . . **27** F2
  Uni Ho, E15 . . . . **27** F2
Uni University of
  Gloucestershire,
  Urban Learning
  Foundation, E14 . . . . **96** C2

Uni University of Greenwich -
  Maritime Greenwich
  Campus, Cooper Bldg,
  SE10 . . . . **154** C4
  Old Royal Naval Coll,
  SE10 . . . . **154** C4
Uni University of London,
  WC1 . . . . **59** D3
  Canterbury Hall of Res,
  WC1 . . . . **37** E5
  Commonwealth Hall of Res,
  WC1 . . . . **37** E5
  Hughes Parry Hall of Res,
  WC1 . . . . **37** E5
  Int Hall of Res, WC1 . . **59** F2
  Stewart Ho, WC1 . . . . **59** D3
  Union, WC1 . . . . **58** C2
Uni University of the Arts,
  W1 . . . . **85** E1
Uni University of Westminster -
  Cavendish Campus,
  W1 . . . . **58** A3
Uni University of Westminster -
  Marylebone Campus,
  NW1 . . . . **56** C3
Uni University of Westminster -
  Regent Campus, W1 . **57** F5
  Gt Portland St, W1 . . . **57** F3
  Little Titchfield St,
  W1 . . . . **58** A4
  Riding Ho St, W1 . . . . **58** A4
University St, WC1 . . . . **58** B2
University Way, E16 . **105** D3
Unwin Cl, SE15 . . . . . . **148** C5
Unwin Rd, SW7 . . . . . . **111** D3
Upbrook Ms, W2 . . . . . . **82** B1
Upcerne Rd, SW10 . . . **162** B2
Upland Rd, E13 . . . . **72** B1
Upnor Way, SE17 . . . . **147** F2
Upper Addison Gdns,
  W14 . . . . **107** E1
Upper Bk St, E14 . . . . . . **97** E5
Upper Bardsey Wk, N1
  off Bardsey Wk **18** B1
Upper Belgrave St,
  SW1 . . . . **113** D3
Upper Berenger Wk, SW10
  off Blantyre St **162** C1
Upper Berkeley St, W1. **84** A1
Upper Blantyre Wk, SW10
  off Blantyre St **162** C1
Upper Brockley Rd,
  SE4 . . . . **176** B5
Upper Brook St, W1 . . . **84** C3
Upper Cheyne Row,
  SW3 . . . . **139** E5
Upper Dartrey Wk, SW10
  off Blantyre St **162** C1
Upper Grosvenor St,
  W1 . . . . **84** C3
Upper Grd, SE1 . . . . **88** C4
Upper Gulland Wk, N1
  off Nightingale Rd . . . **18** B2

Upper Handa Wk, N1
  off Handa Wk......18 B1
Upper James St, W1...86 B2
Upper John St, W1....86 B2
Upper Lismore Wk, N1
  off Mull Wk........18 B2
Upper Marsh, SE1....116 B3
Upper Montagu St, W1.56 A3
Upper N St, E14......97 D2
Upper Pk Rd, NW3...12 A1
Upper Phillimore Gdns,
  W8..............108 C2
Upper Ramsey Wk, N1
  off Ramsey Wk.....18 C2
Upper St. Martin's La,
  WC2..............87 E2
Upper St, N1.........39 D2
Upper Tachbrook St,
  SW1.............114 A5
Upper Thames St, EC4.89 F2
Upper Whistler Wk, SW10
  off Blantyre St....162 B1
Upper Wimpole St, W1.57 E3
Upper Woburn Pl, WC1.37 D5
Upstall St, SE5......169 F4
CollUrdang Acad, The,
  EC1..............39 D5
Urlwin St, SE5......146 A5
Urlwin Wk, SW9.....169 D4
Ursula St, SW11.....163 E4
Usborne Ms, SW8....168 A1
Usher Rd, E3.........46 B2
Usk St, E2...........44 C4
Utah Bldg, SE13
  off Deals Gateway..177 E3
Utopia Village, NW1...12 C5
Uverdale Rd, SW10...162 B2
Uxbridge Rd, W12...106 B1
Uxbridge St, W8.....80 C4

V

Vale, The, SW3......138 C4
Vale Cl, W9..........32 A5
Vale Ct, W9..........32 A5
Valentine Ho, E3
  off Garrison Rd....46 B1
Valentine Pl, SE1....117 E1
Valentine Rd, E9......22 C2
Valentine Row, SE1..117 E2
Valerian Way, E15....49 F5
Vale Royal, N7.......15 E4
SchVale Sch, The, SW7.110 A4
Valette St, E9.......21 F1
Valiant Way, E6......76 A4
Vallance Rd, E1......43 D5
  E2...............43 D5
Valmar Rd, SE5......170 B4
Vanbrugh Cl, E16.....74 C4
Vanbrugh Flds, SE3..156 A5
Vanbrugh Hill, SE3...156 A4

Vanbrugh Hill, SE10..155 F3
Vanbrugh Pk, SE3....180 A2
Vanbrugh Pk Rd, SE3.180 B1
Vanbrugh Pk Rd W,
  SE3.............180 A1
Vanbrugh Ter, SE3...180 B3
Vandome Cl, E16....101 E1
Vandon Pas, SW1....114 B3
Vandon St, SW1.....114 B3
Vandy St, EC2........63 E2
Vane St, SW1.......114 B5
Vanguard Cl, E16.....73 D4
Vanguard Ho, E8......21 F3
Vanguard St, SE8....176 C3
Vanner Pt, E9........22 C2
Vansittart St, SE14...175 F1
Vanston Pl, SW6.....160 C1
Vantage Ms, E14......98 B5
Vantage Pl, W8......109 D4
Varcoe Rd, SE16.....149 F3
Varden St, E1........65 E5
Varley Rd, E16.......73 F5
Varna Rd, SW6......159 F1
Varndell St, NW1.....36 A4
Vassall Rd, SW9.....168 C2
Vauban Est, SE16....120 B4
Vauban St, SE16.....120 B4
Vaughan St, SE16....124 A2
Vaughan Way, E1......92 C3
Vaughan Williams Cl,
  SE8.............176 C2
VAUXHALL, SE11.....143 F3
⇌Vauxhall.........143 F4
⊖Vauxhall.........143 F4
Vauxhall Br, SE1.....143 E3
  SW1.............143 E3
Vauxhall Br Rd, SW1.114 B5
Vauxhall Gdns Est,
  SE11............144 A3
Vauxhall Gro, SW8...144 A4
SchVauxhall Prim Sch,
  SE11............144 B2
Vauxhall St, SE11....144 B2
Vauxhall Wk, SE11...144 A2
Vawdrey Cl, E1.......66 A2
Velletri Ho, E2.......44 C3
Venables St, NW8.....55 D2
Ventnor Rd, SE14....175 D2
Venue St, E14........70 A3
Venus Ho, E3
  off Garrison Rd....46 C1
  E14 off Crews St..124 C5
Venus Rd, SE18.....132 A4
Vera Rd, SW6.......159 F4
Verbena Cl, E16......72 A1
Verdi Cres, W10......29 F3
Vereker Rd, W14....135 F3
Vere St, W1..........85 E1
Verity Cl, W11........79 E1
Verney Rd, SE16....149 D4
Verney Way, SE16...149 E3
Vernon Ms, W14....135 F1
Vernon Pl, WC1......59 F4
Vernon Ri, WC1......38 B4
Vernon Rd, E3........46 B2
  E15..............27 F3
Vernon Sq, WC1.....38 B4

Vernon St, W14......135 E1
Vernon Yd, W11......80 A2
Verulam Bldgs, WC1..60 B3
Verulam Ho, W6
  off Hammersmith
  Gro.............106 A2
Verulam St, WC1.....60 C3
Vesage Ct, EC1.......61 D4
Vesey Path, E14......97 F1
Vesta Ct, SE1
  off Morocco St....119 E2
Vesta Ho, E3
  off Garrison Rd....46 C1
Vestry Ms, SE5......171 E4
Vestry Rd, SE5......171 E4
Vestry St, N1.........40 C4
Viaduct Pl, E2........43 E5
Viaduct St, E2.......43 E5
Vibart Wk, N1........15 F5
Vicarage Av, SE3....181 D2
Vicarage Ct, W8
  off Vicarage Gate...109 E1
Vicarage Cres, SW11.162 C4
Vicarage Gdns, W8....81 D5
Vicarage Gate, W8...109 E1
Vicarage Gro, SE5...171 D3
Vicarage La, E15......27 F5
Vicarage Wk, SW11..162 C4
Vicars Cl, E9.........44 A1
Viceroy Ct, NW8......33 F2
Viceroy Rd, SW8....167 E3
⇌Victoria..........113 F5
⊖Victoria..........113 F5
★ Victoria & Albert Mus,
  SW7.............111 D4
Victoria Arc, SW1
  off Terminus Pl...113 F4
Victoria Av, EC2......63 F4
★ Victoria Coach Sta,
  SW1.............141 E1
Victoria Dock Rd, E16.101 F2
Victoria Embk, EC4....88 A3
  SW1.............115 F1
  WC2.............88 A3
★ Victoria Embankment
  Gdns, WC2.......87 F3
Victoria Gdns, W11...80 C3
Victoria Gro, W8.....110 A3
Victoria Gro Ms, W2...81 D3
Victoria Ho, SW8 off South
  Lambeth Rd......167 F1
Victoria Mans, SW8 off South
  Lambeth Rd......167 F1
Victoria Ms, E8.......20 C1
  NW6............8 C5
Victoria Mills Studios,
  E15..............26 C5
★ Victoria Park, E9...23 E5
Victoria Pk Rd, E9.....43 F1
Victoria Pk Sq, E2.....44 A4
Victoria Pas, NW8.....54 C1
Victoria Pl, SW1.....113 F5
Victoria Rd, NW6.....30 B1
  W8..............110 A4
Victoria Sq, SW1....113 F3
Victoria St, E15.......27 E3
  SW1.............114 A4

Victoria Way, SE7 .... **157** E2
Victoria Wf, E14 ...... **95** F3
Victoria Yd, E1 .... **93** D1
Victory Pl, E14 .... **95** F2
   SE17 .... **118** C5
Sch Victory Prim Sch,
   SE17 .... **118** B5
Victory Wk, SE8 ..... **176** C3
Victory Way, SE16 ... **123** F2
Vigo St, W1 .... **86** A3
Viking Cl, E3 .... **45** F3
Viking Ct, SW6 ..... **137** D4
Viking Gdns, E6 ..... **75** E2
Villa St, SE17 .... **147** D3
Villiers St, WC2 ...... **87** E3
Vince Ct, N1
   off Charles Sq **41** D5
Vincent Cl, SE16 ..... **123** E2
Vincent Ms, E3
   off Menai Pl **46** C2
Vincent Rd, SE18 .... **133** E5
Vincent Sq, SW1 ..... **114** B5
Vincent St, E16 ...... **72** B4
   SW1 .... **114** C5
Vincent Ter, N1 ...... **39** E2
Vince St, EC1 .... **41** D5
Vine Ct, E1 .... **65** D4
Vinegar St, E1 .... **93** E4
Vinegar Yd, SE1 ..... **119** E1
Vine Hill, EC1 .... **60** C2
Vine La, SE1 .... **91** F5
Vine Sq, W14 .... **136** B3
Vine St, EC3 .... **92** A2
   W1 .... **86** B3
Vine St Br, EC1 ...... **61** D2
Vine Yd, SE1 .... **118** B1
Vineyard Wk, EC1 .... **60** C1
★ Vinopolis, SE1 ..... **90** B4
Vintners Ct, EC4 ..... **90** B2
Vintners Pl, EC4
   off Vintners Ct **90** B2
Violet Cl, E16 .... **71** F2
   SE8 .... **152** A4
Violet Hill, NW8 ..... **32** A3
Violet Rd, E3 .... **69** E2
Violet St, E2 .... **65** F1
Virgil Pl, W1 .... **56** A4
Virgil St, SE1 .... **116** B3
Sch Virginia Prim Sch,
   E2 .... **42** A5
Virginia Rd, E2 ...... **42** A5
Virginia St, E1 ...... **93** D3
Visage Apts, NW3 .... **11** D4
Viscount Dr, E6 ...... **76** A3
Viscount St, EC1 ..... **62** A2
Vista Bldg, The,
   SE18 .... **133** D5
Sch Vittoria Prim Sch,
   N1 .... **38** C2
Vivian Ct, W9 .... **31** E2
Vivian Rd, E3 .... **45** E2
Vogans Mill, SE1 .... **120** B1
Voss St, E2 .... **43** D5
Vulcan Cl, E6 .... **105** D1
Vulcan Rd, SE4 ..... **176** A5
Vulcan Sq, E14 ..... **153** D1
Vulcan Ter, SE4 ..... **176** A5

Vulcan Way, N7 ...... **16** B1
Vyner St, E2 .... **43** F2

W

Wadding St, SE17 .... **146** C1
Waddington St, E15 ... **27** D1
Wadeson St, E2 ..... **43** F2
Wades Pl, E14 .... **97** E2
Wadham Gdns, NW3 .. **11** E5
Wadhurst Rd, SW8 ... **166** A3
Wager St, E3 .... **68** A3
Wagner St, SE15 .... **174** A1
Waite St, SE15 ..... **148** A4
Waithman St, EC4 ... **89** E1
Wakefield Ms, WC1 ... **37** F5
Wakefield St, WC1 ... **59** F1
Wakeham St, N1 ..... **18** C2
Wakeling St, E14 ..... **95** E1
Wakelin Rd, E15 ..... **49** E2
Wakeman Rd, NW10 .. **28** C4
Wakerley Cl, E6 ...... **104** A1
Wakley St, EC1 ...... **39** E4
Walberswick St, SW8 . **167** F2
Walbrook, EC4 ...... **90** C2
Walbrook Wf, EC4
   off Bell Wf La **90** B3
Walburgh St, E1 ..... **93** E1
Walcorde Av, SE17 ... **146** B1
Walcot Sq, SE11 ..... **117** D5
Walcott St, SW1 ..... **114** B5
Waldair Ct, E16 ..... **133** E1
Waldair Wf, E16 ..... **133** E1
Waldemar Av, SW6 .. **159** F4
Walden Ct, SW8
   off Wandsworth Rd . **167** D3
Walden St, E1 .... **65** E5
Waldron Ms, SW3 ... **139** D4
Waleran Flats, SE1 ... **119** E5
Wales Cl, SE15 ..... **173** E1
Waley St, E1 .... **67** D3
WALHAM GREEN, SW6. **161** E2
Walham Grn Ct, SW6 . **161** E2
Walham Gro, SW6 ... **160** C1
Walham Yd, SW6 .... **160** C1
Walkers Ct, E8 ...... **20** C1
   W1 .... **86** C2
Walkynscroft, SE15 .. **173** F5
★ Wallace Collection,
   W1 .... **56** C5
Wallace Rd, N1 ..... **18** C5
Waller Rd, SE14 .... **174** C4
Waller Way, SE10 .... **177** F1
Wallgrave Rd, SW5 .. **109** E5
Wallingford Av, W10 . **50** C4
Wallis All, SE1 ...... **118** B1
Wallis Rd, E9 .... **24** B2
Wallside, EC2 .... **62** B4
Wall St, N1 .... **19** D2
Wallwood St, E14 .... **68** B4
Walmer Pl, W1 ...... **56** A3
Walmer Rd, W10 .... **78** B1
   W11 .... **79** E2
Walmer St, W1 ...... **56** A3
Walm La, NW2 .... **6** B2

Walney Wk, N1 ...... **18** B1
Walnut Cl, SE8 ..... **152** B5
Walnut Tree Rd, SE10. **155** F3
Walnut Tree Wk, SE11. **116** C5
Sch Walnut Tree Wk
   Prim Sch, SE11 ..... **116** C5
Walpole Ms, NW8 .... **32** C1
Walpole St, SW3 .... **140** A2
Walsham Rd, SE14 ... **174** C5
Walters Cl, SE17 .... **146** B1
Walters Ho, SE17 ... **145** E5
Walter St, E2 .... **44** C5
Walter Ter, E1 ...... **67** D5
Walterton Rd, W9 .... **52** B2
Walton Cl, SW8 ..... **167** F1
Walton Pl, SW3 ..... **112** A3
Walton St, SW3 ..... **111** F5
WALWORTH, SE17 ... **146** A2
Sch Walworth Acad,
   Upr, SE1 .... **147** F3
★ Walworth Garden Fm -
   Horticultural Training
   Cen, SE17 .... **145** F3
Walworth Pl, SE17 ... **146** B3
Walworth Rd, SE1 ... **118** A5
   SE17 .... **118** A5
Wandon Rd, SW6 .... **161** F2
Wandsworth Br Rd,
   SW6 .... **161** E3
Wandsworth Rd, SW8. **143** E4
Wanlip Rd, E13 ...... **73** E1
Wansbeck Rd, E3 .... **24** B3
   E9 .... **24** B3
Wansdown Pl, SW6 .. **161** E1
Wansey St, SE17 .... **146** B1
WAPPING, E1 .... **93** D4
⊖ Wapping **94** A5
Wapping Dock St, E1 . **93** F5
Wapping High St, E1 . **92** C5
Wapping La, E1 ...... **93** F3
Wapping Wall, E1 .... **94** A4
Warburton Cl, N1 .... **19** E1
Warburton Ho, E8
   off Warburton Rd **21** E5
Warburton Rd, E8 .... **21** E5
Warburton St, E8 .... **21** E5
Wardalls Gro, SE14 .. **174** B1
Warden Rd, NW5 .... **13** D1
Wardens Gro, SE1 ... **90** A5
Wardo Av, SW6 ..... **159** E4
Wardour Ms, W1 ..... **86** B1
Wardour St, W1 ..... **86** C2
Ward Pt, SE11 ...... **144** C1
Ward Rd, E15 .... **26** C5
Wardrobe Pl, EC4
   off St. Andrew's Hill .. **89** F1
Wardrobe Ter, EC4 ... **89** F1
Wards Wf App, E16 ... **130** C1
Wareham Ho, SW8 ... **168** A1
Warfield Rd, NW10 ... **28** C5
Warfield Yd, NW10 ... **28** C5
Warham St, SE5 ..... **169** F1
Warley St, E2 .... **44** C4

Warlock Rd, W9 . . . . **52** C1
Warmington St, E13 . . . . **73** D1
Warndon St, SE16 . . . . **150** B1
Warneford St, E9 . . . . . . **21** F5
Warner Ho, SE13 . . . . . . **177** F5
Warner Pl, E2 . . . . **43** D3
Warner Rd, SE5 . . . . . . **170** A4
Warner St, EC1 . . . . **60** C2
Warner Ter, E14 . . . . . . **69** D4
Warner Yd, EC1 . . . . **60** C2
Warren Ho, E3 . . . . **47** E4
Warren La, SE18 . . . . . . **133** E4
Warren La Gate, SE18 . **133** E4
Warren Ms, W1 . . . . **58** A2
⊖ Warren Street **58** B1
Warren St, W1 . . . . **57** C1
Warriner Gdns, SW11 . **164** B4
Warrington Cres, W9 . . **54** A2
Warrington Gdns, W9 . . **54** A2
Warspite Rd, SE18 . . . **131** E3
Warton Rd, E15 . . . . **26** A4
Warwall, E6 . . . . **77** E5
⊖ Warwick Avenue **54** A2
Warwick Av, W2 . . . . . . **54** A2
 W9 . . . . **54** A2
Warwick Bldg, SW8 . . **165** E1
Warwick Chambers, W8
 off Pater St **108** C3
Warwick Ct, WC1 . . . . . **60** B4
Warwick Cres, W2 . . . . . **54** A3
Warwick Est, W2 . . . . . . **53** E4
Warwick Gdns, W14 . . **108** B4
Warwick Ho St, SW1 . . . **87** D4
Warwick La, EC4 . . . . . . **89** F1
Warwick Pas, EC4 . . . . . **61** F5
Warwick Pl, W9 . . . . **54** A3
Warwick Pl N, SW1 . . . **142** A1
Warwick Rd, SW5 . . . . **108** A5
 W14 . . . . **108** A5
Warwick Row, SW1 . . **113** F3
Warwickshire Path,
 SE8 . . . . **176** B1
Warwick Sq, EC4 . . . . . . **61** F5
 SW1 . . . . **142** A2
Warwick Sq Ms, SW1 . **142** A1
Warwick St, W1 . . . . **86** B2
Warwick Way, SW1 . . **142** A1
Warwick Yd, EC1 . . . . . . **62** B2
Washington Bldg, SE13
 off Deals Gateway . . **177** E3
Washington Cl, E3 . . . . . **47** F4
Watercress Pl, N1 . . . . . **19** F4
Waterford Rd, SW6 . . . **161** F3
Waterfront Studios
 Business Cen, E16 . **100** C4
Water Gdns, The, W2 . . **55** F5
Watergate, EC4 . . . . **89** E2
Watergate St, SE8 . . . **152** C5
Watergate Wk, WC2 . . . **87** F4
Waterhouse Cl, E16 . . . **74** C3
 W6 . . . . **135** D2
Waterhouse Sq, EC1 . . . **60** C4
Wateridge Cl, E14 . . . . **124** C4

Water La, E15 . . . . **27** F1
 EC3 . . . . **91** E3
 NW1 . . . . **13** F4
 SE14 . . . . **174** B1
⇌ Waterloo **116** C1
⊖ Waterloo **116** C1
Waterloo Br, SE1 . . . . . . **88** A3
 WC2 . . . . **88** A3
⇌ Waterloo East **88** C5
Waterloo Est, E2 . . . . . . **44** A2
Waterloo Gdns, E2 . . . . **44** A2
 N1 . . . . **17** E4
Riv **Waterloo Millennium**
 Pier **115** F1
Waterloo Pas, NW6 . . . . **8** B4
Waterloo Pl, SW1 . . . . . **86** C4
Waterloo Rd, SE1 . . . . **116** C1
Waterloo Ter, N1 . . . . . **17** E4
Waterman's Wk, EC4
 off Allhallows La . . . **90** C3
Watermans Wk, SE16 . **123** E3
Waterman Way, E1 . . . **93** E4
Waterside Cl, E3 . . . . . . **24** A5
 SE16 . . . . **121** D2
Waterside Pl, NW1 . . . . **13** D5
Waterside Pt, SW11 . . **163** F1
Waterside Twr, SW6 . . **162** B5
Waterson St, E2 . . . . . . **41** F4
Water St, WC2 . . . . **88** B2
Water Twr Pl, N1 . . . . . . **39** D1
Waterview Ho, E14 . . . . **67** F4
Watford Cl, SW11 . . . . **163** F3
Watford Rd, E16 . . . . . . **73** D4
Watkinson Rd, N7 . . . . . **16** A1
Watling Ct, EC4 . . . . **90** B1
Watling Gdns, NW2 . . . . **7** F2
Watling St, EC4 . . . . **90** A1
 SE15 . . . . **147** F5
Watney Mkt, E1 . . . . . . **93** F1
Watney St, E1 . . . . **93** F1
Watsons Ms, W1 . . . . . . **55** F4
Watson's St, SE8 . . . . . **176** C2
Watts Gro, E3 . . . . **69** E3
Watts St, E1 . . . . **93** F4
 SE15 . . . . **172** B3
Watts Way, SW7 . . . . . **111** D3
Wat Tyler Rd, SE3 . . . . **178** B5
 SE10 . . . . **178** B5
Wavel Ms, NW6 . . . . **9** E4
Waveney Cl, E1 . . . . **93** D4
Waverley Gdns, E6 . . . . **75** F4
Waverley Pl, NW8 . . . . . **32** C2
Waverley Wk, W2 . . . . . **53** D3
Waverton Ho, E3 . . . . . . **24** B5
Waverton St, W1 . . . . . . **85** D1
Wayland Ho, SW9 . . . . **168** C5
Waylett Ho, SE11 . . . . **144** C3
Wayman Ct, E8 . . . . **21** E2
Waynflete Sq, W10 . . . . **78** C2
Weald Cl, SE16 . . . . . . **149** E2
Wear Pl, E2 . . . . **43** E5
Weatherley Cl, E3 . . . . . **68** B3
Weaver Cl, E6 . . . . **105** E2
Weavers Ter, SW6 . . . . **137** D5
Weaver St, E1 . . . . **64** C2
Weavers Way, NW1 . . . **14** C5
Webb Cl, W10 . . . . **50** A2

Webber Row, SE1 . . . . **117** D3
Webber St, SE1 . . . . . . **117** D1
Webb Gdns, E13 . . . . . . **73** D1
Webb Rd, SE3 . . . . **156** B4
Webb St, SE1 . . . . **119** E4
Webheath Est, NW6 . . . . **8** B3
Webster Rd, SE16 . . . . **121** D4
Wedgwood Ho, SE11 . **116** C4
Wedgwood Ms, W1 . . . **87** D1
Wedlake St, W10 . . . . . . **51** F1
Weighhouse St, W1 . . . **85** D1
Weir's Pas, NW1 . . . . . . **37** D4
Welbeck St, W1 . . . . **57** E5
Welbeck Way, W1 . . . . . **57** E5
Welby St, SE5 . . . . **169** F4
Welfare Rd, E15 . . . . . . **27** F3
Welland Ms, E1 . . . . **93** D4
Welland St, SE10 . . . . **154** A4
Wellclose Sq, E1 . . . . . . **93** D2
Wellclose St, E1 . . . . . . **93** D3
Coll **Wellcome Trust**,
 NW1 . . . . **58** C1
Well Ct, EC4 . . . . **90** B1
Weller St, SE1 . . . . **118** A1
Wellesley Ct, W9 . . . . . . **32** A4
Wellesley Pl, NW1 . . . . . **36** C5
Wellesley St, E1 . . . . . . **66** C1
Wellesley Ter, N1 . . . . . **40** B4
★ **Wellington Arch**,
 W1 . . . . **113** D1
Wellington Bldgs,
 SW1 . . . . **141** D3
Wellington Cl, SE14 . . **174** C4
 W11 . . . . **80** C1
Wellington Ct, NW8 . . . **32** C3
Wellington Gro, SE10 . **178** C2
H **Wellington Hosp**,
 NW8 . . . . **33** D3
Wellington Pl, NW8 . . . **33** D4
Sch **Wellington Prim Sch**,
 E3 . . . . **46** C5
Wellington Rd, NW8 . . . **32** C2
 NW10 . . . . **29** D5
Wellington Row, E2 . . . **42** B4
Wellington Sq, N1 . . . . . **16** A5
 SW3 . . . . **140** A2
Wellington St, WC2 . . . **87** F2
Wellington Ter, E1 . . . . **93** E4
 W2 off Notting
 Hill Gate **81** E3
Wellington Way, E3 . . . **46** C5
Wells Ms, W1 . . . . **58** B4
Wells Ri, NW8 . . . . **34** A1
Wells Rd, W12 . . . . **106** A2
Wells Sq, WC1 . . . . **38** A5
Wells St, W1 . . . . **58** A4
Well St, E9 . . . . **21** F4
 E15 . . . . **27** E1
Wells Way, SE5 . . . . . . **147** D4
 SW7 . . . . **110** C3
Welsford St, SE1 . . . . . **148** C2
Welshpool Ho, E8 . . . . . **21** D5
Welshpool St, E8 . . . . . . **21** D5
Welwyn St, E2 . . . . **44** D4
Wendle Ct, SW8 . . . . . **143** E5
Wendle Sq, SW11 . . . . **163** F3
Wendon St, E3 . . . . **24** B5

Wendover, SE17 . . . . . **147** E2
Wenlock Ct, N1 . . . . **41** D3
Wenlock Rd, N1 . . . . . . **40** A2
Wenlock St, N1 . . . . **40** B3
Wennington Rd, E3 . . . **45** D3
Wentworth Cres, SE15. **173** D2
Wentworth Ms, E3 . . . **67** F1
Wentworth St, E1 . . . . . **64** A5
Werrington St, NW1 . . . **36** B3
Wesley Av, E16 . . . . **101** E4
Wesley Cl, SE17 . . . . . **145** F1
★ Wesley's Ho, EC1 . . **62** C2
Wesley Sq, W11 . . . . . . **79** E1
Wesley St, W1 . . . . **57** D4
Wessex Ho, SE1 . . . . . **148** B2
Wessex St, E2 . . . . **44** B5
Wessonmead, SE5
    off Camberwell Rd . . **170** B2
West 12 Shop Cen,
    W12 . . . . **106** C1
West Arbour St, E1 . . . **66** B5
Westbourne Br, W2 . . . **54** A4
Westbourne Cres, W2. . **82** C2
Westbourne Cres Ms,
    W2 . . . . **82** C2
Westbourne Gdns, W2. **53** E5
WESTBOURNE GREEN,
    W2 . . . . **52** C4
Westbourne Gro, W2 . . **81** D1
    W11 . . . . **80** B2
Westbourne Gro Ms,
    W11 . . . . **80** C1
Westbourne Gro Ter,
    W2 . . . . **53** E5
⬤ Westbourne Park . . **52** B3
Westbourne Pk Ms, W2. **53** E5
Westbourne Pk Pas,
    W2 . . . . **53** D4
Westbourne Pk Rd, W2. **53** D4
    W11 . . . . **79** F1
Westbourne Pk Vil, W2. **53** D4
Westbourne Rd, N7 . . . **16** C2
Westbourne St, W2. . . . **82** C2
Westbourne Ter, W2. . . **54** B5
Westbourne Ter Ms,
    W2 . . . . **54** A5
Westbourne Ter Rd,
    W2 . . . . **54** A4
Sch Westbridge Prim Sch,
    SW11 . . . . **163** E3
Westbridge Rd, SW11. **163** D4
WEST BROMPTON,
    SW10 . . . . **137** E4
Ↄ West Brompton . . . **137** D3
⬤ West Brompton . . . **137** D3
Westbrook Rd, SE3 . . . **181** E4
West Carriage Dr, W2. . **83** D5
West Cen St, WC1 . . . . **59** C5
Westcliffe Apts, W2 . . . **55** D4
Westcombe Ct, SE3 . **180** A1
Westcombe Hill, SE3 . **157** D4
    SE10 . . . . **156** C3
⇌ Westcombe Park . . **157** D3
Westcombe Pk Rd,
    SE3 . . . . **155** F5
Westcott Ho, E14 . . . . **97** D2
Westcott Rd, SE17 . . . **145** E4

West Cromwell Rd,
    SW5 . . . . **136** C1
    W14 . . . . **136** A2
West Cross Route, W10. **78** C2
    W11 . . . . **78** C2
West Eaton Pl, SW1 . . **112** C5
West Eaton Pl Ms,
    SW1 . . . . **112** C5
West End La, NW6 . . . . **31** D1
Westerdale Rd, SE10 . **156** C3
Western Beach Apts,
    E16 . . . . **100** C4
Ⓗ Western Eye Hosp,
    NW1 . . . . **56** A3
Western Gateway,
    E16 . . . . **100** C3
Western Ms, W9 . . . . . **52** B2
Western Pl, SE16 . . . . **122** B1
DLR Westferry **96** C2
Westferry Circ, E14. . . **96** C4
Westferry Rd, E14. . . . **96** B4
Westfield Cl, SW10 . . . **162** A2
Westfield London, W12. **78** C4
Westfield St, SE18 . . . **130** C4
Westfield Way, E1 . . . . **45** E5
West Gdn Pl, W2 . . . . . . **83** F1
West Gdns, E1 . . . . **93** F3
Westgate St, E8 . . . . . . **21** E5
Westgate Ter, SW10. . **137** F3
West Gro, SE10 . . . . . **178** B3
Westgrove La, SE10 . . **178** B3
West Halkin St, SW1. . **112** C3
⇌ West Ham. **49** F4
⬤ West Ham. **49** F4
West Ham La, E15 . . . . **27** E4
Ↄ West Hampstead **9** D2
⬤ West Hampstead **9** D2
West Hampstead Ms,
    NW6. . . . . **9** E2
⇌ West Hampstead
    (Thameslink) **9** D1
West Harding St, EC4 . . **61** D5
West India Av, E14. . . . **96** C4
West India Dock Rd,
    E14 . . . . **96** B1
DLR West India Quay . . . **97** E3
⬤ West Kensington . . **136** A2
West Kensington Ct,
    W14 . . . . **136** A2
WEST KILBURN, W9 . . . **30** A4
Westland Ho, E16
    off Rymill St. **104** C5
Westland Pl, N1 . . . . . . **40** C4
West La, SE16 . . . . **121** E2
Coll West London Coll,
    W1 . . . . **85** D1
West Mall, W8 . . . . **81** D4
West Mersea Cl, E16 . . **101** E5
West Ms, SW1 . . . . **141** F1
WESTMINSTER, SW1. . **114** A3
⬤ Westminster **115** F2
★ Westminster Abbey,
    SW1 . . . . **115** E3
Sch Westminster Abbey
    Choir Sch, SW1 . . . . . **115** D3
★ Westminster Abbey
    Mus, SW1 . . . . **115** E3

Sch Westminster Acad,
    W2 . . . . **53** D3
Coll Westminster Adult Ed
    Service, Amberley Rd Cen,
    W9 . . . . **53** E2
    Ebury Br Cen, SW1 . . **141** E2
    Frith St Cen, W1 . . . . . **87** D1
Westminster Br, SE1 . **115** F2
    SW1. . . . . **115** F2
Westminster Br Rd,
    SE1 . . . . **116** B2
Westminster Business Sq,
    SE11 *off Durham St*. **144** A3
★ Westminster Cath,
    SW1 . . . . **114** A4
Sch Westminster Cath Choir
    Sch, SW1 . . . . **114** B4
Sch Westminster Cath RC
    Prim Sch, SW1 . . . . **143** D2
★ Westminster City Hall,
    SW1 . . . . **114** B3
Sch Westminster City Sch,
    SW1 . . . . **114** B3
Westminster Gdns,
    SW1 . . . . **115** E5
Coll Westminster Kingsway
    Coll, Castle La Cen,
    SW1 . . . . **114** B3
    Kentish Town Cen,
    NW5 . . . . **13** E1
    Kings Cross Cen, WC1 . **38** A5
    Peter St Cen, W1 . . . . . **86** C2
    Regent's Pk Cen, NW1. **58** A1
    Vincent Sq Cen, SW1. **114** C5
Riv Westminster Millennium
    Pier **115** F1
Westminster Palace Gdns, SW1
    off Artillery Row. . . . **114** C4
Sch Westminster Sch,
    SW1 . . . . **115** E3
Sch Westminster Under Sch,
    SW1 . . . . **142** C1
Westmoor St, SE7 . . . . **130** B4
Westmoreland Pl,
    SW1 . . . . **141** F3
Westmoreland Rd,
    SE17 . . . . **146** B4
Westmoreland St, W1 . **57** D4
Westmoreland Ter,
    SW1 . . . . **141** F3
Westmoreland Wk,
    SE17 . . . . **147** D4
West One Shop Cen,
    W1 . . . . **85** D1
Weston Ri, WC1 . . . . . . **38** B3
Weston St, SE1 . . . . . . **119** D2
Weston Wk, E8 . . . . . . **21** F4
West Parkside, SE10 . **128** B4
West Pier, E1 . . . . **93** E5
West Pt, SE1 . . . . **148** C2
Westport Rd, E13 . . . . . **73** E2
Westport St, E1. . . . . . . **67** D5
West Poultry Av, EC1 . . **61** E4

West Rd, SW3 . . . .**140** B3
West Row, W10. . . . . .**51** E1
🚇West Silvertown . . . **101** D5
West Smithfield, EC1 . .**61** E4
West Sq, SE11. . . . . . .**117** E4
West St, E2 . . . .**43** F3
WC2. . . . .**87** D1
West Tenter St, E1 . . . .**92** B1
Westview Cl, W10. . . . .**50** B5
West Warwick Pl, SW1.**142** A1
Westway, W2 . . . .**52** C3
W9. . . . .**52** C3
W10 . . . .**51** F5
Westwick Gdns, W14.**106** C2
Westwood Rd, E16. . .**101** E5
Wetherby Gdns, SW5 .**138** A1
Wetherby Ms, SW5. . .**137** E2
Wetherby Pl, SW7. . . .**138** A1
🏫Wetherby Sch, W2 . .**81** D3
Wetherell Rd, E9. . . . .**23** D5
Weybridge Ct, SE16 . .**149** D3
Weybridge Pt, SW11 .**164** B5
Weyhill Rd, E1. . . . . . .**65** D5
Weymouth Cl, E6 . . . .**105** E1
Weymouth Ho, SW8 . .**168** A2
Weymouth Ms, W1. . . .**57** E3
Weymouth St, W1 . . . .**57** D4
Weymouth Ter, E2 . . . .**42** D2
Whalebone Ct, EC2. . . .**63** D5
Whalebone La, E15. . . .**27** E4
Whales Yd, E15. . . . . . .**27** E4
Wharfdale Rd, N1 . . . . .**37** F2
Wharfedale St, SW10 .**137** E3
Wharf La, E14 . . . .**96** A1
Wharf Pl, E2 . . . .**43** D1
Wharf Rd, N1. . . . .**40** A2
N1 (King's Cross). **37** E2
Wharfside Rd, E16 . . . .**71** E4
Wharf St, E16 . . . .**71** E4
Wharton Cotts, WC1
off Wharton St **38** B5
Wharton St, WC1 . . . . .**38** B5
Wheatfields, E6. . . . . . .**77** E5
Wheatley St, W1. . . . . .**57** D4
Wheat Sheaf Cl, E14. .**125** E5
Wheatsheaf La, SW6. .**158** B1
SW8. . . . .**167** F1
Wheatsheaf Ter, SW6.**160** B2
Wheatstone Rd, W10. .**51** F3
Wheeler Gdns, N1. . . . .**15** F5
Wheelwright St, N7 . . .**16** A3
Wheler St, E1. . . . .**64** A2
Whetstone Pk, WC2 . . .**60** A5
Whichcote St, SE1. . . . .**88** C5
Whidborne St, WC1. . . .**37** F5
Whiskin St, EC1. . . . . . .**39** E5
Whistler Ms, SE15. . . .**172** B2
Whistlers Av, SW11 . .**163** D2
Whistler Twr, SW10 . .**162** B1
Whistler Wk, SW10
off Blantyre St **162** B1
Whiston Rd, E2. . . . . . .**42** A2
Whitacre Ms, SE11 . . .**145** D3

Whitby Rd, SE18. . . . .**132** A5
Whitby St, E1 . . . .**64** A1
Whitcher Cl, SE14. . . .**151** E5
Whitcher Pl, NW1 . . . . .**14** A2
Whitchurch Rd, W11 . . .**79** D2
Whitcomb St, WC2
off Whitcomb St. **87** D3
Whitcomb St, WC2 . . . .**87** D3
Whiteadder Way, E14.**125** F5
Whitear Wk, E15. . . . . .**27** E1
Whitebeam Cl, SW9 . .**168** B2
Whitebeam Ho, NW3
off Maitland Pk Rd. . .**12** B1
WHITECHAPEL, E1 . . . .**92** C1
⊖Whitechapel. **65** E3
★ Whitechapel Art Gall,
E1 . . . .**64** B5
Whitechapel High St,
E1 . . . .**64** B5
Whitechapel Rd, E1 . . .**64** C5
White Ch La, E1. . . . . . .**64** C5
White Ch Pas, E1 . . . . .**64** C5
⊖White City **78** B3
White City Cl, W12. . . .**78** B4
White City Rd, W12. . . .**78** A2
White Conduit St, N1. .**39** D2
Whitecross Pl, EC2. . . .**63** D3
Whitecross St, EC1. . . .**62** B1
★ White Cube, N1
off Hoxton Sq. **41** E5
★ White Cube, SW1 . .**86** B4
Whitefriars St, EC4. . . .**89** D1
Whitehall, SW1 . . . .**87** E4
Whitehall Ct, SW1. . . . .**87** E5
Whitehall Gdns, SW1 . .**87** E5
Whitehall Pl, SW1. . . . .**87** E5
White Hart Ct, EC2 . . . .**63** E4
White Hart St, EC4 . . . .**61** F5
SE11 . . . .**145** D2
White Hart Yd, SE1. . . .**90** C5
Whitehaven St, NW8 . .**55** F2
Whitehead's Gro, SW3.**139** F2
White Horse All, EC1 . .**61** E3
White Horse La, E1. . . .**66** C2
White Horse Ms, SE1 .**117** D3
White Horse Rd, E1 . . .**95** E1
White Horse St, W1 . . .**85** E5
White Horse Yd, EC2 . .**62** C5
Whitehouse Apts, SE1
off Belvedere Rd. **88** B5
White Kennett St, E1 . .**63** F5
Whiteleys Shop Cen,
W2. . . . .**81** E1
White Lion Ct, EC3 . . . .**91** E1
White Lion Hill, EC4 . . .**89** F2
White Lion St, N1. . . . . .**38** C3
White Lyon Ct, EC2. . . .**62** A3
White Post La, E9. . . . . .**24** C2
White Post St, SE15 . .**174** A1
White Rd, E15. . . . .**27** F3
Whites Grds, SE1 . . . .**119** F2
Whites Grds Est, SE1
off Whites Grds **119** F1
White's Row, E1 . . . . . .**64** A4
Whitethorn St, E3. . . . .**69** D2
Whitfield Pl, W1 . . . . . .**58** A2
Whitfield Rd, SE3 . . . .**179** D4

Whitfield St, W1 . . . . . .**58** C4
Whitgift Ho, SW11
off Randall Cl. **163** E3
Whitgift St, SE11 . . . .**116** A5
Whitings Way, E6. . . . .**76** C3
Whitley Ho, SW1. . . . .**142** B3
Whitman Rd, E3 . . . . . .**67** F1
Whitmore Est, N1. . . . .**41** F1
Whitmore Gdns, NW10.**28** A2
🏫Whitmore Prim Sch,
N1. . . . .**41** D1
Whitmore Rd, N1 . . . . .**41** E1
Whitstable Ho, W10. . . .**79** D1
Whittaker St, SW1 . . .**140** C1
Whittaker Way, SE1 . .**149** D1
Whittingstall Rd, SW6.**160** B4
Whittington Av, EC3. . .**91** E1
Whittlesey St, SE1 . . . .**88** C5
Whitton Wk, E3. . . . . . .**46** C4
Whitworth Ho, SE1. . .**118** B4
Whitworth St, SE10 . .**155** F2
Wicker St, E1. . . . .**93** E1
Wickford St, E1 . . . . . .**66** A1
Wickham Cl, E1. . . . . . .**66** B4
Wickham St, SE11. . . .**144** A2
Wick La, E3 . . . .**46** C2
Wicklow St, WC1 . . . . .**38** A4
Wick Rd, E9 . . . .**22** C2
Wicksteed Ho, SE1 . . .**118** B4
Wickway Ct, SE15. . . .**148** A5
Widdin St, E15 . . . .**27** D4
Widegate St, E1 . . . . . .**63** F4
Widgeon Cl, E16. . . . . .**73** E5
Widley Rd, W9 . . . .**31** D5
Wigmore Pl, W1 . . . . . .**57** E5
Wigmore St, W1 . . . . . .**84** C1
Wigston Rd, E13. . . . . .**73** E1
Wigton Pl, SE11 . . . . .**145** D3
🏫Wilberforce Prim Sch,
W10. . . . .**29** F4
Wilbraham Pl, SW1. . .**112** B5
Wilby Ms, W11 . . . .**80** B5
Wilcox Cl, SW8 . . . . . .**167** F1
Wilcox Pl, SW1 . . . . . .**114** B4
Wilcox Rd, SW8. . . . . .**167** E1
Wild Ct, WC2 . . . .**60** A5
Wilde Cl, E8. . . . .**20** C5
Wild Goose Dr, SE14. .**174** B4
Wild's Rents, SE1 . . . .**119** E3
Wild St, WC2 . . . .**87** F1
Wilfred St, SW1 . . . . . .**114** A3
Wilkes St, E1. . . . .**64** B3
Wilkins Ho, SW1
off Churchill Gdns . .**142** A4
Wilkinson Rd, E16 . . . .**74** B5
Wilkinson St, SW8. . . .**168** A2
Wilkin St, NW5 . . . .**13** E1
Wilkin St Ms, NW5 . . . .**13** E1
Wilks Pl, N1. . . . .**41** F3
Willan Wall, E16 . . . . .**100** A2
⊖Willesden Green. **6** B1
Willesden La, NW2 . . . . .**6** B2
NW6 . . . .**7** B2
Willes Rd, NW5 . . . .**13** F1
William Cl, SW6 . . . . .**159** F1
🏫William Davis Prim Sch,
E2 . . . .**64** C1

William Dunbar Ho, NW6 . . . . 30 A3
William Ellis Way, SE16 . . . . 121 D4
William IV St, WC2 . . . . 87 E3
William Guy Gdns, E3 . 47 F5
William Henry Wk, SW8 . . . . 142 C5
William Margrie Cl, SE15 . . . . 173 D5
William Ms, SW1 . . . . . 112 B2
Sch William Morris Acad, W6 . . . . 134 C3
William Pl, E3 . . . . 46 A2
William Rd, NW1 . . . . . . 36 A5
William Rushbrooke Ho, SE16 off Eveline Lowe Est. 120 C5
William Saville Ho, NW6 . . . . 30 B3
Williams Bldgs, E2 . . . . 66 A1
Williamson Cl, SE10 . . 156 A2
William Sq, SE16 . . . . . . 95 F3
William St, SW1 . . . . . 112 B2
Sch William Tyndale Prim Sch, N1 . . . . 17 F3
Willis St, E14 . . . . 97 F1
Willoughby Ho, EC2 off The Barbican 62 C4
Willoughby Pas, E14 . . 96 C4
Willoughby St, WC1 . . . 59 E4
Willoughby Way, SE7. 129 E5
Willow Br Rd, N1 . . . . . . 18 A2
Willowbrook Est, SE15 off Shurland Gdns . . 172 B1
Willowbrook Rd, SE15. 148 B5
Willow Ct, EC2 . . . . 63 E1
Willow Ho, NW3 off Maitland Pk Vil . . . 12 B1
Willow La, SE18 . . . . . 132 B5
Willow Pl, SW1 . . . . . . 114 B5
Willow St, EC2 . . . . 63 E1
Willow Tree Cl, E3 . . . . . 45 F1
Willow Wk, SE1 . . . . . . 119 F5
Willow Way, W11 . . . . . 79 D3
Wilman Gro, E8 . . . . 21 D3
Wilmcote Ho, W2 . . . . . 53 D3
Wilmer Gdns, N1 . . . . . 41 E1
Wilmer Ho, E3 . . . . 45 F2
Wilmer Lea Cl, E15 . . . . 26 C4
Wilmington Sq, WC1 . . 38 C5
Wilmington St, WC1 . . 38 C5
Wilmot Cl, SE15 . . . . . 172 C2
Wilmot Pl, NW1 . . . . 14 A3
Wilmot St, E2 . . . . 65 E1
Wilsham St, W11 . . . . . . 79 D4
Wilshaw St, SE14 . . . . 176 C3
Wilson Gro, SE16 . . . . 121 E2
Wilson Rd, SE5 . . . . . . 171 E4
Wilsons Pl, E14 . . . . 96 A1
Wilsons Rd, W6 . . . . . . 135 D2
Wilson St, EC2 . . . . 63 D3
Wilton Cres, SW1 . . . . 112 C2
Wilton Est, E8 . . . . 21 D2
Wilton Ms, SW1 . . . . . . 113 D3
Wilton Pl, SW1 . . . . . . 112 C2
Wilton Rd, SW1 . . . . . . 113 F4
Wilton Row, SW1 . . . . 112 C2

Wilton Sq, N1 . . . . 18 C5
Wilton St, SW1 . . . . . . 113 E3
Wilton Ter, SW1 . . . . . 112 C3
Wilton Vil, N1 . . . . 40 C1
Wilton Way, E8 . . . . 20 C2
Wiltshire Cl, SW3 . . . . 112 A5
Wiltshire Row, N1 . . . . 40 C1
Wimbolt St, E2 . . . . 42 C4
Wimborne Ho, SW8 . . 168 B2
Wimbourne Ct, N1 . . . . 40 C2
Wimbourne St, N1 . . . . 40 C2
Wimpole Ms, W1 . . . . . . 57 E3
Wimpole St, W1 . . . . . . 57 E5
Winchendon Rd, SW6. 160 A2
Winchester Av, NW6 . . . . 7 F5
Winchester Cl, E6 . . . . 104 A1
SE17 . . . . 145 F1
Winchester Ms, NW3 . . 11 D3
Winchester Rd, NW3 . . 11 D3
Winchester Sq, SE1 . . . 90 C4
Winchester St, SW1 . . 141 F2
Winchester Wk, SE1 . . . 90 C4
Wincott St, SE11 . . . . . 117 D5
Windermere Av, NW6 . . 29 F1
Windermere Pt, SE15 . 174 A1
Winders Rd, SW11 . . . 163 E5
Windlass Pl, SE8 . . . . . 151 F1
Windmill Cl, SE1 . . . . . 121 D5
SE13 . . . . 178 B5
Windmill Ct, NW2 . . . . . . 7 F1
Windmill Ho, E14 . . . . 124 C5
Windmill La, E15 . . . . . . 27 D1
Windmill Row, SE11 . . 144 C3
Windmill St, W1 . . . . . . 58 C4
Windmill Wk, SE1 . . . . . 89 D5
Windrose Cl, SE16 . . . . 122 C1
Windsock Cl, SE16 . . . 124 A5
Windsor Gdns, W9 . . . . 52 C3
Windsor Ho, N1 . . . . . . 40 A2
Windsor Pl, SW1 . . . . . 114 B4
Windsor St, N1 . . . . 17 F5
Windsor Ter, N1 . . . . . . 40 B4
Windsor Way, W14 . . . 107 D5
Windspoint Dr, SE15 . 149 E5
Wine Cl, E1 . . . . 94 A3
Wine Office Ct, EC4 . . . 61 D5
Winford Ho, E3 . . . . 24 B4
Winforton St, SE10 . . 178 A3
Wingfield Ct, E14 off Newport Av. 98 C3
Wingfield Ho, NW6 off Tollgate Gdns . . . 31 E2
Wingrave Rd, W6 . . . . 134 B5
Winifred St, E16 . . . . . 104 B5
Winkley St, E2 . . . . 43 E3
Winnett St, W1 . . . . 86 C2
Winsland Ms, W2 . . . . . 54 C5
Winsland St, W2 . . . . . . 54 C5
Winsley St, W1 . . . . 58 A5
Winslow, SE17 . . . . . . 147 E3
Winslow Rd, W6 . . . . . 134 B4
Sch Winsor Prim Sch, E6 . . . . 104 C1
Winsor Ter, E6 . . . . 76 C4
Winter Gdn Ho, WC2 off Macklin St. 59 F5
Wintergreen Cl, E6 . . . . 75 E4

Winterton Ho, E1 . . . . . 93 F1
Winterton Pl, SW10 . . 138 B4
Winthrop St, E1 . . . . . . 65 E3
Sch Winton Prim Sch, N1 . . . . 38 A3
Wise Rd, E15 . . . . 48 B1
Witan St, E2 . . . . 43 F5
Witcombe Pt, SE15 . . . 173 E4
Woburn Ct, SE16 off Masters Dr 149 F3
Woburn Pl, WC1 . . . . . . 59 D1
Woburn Sq, WC1 . . . . . . 59 D2
Woburn Wk, WC1 . . . . . 37 D5
Wodeham Gdns, E1 . . . 65 D3
Wodehouse Av, SE5 . . 172 A3
Wolfe Cres, SE16 . . . . . 122 C2
Wollaston Cl, SE1 . . . . 118 A5
Wolseley St, SE1 . . . . . 120 B2
Wolsey Ms, NW5 . . . . . . 14 A1
Wolsey St, E1 . . . . 66 A4
Wolverley St, E2 . . . . . . 43 E5
Wolverton, SE17 . . . . . 147 D2
Wolverton Gdns, W6 . 106 C5
Wontner Cl, N1 . . . . 18 A4
Woodall Cl, E14 . . . . . . 97 F2
Woodbine Ter, E9 . . . . . 22 B1
Woodbridge St, EC1 . . . 61 E1
Woodchester Sq, W2 . . 53 E3
Woodchurch Rd, NW6 . . 9 D4
Wood Cl, E2 . . . . 64 C1
Woodcocks, E16 . . . . . . 74 B4
Woodcroft Ms, SE8 . . . 151 E1
Woodfall St, SW3 . . . . 140 A3
Woodfield Gdns, W9 . . . 52 B3
Woodfield Pl, W9 . . . . . . 52 B3
Woodfield Rd, W9 . . . . . 52 B3
Woodford Ct, W12 . . . 106 C1
Woodger Rd, W12 . . . . 106 C1
Woodget Cl, E6 . . . . 75 E5
Woodhall, NW1 . . . . 36 A5
Woodhatch Cl, E6 . . . . . 75 E4
Woodhill, SE18 . . . . . . 131 F5
Woodland Cres, SE10. 155 E4
SE16 . . . . 122 C2
Woodland Gro, SE10 . 155 E3
Woodland Hts, SE3 . . . 155 F4
Woodlands Pk Rd, SE10 . . . . 155 E4
Woodland St, E8 . . . . . . 20 B1
Woodland Wk, SE10 . . 155 F3
🚇 Wood Lane 78 B3
Wood La, W12 . . . . 78 B2
Woodlawn Rd, SW6 . . 158 C1
Woodman St, E16 . . . . 105 D5
Woodpecker Rd, SE14. 151 E5
Woodrush Cl, SE14 . . . 175 D1
Wood's Bldgs, E1 . . . . . 65 E3
Woodseer St, E1 . . . . . . 64 B3
Woodsford, SE17 . . . . 146 C2
Woodsford Sq, W14 . . 107 F2
Woodside Rd, E13 . . . . 74 A1
Woods Ms, W1 . . . . 84 B2
Woods Pl, SE1 . . . . 119 F4

Woods Rd, SE15 . . . . . **173** E4
Woodstock Gro, W12 . **107** D1
Woodstock Ms, W1 . . . . **57** D4
Woodstock St, W1 . . . . **85** E1
Woodstock Ter, E14 . . . **97** F2
Wood St, EC2. . . . . **90** B1
Woodville, SE3 . . . . . . **181** F3
Woodville Rd, NW6. . . . **30** B2
Wood Wf, SE10 . . . . . . **153** F4
Wood Wf Apts, SE10
    off Horseferry Pl . . . **154** A4
Wooler St, SE17 . . . . . **146** C3
Woolf Ms, WC1 . . . . . . **59** D1
Sch Woolmore Prim Sch,
    E14 . . . . **98** B2
Woolmore St, E14. . . . . **98** A4
Woolridge Way, E9. . . **22** B3
Woolstaplers Way,
    SE16 . . . . **120** C4
WOOLWICH, SE18 . . . . **133** D3
≈ Woolwich Arsenal . **133** F5
Riv Woolwich Arsenal
    Pier **133** F3
Woolwich Ch St, SE18. **131** E4
≈ Woolwich
    Dockyard **132** A5
Woolwich Dockyard
    Ind Est, SE18 . . . . . **131** F4
Woolwich Ferry Pier,
    E16 . . . . **132** B2
Woolwich Foot Tunnel,
    E16 . . . . **132** C2
    SE18 . . . . **132** C2
Woolwich High St,
    SE18 . . . . **132** C4
Woolwich Manor Way,
    E6 . . . . **76** B2
    E16 . . . . **105** E5
Woolwich Mkt, SE18. . **133** E5
Woolwich Rd, SE10. . . **156** C4
Wooster Gdns, E14. . . . **70** C5
Wooster Pl, SE1 . . . . . **119** D5
Wootton St, SE1 . . . . **117** D1
Worcester Ho, SE11
    off Kennington Rd . . **116** C4
Worcester Ms, NW6 . . . . **9** F1
Wordsworth Rd, SE1 . **148** A1
Worfield St, SW11. . . . **163** F2
Worgan St, SE11. . . . . **144** A2
    SE16 . . . . **123** D4
Coll Working Men's Coll,
    The, NW1 . . . . **36** B2
Worland Rd, E15. . . . . . **27** F3
World's End Pas,
    SW10 . . . . **162** C1
World's End Pl, SW10
    off King's Rd **162** B1
Worlidge St, W6 . . . . . **134** A2
Wormwood St, EC2. . . . **63** E5
Wornington Rd, W10. . **51** E2
Woronzow Rd, NW8 . . . **33** D1
Worship St, EC2 . . . . . . **63** E5
Worth Gro, SE17. . . . . **146** C3

Worthing Cl, E15. . . . . . **49** E1
Wotton Rd, SE8. . . . . . **152** B5
Wouldham Rd, E16. . . . **72** A5
Wren Cl, E16 . . . . **72** B5
Wren Landing, E14. . . . **97** D4
Wren Rd, SE5 . . . . **170** C4
Wren St, WC1 . . . . **60** B1
Wrentham Av, NW10. . **28** C2
Wrestlers Ct, EC3
    off Camomile St. **63** E5
Wrexham Rd, E3. . . . . . **47** D3
Wricklemarsh Rd, SE3. **181** E4
Wrigglesworth St,
    SE14 . . . . **174** C1
Wright Rd, N1 . . . . **19** F1
Wrights La, W8 . . . . . . **109** C3
Wrights Rd, E3 . . . . **46** A2
Wrotham Rd, NW1 . . . . **14** B4
Wyatt Cl, SE16 . . . . . . **124** A2
Wybert St, NW1 . . . . . . **57** F1
Wycherley Cl, SE3. . . . **180** A1
Wyclif Ct, EC1
    off Wyclif St **39** E5
Wyclif St, EC1 . . . . **39** E5
Wycombe Sq, W8 . . . . . **80** C5
Wyfold Rd, SW6 . . . . . **159** E3
Wyke Rd, E3 . . . . **24** C4
Wyllen Cl, E1. . . . . **66** A2
Wymering Rd, W9 . . . . **31** D5
Wynan Rd, E14. . . . . . **153** E2
Wyndcliff Rd, SE7. . . . **157** E3
Wyndham Est, SE5. . . **170** A1
Wyndham Ms, W1 . . . . **56** A4
Wyndham Pl, W1 . . . . . **56** A4
Wyndham Rd, SE5 . . . **169** F2
Wyndham St, W1 . . . . . **56** A3
Wyndham Yd, W1. . . . . **56** A4
Wynford Rd, N1 . . . . . . **38** A2
Wynnstay Gdns, W8 . **109** D3
Wynyard Ter, SE11. . . **144** B2
Wynyatt St, EC1 . . . . . . **39** E5
Wythburn Pl, W1 . . . . . **84** A1
Wythes Rd, E16 . . . . . **103** E5
Wyvil Est, SW8 . . . . . . **167** E1
Sch Wyvil Prim Sch,
    SW8. . . . . **167** F1
Wyvil Rd, SW8. . . . . . **143** E5
Wyvis St, E14 . . . . **69** F3

Y

Yabsley St, E14. . . . . . . **98** B4
Yalding Rd, SE16 . . . . **120** C4
Yardley St, WC1 . . . . . . **38** C5
Yarmouth Pl, W1 . . . . . **85** E5
Yarnfield Sq, SE15 . . . **173** D4
Yarrow Cres, E6 . . . . . . **75** E3
Yateley St, SE18 . . . . . **131** D4
Yates Ct, NW2. . . . . **7** D2
Yates Ho, E2
    off Roberta St **43** D4
Yeate St, N1 . . . . **18** C4
Yeldham Rd, W6. . . . . **134** C3
Yeoman Cl, E6. . . . . . . **105** E2
Yeoman's Row, SW3 . **111** F4

Yeoman St, SE8. . . . . . **123** E5
Yeomans Yd, E1 . . . . . . **92** B2
Yeo St, E3 . . . . **69** E3
Yoke Cl, N7 . . . . **15** F1
York Br, NW1 . . . . **56** C1
York Bldgs, WC2 . . . . . . **87** F3
York Cl, E6. . . . . **104** A1
York Gate, NW1. . . . . . **56** C2
York Gro, SE15 . . . . . . **174** A4
York Ho Pl, W8 . . . . . . **109** E1
York Pl, WC2 . . . . **87** F3
York Rd, SE1 . . . . **116** B1
Yorkshire Grey Yd,
    WC1. . . . . **60** A4
Yorkshire Rd, E14. . . . . **95** E1
York Sq, E14 . . . . **95** E1
York St, W1 . . . . **56** B3
York Ter E, NW1. . . . . . **57** D2
York Ter W, NW1. . . . . . **56** C2
Yorkton St, E2 . . . . **42** C3
York Way, N1 . . . . **15** D1
    N7 . . . . **37** F1
York Way Est, N1 . . . . . **37** F1
York Way Est, N7
    off York Way **15** E2
Young Rd, E16 . . . . **74** A4
Young's Bldgs, EC1. . . . **62** B1
Youngs Ct, SW11 . . . . **165** D4
Young St, W8 . . . . **109** E2

Z

Zampa Rd, SE16 . . . . . **150** A3
Zander Ct, E2 . . . . **43** D3
Zealand Rd, E3 . . . . **45** E2
Zetland St, E14. . . . . . . **69** F4
Zion Ho, E1 . . . . **66** A5
Zoar St, SE1 . . . . **90** A4